# Barron's Review Course Series

# Let's Review:

# Global History and Geography

## Fifth Edition

**Mark Willner**
*Brooklyn College, City University of New York*
*Brooklyn, New York*
*Former Assistant Principal and Chairman, Social Studies Department*
*Midwood High School at Brooklyn College*
*Brooklyn, New York*

**Mary Martin**
*Greene Central School*
*Greene, New York*
*ARC Otsego, Individual Program Coordinator*
*Oneonta, New York*

**Jerry Weiner**
*Kean University*
*Union, New Jersey*

**David Moore**
*Webster Central School*
*Webster, New York*

**George Hero**
*Midwood High School at Brooklyn College*
*Brooklyn, New York*

**BARRON'S**

*All inquiries should be addressed to:*
Barron's Educational Series, Inc.
250 Wireless Boulevard
Hauppauge, New York 11788
**www.barronseduc.com**

Library of Congress Catalog Card Number: 2012938916

ISBN: 978-1-4380-0016-9

PRINTED IN CANADA

9 8 7 6 5 4 3 2

**10%**
**POST-CONSUMER**
**WASTE**
Paper contains a minimum
of 10% post-consumer
waste (PCW). Paper used
in this book was derived
from certified, sustainable
forestlands.

# About the Authors

**MARK WILLNER** was the assistant principal and chairman of the social studies department at Midwood High School in Brooklyn, New York, from 1973 to 2005. He was selected as the Outstanding Social Studies Supervisor in the United States for the year 2000. Similar outstanding supervisory honors were bestowed on him in New York State (1991) and in New York City (1984, 1988). In 1997, New York State chose him as its Distinguished Social Studies Educator. In 1995, New York State also selected him to receive the Louis E. Yavner Teaching Award for Outstanding Contributions to Teaching About the Holocaust and Other Violations of Human Rights. In 2004, he was the winner of the Spirit of Anne Frank Outstanding Educator Award, presented by the Anne Frank Center, U.S.A. His most recent honor was in 2006, when he was given the Consul General's Commendation by the Japanese Consulate in New York City.

Mr. Willner is the lead author of three Barron's publications: *Global Studies* (Vol. II), *Global History*, and *Let's Review: Global History and Geography*. He has also contributed to Barron's *Regents Exams and Answers: Global History and Geography, Regents Exams and Answers: U.S. History and Government,* and *CLEP (How to Prepare for the College Level Exam Program).* He is currently a member of the adjunct faculty at Brooklyn College, and has served as an educational coordinator with the Gilder Lehrman Institute of American History and a consultant with New Visions for the Public Schools.

**MARY MARTIN** has taught social studies and was Social Studies Department Chairperson at Greene Central School in Greene, New York. She was a contributing author to Barron's *Regents Exams and Answers, Global History and Geography,* for which she wrote the Introduction and Glossary sections. She contributed to the development of several Global Studies, Global History and Geography, and U.S. History and Government regents and competency exams. She is presently an Individual Program Coordinator for the ARC Otsego in Oneonta, New York.

**JERRY WEINER, Ph.D.**, is a professor at the College of Education at Kean University in New Jersey, where he is the Coordinator of European Programs and Studies and Coordinator of Secondary Education Programs. He also works as a visiting professor at the Ecole Superieure de Commerce in France and the Universidad de Deusto in Spain. Dr. Weiner is a retired New York City high school administrator and supervisor who specialized in social studies education. He was awarded a Fulbright fellowship for study in Brazil. He was also a New York City Supervisor of the Year and was a winner of the John Bunzel Award for supervisors.

**DAVID MOORE** retired from teaching in June 1999 after a 32-year career in the New York State public schools, most of it focusing on Afro-Asian/Global Studies and Humanities. A graduate of Oberlin College (B.A.) and Kent State University (M.Ed.), Mr. Moore taught at the Webster Central School from 1970 after 3 years in the Herricks District. His overseas teaching experience included exchange years in England at the Jack Hunt School in Peterborough (1980–1981) and the Westfield School in Watford (1988–1989) as well as a year at the American Embassy School in New Delhi, India (1973–1974). In addition, he has participated in travel-study programs in India (1971), Indonesia (1978), Jamaica (1984), and Ireland (1997). Mr. Moore served as editor of *Global Studies Resource Guide* for the New York State Council for the Social Studies. He has also worked as a college supervisor of student teachers for SUNY Geneseo.

**GEORGE A. HERO** has been a teacher in the social studies department of Midwood High School at Brooklyn College since 1984. He has taught Global History, European History Advanced Placement, and Social Science Research, as well as electives in Greco-Roman, Byzantine, and Russian history. He is the founder and director of the Social Science Research Program at Midwood and has also taught at Brooklyn College and Long Island University (Brooklyn Campus). He is the coauthor of *Global Studies* (Vol. II) and *Global History* (2 volumes), both published by Barron's. In 2004, he won the Bunzel Award as the outstanding high school teacher of social studies in New York City.

# Table of Contents

# Preface

This book is designed to be used as a review text for the New York State two-year course in Regents Global History and Geography. The material follows the syllabus of the course as taught throughout New York State on the secondary level. Although the material has been prepared to meet the needs and standards of New York State students, it can also be helpful to students in any Global History or World History course anywhere in the United States.

## • Special Features of This Book

The information in this book parallels the New York State syllabus in Global History and Geography. It serves as an excellent guide for students in two ways: (1) as they take each of the four required terms of Global History, and (2) as they prepare for the Regents Examination in Global History. The book begins with an introductory unit that provides important information about the social sciences and about the general features and geography of Africa, Asia, Europe, and Latin America. These are the four parts of the world that are studied in the Global History and Geography course sequence. Following the introductory unit are eight units that cover specific time eras in a chronological pattern. Each unit highlights the significant people and events in the era.

This book also contains references to various global concepts, themes, and issues that appear in the New York State syllabus, and which are used in making up the Regents Exam questions.

1. The ones focused on history are as follows: belief systems, change, choice, citizenship, conflict, culture, diversity, empathy, environment, human rights, identity, imperialism, interdependence, justice, movement of people and goods, nationalism, political systems, power, scarcity, technology, and urbanization.

2. Those focused on geography are as follows: the world in spatial terms, places and regions, physical systems, human systems, environment and society, and the uses of geography.

3. The major world issues are: population, war and peace, terrorism, energy—resources and allocations, human rights, hunger and poverty, world trade and finance, environmental concerns, political and economic refugees, economic growth and development, and determination of political and economic systems.

References to these items are noted in the margins of the book, by icons and call-outs.

Complementing the text in each unit you will find maps, tables, charts, and illustrations. Also included are review questions that are similar to those that appear on the Regents Exam. These are characterized as multiple-choice questions, thematic essays, and document-based questions (DBQs).

## • Taking the Regents Examination

1. Preparation for the Regents Exam begins the first day of class. Good study habits, effective note-taking, completion of all assignments, and a positive attitude throughout the year will make succeeding on any exam an easy task.

2. You will have three hours to complete the exam. The exam will consist of three types of questions.
   A. Multiple-Choice Questions—There will be 50 multiple-choice questions, accounting for 55 percent of the 100 points on the exam. Each question will have four choices, only one of which will be correct. Use the process of elimination if necessary to determine the best answer.
   B. Thematic Essay Question—The exam will have one thematic essay question. It will be worth 15 percent. It will be based on one of the themes, concepts, or issues previously described .
   C. Document-Based Question—There will be one DBQ, worth 30 percent. In answering this question, you will be asked to look at several documents on a single topic. The documents may be written items (for example, speeches, letters, diaries, news articles) or non-written items (for example, maps, cartoons, photographs, paintings, tables, graphs). After each document, there will be a question called a scaffolding question. The answer to these questions will be worth 15 percent and will be labeled as Part A of the DBQ. The remaining 15 percent of the DBQ, Part B, will be an analytical essay. The essay will require an answer built on evidence from the documents as well as from knowledge of global history and geography. Samples of all of these types of questions are present in this book. The questions may be about a single person, place, or time, or may call for connections to be made. Questions that call for making connections across time and place will require you to make comparisons and contrasts.

3. Directions for answering each of the question types will be indicated on the exam itself. The directions will probably use such key skill terms as define, show, discuss, describe, evaluate, and explain.

4. Save all of your notes from your Global History courses. Although you will be taking the Regents after the Global History 4 class, you will still have to know material from the other Global History classes you have taken.

## • Conclusion

As you use this book to help with daily lessons and homework assignments, as well as for your Regents Exam preparation, you are certain to find it to be very helpful. Good luck in your studies!

Mark Willner

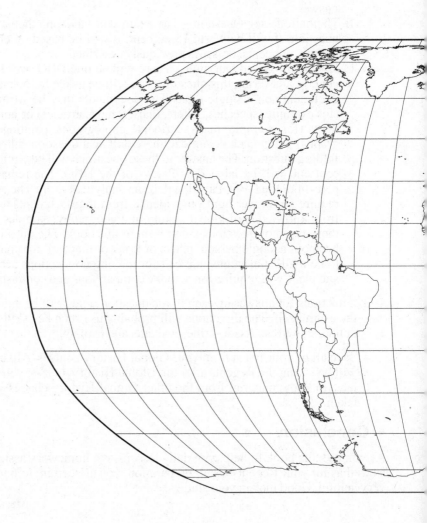

# Introduction to Global History and Geography

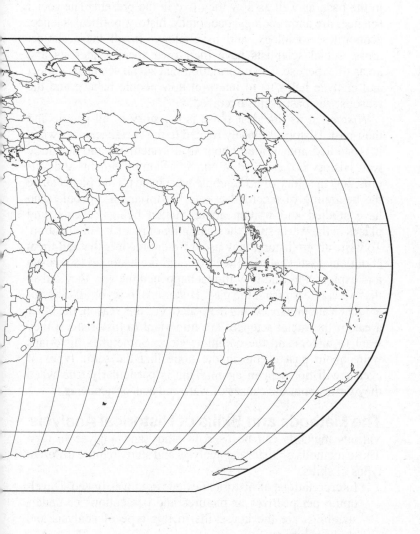

# Part A: The Social Sciences

*Social science* is the term used for all or any of the branches of study that deal with humans in their social, economic, and political relations. These studies are referred to as the social sciences. Modern social sciences use the scientific method, an organized and systematic way of research that dates from the 18th century. Social sciences use quantitative methods and statistical techniques to analyze humans and their behavior toward each other.

The social sciences are sometimes called the people sciences. Social sciences help us to understand how people lived and acted in the past, as well as how they live in the present. The social sciences are anthropology, geography, history, political science, economics, sociology, and psychology. In all these subject areas, social scientists have their own special interests and areas of expertise. The information that social scientists collect and analyze helps us to interpret how people behave and the reasons why past events occurred.

*History* in its broadest sense is the story of all people and their past. History is closely related to the social sciences when it is studied and written about in a systematic and scientific way. History is the record of human accomplishments and failures. It is the story of how people have lived on our planet since the beginning of recorded events. Historians are people who have studied and written about human beings, events, and places in the world since the beginning of recorded civilization. To write about history, they use different records that tell them about our past. Historical records help the historian to analyze and explain how and why things happened the way they did so that we can learn from the past. Historians look for all kinds of evidence about why events happened. For this reason, the other areas of the social sciences are important to historians if they want to understand the complete story. Sometimes historians write about past events in the hope that the same types of events will not happen again. This is particularly true when they write about the causes of wars and acts of genocide.

## The Methods and Skills of Historical Analysis

Various methods can be used to study and analyze history. These methods of historical analysis and study require different types of skills.

- Interpretations of historical events are investigated. Developing perspectives or pictures and perceptions or understandings are the key skills in this type of analysis and study of history.

- Hypotheses about interpretations of historical events are investigated. The skill of constructing hypotheses that work is essential in this method of study and analysis.
- Examination of primary historical evidence leads to explanation and analysis. Finding differences and classifying types of evidence are crucial in this method.
- Concepts or ideas and themes are studied over a period of time. Skills in developing a conceptual or thematic framework are important in this method.
- Comparisons and contrasts are made concerning similar types of historical events. Skills in making proper comparisons and contrasts are essential in this method of analysis and study.

*Economics* is the study of how human beings use resources to produce various goods and how these goods are distributed for consumption among people in society. Throughout human history, people have lived and worked under different economic systems. These economic systems include barter, capitalism, fascism, socialism, and communism. Economists use complex mathematical techniques and statistical data in economic forecasting and analysis and management of resources.

*Sociology* is the scientific study of human behavior. As the study of humans in their collective or group aspect, sociology is concerned with all group activities—economic, social, political, and religious. Sociologists seek to determine the laws governing human behavior in social contexts. With this objective in mind, they investigate a selected group of social facts or relations.

*Psychology* is the science or study of living things and their interactions with the environment. Psychologists study processes of how people sense other people, things, and their own feelings. They concentrate on the development of learning, motivations, personality, and the interactions of the individual and the group. Psychology is concerned with human behavior and its physiological and psychological bases.

*Anthropology* is the study, classification, and analysis of humans and their society—descriptively, historically, and physically. Its unique contribution to studying the links between human social relations has been the special concept of culture. Its emphasis is on data from nonliterate peoples and explorations of archeological remains. Anthropologists study the characteristics, customs, and cultures of people.

*Political science* is the study of government, political processes, institutions, and political behavior. Political scientists study and comment on fields such as political theory, national and local government, comparative government, and international relations. Political scientists are often called on to make predictions about politics, such as elections and people's reactions to different events.

## Geography—The Physical World

Human beings and societies in all regions of the earth share a common global environment. This environment is a closed system consisting of a variety of physical features—landforms, bodies of water, vegetation and animal species, and climatic regions. These physical features are the result of several natural processes including the rotation and revolution of the earth, geological activity, the water cycle, and biological interactions.

The environment provides humans with a variety of renewable and nonrenewable resources, which can be used to meet the needs of both individuals and societies. Though these needs are basic to all humans, the different ways in which they are met are determined by the differences in environments that exist from one part of the earth to another.

The land surface of the earth is generally divided into seven large landmasses called continents—North America, South America, Asia, Africa, Europe, Australia, and Antarctica. Large bodies of water, called oceans—Atlantic, Pacific, Indian, and Arctic—and smaller ones called seas cover about 70 percent of the earth's surface. These bodies of water separate some continents from one another.

In recent centuries, humans have improved their abilities to use more of the earth's limited resources, and technology has created closer contacts among peoples of different cultures. This global interdependence has made it increasingly important to understand the similarities and differences among cultures. It is hoped that such understanding will aid in solving shared problems and resolving disputes between peoples of different cultures.

## Maps and Their Uses

We can illustrate much information about the world with maps, but we must be aware of their limitations and distortions. Projecting the features of a sphere (the globe) on a flat surface (a map) can distort sizes and distances, especially when we attempt to show the entire world.

Attempting to illustrate the shapes of landmasses correctly can distort the sizes of the landmasses. On the other hand, trying to show size can distort shape, as in the Gall-Peters projection. Thus, maps can convey inaccurate impressions of the importance and influence of certain areas of the world.

Placement or location can give false impressions of the relationships among regions or the relative importance of an area. For example, in the Mercator projection, with the Atlantic Ocean in the middle, North America and Europe are located top center. This seems to illustrate both the importance and the closeness of their relationship. Compare the Mercator projection and the Japan Airlines map. The Japan Airlines map centers on the Pacific Ocean and therefore islands in the Pacific become important. If you look at the Macarthur corrective map, which was created by Australians, you will see a different story and emphasis in which land areas in the South Pacific are prominent.

Reading maps requires an understanding of their language. The scale provides a tool for determining distances. A map's legend or key provides information about the meaning of lines, symbols, colors, and other markings found on the map itself.

Modern technology has changed how we think about the size of the world. Actual (or absolute) distance has become less important than relative distance—how quickly communication and transportation can move ideas and people from one part of the world to another. Cultural regions once separated by thousands of miles or formidable physical barriers now interact with one another.

Maps can present information in many ways. A topographical map attempts to show physical features, a political map focuses on the way humans divide up the world (the boundaries of nations), and an economic map illustrates the ways in which people use the environment and resources. Comparing specific maps, such as those showing rainfall patterns and population distribution, can be useful in understanding ways of life and the relationships between humans and the world in which they live.

## FOUR PARTS OF THE NATURAL ENVIRONMENT

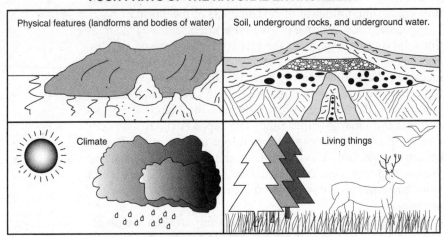

Physical features (landforms and bodies of water)

Soil, underground rocks, and underground water.

Climate

Living things

## CONTINENTS AND OCEANS

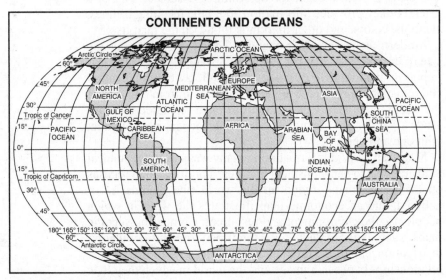

## MERCATOR PROJECTION

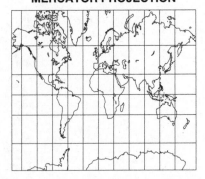

## GALL-PETERS PROJECTION

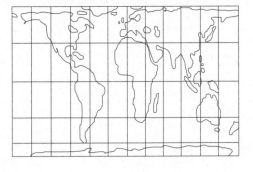

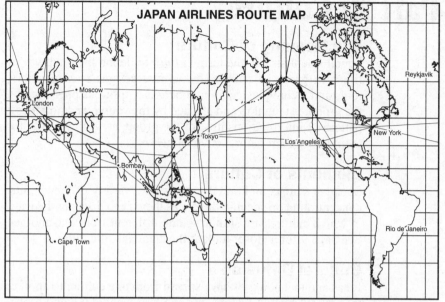

**JAPAN AIRLINES ROUTE MAP**

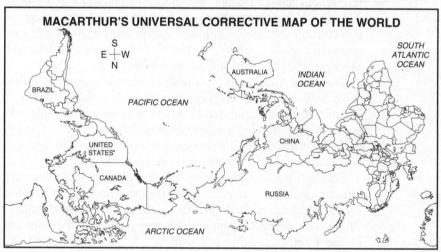

**MACARTHUR'S UNIVERSAL CORRECTIVE MAP OF THE WORLD**

7

# Part B: Culture

## The Meaning of Culture

Social scientists use the term *culture* to define the total way of life of a group of people. It includes actions and behaviors, tools and techniques, ideas and beliefs. Culture is preserved by the group, is taught to and learned by the young, and provides a pattern of interrelationships for the group, as well as a way for them to use their natural environment.

## Elements of Culture

Social scientists look at cultures from a variety of viewpoints, concentrating on specific factors as they try to discover the ways in which cultures are similar to and different from one another. See page 9 for a closer look at the elements of culture.

## Cultural Diffusion

Ideas and technologies have spread from one culture to another throughout human history, but modern technology and global interdependence have increased both the speed and extent of this cultural diffusion. Some see these recent developments as creating a global culture in which similar styles, tastes, and products will be universally acknowledged.

Trade, aid, migration, conquest, slavery, war, and entertainment have all promoted this process, with both positive and negative results. Useful traditions can be destroyed or replaced; social and economic patterns can be disrupted. But new technology can also bring improvements in standards of living, and new ideas can bring variety and enrichment to any culture.

Through the first decade of the 21st century this increased international and intercultural contact has been greatly enhanced by the rapid escalation of electronic communication. Widespread computer and cellular phone usage and expansion of the Internet provide opportunities for both good and ill. Knowledge of other cultures is more readily available to more people with the potential for greater tolerance and understanding. At the same time, these devices enable the spreading of grievances, hatred, prejudices, and intolerance while enabling those who would put these feelings into action. The relative ease of communication can facilitate planning of violence and terrorist acts as well as aid those who would organize and protest peacefully.

Increased contact between cultures can also bring about exploitation and help to create or at least emphasize differences in prosperity and standards of living from one culture region to another. The "developed" regions—Europe (East and West), Anglo-America, Japan, and Australia/Oceana—have been greatly influenced by the Industrial Revolution. The people of these regions have a more abundant supply of material goods and personal services.

In the "developing" (once called "less developed" or "Third World") regions, the populace generally has fewer comforts and

---

### ELEMENTS OF CULTURE
*How a group of people react to some or all of the following:*

#### CONFLICT
Causes and Effects • Competition: Human vs. Nature • Human vs. Human • Philosophical • Physical • International • Domestic Resolution • War • Peace • Compromise • Cooperation • Control • Change • Violence • Prejudice

#### ENVIRONMENT
Geography • Geology • Landforms • Weather/ Climate • Natural Resources • Vegetation • Soil • Bodies of Water • Minerals • Land Use • Latitude • Elevation • Time/Space Patterns • Ocean Currents • Tectonic Activity • Wildlife

#### TECHNOLOGY
Tools • Shelter/Housing • Resource Extraction • Machinery • Production Systems • Energy Use • Clothing • Science • Medicine • Electronics • Simplicity to Complexity • Training • Skills • Industrialization

#### MODES OF EXPRESSION
Language • Communication • Spoken • Written • Physical • Electronic • Music • Art • Literature • Dress • Entertainment • Education • Transportation • Travel • Migration • Diffusion

### CULTURE

#### SOCIAL ORGANIZATION
Groups: Role/Status • Rules • Clan • Tribe • Race • Social Class • Age • Occupation & Peer Groups • Hierarchies • Ethnicity • Lineage • Family Structure • Generation • Household

#### VALUES/RELIGION
Origins: Human/Divine • Superstitions • Answers • Questions • Major Belief Systems • Mythology • Theology • God • Founders • Scriptures • Doctrines • Animism • Monotheism • Polytheism • Atheism • Secular Humanism

#### POLITICS/LAWS
Rules • Power/Influence • Government • Bureaucracy • Monarchy/Oligarchy/ Autocracy/ Democracy/ Dictatorship/Totalitarianism • Constitutions/Rights • Parties/Elections • Leadership • Citizenship/Nationalism • Authority • Legitimacy • Sovereignty

#### ECONOMIC ORGANIZATION
Agriculture/Industry • Labor Scarcity: Needs & Wants • Resource Base • Carrying Capacity • Goods & Services • Money/Trade • Poverty/ Prosperity • Capital Supply & Demand • Distribution • Capitalism/Socialism/ Communism • Markets

RESULTS | IN

The distinctive CULTURE of that group

The existence and operation of these factors in a culture's past makes up its *History*

conveniences, and significant numbers of people may survive at a subsistence level. A major goal for most countries in these areas is *economic development*—an increase in the capacity to produce goods and services in order to make life safer and healthier.

In the last decades of the 20th century and the early years of the 21st century, significant numbers of people in some "developing" nations, particularly China, India, and several countries in Southeast Asia have benefited from increased standards of living. The growth of a vigorous middle class in these countries has been based on enhanced educational opportunities and access to more complex technology and communication. In many cases it has also accentuated economic discrepancies within these nations.

# Part C: World Regions

We can view the world as being divided into different regions based on cultural, economic, political, and physical features. This means that large sections of the globe can be classified as regions depending on what type of culture, economic and political systems, or physical characteristics they have. The identification of factors shared by most people in a regional area provides a tool for studying similarities and differences among regions. It can also be a basis for understanding relationships within a given region, as well as contacts between regions.

In *Let's Review: Global History and Geography* we study major regions including the Middle East, South Asia, Southeast Asia, East Asia, Sub-Saharan Africa, Latin America, Western Europe, Eastern Europe, and Russia in terms of their cultural characteristics, economic and political systems, and physical features.

Specific factors help us to define a region by its cultural characteristics. Examples of cultural characteristics are religion and language. The Middle East is often identified by its cultural characteristics: Islamic religion and Arabic language. Latin America can be identified by its cultural characteristics: Roman Catholic religion and Spanish language.

The physical features of an area are another way to identify a region. For example, such physical characteristics as mountains, deserts, bodies of water, fertile river valleys, and coastal plains are identifying characteristics of different regions. Bodies of water may also unite groups of islands or coastal areas. For example, the islands of the Caribbean basin can be called a subregion. Climate patterns and resource bases help to determine lifestyles within regions and often help to determine social structures. The Arctic can be classified as a region based on its extreme climate conditions and physical features. The lifestyle of the Eskimo people is greatly influenced by the region's physical apects.

Economic and political systems are other characteristics that help us to determine a region's identity. For example, Western Europe can be studied as a region known for democratic-type governments and capitalist economic systems.

## Classification of World Regions by Common Characteristics

Each region possesses a set of common characteristics that sets it apart from other regions. The world regions defined below share a number of classification factors. These regions have their own special combinations of characteristics. Some characteristics may not be typical of all nations in a specific region because these countries have their own special features.

**Western Europe.** Judaic-Christian religious ethic, Greco-Roman traditions, industrial economies, temperate-type climate, Latin and Germanic languages, members of the European Union.

**Central and Eastern Europe.** Primarily Slavic languages, Orthodox Christian religious ethic, formerly communist/socialist economies, developing capitalist economies, recently obtained membership in or candidates for admittance to the European Union.

**Latin America.** Primarily Roman Catholic religion, Latin-based languages (Spanish/Portuguese), heritage of European colonialism, Native American cultural influences.

**Sub-Saharan Africa.** Tropical or semitropical climate, multiple religious traditions (animism, Christianity, Islam), strong tribal identities and ethnic-group social organizations, agricultural.

**Middle East.** Islamic religious ethic, crossroads location with connecting waterways, Arabic language and culture, arid climate, abundance of oil, birthplace of three major religious systems (Judaism, Christianity, and Islam), authoritarian governments.

**South Asia and Southeast Asia.** Monsoon climatic conditions, Hindu, Buddhist, and Islamic religious traditions, floodplain agriculture, colonial experiences, transition to more industrial economies from agricultural economies.

**East Asia.** Confucian/Taoist/Buddhist traditions and ethic, hierarchical social systems, character-based alphabet, developing industrialized economies based on trade priorities.

**West Asia.** Former republics of the Soviet Union, Islamic religious ethic, authoritarian secular governments, mineral resources (particularly oil).

Within individual regions there are often great differences among the individual countries and peoples. For example, in the Middle East the nation of Israel has a Judaic tradition and a democratic government. Turkey and Iran are Islamic but do not have Arabic cultures. In Latin America, the climate varies from tropical in the Amazon basin to temperate further south in the Argentine pampas. Sub-Saharan Africa has hundreds of distinct ethnic groups with a wide variety of cultural characteristics.

Muslims make up the majority in some South Asian and Southeast Asian countries, thereby giving nations such as Pakistan, Bangladesh, and Indonesia a cultural tradition strongly influenced by Islamic traditions. This is not true of other nations in this region. In Eastern Europe, Poland has a Christian yet non-Orthodox religious tradition, and Bosnia and Albania have primarily Islamic cultures.

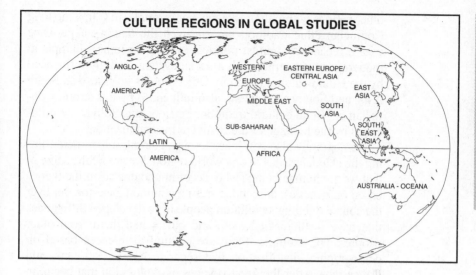

In addition there are transition or diffusion zones between regions that are hard to define by distinct cultural characteristics. In these zones or areas, cultures meet, mix, and produce unique combinations. The area of the former Soviet Union known as the Trans-Caucasus is such a subregion, having traditions from both the Orthodox and Islamic cultures. The Caribbean subregion of Latin America combines Latin, African, and Anglo-European traditions.

There has been a recent development of more integrated global economic systems that transcend regions. For example, the European Union and the North American Free Trade Association (NAFTA), which operate as integrated economic systems, are creating bridges and interconnections between different world regions. This is particularly true in Central and Eastern Europe where many nations are joining or seeking to join the European Union. Even Turkey, a nation that is mostly Middle Eastern and Islamic, is a candidate for membership in the European Union. Heavy immigration to the more industrialized nations is also leading to changes in the cultural characteristics that traditionally defined these nations. This is particularly true in Western Europe and the United States. The end of communism and the trend away from military-led governments have led to fundamental changes in the political systems that characterized some world regions.

## The Impact of Resources, Demography, and History

The history, demography, and resources of any region influence the characteristics of that defined world region. The nations of India, China, Peru, and Egypt have long historical traditions that influence their national characteristics and the cultural traits of

13

other nations within their regions. For example, in China the long Confucian ethic tradition has survived the nation's experience with a recent communist political system. In India, attempts at modernization conflict with a social system strongly influenced by the Hindu cultural tradition. Other nations in East Asia, South Asia, and Southeast Asia are also influenced by this strong Confucian or Hindu cultural tradition. Ecuador and Bolivia are influenced by the heritage of the Peruvian Inca civilization.

Demography also continues to play a strong role in determining the characteristics of any world region. We are all the same in that we are human beings who, according to one scientific theory based on genetics, descended from a common ancestor. Yet over the course of human evolution people have developed differences that have distinguished them and others like them from other peoples. For example, there are cultural differences based on demographic identification that separate Asians, Africans, and Caucasians. After the great voyages of exploration that began in the 1400s, the identification of certain demographic groups became more complex. The European-inspired global trading and colonial connections among world regions led to greater mixing of peoples. In the later part of the 20th century the process accelerated as increasing numbers of people immigrated to world regions where they have a greater chance to prosper economically, practice their religion, or gain political freedom.

Resources also help us to define world regions. For example, in the Middle East there are large deposits of oil. When we think of the Middle East, oil is one of the resource characteristics that we use to identify this region or the nations that comprise this area. When we study about the subregion of the Caribbean, agricultural resources such as sugar and tobacco help us to identify the type of economy of this area and the countries in it. Abundant resources and a scarcity of resources are ways of defining world regions. Sometimes the scarcity of resources influences the development of a world region. This is true when we look at the history of Western Europe where during the Age of Exploration nations went to other world regions to gain access to resources. The rise of European industry is tied to this development of trade and colonialism, which heavily influenced all the regions that the Europeans penetrated. In East Asia, the economic and political history of Japan continues to be greatly influenced by the lack of natural resources in this island nation. It seems safe to say that the issue of resources, for example, oil, water, and timber will continue to influence the development of different world regions and the nations within them in the years to come.

Next we will briefly examine different regions, by learning about each one's physical, economic, and human geographical features.

*Multiple Choice.* Select the letter of the answer that correctly completes each statement.

1. Which phrase best describes the meaning of the term "culture"?
   A. the advancement and progress of a nation
   B. the ability of humans to appreciate art and music
   C. all the ways in which a group of people lives
   D. all the products that a group of humans makes and uses

2. Social scientists who study human culture are called anthropologists. Their work would most likely involve
   A. examining the environment in which people live
   B. determining the operating principles of modern machinery
   C. learning the reasons that certain groups of people live as they do
   D. discovering the influence of climate upon types of plants and animals

3. Which aspect of culture is most directly affected by the physical geography of an area?
   A. religion
   B. language
   C. food
   D. music

4. In dividing the world's population into culture groups, social scientists are most concerned with
   A. weather and climate patterns of different regions
   B. political boundaries separating countries
   C. similarities and differences in styles and patterns of living
   D. present political systems in various nations

5. Below are three proverbs.
   "Mighty oaks from tiny acorns grow." (United States).
   "The journey of 1,000 miles begins with a single step." (China)
   "A little rain each day will fill the river to overflowing." (West Africa)

   Which conclusion is best supported by these proverbs?
   A. Humans in all cultures make excuses for their shortcomings.
   B. All cultures are concerned with transportation and conservation.
   C. Natural resources are a major concern for people in all cultures.
   D. Though cultures may differ humans view many situations in similar ways.

6. The popularity of baseball in Japan and karate in the United States are examples of
   A. cultural diffusion
   B. technological development
   C. ethnocentrism
   D. cultural isolation

7. Which of the following statements about maps is *not* correct?
   A. A topographical map would show mountains and water bodies.
   B. Political maps emphasize boundaries between countries.
   C. An economic map might show areas of agricultural production.
   D. Demographic maps generally show types of governments.

8. Culture regions as defined in this course
   A. are for the most part quite small and isolated
   B. usually contain very little cultural variety
   C. have developed as a result of geographic and historical factors
   D. change frequently as political parties and governments change

9. The so-called developing regions of the world are generally located on which continents?
   A. Asia, Africa, and South America
   B. Europe, Africa, and Australia
   C. North America, South America, and Asia
   D. North America, Australia, and Europe

# SECTION 1: THE MIDDLE EAST

## I. PHYSICAL GEOGRAPHY OF THE MIDDLE EAST

### Overview

The region known as the Middle East includes parts of three continents—Europe, Africa, and Asia. Because all three continents seem to intersect here, the region has also been called "the crossroads of the world." However, these names, as well as another commonly used name, the Near East, seem appropriate only when one looks at a world map with Western Europe at the center. The African portion of the Middle East includes the area known as North Africa, while the Asian portion includes what might be called SWASIA (Southwest Asia).

The North African portion of the Middle East is made up of five nations—Morocco, Algeria, Tunisia, Libya, and Egypt.

The Southwest Asian portion includes fifteen nations— Turkey, Syria, Lebanon, Israel, Jordan, Saudi Arabia, Yemen, Oman, the United Arab Emirates, Bahrain, Qatar, Kuwait, Iraq, Iran, and Afghanistan.

GLOBAL CONCEPTS

**Diversity**

CONCEPTS GLOBAL

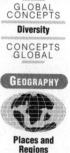

**GEOGRAPHY**

**Places and Regions**

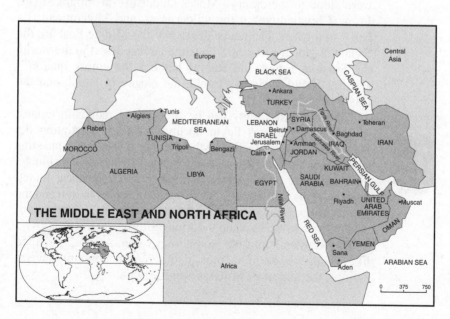

**THE MIDDLE EAST AND NORTH AFRICA**

The European portion of the Middle East consists of the part of Turkey that lies across the Dardanelles from the Asian part and that contains the famous city of Istanbul (formerly Constantinople). The Asian part of Turkey is often referred to as Asia Minor. (This reference is a geographical one, not a political one.)

## Topography

**Physical Settings**

GLOBAL CONCEPTS

**Empathy**

CONCEPTS GLOBAL

Throughout the Middle East, which is about twice the physical size of the United States, the most common landform is desert. The aridity (dryness), lack of vegetation, and barrenness of its desert territories have had profound effects on the history and culture of the Middle East. The nomadic (wandering) lifestyles of such people as the Bedouins, Arabs, and early Israelites put an emphasis on sharing, group values, and conformity over individual values. Close family and clan ties and frugality (thriftiness) were also important. As deserts make up over 80 percent of the land area, population distribution has been uneven. Human settlements were and are still found mainly near the precious water bodies. Armed struggles have occurred throughout history for access to and control over water. The emptiness of the deserts may also have had an impact on the growth of strong religious feelings in the Middle East. A society's religious devotion may become heightened when people live amid harsh natural conditions. Scholars also note that three central religious figures had profound experiences when they were alone in the desert—Moses (Judaism—at Mount Sinai), Jesus (Christianity—in the wilderness), and Muhammad (Islam—in a cave). The major deserts of the Middle East are the Sahara in North Africa, which is the largest desert in the world, the Sinai in Egypt, the Rub-al Khali ("the empty quarter") and the Nafud in Saudi Arabia, the Negev in Israel, and the Dasht-i-Kavir in Iran.

**Places and Regions**

Topographical variety can be seen in the mountain ranges. The Atlas Mountains lie in northwest Africa, separating the Sahara Desert from land near the Mediterranean Sea. Since this land area is arable and has a comfortable Mediterranean climate, there are large cities located here, such as Casablanca, Rabat, Algiers, Tunis, and Tripoli. The Elburz Mountains in Iran and the Taurus Mountains in Turkey are a link between the Himalayas of Central Asia to the east and the Alps of Europe to the west.

The Arabian Peninsula, sometimes called Arabia, is shaped like a huge boot. It is mostly desert and contains several nations, the largest of which is Saudi Arabia.

# Water Bodies

The scarcity of water in the Middle East is an important fact of life and is crucial to understanding the region's history. Apart from their life-sustaining importance, water bodies have also had vital maritime and strategic influences.

GLOBAL
CONCEPTS

Scarcity

CONCEPTS
GLOBAL

The largest bodies of water in the area are the five surrounding seas—the Caspian, Black, Mediterranean, Red, and Arabian. They have always been a source of fish. The "pathway" provided by the Mediterranean and its Suez Canal link to the Red Sea and then to the Gulf of Aden has brought Europe "closer" to the southwestern, southern, and eastern parts of Asia. The Mediterranean has served as a highway of conquest, commerce, and culture. In ancient times, Roman legions traveled across the Mediterranean eastward to the Levant (lands touching the eastern Mediterranean, such as modern-day Syria, Lebanon, and Israel), and Phoenician traders traveled westward from the Levant to North Africa. The Persian Gulf, which leads into the Arabian Sea, was a crucial battleground in the Iran-Iraq War of the 1980s. It was also important in 1991 during Operation Desert Storm (also known as the Persian Gulf War), which involved a U.S.-led coalition against Iraq. The Persian Gulf area contains most of the world's oil reserves, and so it is a strategic route through which oil tankers pass, many bound for Japan, the United States, and Europe. Finally, the Bosporus–Sea of Marmara–Dardanelles Strait route from the Black Sea to the Aegean Sea and Mediterranean Sea is of paramount importance to Russia and the Ukraine. As it was for ships of the former Soviet Union, it is the only way for ships of these nations to reach the warm navigable waters of the Mediterranean Sea.

GLOBAL
CONCEPTS

Culture

CONCEPTS
GLOBAL

GEOGRAPHY

Use of Geography

WORLD ISSUES

War and
Peace

From ancient times until today, the four major rivers of the Middle East have greatly affected patterns of settlement. They are the Tigris, Euphrates, Nile, and Jordan. Because of the region's arid climate, these water bodies are very valuable. Except for the coasts of Turkey and the Levant, rainfall is practically nonexistent in the Middle East.

GEOGRAPHY

Physical Settings

1. The Tigris and Euphrates rivers originate in the Taurus Mountains of Turkey and flow southeastward a few miles from each other. They converge (meet) in Iraq and flow as one, the Shatt-al-Arab, past the Strait of Hormuz into the Persian Gulf. The Shatt-al-Arab region, like all delta areas, has rich soil. It is also of strategic value because of the nearby oil deposits and ports. Consequently, it was the scene of much fighting during the 1980s Iran-Iraq War and the 1991 Persian Gulf War.

The area between the Tigris and Euphrates rivers was referred

WORLD ISSUES

World
Trade and
Finance

**GEOGRAPHY**

Spatial Terms

to in ancient times as Mesopotamia ("land between the two rivers"). Because it was well irrigated and able to support large numbers of people, it was the site of one of the early river valley civilizations. It was part of an arc-shaped region called the "fertile crescent," which extended from the eastern shores of the Mediterranean Sea to the Persian Gulf. The ancient city of Babylon was in Mesopotamia. Modern-day Baghdad, the capital of Iraq, lies on the Tigris River, just north of the ruins of Babylon.

GLOBAL
CONCEPTS

Environment

CONCEPTS
GLOBAL

**GEOGRAPHY**

Physical Settings

2. The other major river valley civilization in the Middle East arose in ancient Egypt, along the Nile River, the world's longest river. The Blue Nile, with its source in Central Africa, and the White Nile, with its source in East Africa, converge in the Sudan and flow northward into the Mediterranean Sea. When the Nile overflows its banks, the waters deposit silt and make the nearby land very fertile. The Aswan High Dam was built in 1970 to control the Nile's floodwaters. Since over 95 percent of Egypt is desert, the vast majority of Egyptians live along the narrow strip of land along the Nile River. The ancient cities of Thebes and Alexandria (in the delta) are on the river, as are the present-day Egyptian capital of Cairo and the Sudanese capital of Khartoum.

**GEOGRAPHY**

Environment
and Society

3. The Jordan River is smaller than the other three rivers, but it is vital to the peoples of Lebanon, Syria, Jordan, and Israel. It flows southward from highland areas in Lebanon, Syria, and Israel and makes irrigation possible along its banks. However, use of its waters has led to political quarrels between the nations through which the Jordan River runs.

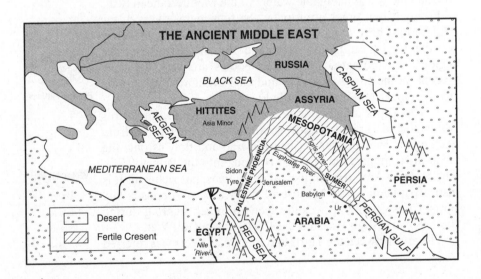

THE ANCIENT MIDDLE EAST

The Jordan River has had historical and political significance. It was an important source of water in ancient times. Jericho, one of the earliest urban sites in the world, lies only six miles west of the Jordan River. The land portion just west of the river, administered by Israel and the PA (Palestine Authority), is called the West Bank as well as by its biblical names—Judea and Samaria. It was under illegal Jordanian control until Jordan's attack on Israel during the Six-Day War of June 1967. (See Era VII, Part D.) The river is also important because of its biblical significance. For Jews and Christians, the Jordan River is especially noteworthy for beliefs about events that occurred near it concerning such figures as Moses, Joshua, and Jesus.

The Jordan is also economically significant. Its waters flow into the Sea of Galilee and, farther south, into the Dead Sea. The Sea of Galilee has been a source of fish from ancient days until the present. The Dead Sea is the lowest point on the earth and is the end point for the Jordan's waters. Unique natural conditions have made the Dead Sea area a valuable source of chemicals, such as potash and phosphates. Israel has constructed a major chemical complex there and has invited Jordan's participation. Both Israeli and Jordanian companies have speeded up natural evaporation in order to extract valuable mineral salts from the Dead Sea.

## REVIEW QUESTIONS

*Multiple Choice.* Select the letter of the answer that correctly completes each statement.

1. Which phrase refers to only one continent?
   A. Near East
   B. Middle East
   C. SWASIA
   D. "crossroads of the world"

2. Which pair of water bodies is incorrectly matched?
   A. Tigris River–Persian Gulf
   B. Persian Gulf–Strait of Hormuz
   C. Nile River–Arabian Sea
   D. Jordan River–Dead Sea

3. The "fertile crescent" was known historically for the early growth of
   A. manufacturing
   B. civilizations
   C. architecture
   D. water conservation

4. The Rub-al Khali refers to a
   A. city
   B. desert
   C. seaport
   D. mountain

5. The Middle East has been described as the "crossroads of the world." Which fact would best support this statement?
   A. Most of the world's oil reserves are there.
   B. The Suez Canal is an important waterway.
   C. Parts of three continents intersect there.
   D. Water bodies surround the region.

6. The area between the Tigris and Euphrates rivers was once known as
   A. Arabia
   B. Palestine
   C. Asia Minor
   D. Mesopotamia

## II. ECONOMIC GEOGRAPHY OF THE MIDDLE EAST

### Agriculture

It is important to remember that barely 15 percent of the land in the Middle East is arable (good for farming). Moreover, inadequate rainfall, large desert areas, and a scarcity of water are obstacles to agricultural development. In addition to these natural obstacles, the traditional system of landownership, with only a very small number of people controlling the little arable land, has also made it difficult to grow enough food to support the increasing population. The major crops are cereal grains, such as wheat and barley, and olives, grapes, and dates, which have been cultivated since ancient times.

Israel's ability to grow oranges and other citrus fruits while "making the desert bloom" has enabled it to export food. Its "drip irrigation" system has been very successful. Egypt has built up a substantial cotton industry. The Aswan High Dam along the Nile has added to Egypt's agricultural productivity.

Over 75 percent of the people in Arab countries are farmers (fellahin), who have traditionally leased the land as tenants from wealthy landowners. However, land-reform laws in several countries, including Egypt, Syria, and Iraq, have redistributed the land so that more farmers have become landowners. Nevertheless, primitive farming techniques prevent farmers from getting high crop yields from their lands.

In Israel's kibbutz movement, land is held collectively by a large group of people who work the land. There are few private landowners. Advanced farming techniques used in Israel have resulted in food surpluses.

Ever since biblical times, sheep herding has been carried on. Consequently, lamb has been a basic part of the diet of the people of the Middle East.

### Industrial Production

The major natural resource in the Middle East is oil. Most of this precious resource is found in nations such as Saudi Arabia, Iraq, Kuwait, and Iran, which border the Persian Gulf. It is estimated that most of the world's oil reserves are in the Middle East. Since the oil-rich nations produce more than they need, they are able to export millions of barrels a year. From these exports, the oil-rich nations have become very wealthy.

GEOGRAPHY

Physical Settings

WORLD ISSUES

Economic
Growth and
Development

GLOBAL
CONCEPTS

Change

CONCEPTS
GLOBAL

INTRODUCTION

WORLD ISSUES

Economic
Growth and
Development

GLOBAL
CONCEPTS
Interdependence

CONCEPTS
GLOBAL

**Growth of the Oil Industry.** From about 1900 to 1970, oil production in the Middle East was dominated largely by foreigners—British, French, Dutch, and American. The chief reason for this was that foreigners were able to supply most of the factors of production. (The four factors of production are land, labor, capital, and management—those things that are necessary to make a product.) While the Middle Eastern nations had the land on which oil was first discovered in the early 1900s, they did not have enough of the other three factors of production to produce the oil themselves. Foreigners supplied the other three factors: labor (skilled workers), capital (this refers to both money and capital goods, such as oil wells and drills,

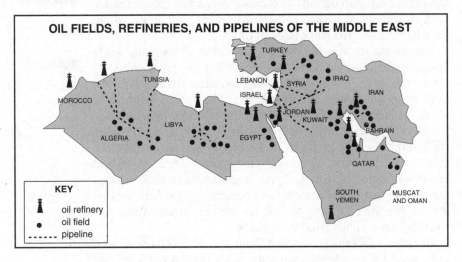

OIL FIELDS, REFINERIES, AND PIPELINES OF THE MIDDLE EAST

KEY
oil refinery
oil field
pipeline

necessary to produce the oil), and management (skilled managers and engineers).

In any economic relationship, both sides agree to give certain things to each other. By providing labor, capital, and management, the foreigners received concessions (permission to use the land) from the oil-rich nations. The foreigners also promised to produce and sell the oil and to give royalties (a percentage of the money earned by selling the oil) to the oil-rich nations. Some foreign companies also agreed to train people from these nations in oil-production techniques.

By the 1970s, these nations wanted higher royalties and more control over the oil industry. Some of them nationalized (took over) the oil fields. Creation of OPEC (Organization of Petroleum Exporting Countries)—an organization of major oil-rich nations in Asia, Africa, and Latin America that is domi-

WORLD ISSUES

Energy:
Resources and
Allocations

nated by the Arab nations—was another step in reducing foreign influence in the oil industry. By the 1990s, the oil-rich nations had achieved complete control over their oil and had become very wealthy.

**Impact of Wealth Gained by Oil.** The Arab nations became very wealthy from the large amount of money ("petro dollars") paid to them by countries that had to import oil. Because they controlled so much oil, the OPEC nations were able to charge almost any price they wanted. The acquisition of vast amounts of money has had important consequences both internally (inside these nations) and externally (relations with other countries).

**GEOGRAPHY**

**Use of Geography**

1. *Internal impact.* Although some Arab rulers have used the newly acquired money for themselves, an increasing tendency has been to use this wealth in ways that would benefit their people. As a result, a dramatic increase in the standard of living has occurred in such nations as Saudi Arabia, where new highways, houses, hospitals, and schools have been built. This rapid increase in modernization has, however, clashed with some traditional values regarding marriages, child-rearing practices, and attitudes toward women in the region. The increased emphasis on material comforts and secular (worldly, nonspiritual) concerns associated with increasing wealth has been one reason for the growing influence both of modernization and of Western values on traditional Islamic culture.

GLOBAL CONCEPTS
**Diversity**
CONCEPTS GLOBAL

2. *External impact.* The oil-rich nations of the Middle East have gained more power and respect in international affairs because of their control of oil and because of their newly acquired wealth. For example, by refusing to export oil or by increasing its export of oil to a given nation, an Arab nation can "pressure" that nation to do things a certain way. (Saudi Arabia's embargo [denial] of oil shipments to the United States in 1973 to 1974 was designed to get the United States to behave in a certain way towards Israel.) Many "petro-dollars" have been used by Arab investors to buy up property and businesses in other nations. (An increasing amount of land in New York City and London was sold to Arabs.)

GLOBAL CONCEPTS
**Interdependence**
CONCEPTS GLOBAL

**WORLD ISSUES**

World Trade and Finance

3. The rich oil deposits in the Caspian Sea will be transmitted, most likely, via pipelines to ports on the Black Sea and the Mediterranean Sea.

## MAJOR CITIES IN THE MIDDLE EAST

| Country | City |
| --- | --- |
| Algeria | Algiers |
| Egypt | Cairo |
| | Alexandria |
| Iran | Teheran |
| | Isfahan |
| Iraq | Baghdad |
| | Basrah |
| | Mosul |
| Israel | Jerusalem |
| | Tel Aviv |
| | Haifa |
| Jordan | Amman |
| Lebanon | Beirut |
| Libya | Tripoli |
| | Benghazi |
| Morocco | Casablanca |
| | Rabat |
| Saudi Arabia | Riyadh |
| | Jidda |
| | Mecca |
| Syria | Damascus |
| | Aleppo |
| Tunisia | Tunis |
| Turkey | Istanbul |
| | Ankara |
| | Izmir |

# Current Economic Issues

1. Many Middle Eastern nations need foreign aid to help them meet economic problems. Egypt is among the five largest recipients of U.S. aid.

2. Overpopulation and a growth in cities have put a strain on the economy in some areas. Growing numbers of people are demanding that their governments do more to improve living standards. These demands are part of the movement described as a "revolution of rising expectations." They are also some of the reasons for the 2011 protests known as the "Arab Spring." These protests occurred in most of the Arab countries from Tunisia to Syria.

3. Extensive spending on military weapons, especially in Libya, Egypt, Syria, Saudi Arabia, Iran, and Iraq (prior to the war beginning in 2003), has taken away funds needed for economic and social development. With the exception of Egypt, the military threat posed by these nations to Israel has forced Israel to spend large amounts of money on arms for defense.

4. Greater regional cooperation could help the nations of the Middle East in finding solutions to common problems. For example, removal of political barriers between Israel and all the Arab nations, as well as those between some of the Arab nations themselves, could lead to increased trade, reduction of arms spending, and improved desalinization projects. (These projects would purify sea water and make it drinkable by removing the salt content.)

5. The frequent changes in world oil prices often lowers the income received from "petro-dollars" and affects the region's economy. Also, the search for alternative sources of energy combined with energy-conservation measures may affect the global demand for oil. Thus, in 1994, when a surplus of world oil supplies led to a drop in oil prices, Saudi Arabia cut its budget by 20 percent. This meant that the government would have to reduce spending on medical care, fuel, and food for its people. These reductions could result in political tension, since the Saudi Arabian population had grown accustomed to large government expenditures for these items.

6. Political tension linked to an economic issue can also be seen in a decision by Turkey to build a series of twenty-two dams in Anatolia, its southeastern region. The dams, part of the GAP project and including the massive Ataturk Dam, would aid irrigation and produce great amounts of energy in Turkey. GAP, an abbreviation for Turkish words, is the name for Turkey's massive agricultural and hydroelectric power project. The project would, however, affect the flow of water along the

**WORLD ISSUES**

Population

GLOBAL CONCEPTS

**Choice**

CONCEPTS GLOBAL

GLOBAL CONCEPTS

**Interdependence**

CONCEPTS GLOBAL

**WORLD ISSUES**

Energy:
Resources and
Allocations

Tigris and Euphrates rivers, whose sources are in Turkey. Both Syria and Iraq are worried about the project's impact on water in their countries and have voiced their concerns to the Turkish government.

7. Israel's economy has improved during the 1990s and early 2000s, particularly with the growth of high-tech industries. Of significance has been the emigration of Jews from the former Soviet Union, many of whom are highly skilled engineers and scientists. This growth, from what was once an agriculture-based economy, has been described as going from "Jaffa to Java" (Jaffa oranges to a computer program). Israel has become a very attractive place for foreign investment. It is the world leader in the percentage of the economy that is spent on research and development. Yet Israel must find ways of housing these immigrants as well as those from Ethiopia.

8. Since the end of the Lebanese Civil War in 1990, the capital city of Beirut has slowly regained its status as a major commercial center. Evidence can be seen in the increasing number of banks, businesses, hotels, skyscrapers, and restaurants.

9. Tourism continues to be a prime source of income for those Middle Eastern nations that have sites of religious and historic importance. Among them is Egypt, where the government has been concerned about attacks on foreigners by Islamic militants as well as the protests and political changes in 2011.

10. Much of the Arab world faces great challenges, as noted in the United Nations' Arab Human Development Report. Produced in 2005 by a group of Arab scholars led by Egypt, it concluded that the Arab people suffer from three severe problems: a lack of freedom, a deficit of knowledge, and a lack of women's empowerment.

In the last few years, discovery was made of a potentially abundant source of natural gas in the eastern Mediterranean Sea. Israel, Lebanon, and Turkey, along with Cyprus and Greece, have expressed great interest in developing this source.

# REVIEW QUESTIONS

*Multiple Choice.* Select the letter of the answer that correctly completes each statement.

1. During the first half of this century, foreign oil companies provided all the factors of production needed in the oil industry except for
   A. labor
   B. capital
   C. land
   D. management

2. What did these foreign companies expect in return for their supplying important factors of production?
   A. "petro-dollars"
   B. territory
   C. pensions
   D. concessions

3. Arable land is land that is good for
   A. growing food
   B. producing oil
   C. manufacturing steel
   D. building highways

4. The Aswan High Dam has increased the agricultural productivity of
   A. Syria
   B. Iran
   C. Egypt
   D. Israel

5. Which action by OPEC nations would most upset foreign oil companies?
   A. desalinization
   B. nationalization
   C. modernization
   D. Westernization

6. The decision by Arab governments on how best to use their "petro-dollars" is an issue that can be described as
   A. human
   B. cultural
   C. physical
   D. economic

7. Most of the oil-producing regions of the Middle East are located around the
   A. Dead Sea
   B. Mediterranean Sea
   C. Persian Gulf
   D. Suez Canal

8. Turkey's dam project is of grave concern to people in those nations whose capital cities are
   A. Cairo and Riyadh
   B. Baghdad and Damascus
   C. Teheran and Kuwait City
   D. Amman and Beirut

# III. HUMAN AND CULTURAL GEOGRAPHY OF THE MIDDLE EAST

## Overview

As a region covering parts of three continents and often described as "the crossroads of the world," the Middle East contains a variety of people. Three major religions developed here— Judaism, Christianity, and Islam. People live in both small villages and large cities. Over 90 percent of the people of the Middle East can be described as Semites or Semitic. These terms describe a family of languages that includes Arabic and Hebrew. The terms are also used to refer to anyone who speaks one of these languages and who belongs to an ethnic group that follows certain customs. An Arab is a person who speaks Arabic and who follows traditions associated with an Arab way of life, that is, traditions connected with existence in a desert environment in the Middle East. Although most Muslims in the Middle East are Arabs, the word "Arab" does not refer to a particular religious group. (A small number of people in Egypt, Israel, and Lebanon consider themselves to be Christian Arabs. Muslims in Turkey and Iran do not consider themselves to be Arabs.)

The population of the Middle East continues to grow at a very fast pace. Saudi Arabia, for example, had a population growth rate in 2004 of 2.3 percent (or twenty-three people per thousand). This is one of the highest rates in the world. (The growth rate of a nation is based upon the difference between both the number of births and migrants entering and the number of deaths and people leaving the nation.) Egypt also has a high population growth rate. As these rates continue to increase, high population density or severe overcrowding in cities occurs. The demands for electricity, food, telephone service, and other daily needs can easily outpace what a government can provide.

GLOBAL CONCEPTS
**Diversity**
CONCEPTS GLOBAL

GLOBAL CONCEPTS
**Identity**
CONCEPTS GLOBAL

**WORLD ISSUES**

Population

## Islam: The Main Religion in the Middle East

Islam is the religion practiced by over 90 percent of the people in the Middle East. It was the third major religion to develop in the area, Judaism being the first and Christianity the second. Many Islamic beliefs come from Judaism and Christianity. The most important element common to all three religions is monotheism, or the belief in the existence of one God, which was first stated by the Jews. The followers of Islam call this one God Allah. People who are followers of Islam submit themselves to the will of Allah and are called Muslims. The word "Muslim"

GLOBAL CONCEPTS
**Culture**
CONCEPTS GLOBAL

31

is a religious term, while the word "Arab" is a cultural term. The word "Islam" is defined as "submission."

**The Importance of Muhammad.** Muhammad lived from 570 to 632 in what is now Saudi Arabia. Muslims believe that he was the fourth and most important prophet chosen by God (Allah) to teach and spread holy ideas and thoughts. Muslims accept most of the teachings of Judaism and Christianity and therefore accept the existence of Abraham, Moses, and Jesus as prophets. However, Muslims view these leaders as simply preparing the way for Muhammad. The life of Muhammad is essential for understanding Islam, as the lives of Abraham and Moses and Jesus are essential for understanding Judaism and Christianity. All four leaders are considered to have had direct communication with God at specific moments when each was alone. Events in the lives of each have profound religious meaning for the faithful; for example, Abraham with Isaac at Mt. Moriah, Moses at Mt. Sinai, the birth and crucifixion of Jesus.

Muhammad, who was born in Makkah (formerly spelled "Mecca"), claimed to have had revelations from God and visions while sleeping in a cave. These revelations, received through the angel Gabriel, were collected and written down in the Quran (formerly spelled "Koran"). The Quran—"the recitations"—became the holy book of Islam. Muhammad began to preach, but he was scorned and driven from Makkah.

GLOBAL CONCEPTS

**Empathy**

CONCEPTS GLOBAL

He fled to Medina in 622. This flight from Makkah to Medina is called the Hijra (formerly spelled "Hegira"), and it is considered a very holy event by Muslims. The year 622 marks the first year in the Muslim calendar. Muhammad gained many followers in Medina, raised an army, and was able to take over Makkah. Makkah was an important city because of its economic activity and because it contained a holy shrine called the Kabbah. The Kabbah is a black stone building, approximately 45 feet high. Muslims believe that it stands on the site where God commanded Abraham and Ishmael, one of his sons, to build a place of worship. Today, the Kabbah lies within the Great Mosque at Makkah. Muslims thus consider Makkah to be their holiest city, with the Kabbah their holiest site.

Muhammad died in Medina, which is Islam's second holiest city. Muslims also believe that one night, Muhammad rode to Jerusalem on a winged mare and stepped on a rock before going to heaven. He then returned to the rock and rode back to Makkah by dawn. (This rock is the one on which Jews believe Abraham was going to sacrifice his other son, Isaac.) In 637 Muslims conquered Jerusalem and soon thereafter built a shrine over this rock. This building is called the Dome of the Rock. Consequently, Jerusalem is considered Islam's third holiest city.

**Basic Beliefs of Muslims.** The five basic obligations, or "pillars," of Islam, are described in the chart below, with corresponding similarities in Judaism and Christianity.

| The Five Obligations | Islam | Judaism | Christianity |
|---|---|---|---|
| Proclamation of faith | "There is no God but Allah, and Muhammad is his prophet." | "Hear oh Israel, the Lord our God, the Lord is one." | "There is but one God, creator of heaven, earth, and all things." |
| Prayer | Five time a day, facing Makkah. | Three times a day for some Jews, facing Jerusalem. | Some Christians in the Middle East pray seven times a day. |
| Fasting | During Ramadan, fasting from sunrise to sunset. (Ramadan was the month when the Quran was revealed to Muhammad.) | Fasting on specifically designated days during the year (i.e., Yom Kippur). | Abstinence from certain foods on specifically designated days during the year (for example, Lent, Advent). |
| Almsgiving (charity) | "Whoever does not know that his need of the reward for giving is greater than the poor man's need of the gift is donating his charity in vain." | "The poor person does more for the giver than the giver does for the poor man." | "It is more blessed to give than to receive." |
| Pilgrimage (visit to a holy area) | An obligation to make the *haj* (a visit to Makkah) once in a lifetime. One who makes the haj is called a haji. | Jerusalem is holy because it is the site of the first two Jewish temples and contains the Western Wall. | Bethlehem is holy as the birthplace of Jesus; Jerusalem is important as the site of his crucifixion. |

## Other Items

| | | | |
|---|---|---|---|
| Holy Books | Quran contains 114 suras or chapters. The Shari'a is a code of law based upon the Quran. | Old Testament (also called the Tanach, containing the Torah and other writings). The Talmud has commentaries on the Tanach. | The Bible (contains the Old Testament and the New Testament.) |
| Groupings | Sunni Muslims and Shi'ite Muslims. Sunnis are the larger group. Shi'ites live mostly in Iran. | Orthodox, Conservative, and Reform. | Catholic, Protestant, and Eastern Orthodox. |

## Important Information About Islam

GLOBAL CONCEPTS

**Identity**

CONCEPTS GLOBAL

1. Shi'ite Muslims in Iran, as well as scattered groupings of Muslims in other countries, claim that many traditional Islamic values are being lost in the current world. They would like to see a return to traditional, fundamental values and thus have been called Islamic fundamentalists or Islamists. They are worried about such things as the growth of materialism, introduction of Western values, and changing the role of women. Their protests against some Arab governments as well as their preaching have been a source of concern. An example of an Islamic fundamentalist was the former leader of Iran, Ayatollah Khomeini. Another example was the former Taliban rule in Afghanistan.

2. The crescent and the star, symbols of Islam, are found in the flags and currencies of many Islamic nations.

3. There is no central controlling figure for all Muslims, similar to the position of pope for Catholics.

4. Muslims believe that the Quran was revealed to Muhammad in Arabic, and translations were not allowed. In order to read the Quran, one had to know Arabic. Therefore, Arabic became a common language for all Muslims, whether they were Arab, such as people in Egypt, or non-Arab, such as people in Pakistan and Indonesia.

5. Although Islam began in the Middle East, the largest Islamic nations are not there. They are Indonesia, Pakistan, and Bangladesh. While most Arabs are Muslim, not all Muslims are Arabs.

6. Islam is the official state religion of Egypt, as declared in its constitution. The same is true of Saudi Arabia, although it is much less tolerant of other faiths. For example, no Christian churches or Jewish temples are allowed to exist there. Christian and Jewish members of the American armed forces stationed there were told not to wear any religious symbols. Non-Muslims may not enter Makkah. Turkey, however, although a majority Muslim nation, allows religious diversity. Israel, although a majority Jewish nation, is a democracy, and permits religious freedom for all faiths. Christians live freely in Turkey and Israel, but have suffered persecution in Egypt and the Palestinian territories.

## Language

As you read previously, Arabic is the most widely spoken language in the Middle East. Along with Hebrew, spoken mainly in Israel, it is a Semitic language. Several other languages are also spoken in the Middle East. Farsi, or Persian, is spoken mainly in Iran. Turkish is spoken in Turkey. The Turkish script is written in Latin letters instead of Arabic, the result of a change made by the Turkish leader Kemal Ataturk in 1928. This was a break with tradition, as was his decision to translate the Quran from Arabic into Turkish. European languages are spoken mostly in areas that were under European influence. Thus, English is used in Egypt, while French is used in Lebanon and Syria. (As of today, the Quran has been translated into many languages.)

GLOBAL
CONCEPTS

**Change**

CONCEPTS
GLOBAL

# REVIEW QUESTIONS

*Multiple Choice.* Select the letter of the answer that correctly completes each statement.

1. Which pair of languages has the most in common?
   A. Arabic and Turkish
   B. Turkish and Hebrew
   C. Hebrew and Arabic
   D. Turkish and Farsi

2. Shi'ites and Sunnis refer to groupings of people who are
   A. Catholics
   B. Jews
   C. Muslims
   D. Protestants

3. Many Egyptians speak English, whereas many Lebanese speak French. The reasons are the result of history and
   A. political systems
   B. cultural diffusion
   C. belief patterns
   D. increased interdependence

# SECTION 2: SOUTH ASIA

## I. PHYSICAL GEOGRAPHY OF SOUTH ASIA

### Overview

The region known as South Asia is also called the Indian or Asian subcontinent. It is a very large area, bigger in size and population than all of Western Europe. Consequently, it could be called a continent by itself except for the fact that it is attached to the Asian mainland. The subcontinent is slightly less than half the size of the United States. India, called "Bharat" in that country, is the seventh largest nation in the world in area. The subcontinent contains six nations: India, Pakistan, Bangladesh, Bhutan, Nepal, and the island nation of Sri Lanka.

**GEOGRAPHY**

**Spatial Terms**

GLOBAL
CONCEPTS

**Environment**

CONCEPTS
GLOBAL

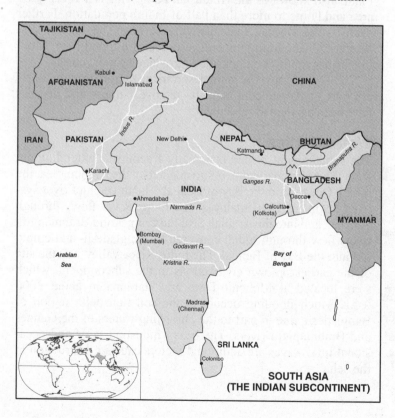

**SOUTH ASIA
(THE INDIAN SUBCONTINENT)**

## Topography

The region's topography has had a dramatic impact on political, economic, and cultural patterns. Its land features are one reason for the area's being open to greater foreign influences from the west than from the north and east. The Himalaya Mountains in the north contain Mount Everest, the highest peak in the world. The presence of these mountains has acted as a barrier to contact with peoples to the north and northeast of the region, separating the subcontinent from the rest of Asia. In the northwest, openings in the mountains, such as the Khyber Pass, have resulted in the movement of peoples, goods, and ideas. This movement, an example of cultural diffusion, has generally been from west to east and has included the Aryans (2000 B.C.E.), Alexander the Great (327 B.C.E.), Muslims (1000 C.E.), and Afghan refugees (1980s). As a result, a traveler to the subcontinent today would find a mixture of many ethnic groups, religions, and languages. The northern part of the region is subject to severe earthquakes and mudslides such as those that occurred in 2005.

South of the Himalaya Mountains lies the Indo-Gangetic Plain, also known as the Hindustan Plain. This is a very fertile area and home to more than half of India's population. Farther south is the Deccan Plateau, lying between the Eastern and Western Ghats. Many mineral resources are found here. Moving farther south, one finds good farm land near the coasts.

The Thar Desert, the main desert in the region, is in the western part of the subcontinent. Its relative flatness and dryness have been barriers to settlement.

## Water Bodies

The subcontinent, which is actually a peninsula extending out from the Asian mainland, is surrounded by the Arabian Sea, the Indian Ocean, and the Bay of Bengal. The three chief river systems begin in the Himalayas: the Indus River flows through Pakistan and into the Arabian Sea; the Ganges and Brahmaputra rivers flow through India, converge in Bangladesh, and empty out into the Bay of Bengal. The Indus River Valley was the site of the earliest known civilizations in the subcontinent, which were located at Mohenjo-Daro and Harappa in about 3000 B.C.E. Much flooding occurs in the soil-rich delta region of Bangladesh, due in part to the onrushing waters of the Ganges and Brahmaputra rivers. The heavy monsoon rains and occasional tidal waves are additional factors causing destruction in the delta.

## Impact of the Monsoon

The monsoon rains occur from June to September, bringing to the subcontinent 90 percent of its annual rainfall. They can be a blessing, bringing crop surpluses, or a curse, bringing famine, flooding, and drought, depending on their timing and the amount of rain that falls. The monsoon's direction is generally northeasterly, coming across the Arabian Sea and affecting mainly northcentral India and Bangladesh.

**WORLD ISSUES**

Environmental
Concerns

**GEOGRAPHY**

**Environment
and Society**

**INTRODUCTION**

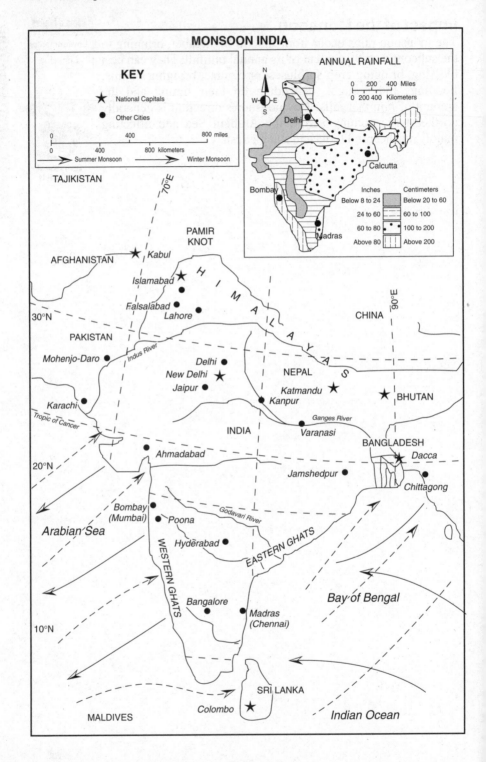

# MONSOON INDIA

### KEY

★ National Capitals

● Other Cities

0 — 400 — 800 miles
0 — 400 — 800 kilometers

→ Summer Monsoon  → Winter Monsoon

## ANNUAL RAINFALL

0 — 200 — 400 Miles
0 — 200 400 Kilometers

Delhi

Bombay

Calcutta

Madras

| Inches | Centimeters |
|---|---|
| Below 8 to 24 | Below 20 to 60 |
| 24 to 60 | 60 to 100 |
| 60 to 80 | 100 to 200 |
| Above 80 | Above 200 |

TAJIKISTAN

70°E

PAMIR KNOT

AFGHANISTAN  ★ Kabul

★ Islamabad

Falsalabad ●
● Lahore

HIMALAYAS

CHINA

90°E

30°N

PAKISTAN

Mohenjo-Daro ●

Indus River

● Delhi
New Delhi ★
Jaipur ●

NEPAL

Katmandu ★
● Kanpur

★ BHUTAN

Karachi ●

Tropic of Cancer

INDIA

Ganges River

Varanasi ●

BANGLADESH

★ Dacca

20°N

Ahmadabad ●

Jamshedpur ●

Chittagong

Bombay
(Mumbai) ●
● Poona

Godavari River

Arabian Sea

Hyderabad ●

WESTERN GHATS

EASTERN GHATS

Bay of Bengal

10°N

Bangalore ●

● Madras
(Chennai)

SRI LANKA

MALDIVES

Colombo ★

Indian Ocean

## REVIEW QUESTIONS

*Fact or Opinion.* If the statement is a fact, write F. If the statement is an opinion, write O.

1. India has been more influenced from the west than from the east.

2. A good monsoon is proof of God's blessings upon the Indian subcontinent.

3. A drought will occur if there is a poor monsoon and little water in reserve in India's dams.

4. The largest nations in physical size on the subcontinent are India and Pakistan.

# II. ECONOMIC GEOGRAPHY OF SOUTH ASIA

## Agriculture

In recent decades, food production in India has increased. Self-sufficiency has been achieved, at least temporarily, despite some bad monsoon years. Consequently, imports from nations such as the United States have declined. Crop production focuses mainly on rice, wheat, cotton, tea, jute, and sugar cane.

Much of this agricultural development has resulted from the Green Revolution, that is, the use of modern science and technology to improve agricultural productivity. Examples of modern technology include laboratory-produced fertilizers, insecticides, and improved seeds, which are high-yielding and drought-resistant, such as IR-8. Scientists involved in these efforts are known as agronomists. A leading figure in this work has been the American agronomist Dr. Norman Borlaugh (winner of a Nobel Peace Prize in 1970). Critics, however, have noted some negative aspects of the Green Revolution:

1. Resistance among farmers to new planting and landholding patterns.

2. Higher financial costs when using new technology and machinery (more readily used by "agribusiness," or large landholders, rather than small farmers).

3. Need for better nationwide infrastructure, such as storage facilities, dams, and highways.

4. The taste of the food produced is different from traditional crops.

## Industrial Production

India has some of the world's largest steel mills and is a major producer of bauxite. Other major industrial products include textiles, machinery, cement, and scientific instruments. Recently, Indian scientists have made advances in nuclear energy and in developing space satellites. India is the most industrially advanced nation in the subcontinent and has one of the world's ten highest GNPs. Nevertheless, as is true of all industrialized societies around the globe, India must find ways of coping with the environmental consequences of industrialization. The tragic accident involving the Union Carbide Company at Bhopal in 1984 and the destructive effects of air pollution on the Taj Mahal, for example, have been of great concern to India.

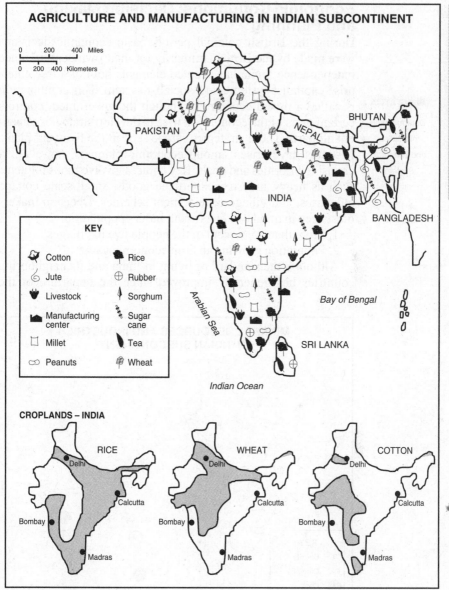

## AGRICULTURE AND MANUFACTURING IN INDIAN SUBCONTINENT

0   200   400   Miles

0   200   400   Kilometers

PAKISTAN

NEPAL

BHUTAN

INDIA

BANGLADESH

Arabian Sea

Bay of Bengal

SRI LANKA

Indian Ocean

### KEY

- 🌸 Cotton
- 🍃 Jute
- 🐃 Livestock
- 🏭 Manufacturing center
- ⬜ Millet
- 🥜 Peanuts
- 🌳 Rice
- ⊕ Rubber
- ↟ Sorghum
- ⚒ Sugar cane
- 🍂 Tea
- 🌾 Wheat

### CROPLANDS – INDIA

RICE

Delhi

Calcutta

Bombay

Madras

WHEAT

Delhi

Calcutta

Bombay

Madras

COTTON

Delhi

Calcutta

Bombay

Madras

43

# Economic Conditions: Decision Making and Planning

During the British colonial period, basic economic decisions were made by the British, primarily for their own benefit. Since independence, India has adopted elements both of a free enterprise/capitalist system and a socialist system. This combination is called a mixed economy. Although the government controls certain parts of the economy, it tries to develop strategies to benefit all parts. These strategies can be seen in the five-year plans. Disputes have arisen among economic planners, however, in choosing priorities and goals. Key choices involve funds for items such as heavy industry, exportable goods, small-scale cottage industries, and village development schemes. Decision makers must keep in mind two facts about India's population:

1. More than 75 percent of the people live in villages.

2. Population growth can limit economic gains.

Although the standard of living in India and its neighboring countries has generally improved since the departure of the

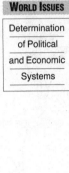

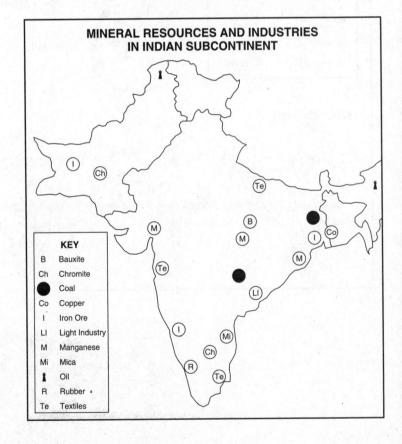

**MINERAL RESOURCES AND INDUSTRIES IN INDIAN SUBCONTINENT**

KEY

| | |
|---|---|
| B | Bauxite |
| Ch | Chromite |
| ● | Coal |
| Co | Copper |
| I | Iron Ore |
| LI | Light Industry |
| M | Manganese |
| Mi | Mica |
| ♦ | Oil |
| R | Rubber |
| Te | Textiles |

44

British, severe poverty and malnutrition still exist in many areas. These features are evident in such large cities as Calcutta as well as in the villages.

The attempts by nations such as India to raise sharply the standard of living for all citizens, as well as promote economic growth, have necessitated borrowing money from overseas and importing needed goods. Consequently, India continues to face a large foreign debt and a trade imbalance (where the value of imports exceeds that of exports).

Since the 1990s India has made significant moves to boost its economy. It has attracted Western support by approving more foreign investment projects. It privatized some state-controlled companies, cut interest rates, and raised the ceiling on executive pay. The last move was designed to induce talented Indian managers to stay in India, and thereby reduce India's "brain drain" (migration by one nation's skilled and educated people to another nation, where they hope to gain better positions and more money). Many observers have noted that the economy would benefit if India could find ways to end the frequent scandals and corruption that have involved some businesspeople and government officials. Another benefit would be a reduction in the vast bureaucracy (large number of offices where permission is needed for commercial ventures). One economist has commented on how this "license-permit-raj" system can slow down investment and invite bribery.

Since the late 1980s successive Indian administrations have focused on encouraging economic reform and foreign investment, bringing the nation's economy more extensively into the network of world trade. The world's leading economic and political powers, including frequent antagonist China, now seek expanded trade and exchange relations with India. The growing urban middle class provides a large, skilled workforce, fostering growth in fields like information technology and software development in areas like Bangalore's "Silicon Valley," making it a popular choice for international companies seeking to outsource work. All this has turned India's stock market into one of the world's fastest rising indicators of economic progress.

The 2004 electoral victory by the Indian National Congress Party and the selection of Manmohan Singh to serve as prime minister created optimism that the pace and nature of reforms would continue and even accelerate. A well-respected economist credited with India's early 1990s economic liberalization plan that forestalled an impending national monetary crisis, Singh and his party nevertheless campaigned on a platform of creating jobs in government-owned companies and production units.

**WORLD ISSUES**

Economic
Growth and
Development

Mr. Singh's government has ushered in a new level of prosperity for many sectors of the Indian economy. Along with Brazil, Russia, and China (the so-called BRIC countries), the nation is now considered a "new economic powerhouse." A burgeoning information technology sector, a newly revitalized industrial capacity, and rising educational levels have contributed to a growing middle class. Internationally, Prime Minister Singh has been hailed for his leadership at meetings of the major economic powers, but at home he has his critics. Some analysts and some very active protestors have criticized the alleged rampant corruption, incompetence, and overstaffing in government.

Thus, only a few years after being considered a near "basket case," India occupies an increasingly influential role in the global economy. Severe problems still exist—poverty, ethnic conflict, inequality, environmental degradation, lagging productivity, high tariffs—and continue to hinder improvements in the standard of living for millions.

Each of India's neighboring nations has its own set of strengths and problems. Internal social and political conflict can short-circuit productive economic decision making. Over 40 percent of Pakistan's labor force is employed in agriculture— the nation is a major exporter of rice, for instance. Its textile industry is a major source of foreign exchange. Other significant industrial products include construction materials, pharmaceuticals, and fertilizer. The country is dependent on imports for many other manufactured goods as well as petroleum products. Significant increases in energy output based on hydroelectric and thermal power have contributed to a more useful and efficient infrastructure. The economy of Sri Lanka, a nation recovering from a long and bloody civil war, is built upon agriculture and tourism. Textiles and apparel, tea and spices, precious gems, and rubber products are among its exports. Impoverished Bangladesh is another agriculture-dependent nation. Principal products are rice, jute, tea, wheat, sugarcane, and tobacco. Most heavy industrial and other manufactured goods must be imported.

*Multiple Choice.* Select the letter of the answer that correctly completes each statement.

1. Agronomists are important individuals in India's economic development plans because they
   A. are knowledgeable about uses of the Internet
   B. have helped build the nation's industrial capacity
   C. support efforts to make the nation more democratic
   D. can help to increase food production

2. Which of the following has the greatest effect on limiting/decreasing per capita food consumption in India?
   A. monsoons
   B. inadequate funds
   C. population increase
   D. government spending

3. To say that India is self-sufficient in agriculture means that it
   A. needs foreign aid
   B. can pay back other nations for food shipments
   C. grows enough food for its people
   D. can avoid famines

4. Norman Borlaugh would be most pleased with India's added production of
   A. space satellites
   B. steel
   C. fertilizer
   D. airplanes

5. In the 1990s, which condition was probably most responsible for stimulating economic growth in India?
   A. a small urban population
   B. an increasing infant mortality rate
   C. a diversity of languages
   D. an increased investment of capital

## III. HUMAN AND CULTURAL GEOGRAPHY OF SOUTH ASIA

### Overview

The most important human feature of South Asia, and in particular of India, is the size of the population. With nearly 1.1 billion people, India ranks as the second largest nation on earth and is the world's most populous democracy. Pakistan and Bangladesh, after Indonesia, are the second and third largest Muslim nations in the world. The study of population patterns in these and other nations is what demography is all about. The ways in which a population views itself and practices certain lifestyles, along with the human values it holds to be important, may be thought of as its culture.

### Demography

India's population is close to four times that of the United States; yet India is only about one-third the physical size of the United States. Consequently, India has a higher population density (population density is determined by dividing a nation's population by its area). This greater crowding can be seen in such large cities as Bombay, Calcutta, Madras, and New Delhi. However, most of India's people live in rural areas. Roughly 75 percent of the population lives in the hundreds of thousands of villages. To "know the village," therefore, is to know India. (See below for more data about villages.)

**WORLD ISSUES**

Population

**GEOGRAPHY**

**Human Systems**

1. *Growth rates.* A nation's annual population growth rate tells us about how fast the nation's population grows each year. The rate is expressed as a percentage and is determined by subtracting the number of deaths per thousand in a given year from the number of births per thousand in the same year. For example, India's birth rate continues to decline, down from twenty-eight per thousand in the 1990s to an estimated twenty-two in 2010; subtract from this figure the death rate of eight per thousand to arrive at a growth rate of fourteen per thousand, or 1.4 percent. (The growth rate in the United States at the same time was less than 0.7 percent.) The growth-rate figure for India is very high and is crucial in that it adds to already existing problems of housing, food, and employment. Indian government officials are very concerned about the high growth rate and try, therefore, to determine ways of reducing it. Present estimates of the nation's population are nearly 1.2 billion; expert projections

have India surpassing China as the world's most populous country by 2025, with its population reaching 1.6 billion by 2050.

### POPULATION GROWTH IN INDIA

| | |
|---|---|
| 1948—345 million | |
| 1957—392 million | |
| 1961—439 million | |
| 1967—501 million | |
| 1971—548 million | |
| 1977—615 million | Growth rate: 1.8% a year |
| 1989—835 million | |
| 1993—897 million | |
| 2001—1.03 billion | |
| 2010—1.21 billion (estimated) | |

2. *Birth rate.* The reasons for a high birth rate in India are generally the same as those for high rates in Pakistan, Bangladesh, and other developing nations that are predominantly rural and agricultural. An agrarian society requires much manual labor, and therefore families tend to have many children to help work the land. Additional factors contributing to a high birth rate include: arranged marriages at an early age; a high infant-mortality rate; children seen as a form of "social security" for their parents in old age; desire for sons to pass on the family name and caste; the low status of women; religious motivations; joint/extended family patterns; and failure to use birth control measures.

GLOBAL
CONCEPTS
**Culture**
CONCEPTS
GLOBAL

3. *Death rate.* The reasons for a decreasing death rate in India are generally the same as those for decreasing death rates throughout the world. These include: increase in food production; better hygienic and sanitary conditions; and the introduction of modern medicine. (A dramatic and welcome example of the last item was the declared eradication of smallpox in India. This disease had long been a leading cause of death among Indians.) The result of a lower death rate means an increase in life expectancy. This has special significance for India, in light of the fact that 36.4 percent of its current population is under fourteen years of age according to the census of 2001.

4. *Attempts to lower the growth rate.* The Indian government has been moderately successful in some regions with the introduction of family-planning programs. These include birth-control clinics, monetary incentives for sterilization, and "Madison Avenue" advertising campaigns advocating the advantages of having a small family. (The few instances of government-mandated birth-control tactics have met with controversy and were considered undemocratic.) Additional national strategies involve improving literacy and education rates, improving

GLOBAL
CONCEPTS
**Choice**
CONCEPTS
GLOBAL

GLOBAL
CONCEPTS
**Citizenship**
CONCEPTS
GLOBAL

employment opportunities for women, and implementation of the Hindu Marriage Act. (This act requires a minimum age of eighteen for men and of fifteen for women to marry.) As India becomes more industrialized and urbanized, its birth rate may decline. Such reduction would follow a pattern that occurred in other nations in the 20th century, such as in Japan, the United States, and Germany.

GLOBAL
CONCEPTS
**Diversity**
CONCEPTS
GLOBAL

## Languages of South Asia

A great diversity of languages is found in India. Sixteen languages are recognized. Of these, the one spoken by the largest number of Indians is Hindi. However, it is spoken by less than half of the population, and mainly in the north. Southern Indians have local languages, such as Tamil, and have objected to any imposition of a uniform national language. Disputes over language have harmful political effects, and in many cases they have fostered stronger ties to people's locality than to their national government. Other principal languages in South Asia include Bengali (Bangladesh), Urdu (Pakistan), and Sinhalese (in Sri Lanka). English is understood by small numbers of people, mainly in urban areas, throughout all nations in South Asia. Among educated people it is a unifying focus. However, many people are wary of using it as an official language because of its link to the age of imperialism.

GLOBAL
CONCEPTS
**Identity**
CONCEPTS
GLOBAL

**PRINCIPAL LANGUAGES OF INDIA AND PAKISTAN**

| India | Pakistan |
|---|---|
| Hindi | Punjabi |
| Telugu | Pushto |
| Bengali | Sindhi |
| Marathi | Saraiki |
| Tamil | Urdu |
| Urdu | |
| Gugerati | |
| Kannada | |
| Malayalam | |
| Oriya | |
| Punjabi | |
| Rajasthani | |
| Assamese | |
| Kashmiri | |

GLOBAL
CONCEPTS
**Empathy**
CONCEPTS
GLOBAL

## The Village

The village is central in understanding India's social structure, as villages contain such a high proportion of India's population. A council of elders in each village, called the panchayat, usually makes rules for the people about local issues, such as sanitation, streets, and family disputes. Families arrange marriages so that young people will marry within their own social group, or caste. This practice is called endogamy. Another village practice is seen in sons' assuming the occupations held by their fathers. This custom, along with the jajmani system, has created self-sufficient communities. (Under the jajmani system, an economic pattern was followed whereby a jajman—a landowner—and members of a caste group would inherit the service relationships and mutual obligations that their immediate ancestors had.)

These customs, along with other traditional practices such as the limited, designated household roles for women, may undergo change as the villages become less isolated from the outside world. Historically, this isolation was the result of poor transportation and communication links. However, the increase in paved roads, electricity, and schools and the introduction of radio and television are making villagers more aware of the world around them and of modern 21st-century cultural patterns. The social changes in village life that these forces have brought about are proceeding slowly. It is uncertain as to which traditional cultural patterns will remain the same, which will be modified, and which will be changed completely.

## Hinduism: The Main Religion in India

As with all the world's great religions, Hinduism is a system of beliefs that provide answers to some of the perennial questions humans have asked. These questions concern the origins and meaning of life and proper conduct toward others.

GLOBAL CONCEPTS

**Identity**

CONCEPTS GLOBAL

Over 80 percent of the people of India consider themselves Hindus. Even though there are differences in some beliefs and practices among Hindus, certain basic ideas are accepted.

1. Each human being occupies a place on the wheel of life (mandala). A person's place on the mandala is determined by the law of karma. According to this law, what happened to a person's soul in a previous life (incarnation) will affect the person's current status. The soul undergoes a process of rebirth, or reincarnation (samsara). Whether reincarnation results in the soul's moving "up" or "down" depends on how a person performed his or her dharma (obligation and behavior based on family and caste).

2. The goal of a Hindu is to achieve moksha (release of the soul from the cycle of birth and rebirth on the mandala).

3. There are many gods and goddesses in Hinduism. However, it could be said that each of these deities is but one form or manifestation of a single God. From its origin in about 3000 B.C.E. until now, the three chief Hindu deities have been Brahma (associated

with creation), Vishnu (associated with preservation), and Shiva (associated with destruction). The most popularly worshiped today are Vishnu and Shiva, either in their own form or in the different male and female forms they take. For example, Vishnu is often worshiped in the form of Rama or Krishna; Shiva is sometimes worshiped as an ascetic doing yoga (a form of meditation) or in the form of Kali or Durga.

4. There is no one specific holy text or bible in Hinduism. Rather, there are several writings that are looked to for guidance and inspiration. The *Vedas* were written somewhere between 1500 B.C.E. and 800 B.C.E., and they contain hymns dealing with creation and reverence for nature. The Upanishads were written about 500 B.C.E., and they include discussions about the soul and proper ways of behavior. The Ramayana, a very popular long epic poem written between 400 B.C.E. and 100 B.C.E., is about Prince Rama (an incarnation of Vishnu) and his wife Sita. The story is performed and read throughout India and Indian communities all over the world. It is viewed as a guide for dharma, love, and devotion. The Mahabharata, which contains the Bhagavad Gita, is one of the longest and best-known poems in the world. It describes the conflict between related families and kingdoms, involving exile, wars, and conquest. It is revered for its pronouncements on morality and proper behavior.

5. The caste system evolved as a hierarchy or ranking of social groups based on heredity and occupation. There have been four major groupings, more accurately referred to as varnas than as castes: Brahmans (priests), Kashatriyas (soldiers), Vaishyas (merchants), and Shudras (laborers). The Untouchables were considered to be outside of and beneath the caste system. In the 21st century, a Hindu is more likely to describe himself or herself as belonging to a jati (subcaste) rather than simply to one of the larger varna groupings. A varna may contain dozens of jatis. With the growth in educational opportunities and of newer and more technological occupations, especially in urban areas, the link between varna and occupation is disappearing. For example, someone whose ancestry has been in a jati within Shudras may become educated and hold down a job as a computer engineer.

Additional things to remember about the caste system are:

1. Ritual purity and avoidance of pollution, endogamy, and observance of religious taboos are the elements that keep one attached to his or her jati.

2. The Indian constitution prohibits discrimination against a person because of his or her jati. Nevertheless, in many villages, tensions between people of different jatis still exists.

GLOBAL CONCEPTS
**Identity**
CONCEPTS GLOBAL

GLOBAL CONCEPTS
**Justice**
CONCEPTS GLOBAL

3. A jati lower in social ranking may rise in status by adopting more pure ideals, such as becoming vegetarian. This process is called sanskritization. Another example would be for a lower-ranking jati to refrain from making leather items from a cow. Because of cow reverence in India among Hindus, working with leather is considered a polluting activity.

## Islam as a Major Religion in South Asia

Islam is the major religion of Pakistan and Bangladesh, the next two most populous nations in South Asia after India. The Islamic community in India, although in the minority, is very large. Muslims in India number over 80 million, constituting about 11 percent of the total population. This figure is larger than that of any Muslim nation in the Middle East and would be sufficient to rank among the four largest Islamic populations in the world if the Muslims in India were to make up a nation. Islam came to South Asia from its birthplace in the Middle East and has had a profound impact. For example, even though India is primarily a Hindu nation, its most famous building, the Taj Mahal, was built by a Muslim ruler in the 17th century.

The history of Hindu-Muslim relations in South Asia has been at times peaceful and at times violent. The term communalism describes those instances when serious tensions have arisen between the two groups. Respect by each group for the other begins with an appreciation of basic beliefs, practices, and differences. It also includes shared concepts. A checklist of some of these appears in the table below:

|  | Hinduism | Islam |
| --- | --- | --- |
| Holy sites | Benares (Varanasi) Ganges River | Makkah, Medina, Jerusalem (No holy rivers) |
| Buildings | Carved images of deities, ornate and decorative | Carved images of Allah and Muhammad are not permitted; writings from the Quran |
| Holy books | *Vedas,* Upanishads, Ramayana, Mahabharata | Quran |
| Dietary taboos | Beef | Pork |
| Obligations | Dharma | Five Pillars |
| Deity beliefs | Belief in different gods is acceptable | Monotheistic |
| Life after death | Reincarnation, moksha, depending on karma | Heaven for true believers and those who act righteously |

| cont. | Hinduism | Islam |
|---|---|---|
| Divisions | Stratification/hierarchy based on caste | Equality of all before Allah; schism between Sunni and Shi'ite sects |
| Attitude on life | Ahimsa—doctrine of nonviolence | Jihad—concept of holy wars |
| Political attitudes | Democratic; separation between civil and religious authority | Theocratic—Quran as basis for laws in society |

Serious incidents of Hindu-Muslim communal violence have increased in recent decades. A dispute over the location of the four hundred-year-old Babri Masjid mosque at a site sacred to the memory of a Hindu deity led to the destruction of the building by a huge mob of fundamentalist Hindus in 1992. Further outbreaks of anti-Muslim violence in several Indian states have occurred in the decades since causing thousands of casualties. Islamist terrorists attacked the Indian parliament building in 2001 and battled with police at the Babri Masjid site in 2005. A series of bombings in and around the western Indian port of Mumbai (Bombay) preceded a three-day rampage of shooting and bombing attacks in November 2008. Blame fell upon a militant Pakistani Islamist organization called Lashkar-e-Taiba. Elements of Pakistan's security forces were alleged to have provided support for the attacks.

## Buddhism in South Asia

GLOBAL CONCEPTS

**Change**

CONCEPTS GLOBAL

Buddhism grew out of Hinduism as a result of the teachings of the Buddha, born as Siddhartha Gautama. Gautama was born as a high-caste Hindu in 560 B.C.E. However, he and his disciples wished to keep some ideas (such as the mandala) of Hinduism while seeking to change other ideas (such as end the caste system). Buddhism became popular in India during the rule of Ashoka (250 B.C.E.). However, its influence gradually diminished because some of its ideas were accepted by Hindus and became part of the Hindu religion and also because of the destructive impact of Muslim invasions after 800 C.E. It is estimated that there are about one million Buddhists today in India. However, the population of Sri Lanka is mostly Buddhist. Buddhism became much more popular in Southeast Asia and in East Asia.

## Sikhism

Sikhs form about 2 percent of India's population and are concentrated in the northwestern region known as the Punjab. The religion was founded around 1500 by Guru (teacher) Nanak, born as a Hindu but raised with Islamic ideas. The Sikh (disciple) faith has aspects of both Hinduism and Islam. However, it has no caste system. Sikhs have a reputation as successful businesspeople and good soldiers. Sikhs vow never to cut their hair or beards and to carry a dagger or saber with them at all times. Their attempt to break away from India and form a separate state led to conflicts with the Indian government in the 20th century. In the early1980s, separatists occupied and fortified the Golden Temple of Amritsar, the most sacred and central of Sikh temples. By mid-1984, Prime Minister Indira Gandhi had decided to end the occupation; army forces did so with much destruction and loss of life. In October of the same year, Mrs. Gandhi was assassinated by two of her Sikh bodyguards. Retaliatory rioting resulted in the deaths of thousands of Sikhs.

GLOBAL
CONCEPTS

**Identity**

CONCEPTS
GLOBAL

## Jainism

Jains, who make up less than 1 percent of India's population, follow the beliefs set down by guru Mahavira in about 500 B.C.E. He was born a Hindu, as were Gautama and Nanak, and also rejected certain Hindu doctrines while accepting others.

The main Jain doctrine is that all of nature is alive. This belief led to the refusal to kill any living thing and to a strict notion of nonviolence, the ideal of ahimsa. This idea was gradually incorporated into Hinduism.

Christians, Jews, and Parsees are also found in India. Their total numbers are very few, and they make up no more than 3 percent of the population.

# REVIEW QUESTIONS

*Multiple Choice.* Select the letter of the answer that correctly completes each statement.

1. In India the traditional role of women changed during the 20th century mainly because of the
   A. impact of increased urbanization
   B. growth of political unrest
   C. use of passive resistance
   D. effects of religious persecution

2. Demographers are most concerned with studying trends in
   A. religion
   B. culture
   C. dress
   D. population

3. The most widely spoken language in India is
   A. Tamil
   B. Hindi
   C. Bengali
   D. Urdu

4. The practice of endogamy results in married couples who
   A. will have many children
   B. have come from village communities
   C. have had their marriage arranged by their families
   D. come from different castes

5. Which does NOT belong with the others?
   A. Krishna
   B. Vishnu
   C. Shiva
   D. Mandala

6. The duties and obligations of a caste member are known as his or her
   A. dharma
   B. karma
   C. moksha
   D. reincarnation

7. The Bhagavad Gita is the name of a famous
   A. battle
   B. family
   C. poem
   D. city

# SECTION 3: CHINA

## I. PHYSICAL GEOGRAPHY OF CHINA

### Overview

Until the age of exploration in the 1500s, China was largely isolated from other regions of the world by the ocean, the deserts, and the mountains along its borders. For the most part, Chinese civilization developed independent of external influences and in a unique Chinese fashion. As a result, the Chinese developed a strong ethnocentric attitude, believing that their civilization was

GLOBAL
CONCEPTS
**Environment**
CONCEPTS
GLOBAL

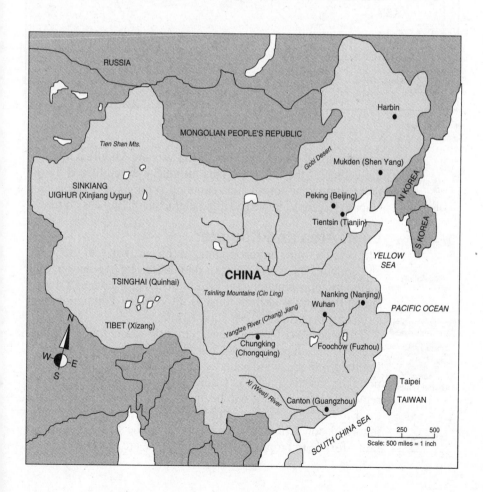

RUSSIA

Harbin

MONGOLIAN PEOPLE'S REPUBLIC

Tien Shan Mts.

Gobi Desert

Mukden (Shen Yang)

SINKIANG
UIGHUR (Xinjiang Uygur)

Peking (Beijing)

N KOREA

Tientsin (Tianjin)

S KOREA

YELLOW
SEA

TSINGHAI (Quinhai)

**CHINA**

Tsinling Mountains (Cin Ling)

Nanking (Nanjing)

Wuhan

PACIFIC OCEAN

TIBET (Xizang)

Yangtze River (Chang) Jiang

Chungking
(Chongquing)

Foochow (Fuzhou)

N

W E

S

Xi (West) River

Canton (Guangzhou)

Taipei

TAIWAN

SOUTH CHINA SEA

0    250    500

Scale: 500 miles = 1 inch

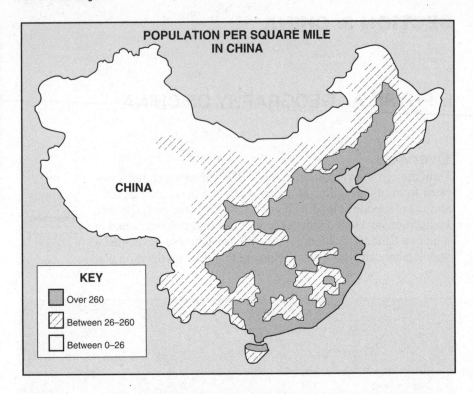

POPULATION PER SQUARE MILE
IN CHINA

CHINA

KEY

Over 260

Between 26–260

Between 0–26

superior to all others and that China was the Middle Kingdom, the center of the universe. This attitude was reinforced by the fact that most cultures China came into contact with in the area (Japan, Korea, Vietnam) adapted elements of Chinese culture.

## Land Area and Climate

China is the third largest country in physical size in the world and contains the world's largest population. Its population, estimated at approximately 1.3 billion in 2010, is concentrated in China Proper, the eastern third of the country. Population density is estimated at 360 per square mile.

The land area of China is over 3 million square miles. Its long, irregular coastline provides China with many excellent harbors. Latitude, altitude, wind patterns, and distance from the sea determine the varied climates of China. In general, the farther north a region lies, the cooler it will be; the farther west a region lies, the drier it will be because it is farther from the source of the summer monsoon. Chinese farmers depend on the summer monsoon rains for their crops, but the monsoons are not dependable.

# The Monsoon

The monsoon is a seasonal wind reversal caused by land and sea temperature differences. In Asia, in the spring-time, as the direct rays of the sun move toward the Tropic of Cancer, the land warms more rapidly than the oceans. This creates a low-pressure system over the huge Asian land mass and a high-pressure system over the oceans. As the warm air over the land rises, the cool, moist ocean air rushes in to replace it, creating the summer monsoon system. In the fall, as the direct rays of the sun move south to the Tropic of Capricorn, the Asian land mass cools more rapidly than the water, the positions of the high- and low-pressure systems are reversed, the warm air over the ocean rises, and the winds reverse direction. This creates the winter monsoon system, which in most of Asia is a dry monsoon, since it originates over land.

**GEOGRAPHY**

**Environment and Society**

The summer monsoon is the major source of rainfall for most of South, Southeast, and East Asian farmers. In a good year, the monsoon may bring adequate rains to most of the farmers who depend on it. However, if the monsoon is too strong it may pass over an area very rapidly and not drop enough precipitation, thus causing crops to fail due to a lack of moisture. The monsoon may continue carrying an excessive amount of moisture; thus, when it hits a mountain wall farther inland, it creates a flood problem in that area. A weak monsoon may stall in an area fairly near the coast and create terrible flooding there, while at the same time causing a drought in areas farther inland because the moisture has fallen elsewhere. In general, the average amount of rainfall a region receives is determined by its nearness to the sea and its location in relation to hills and mountains, which will cause the winds to rise and precipitation to fall. Areas on the windward side of hills and mountains receive higher amounts of precipitation than other regions.

For most of Asia, the winter monsoon is dry. It originates over the lands to the north of India and China, and therefore the only regions that receive significant amounts of rainfall are those that lie on the northern and western coasts and slopes of mountains.

The summer monsoon is the southeast or southwest monsoon, and the winter monsoon is the northwest monsoon. The systems are named, like other winds, for the region in which they originate.

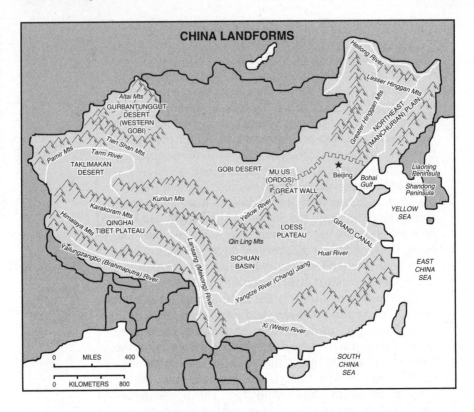

# CHINA LANDFORMS

Altai Mts

GURBANTUNGGUT DESERT (WESTERN GOBI)

Tien Shan Mts

Pamir Mts

Tarm River

TAKLIMAKAN DESERT

Karakoram Mts

Kunlun Mts

Himalaya Mts

QINGHAI TIBET PLATEAU

Yalungzangbo (Brahmaputra) River

Lansang (Mekong) River

GOBI DESERT

MU US (ORDOS)

GREAT WALL

Yellow River

Qin Ling Mts

LOESS PLATEAU

SICHUAN BASIN

Yangtze River (Chang) Jiang

Xi (West) River

Heilong River

Lesser Hinggan Mts

Greater Hinggan Mts

NORTHEAST (MANCHURIAN) PLAIN

Beijing

Bohai Gulf

GRAND CANAL

Hual River

Liaoning Peninsula

Shandong Peninsula

YELLOW SEA

EAST CHINA SEA

SOUTH CHINA SEA

```
0        MILES      400

0      KILOMETERS    800
```

**GEOGRAPHY**

**Places and Regions**

Sometimes the rains fail and the crops suffer drought. Sometimes the rains are excessively heavy and the crops suffer floods.

China has five major geographic and climatic regions:

1. Southern China, which is warm and moist year-round, is a major rice-growing region and contains the southern hills region and the Xi and Chang (Yangtze) river valleys.

2. North China, a cold, relatively dry region, is a major wheat-growing region and contains the Huanghe (Yellow) River Valley and the North China Plain.

3. Manchuria lies in northeastern China, a large region of lowland plains, and contains vast mineral resources.

4. Inner Mongolia and Xinjiang (Sinkiang), in northcentral and western China, are largely desert and dry steppe.

. 5. Tibet, in the southwest, is a vast, cold plateau with an average elevation of 15,000 feet.

**GEOGRAPHY**

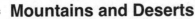

**Physical Settings** ## Mountains and Deserts

The Gobi Desert stretches across most of northcentral China (Inner Mongolia). Some of the world's highest mountains are located in and adjacent to the borders of China. To the northwest are the Altai and Tien Shan and to the southwest the Himalayas, the highest mountains in the world. The Qin-ling (Tsinling), in central-eastern China, separate the dry, cold northern region from the wet, warm southern region and serve as a cultural dividing line in China.

The difficult terrain (hills, plateaus, mountains, and deserts) has resulted in sparse population in both north and west China. However, the eastern third of China, known as China Proper, is very heavily populated, containing about 90 percent of China's people.

## The River Valleys

The heaviest concentrations of population in China Proper are in the great river valleys—the Huanghe (Hwang-ho or Yellow), the Chang (Yangtze), and the Xi (Hsi or West).

The northernmost of the three, the Huanghe, is the major farming region of China. It flows through the great loess (fertile yellow soil) region of northern China and picks up and carries a vast amount of topsoil, which is deposited in the bed of the river and on the flood plains of the North China Plain. The river carries so much silt that the riverbed has been built up to an elevation higher than the surrounding plains and must be controlled by dikes. When the dikes fail, the river floods, destroying crops and homes and killing people. For this reason, the river has become known as "China's sorrow" and the North China Plain, the "famine region of China."

The Chang (Yangtze), China's longest river, flows through some of China's most productive farmland. The rich deposits of topsoil from floods encourage farming, and many of China's most important industrial cities, such as Nanjing (Nanking), Wuhan, Hankow, Chongqing (Chungking), and Shanghai, are located along it.

The Xi (Hsi or West) River, in the far south of China, is an important source of irrigation, and at its mouth lies the city of Guangzhou (Canton) and, nearby, the Special Administrative Region of Hong Kong.

GLOBAL CONCEPTS

Environment

CONCEPTS GLOBAL

GEOGRAPHY

Human Systems

WORLD ISSUES

Environmental Concerns

GEOGRAPHY

Environment and Society

# REVIEW QUESTIONS

*Multiple Choice.* Select the letter of the answer that correctly completes each statement.

1. The majority of China's over 1 billion people live in the
   A. Manchurian Plains
   B. river valleys of eastern China
   C. Kweichow Plateau
   D. Takla Makan of western China

2. A population density map shows us the
   A. distribution of ethnic groups in China
   B. location of villages in a region
   C. approximate number of people per square mile
   D. location of industrial centers in a given nation

3. The direction of the flow of China's major rivers indicates that
   A. eastern China is cooler than western China
   B. western China is at a higher elevation than eastern China
   C. northern China receives more rainfall than southern China
   D. the monsoons originate in the southwest

4. North China raises large crops of wheat. South China raises large crops of rice. This is largely because of a difference in
   A. elevation
   B. rainfall
   C. cultural development
   D. technological development

5. Chinese farmers use terracing because they
   A. fear technological change
   B. must use all available land to feed the people
   C. prefer farming on the hills and plateaus
   D. can farm without irrigation

6. Over 90 percent of China's people live on less than half the land. The major reason for this is
   A. fear of the "barbarians" in the border regions
   B. the other half is disputed territory
   C. the rain forest prevents human habitation
   D. most of China's arable land is found in the east

7. Physical geography and history combined to give the early Chinese
   A. a deeply religious attitude
   B. an ethnocentric view
   C. a desire for modernization
   D. motivation to establish trade to gain knowledge

8. As one travels from eastern to western China, one is less likely to find
   A. sparse population
   B. mountains
   C. deserts
   D. agricultural centers

9. The most important influence on farming in China is
   A. the diurnal temperature change
   B. the availability of heavy machinery
   C. the winter monsoon
   D. the summer monsoon

10. The Yellow River is also known as the
    A. Chang
    B. Xi
    C. Huanghe
    D. Amur

# II. ECONOMIC GEOGRAPHY OF CHINA

## Resource Potential

China has adequate supplies of coal, iron ore, petroleum, natural gas, tin, antimony, tungsten, uranium, and many other minerals. It also has enormous hydroelectric-power potential, and China has constructed some dams and hydroelectric power plants. Most of China's petroleum reserves are located in the sparsely populated western regions, but pipelines transport crude oil to refineries and the densely inhabited eastern areas. Enough oil is produced for export. Most of the exported oil goes to Japan. China has major deposits of iron ore and coal in Manchuria. This iron has made possible the development of a sizable steel industry and has also made Manchuria a center of other types of heavy industry, such as locomotive production.

The majority of the Chinese people are still engaged in agriculture, and the capital for investment in developing industries must come from the sale of agricultural products. Since only one third of China's land is arable, peasants must overproduce to feed the vast Chinese population and also have products to sell abroad. The intensive agriculture employed by the Chinese farmers (hand labor, terracing, irrigation, and so on) and the new incentives under the "responsibility system" have increased production, but the growing population demands ever more goods and services. China's economy has been the world's most rapidly growing in recent years and China is becoming an industrial power. To achieve this goal, the Chinese are using technology to overcome the scarcity of both food and consumer goods.

## Changes in the Economic System Under Mao Zedong

For generations, China was an agrarian nation. The majority of the people were tenant farmers who rented their land from the landed gentry, who made up 10 percent of the population but owned 70 percent of the land. Rent and taxes kept the vast majority of tenant farmers impoverished. They lived on a subsistence level, providing their families with the necessities of life—food, clothing, and shelter—unless the monsoons failed them, and then many of them starved. The peasants were constantly faced with the threat of famine, starvation, and exploitation by the landlords and the government.

After the establishment of the People's Republic of China in 1949, Mao Zedong made drastic changes in China's economy. Those changes included:

1. Foreign-owned industries were almost immediately nationalized, and Chinese-owned industries were also gradually nationalized.

2. Banks, transportation, and mining also came under government control.

3. Production goals and methods to meet China's economic goals were set by Communist leaders through five-year plans.

4. The Communists carried out land reform, and the peasants were given small plots of land of their own.

Under Mao's leadership, the Communists were determined to industrialize China. The capital for investment had to come from the sale of agricultural products. However, since the peasants on their small plots simply were not producing enough to provide that capital, the communist government began to take control of the land and agricultural production.

Cooperative farms were formed where individual farmers still owned the land but shared the ownership of machinery, tools, and work animals, and the farmers worked the land collectively. However, cooperatives also did not provide the desired increase in production.

The next step was the collective farm, where the land, the tools, machinery, and animals belonged to the collective (the state) and decisions on production were made by government officials. Individuals were paid wages, and the goods produced and the profit from that production now belonged to the state. Individuals were still allowed to own their homes, and they still enjoyed a private family life.

During the Second Five-Year Plan (1958–1962), called the Great Leap Forward, all the country's resources were to be directed toward greater industrialization. Communes—huge state-owned farms which were economic, political, and social units—were formed. The commune managed local schools, hospitals, power plants, radio stations. Agricultural planning was done by Communist Party members, as was the planning for the industry the commune was engaged in. Ownership of private property ended. The communes had communal dining halls, nurseries, and dormitories. The plan called for increasing grain production by 100 percent in one year. Instead, it decreased by 20 percent in two years. Drought, peasant resistance, and inefficient central planning caused the failure of the

WORLD ISSUES

Determination of Political and Economic Systems

GLOBAL CONCEPTS

Choice

CONCEPTS GLOBAL

WORLD ISSUES

Determination of Political and Economic Systems

Great Leap Forward. As a result, the government divided the communes into production brigades to set goals and production teams to perform the labor. Most of the decisions were made by the commune members themselves. The government gave them quotas, but they decided how to meet those quotas and what to do with any surplus. Although production increased, it did not meet the needs of the growing Chinese population. The Great Leap Forward proved to be a disaster, with millions dying of starvation.

## Economic Development Under Deng Xiaoping

After the death of Mao in 1976, Deng Xiaoping was the most powerful figure in China until his own death in 1997. In 1978 he began a program known as the Four Modernizations in agriculture, industry, defense, and science and technology, which made significant changes in China. Deng believed there should be less government control and planning. To carry out this program, Deng introduced elements of capitalism (free enterprise), and as a result China now has a mixed economy rather than a strict command economy. (In a command economy, the government makes all the basic economic decisions.)

Beginning in 1979, the communes were dismantled and the "responsibility system" was started, under which the land still belongs to the state but individual families lease plots. The peasants decide what to raise on the land and how to raise it. They contract with the state for a certain amount of their produce. Anything produced above that amount belongs to the peasant, who can choose what to do with the surplus. Free markets were established to sell the extra produce. Production has increased considerably. Estimates are that the average peasant's income more than doubled and production grew by over 7 percent per year.

The responsibility system was extended to state-owned industries in 1984. Managers are now allowed to make production decisions. They must still meet quotas set by the state but can decide what to do with surplus production. The factories and the machinery belong to the state, and the state still controls raw materials, but managers are free to obtain raw materials themselves. The industries pay a tax on the profit of sales of surplus goods, but the rest of the income can be used for reinvestment or to reward workers.

Some private enterprise has also been encouraged. The government offered tax breaks and low-interest loans to people to organize small businesses, such as fast food, beauty shops, brick-making, carpentry, and so on. The number of workers who can be employed in these private enterprises is limited by the government.

The production of consumer goods has also been stressed. There has been a push to raise the standard of living of the average Chinese, and there has been much greater production of radios, bicycles, cameras, TVs, and other consumer goods. Other major economic changes have been the encouragement of foreign investment in Chinese industries and allowing foreign industries to locate in China.

Joint ventures between Chinese and foreign businesses have been encouraged, but, in addition, foreign companies have been encouraged to locate in Special Economic Zones (SEZ) located in coastal southeastern China. Here almost none of the restrictions placed on Chinese businesses apply, and private enterprise is the order of business. The foreign businesses receive tax benefits, raw materials can be imported, workers can be hired and fired at will, and profits can be kept. These Special Economic Zones are capitalist enclaves in China. The Chinese have also reached agreements with several foreign countries for scientific and technological exchange. The major foreign investments are from Britain, the United States, Germany, France, and Japan.

With the dawn of the current century, China's role on the world stage in terms of economics has grown remarkably. Its influence is rising, whereas that of the United States, particularly in East Asia, is declining. Japan imports more from China than it does from the United States. By 2011 the Chinese economy has outstripped Japan and become the second largest in the world.

| WORLD ISSUES |
| --- |
| World |
| Trade and |
| Finance |

## New Educational and Cultural Policies

As part of the Four Modernizations program, the government tried to improve education. The closing of schools during the Cultural Revolution and the persecution of teachers caused a major weakness in scientific and technical skills in China. To bridge this gap the government began to allow Chinese students to study abroad, and there were several thousand foreign advisers and many foreign students studying in China.

There was less emphasis on the use of art to further socialist ideals. During the Cultural Revolution artistic expression was severely restricted. Under Deng, Western television and music were allowed into China.

GLOBAL
CONCEPTS

Change

CONCEPTS
GLOBAL

Many leaders of the Chinese Communist Party believed Deng went too far in allowing capitalism into the Chinese economy. They feared corruption and the exploitation of workers. They also feared that the party would lose social and political control. The new freedom in education and culture was also seen by many government leaders as dangerous. But Deng and his supporters felt it was essential in order to advance science and technology. Indeed, the student "democracy" movement of May and June 1989 indicated that those who foresaw danger were right, and Western influences were blamed for the student rebellion that began in Beijing. Deng ordered a military crackdown on the democracy movement. In 1989, the democracy movement that was based in Tiananmen Square in Beijing was crushed by the Chinese police and army.

Censorship continues to be a firm policy of the government. Evidence can be seen in restrictions on use of the Internet as well as on the content of newspapers and official government publications. In 2010 Google ended cooperation with Chinese Internet censors when it discovered that there had been cyberattacks on its computer systems that had originated in Chinese universities. American secretary of state, Hillary Rodham Clinton, condemned the attacks and said that the attacks threatened freedom of information. The Chinese government counteracted by saying that they felt that an unrestricted Internet was an American plot to control international information. Google eventually shut down its mainland servers and directed its Chinese users to log onto its Hong Kong servers, but these servers were also censored.

In the area of science and mathematics education, China has made great strides. Increasing numbers of students are majoring in various scientific and mathematical areas and in related fields such as engineering. Several American observers of these trends are wary of the perceived growing gap between American and Chinese education in these and other disciplines.

## Conditions Posing Problems in Achieving Goals

In spite of the many hindrances to development in China, progress has been made and the majority of the Chinese people enjoy a higher standard of living than before the Communist Revolution. Nonetheless, several factors make it difficult for the Communists to achieve their economic goals.

**WORLD ISSUES**

Economic
Growth and
Development

Since China's economy still has an agricultural base, most of the capital for investment still must come from agriculture. Secondly, economic development has been uneven since regional differences present problems for development. Southeast China has excellent conditions for agriculture and has made economic gains. However, the North China Plain suffers recurring floods and drought, and much of the western regions are desert. Northeastern China (Manchuria), with its major iron and coal resources, has seen major industrial development. Uneven regional economic development creates another problem. The regions are inhabited by diverse ethnic groups, and the economic development, or lack of it, serves to prolong ethnic differences and conflicts. Moreover, attempting to provide at least an elementary education for the Chinese people has put enormous strains on the economic resources of the state. China's large population and level of education are both important factors in determining the level of development in the country and, for the time being, serve to hinder that development.

# REVIEW QUESTIONS

*Multiple Choice.* Select the letter of the answer that correctly completes each statement.

1. The Great Leap Forward was expected to produce gains in China's
   A. imports
   B. birth rate
   C. army
   D. gross national product

2. An example of government-organized collectivist and group ideology was seen in China's
   A. foreign relations
   B. military
   C. commune system
   D. maritime trade

3. Since World War II Manchuria has become important as a center of
   A. heavy industry
   B. rice cultivation
   C. nomadic herding
   D. mining for gold

4. Arable land can be described as land that is
   A. dry and windblown
   B. composed of loess
   C. affected by earthquakes
   D. fertile and can be farmed

5. The best example of a command economy is
   A. China under Mao during the 1950s
   B. the responsibility system in China
   C. tenant farming in pre-civil war China
   D. subsistence farming in ancient China

6. Many nations have mixed economies. This means they have
   A. combined elements of democracy and dictatorship
   B. adopted both socialist and capitalist elements
   C. government ownership of all mines
   D. individual ownership of all industries, resulting in monopolies

7. Five-year plans in China have been used primarily to
   A. set economic production goals
   B. limit population growth
   C. increase adult literacy
   D. decrease infant mortality

8. The nationalization of industry refers to
   A. employing only native inhabitants
   B. government takeover of private industry
   C. government subsidies for industries
   D. providing government contracts to defense industries

9. The Four Modernizations program of Deng Xiaoping was designed to make specific changes in all of the following except
   A. agriculture
   B. industry
   C. science and technology
   D. family structure

10. The student rebellion and demonstration in Tiananmen Square in 1989 led to
   A. the establishment of a democratic government
   B. a military crackdown on the participants
   C. greater emphasis on individual rights
   D. decreased government restraint on political freedom

11. Google shut down its search engine in China because
   A. the Chinese people failed to employ its services
   B. so many Chinese were using the system that it slowed worldwide
   C. there were Chinese cyberattacks and Chinese censorship
   D. the Chinese had free access through Hong Kong

# III. HUMAN AND CULTURAL GEOGRAPHY OF CHINA

## Confucianism

Confucian thought, the foundation of Chinese civilization, influenced social organization, political structure, and the educational system. Confucius, or Kung Fu-tzu (551 B.C.E.–479 B.C.E.), lived during a time of great turmoil in China, marked by constant civil war. Confucius believed he knew how to bring about peace and harmony. His teachings became the basis of Chinese society during the Han dynasty (202 B.C.E.–220 C.E.).

GLOBAL
CONCEPTS

**Culture**

CONCEPTS
GLOBAL

Confucius was not concerned with religion and did not teach about a divine being or salvation. He taught ethics (good and bad conduct), or moral precepts. A conservative, he believed the Chinese should follow ancient ways that had worked well in the past. Confucius taught that one should *not* do to others what one would *not* want done to oneself, stressing actions *not* to be taken against others.

GLOBAL
CONCEPTS

**Identity**

CONCEPTS
GLOBAL

Confucius believed there was a basic order to the universe and that people must live in society to fulfill their potential. To achieve a peaceful and harmonious relationship in society, Confucius taught five basic relationships. All the relationships were based on the principle of reciprocity. Each person, according to Confucius, had a place in society, and if each person accepted the duties and obligations of his or her role, society would function properly. In each relationship there is a superior and an inferior. The superior shows love for and responsibility for the inferior. The inferior owes loyalty and obedience to the superior.

---

### Five Relationships:

1. **Ruler and subject**
2. **Father and son**
3. **Husband and wife**
4. **Older brother and younger brother**
5. **Friend and friend.** This is the only relationship not based on a superior/inferior foundation. Friends were to respect and honor each other.

---

.For many centuries China was ruled by imperial dynasties. Confucianists believed that the ruler held the mandate of heaven (the right to rule granted by the will of heaven). If he was a just ruler and cared for his subjects, he and his family would continue to hold the mandate. But if he was not, the people had the right to rebel and overthrow the ruler and the dynasty. The success of their rebellion would be proof that the ruler had lost the mandate.

GLOBAL
CONCEPTS
**Power**
CONCEPTS
GLOBAL

## The Traditional Chinese Family System

The extended, patriarchal, and patrilineal family was the traditional ideal in China and was the basic social unit, although usually only the wealthy could actually afford to live in such large households. A person gained his position in society as a member of his family. To be without family was to be without position. The family was also the basic economic unit. Most families lived on farms. Domestic handicraft was the major type of manufacturing. With few exceptions a son learned the trade of his father. There was a single family budget. Upon his death, a man's property would be divided equally among his sons, who would begin to build their own extended families.

GLOBAL
CONCEPTS
**Citizenship**
CONCEPTS
GLOBAL

Two well-defined, unwritten rules determined relationships within the family. Those rules were:

1. The superiority of males over females.
2. The superiority of the old over the young.

Strong-willed, older females were likely to exercise considerable influence over family decisions, although most females were reluctant to do so, simply because they had learned to accept their inferiority as a matter of custom and tradition.

The most important virtue in China was filial piety, which might be defined as reverence, love, and devotion to family and respect and obedience to parents. Individuals had a lifelong obligation to their parents, and were expected to serve them during their worship. Ancestor worship actually reduced the mobility of Chinese families. One had to remain near the graves and the spirits of one's ancestors, so that the proper sacrifices could be made to the spirits at the appropriate times. It was believed that the spirits of the ancestors watched over the activities of the living, and that the spirits were to a large degree responsible for the prosperity or lack or prosperity experienced by the living. Ancestor worship was practiced by nearly everyone in China.

GLOBAL
CONCEPTS
**Identity**
CONCEPTS
GLOBAL

The individual was subordinate to the family. What was good for the family was allowed; what was not good for the family was not allowed. The success or failure of the individual reflected on the family, and vice versa. The head of the family was expected to punish infractions of societal mores and values to save "face" and preserve the family's good name. Government officials often dealt with the head of the family rather than with the individual who had committed crimes. The patriarchal clan cared for the aged and orphans. If a person had family, they would always be cared for.

The oldest living male was the head of the family and the chief authority figure. He was responsible for the actions of all members of the family, and, ideally, his authority was unquestioned.

The traditional inferiority of the female made the female role in China unenviable, particularly for young women. A woman's role was to provide her husband with sons to carry on the family name, and she had virtually no position in her husband's family until this was accomplished. Indeed, failure to produce sons was one of the most shameful things for a woman. The feet of upper-class females were bound because small feet were considered necessary for making "good" arrangements for marriage. Female children were often abandoned to die (female infanticide) during times of famine so that older members of the family might survive.

GLOBAL
CONCEPTS

**Human Rights**

CONCEPTS
GLOBAL

Marriages were arranged, and were considered social and economic arrangements between families. It was common for the couple not to see each other until the marriage actually took place. It was an important means of maintaining the existing social order. Arrangements were made between families with the assistance of a go-between who researched the background of the families and the two being married, including horoscopes and astrology. Most important were the family's social and economic status. The marriages were made to enhance the standing of the two families, not to satisfy the couple. The most important product of the marriage would be sons to carry on the family name and the family business, and to care for the parents when they were too old to care for themselves.

The rules worked because they were based on the principle of reciprocity derived from Confucianism, on mutual responsibilities and obligations. The head of the family had a duty to care for and protect the other members of the family, and the young and the females had a duty to respect and obey the head of the family in return. The subordinate members of the family trusted in the impartiality of the head of the family and in the belief that he would do what was best for the family (the group) and, therefore, what was best for the individual.

The system provided psychological and economic security. It created a sense of lifelong belonging. As long as the family existed and one did not shame the family, one would always be cared for. In a nation where political conflict and economic insecurity were common, the family provided an ongoing sense of social security. These were the advantages of the system. The disadvantages included: spreading the family income very thin, jealousy in the extended family, particularly if there were joint households; in-law problems; mistreatment of young wives by mothers-in-law, who were finally superior to someone and whose sons were duty bound to support them in disagreements; during times of famine, sacrifice of young for the old. The status of women has undergone a slight change. This can be seen in an increasing rate of divorce, usually initiated by women, and a changing view of marriage. Although these trends are found mainly in urban areas, they are typical of developing countries that are rapidly modernizing, gaining affluence, and being exposed to Western influences.

GLOBAL CONCEPTS

**Empathy**

CONCEPTS GLOBAL

## The Four Chinese Social Classes

1. Scholars, who made up a very small portion of society, held the highest position in Chinese society. They were the only ones eligible to take the civil service examinations and serve in government.

2. Peasants, who made up the largest portion of society, were the second highest class because they were the primary producers, providing the grains and textiles necessary for food and clothing.

3. Artisans, or craftspeople, were skilled workers who made up the third group. They were secondary producers.

4. Merchants, the lowest socially, though often the wealthiest, made their profits from the labor of others.

The nobility were above the class system. Soldiers and a group called "chien-min" (barbers, entertainers) were below the system.

## Taoism (Daoism)

Taoism, a Chinese philosophy traditionally attributed to Lao-tzu ("old master"), originated in the 6th century B.C.E., about the same time as Confucianism. Taoism teaches the necessity of the individual's having a sense of nature, understanding his or her part in it, and adapting to it.

The Taoists believed there was a natural order to existence and that people should do as little as possible to change that natural order. By accepting things as they are, people could live in harmony with the natural laws. Taoists opposed the existence of a large bureaucratic government and many governmental laws. Individuals should seek to find their own nature and place in the natural world and act according to instinct, since human instincts are good, and it is learning and custom that have taught them to be bad. Once people rid themselves of the burden of unnatural laws and customs, they could find the tao (or way) of the universe.

Like Confucianism, Taoism was not immediately widely accepted. However, over the years it underwent major changes. It borrowed heavily from old Chinese folk religions and became a religion with a priesthood, ceremonies, and elaborate rituals. Some Taoists practiced alchemy (trying to change inferior metals to gold), some practiced magic, and others did ritual exercises.

## Legalism

The Legalist philosophy originated in the same period as Confucianism and Taoism. The Legalists assumed that human nature was evil and that people must be restricted by laws. They believed that through harsh punishment people would be forced to obey those laws. They taught that a strong central government was essential to maintain peace and order, and that the ruler should have unquestioned authority. They also believed that only two occupations should be allowed: farmer (to provide sustenance) and soldier (to support the ruler).

## Buddhism

Buddhism originated in India in the 6th century B.C.E. and was carried to China by Indian merchants during the 1st century C.E. (See section on Southeast Asia for a discussion of Buddhism.)

GLOBAL
CONCEPTS

**Change**

CONCEPTS
GLOBAL

The first Chinese converts were from the upper class. The complex philosophy and elaborate rituals appealed to them. Buddhism was greatly changed by the Chinese, who translated difficult Buddhist concepts into traditional Confucian ethics. They stressed the obligations of children to parents. They inter-

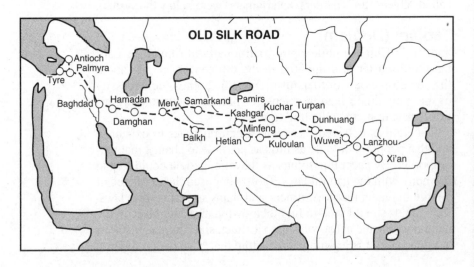

OLD SILK ROAD

Antioch
Palmyra
Tyre
Baghdad    Hamadan    Merv    Samarkand    Pamirs
                                             Kuchar    Turpan
           Damghan                     Kashgar
                                                      Dunhuang
                Balkh              Minfeng
                     Hetian    Kuloulan    Wuwei    Lanzhou
                                                    Xi'an

preted nirvana not as a place empty of human thought and desire but as a continuation of life on earth, without the usual suffering. In the period of disorder after the fall of the Han dynasty, many Chinese began to accept Buddhist beliefs. Buddhist temples and monasteries became centers of education, and monasteries became economically and socially powerful.

The Chinese saw no contradiction in being a Buddhist-Confucianist-Taoist-Legalist. Buddhism offered optimism and hope for a better existence; Confucianism offered order and harmony and strong family relationships; Taoism offered rituals and ceremonies; and Legalism offered control. So a Chinese could be all these things.

## Chinese Contributions

Historically, China was one of the world's leading civilizations in technological development. The Chinese contributed much to the world: silk, tea, porcelain (china), paper, block printing, gunpowder, the mariner's compass, and many plants and plant products. Most of these early Chinese inventions and products were diffused to the West (Europe) between 200 B.C.E. and 1800 C.E. by one of two routes—the Old Silk Road, which led from China through Central Asia into the Middle East and from there to Europe, or by the southern sea route, from China to India and onward to the Middle East and again from there to Europe.

GLOBAL CONCEPTS

**Technology**

CONCEPTS GLOBAL

## Chinese Influence upon Other Peoples in East Asia

The original Chinese writing was a system of pictographs. Each symbol was a recognizable picture of an object. Eventually the Chinese developed a system of ideographs—symbols used for expressing ideas. The writing system includes more than fifty thousand symbols. This elaborate system of writing spread to Korea, Japan, and Vietnam.

GLOBAL CONCEPTS

**Culture**

CONCEPTS GLOBAL

Buddhism was adapted to the Chinese civilization, and Chinese Buddhism spread from China to Korea, Japan, and Vietnam. The Zen Buddhism practiced in Japan is said to have originated in China and entered to Japan by way of Korea.

The Confucian tradition of ancient China also influenced the cultures of Korea, Japan, and Vietnam. Confucian influence can be seen in their family systems, ethical systems, and class systems, which are adaptations from the Chinese. Confucianism can also be seen in the dominance of the idea that there should be harmony between the individual and nature and in the importance given to the peasant in all three societies. Japanese and Korean art also reflect Confucian influence.

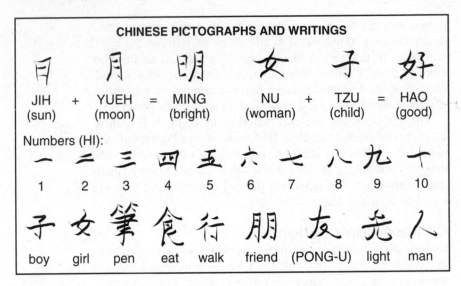

**CHINESE PICTOGRAPHS AND WRITINGS**

JIH + YUEH = MING     NU + TZU = HAO
(sun) (moon) (bright)     (woman) (child) (good)

Numbers (HI):

| 一 | 二 | 三 | 四 | 五 | 六 | 七 | 八 | 九 | 十 |
|---|---|---|---|---|---|---|---|---|---|
| 1 | 2 | 3 | 4 | 5 | 6 | 7 | 8 | 9 | 10 |

boy   girl   pen   eat   walk   friend   (PONG-U)   light   man

---

**WORLD ISSUES**

Population

GLOBAL
CONCEPTS

**Scarcity**

CONCEPTS
GLOBAL

## China's Population

A large population requires large amounts of resources for sub-sistence and therefore makes development difficult. China has a huge population and a limited amount of arable land. The people themselves are perhaps China's most important resource and the cheapest factor in production, but their numbers are one of its greatest problems. To counteract this population problem, the Chinese government encourages a "one-child policy." This policy is relatively ineffective in the countryside but has had success in urban areas. China's goal is not just to decrease the birth rate but to actually decrease the population growth rate. The government also encourages late marriage.

*Multiple Choice.* Select the letter of the answer that correctly completes each statement.

1. On which Asian nation did Chinese culture have the greatest impact?
   A. India
   B. Thailand
   C. Japan
   D. Pakistan

2. A goal common to Confucianism, Taoism, and Buddhism is to
   A. establish peace and harmony
   B. provide the basis for democratic government
   C. return the power of emperors
   D. promote individual artistic activity

3. The traditional Chinese writing system makes use of
   A. letters
   B. ideographs
   C. phonetics
   D. an alphabet

4. The "Five Relationships" were part of the philosophy of
   A. Lao-tzu
   B. Confucius
   C. Sun Yat-sen
   D. Mao Zedong

5. Of the world's total population, China contains about
   A. one half
   B. one third
   C. one fourth
   D. one fifth

6. The one word that would best describe five relationships of Confucius
   A. manorial
   B. ethnic
   C. disorderly
   D. reciprocal

7. The two groups in China whose social and economic positions most improved since the Communist victory in 1949 are
   A. students and government workers
   B. the aged and industrial employees
   C. factory managers and soldiers
   D. women and peasants

8. A Chinese emperor ruled through the mandate of heaven. This meant he was
   A. chosen by the gods to rule
   B. descended from the gods
   C. a god himself
   D. able to communicate directly with the gods

9. The major purpose of China's one-child policy is to
   A. lower the infant mortality rate
   B. increase the amount of agricultural production
   C. decrease the population growth rate
   D. improve the literacy rate

# SECTION 4: SOUTHEAST ASIA

# I. PHYSICAL GEOGRAPHY OF SOUTHEAST ASIA

## Overview

The region known as Southeast Asia consists of ten nations. Six are on the Asian mainland: Cambodia (Kampuchea), Laos, Malaysia, Myanmar (Burma), Thailand, and Vietnam. The other four are island nations: Brunei, Indonesia, the Philippines, and Singapore. In the past, parts of the region have been known by other names,

GLOBAL
CONCEPTS
**Diversity**
CONCEPTS
GLOBAL

**SOUTHEAST ASIA**

81

such as the Spice Islands, the East Indies, and Indochina. The land portions of this region total about half the area of the United States.

## Topography and Geology

Most of mainland Southeast Asia is located on two peninsulas—the Indochina Peninsula and the Malay Peninsula. The island nations of Indonesia and the Philippines form archipelagoes. The soil found on these islands, much of it from volcanic ash, is very rich. Mountain chains on the mainland divide the land area into river valleys, in which most of the population lives. Many tropical jungles and swamps exist here. Geography has tended to isolate some peoples from others and is partially responsible for the great diversity of cultures found in Southeast Asia.

Many areas of Southeast Asia lie along the edges of tectonic plates, regions of frequent volcanic and earthquake activity. In December 2004, a massive undersea quake caused a destructive tsunami (giant wave) that devastated the west coasts of the island of Sumatra and the Malay Peninsula and wreaked death and destruction as far away as Sri Lanka and southern India. Estimated death tolls approached 300,000 people, and economic damages and costs soared into the hundreds of millions of dollars.

## Water Bodies

The two oceans that sandwich the region, the Indian and Pacific, have acted as "highways," bringing foreigners from South Asia, East Asia, Europe, and the United States. This foreign contact has continued for over five hundred years and has contributed to the "patchwork quilt" of cultures found in the ten Southeast Asian nations. The Strait of Malacca, lying between Indonesia, Malaysia, and Singapore, is a vital strategic and economic link between the Indian and Pacific oceans, in the way that the Panama Canal is a link between the Pacific and Atlantic oceans.

The major rivers are the Irawaddy, Chao Phraya (Menam), Mekong, and Red. They flow southward, forming fertile river valleys and providing transportation routes for the movement of goods and people. The largest lake in Southeast Asia is the Tonle Sap (Great Lake) located in Cambodia. The rivers and straits in the area, along with the major seas, including the Java Sea and the South China Sea, make up half the size of the region. As a result, it is easy to see why water bodies have had such an enormous effect on the diet, commerce, transportation, and history of Southeast Asia. It is also estimated that Indonesia and the Philippines together contain over 20,000 islands.

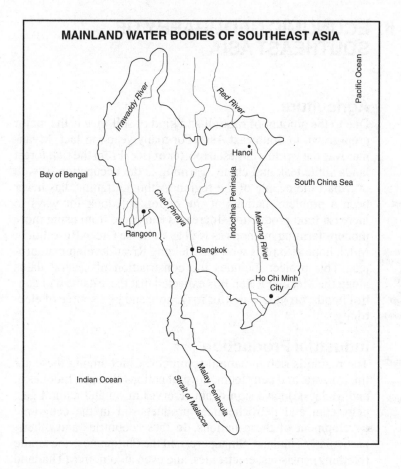

MAINLAND WATER BODIES OF SOUTHEAST ASIA

## Climate

The climate is tropical, characterized by much humidity and heavy rainfalls, especially in the summer. These features are similar to those found in the Caribbean Sea area in the West Indies, Haiti, the Dominican Republic, and Puerto Rico. The winds that cause the heavy rainfall are referred to as the summer monsoons. As in South Asia, the monsoons can make the difference between a good or a bad harvest.

## II. ECONOMIC GEOGRAPHY OF SOUTHEAST ASIA

### Agriculture

GLOBAL
CONCEPTS
**Environment**
CONCEPTS
GLOBAL

**GEOGRAPHY**

**Human Systems**

Due to the amount of rainfall and kind of soil, rice is the major crop grown in Southeast Asia. For many years, in fact, Myanmar was the world's largest exporter of rice. From the rich forest lands come teak and ebony. Farming is the occupation of well over half the people of the region. Although famine has never been a problem, nations of the region still look for ways to increase food production. Increases can come from using more modern farming methods as well as from the Green Revolution. Much hope also rests with the Mekong River development project. This project includes the construction of several dams along the Mekong River. It is expected that these dams will control floods, provide water for irrigation, and be a source of electricity.

### Industrial Production

**WORLD ISSUES**

Economic
Growth and
Development

The region is rich in natural resources. Chief among these are tin, iron ore, and petroleum. Several nations (Brunei, Indonesia, and Malaysia) have significant reserves of oil and natural gas; petroleum and petrochemical products aid in the economic development of these nations. In these countries and others, particularly Thailand, Singapore, and the Philippines, the textile (clothing), plastics, electronics, and even automotive (Thailand has begun manufacturing vehicles) industries promote modernization and help raise skill and educational levels. These manufacturing sectors, along with more traditional industries based on renewable resources in agriculture (rubber, sugarcane, lumber) and aquaculture (fishing), have enhanced the standing of Southeast Asian countries in the world economy. Expansion of tourism, given the region's natural features and historic sites, has also served to generate income.

These nations, along with several other strong Asian economies, have been referred to as "Economic Tigers," reflecting their rapidly growing industrial and export sectors and increasingly significant role in world trade. Growth rates in these "Tiger" economies reached 6 percent from the 1960s through the 1990s, raising standards of living but creating new issues for their governments to deal with. Nations depending on only a few export products are vulnerable to changes in global demand, overuse of agricultural land, and careless industrial development causing degradation of the environment. Political and social issues can arise over competing land use demands.

## ASEAN

The Association of Southeast Asian Nations, which is made up of Brunei, Malaysia, Thailand, the Philippines, Indonesia, and Singapore, was formed in 1967 to promote cooperative economic advancement. It seeks to increase exports and gain more help from nations such as Japan.

## Economic Decision Making

Different economic systems are found in the countries of Southeast Asia. Capitalist features predominate in Singapore, Brunei, Indonesia, Malaysia, and the Philippines. Greater centralized control of the economy is found in Myanmar, Laos, Cambodia, and Vietnam.

In 2004, ASEAN nations signed an accord with China aimed at creating the world's largest free trade area by 2010. The agreement seems to signal ASEAN's intention to create a unified economy similar to the European Union. It would also give China access to new markets that would reduce, and possibly eventually challenge, the influence of the United States in Asia.

Japan has also explored "heightened partnerships" with ASEAN and its member nations in trade, investment, and disaster prevention and relief. As of 2011 the ASEAN nations themselves were in the midst of implementing a cooperative seven-year "Economic Blueprint" dealing with the same issues as well as commerce, agriculture and forestry, infrastructure development, and the free flow of goods, labor, and services. The organization has also considered the 2011 membership application of recently independent East Timor. Acceptance of this impoverished and frequently violence plagued former Portuguese colony has drawn the opposition of at least one of ASEAN's more prosperous members.

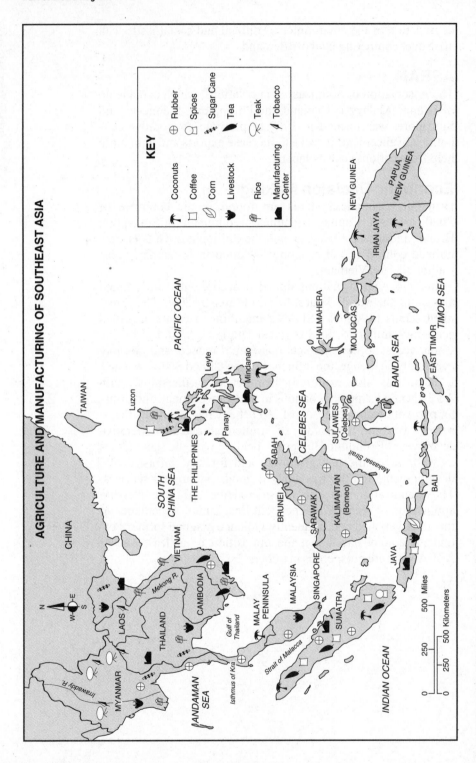

AGRICULTURE AND MANUFACTURING OF SOUTHEAST ASIA

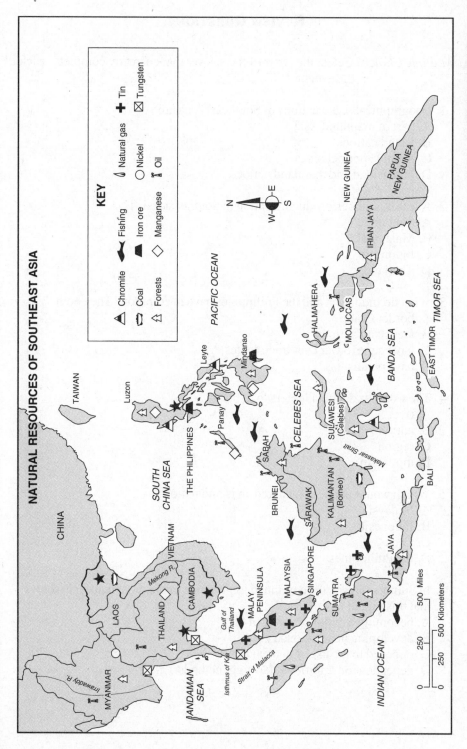

# NATURAL RESOURCES OF SOUTHEAST ASIA

**KEY**

- ◭ Chromite
- ◢ Coal
- △ Forests
- ⌐ Fishing
- ◼ Iron ore
- ◇ Manganese
- ✚ Tin
- ⏚ Natural gas
- ○ Nickel
- ⛽ Oil
- ⊠ Tungsten

N
W—E
S

87

## REVIEW QUESTIONS

*Multiple Choice.* Select the letter of the answer that correctly completes each statement.

1. Geographically, the nations of Southeast Asia are
   A. part of mainland Asia
   B. island nations
   C. mostly archipelagoes
   D. both island and mainland nations

2. A leading rubber-producing nation in Southeast Asia is
   A. Singapore
   B. Malaysia
   C. Indonesia
   D. Thailand

3. What do Indonesia and the Philippines have in common? They both
   A. border China
   B. are island nations
   C. have gone to war over trade routes
   D. have peninsulas

4. The word "Indochina" refers to a
   A. river
   B. nation
   C. region
   D. mountain

5. Which would not be considered an island nation?
   A. Malaysia
   B. Indonesia
   C. Laos
   D. the Philippines

6. In Southeast Asia, the continued importance of the monsoon cycle shows that this region is
   A. becoming a major exporter of oil
   B. developing heavy industry
   C. opposed to the use of nuclear power
   D. dependent on traditional farming methods

# III. HUMAN AND CULTURAL GEOGRAPHY OF SOUTHEAST ASIA

## Overview
The most striking feature of Southeast Asia's population is its variety. This variety can be seen in the different languages, religions, and ethnic groups. Therefore, the region can be described as a "patchwork quilt" of peoples. With a total population of slightly over 400 million, the ten nations have more people than in all of North America. Indonesia, with 205 million people, is the fourth largest nation in the world.

GLOBAL CONCEPTS
**Diversity**
CONCEPTS GLOBAL

## Demography
Although the majority of people live in the villages and the mountains, there are several large cities in Southeast Asia. The population density is uneven. The Indonesian island of Java, for example, has over 1,500 people per square mile, while the whole nation of Indonesia has 225 people per square mile. Most other areas have less than 125 people per square mile.

## Language
The many languages spoken in Southeast Asia are primarily a reflection of the area's history. Several of these can be traced to nations from outside that have had great influence here. French is spoken in Cambodia, Laos, and Vietnam; Spanish in the Philippines; English in the Philippines, Myanmar, Malaysia, and Singapore; and Dutch in Indonesia. Migration of people from India and China have brought Tamil and Chinese to parts of mainland Southeast Asia. Languages native to the region are Thai, Vietnamese, Burmese, Lao, Malay, Pilipino, and Tagalog.

GLOBAL CONCEPTS
**Identity**
CONCEPTS GLOBAL

## Religion
A diversity of religions exists, basically for the same historical reasons that a variety of languages exists. Animism, a form of nature worship, is native to the region. The five major "outside" faiths include Buddhism, Confucianism, Christianity, Hinduism, and Islam. The number of Muslims in Indonesia make it the largest Islamic nation in the world. However, the religion with the greatest number of followers in the mainland nations is Buddhism. Buddhism began in India. Some of the main ideas about Buddhism are:

GLOBAL CONCEPTS
**Culture**
CONCEPTS GLOBAL

1. Siddhartha Gautama became the Buddha or the "Enlightened One."

2. The Four Noble Truths are from Gautama's teachings: Suffering is part of life; Selfish desires cause suffering; To end suffering, one must give up these desires; To end these desires, one must follow the Eightfold Path.

The Eightfold Path consists of a series of words and acts, such as right speech, right occupation, right thought, and right conduct; following the "middle way" between extremes, such as denial or indulgence.

3. The goal of Buddhists is to reach enlightenment and then nirvana. Nirvana results in a release from the mandala (wheel of life) and extinction of the soul.

4. Two major schools, or sects, of Buddhism are found in Southeast Asia. The Hinayana ("Little Vehicle") Buddhists are found in Myanmar and follow a more strict and traditional form of practice. The Mahayana ("Greater Vehicle") practitioners are more liberal and have adopted certain ideas such as that of the bodhissatva. (A bodhissatva is someone who has achieved buddhahood but has given up this status to return to earth and be of help to human beings.)

## Ethnic Groups

GLOBAL
CONCEPTS

**Diversity**

CONCEPTS
GLOBAL

**WORLD ISSUES**

Economic
Growth and
Development

There is a great variety of ethnic groups in Southeast Asia. These include both those native to the region and those that have ancestral ties to foreign areas. Among the ethnic groups native to Southeast Asia are the Khmers (Cambodia), Chams (Vietnam), and Malays (Indonesia, Malaysia, Philippines). "Outside" groups include Europeans, Indians, and Chinese. Of these, the Chinese are the most numerous. Referred to as the hua-chiao ("overseas Chinese"), they have usually settled in urban areas and have had a major economic impact in several nations, such as Singapore. However, they have also been the target of prejudice on occasion, especially in Indonesia and Malaysia. The various ethnic groups have slowly made progress in learning to live with each other and in adapting traditional customs to modernization and to Westernization.

# REVIEW QUESTIONS

*Multiple Choice.* Select the letter of the answer that correctly completes each
statement.

1. The "hua-chiao" are Chinese who
   A. control Singapore
   B. live outside of China
   C. live in coastal areas of Southeast Asia
   D. fought the Indonesian government

2. Siddhartha Gautama is known as "the Buddha" because
   A. his Four Noble Truths inspired many followers
   B. the Eightfold Path was an entirely new idea
   C. of his teachings concerning the "middle way"
   D. he gained "enlightenment" through meditation

3. Indonesia's place as the most populous of the Southeast Asian nations is
   most likely due to its
   A. fertile volcanic soil and long coastlines
   B. huge, flat, fertile plains and a temperate climate
   C. vast mineral resources and a mostly industrialized
      economy
   D. extensive immigration and a large tourist industry

4. Mahayana Buddhism differs from Hinayana Buddhism in
   A. believing in karma and reincarnation
   B. following only some of Siddhartha Gautama's teachings
   C. accepting enlightened bodhisattvas as earthly helpers
   D. worshiping numerous gods and goddesses

# SECTION 5: JAPAN AND KOREA

## I. PHYSICAL GEOGRAPHY OF JAPAN

### Overview

Japan is a chain of islands (archipelago) lying off the east coast of the Asian mainland in the northern Pacific Ocean, separated from the mainland by the Sea of Japan and the Korean Strait. Because it has no land borders with the rest of Asia, Japan has been able to maintain its insular (separate) quality, develop a sense of identity, and borrow selectively from the cultures of

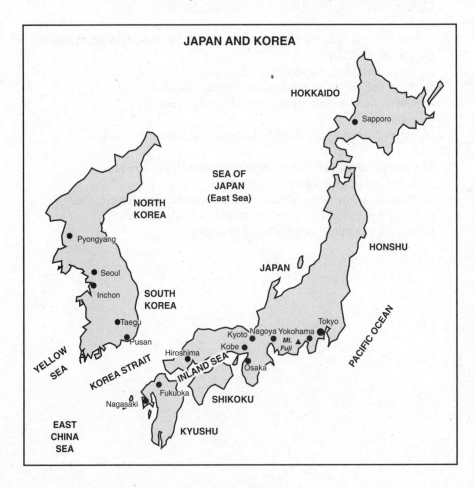

JAPAN AND KOREA

the nations near it. Through the processes of cultural borrowing, adaptation, and assimilation, Japan has created a uniquely Japanese society. Korea (a "land bridge" to Japan) served as a cultural bridge between Japan and China.

Japan's land area is approximately 143,000 square miles, and it has a coastline of over 16,000 miles, with many excellent harbors. The four main islands of Japan are Hokkaido, Honshu, Shikoku, and Kyushu. Hokkaido, the northernmost and second largest of the islands, has a difficult terrain, a somewhat severe winter climate, and the smallest population. Hokkaido is Japan's frontier. Honshu, the largest island, contains 60 percent of Japan's total land area and the vast majority of Japan's 123 million people. Most of Japan's best farmland, its major cities, and its industry are located here. The island of Kyushu is second in importance to Honshu. Across the Inland Sea lies Shikoku. These three southern islands were the region where Japanese civilization developed. Japan also contains some 3,400 smaller islands, many of which are uninhabited.

**Spatial Terms**

## Topography, Climate, and Resources
Because 85 percent of the total land area of Japan is mountainous, only 11 percent of the land is arable. The highest mountain, Mount Fuji, or Fujiyama (over 12,000 feet), is an extinct volcano, conical in shape, and snow-covered year round. To overcome the shortage of arable land, the Japanese have practiced intensive agriculture for generations—reclaiming land from the sea, terracing hillsides, building irrigation canal systems, and employing human labor to make the best possible use of the land.

GLOBAL
CONCEPTS
**Environment**
CONCEPTS
GLOBAL

**Environment
and Society**

Japan has only a few small areas of plains squeezed between the seacoast and the foothills of the mountains. The most important plains region is the Kanto, which is located on the island of Honshu in the region of Tokyo-Yokohama.

Japan has many rivers. They are of very limited use in navigation, but they do provide a source of hydroelectric power and irrigation.

The most important factors in determining the climate of Japan are its island location (ocean currents), latitude, nearness to the Asian continent, and elevation. The climate is similar to that of the United States along the Atlantic Coast, as it lies in much the same latitude zone, and the Japanese enjoy four seasons. The northern Japan summers are warm, and winters long, snowy, and cold. Most of the rest of Japan enjoys a mild winter with little or no snow. Summers, with the exception of the subtropical southeast, are generally warm, with adequate rainfall. In fact, nearly all of Japan receives at least 40 inches of rain per year.

**GEOGRAPHY**

**Environment and Society**

GLOBAL
CONCEPTS

**Scarcity**

CONCEPTS
GLOBAL

Japan lies at the northern edge of monsoon Asia. In summer the moist, cool winds bring rains to the southeastern coasts of Japan. The winter monsoon drops heavy snowfall on the northwestern slopes of Honshu and Hokkaido. September and October in Japan can be a dangerous time as it is the season of typhoons (tropical wind storms much like hurricanes). Typhoons can cause severe damage to buildings, crops, and people and very often result in flooding and tidal waves, which do even more damage.

Japan's resource base, like its arable land, is severely limited. Deposits of iron ore and petroleum are limited. Deposits of coal are extensive, but the coal is low grade. The Japanese must import the raw materials needed for industrial production.

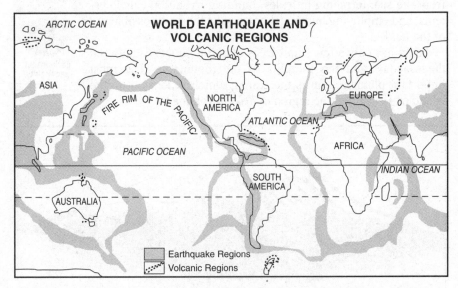

Japan is located in a volcano and earthquake-prone area known as the "Fire Rim of the Pacific."

Japan lies in what is often referred to as the fire rim of the Pacific, or the ring of fire, an earthquake and volcano zone. More than half the world's active volcanoes lie in this zone. Most of Japan's volcanoes are inactive, though there is an occasional eruption. Earthquakes occur much more frequently. An average of four earthquakes a day strike Japan. Most are slight tremors, but every few years a major quake occurs.

The sea plays an enormous role in the lives of the Japanese. They depend on it as a source of livelihood, food, transportation, and in recent years, commerce. For many years the sea also served as an effective barrier to invasion by other countries.

**INTRODUCTION**

# REVIEW QUESTIONS

*Multiple Choice.* Select the letter of the answer that correctly completes each statement.

1. Which statement best characterizes Japan?
   A. part of the Asian mainland
   B. the longest archipelago in the world
   C. an island nation
   D. flat topography

2. Honshu contains 60 percent of Japan's population because
   A. it is the only island that is not mountainous
   B. it is the home of the Ainu
   C. it contains most of Japan's best farmland
   D. it doesn't experience earthquakes

3. Japan's most valuable resource is
   A. petroleum
   B. coal deposits
   C. gold
   D. its people

4. The Japanese must use their land carefully and wisely because
   A. very little is arable
   B. most of it is desert
   C. the topography is uneven
   D. much flooding occurs

5. Which Japanese industry would be most severely affected by a maritime disaster such as a typhoon?
   A. coal mining
   B. electronics
   C. cameras
   D. fishing

6. A nation like Japan, consisting of a chain of islands, is
   A. a peninsula
   B. an isthmus
   C. an archipelago
   D. a promontory

7. The most important geographic influence of the cultural development of Japan was
   A. the mountainous nature of the islands
   B. the shortness of the rivers
   C. the frequent occurrence of flood and drought
   D. its location in relation to the Asian mainland

8. The best description of Japan's climate is
   A. tropical
   B. desert
   C. variable
   D. polar

9. Which of the following types of natural disasters is *not* common in Japan?
   A. earthquake
   B. typhoon
   C. drought
   D. flood

10. Which phrase would best describe the resource base of Japan?
   A. adequate for heavy industry
   B. much like that of the United States
   C. severely limited
   D. equal to that of China

# II. ECONOMIC GEOGRAPHY OF JAPAN

## Economic Recovery after World War II

At the close of World War II, Japan lay in ruins. More than 3 million people had been killed; 10 million were homeless. One fourth of Japan's industry and manufacturing facilities had been destroyed. Communications and transportation lines had been badly damaged. Nearly the whole maritime fleet had been destroyed, and harbor and port facilities were in ruins. The Japanese empire had been reduced to the four main islands, and as a result it had lost its source of raw materials.

The leaders of the occupation realized that to build a democratic nation, there would also have to be economic reform. A program of land reform to increase food production by providing greater incentives to farmers, who now owned the land, was the most successful and long-lasting program. A second step in economic reform was to destroy the zaibatsu (monopolies). However, since the financial resources of the zaibatsu could help rebuild Japan, the effort to break them up was eventually dropped. The zaibatsu still exist in Japan today (for example, Mitsui, Mitsubishi, Fuji, Sumitomo). A third effort at economic reform was to organize and encourage the organization of labor unions.

**WORLD ISSUES**

Economic
Growth and
Development

## Characteristics of the Japanese Economy

There has been tremendous growth in the Japanese economy since 1950. Today its GDP is over $4.137 trillion. Japan's GDP has fallen behind that of China in the early 21st century. Per capita income is nearly $32,600, and the unemployment rate is 4.8 percent. (GDP, gross domestic product, is the dollar amount of all goods and services produced by a nation in a given year.)

Though Japan's economic recovery after World War II was remarkable, in the 1990s Japan experienced an economic downturn fueled by scandal involving government, banking, and industrial officials. In the late 1990s it experienced its worst recession since the war. Japan's economy grew worse again in 2001, but then rebounded. However, in 2008–2009 the worldwide recession hit Japan hard. Exports fell, and the economy declined again. Because of the recession, it is probably inevitable that more young people will face unemployment in Japan in the near future. College graduates will find themselves competing for fewer and fewer job openings.

Japan is the world's leading shipbuilding nation. It is a leader in producing textiles, cameras, microscopes, and electronic goods. By the 1980s it had become one of the leading producers of cars and trucks. It exports steel and machinery. It is second only to the United States in the manufacture of computers. In 2003 its trade surplus was $100.5 billion.

How did the Japanese make such incredible economic gains after the almost total destruction of World War II?

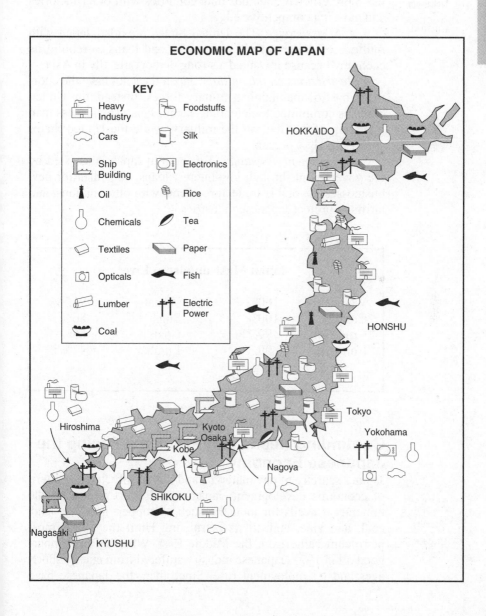

## ECONOMIC MAP OF JAPAN

**KEY**

Heavy Industry
Cars
Ship Building
Oil
Chemicals
Textiles
Opticals
Lumber
Coal

Foodstuffs
Silk
Electronics
Rice
Tea
Paper
Fish
Electric Power

HOKKAIDO

HONSHU

Tokyo

Yokohama

Hiroshima

Kyoto
Osaka

Kobe

Nagoya

SHIKOKU

Nagasaki

KYUSHU

Japan's economic recovery was aided by:

1. *Its people.* The Japanese people were disciplined and hard-working. The labor force was highly skilled, receptive to on-the-job training, and well educated. For many years they accepted low wages, which gave Japanese industry a competitive edge in the world market.

2. *Technology.* When industry was rebuilt after World War II, the latest in technology was used. This allowed the Japanese to use more efficient methods than countries with older factories and gave it a competitive edge.

GLOBAL
CONCEPTS

**Technology**

CONCEPTS
GLOBAL

3. *U.S. assistance.* The United States provided Japan with millions of dollars of aid, assistance, and loans to rebuild its economy because it wanted a strong democratic ally in Asia.

4. *Restrictions on the military.* Japan does not have the enormous cost of maintaining military forces. Instead, the United States is committed to defending Japan. Japan spends less than 1 percent of its GDP on the military, while the United States spends nearly 4 percent.

5. *Government assistance.* Business in Japan is assisted by the government through low-interest loans, subsidies for new businesses, favorable trade agreements with other nations, and tariffs to protect Japanese industries.

| **Japan Must Import to Live** | | | |
|---|---|---|---|
| Wool | 100% | Wheat | 91.7% |
| Cotton | 100% | Sugar | 86% |
| Crude Oil | 99.7% | Coal | 65% |
| Iron Ore | 99.3% | Lumber | 47% |

## Continuing Needs and Problems Facing the Japanese Economy

Japan's scarcity of raw materials and oil has affected its pattern of economic development. Japan must import almost all the minerals it needs for industry, such as copper, iron ore, lead, coal, and zinc, and all its petroleum. Until the 1970s most petroleum came from the Middle East. When OPEC embargoed oil in 1973, Japanese industry suffered from energy shortages and unemployment rose. Since then, the Japanese have

GLOBAL
CONCEPTS

**Scarcity**

CONCEPTS
GLOBAL

found a new source of oil in China, although they are still highly dependent on Middle Eastern oil. Japan's economic life depends on its ability to import raw materials and its capacity to maintain and expand its exports to pay for those raw materials.

Although arable land in Japan is scarce, by making use of the advanced farming technology of the Green Revolution, Japanese farmers provide about 70 percent of the nation's food supply. Most of the rest comes from the United States, China, Australia, and Canada.

## United States-Japanese Economic Interactions

Since the 1970s the balance of trade between the United States and Japan has run heavily in favor of Japan. The United States buys about 18 percent of Japanese exports. The United States feels that the Japanese government's restrictions on the import of foreign goods is largely responsible and that Japanese tariffs keep U.S. goods from selling in Japan. Japanese investments are welcomed in the United States, but the Japanese government restricts foreign investments in Japan. The U.S. government has accused Japan of employing unfair trade practices.

GLOBAL CONCEPTS
**Interdependence**
CONCEPTS GLOBAL

Japan needs to maintain its high level of exports to pay for imported raw materials, and the United States needs to increase its exports to Japan to decrease its trade deficit. Consequently, the United States has asked Japan to voluntarily decrease some exports to the United States, to open their markets to more American goods, and to allow American companies to operate in Japan on an equal basis with Japanese companies. The United States has threatened to increase tariffs and place import quotas on Japanese goods unless Japan ends its unfair trade practices. Japan has promised to increase its defense spending, relax trade barriers, and export less. Some concessions have been made, but American policy makers continue to demand further concessions. In 1992 Japan agreed to concessions in the areas of paper, computers, auto sales and parts, and so on. In 1993 they agreed to open construction contracts to American bidding. Since then, Japanese prime ministers have been expected to attempt to improve trade relations, but they have found themselves pressured by entrenched financial interests in Japan. Most Japanese in a position to influence government decisions do not really wish to allow Americans free access to the Japanese market, and American businesspeople and politicians will continue to demand that Japanese markets be more open to foreign competition.

**WORLD ISSUES**

World Trade and Finance

## Japan's Role in the Global Economic Picture

**WORLD ISSUES**

World
Trade and
Finance

While Japan may be dependent on other countries for resources, its economic strength gives it power in international relations. While it has not played an international political role consistent with its economic strength, its influence has been felt through its trade policies. Beginning in the 1980s Japan has participated in a series of economic summits with the world's leading non-Communist economic powers. The Japanese have promised to increase foreign access to Japan's domestic markets at these economic summits, but so far no major changes have been made. Also in recent years, there has been a large increase in Japanese economic investment in the United States.

*Multiple Choice.* Select the letter of the answer that correctly completes each statement.

1. Japan has overcome its shortage of mineral resources by relying on
   A. Shinto spirits
   B. allies
   C. imports
   D. the United Nations

2. In Japan, the word "yen" refers to
   A. transistors
   B. money
   C. sushi
   D. architecture

3. Japan is considered an economic giant because
   A. most of its labor force is engaged in agriculture
   B. it exports raw materials to the rest of the world
   C. it has one of the highest GDPs in the world
   D. 11 percent of its land area is arable

4. Japanese-American interdependence is characterized most by
   A. America's wish for Japan's goods and Japan's need for American markets
   B. America's need for foreign investment and Japan's need for American surplus goods
   C. America's dependence on agricultural imports and Japan's need for electronics
   D. America's need for nuclear arms and Japan's ability to supply material for that need

5. Japan's economic recovery after World War II was highly successful because
   A. the Chinese government provided scientific and technical support
   B. the latest technology was used to replace factories destroyed during the war
   C. the Soviet Union provided assistance in an effort to build a strong Asian ally
   D. the American government used tariffs to protect Japanese industries

6. Japanese farmers today
   A. are very efficient
   B. are mainly subsistence farmers
   C. are mostly tenant farmers
   D. use no artificial fertilizers

7. Japanese tariffs
   A. are considered unfair trade barriers by many of its trading partners
   B. are the only reason Japan has had such economic success since World War II
   C. have protected Japanese defense industries from competition
   D. have made Japan the largest producer of petroleum products in the world today

8. The zaibatsu in Japan
   A. were ancient warriors
   B. are industrial monopolies
   C. were emperors
   D. were labor unions

9. Japan is a leading producer of
   A. cars
   B. gold
   C. oil
   D. corn

10. The United States Occupation reforms included
   A. land reform
   B. discouraging the creation of labor unions
   C. destruction of the zaibatsu
   D. rearming the military

# III. HUMAN AND CULTURAL GEOGRAPHY OF JAPAN

## The Japanese People

The early inhabitants of Japan migrated from northern Asia, Korea, China, and Southeast Asia over hundreds of years. These peoples gradually intermingled and intermarried and became the Japanese people we know today. The Japanese people are ethnically homogeneous (alike), and the only really distinct group of people who remained were the Ainu (the original inhabitants of Japan), who were pushed northward, finally, to the island of Hokkaido by the people we call Japanese.

The Japanese tend to think of themselves as a racially pure people. As a result, they seldom accept foreigners as full members of their society. Japan's strong sense of cultural unity is a result of Japan's relative isolation from foreign influence for many centuries and its cultural homogeneity for at least 1,000 years.

GLOBAL CONCEPTS
**Identity**
CONCEPTS GLOBAL

## Early Traditions—Shinto, the "Way of the Gods"

Shinto, the native religion of Japan, began as a simple form of nature worship. The Shintoist believed that all natural things— trees, rocks, storms, ocean waves—contained *kami* (the spirits of the gods). Later on, Shinto came to include hero, ancestor, and emperor worship.

GLOBAL CONCEPTS
**Culture**
CONCEPTS GLOBAL

Shinto teaches no moral precepts, no ethical code. It teaches that the Japanese should be thankful for and reverent to all aspects of nature; grateful for life, birth, fertility. Shinto teaches that physical purity, not moral, is of the utmost importance. Shinto therefore is an example of a type of religion called animism.

Because Shinto has no concept of a single god and no moral precepts, it has been relatively easy for the Japanese to accept other religious teachings. Buddhism and Shinto have existed side by side for over 1,000 years.

## Buddhism

Buddhism was introduced from Korea in 552 C.E. At first, it was popular only among the nobility and upper classes. Buddhist teachings were too complicated and its outlook too pessimistic to appeal to the common people. During the Kamakura period, Buddhism in Japan underwent basic changes, however, and its teachings were made easier to understand and accept. Consequently, Buddhism began to be accepted by the lower classes, who combined Shinto and Buddhism. Happy events such as birth and marriage were observed with Shinto ceremonies and funerals with Buddhist rites.

One of the Buddhist sects, which became especially popular with the samurai (warriors), is Zen. Zen teaches that each person must seek enlightenment individually through meditation and that no others can help an individual achieve enlightenment. The meditation requires great self-discipline and the ability to conquer oneself. The self-discipline learned in Zen was later applied to the code of the warrior, Bushido. The simplicity taught by Zen is revealed in Japanese painting, poetry, and the tea ceremony.

# Chinese Influence

The first contacts between the Japanese and Chinese took place through Korea. Chinese civilization was much more advanced than that of the Japanese, and some powerful Japanese determined that elements of Chinese civilization should be introduced in Japan. By the 10th century, Japan had been transformed, but it was not just an imitation of China. Chinese culture was adapted to suit Japanese needs.

GLOBAL CONCEPTS

**Change**

CONCEPTS GLOBAL

During the rule of Prince Shotoku in the late 6th and early 7th centuries, Japanese students were sent to China to study religion, philosophy, art, architecture, and government administration. The greatest flowering of Chinese culture in Japan occurred during the Nara period (710–794). The Yamato rulers established a central government based on that of the Chinese, and officials were appointed to govern administrative units, but no civil service was established. Japanese officials were chosen, instead, because of their connections and families. The Chinese emperor ruled by the mandate of heaven, but the Japanese emperor held the throne because he was considered divine.

GLOBAL CONCEPTS

**Political Systems**

CONCEPTS GLOBAL

The traditional Japanese family was much like the traditional Chinese family. The Japanese had been strongly influenced by Confucianism from China. The ideal family in traditional Japan was the extended patriarchal and patrilineal family. The eldest male was the head of the household, and was legally responsible for every member of the household. Women and the young were subordinate, and marriages were arranged. Filial piety determined relationships within the family.

The family was the basic social and economic unit, and the individual existed only as a member of this socially accepted group. Children were officially registered with the local authorities, and a family could disown a member by removing his or her name from the register. If this happened, the person was no longer socially accepted, and they might just as well be dead. Everything an individual did was supposed to be considered in light of how it would reflect on the family.

The Chinese writing system was adopted, but it presented problems, so the Japanese eventually developed a writing system of their own based on the Chinese. It is a mixture of Chinese characters for words and symbols that stand for sounds. The phonetic (for sound) symbols are called kana; there are fifty of them.

GLOBAL CONCEPTS

**Culture**

CONCEPTS GLOBAL

In 708 the Japanese built their first permanent capital city, Nara, modeled after the Chinese capital. Later in the 8th century, a new capital city was built at Heian (now Kyoto), which remained the imperial capital until 1868.

During the Heian period (794–1185), contact with China was decreased. Japan stopped sending students and envoys to China to study. They believed that they had advanced to the point where they could develop their own arts and culture without Chinese influence. Japanese art and literature blossomed. The world's first novel, *The Tale of Genji*, describing Heian court life, was written by Lady Murasaki about 1000 C.E. Painting, sculpture, poetry, architecture, and landscape gardening flourished. The literacy rate increased considerably. During their long period of isolation, the Japanese developed a strong feeling of their own uniqueness.

## Cultural Developments During the Feudal Period

GLOBAL
CONCEPTS

**Identity**

CONCEPTS
GLOBAL

Zen Buddhism was introduced to Japan at about the same time the first shogunate was established. Zen influenced the development of chanoyu (tea ceremony), ikebana (flower arranging), and landscape gardening. Literature and poetry flourished. Haiku poetry was developed and refined during shogunal rule. Japanese Noh drama, Bunraku (puppet plays), and Kabuki drama developed. Landscape painting achieved remarkable refinement. Japanese arts reflected cultural refinement (haiku, landscape painting, tea ceremony). Their art also reflected the times, with drama often depicting their present way of life as well as the conflict of the changing times.

---

Haiku is the simplest form of poetry. It consists of one verse with seventeen syllables, spaced over three lines in a 5-7-5 pattern. A good haiku sets a mood, then flashes a sudden understanding of life—all in three lines.

**The Pond**
The ancient pond
A frog leaps in
The sound of water
BASHO

**Mist**
Above the veil
of mist, from time to time
there lifts a sail . . .
GAKOKU

**A Remembrance**
Show that we two
looked at together—this yew
Is it fallen anew?
BASHO

**The Crow**
On a leafless branch
a crow has settled:
autumn nightfall.
BASHO

---

## Population Characteristics of Japan Today

Japan's population in 2004 was estimated at just over 127 million. The country itself is slightly smaller than California. With a population density of about 873 people per square mile, Japan is one of the most crowded nations in the world, and living space for urban Japanese is incredibly limited. About 95 percent of the Japanese people are employed in manufacturing, mining, and service industries. Approximately another 6 percent are engaged in agriculture. The birth rate has decreased in recent years, but because of improved health care and increased life expectancy, the population continues to grow slowly. By the year 2030, Japan's population is expected to stabilize, or cease to grow.

**WORLD ISSUES**

Population

The Japanese population is one of the most homogeneous in the world. Over 99 percent of the people are ethnic Japanese. The largest minority group are the Koreans. Only one major language, Japanese, is spoken in the country, and over 80 percent of the people belong to the same religious grouping—a blend of Shinto and Buddhism.

### THE LARGEST CITIES

| Urban Area | Population (millions of people) |
| --- | --- |
| Tokyo-Yokohama, Japan | 33.4 |
| Mexico City, Mexico | 21 |
| São Paulo, Brazil | 10.4 |
| Seoul, South Korea | 9.9 |
| New York, United States | 21.2 |
| Mumbai (Bombay), India | 16.4 |
| Osake-Kobe-Kyoto, Japan | 5.6 |
| Calcutta, India | 4.6 |
| Rio de Janeiro, Brazil | 14.4 |
| Tehran, Iran | 6 |

SOURCE: U.S. BUREAU OF THE CENSUS, 1998
NOTE: Population figures based on metropolitan areas.

## Education System

The importance of education in Japan is unmatched in any other country. Entrance to the top-ranking universities is highly competitive. Only one of six applicants is accepted. As a result, the pressure on a Japanese student to achieve is incredible.

Education is compulsory through age 15. Entrance exams must be passed to enter high school and university. Some of the better schools even have entrance exams for kindergarten. Since good jobs and the right education are so closely linked, the competition in schools is fierce, especially today when good jobs are harder and harder to find. More graduates find themselves unemployed and living with their parents like their counterparts in the United States.

The school day, the school week, and the school year are longer in Japan than in the United States. Discipline is strict, and all the students are expected to study a foreign language. Most students receive outside tutoring and/or attend "cram" schools, even during vacations. Teachers are considered responsible for students' behavior both inside and outside the school.

## Urban Issues and Problems

WORLD ISSUES

Environmental
Concerns

Many of Japan's cities are clustered together in a megalopolis (one city blends into the edges of another). Because of the size of Japan's urban areas and its industries, Japan has one of the highest rates of pollution in the world. Smog is a serious problem. Rivers and coastal waters are being polluted by industrial wastes. The increasing use of insecticides and chemical fertilizers by farmers adds to the pollution problem.

Japan's cities are terribly overcrowded. There is a severe housing shortage. Transportation, while among the best in the world (Japan's "bullet" trains travel as fast as 160 mph), is inadequate to meet the needs of the enormous urban populations.

## Evolving Role of Women

Since the end of World War II, the roles and status of women have changed. Much of this is due to the constitution, which gave women equal rights. They were allowed to vote, to own property, to hold political office, and to seek divorce. They must receive an education, and more and more of them go on to receive a university education. Nearly 40 percent of the Japanese work force is female, though the majority of them have low-status, service-oriented jobs. Many of them earn less money than men doing the same job. The man's authority as head of the family has decreased somewhat. In addition, about six of ten working women are married. They share not only economic responsibility but authority as well. Arranged marriages are still common, however.

## Treatment of Minorities

There are only a few non-Japanese people in the country. About 12,000 Ainu, the original inhabitants of Japan, live on the northern island of Hokkaido. Most of them have been integrated into rural life on Hokkaido.

GLOBAL
CONCEPTS
**Human Rights**
CONCEPTS
GLOBAL

The second major group of non-Japanese people are the Koreans, most of whom came during World War II to work in wartime industries. Koreans are discriminated against in employment, housing, and social life. They were not allowed to become Japanese citizens until 1985.

A third minority group are the burakumin people, descendants of people who did jobs considered unclean by the Japanese, such as butchering. They used to live separately in small villages and were considered outcastes. Today they live in segregated slums in the cities and are discriminated against in housing, employment, education, and social life. There may be as many as 3 million burakumin.

## Social and Work Relations

The Japanese share an intense loyalty to groups, such as the family or the company. Group loyalty means putting the interests of the group before one's own interests, being willing to accept the decisions of the group, and avoiding situations that might shame the group. This loyalty concept extends to the workplace. Employers provide many benefits to their employees and expect loyal service in return. Japanese employees take great pride in their company and do not change jobs often because it would be disloyal to the company.

The Japanese do not like emotional confrontations and blunt speech, which might hurt feelings or cause one to lose "face" (pride). They reach decisions in business as they do in government, by consensus; they negotiate until everyone agrees on a decision. Consensus may take a long time, but for the Japanese it means that everyone is satisfied with a decision.

Most probably the great emphasis on conformity grew out of the problem of accommodating too many people on too little land. People had to learn to cooperate and restrain themselves because the Japanese have had to live uncomfortably close to each other physically. Only harmony in human relationships would make such close physical proximity bearable.

## Impact of Japan's Aesthetic Ideas

The Japanese still maintain their identity through traditional values and activities. They have a strong love of nature, which is expressed in activities such as hiking and skiing and in landscape gardens and flower arranging. The Japanese still use haiku as a creative medium. Millions of Japanese write haiku, and there are national poetry contests each year. Most Japanese are skilled in at least one of the traditional arts: music, dance, drama, painting, calligraphy.

## REVIEW QUESTIONS

*Multiple Choice.* Select the letter of the answer that correctly completes
each statement.

1. The most populated part of Japan is
   A. Honshu
   B. Kyushu
   C. Hokkaido
   D. Shikoku

2. Even though Japan has few natural resources, it has a high standard of
   living mainly because it has
   A. developed technology that can be exchanged for the resources it needs
   B. printed more money whenever living standards have started to decline
   C. imported manufactured goods
   D. produced goods and services without obtaining resources

3. Which statement best describes Japan today?
   A. Japan has become an urban society that has adopted Western values
      in nearly every aspect of life.
   B. Japan has continued to rely on China and Korea for its cultural values
      and technological development.
   C. Japan has remained primarily an agrarian society with an emphasis
      on maintaining traditional values.
   D. Japan has adopted modern technological advances while maintaining
      aspects of the traditional culture.

4. Birth and marriage ceremonies are celebrated with rituals associated with
   A. Zen
   B. Bushido
   C. Shintoism
   D. Buddhism

5. Nara, Kyoto, and Tokyo are cities that have all been
   A. centers of heavy industry
   B. conquered by the Chinese
   C. capitals of Japan
   D. populated by the Ainu

6. Haiku is a form of
   A. painting
   B. poetry.
   C. furniture
   D. architecture

7. An example of the type of religion called animism is
   A. Judaism
   B. Christianity
   C. Shinto
   D. Islam

8. As a result of cultural diffusion, many aspects of Japanese culture were adapted from the Chinese. An example of this is
   A. the Japanese writing system
   B. Shinto
   C. the tea ceremony
   D. ikebana

9. Which of the following statements about the people of Japan is *not* true?
   A. The people of Japan are ethically homogeneous.
   B. Most Japanese practice a mixture of Shinto and other religions.
   C. Most Japanese are not well educated.
   D. Japanese people feel strong group loyalties.

10. Which of the following is *not* associated with Zen?
    A. ikebana
    B. landscape gardening
    C. the tea ceremony
    D. zaibatsu

11. Buddhism in Japan is an example of
    A. imperialism
    B. cultural diffusion
    C. isolationism
    D. nativism

12. The strongest example of Chinese influence in Japan can be seen in
    A. Bushido
    B. Shinto
    C. Noh drama
    D. the written language

13. The Japanese constitution
    A. guarantees equal rights for minorities
    B. gives women the right to vote
    C. guarantees equal education for all
    D. establishes a totalitarian government

14. Education in Japan
    A. is available only to the upper classes
    B. is highly competitive
    C. does not include technical skills
    D. has failed to decrease the illiteracy rate since 1945

# IV. PHYSICAL GEOGRAPHY OF KOREA

## Overview

The Korean peninsula, bordered by the Yellow Sea, the Sea of Japan, and the Korea Strait, lies between China and historic Russia, and Japan. Its strategic location between these three regions has had a profound effect on its history. China has often seen fit to extend its influence into the region in order to maintain some control over what it has seen as a strategic outpost on its northeastern borders. Indeed, for many years, Korea was one of the Chinese tribute states. Russia's interest was mainly in the warm water ports to be found in Korea. Korea has also served as a cultural bridge between China and Japan. Japan often used Korea as a launching point for invasions of the Asian continent.

**GEOGRAPHY**

**Spatial Terms**

GLOBAL
CONCEPTS
**Environment**
CONCEPTS
GLOBAL

Korea, known as "the land of the morning calm," is a peninsula approximately half the size of California, and is home to over 67 million people and the site of two countries, the Democratic People's Republic of Korea, and the Republic of Korea. The Democratic People's Republic of Korea is also known as North Korea, and the Republic of Korea is known as South Korea. In the 1950s Korea was a battleground in the Cold War between the United States and the Soviet Union. As a result it was divided. The division of the peninsula deprived each region of the other's resources, therefore limiting the economic future of each. Much of the peninsula is hilly and mountainous, limiting the amount of arable land to approximately one fifth of the land area. The most extensive farming regions are found in the southwest and in the coastal plains throughout the peninsula. Most Koreans live in the plains found in southern Korea, along the west coast, and in the northeast. The Republic of Korea, or South Korea, contains the largest amount of arable land, but the Democratic People's Republic, or North Korea, has the most extensive deposits of natural resources, including coal, iron, tungsten, copper, and zinc.

**GEOGRAPHY**

**Physical Settings**

Korea has a long coastline of nearly 6,000 miles. Many Koreans are fishermen. South Korea, especially, has a thriving fishing industry.

Korea has a temperate climate. The summers are hot, the winters cold. Winters are colder in the north than in the south. There is a longer growing season in the south. The South Koreans have one of the highest rice yields in the world.

# V. ECONOMIC GEOGRAPHY OF KOREA

## Agriculture

Traditionally, agriculture was the chief economic activity in Korea. Industrial activity was on a low level and was severely hurt during the Korean War (1950–1953).

However, since the war, both North and South Korea have made significant economic strides. Since the early 1960s South Korea has seen a spectacular increase in its GDP, which has increased from just over $2 billion to over $1.4 trillion. Per capita GDP is over $28,000. Major industrial products include telecommunications, chemicals, ships, automobiles, electronics equipment, and steel, much of which is exported to the United States, China, and Japan. Approximately 80 percent of the population is urban. The literacy rate is 98 percent. North Korea's GDP is over $40 billion, and its per capita GDP over $1,900. Its major trading partners are China and Japan. The government has concentrated on the development of heavy industry rather than on consumer products. Its major industrial products include machines, military products, textiles, and chemicals. Approximately 61 percent of the North Korean population is urban.

| WORLD ISSUES |
| --- |
| Economic |
| Growth and |
| Development |

# VI. HUMAN AND CULTURAL GEOGRAPHY OF KOREA

## The Korean People

The Korean people are of Mongoloid origin, probably originating in Siberia, Manchuria, and northeastern China and migrating to the peninsula in prehistoric times. These people mingled and intermarried, and the resultant people are the Koreans. The Koreans are a homogeneous grouping, speaking a single language. Their written script, hangul, originated in the 15th century, and replaced many Chinese characters that had been used previously. Hangul consists of ten vowels and fourteen consonants, which are combined to form syllables. It is perhaps one of the most scientific writing systems in the world and because it is also one of the simplest it helps to account for the high literacy rates in both North and South Korea. Koreans also still use some Chinese characters.

As a result of its geographic location, Korea has been strongly influenced by Chinese culture. The Chinese influence can be seen in the traditional family, social, and government systems that indicate diffusion of Confucian philosophy. Buddhism, architecture, ceramics, painting, sculpture, and historical writing also reflect Chinese influence. Korea served as a cultural bridge between China and Japan. The Koreans, much like the Japanese after them, would adapt the Chinese cultural contributions to their own system, making them their own before passing them on to Japan.

The oldest religious belief is Shamanism. It is a form of nature worship, or animism. A key figure is the shaman, a person who is believed to act as an intermediary with the spiritual world. A shaman may be called upon to perform a kut, a ritual to get rid of evil spirits. In South Korea the major religions are Buddhism (23 percent of the population) and Christianity (26 percent). In North Korea religious activities are almost nonexistent as they are discouraged by the government. There are some government-sponsored religious groups, but they exist only to give the illusion of religious freedom.

GLOBAL
CONCEPTS
**Identity**
CONCEPTS
GLOBAL

GLOBAL
CONCEPTS
**Choice**
CONCEPTS
GLOBAL

GLOBAL
CONCEPTS
**Environment**
CONCEPTS
GLOBAL

GLOBAL
CONCEPTS
**Diversity**
CONCEPTS
GLOBAL

# REVIEW QUESTIONS

*Multiple Choice.* Select the letter of the answer that correctly completes each statement.

1. Korea, a peninsula, lies between
   A. China, Russia, and Japan
   B. China, Mongolia, and Japan
   C. Japan, Taiwan, and China
   D. Taiwan, Russia, and China

2. Korea has been a divided nation since the 1950s as a result of
   A. World War II
   B. the Cold War
   C. the Japanese occupation
   D. religious conflict

3. The strongest cultural influence in Korea has been that of the
   A. Japanese
   B. Indians
   C. Chinese
   D. Russians

# SECTION 6: AFRICA

# I. PHYSICAL GEOGRAPHY OF AFRICA

## Overview

The geography and climate of Africa have played an important role in its historical, economic, and cultural development. For

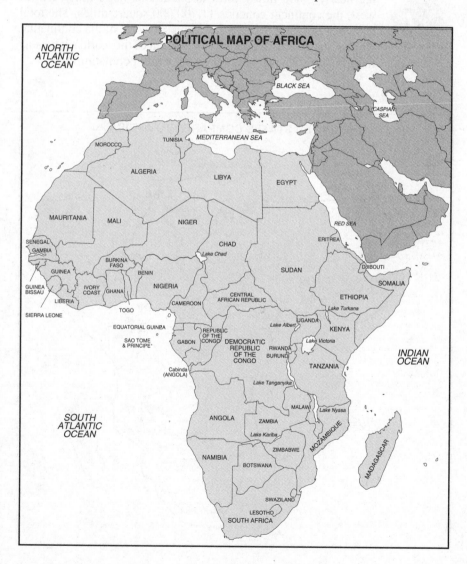

POLITICAL MAP OF AFRICA

NORTH ATLANTIC OCEAN

BLACK SEA

CASPIAN SEA

MOROCCO

TUNISIA

MEDITERRANEAN SEA

ALGERIA

LIBYA

EGYPT

MAURITANIA

MALI

NIGER

RED SEA

ERITREA

SENEGAL

GAMBIA

CHAD

Lake Chad

DJIBOUTI

BURKINA FASO

GUINEA

BENIN

SUDAN

SOMALIA

GUINEA BISSAU

IVORY COAST

GHANA

NIGERIA

LIBERIA

CAMEROON

CENTRAL AFRICAN REPUBLIC

ETHIOPIA

Lake Turkana

SIERRA LEONE

TOGO

UGANDA

Lake Albert

KENYA

EQUATORIAL GUINEA

SAO TOME & PRINCIPE

GABON

REPUBLIC OF THE CONGO

DEMOCRATIC REPUBLIC OF THE CONGO

RWANDA

BURUNDI

Lake Victoria

INDIAN OCEAN

Cabinda (ANGOLA)

TANZANIA

Lake Tanganyika

MALAWI

Lake Nyasa

SOUTH ATLANTIC OCEAN

ANGOLA

ZAMBIA

Lake Kariba

ZIMBABWE

MOZAMBIQUE

MADAGASCAR

NAMIBIA

BOTSWANA

SWAZILAND

LESOTHO

SOUTH AFRICA

GLOBAL
CONCEPTS
**Diversity**
CONCEPTS
GLOBAL

many years Africa was known as the "Dark Continent" because Western Europeans and Americans knew so little about it. The smooth coastline with few natural harbors, the falls and rapids near the mouths of rivers that made interior navigation difficult, and the deserts isolated Africa south of the Sahara. It was not until modern times that Westerners began to learn of Africa's early civilizations and its many diverse cultures.

## Size and Location

**Spatial Terms**

The African continent is the second largest in the world. Stretching nearly 5,000 miles north to south and 4,500 miles east to west, the continent contains 11,700,000 square miles. The total land area is approximately three times the size of the continental United States. Africa contains 20 percent of the world's land surface, but only 12 percent of the total world population.

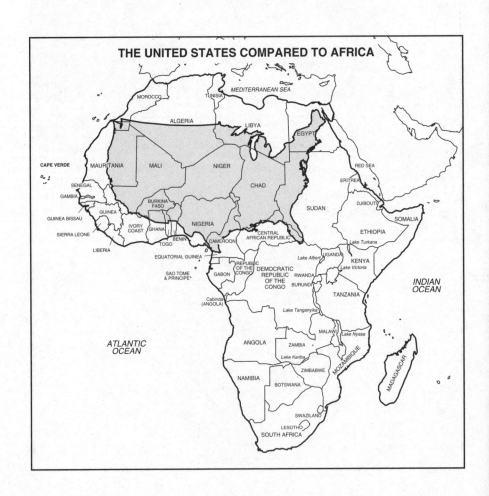

THE UNITED STATES COMPARED TO AFRICA

The African continent is divided nearly in half by the equator, and it stretches from approximately 38° north latitude to about 35° south latitude. Because of this, the central portion of Africa lies within the tropics.

The Mediterranean Sea lies to the north and has served as a link between Africa and European culture. To the west is the Atlantic Ocean, and to the east lies the Indian Ocean, which served as a trade route between Africa and India, Southeast Asia, and China. On the east coast is the Red Sea, which served as a trade route between Africa and Arabia and as a route for cultural diffusion, especially the diffusion of Islam. In the northeast is the Suez Canal, which is a major route for the transport of crude oil between the Persian Gulf nations and Europe.

## Mountains

Much of Africa is a great plateau or a series of plateaus interspersed with many great river basins. The central plateau makes the average elevation of Africa higher than that of any other continent. About 90 percent of sub-Saharan Africa (Africa south of the Sahara) is over 500 feet in elevation. The plateau is interrupted by various mountain ranges. The Atlas Mountains are located in the northwest. The Ethiopian Highlands in the northeast contain Lake Tana, the source of the Blue Nile. In the central region are the Ruwenzori (Mountains of the Moon) Mountains. The Drakensberg Mountains are found in South Africa. The Tibesti Mountains, the Ahaggar Mountains, and the Tassili-N-Ajjer are in the Sahara Desert.

**Physical Settings**

## Great Rift Valley

In the east the plateau is sliced by the Great Rift Valley, a great trough, or canyon, created by upheavals and disturbances in the earth's surface millions of years ago. The Eastern Rift Valley is about 4,000 miles long, while the Western Rift is about 1,000 miles long. The sides of the rift are as much as 100 miles apart and the depth of the valley varies from hundreds of feet to a mile. The rift influenced migration in East Africa, forcing people to move in a north-south direction.

GLOBAL
CONCEPTS
**Environment**
CONCEPTS
GLOBAL

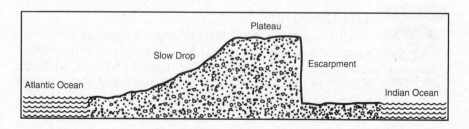

# Rivers

The great central plateau region drops sharply near the coast, creating a series of waterfalls and rapids on most of Africa's great rivers. As a result, Africa has a narrow coastal plain, and interior navigation is difficult. However, many of the rivers are navigable once the falls and rapids have been traversed. For example, the Congo River is navigable from the Atlantic Ocean for only 85 miles, but beyond the falls and rapids it becomes a major transportation route for Central Africa. The falls and rapids mean that Africa has great hydroelectric power potential. Much of this potential, however, goes untapped because of a lack of capital as well as little call for electricity in the villages.

The Nile River, at over 4,100 miles long, is the longest river in the world. The White Nile, which has its source in Lake Victoria, joins the Blue Nile, which has its source in Lake Tana in Ethiopia, at Khartoum in Sudan. The river flows north and empties into the Mediterranean Sea at Alexandria in Egypt, where it forms the Nile delta, an important agricultural area. Egypt is desert except for a strip, approximately ten miles wide, along the Nile. The predictable Nile flood provides a fresh deposit of alluvial soil each year and makes irrigation, transportation, and communication possible. In Sudan aquatic vegetation creates a region known as the Sudd, where the vegetation is so thick that travel becomes difficult and channels must be cut through the vegetation. Lake Nasser, created by the construction of the Aswan High Dam, is located in Egypt on the Nile.

The second longest river in Africa is the Congo. With its tributaries it drains an area of 1.4 million square miles. The Zambezi River contains Victoria Falls. Below the falls, a dam and lake (Lake Kariba) have been created to provide hydroelectric power. The Niger River rises in the Guinea Highlands, flows northeast through Mali, turns to the southeast and joins the Benue in Central Nigeria, then flows south to empty into the Gulf of Guinea in Nigeria, where it forms the Niger delta. The Niger, like the Nile, flows through a desert region, and many of the early West African kingdoms or civilizations developed along the Niger.

# The Deserts

The Sahara, the largest desert in the world, covering 3.5 million square miles, was not a total barrier to migration and trade. Arab traders set up camel caravan routes in the west, while the Nile River and coastal waters in the north and east provided routes of trade and cultural diffusion.

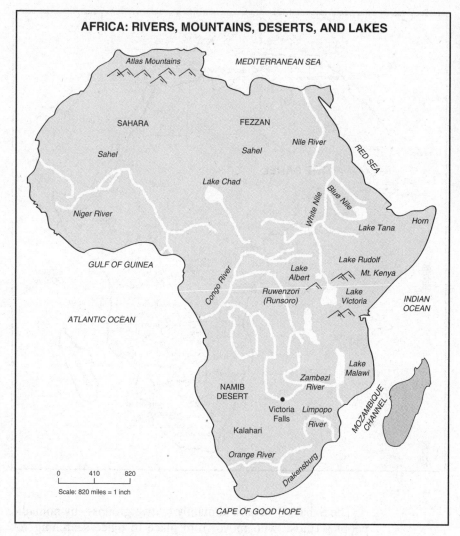

### AFRICA: RIVERS, MOUNTAINS, DESERTS, AND LAKES

Atlas Mountains

MEDITERRANEAN SEA

SAHARA

FEZZAN

Sahel

Sahel

Nile River

RED SEA

Lake Chad

Niger River

White Nile

Blue Nile

Lake Tana

Horn

GULF OF GUINEA

Congo River

Lake Albert

Lake Rudolf

Mt. Kenya

Ruwenzori (Runsoro)

Lake Victoria

INDIAN OCEAN

ATLANTIC OCEAN

Lake Malawi

NAMIB DESERT

Zambezi River

MOZAMBIQUE CHANNEL

Victoria Falls

Limpopo River

Kalahari

Orange River

Drakensburg

CAPE OF GOOD HOPE

0    410    820
Scale: 820 miles = 1 inch

The Sahara was not always a vast wasteland. Archeological discoveries indicate that at one time it was a well-watered grassland and that streams, lakes, and animals abounded. Climate changes, resulting from the Ice Age, are largely responsible for the changes.

Today the Sahara is largely uninhabited, with heavier population settlements in the areas where oases (places in the desert where there is enough ground water to make cultivation possible) or rivers are found, such as the Nile River Valley. The Niger River in the western Sahara made the development of the early kingdoms of Ghana, Mali, and Songhai possible.

GLOBAL CONCEPTS
**Environment**
CONCEPTS GLOBAL

123

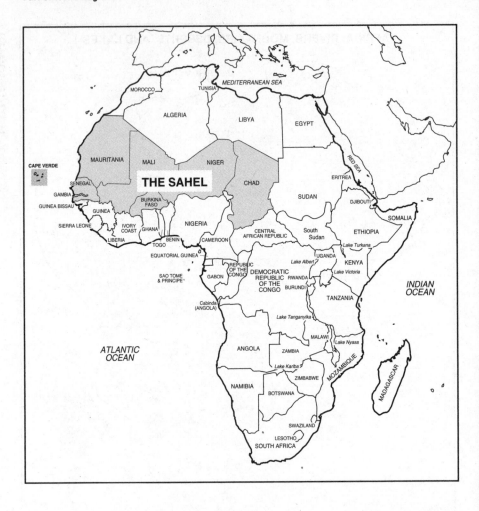

The Sahara is inhabited mainly by two groups—by nomadic peoples (those who move from place to place searching for grazing land for their animals) and seminomadic peoples and by people who have settled in the oases and are engaged in agriculture, raising date palms, vegetables, and grains. In recent years, mineral deposits, such as petroleum, natural gas, iron, phosphates, manganese, and copper, have been discovered in the desert.

The southern edge of the Sahara is bordered by a region known as the Sahel. It is a region of steppe, a marginal zone between the deserts to the north and the savanna to the south. The Sahel has long been inhabited by animal grazers and farmers. As long as the number of inhabitants remained relatively small, the Sahel could support human population. However, as

**WORLD ISSUES**

Environmental
Concerns

the numbers of both people and animals have increased, the strain on the land and its water resources has increased. As a result, the process of desertification (the process by which arable land becomes a desert) is taking place, and the Sahara is inching slowly southward into the Sahel.

Other major desert regions in Africa include the Namib, the Kalahari, and the deserts of southeastern Ethiopia and Somalia. The Kalahari has been inhabited by the Bushmen (Khoisan peoples) for hundreds of years.

## The Lakes

East Africa and the area of the Great Rift Valley are often referred to as the lakes region since many of Africa's great lakes are located there. Lake Victoria, the largest lake in Africa, the world's second largest fresh water body, and the world's third largest lake, is located between the two rift valleys and is very shallow. Lake Tanganyika in the Western Rift Valley, one of the deepest lakes in the world, reaching a depth of about 4,800 feet, is the second largest lake in Africa and the seventh largest in the world. The third largest lake in Africa is Lake Malawi (Nyasa). Lake Chad is located on the southern edge of the Sahara and in the Sahel, making it a very important source of water. Unfortunately, the lake is prone to evaporation and varies in size and volume throughout the year. Africa's lakes are an important source of fish, one of the major sources of protein in Africa.

## Climate and Vegetation Zones

The three most important factors in determining the climate of Africa are latitude, altitude, and wind patterns. Since the equator divides Africa nearly in half, climatic zones are similar in the north and south.

Extending north and south of the equator in Central or Equatorial Africa and in West Africa is a rain forest region, which makes up about 15 percent of Africa. It is characterized by high humidity, daily rainfall (60 to 80 inches average per year), and high temperatures (90°F) year round. Vegetation is basically on three levels. The ground cover consists of ferns and creeping plants. There is a second level of middle-growth trees and a third layer of tall trees. The last layer forms what is known as a canopy and prevents sunlight from reaching the rain forest floor.

The rain forest region is inhabited by some settled farmers, by some people who practice shifting cultivation, and by hunting-and-gathering groups such as the Pygmies. It is sparsely populated in Central (Equatorial) Africa and heavily populated in the coastal regions of Nigeria, Benin, Togo, and Ghana. The characteristics of the rain forest region discouraged European settlement.

North and south of the rain forest are the savanna zones, which cover about 40 percent of Africa. In the north the region is called the Sudan, and in the south, the Veldt. The savanna is characterized by a distinct wet season and a dry season. Rainfall varies from 20 to 60 inches per year. Vegetation consists of tall grasses, brush, and scattered trees. It is useful for grazing livestock and for shifting cultivation, and it is the home of much of Africa's wildlife. For the most part, the savanna is sparsely populated and did not attract European settlers. However, Zambia and Zimbabwe were heavily settled by Europeans because the winds and altitude moderated the climate.

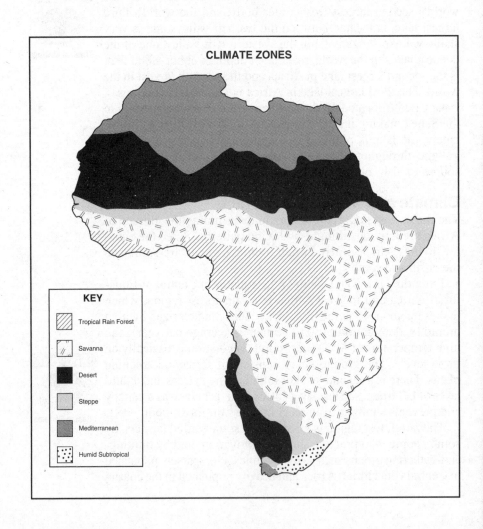

**CLIMATE ZONES**

**KEY**

- Tropical Rain Forest
- Savanna
- Desert
- Steppe
- Mediterranean
- Humid Subtropical

North and south of the savannas are the steppe regions, the so-called marginal lands. Rainfall here varies from 10 to 20 inches per year. Vegetation consists of short, scattered grasses. Grazing and some settled agriculture and shifting cultivation are possible. In general, this region is sparsely inhabited and did not attract European settlement.

North and south of the steppes are the desert regions, which receive less than 10 inches of rain per year. The desert regions make up another 40 percent of Africa. The Sahara lies to the north and the Namib and Kalahari to the southwest. Vegetation in the Sahara is mostly scattered desert grasses, often called cram-cram. These regions are very sparsely inhabited.

**GEOGRAPHY**

**Human Systems**

GLOBAL
CONCEPTS

**Scarcity**

CONCEPTS
GLOBAL

North and south of the deserts, in the northwest and southeast coastal regions, is a Mediterranean climate zone. There the summers are warm and dry; winters are cool and moist. Settled agriculture is possible, and olives and citrus fruits are raised. This is one of the climate zones that Europeans found attractive.

In the highlands of southern and eastern Africa, there is a vertical climate—that is, within a relatively short distance, because of changes in elevation, several climate types are found. These highlands attracted European settlement because of the fertile soils and more moderate temperatures.

| WORLD ISSUES |
| --- |
| Hunger |
| and |
| Poverty |

Many regions of Africa suffer from shortages of water. Twenty inches of rain may fall one year, none the next year, and 40 inches the next. Farmers, who rely on rainfall for their livelihood, have a very uncertain existence in Africa.

# REVIEW QUESTIONS

*Multiple Choice.* Select the letter of the answer that correctly completes each statement.

1. What part of Africa are the rift valleys in?
   A. northern
   B. southern
   C. eastern
   D. western

2. Which is the most valid description of Africa's topography?
   A. a relatively tilted plateau
   B. all rivers navigable for their entire lengths
   C. mountain ranges extending east and west
   D. savanna areas unfit for human habitation

3. The famine conditions in the Sahel region of Africa have been worsened by all the following *except*
   A. desertification
   B. overpopulation
   C. overgrazing
   D. international relief efforts

4. The Sahara
   A. prevented cultural diffusion in North Africa
   B. is a major source of agricultural products
   C. is home to many nomadic groups
   D. prevented migration in North Africa

5. Africa was once known as the Dark Continent, largely because of its
   A. nearness to the equator
   B. people
   C. geography
   D. lack of resources

6. A major reason for the north/south migration trend in East Africa is the location of the
   A. Atlas Mountains and Congo Basin
   B. Atlantic Ocean and Orange River
   C. Mediterranean Sea and Lake Chad
   D. Great Rift Valley and Nile River

7. European settlers in Africa tended to claim areas
   A. in the equatorial zone
   B. along the upper reaches of the Nile River
   C. adjacent to the Great Rift Valley
   D. in the cool highlands

8. Africa's geography
   A. helped to ensure cultural uniformity on the continent
   B. helped to create cultural diversity on the continent
   C. prevented foreign contact until the 19th century
   D. created insurmountable barriers to north/south migration

9. The Sahara Desert was not a total barrier to communication between
   North Africa and the West African kingdoms because of the existence of
   A. several north-/south-flowing rivers
   B. an early railroad system
   C. trans-Saharan camel trade routes
   D. a paved highway system

10. The most urgent problem in the Sahel of Africa is the
    A. process of desertification
    B. loss of the rain forest
    C. lack of farm machinery
    D. annual flooding of rivers

11. Africa's smooth coastline
    A. forced the Africans to develop deepwater fishing
    B. limits the number of good natural harbors
    C. prevented European conquest of the interior of the continent
    D. is caused by river runoff and deposits

12. Europeans who settled in Africa chose the highlands of the east largely
    because
    A. the people there were culturally similar to the Europeans
    B. natives of the area were mostly Christian
    C. the languages spoken there were similar to European languages
    D. the climate was similar to what they were used to in Europe

13. Egypt has been called the Gift of the Nile because
    A. transportation on the Nile made building the pyramids possible
    B. the Nile provides water for irrigation and deposits of alluvial soil
    C. the falls and rapids of the Nile prevented foreign invasion of Egypt
    D. the water of the Nile provide hydroelectric power for industry

14. The Great Rift Valley
    A. improved east/west travel in Africa
    B. is the location of many of Africa's great lakes
    C. was a major avenue of trade in ancient Africa
    D. contains Africa's richest farmland

# II. ECONOMIC GEOGRAPHY OF AFRICA

## Resources

The soils of Africa are generally poor, oxidized, and hard. Much of the soil contains laterite, which is not useful for agriculture. The soil of the tropical rain forest appears to be rich but is not. It is leached; the heavy rainfall forces the minerals so deep into the ground that plant roots cannot reach them, and the heavy vegetation is actually supported by the decay of humus on the forest floor. When the rain forest is cut down, heavy erosion occurs and desertification begins.

Africa is rich in mineral resources. In the countries of the Sahara and Nigeria, petroleum is an important source of revenue. Congo, Zambia, and Zimbabwe have enormous copper deposits. South Africa is a leading producer of gold and the world's major source of diamonds. The continent produces about 80 percent of the world's diamond supply. Other important minerals found in Africa include bauxite, uranium, tungsten, cobalt, tin, and zinc.

**WORLD ISSUES**

World
Trade and
Finance

## Barriers to African Development

Because of geographic, climatic, and economic factors, Africans have had to make major adjustments to suit the environment. In the process, distinct hunting, farming, herding, and fishing societies have developed in various regions of Africa. These groups have long traded with one another, making them interdependent.

Many factors combined to slow development in Africa and to limit the Africans' ability to live in certain regions and provide enough food. One factor is that about 75 percent of the region south of the Sahara is short of water. This is a result of the unpredictability of rainfall, the few great river systems for a continent of this size, and the concentration of lakes in the rift valleys. A lack of capital has made it difficult for many African nations to construct major irrigation projects.

GLOBAL CONCEPTS

**Scarcity**

CONCEPTS GLOBAL

The Africans have made limited use of available natural resources. Historically, the major reason was that resources were located far from market centers. Today they lack the technology to develop these resources, and they also lack the capital for investment in mining and processing industries. Since the resources are located far from market centers, the lack of capital makes it difficult to construct new transportation facilities and to maintain existing ones. Moreover, rivers are not naviga-

**GEOGRAPHY**

**Human Systems**

GLOBAL CONCEPTS

**Technology**

CONCEPTS GLOBAL

ble all the way to the trade centers because of falls and rapids, and certain climate zones (desert, rain forest) also make it difficult to construct transportation routes.

In sub-Saharan Africa the tsetse fly, which attacks livestock, made the use of horses and oxen impossible, so the Africans developed farming techniques that relied on human labor. Reliance on traditional methods of agriculture and a lack of agricultural equipment make the exploitation of soils, trees, and minerals difficult.

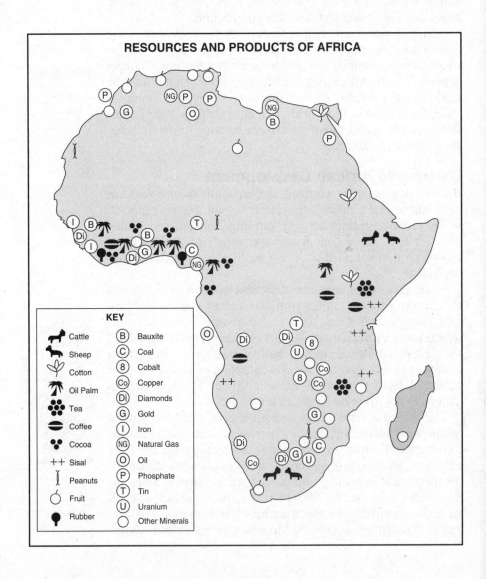

RESOURCES AND PRODUCTS OF AFRICA

KEY

| | | | |
|---|---|---|---|
| Cattle | | B | Bauxite |
| Sheep | | C | Coal |
| Cotton | | 8 | Cobalt |
| Oil Palm | | Co | Copper |
| Tea | | Di | Diamonds |
| Coffee | | G | Gold |
| Cocoa | | I | Iron |
| Sisal | ++ | NG | Natural Gas |
| Peanuts | | O | Oil |
| Fruit | | P | Phosphate |
| Rubber | | T | Tin |
| | | U | Uranium |
| | | ○ | Other Minerals |

# Economic Development Since Independence

The colonial powers followed a policy of mercantilism (colonial powers required their colonies to buy and sell only to them, thus enabling them to export more than they imported and build up economic profit). As a result, some of Africa's resources were developed, but the profits went to the colonial powers. Since Africans were encouraged to raise cash crops and forced to buy more expensive finished products from the mother country, most African nations did not accumulate any capital reserves.

**WORLD ISSUES**

Economic
Growth and
Development

When the African nations became independent, they needed capital to continue the development of their resources and to build industries and modernize. As a result, African nations were forced to borrow heavily from the superpowers (the United States and the Soviet Union) and from their former colonial rulers. They also turned to international organizations such as the World Bank. However, they have borrowed so heavily from such organizations that, with their current economic problems, these organizations are reluctant to lend them more.

**WORLD ISSUES**

World
Trade and
Finance

Current economic problems of African nations are a result of many factors:

1. With the capital from international loans, some gains were made, but often local conditions were not considered. Factories have been built in areas where the climate makes work difficult, both for people and machines. Dams that were built to supply hydroelectric power sometimes ruin the ecological balance of a region and are therefore harmful to farmers.

2. Capital investment in most countries has been concentrated in the industrial sector. Since most of Africa is still rural, this has not given Africans greater purchasing power, and there is little domestic market for manufactured products.

3. Africa lacks skilled workers. Colonial education was designed to provide lower-level government workers, and those who can afford higher education today are more interested in law, medicine, and so on—education that provides prestige or entry into politics and government.

4. Transportation and communications systems in Africa are still inadequate. Roads are difficult to build and maintain in the tropical climates. It is difficult to transport resources to the sites of manufacturing plants.

5. To achieve progress, people must work together, and this is difficult in nations where ethnic rivalries are prevalent.

GLOBAL
CONCEPTS
**Choice**
CONCEPTS
GLOBAL

**WORLD ISSUES**

Determination
of Political
and Economic
Systems

**WORLD ISSUES**

Economic
Growth and
Development

**WORLD ISSUES**

Political and
Economic
Refugees

6. Much of the money from international loans and foreign aid has been squandered in schemes designed to promote national pride (such as huge government buildings, statues, and so on) or simply confiscated by corrupt leaders.

7. World economic conditions have also affected Africa. During the 1970s many African nations were forced to pay high prices for petroleum. During the 1980s countries like Nigeria, which export oil, suffered from low oil prices. Prices for many of Africa's cash crops have dropped in the world market.

The heavy debt burden and the export of cash crops create an economic dependency for trade, capital, and food, which is deeply resented by many African peoples and interpreted as neo-colonialism (establishing colonial-type political and economic control in independent developing nations). Many countries in Africa have nationalized (placed under state control) industries, and the presence of multinational corporations (companies with branches in several nations) has been encouraged, even though many Africans resent the foreign ownership and fear a loss of control.

Various attempts at economic development have included the introduction of socialism or mixed economic activities. When Julius Nyerere became president of Tanzania with Tanzania's independence in the 1960s, he introduced a socialist system called ujamaa (familyhood, sharing). In 1967 a program of nationalizing industries and plantations and creating cooperative farms began. Villages in the rural areas were formed into cooperatives, schools and clinics were established, and new farm machinery and techniques were introduced. In the 1970s the rising cost of petroleum products hurt Tanzania, and there were some problems with ujamaa. Hit by drought in 1980 to 1984, Tanzania had to appeal for international aid. Nyerere was replaced in 1985. Privatization of the economy was undertaken in the 1990s. The per capita GDP is only $600.

Nigeria has a mixed economy—major industries and oil production are nationalized, while small industries and agriculture remain in private hands. Multinational corporations are required to serve local needs as well as their own interests. Nigeria has experienced success in industrial and petroleum output, but agricultural production still lags, and food must be imported. Many other nations have a mixed economy, such as Kenya, Angola, Zambia, Uganda, Algeria, and Egypt.

The trend has been to invest in the urban, industrialized areas and to neglect the rural sector of the economy, and most Africans still live at or near the poverty level. So many Africans have moved to the cities in search of work that the cities are overcrowded, and shantytowns have sprouted up on their outskirts. The unemployment rate is high since there are not enough jobs for all the Africans who have migrated to the cities. City services have proven inadequate to handle the needs of the rapidly expanding population, and pollution and unsanitary conditions are a problem. There is also a notable difference between the "haves" (the rising middle class) and the "have nots" (unemployed rural immigrants), which emphasizes the inequality that still exists in Africa.

## Agriculture

Approximately 60 percent of the African people are still engaged in agriculture. Most African farmers are subsistence farmers, raising just enough to support their families. Many of these farmers use a method known as bush-fallow (the same crop is planted until the land loses its fertility, and then the land is allowed to lie fallow until the fertility is naturally renewed). In order to gain capital, many governments have encouraged the raising of cash crops, such as coffee, peanuts, cotton, cocoa, and palm products, for export. Major food products include maize, cassava, and yams. Because of the demand for cash crops, African farmers do not raise enough food for themselves, and many food products must be imported. In addition, food production is unable to keep up because the population is increasing so rapidly. But there are other reasons:

1. *Deforestation and erosion.* Most Africans still use wood as a source of fuel, and forests are being destroyed. The loss of forest cover leads to soil erosion and loss of topsoil.

2. *Lack of government encouragement and assistance.* Many African governments are interested in the export of cash crops and accumulation of capital and have failed to provide programs to encourage greater food production.

3. *Desertification.* Overgrazing and overcultivation in the marginal lands (particularly in the Sahel) have increased the rate at which the desert is advancing into what was once agricultural land.

4. *Scarcity of water and erratic rainfall.* African farmers, without government assistance, simply cannot afford the high cost of sinking wells and building irrigation systems.

5. *Failure to fertilize the land.* Many Africans use natural fertilizer for fuel. Most farmers cannot afford artificial fertilizers, and African soils are not naturally rich.

6. *Civil wars.* Civil wars in some countries (notably Ethiopia, Sudan, Mozambique, Chad, Somalia, Liberia, Sierra Leone)

**WORLD ISSUES**

Economic
Growth and
Development

have resulted in a great decrease in food production and contributed to famine in those countries.

**WORLD ISSUES**

Environmental Concerns

7. *Drought.* Over twenty countries in Africa suffered repeated drought over the last forty years. The drought was particularly severe in the countries of the Sahel (though drought has affected Tanzania, Mozambique, Kenya, Somalia, and others). It has been particularly severe in eastern Africa in 2010 and 2011. Food production dropped and millions of people died.

**WORLD ISSUES**

Population

The birth rate in Africa remains high because people in rural areas have little access to education and health services. Rural Africans have many children because children can assist in the fields, provide social security (eventual care for their elders), and assure continuance of the family lineage. At the same time, better medical care has decreased the death rate and increased life expectancy.

GLOBAL CONCEPTS

**Change**

CONCEPTS GLOBAL

The Green Revolution, with its hybrid seed and new fertilizers and methods, promises great hope. However, African farmers need government encouragement and assistance to benefit from the Green Revolution. They must be convinced that the new technology is better than traditional methods, and they need financial assistance to purchase the expensive new seeds and fertilizers. They also need education to avoid the pitfalls (overuse of pesticides and chemical fertilizers resulting in human illnesses) that have occurred in India.

# REVIEW QUESTIONS

*Multiple Choice.* Select the letter of the answer that correctly completes each statement.

1. South Africa is one of the world's greatest sources of
   A. oil
   B. gold
   C. iron
   D. timber

2. Which factor of production do poorer African nations need from the World Bank?
   A. labor
   B. capital
   C. land
   D. management

3. An increase in cash crops would directly increase a nation's
   A. imports
   B. exports
   C. population
   D. territory

4. A family that grows only enough food to feed itself is engaged in farming that is known as
   A. single crop
   B. cash crop
   C. subsistence
   D. modernized

5. A country with a one-crop economy is
   A. self-sufficient
   B. economically dependent on others
   C. unaffected by world market fluctuations
   D. independent of international economic trends

6. Europeans colonized Africa for all the following reasons *except*
   A. to provide markets for their own industrial products
   B. to gain control of natural resources
   C. to expand their own empires
   D. to study the languages and religions of the Africans

137

7. Which of the following beneficial results of colonial rule has actually helped to create one of the major modern problems in emerging African nations?
   A. European technology led to the development of new African industries.
   B. European settlers introduced modern farming methods in Kenya.
   C. Missionaries established elementary schools in the Congo.
   D. New medicines increased life expectancy and decreased the infant mortality rate.

8. Which type of nation is most dependent on world economic trends?
   A. one with a cash-crop economy
   B. one with a subsistence economy
   C. one with a command economy
   D. one with a capitalist economy

9. Vegetation zones in Africa
   A. have strongly influenced regional land use
   B. are much like those in North America
   C. run parallel to the prime meridian
   D. have not affected cultural development

10. Africa is best known for its
    A. mineral resources
    B. food surpluses
    C. democratic governments
    D. health care facilities

11. Leached soil
    A. has high levels of minerals and nutrients
    B. does not support profitable agriculture
    C. results from overgrazing
    D. occurs in desert regions

12. European powers required their colonies to buy from and sell to only them. This practice is known as
    A. imperialism
    B. nationalism
    C. mercantilism
    D. nationalization

13. A country in which the government owns mines and rail lines and private citizens own major industries and the land has an economy known as
    A. communism
    B. utopian
    C. mixed economy
    D. traditional

14. All the following have contributed to famine conditions in Africa *except*
    A. civil disturbances and warfare
    B. erosion
    C. desertification
    D. excess rainfall

15. Many early sub-Saharan societies did not use horse and oxen power because
    A. the tsetse fly and sleeping sickness were present
    B. they made use of the camel as a source of labor instead
    C. they had no domesticated animals
    D. their animistic beliefs denied them the use of animal power

16. The majority of sub-Saharan nations do not have the necessary capital to invest in industrial development largely because
    A. colonial powers made no efforts to develop African resources
    B. they are spending most of their money cleaning up the environment
    C. too much is spent providing social services for rural inhabitants
    D. the majority of sub-Saharan Africans are subsistence farmers with little or no cash income

17. Which of the following is a result of the fact that approximately 70 percent of all Africans live in rural areas and depend on agriculture for a living?
    A. Africa has one of the most rapidly growing populations of any of the continents.
    B. There is a problem of unemployment in African urban areas.
    C. Most African governments have concentrated on building roads and electric plants in rural areas.
    D. The increase in population growth has been matched by increasing food production.

# III. HUMAN AND CULTURAL GEOGRAPHY OF AFRICA

## The People of Africa

A 2005 estimate of Africa's population puts it at 900 million, approximately 14 percent of the world's population. The people of Africa may be more diverse than the people of any other continent. They differ from one another both culturally and physically for two main reasons. First, Africans have intermingled and intermarried with others for generations. Second, because of geography many African groups developed in relative isolation. In fact, there are over 2,000 distinct cultural or ethnic groups.

Anthropologists seem to agree that most of the people of sub-Saharan Africa reveal physical characteristics of the Negroid race. Physical characteristics vary from group to group, however. Skin color ranges from very dark to light, hair texture varies, and the world's tallest as well as the shortest peoples are found in Africa. The people of North Africa reflect Caucasian characteristics. Many Europeans have settled in South Africa, Kenya, and Zimbabwe. East Africa and the Republic of South Africa also have many Asian peoples.

GLOBAL CONCEPTS
**Diversity**
CONCEPTS GLOBAL

## African Languages

Over 2,000 languages are spoken on the African continent. The Bantu languages of sub-Saharan Africa are the most widely spoken. Swahili, a mixture of Arabic and Bantu, is spoken in East Africa. The Khoisan (click) languages are spoken by the Bushmen and Hottentots. Hausa is common in West Africa, and Arabic is common in North Africa. In addition, many European languages are spoken and reflect the colonial heritage. For example, in many African countries, English and French were the colonial European languages widely spoken there before independence. Today they are used as official languages.

GLOBAL CONCEPTS
**Change**
CONCEPTS GLOBAL

## Traditional Beliefs

Traditional African religions were as varied as the ethnic groups that created them, and there are over 2,000 ethnic groups on the African continent. In spite of this, there are certain beliefs that most of the traditional African religions have in common. These include belief in ancestral spirits, belief in continuity of the clan and ethnic group, and belief that the land is held in ancestral trust. Traditional religions developed a philosophy of the individual's relation to the natural world and of the individual's place in that world. They helped to provide each clan and ethnic group with an identity.

In traditional Africa the individual was a member of a family, which was a part of a clan, which in turn was part of an ethnic group or tribe. It is common belief that the African is part of an unbroken chain that includes dead ancestors, living relatives, and unborn relatives, and that a person's spirit lives as long as he or she is remembered by future generations.

GLOBAL
CONCEPTS

**Culture**

CONCEPTS
GLOBAL

Also common in sub-Saharan traditional religious belief is the idea that ancestral spirits are involved in the lives of the present generation. It is believed that the ancestral spirits watch over the living. The spirits of ancestors are helpful as long as they are respected, but when they are not, they will bring harm to their descendants. As a result, prayers, ceremonial rites, and even sacrifices are necessary to show respect for ancestors.

GLOBAL
CONCEPTS

**Identity**

CONCEPTS
GLOBAL

According to tradition, the land was held in trust by the ancestors and could not be owned. The African only had the right to use it. The land belonged to the family, the clan, and the ethnic group, and the right to work or use it was handed down from generation to generation.

Also common in traditional African religion is belief in a supreme God who created the world and then withdrew and in lesser gods whose spirits inhabit natural things (animism). These spirits determine everything that happens; they control life and death, good and evil. Most Africans do not worship rivers, trees, animals, and so on; instead, they worship the spirits they represent.

Among some traditional African groups, there was also a belief that the chiefs or kings were divine. In others, the chief was considered the custodian of the land, and he could assign the right to use it.

## Islam in Africa

Islam, the religion of the prophet Muhammad, originated in the deserts of the Arabian Peninsula in the 7th century. Shortly thereafter, Muslim conquerors swept across North Africa in search of converts to Islam and also arable land. They offered the conquered peoples three choices: fight, convert, or pay tribute. Conversion to Islam was the easiest and most practical response. Many of the teachings of Islam were similar to those of traditional African beliefs and were liberal enough to allow an African to become a Muslim and still retain many traditional beliefs and customs.

Islam spread to West Africa as a result of the trade carried along the trans-Saharan trade routes by the Arabs. In time, Islam spread to the kingdoms of Ghana, Mali, and Songhai, which became theocracies (where religious leaders are also govern-

GLOBAL
CONCEPTS

**Change**

CONCEPTS
GLOBAL

ment leaders). Muslims established universities, religious centers of learning, and research, which enriched the lives of the people of West African kingdoms. In the eastern coastal regions of Africa, Islam was spread by Arab traders, who controlled the trade between Africa and the Far East and who settled in coastal cities and towns.

GLOBAL
CONCEPTS

**Identity**

CONCEPTS
GLOBAL

In a region of great ethnic diversity, Islam has provided a focus for unity, and in some of the North and West African countries, it was used as a rallying point for independence movements. The Arabic language also provided unity and in many areas, the first written language. Koranic (Quran, the holy book of Islam) studies led to a new class of educated leaders. Islamic law (which exists along with traditional African law) and laws established during the colonial period in most of North Africa provided a uniform system of justice, while Muslim traders increased the amount of trade and market activity.

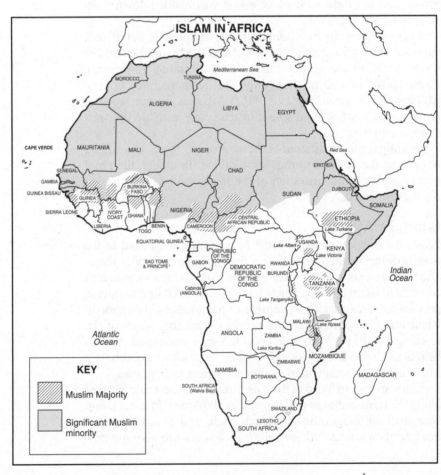

ISLAM IN AFRICA

KEY

Muslim Majority

Significant Muslim minority

142

Fundamentalist Islamic movements in some African countries created tension and violence in the 20th century. The assassination of Egyptian President Anwar Sadat in 1981 is one example. The political unrest in Sudan as a result of an attempt to institute Islamic law in the 1980s is another. And the civil war in Algeria where an estimated 80,000 people have died is still another. There are approximately 360 million practicing Muslims in Africa today.

## Christianity in Africa

The Coptic Christian Church was established in Egypt in the 1st century A.D. as a result of Greek influence. Coptic Christianity was brought to the Sudan or Nubia by Egyptian missionaries and made its way to Axum in the 4th century, where it was adopted as the official religion.

In the 1400s and 1500s, Portuguese and Spanish explorers who came to Africa were accompanied by Christian missionaries. Numerous missions were established along the west coast, but not many Africans converted to Christianity. In the late 19th century, missionaries followed the explorers into the interior of Africa, where they established schools to teach the doctrines of Christianity. By the end of the 19th century, Europeans had carved Africa into colonial empires, and Christianity came to be associated with colonial regimes. Nevertheless, millions of Africans converted to Christianity, both for spiritual and practical reasons. As with Islam, there were certain similarities between Christianity and traditional African beliefs, such as the African belief in a supreme God and the Christian belief in a single God, that enabled many Africans to adopt Christianity. Moreover, Africans soon learned that training at the mission schools was necessary if they wanted to take part in the economic activities and administration of government under their colonial rulers. Many of them used the knowledge of scientific theory, human rights, and self-determination they learned in the mission schools to become leaders of independence movements in their nations. There have been movements to establish independent African Christian churches and to make Christianity more African in form. Many Africans believe that Christianity can be adapted to African life and tradition without sacrificing its major teachings. There are approximately 400 million practicing Christians in Africa today.

## Role and Expression of Traditional African Art

Two of the dominant and most famous of the traditional African art forms are sculpture and masks. African sculpture served rit-

GLOBAL
CONCEPTS
**Justice**
CONCEPTS
GLOBAL

**WORLD ISSUES**

Terrorism

GLOBAL
CONCEPTS
**Change**
CONCEPTS
GLOBAL

GLOBAL
CONCEPTS
**Culture**
CONCEPTS
GLOBAL

ual purposes and was often designed with the intent of social control. African sculpture includes figurines, fetishes (objects thought to have magical powers to bring good or evil and protect the owner from evil forces), and stools. A piece of sculpture was not designed to be looked at and enjoyed as a beautiful creation. Instead, it was designed for use in ceremonies, to represent spirits of ancestors or gods, or even to house spirits of unborn babies. Some, usually those of animals, were carved to represent admirable qualities, such as strength, speed, or endurance. Some represented fertility. Since these sculptures were often representations, it was not considered proper for them to be too realistic. As a result, African art was often abstract or exaggerated. The most favored material for sculpture was wood, but bronze, brass, gold, clay, ivory, and soapstone were also used.

African masks, which can be considered a form of sculpture, were worn in ceremonies of ritual dance. The mask, which was often worn with a costume, was part of a spiritual disguise. Often the masks were hidden, except when the ceremonies took place. When used in ceremonial rites, worn by rapidly whirling and swaying dancers, the masks became powerful representations of the spirits and gods.

African dance is generally symbolic and has strong ties to traditional religions. Dance was used at initiation ceremonies, funerals, and before going into conflict with other groups. There are dances for a good harvest, a successful hunt, and so on. There are dances to thank, appease, and make requests from the spirits. Dance is also performed for entertainment. Dance is most often accompanied by music. Instruments include drums, gourd rattles, horns, flutes, stringed instruments, and xylophones, depending on the region. African music is polyrhythmic, consisting of as many as five rhythms being played at the same time.

## African Cultural and Social Institutions

The diffusion of Western ideas and institutions resulted in significant changes in African lifestyles and world views of Africans.

Perhaps the most significant change taking place in Africa is the development of many major urban areas. With its rapidly growing population, there isn't enough arable land to support the people, causing many young Africans to migrate to urban areas in search of jobs. Here their lives undergo dramatic change.

In traditional Africa and in the rural areas even today, an African is a member of an extended family, a clan, a lineage, and an ethnic group. As members of an extended family and clan, Africans have social security and are assured of support.

GLOBAL CONCEPTS
Identity
CONCEPTS GLOBAL

GLOBAL CONCEPTS
Culture
CONCEPTS GLOBAL

GLOBAL CONCEPTS
Change
CONCEPTS GLOBAL

In the cities, the extended family becomes a luxury young people can no longer enjoy. Also, in urban life arranged marriages become less and less common. Moreover, since urban Africans no longer depend on the land, the old ethnic authority structure is breaking down. The influence and authority of chiefs or elders is no longer so strong and is seldom felt in the cities.

In much of traditional Africa and in some rural areas today, polygamy was (or is) practiced. In urban areas this is no longer practical for most Africans, and more and more Africans practice monogamy. However, some urban dwellers, who can afford to, still practice polygamy.

African women have traditionally played an important role in society. Among many ethnic groups, division of labor meant that men were hunters and/or warriors; among most herders, men were responsible for the herds. This left women to tend the fields, and they were often responsible for marketing the produce. Several ethnic groups practiced matrilineal descent, in which inheritance is carried through the mother's family line. Urban African females are active today in politics, law, medicine, and other professions. In rural areas, the traditional female role is still strong, though more and more men engage in cultivating the fields.

The majority of Africans still live in rural areas and depend on the land for subsistence. The rural areas retain traditional values, attitudes, and practices. There is strong loyalty to the ethnic group and the traditional authority system. The influence of the council of elders is strong, and there is a strong community spirit. Women are largely engaged in traditional roles, and the birth rate is high.

These traditional values and the traditional morality are often in conflict with the changing attitudes of the urban dwellers. The conflict is compounded by the increasing role played by the media and education. Through the mass media and the education process, Africans gain knowledge of Western ideas of mass democracy, socialism, majority rule, and minority rights, and they wish to adopt these concepts. Industrialization and modernization are bringing new technology to Africa, which in turn requires some change in traditional roles and relationships. Women who are wage earners are no longer willing to accept subordinate roles, for example.

Although there have been major changes in the lifestyles of many Africans, tradition still has a strong hold in Africa. Many urban Africans return to the rural areas for ceremonies such as marriage, birth, death, and circumcision. In urban areas, members of ethnic groups often band together to provide support.

GLOBAL
CONCEPTS
**Choice**
CONCEPTS
GLOBAL

GLOBAL
CONCEPTS
**Identity**
CONCEPTS
GLOBAL

GLOBAL
CONCEPTS
**Change**
CONCEPTS
GLOBAL

# REVIEW QUESTIONS

*Multiple Choice.* Select the letter of the answer that correctly completes
each statement.

1. The largest language group in Africa is
   A. Swahili
   B. Bantu
   C. Arabian
   D. Hausa

2. Which of these groups has African society been organized around for
   thousands of years?
   A. occupational
   B. ethnic
   C. economic
   D. national

3. The spread of Islam throughout Africa is an example of
   A. national security
   B. socialism
   C. self-determination
   D. cultural diffusion

4. Animistic beliefs emphasize
   A. monotheism
   B. ancestor worship
   C. nature worship
   D. patriotism

5. The influence of traditional African cultures is best seen today in Western
   A. art forms
   B. technological advances
   C. family patterns
   D. political ideas

6. Racial and family patterns have been studied mostly by
   A. economists
   B. biologists
   C. anthropologists
   D. archeologists

7. Cultural change will occur most rapidly in a region that is
   A. geographically isolated
   B. ethnocentric
   C. industrializing
   D. self-sufficient

8. The greatest advantage for the Africans of the colonial period was that
   A. natives who received a Western education shared a common language
   B. African resources were exploited
   C. through mercantilism the natives had a market for their industrial products
   D. the European countries sold manufactured products to the Africans

9. The effects of urbanization and industrialization on the traditional family include
   A. the strengthening of patriarchal authority
   B. increase in family size
   C. the loss of the eldest male's authoritative control
   D. increased subordination of women

10. The introduction of Western education during the colonial period in Africa
    A. led to the development of nationalist movements in the colonies
    B. ensured that the emerging African nations would have a surplus of technically trained workers
    C. resulted in democratic governments in all the former colonies
    D. resulted in equality of the sexes in the independent African countries

11. Young Africans who move to the city seeking employment are likely to find
    A. they miss the sense of security they had as members of a rural community
    B. their lack of education is not a problem because African industry already has plenty of skilled workers
    C. housing in the cities is readily available and fairly cheap
    D. other recently arrived workers are eager to help them adapt to urban living

12. As African nations become more urbanized
    A. traditional ties to the family become stronger
    B. clan and family loyalties weaken
    C. nuclear families become less popular
    D. ancestor worship becomes increasingly important

13. The term Bantu refers to
    A. a tribal grouping in Africa
    B. a linguistic group
    C. religious groups
    D. village organization in Tanzania

14. In which of the following areas would one find the people most strongly affected by traditional attitudes and values?
    A. suburban area with many middle-class factory workers
    B. an urban, upper-class neighborhood inhabited by doctors and lawyers
    C. a rural area where the majority have always been subsistence farmers
    D. a lower-class city neighborhood inhabited by people from many different ethnic backgrounds

# SECTION 7: LATIN AMERICA AND THE CARIBBEAN BASIN

## I. PHYSICAL GEOGRAPHY OF LATIN AMERICA AND THE CARIBBEAN BASIN

The physical geography of Latin America and the Caribbean basin has had a great impact on the economic life, political events, and human/cultural geography of the nations and peoples in the region.

### A Definition of Latin America and the Caribbean Basin

Latin America refers to the region in the Western Hemisphere that is south and southeast of the United States. The region has interesting geographical characteristics and contrasts. Latin America is a physical area that includes the southern part of North America and almost all the land area of South America and Central America and islands in the Caribbean Sea.

Latin America can be divided into three geopolitical subregions: South America, Middle (Meso) America (Mexico and Central America), and the Caribbean Islands that are classified as Latin American. There are a total of twenty-four Latin American nations and dependent lands. In addition, there are nations, areas with countries and dependent lands, that have an English, American, and Dutch heritage.

Latin America and the Caribbean basin, which comprise one sixth of the earth's land surface, is approximately 8 million square miles. From the northern border of Mexico to the southern tip of Chile, it is 6,000 miles. At its widest point from Brazil on the Atlantic Ocean to Peru on the Pacific Ocean, the region is 3,000 miles wide. The nations of the region range in size from Brazil, the world's fifth largest country, to small island nations in the Caribbean Sea.

Latin America and the Caribbean basin lie between latitudes 33° north and 56° south. The geographical location of most of the region within the tropics and subtropics determines its climate, rainfall, and vegetation. Other geographical factors also influence and help determine the region's agricultural production, political, economic, and social patterns.

The Caribbean basin subregion includes islands in the Caribbean Sea and land areas in Central America and South

149

America. This subregion has a number of larger and smaller islands. Among these are the Greater Antilles and the Lesser Antilles. Some of the countries of these islands, Cuba, the Dominican Republic, Puerto Rico, and Haiti, are part of Latin America. Within this subregion, there are other islands and lands that are not defined as Latin American. For example, Jamaica, Aruba, Belize, and Barbados are nations with an English or Dutch colonial heritage.

**LATIN AMERICA POLITICAL MAP**

The national languages of Latin America are mostly Romance languages: Spanish, Portuguese, and French. There are islands and land areas in the Caribbean basin and countries in Central America and South America that have English or Dutch cultural and language traditions. Also, there are nations in which Native American peoples speak a number of languages including Guarani, Quechua, and Amayra. In Haiti, the use of Creole is widespread, and English is often used in Puerto Rico.

The nations of Latin America and the Caribbean basin all have a European colonial heritage. Spain, Portugal, France, England, Holland, and Denmark all had colonies in this region. Christianity is the major religion in Latin America, and most people are Roman Catholic or Protestant. There are also nations such as Brazil (spiritualism) and Haiti (voodoo) where African religious influences are strong.

### LANGUAGES OF LATIN AMERICA

| South America | Central America | Caribbean |
|---|---|---|
| Brazil (Portuguese) | Mexico (Spanish) | Cuba (Spanish) |
| Argentina (Spanish) | Guatemala (Spanish) | Dominican Republic (Spanish) |
| Uruguay (Spanish) | El Salvador (Spanish) | Haiti (French, Creole) |
| Paraguay (Spanish, | Honduras (Spanish) | Puerto Rico (English, Spanish) |
| Tupi-Guarani) | Nicaragua (Spanish) | Martinique (French) |
| Bolivia (Spanish, | Costa Rica (Spanish) | Guadeloupe (French) |
| Quechua, Aymara) | Panama (Spanish) | |
| Chile (Spanish) | | |
| Peru (Spanish) | | |
| Ecuador (Spanish) | | |
| Colombia (Spanish) | | |
| Venezuela (Spanish) | | |
| French Guiana (French) | | |

The process of cultural diffusion continues to play an important role in shaping society within Latin America and the Caribbean basin. Recent immigration from Asia and the Middle East has had a significant impact. For example, in São Paulo, Brazil, the influence of Japanese immigrants is strongly felt in agriculture. In Costa Rica, increased North American immigration by retired persons seeking a less expensive environment and year-round warmer climate has caused a different cultural diffusion.

## Mountains, Plateaus, Highlands, and Water Bodies

The region has two major physical characteristics: enormous mountain ranges and vast river systems. The large mountain

151

ranges are found in Mexico, in the three Sierra Madre chains, and in South America where the 4,000-mile-long Andes chain stretches along the western coast of the continent from Venezuela south to Tierra del Fuego. There are some mountains with peaks as high as 22,000 feet. The mountains separate regions in Mexico and the nations of South America, making trade and communication more difficult.

There are also three large river systems in South America. They are the Amazon, Orinoco, and Rio de la Plata river systems, which spread out over much of the South American continent. The Amazon River and its tributaries in the tropics spread out over much of the northern part of South America and make up the largest tropical river system in the world. The Amazon has both helped and made difficult the development of transportation and human settlement in the tropics. It provides water for irrigating farmland and offers the possibility of river transportation during the drier seasons. However, when the rainy season comes, the Amazon and its tributaries overflow, causing widespread flooding of farmland and making river and road transportation often impossible. Only in recent times, with the development of modern technology, airplanes, and telephone and Internet communication, has the geographical isolation of this part of South America been partly overcome. The Orinoco River system is found in the northwestern part of the South American continent. Much of this river system flows through Venezuela and Colombia. The Rio de la Plata River system, which includes the Uruguay, Paraguay, and Parana rivers, is located in the southeastern part of South America, in Argentina, Paraguay, Uruguay, and southern Brazil. The Caribbean Sea has also had a major influence on the development of the nations, peoples, and lands in the Caribbean basin.

## Climates in Latin America

Latin America and the Caribbean have a varied climate. There are five different climatic subregions: high mountains, tropical jungles, deserts, temperate coastal plains, and temperate highlands. The first three areas are not very populated because the climatic conditions make life more difficult. In these climatic zones it is either too hot, cold, dry, or wet. Most people in Latin America live on the temperate coastal plains and highlands of Mexico, Central America, South America, and the Caribbean Islands. In these climatic zones the temperature and rainfall are moderate, and it is easier to raise crops and develop urban centers where people can live and work.

## CLIMATES OF LATIN AMERICA

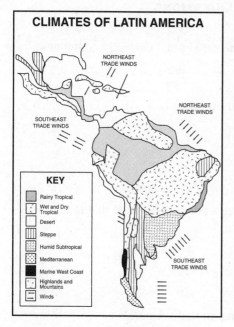

NORTHEAST TRADE WINDS

NORTHEAST TRADE WINDS

SOUTHEAST TRADE WINDS

SOUTHEAST TRADE WINDS

### KEY

- Rainy Tropical
- Wet and Dry Tropical
- Desert
- Steppe
- Humid Subtropical
- Mediterranean
- Marine West Coast
- Highlands and Mountains
- Winds

## CURRENTS OF LATIN AMERICA

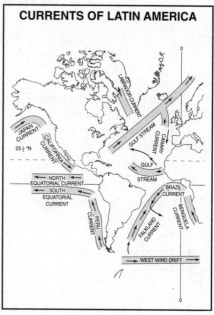

LABRADOR CURRENT

GULF STREAM

CANARY CURRENT

JAPAN CURRENT

CALIFORNIA CURRENT

23½°N

GULF STREAM

NORTH EQUATORIAL CURRENT

SOUTH EQUATORIAL CURRENT

BRAZIL CURRENT

PERU CURRENT

FALKLAND CURRENT

BENGUELA CURRENT

WEST WIND DRIFT

The amount of rainfall varies throughout Latin America and the Caribbean. In northern Mexico few permanent river systems exist. The lack of rainfall makes life difficult for farmers. Only about 10 percent of the land area of Mexico has enough water to support cultivation. Droughts are very common, particularly in the northern desertlike states. In Brazil and Central America there can be too much rainfall. During the rainy season, more rainfall than needed can cause floods and wash away the top soil, which also can hurt the growing of crops.

# REVIEW QUESTIONS

*Multiple Choice.* Select the letter of the answer that correctly completes each statement.

1. The major religion in most of Latin America is
   A. Roman Catholicism
   B. Protestantism
   C. Islam
   D. Buddhism

2. Most nations of Latin America have a colonial heritage that is
   A. Spanish
   B. Portuguese
   C. French
   D. British

3. The nation with the largest land area in Latin America is
   A. Brazil
   B. Argentina
   C. Mexico
   D. Peru

4. Most of Latin America lies within the climatic zone known as the
   A. tropics
   B. tundra
   C. Arctic circle
   D. humid continental

5. The term "Latin America" refers to the three geopolitical regions: South America, Meso (Middle) America, and the
   A. Caribbean Sea islands
   B. Sahel region
   C. Indian subcontinent
   D. East Indies islands

6. All the following are examples of cultural diffusion *except*
   A. Japanese immigrants in Brazil speaking Portuguese
   B. Native Americans listening to rock music
   C. French missionaries in Haiti learning Creole
   D. Mexican citizens in Spain speaking Spanish

# II. ECONOMIC GEOGRAPHY OF LATIN AMERICA

## Economic Development in Latin America

Latin America has had a history of economic dependence dating from the colonial period. During the colonial period, because of the mercantilist policies of Spain and Portugal, the future Latin American nations were primarily exporters of raw materials and importers of manufactured goods. The Dutch, French, and most notably the British dominated trade within Latin America in the 1800s.

The economies of the newly independent Latin American nations continued to have a colonial character. Latin America was heavily dependent on imported consumer goods, food, and machinery and on the export of raw materials as payment for these imports. The dependence on one or two commodities made many smaller Latin American countries vulnerable to economic pressure. Even large countries like Brazil (coffee and sugar) and Argentina (cowhides, wheat) were dependent on the prices that their major exports earned.

In the second half of the 19th century, first Germany and then the United States began to trade with and invest in Latin America. This was a challenge to Britain's economic dominance of the region. The Latin American countries continued to export agricultural products and raw materials. Coffee, tobacco, sugar, copper, and nitrates paid for the increased imports of luxury goods, machinery, and other manufactured products.

Before World War I, the European nations accounted for 60 percent of the foreign investment in Latin America. U.S. trade and investment grew substantially between the wars. North American capital investment concentrated on mines and railroads, which stimulated the import of American machinery. Although German and British trade and investment resumed after World War I, the United States' dominance, particularly in the Caribbean, Mexico, and northern South America, continued. During these years, the Latin American nations faced increased competition to sell their raw materials in Europe because of new sources of these raw materials in Asia and elsewhere.

Since World War II, Latin American trade has undergone rapid changes in volume and direction. By the end of the 1960s, the region's economic giants—Brazil, Mexico, Argentina, and oil-rich Venezuela—accounted for 56 percent of the total value of Latin American trade. These nations began to produce more manufactured goods. By the late 1980s, Brazil had become the world's eighth largest economy. Mexico, Venezuela, Peru, Argentina, and other nations to a lesser extent became more industrialized because of foreign investment and loans. Foreign capital was also used by the Latin American nations to develop their infrastructures and establish credit to buy needed technology. However, in the 1970s the foreign debt of the Latin American nations increased enormously, and in the late 1980s it began to have a negative impact on their economies.

In the 1990s the United States, Mexico, and Canada signed the North American Free Trade Agreement (NAFTA). These nations were already trading partners, and with NAFTA they sought to increase their economic interdependence by abolishing tariffs on most goods traded among them and also develop ideas and mechanisms that would make this block of nations more open and competitive economically at a time when globalization of the world economy was increasing. The agreement was designed to improve how these three nations resolve issues relating to industrial and agricultural production, transportation of goods, and labor markets.

On January 1, 2004, the United States, Canada, and Mexico marked the tenth anniversary of implementation of the NAFTA agreement. The successes and failures of NAFTA are still being debated today. The promoters of the agreement argue that it has created hundreds of thousands of jobs, raised the living standards in all three nations, and improved environmental conditions. The opponents of NAFTA have argued that the agreement has led to reduced wages, destroyed hundreds of thousands of high-paying U.S. and Canadian jobs, and led to a worsening of environmental standards and conditions.

In 2012, one thing is certain about the trade agreements that have been made throughout the Americas. NAFTA, the recent U.S. trade agreements with Colombia and Panama, and other agreements such as the General Agreement on Tariffs and Trade (GATT), the CARICOM trade agreement among Caribbean nations, and the MERCOSUR agreement among Brazil, Argentina, Paraguay, and Uruguay are a growing recognition that there is a need to develop multination trade agreements and relationships at a time when globalization of the world economy is increasing.

## Industry

Industrial development started in the late 19th century. In Argentina, Brazil, and Mexico, the first manufacturing involved small workshops and factories that produced textiles and food products. There was also some production of machine tools and spare parts for the operation of sugar-refining mills, railroads, and other service needs. Before World War I industrial growth took place in the larger Latin American nations. The types of industries that developed were import-substitutive because they sought to replace imports for an already existing market. Factories producing textiles, food products, and other light consumer goods expanded their output. In the 1930s there were also attempts to develop heavy industry. For example, in Brazil, steel production began.

World War II encouraged the growth of industry because it became difficult to import manufactured goods. Existing factories were used to capacity, and new plants were added. After World War II, Latin American governments promoted industrialization, which was financed largely by American capital. Various methods used to promote industrialization were protective tariffs, preferential exchange rates for fuels and industrial raw materials, government construction of infrastructure projects (transportation and power facilities), and government investment in some heavy industries such as steel and petroleum.

In Argentina, Chile, and Venezuela, consumer-goods industries were first encouraged. Heavy industry for such products as steel and chemicals came later. In Mexico and Brazil, the governments sought to promote consumer and capital goods at the same time. By the late 1960s, in Argentina, Brazil, and Mexico, industry produced about 30 percent of the gross national product (GNP). Steel output increased enormously, and automobile production in these nations rose to a combined total of over 1 million cars.

By the 1980s Brazil was in the top ten nations in terms of industrial production, producing airplanes, computers, automobiles, and military goods that competed in global markets. Mexico City was a great center of industrial production, while Venezuela developed an important petroleum industry. In 2011, Mexico was ranked as the world's fifteenth biggest economy.

The stress on industrialization has had mixed results. On the positive side, many new jobs for the increasing population have been created; national pride increased because of reduced dependence on foreign imports; manufacturing centers developed and spurred the growth of cities; and an industrial class of manufacturers and factory workers grew. Moreover, new wealth has been created, which has stimulated overall economic growth, and national financial institutions have grown. However, there have also been negative aspects to industrialization. The stress on manufacturing has led to a neglect of agricultural exports, which

157

traditionally accounted for much of the foreign exchange earned. Industry has not been able to employ all the rural workers who have left agriculture. Moreover, some industries are not competitive, are too costly to run profitably, and have been a drain on the national budget. Pollution, urban squalor, and crime have often been byproducts of industrial growth.

The money borrowed to finance this industrialization created crises in Brazil, Mexico, Venezuela, Argentina, Peru, and smaller economies that could not repay their growing foreign public and private debt. This debt crisis seriously affected growth rates, destroyed national currencies due to spiraling inflation, and led to political instability in some nations. Argentina resorted to linking its national currency, the austral, to the American dollar in order to stabilize its economy. Mexico relied on a major loan from the United States to restore confidence in the peso. The loan was repaid when the Mexican economy stabilized. In 1999, Brazil, which is Latin America's largest economy, agreed to the recommendations of the International Monetary Fund (IMF) and began a painful process of austerity in its national budget in an effort to prevent a collapse of its economy and restore faith in its currency.

In the 1990s Latin American nations hoped for increased economic growth. Their hopes rested on each nation's ability to combat inflation and ease the debt crisis. Foreign banks and governments wanted to be repaid the billions owed to them. The International Monetary Fund also set conditions for future lending. For example, the IMF wanted an end to price-support systems and subsidies to lower food costs. Unless the demands of investors were met, Latin American nations did not receive the necessary funding to support their economic plans.

During the 1990s and into the first years of the 21st century, economic growth and industrial development in Latin America was volatile and tended to follow economic cycles. There was a rise in exports, an upsurge in trade, and an increase in investment within the region. Regional free trade agreements among Latin American nations increased overall trade. However, there is a lack of export diversification, which continues to limit trading possibilities. Most nations in Latin America remain dependent on the export of raw materials or agricultural goods. Only Brazil and to a certain extent Mexico and Chile have diversified industrial and agricultural economies.

## Agriculture

Since the pre-Columbian period, agriculture has been the most important part of the economy in the Latin American nations.

More than half the population is employed in agriculture in almost all Latin American countries. However, in proportion to the population employed, agriculture produces a small percentage of the gross national product. The region produces large crops of coffee, bananas, cacao, sugar, and cotton, but their export value often does not justify the amount of labor and investment. Agriculture supplies both food and raw materials for the region, and most Latin American countries depend heavily on the export of agricultural products to earn foreign currency. Latin America suffers from cultural and physical obstacles that hold back the development of more modern agriculture.

Even before the discovery of America, the slash-and-burn method of bringing new lands under cultivation has been used. For example, even today in the Amazon region huge areas of virgin forest are being destroyed by burning to create land for cattle ranching and farming. Often, lands have been overused until the effects of erosion, mineral depletion, and single-crop usage soon make the land increasingly incapable of production. Climate and topography have played important roles in reducing the fertility of arable lands. For example, in pre-Columbian times, Native Americans in the Andes region used a terrace farming system to lessen the effects of erosion, but during the colonial period this system was abandoned.

**GEOGRAPHY**

**Environment and Society**

The arrival of the Europeans changed the land holding system. Large landed estates, latifundio, were created, which were inefficiently operated. Absentee landlords still control huge tracts of land. In contrast, millions of Latin American families are subsistence farmers, growing a handful of food staple crops such as corn, beans, potatoes, plantains, manioc, and rice. The growing demand for land reform has been strongly resisted by the traditional landed elite.

Commercial agriculture, however, is increasing throughout Latin America. Crops for export began to be grown in the colonial period, especially in Brazil and the Caribbean, where sugar and cacao became important. In the 1800s coffee, wheat, wool, and beef made the agricultural exports of Brazil, Argentina, and Uruguay increasingly important. In the 20th century the development of refrigerated transportation made bananas and other fruits valuable exports. However, the heavy reliance on one-crop economies in Central American nations such as Honduras has had a negative effect on commercial agriculture. By contrast, in Brazil, where agricultural diversification is possible, export crops such as soy beans have earned needed foreign currency.

Latin America needs to increase its agricultural production to meet its high rate of population growth. In the Andean region

**AGRICULTURAL PRODUCTS OF LATIN AMERICA**

KEY

Bananas
Beef Cattle
Cacao
Cassava
Coffee
Corn
Cotton
Fish
Potatoes
Soybeans
Sugarcane
Timber
Wheat
Corn zone
Rice zone
Wheat zone

and elsewhere, farmers have turned to the growing of coca leaves, marijuana, and poppy plants to escape the endless cycle of poverty. Without land reform, agricultural productivity will continue to be held back by culture and physical problems. Many of these subsistence farmers are the one who are fleeing the rural areas for the cities.

## Mineral and Energy Sources

During the conquest of Latin America, the Europeans searched for precious metals, especially gold and silver. Much of the mineral wealth, primarily gold and silver objects taken from the more advanced pre-Columbian peoples, was shipped to

**RESOURCES OF SOUTH AMERICA**

KEY

| | |
|---|---|
| M | Manganese |
| ▼ | Iron Ore |
| ● | Coal |
| △ | Natural Gas |
| C | Copper |
| ▲ | Petroleum |
| ▢ | Tin |
| ▱ | Gold |
| △ | Silver |
| ✈ | Fishing |
| ⌗ | Lumbering |
| ⚡ | Hydroelectric plants |
| ◣ | Bauxite |

| 0 | 400 | 800 Miles |
|---|---|---|
| 0 | 400 800 | Kilometers |

Europe. From the 1500s to the 1700s, new deposits of gold, silver, and diamonds were found in Mexico, Peru, Bolivia, and Brazil. Although other mineral deposits—for example, iron ore, lead, tin, copper, and zinc—were discovered, they were not used to any great extent.

In the late 19th century, mining activities were extended to new areas. Increased foreign investment from Western Europe and the United States provided capital, technology, and management. In the 20th century, in Peru, Chile, Bolivia, Mexico, Brazil, and elsewhere, mining production increased and contributed significantly to the GNPs of these nations. Certain nations became increasingly dependent on their mineral wealth.

For example, Bolivia (tin), Chile (copper), Peru (bismuth), and Brazil (manganese and iron ore) became major centers of the world production of these metals. Today, prospects for mining should continue to increase in many Latin American countries.

Energy resources are less abundant in Latin America. Mexico is the leading producer of oil; *Petroleos Mexicanos* (Pemex) controls the distribution from Mexico's oil fields. Newly discovered fields in the Gulf of Mexico have increased Mexico's known reserves.

In South America, Venezuela is the leading producer of petroleum. In 1970 Venezuela produced approximately 70 percent of Latin America's petroleum. Argentina, Brazil, Colombia, Peru, Educador, and Chile are all petroleum-producing nations, but most of the oil produced by these nations is used to meet their own energy needs. Recent finds by Brazil in the Atlantic Ocean and by Peru and Ecuador in their Amazon lands have raised hopes of exporting oil; however, in comparison with other regions, particularly the Middle East, the proven reserves are very limited. The lack of large oil reserves could handicap the long-term development of Latin America's industrial base.

### MINERALS IN LATIN AMERICA

| Mineral | Produced in |
| --- | --- |
| Silver | Mexico (first in the world), Argentina, Colombia, Peru, Bolivia, Costa Rica, Ecuador |
| Tin | Bolivia |
| Copper | Chile (Atacama Desert), Argentina, Bolivia, Colombia, Cuba |
| Nitrates (fertilizer) | Chile (Atacama Desert) (first in the world) |
| Oil | Brazil, Venezuela, Mexico, Colombia, Argentina, Trinidad, Peru |
| Iron ore | Venezuela, Peru, Chile, Brazil, Argentina, Guatemala |
| Aluminum (bauxite) | Suriname (first in the world), Guyana (second in the world), Jamaica |
| Iodine | Chile |
| Manganese | Brazil, Cuba |
| Antimony | Bolivia, Mexico, Peru |
| Platinum | Colombia (third in the world) |
| Diamonds | Brazil (second in the world) |
| Uranium | Brazil |

# The Quest for Development in Latin America

Few areas of Latin America have the proper combination of industrial capacity, capital for investment, raw materials, energy resources, and technology needed for developing their economies. Brazil comes the closest to having all the necessary factors. However, even Brazil, which has increased its industrial capacity, encountered enormous problems in the 1990s.

The desire to satisfy the demand for consumer goods while providing manufactured goods and agricultural products for export led to a substantial increase of foreign investment capital. Today Brazil is the nation in Latin America that has achieved the greatest success in developing its industry and agriculture. In 2011, Brazil was ranked as the world's seventh biggest economy. In addition, Brazil was selected to host the Summer Olympic Games in Rio de Janeiro in 2016.

In Latin America, modernization and industrialization have resulted in many new and difficult problems. Mexico, Argentina, Peru, Colombia, and Venezuela face enormous economic uncertainties. Economic problems have led to increasing migration from rural to urban areas, and the search for economic opportunity has led people to migrate to other nations.

Multinational corporations have been established in Latin America that seek to profit from the cheap labor, available raw materials, and the need for investment capital for industrialization. Often they have a competitive advantage over national industries. Multinational corporations show the growing interdependence of the more industrialized and less-developed regions of the world. In Latin America multinationals take as profit the capital that is much needed instead of reinvesting it. This is a serious problem.

Some Latin American nations have sought to work together in regional projects in order to better develop their economies. Brazil and Paraguay are jointly building the Itaipu Dam to harness the energy of the Paraná River system for electrical power. There have been several attempts at regional economic cooperation by Andean nations, some Caribbean countries, and Brazil and Argentina. In the Caribbean region, nations of the Caribbean Community and Common Market (CARICOM) are working on policies to liberalize trade among the organization's members. A more open trading system would stimulate economic growth and development. This is particularly important since economic trading blocs, such as NAFTA and the EU, will favor trade among their member nations.

Many countries that lack natural resources have turned to tourism. This is particularly true of the Caribbean island nations of the Dominican Republic and Jamaica. Even the more diversified economies of Mexico and Brazil have come to depend on tourism as a source of needed foreign currency. Tourism can be a mixed blessing in some situations, but it is one path to development in Latin America that is increasingly being tried.

## Latin America in the Global Context

Today Latin American nations have ever more global trading relationships. For example, Japan's economic investment in and trade with Latin America have recently expanded. The more industrialized nations such as Brazil export such manufactured products as automobiles, military equipment, and commercial aircraft as well as agricultural products to Africa and the Middle East. The petroleum industries of Latin America, most notably that of Venezuela, are increasingly a part of the global oil network. U.S. economic relations with Latin America remain strong. However, global interdependence has led to more diversified economic relationships.

Latin America has achieved a higher degree of political and social stability and made considerable progress in trade reform in the past decade. However, in Latin America as a whole, the main regional connection within the global economy remains each individual nation's export of resource-processing primary goods including energy. In order for the nations of Latin America to further integrate their economies into global markets, a greater emphasis will have to be given to a higher level of technical education and investment in research and development as the 21st century progresses.

*Multiple Choice.* Select the letter of the answer that correctly completes each statement.

1. The nation that dominated trade in Latin America during the 1800s was
   A. Great Britain
   B. France
   C. Germany
   D. the United States

2. By the 1980s the Latin American nation that was among the top ten nations in terms of industrial production was
   A. Brazil
   B. Mexico
   C. Argentina
   D. Peru

3. Large landed estates in Latin America are called
   A. latifundio
   B. terraced farms
   C. subsistence farms
   D. minifundia

4. Increased foreign investment from Western Europe, the United States, and Japan has provided Latin American nations with all the following *except*
   A. capital
   B. technology
   C. management
   D. raw materials

5. Brazil's foreign debt problem has caused all the following *except*
   A. hyperinflation
   B. high debt interest payments
   C. a rising standard of living
   D. a favorable balance of trade

6. The NAFTA nations are
   A. United States, Mexico, and Chile
   B. United States, Mexico, and Canada
   C. Mexico, Canada, and Chile
   D. Mexico, Canada, and Brazil

# III. HUMAN AND CULTURAL GEOGRAPHY OF LATIN AMERICA AND THE CARIBBEAN BASIN

There is a very uneven distribution of population in Latin America and the Caribbean Islands. Compared to other world regions, Latin America and the Caribbean Islands are not overpopulated, although there are major cities with very large urban populations. In Latin America, Mexico City and Sao Paolo, Brazil, are among the largest cities in the world in terms of population. Nevertheless, the huge Amazon basin with its tropical forests and the vast deserts of Patagonia in southern Argentina and desert wastelands of northern Mexico have never been well populated. This is because it is difficult to live in these areas.

Most of the people in Latin America and the Caribbean are concentrated in the more temperate climatic coastal plains and highland plateaus. The heaviest concentrations of people are found in the inland plateaus in western South America, primarily Bolivia, Peru, and Colombia. Most people live on or close to the coast of Brazil, Argentina, and Uruguay. In Mexico, the central plateau has the greatest concentration of people. In the larger islands of the Caribbean—Cuba, the Dominican Republic/Haiti, and Puerto Rico—the greatest concentration of population are found in coastal cities.

## Overview of the Culture, Geography, and Political History of Latin America

The earliest people who arrived in this part of the world came from Asia, migrating to the Americas perhaps as early as 40,000 years ago. They came to the Americas across the Bering Sea islands. The sea was frozen at the time because of the Ice Age and formed a bridge between the two continents: Asia and North America. They came in more than one migratory wave because the ice melted and refroze during this time period of dramatic climatic changes. The last Ice Age ended about 9,500 years ago. After this time the people who migrated to the Americas became isolated from the changes that were taking place in other parts of the world. They lived and developed their societies and cultures without contact with other regions of the world until almost 1500 C.E.

It was only after the voyages of exploration that great numbers of Europeans and Africans came to the Americas. The colonial impact on the Native American people and cultures was enormous. Many Native American peoples and cultures disappeared after the Europeans came to the Americas. Those that survived experienced great changes in their way of life. Africans were brought to the Americas to work. This led to the development of new groups of peoples who share the heritage of the different peoples and cultures that make up the present populations in Latin America and the Caribbean. Today many people in Latin America are classified as mestizo or mulatto because of the mixture of peoples.

Latin American societies are very hierarchal in structure. At the top of the hierarchal pyramid is a wealthy class of land-owners, industrialists, bankers, and businesspeople. This wealthy group is small in number but controls the important political, economic, and social institutions of their nations and cultures. This social class is made up mostly of the descendants of European peoples. They have ruled and controlled the other social groups in Latin American societies since the 1500s. A middle class made up of professionals, government workers, and military officers has begun to develop in some countries, but it remains small in number in comparison to the United States and developed European nations. The vast majority of people make up the lower social classes of Latin American societies. These people are primarily of Native American, African, mestizo, or mulatto origin; however, not all the descendants of Europeans are in the upper and middle classes. One of the important challenges facing Latin American and Caribbean nations is to find a way to offer the less privileged classes in their countries a better life. They are too often limited by poverty and the lack of educational opportunities. Improvements in health care, education, job opportunities, and basic necessities such as clean water and electricity are needed if the poorer classes are to improve their lives and climb the social pyramid.

The people who live in Latin America speak mostly Romance languages. Spanish is the most widely spoken language in almost all the nations of Latin America. Portuguese is spoken in Brazil, which is the country with the largest population in South America. French is the key language on the islands of Martinique and Guadeloupe. Native American languages are still spoken in some nations. In Paraguay, most people still use the Tupi-Guarani language in their daily lives. In Bolivia, Peru, and Ecuador many people speak Quechua and Aymara.

The first people who inhabited the region called Latin America were polytheistic in their religious beliefs. They worshipped the objects and forces of nature, spirits, and other human beings. Today these religious beliefs survive mainly among the small number of Native American tribes and peoples. After the arrival of the Europeans, Christianity, primarily Roman Catholicism, became the religion of most people in Latin America. In the 20th century, Protestantism, especially evangelical sects, began to expand throughout Latin America. In most Latin American countries today, there are also small groups of people who follow Islamic, Jewish, and Buddhist traditions. Some people, particularly in Brazil and Haiti, follow religious practices that have African origins such as voodoo and condomble.

Latin American societies followed an agricultural pattern of society organization until the 20th century brought great changes to many countries. Most people lived in the countryside in agricultural communities and engaged in farming of one kind or another. Capital and provincial cities existed, but they were not as well populated as they are today. The growth of populations in Latin America and the inability of people to survive as farmers have led to a migration to the cities. Today most of the cities of Latin America have experienced enormous population growth. Latin America is becoming increasingly urban as people come to the cities to find work and establish new lives. Many cities and towns in Latin America do not have adequate housing, fresh water, sewage, and educational facilities to meet the demands of the rising urban populations. Latin American nations face great challenges to bring the benefits of modern society to all the people living in the country.

*Multiple Choice.* Select the letter of the answer that correctly completes each statement.

1. Demographic growth in Latin America is the result of all of the following factors *except*
   A. the Roman Catholic Church's stand against abortion
   B. improvements in public health services
   C. a persistent tradition that values high birth rates
   D. the trend toward urbanization in many countries

2. A group of Latin American nations whose population is of primarily European heritage is
   A. Argentina, Costa Rica, Uruguay
   B. Guatemala, Nicaragua, Ecuador
   C. Mexico, Cuba, Bolivia
   D. Colombia, Venezuela, Peru

# SECTION 8: WESTERN EUROPE

# I. PHYSICAL GEOGRAPHY OF WESTERN EUROPE

## Overview

Europe is often called a continent, although in reality it is a large peninsula lying in the western portion of the Eurasian continent. Western Europe makes up approximately 1.4 million square miles (3.6 million square kilometers) of the entire region. The region known as Western Europe consists of twenty nations. These nations may be grouped in the following ways:

**Spatial Terms**

1. Northwestern Europe, which consists of Ireland, the United Kingdom (England, Scotland, Wales, and Northern Ireland), France, and the Benelux countries (Belgium, the Netherlands, and Luxembourg).

2. Southern Europe, consisting of Portugal, Spain, Italy, and Greece.

3. Middle (Central) Europe, which consists of Germany, Switzerland, Austria, and Liechtenstein.

4. Scandinavia, made up of Iceland, Norway, Sweden, Finland, Denmark, and Greenland.

## Topography

Western Europe has many different kinds of landforms, which have affected political, economic, and cultural ways of life. The major mountains are the Alps, Apennines, and Pyrenees. The Pyrenees have restricted movement between France and Spain, thereby separating the Iberian Peninsula (Spain and Portugal) from the rest of the region. The mountainous terrain in Greece was responsible for the growth of separate city-states in Ancient Greece. The lowlands in the Netherlands made that country concerned about frequent flooding from the North Sea, and many dams and canals have been built for protection. The low plains in the other Benelux nations as well as in northeastern France have been the sites of invasions and battlegrounds throughout European history.

GLOBAL
CONCEPTS

**Environment**

CONCEPTS
GLOBAL

**Environment
and Society**

# WESTERN EUROPE

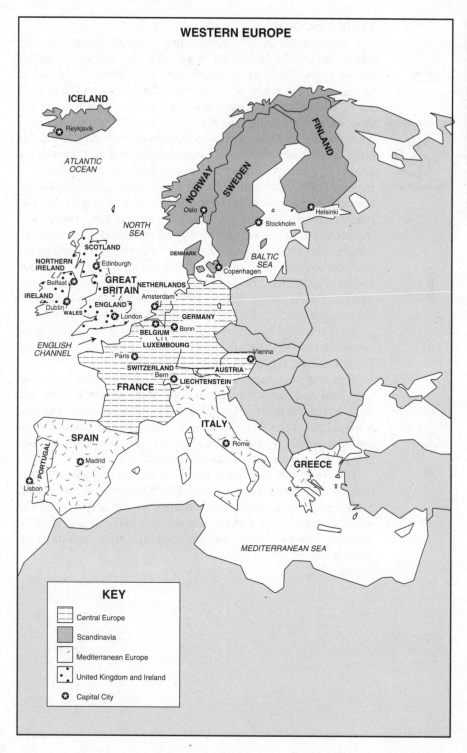

ICELAND

Reykjavík

ATLANTIC
OCEAN

NORWAY

SWEDEN

FINLAND

Oslo

Stockholm

Helsinki

NORTH
SEA

SCOTLAND

Edinburgh

DENMARK

BALTIC
SEA

Copenhagen

NORTHERN
IRELAND

Belfast

GREAT
BRITAIN

NETHERLANDS

Amsterdam

IRELAND

Dublin

WALES

ENGLAND

London

GERMANY

Bonn

BELGIUM

LUXEMBOURG

Vienna

ENGLISH
CHANNEL

Paris

SWITZERLAND

Bern

AUSTRIA

LIECHTENSTEIN

FRANCE

ITALY

Rome

SPAIN

Madrid

PORTUGAL

GREECE

Lisbon

MEDITERRANEAN SEA

## KEY

Central Europe

Scandinavia

Mediterranean Europe

United Kingdom and Ireland

Capital City

## Water Bodies

The major water bodies surrounding Western Europe are the Baltic Sea and the North Sea in the north, the Atlantic Ocean in the west, and the Mediterranean Sea in the south. The Atlantic Ocean has been a highway of commerce and a migration path for peoples between Europe and the Americas, particularly for those nations touching the Atlantic, such as Britain, France, Ireland, and Spain. The nearness to large bodies of water led to the build-up of fishing fleets and eventually to great naval power for several nations. At different times in history, these nations— Britain, France, Holland, Portugal, and Spain—established overseas colonial empires. Historically, the Mediterranean Sea has made cultural diffusion possible between Europe, Africa, and the Middle East, especially by way of the Italian Peninsula. In the 20th century, the North Sea has been developed as an important source of oil. The many warm-water ports on these major bodies of water have helped in the movement of goods and people. The Dutch port of Rotterdam, for example, is the largest in Europe and handles more cargo than New York City.

Several navigable rivers are found in the region, providing ease of transportation and trade. Among these are the Rhine, Po, Seine, Danube, and Thames.

The English Channel separates Britain from the European mainland and, consequently, has provided protection for the British Isles for most of British history. However, times change; a tunnel has been built underneath the English Channel that provides for the passage of trains and cars. It opened in May 1994 linking mainland Europe to Britain.

The North Atlantic Drift brings moderate temperature patterns to the Atlantic coast nations. Much of southern Europe has a Mediterranean climate. The summers are hot and dry, and the winters are mild and rainy. There are also mountainous areas in Western Europe where the temperature varies according to altitude.

# REVIEW QUESTIONS

*Multiple Choice.* Select the letter of the answer that correctly completes each statement.

1. Which of the following is in Scandinavia?
   A. Germany
   B. Switzerland
   C. Sweden
   D. Spain

2. Spain and Portugal are in a region known as
   A. Central Europe
   B. the Iberian Peninsula
   C. the lowlands
   D. Scandinavia

3. In recent years, the area that has been developed as a source of oil is the
   A. North Sea
   B. Baltic Sea
   C. Mediterranean Sea
   D. Atlantic Ocean

# II. ECONOMIC GEOGRAPHY OF WESTERN EUROPE

## Agriculture

Europe's farmers, although declining in number, produce large amounts of food. Careful use of land, along with pesticides and modern technology, have contributed to food surpluses in many areas. The major agricultural products are wheat, potatoes, meat, wine, and dairy products.

## Industrial Production

Western Europe has long been one of the world's leading areas in manufacturing and industrial development. The large deposits of coal in Britain and Germany and scientific technology (beginning with the 19th-century Industrial Revolution) have been primary factors in this development. Major industrial products are automobiles, chemicals, electronics, steel, and machinery.

Advances in agricultural and industrial production have resulted in a high standard of living for Western Europe's people. Germany has the highest GDP (gross domestic product) on the European continent.

## The Marshall Plan

**WORLD ISSUES**

Economic
Growth and
Development

The Marshall Plan is named after George C. Marshall, U.S. secretary of state, who proposed a way in which the United States could help build up Europe's economy after World War II. His plan, passed by Congress in 1947, was officially known as the European Recovery Act. It made about $12.5 billion in aid available to countries that suffered damage and devastation from the war and called upon the European countries to draw up their own plans for recovery. Most noncommunist European nations accepted the aid offered by the Marshall Plan and as a result achieved much economic progress.

Although the plan included all the European nations, the aid was refused by the communist nations. Instead, they accepted aid from the Council of Mutual Economic Assistance, a Soviet version of the Marshall Plan.

## Economic Systems and Decision Making

Today, different types of economic systems exist in the Western European nations. An economic system is a way of making decisions about such basic economic questions as: What should be produced? Who should produce it? How should it be produced? What should the price be? Who should own the land and the means of production? How is the product to be distributed? To whom should it be distributed?

In a capitalist system, most of these economic questions are decided privately and freely by individual citizens. Under capitalism, a society's government has very little to do with making economic decisions. This kind of system permits a free market economy to exist. Societies that have a market economy and economic freedom also allow other kinds of freedom, such as freedom of religion, speech, the press, etc. In *The Wealth of Nations,* written in 1776, Adam Smith provided a good description of a capitalist system.

In a socialist system, most of the basic economic issues are decided by the government. A socialist government is freely elected by the people, and its main goal is to improve the conditions of workers. Democratic freedoms are allowed, as are many political parties.

In a communist system, the government makes all the economic decisions. Communist governments come to power as a result of violence and revolution. Only one party, the Communist Party, is allowed to exist. *The Communist Manifesto,* written by Karl Marx and Friedrich Engels in 1848, explained certain aspects of communist theory.

The countries in Western Europe today are said to have a mixed economy; that is, they have elements of both capitalism and socialism. Each nation has a different degree of government ownership (nationalization) of industries. In the field of health and other social services, some nations, such as England, Denmark, and Sweden, have extensive social welfare programs. For example, the British National Health Service provides free dental and medical benefits. The costs of these programs are paid for by taxes on employers and workers.

GLOBAL CONCEPTS
**Diversity**
CONCEPTS GLOBAL

Although communist parties have existed in almost every Western European nation, the Communists have been weak and have never won control of a government.

## Attempts at Economic Cooperation

World War II brought economic ruin to Western Europe and also signaled an end to almost 500 years of European economic dominance in the world. During these many centuries, economic rivalry and competition grew among European nations. Since World War II, however, there has been a movement to promote economic unity and cooperation.

# EUROPE

*ATLANTIC OCEAN*

*B A R E N T S SEA*

Reykjavik
ICELAND

Narvik

Murmansk

Luleå

FAEROE ISLAND
(DEN.)

Trondheim

SWEDEN

Oulu

Vaasa

NORWAY

FINLAND

SHETLAND ISLANDS
(U.K.)

Bergen

Helsinki

Oslo

Leningrad

Göteborg

Edinburgh

DENMARK

Stockholm

Alborg

Moscow

RUSSIA

Belfast

Kiel

Copenhagen

Gdansk

Minsk

IRELAND

Manchester

C.I.S.

Dublin

NETHERLANDS

Berlin

POLAND

BRITAIN

Amsterdam

GERMANY

Warsaw

Chernobyl

London

BELGIUM

Bonn

CZECH REPUBLIC

Kiev

Brussels

LUXEMBOURG

Prague

UKRAINE

ENGLISH CHANNEL

SLOVAKIA

Brest

Paris

Vienna

Rostov

Nantes

FRANCE

Munich

AUSTRIA

Odessa

Bern

Budapest

Geneva

SWITZ.

HUNGARY

Milan

Venice

ROMANIA

ANDORRA

Genoa

Belgrade

Bucarest

Yalta

MONACO

San Marino

SERBIA

BLACK SEA

Bilbao

Marseille

*ADRIATIC SEA*

BULGARIA

PORTUGAL

CORSICA
(FR.)

Vatican
City

Rome

Sofia

Istanbul

Samsun

Barcelona

Trana

Madrid

SARDINIA
(IT.)

ALBANIA

Izmir

TURKEY

Ankara

Lisbon

SPAIN

ITALY

GREECE

Adana

Malaga

BALEARIC ISLANDS
(SP.)

Palermo

Athens

GIBRALTAR
(U.K.)

SICILY
(IT.)

RHODES (GR.)

CYPRUS

CRETE (GR.)

MALTA

*M E D I T E R R A N E A N   S E A*

## KEY

| | | | | |
|---|---|---|---|---|
| Cattle | Corn | Industry | Oil | Sheep | Wheat |
| Citrus | Fish | Iron Ore | Olives | Sugar beets | Wine |
| Fruits | Flax | Lumber | Potatoes | Water power | Capital |
| Coal | Grapes | miles 0     500 | | | Other city |
| | | km 0     500 | | | |

176

**The European Union.** Once known as the Common Market, this organization was originally created in 1951 as the ECSC (European Coal and Steel Community). Its aim, as stated by French Foreign Minister Robert Schuman in his Schuman Plan, was to bring together the coal and steel industries of six nations—Belgium, France, Italy, Luxembourg, the Netherlands, and West Germany. This group was also known as the Inner Six.

1. In 1957 the Inner Six agreed to bring together their economies and reduce economic barriers such as tariffs. As a result, there was more free trade among these nations, and they changed their name from the ECSC to the EEC (European Economic Community). They also created Euratom to tie together the six nations' research in nuclear power.

2. The EEC came to be known as the European Community (EC) and was very successful in increasing economic activity among its members. By 1985, six other nations were accepted for membership—Denmark, Ireland, England, Greece, Portugal, and Spain.

3. In 1987 the twelve nations of the EC agreed to bring their economies even closer together by 1992 and to create a frontier-free Europe. This plan called for one large common market in which nations could sell their goods more easily to other members; it would allow citizens of a member nation to work in any member nation of the EC; and it would subject goods coming into the EC from outside to a high tax (tariff). The EC's twelve nations would thus make up a single economic unit, with 330 million citizens that could compete with the world's two current economic giants—the United States and Japan. Eventually, the twelve nations might join together politically, creating a United States of Europe. Discussions about this took place in Dublin and Rome in 1990.

The hopes described above, for greater economic unity by 1992, received a boost with the signing in that year of the Maastricht Treaty. Although the treaty sparked debate in many countries, notably Denmark, England, France, and Germany, it was approved by all members by 1993. These nations were concerned about their voting rights under the treaty as well as the extent to which regulations would affect their sovereignty and the lives of their citizens. The treaty became effective in November 1993. The EC is now known as the European Union. In March 1994 the foreign ministers of the twelve member nations voted to admit four more nations—Austria, Finland, Norway, and Sweden. These four nations became members on January 1, 1995. By treaty, the members agreed to establish a single European currency by 2002. It is called the euro. By

GLOBAL
CONCEPTS
**Change**
CONCEPTS
GLOBAL

GLOBAL
CONCEPTS
**Interdependence**
CONCEPTS
GLOBAL

**WORLD ISSUES**

Determination
of Political
and Economic
Systems

February 2002, the euro had replaced the national currencies in Austria, Belgium, Finland, France, Germany, Ireland, Italy, Luxembourg, Netherlands, Portugal, Spain, and Greece.

**The European Free Trade Association (EFTRA).** Also known as the Outer Seven, this organization, which came into existence in 1960, contained seven member nations—Austria, Finland, Iceland, Liechtenstein, Norway, Sweden, and Switzerland. EFTRA did not establish as strong links as the EU, but it had similar economic goals. In 2004, the member nations were Iceland, Liechtenstein, Norway, and Switzerland.

## Economic Issues

The term post-industrial society refers to a society in which more people work in service industries (accounting, health) than in production industries (steel, textiles). This situation is becoming more and more common in Western Europe, as it is in the United States.

Inflation refers to rising prices, which have caused a decrease in the value of the European currencies. The increase in oil prices charged by the Middle Eastern nations during the 1970s was one reason for inflation in Western Europe. Another reason was the attempt by the United States to cut down the flow of European imports into the United States and to increase the flow of American exports. Most Western European nations are dependent on outside areas for raw materials, such as oil from the Middle East.

Of increasing importance to Western Europe in the opening years of the 21st century will be its economic relations with Japan and the United States, as well as with the former Soviet Union and Eastern European nations, and the former European colonies in Africa and Asia.

# REVIEW QUESTIONS

*Multiple Choice.* Select the letter of the answer that correctly completes each statement.

1. An aspect of socialism that can be found in some Western European nations is
   A. a ban on government participation in the economy
   B. free dental and medical benefits
   C. only one political party
   D. no free elections

2. The Marshall Plan provided aid that was
   A. cultural
   B. military
   C. financial
   D. agricultural

3. The person most responsible for the growth of the European Common Market was
   A. Karl Marx
   B. Robert Schuman
   C. Friedrich Engels
   D. George Marshall

## III. HUMAN AND CULTURAL GEOGRAPHY OF WESTERN EUROPE

### Overview

Western Europe, with over 300 million people, has a variety of religious, ethnic, and linguistic groups. The largest nations are Germany (82 million), Italy (58 million), and France (60 million). Overpopulation and overcrowding (high population density) are not problems in Western Europe. In fact, population growth rates are among the lowest in the world. One reason for the absence of demographic (population) problems is that Western Europe is very industrialized and has high standards of living and modern health care. Compared with people in less industrialized areas, such as South Asia and sub-Saharan Africa, Western Europeans tend to live longer, marry later, and have smaller families. In addition, more women are in the work force. Urbanization—the movement of people from rural to city areas—is also characteristic of Western Europe.

### Religion

GLOBAL
CONCEPTS

**Culture**

CONCEPTS
GLOBAL

Christianity is the predominant religion in Western Europe. The majority of people are Catholic, with the largest concentrations in the south, in Spain and Italy. Members of Protestant denominations are found mainly in the north, in nations such as England and Sweden. Greece belongs to the Eastern or Greek Orthodox Church.

Jews have been a minority in the Western European nations for centuries. They share some basic beliefs with Christians, such as the belief in one God and in the Ten Commandments. The combined basic beliefs and ideals of Jews and Christians make up the Judeo-Christian tradition. This tradition has influenced life in Western Europe for the last 2,000 years. It has also influenced life in areas that had the greatest amount of overseas European settlement, such as North and South America. Jews accept the part of the Bible popularly known as the Old Testament (known to Jews as the Tanach); Christians accept both the Old and New Testaments. (For a comparison of Judaism, Christianity, and Islam, see the section on the Middle East.)

A growing number of Muslims and Hindus today live in some Western European nations, mostly those nations that once had colonies in Africa and Asia. France's Islamic community comes mainly from Algeria and Morocco. Most Hindus and Muslims in England come from the Indian subcontinent (India, Pakistan, and Bangladesh). The Muslims in Germany are mainly Turks who have immigrated for economic reasons.

# Ethnic Minority Groups

**From Outside Europe.** Besides the groups listed, people from other areas of the world are found throughout Western Europe. They include people from the Caribbean, Africa, the Middle East, and East Asia. The British have mixed feelings about whether to admit great numbers of Chinese and other non-British people to their nation. Some of this concern in England (as well as in other European nations such as France and Germany) results from prejudice against foreigners. This prejudice is rooted in the issues of race as well as competition for employment, and at times it has even led to riots.

**From Inside Europe.** The more industrialized nations, such as Germany and France, have guest workers from other parts of Europe. These workers often take jobs for short periods of time and send money back to their families. Such workers are from Turkey, Greece, Serbia and the other nations that had comprised the former country of Yugoslavia, Italy, and Portugal. Although there have been attempts by the host countries to assimilate these workers and provide education, instances of ill feeling and prejudice have also been evident.

GLOBAL
CONCEPTS

**Empathy**

CONCEPTS
GLOBAL

# Languages

While a variety of languages exists in the Western European nations, many have striking similarities. All languages in Western Europe except for Greek are written using the Roman alphabet. There are also similarities in the ways some words are put together and are spoken. As a result, people in one nation are frequently able to understand the language of another nation. Because of the similarities between the languages, many Europeans are multilingual. Other reasons for the large numbers of Europeans who are multilingual are the nearness of nations to one another and the frequent travel and economic exchanges between them.

GLOBAL
CONCEPTS

**Diversity**

CONCEPTS
GLOBAL

French, Spanish, Portuguese, and Italian are Romance languages and have words constructed in a similar pattern. English is a Germanic language. German and Dutch have much in common, while the Scandinavian languages, except for Finnish, are similar. Some nations are officially bilingual because large segments of their populations speak distinct languages. For example, in Switzerland, French and German are spoken, while in Belgium, Flemish and French are used.

# REVIEW QUESTIONS

*Multiple Choice.* Select the letter of the answer that correctly completes
each statement.

1. Which nation has the largest population in Western Europe?
   A. France
   B. Ireland
   C. Germany
   D. Italy

2. In which pair of nations is Catholicism the predominant religion?
   A. England and Italy
   B. France and Denmark
   C. Spain and Portugal
   D. Sweden and Holland

3. Which pair of nations have Romance languages?
   A. Italy and Spain
   B. England and Germany
   C. France and Holland
   D. Norway and Austria

4. A nation that is officially bilingual is
   A. Finland
   B. Belgium
   C. Sweden
   D. Austria

# SECTION 9: EASTERN EUROPE

## I. PHYSICAL GEOGRAPHY OF EASTERN EUROPE

### Overview

Eastern Europe consists of nations located between Western Europe and the Commonwealth of Independent States. Common religious, ethnic, and/or cultural ties distinguish the Eastern European countries. Despite a diverse mixture of peoples and influences, the Eastern European nations of Albania, Bulgaria, the Czech Republic, Hungary, Poland, Romania, Slovakia, and the countries that formerly constituted Yugoslavia (Bosnia-Herzegovina, Croatia, Montenegro, Serbia, Slovenia, and Macedonia, known officially as the Former Yugoslav Republic of Macedonia) have similar historical roots and have had similar experiences. Containing approximately 126 million people, with a wide range of languages and religions, these countries seem to have been brought together many times over the centuries by historical events.

**GEOGRAPHY**

**Places and Regions**

### Topography

Its topography and location have made Eastern Europe an invasion route throughout history. This has resulted in the mixing of many peoples, languages, and cultures. Mountains have played the most influential role in the development of Eastern Europe's nations. They have acted as barriers and trade routes, both protecting and/or unifying peoples in this region. Eastern Europe's mountains are low and relatively accessible when compared with other ranges in the world. The Carpathians are the longest mountain range (stretching through Romania, Hungary, the Czech Republic, Slovakia, and Poland), followed by the Balkans (which run from northern Bulgaria to eastern Serbia). Other important ranges are the Rhodopes (in southern Bulgaria), the Bohemian and Sudetens (in the Czech Republic), and the Julian and Dinaric Alps (running through Slovenia, Croatia, and Bosnia-Herzegovina, and the Transylvanian Alps in Romania).

**GEOGRAPHY**

**Physical Settings**

Plains have also had a profound effect on the history of Eastern Europe. The Northern Plain stretches from the Atlantic Ocean across Western Europe through the north of Germany into Poland and continues across Eastern Europe into Russia (see Physical Geography in Part I). This has served as a major invasion route for armies from both the east and west for centuries. The Great Hungarian Plain, located in the center of Eastern Europe, is both an agricultural and horse-breeding region and has also attracted invaders.

## Bodies of Water

Rivers have played an important role in the development of Eastern Europe. They have served as major trade routes, linking the nations of Eastern Europe with the rest of Europe, particularly with Byzantium. The Danube is the most important of these waterways, connecting Hungary, Slovenia, Croatia, Serbia, Bulgaria, and Romania. In addition to trade, it has always been a source of fish, irrigation, and, in modern times, hydroelectric power. Other important rivers are the Morava (linking the Czech Republic, Slovakia, Hungary, Croatia, and Serbia), the Drava (flowing from Hungary to Croatia), the Drina (flowing from Serbia through Bosnia-Herzegovina to Montenegro), the Vandar (connecting Macedonia with Greece), the Prut (which links Romania to Moldova and Ukraine), and the Bug (running from Poland through Belarussia into Ukraine). There are also several rivers that have been essential to trade and communication within countries: the Tisza (Hungary), the Vitava (the Czech Republic and Slovakia), the Vit (Bulgaria), the Sava (Yugoslavia), and the Vistula (Poland).

There are many scenic lakes throughout Eastern Europe, the most important of which is Lake Balton in Hungary. Slovenia, Croatia, Bosnia-Herzegovina, Monetenegro, and Albania are located on the coast of the Adriatic Sea, a rich source of fishing and tourism for all these nations except Albania. Bulgaria and Romania, which have access to the Black Sea, have experienced the same problems as the Russians—their only access to the Mediterranean is the Turkish-controlled Dardanelles. Poland's access to the Baltic has been limited since the 18th century, due to Russian expansion.

## Vegetation Belts

As a whole, the region of Eastern Europe is mountainous. Yet, there are areas of abundant vegetation: the Pannonian Plain (located in Serbia and Montenegro); in Hungary, parts of the Great Hungarian Plain (particularly near Debrecen on the Romanian border); in the Danube Valley, the Czech provinces of Moravia and Bohemia, and Slovakia, in Bulgaria, the Maritsa Valley, known as Bulgaria's California (located between the

Balkan and Rhodope mountains), and the Balkan Plateau (in the north bordering Romania); in Romania, western Transylvania as well as the river valleys of the Danube and Prut; and in Poland, the Silesian region (southern plain).

There are also extensive forests in the uplands of Bosnia and Croatia (along the coast of the Adriatic) and the northern plain of Poland. The exception is Albania, whose poor soil and lack of resources have only compounded other problems, making it an extremely poor nation.

## Climate

The harshest climates of Eastern Europe are in the Czech Republic, Slovakia, and Poland, where very cold winters and cool summers have traditionally shortened growing seasons and lengthened people's endurance. There are less severe winters and warmer summers in Hungary, Bulgaria, and Romania. With hot, dry summers and milder winters (especially by the Adriatic coast), the former nations of Yugoslavia have benefited from the climate by expanding agriculture.

**GEOGRAPHY**

**Environment and Society**

# II. ECONOMIC GEOGRAPHY OF EASTERN EUROPE

## Agriculture

Eastern Europe's economy was almost completely agricultural until the 20th century. Due to larger growing areas and richer soil, Serbia and Montenegro, followed by Bulgaria and Romania, provide the greatest agricultural output. Serbia and Montenegro also produce grains, fruits, tobacco, and wood; Bulgaria provides grains, fruit, rose oil, and tobacco; and Romania grows corn, wheat, and timber. Poland produces limited grain and timber, while Hungary provides grain and wine. The Czech Republic, unlike Slovakia, was almost completely industrial until recently. Albania's former rigid communist system, combined with its new problems, created by its transition to democracy and capitalism, made its agricultural output barely self-sufficient.

## Industrial Production/Resources

The Czech Republic is Eastern Europe's most industrialized nation. Rich in coal and ores used in the production of atomic energy, it also produces beer, glass, china, machinery, and light aircraft. Poland, with its wealthy deposits of iron ore, coal, zinc, and sulphur, provides iron, automobiles, textiles, and chemicals. Romania, rich in oil (for which it became a target in World War II), produces textiles, machinery, and metals in addition to oil, its greatest resource. Hungary provides steel, iron, aluminum, machinery, and railway equipment. Among the nations of the former Yugoslavia, Slovenia and Croatia were the most industrialized, producing steel, copper, lead, zinc, chrome, and wood products. Bulgaria's production is limited to machinery and chemicals. Albania's industrial production was limited to domestic consumption under communist domination but is now in the process of changing.

**WORLD ISSUES**

Economic Growth and Development

## "Guns vs. Butter" Controversy

As in the former Soviet Union, the guns versus butter controversy also raged in Eastern Europe. The question of whether to produce consumer goods or weapons for the military and defense had become very important, especially when most Eastern European nations started to reject communist economic doctrines and develop democratic governments.

# REVIEW QUESTIONS

*Multiple Choice.* Select the letter of the answer that correctly completes the statement.

1. Eastern Europe's topography and location have made it
   A. well protected from invaders
   B. an invasion route throughout history
   C. isolated and culturally homogeneous
   D. dominant in the affairs of Western Europe

2. All of the following are important Eastern European rivers *except* the
   A. Danube
   B. Don
   C. Vistula
   D. Seine

3. The nations of Eastern Europe that provide the largest agricultural output are
   A. Serbia, Montenegro, Bulgaria, and Romania
   B. Poland, Romania, Serbia, and Montenegro
   C. Bulgaria, Hungary, the Czech Republic, and Slovakia
   D. Albania, Bulgaria, Croatia, and Slovenia

4. The most industrialized Eastern European nation is
   A. the Czech Republic
   B. Hungary
   C. Poland
   D. Romania

5. Which is *not* true of Eastern Europe?
   A. It consists of nations located between Western Europe and the Middle East.
   B. There is a diverse mixture of peoples.
   C. It contains approximately 126 million people.
   D. There is a unity of religious belief.

# III. HUMAN AND CULTURAL GEOGRAPHY OF EASTERN EUROPE

## Demography

The population of Eastern Europe is approximately 126 million people. A comparison of the population and area of each individual nation illustrates the breakdown: the Czech Republic and Slovakia, about the size of New York State, have a population of about 16 million; Albania, slightly larger than Maryland, has roughly 3 million; Bulgaria, as large as Ohio, has a population of about 8 million; Romania, twice the size of Pennsylvania, has a little over 23 million; Hungary, about the size of Indiana, has 10 million inhabitants; and Poland, roughly the size of New Mexico, has a population of about 39 million. Due to the present disputes about borders and the conflict over territory in the former Yugoslavia, a breakdown for the nations of Bosnia-Herzegovina, Croatia, Montenegro, Serbia, Slovenia, and Yugoslavian Macedonia is not possible. The former nation of Yugoslavia was about the size of Wyoming and had approximately 20 million people.

## Ethnic Groups and Languages

While many ethnic and linguistic groups make up the population of Eastern Europe, the largest and most dominant ethnic group are the Slavs (approximately 85 million), which include Great Russians, Belarussians, Ukrainians, Poles, Serbians, Croatians, Bulgarians, Slovenes, Slovaks, and Czechs. The larger non-Slavic groups of Eastern Europe are the Magyars (proper name for Hungarians), Romanians, Albanians, Greeks, Germans, Turks, and Gypsies. Each nation is divided linguistically as follows:

| Country | Languages |
|---|---|
| Albania | Albanian, Greek |
| Bulgaria | Bulgarian, Turkish, Greek |
| Czech Republic and Slovakia | Czech, Slovak, Magyar, German, Ukrainian, Polish |
| Hungary | Magyar, German, Serbian, Croatian, Slovak, Romanian |
| Poland | Polish, Ukrainian, Byelo-Russian |

| Country | Languages |
|---------|-----------|
| Romania | Romanian, Magyar, German |
| Serbia | Serbian, Croatian, Slovenian, Albanian |
| Croatia | Croatian, Serbian, Albanian |

# Religion in Eastern Europe

The majority of Eastern Europeans are Eastern Orthodox Christians. The peoples of Albania, Bulgaria, the Czech Republic, Montenegro, Romania, and Yugoslavian Macedonia were Christianized by the Eastern Orthodox Church and came under the influence of the Byzantine Empire. (The majority of Czechs became Roman Catholic while under Austrian rule and the majority of Albanians became Muslim under Turkish domination.) Croatia, Hungary, Poland, Slovakia, and Slovenia were converted to Christianity by Roman Catholic missionaries. Large groups of Uniates (Orthodox in practice while nominally under the Pope), Protestants, Muslims, and Jews also exist in Eastern Europe. Each nation is divided along religious lines as follows:

GLOBAL CONCEPTS

**Culture**

CONCEPTS GLOBAL

| Country | Religion |
|---------|----------|
| Albania | Muslim 60% |
| | Eastern Orthodox 30% |
| | Roman Catholic 10% |
| Bulgaria | Eastern Orthodox 90% |
| | Muslim 10% |
| Czech Republic and Slovakia | Roman Catholic 65% |
| | Eastern Orthodox and Uniate 35% |
| Hungary | Roman Catholic 70% |
| | Protestant 25% |
| Poland | Roman Catholic 94% |
| | Eastern Orthodox 6% |
| Romania | Eastern Orthodox 85% |
| | Roman Catholic 10% |
| | Muslim 5% |
| Serbia, Montenegro | Eastern Orthodox 90% |
| | Muslim 10% |
| Croatia, Slovenia | Roman Catholic 90%, |
| | Eastern Orthodox 8% |
| Bosnia | Muslim 60% |
| | Eastern Orthodox 30% |
| | Roman Catholic 9% |
| Macedonia | Eastern Orthodox 55% |
| | Muslim 40% |

## REVIEW QUESTIONS

*Multiple Choice.* Select the letter of the answer that correctly completes the statement.

1. The largest and most dominant ethnic group in Eastern Europe are
   A. Romanians
   B. Slavs
   C. Magyars
   D. Albanians

2. Uniates are
   A. Roman Catholics who support the union of all Christian churches
   B. Eastern Catholics who are Orthodox in practice but nominally under the Pope
   C. Christians married to Muslims
   D. Protestants who want union with Roman Catholics

# SECTION 10: COMMONWEALTH OF INDEPENDENT STATES (C.I.S.)

## I. PHYSICAL GEOGRAPHY OF THE C.I.S.

### Overview

The Commonwealth of Independent States (C.I.S.), formerly the Union of Soviet Socialist Republics or U.S.S.R., is an immense federation of countries that is more than two and one-half times the size of the United States. It is located in both Europe and Asia, occupying two-fifths of the continent or land mass referred to as Eurasia. Its geographic location in two continents, particularly that of Russia, was often reflected in the political and cultural developments of the region. Before 1917, the Soviet Union was called the Russian Empire. Today Russia is the largest country in the Commonwealth of Independent States. The Baltic nations and Georgia, formerly part of both

GEOGRAPHY

Spatial Terms

GLOBAL
CONCEPTS
Diversity

CONCEPTS
GLOBAL

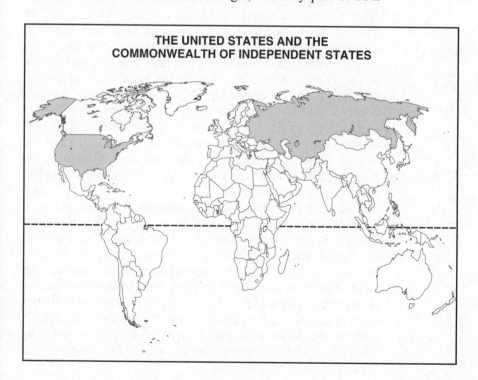

THE UNITED STATES AND THE
COMMONWEALTH OF INDEPENDENT STATES

the Russian Empire and the U.S.S.R., are not currently members of the C.I.S. Russia's great size (more than a quarter of the globe) has brought both problems and advantages to its inhabitants. With over 293 million people, the population of the C.I.S. is made up of more ethnic groups than any other area. Over a hundred languages are spoken there.

## Topography

**Physical Settings**

GLOBAL
CONCEPTS
**Environment**
CONCEPTS
GLOBAL

The topographical diversity of Russia has had an enormous impact on its political, economic, and cultural development. Originally, Russia was a much smaller country, landlocked (no access to the sea) and isolated by the Eurasian land mass. The desire to gain access to the sea for trading purposes led many Russian rulers to adopt a policy of expansion. This goal of gaining warm-water ports has always been central to Russian foreign policy. The numerous rivers that run throughout Russia long served as its only connections to the outside world. It was through these water trade routes that the Kievan princes made contact with the Byzantine or Eastern Roman Empire, which eventually gave Russia its religion and culture. Invasions from both Europe and Asia made it clear to later Russian rulers that if Russia did not gain access to the sea, it would be absorbed by other nations and cease to exist as a nation. As a result, the Russian kings, called tsars, followed an expansionist policy. First they set out on a path of conquest to the North and White seas, then south to the Black Sea, and finally east through Siberia to the Pacific Ocean. Yet, despite the acquisition of several thousand miles of coastline by the early 20th century, Russia's access to the Mediterranean, which carried the great bulk of commerce, was limited. Russian ships must leave from a port on the Black Sea and travel through the Dardanelles and the Sea of Mamara to reach the Mediterranean. Moreover, the ports gained by the Soviet Union were cold-water ports locked in ice during the winter.

The plain of northern Eurasia consists of several thousand miles of flat land, often referred to as the Northern European Plain. This area stretches from the Atlantic Ocean, across Western Europe and Eastern Europe until it reaches Russia, where it becomes the Siberian Plain. Only some mountain ranges, such as the Urals (the traditional dividing line between Europe and Asia), interrupt the plain. The geographic feature made Russia open to invasion. For example, during the Middle Ages, Russia suffered attacks by the Teutonic (German) knights as well as by Swedish and Polish armies from the west, while Mongols and Tartars invaded from the east.

The Great Caucasus, the highest mountains in the European part of Russia, stretch between the Black and Caspian seas. This series of mountain ranges, which run eastward from the Great Caucasus along the borders of Iran, Afghanistan, Pakistan, and India and then north along Tibet and China, separates Russia from its southern neighbors. Although these mountains are an obstacle, they have not prevented Russian attempts at expansion.

**Physical Settings**

## Bodies of Water

As you have read, the rivers of Russia have played an important role in its history and development. In the European part of Russia, the Volga (the longest river in Europe), Dneiper, Dvina, and Don rivers were essential for internal trade and commerce. The Neva River still serves as an important link between Russia's industrial centers and the Baltic Sea. In the Asian part of Russia, the Ob, Yen, and Lena rivers have recently become valuable as sources for hydroelectric industrial power.

**Use of Geography**

Russia's seas and lakes also have great importance. The Caspian Sea (the largest inland body of water in the world) provides food and a passageway for commerce. The Black Sea also provides an important trade route. Russia's freshwater lakes, such as Lake Baikal (the deepest lake in the world) and Lake Ladoga (the largest inland body of water in Europe), also provide important links in a generally landlocked country.

## Vegetation Belt

The vegetation belts of the region consist of three zones: the tundra, the taiga, and the steppes. The northern rim, including the islands of the Arctic Circle, is known as the tundra and covers about 10 percent of the country. It consists of a thick layer of permanently frozen ground, called permafrost. Its severe climate makes the tundra uninhabitable.

**WORLD ISSUES**

Population

The taiga, which covers nearly half of Russia, is a great forest that provides wood and limited crops. These conditions have kept the population there small.

The steppes is a very fertile region that has attracted both farmers and nomadic tribes. The southwestern region of the steppes, now the nation of Ukraine, is an important agricultural area that was known as the breadbasket of Russia. It has the most fertile land in the C.I.S. As it has no natural barriers, the steppes has always served as an invasion route for armies from both the west and the east.

**Physical Settings**

GLOBAL
CONCEPTS
**Environment**
CONCEPTS
GLOBAL

The territories between the steppes and frontier mountains of the southeast are mainly uninhabited desert. The majority of people in the Russian Empire lived in European Russia, particularly

**Human Systems**

GLOBAL
CONCEPTS

**Culture**

CONCEPTS
GLOBAL

in the steppes. It was only during the Soviet period that large numbers of people moved north and east, largely to exploit the natural resources in these areas. Russia's vast size has always presented great obstacles for travel, communication, and trade. However, it has also helped to save the Russians from invaders. For example, the invasions of both Napoleon's and Hitler's armies were defeated by Russia's vast size and harsh climate. The relative isolation of much of the population has resulted in the often stubborn and conservative nature of the Russian people.

## Climate

**Environment and Society**

The climate of Russia has played an important role in shaping the character of its people. The lack of warming ocean winds and the cool Arctic blasts make Russia's winters the coldest in the populated world. Even Russia's warmest areas have a climate similar to that of the Great Lakes or Canada. The harsh winters and short growing season have made the Russians both patient and able to endure great hardships.

*Multiple Choice.* Select the letter of the answer that correctly completes the statement.

1. The area of the former Soviet Union is physically
   A. twice the size of the United States
   B. more than two and a half times the size of the United States
   C. half the size of the United States
   D. larger than Europe but smaller than the United States

2. Until the 18th century, Russia
   A. was landlocked and isolated by the Eurasian land mass
   B. only had ports on the Black Sea
   C. had Baltic ports with limited use
   D. had easy access to the Mediterranean via the Black Sea

3. The most fertile region of Russia that attracted both farmers and nomadic tribes is the
   A. taiga
   B. steppe
   C. tundra
   D. plain

4. Covered with permafrost and uninhabitable, Russia's northern rim is known as the
   A. taiga
   B. tundra
   C. steppe
   D. plain

5. Which of the following rivers has not been important in the development of Russia?
   A. Dnieper
   B. Neva
   C. Sava
   D. Volga

# II. ECONOMIC GEOGRAPHY OF THE C.I.S.

## Agriculture

Until the 20th century, Russia's economy was almost completely agricultural. Ukraine was the primary source of crops. Called the breadbasket of Russia, Ukraine was able to grow enough grain to supply the entire Russian Empire with enough surplus to make it a major food-exporting nation. Now an independent nation, Ukraine still produces wheat, rye, barley, cabbage, and potatoes. The Caucasus region supplies cotton, tea, and subtropical fruit such as oranges and grapes.

WORLD ISSUES

Environmental
Concerns

However, certain geographic conditions have been harmful to Russia's agricultural production. These include droughts that severely affect crop production and Russia's vast size, which makes the transportation of crops difficult.

In addition to these geographic factors, other conditions have affected agricultural production in the region. The policy of Collectivization (a Soviet government policy that forced farmers to work together on state land in accordance with communist philosophy) under Stalin reduced agricultural output. State control of the Soviet economy (the government decided what was produced, who should produce it, and how much it should cost) interfered with the farmers' free choice and did not respond to the demands of the population. In 1986 the nuclear power plant at Chernobyl near Kiev (the capital city of Ukraine) exploded. As a result, much of the soil in Ukraine was contaminated, and the produce was not safe for humans. For that reason, the Soviet Union was dependent on outside sources, especially the United States, for much of its wheat.

WORLD ISSUES

Determination
of Political
and Economic
Systems

GLOBAL
CONCEPTS
Interdependence
CONCEPTS
GLOBAL

## Industrial Production Resources

**Major Resources.** Southwest Russia and Ukraine are rich in coal, iron ore, manganese, natural gas, and other minerals, especially metallic ores and precious and semiprecious stones. It is also a major source of oil. Siberia supplies the C.I.S. with 90 percent of its coal and half its natural gas. Siberia also has a huge supply of oil and immense deposits of iron and other minerals. However, the severe climate conditions make these resources difficult to obtain. In addition, Siberia provides over 60 percent of the Commonwealth's hydroelectric power. The rich forests of the taiga provide the C.I.S. with timber and fur.

WORLD ISSUES

Energy:
Resources and
Allocations

The Pacific Ocean in the Far East yields one-third of the Soviet fish supply, while the Baltic and Black seas provide the balance.

**Major Industries.** The C.I.S. is the world's largest producer of coal. The most important centers of this production are in Ukraine, the Urals, and eastern Siberia. Petroleum is also an important part of the Russian economy. The largest oil-producing area is the Volga-Ural region, which provides over 70 percent of the C.I.S.'s oil, followed by Azerbaijan and western Siberia. Most natural gas is produced in the Volga-Ural region as well. The C.I.S. is also the world's largest producer of iron and manganese, with Ukraine serving as the major center of this industry. The production of chemicals, essential to Russian technology, is also centered in the Volga-Ural region.

**Guns vs. Butter Controversy.** The GNP, or gross national product (total value of goods and services produced in a country) of the nations of the C.I.S., was severely strained during the years of Soviet rule. In the former U.S.S.R., it was estimated that between 16 and 20 percent of the GNP was spent on national defense. This led to a guns vs. butter controversy, that is, a disagreement over whether more of the GNP should be spent on the military or on food production and consumer goods. For example, much of the iron produced in the C.I.S. nations was used to manufacture tanks rather than consumer goods. As a result, few consumer goods were available. This lowered the general standard of living for most Soviet citizens.

WORLD ISSUES

Economic Growth and Development

**Perestroika.** In the 1980s the former Soviet Union faced an enormous economic crisis. It had become evident that the communist system had failed. In an effort to revive the Soviet economy, President Gorbachëv (who had taken power in 1985) began a series of economic reforms known as *Perestroika* (restructuring). Beginning with an attempt to improve the quality of products, Gorbachëv decentralized Soviet industrial and agricultural management (the Enterprise Law of 1987). Factory and farm managers were given greater control over determining both production and distribution of profits. Worker incentives, such as a pay increase for greater individual productivity, were adopted. The goal of this law was to make factories and farms independent, self-sufficient, and profitable so that they no longer needed government subsidies (money to make up losses). The Law of Cooperatives of 1987 allowed Soviet citizens to set up private businesses free of state control and keep the profits. The goal of this law was to encourage

GLOBAL CONCEPTS

**Choice**

CONCEPTS GLOBAL

WORLD ISSUES

Economic Growth and Development

197

more production and better products or services by beginning a system of individual enterprise. The Agricultural Reform Law of 1988 broke up the state and collective farms, replacing them with a private leasing system. Individual farmers could own and profit from their farms after paying off a long-term lease. The goal of this reform was to promote greater productivity through private ownership of land.

While the purpose of Perestroika was to "restructure" and thereby improve the Soviet economy, it faced many problems. These included:

1. The Soviet people had been used to a state-dependency system that provided security and undemanding work, not individual initiative and productivity.

2. Consumers expected immediate improvements (greater availability of goods and services), while Perestroika needed time in order to be effective.

3. Opposition by conservatives, especially government officials and party members who had benefited from the communist system, made it difficult to carry out the reforms.

## Economic Reforms in the Post-Soviet Period

With the collapse of the Soviet regime in 1991, the economic controversy started to resolve itself, as the newly independent nations began reforms to develop capitalist economies. However, the political instability and ethnic/religious conflicts in many regions of the C.I.S. threaten these changes as well as attempts to establish democratic governments. A further problem faced by the nations of the C.I.S. was to dismantle the huge Soviet nuclear and military arsenals and reduce the armed forces.

# REVIEW QUESTIONS

*Multiple Choice.* Select the letter of the answer that correctly completes the statement.

1. Originally called the breadbasket of Russia, the greatest agricultural output has always come from
   A. Belarussia
   B. Georgia
   C. Siberia
   D. Ukraine

2. The Soviet government's policy of forcing farmers to work on state farms was known as
   A. collectivization
   B. cooperatives
   C. Russification
   D. Perestroika

3. The guns vs. butter controversy was a disagreement over
   A. the quality of arms and food production
   B. whether or not to nationalize heavy and light industries
   C. whether or not to decentralize industry
   D. the amount of the GNP spent on arms as opposed to consumer goods

4. In 1986 Mikhail Gorbachëv began a series of reforms designed to restructure the Soviet economy. It was known as
   A. Glastnost
   B. Perestroika
   C. N.E.P.
   D. collectivization

5. Both the Enterprise Law of 1987 and the Law of Cooperatives are examples of
   A. capitalist incentives
   B. Marxist economic principles
   C. a command economy
   D. economic nationalism

# III. HUMAN AND CULTURAL GEOGRAPHY OF THE C.I.S.

## Demography

The population of the C.I.S. is approximately 293 million, slightly more than that of the United States. However, when one considers that Russia is two and one-half times the size of the United States, it is really underpopulated. In fact, the Commonwealth's population density is only 33 people per square mile, compared with 68 people per square mile in the United States and over 288 people per square mile in China. Yet, most of the population is located in European Russia and Ukraine. The small populations in Siberia, the Taiga, the Central Asian nations, and the countries of the Caucasus have grown only slightly in the last century. Most of this increase is due to industrialization of these areas.

## Ethnic Groups, Languages, and Religion

There are many ethnic groups in the C.I.S. and its surrounding regions. (The Baltic nations and Georgia, which are not presently C.I.S. members, are included because of their historical importance as part of both the Russian Empire and the U.S.S.R.) The largest of these groups, the Great Russians, Ukrainians, and Belarussians (White Russians), share a common culture and religious heritage. They also have common

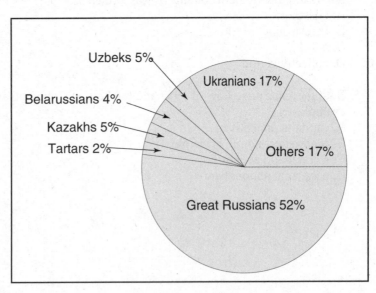

linguistic roots in Slavonic, the ancient language of the Slavic Eastern Orthodox churches. The Georgians, while distinct in their cultural and linguistic origins, also share the Orthodox Christian faith. The Armenians, who share a cultural and linguistic heritage with the Georgians, come from an eastern Anatolian nation that was forced into Russia by Turkish genocide between 1915 and 1923. The Armenians are also Eastern Orthodox Christians, but have their own church that differs slightly in ritual and practice. The Azerbaijanis, Turkmen, Uzbeks, and Kazahks are descended from the Turkish invaders of Russia in the Middle Ages. The Tartars are descendants of the Mongols, who ruled Russia from 1237 to 1450. Among the peoples of the Baltic region, the Latvians and Lithuanians share a common linguistic, cultural, and religious heritage, while the Estonians speak a language closely related to Finnish and Hungarian.

## The Orthodox Church

Christianity came to Eastern Europe and Russia from the Byzantine Empire. It played an essential role in the development of the Russian language, culture, art, and architecture.

In 988 Prince Vladimir of Kiev adopted Eastern Orthodox Christianity and had the people of Ukraine, Russia, and Belarussia baptized along with him. The Russian Orthodox Church dominated the culture of Russia until the 18th century. It continued to play a major role in the life of most Russians until the Communist Revolution in 1917. The Russian language is written in Cyrillic letters and was influenced greatly by the Slavonic language used by the church. Russian folk music and polyphony (using four-part harmony) were incorporated into church hymns. The building of churches became the chief objective of Russian architects, who developed a distinctive onion dome style. The painting of holy pictures, or icons, depicting Jesus, the Mother of God (Virgin Mary), and the saints, became Russia's major art form. Monasticism became very popular in Russia, and large monasteries were centers of spirituality and pilgrimages.

The Russian Orthodox Church is an independent institution with strong ties to the other Orthodox churches throughout the world. It is headed by a bishop known as the Patriarch of Moscow. Unlike the Pope of the Roman Catholic Church, who is supreme in religious matters, the patriarch is one of many bishops who consult together regularly to decide important church matters. Ukraine and Georgia have their own patriarchs as well.

Historically, the Russian Orthodox Church was often pressured and controlled by the tsars. Following the Russian Revolution of 1917, it was subjected to violent persecution by the Soviet government. In the Soviet regime's last years, the hostility of Communist authorities to the church lessened and a small measure of religious freedom was allowed. Despite years of great persecution, many Russians remained faithful. While precise figures are difficult to obtain, the majority of Russians, Ukrainians, Belarussians, and Georgians remained Orthodox Christians.

## Other Religions in Russia

GLOBAL
CONCEPTS
**Diversity**
CONCEPTS
GLOBAL

The Armenians, who are also Eastern Christians, have their own church that differs slightly in ritual and practice. The majority of Roman Catholics in Russia are Uniates, or Eastern Rite Catholics (Orthodox in ritual but officially under the authority of the Pope). Most Uniates are located in Ukraine. Otherwise, Lithuania has the only large Roman Catholic population. The other Baltic states, Estonia and Latvia, are primarily Lutheran (Protestant). The Azerbaijanis, Turkmen, Uzbeks, Kazakhs, Tartars, and other peoples of Turkish or Mongol origin are mainly Muslims. Finally, there is a sizable minority of Jews living in the C.I.S.

## Cultural Achievements

GLOBAL
CONCEPTS
**Culture**
CONCEPTS
GLOBAL

Russia's culture had two great influences—Byzantium and Western Europe. From the 10th to the 17th centuries, the Byzantine Empire, and consequently the Orthodox Church, were the main influences on Russian art, architecture, music, and literature. Religion played the key role in the early development of these forms. Most art was religious, usually in the form of icons, while Russian architects distinguished themselves building churches. (See "The Orthodox Church" on previous page.) Russian composers were usually monks who devoted themselves to writing church hymns, often based on traditional folk music. The ban on the use of musical instruments by the Orthodox Church encouraged the development of a cappella (without instrumental accompaniment) choirs. Literature written in Slavonic, the language of the Church, consisted for the most part of chronicles (narratives that combined history and legend) and hagiography (the lives of saints). As with music, literature was also written almost exclusively by monks.

GLOBAL
CONCEPTS
**Choice**
CONCEPTS
GLOBAL

At the beginning of the 18th century, Tsar Peter the Great carried out a policy of Westernization that drastically changed the direction of Russian culture. Combining traditional Russian themes while imitating Western European styles, uniquely Russian schools of art, architecture, music, and literature developed.

Artists painted portraits and landscape series as well as icons, while architects created lavish palaces and churches that combined the best of Western European and Russian styles. It was, however, in music and literature that the Russians most distinguished themselves.

Russia's best-known composers in the Tsarist period were Aleksandr Borodin (1833–1887), Modest Moussorgskii (1839–1881), Piotr Illich Tchaikovskii (1840–1893), and Nikolai Rimskii-Korsakov (1844–1908). These musical giants composed operas, choral works, symphonies, concertos, and chamber music that featured traditional Russian melodies. This tradition was continued in the Soviet period by composers such as Sergei Prokofiev (1891–1953), Dimitrii Shostakovich (1906–1975), and Aram Kachaturian (1903–1978). Certain composers, such as Sergei Rachmaninov (1873–1943) and Igor Stravinskii (1882–1971), forced into exile by the Russian Revolution in 1917, continued to create music and win acclaim for their work.

Russia's literary giants also brought a unique perspective to their work. These include: Aleksandr Pushkin (1799–1837), best known for his poetry and short stories; Nikolai Gogol

Count Lev Tolstoi

(1809–1852), noted for his short stories and the novel *Dead Souls* (which criticized serfdom); Ivan Turgenev (1818–1883), famous for his novels, particularly *Fathers and Sons*; Theodor Dostoievskii (1821–1881), whose psychological novels *Crime and Punishment* and *The Brothers Karamazov* won him world-wide acclaim; Count Lev Tolstoi (1828–1910), author of the masterpiece novels *Anna Karenina* and *War and Peace*; and Anton Chekhov (1860–1904), whose plays (*The Cherry Orchard*, *The Seagull*, *The Three Sisters*) have become world theater classics. In the Soviet period, most distinguished writers were dissidents, often punished for their work. One of the most famous, Boris Pasternak (1890–1960), was forced by the government to reject the Nobel Prize in Literature for his novel *Doctor Zhivago*. Another is Aleksandr Solzhenitsyn (1918–2008), whose stories ("One Day in the Life of Ivan Denisovich"), novels (*Cancer Ward*), and history of the Stalinist concentration camps (*The Gulag Archipelago*) brought him exile. However, as times and attitudes have changed, Solzhenitsyn was able to return to Russia in 1994.

# REVIEW QUESTIONS

*Multiple Choice.* Select the letter of the answer that correctly completes the statement.

1. Most of the population in the nations of the former Soviet Union lives in
   A. Central Asia
   B. European Russia and Ukraine
   C. Siberia
   D. the Far East

2. The largest ethnic group in the nations of the former Soviet Union is the
   A. Kazakhs
   B. Georgians
   C. Slavs
   D. Armenians

3. In 988 Russia adopted
   A. Eastern Orthodox Christianity and Medieval Latin culture
   B. Roman Catholicism and Medieval Latin culture
   C. Eastern Orthodox Christianity and Byzantine culture
   D. Roman Catholicism and Byzantine culture

4. The spiritual leader of the Russian Orthodox Church is the
   A. Patriarch of Constantinople
   B. Pope of Rome
   C. Patriarch of Kiev
   D. Patriarch of Moscow

5. Russia's most notable cultural achievements were in
   A. art and architecture
   B. literature and art
   C. music and art
   D. literature and music

6. Select the correct match of author and work.
   A. Nikolai Gogol—              *War and Peace*
   B. Count Lev Tolstoi—          *Dead Souls*
   C. Theodor Dostoievskii—       *The Brothers Karamazov*
   D. Aleksandr Solzhenitsyn—     *Father and Sons*

7. Russia's architecture is characterized by the
   A. baroque style
   B. basilica style
   C. onion dome style
   D. classical style

# THEMATIC ESSAYS

**Essay #1 Theme: Geography**
The physical geography of a region greatly influenced the way societies developed in different countries of the world.

Task:

1. Define the term "physical geography."

2. Select two societies or nations in different regions of the world and explain how the development of each society or nation was influenced by its physical geography.

Directions: Write a well-organized essay with an introduction stating the topic, a body that accomplishes the task, and a summarizing conclusion.

*Hint:* You may choose any two societies or nations and discuss the influence of factors such as topography, climate, and water bodies.

**Essay #2 Theme: Belief Systems**
Religious systems vary in different regions of the world and influence the cultural beliefs of people in the countries of these world regions.

Task:

1. Define religious belief system.

2. Select two religious belief systems in countries in two different world regions and describe how they have influenced the cultural developments in these nations.

Directions: Write a well-organized essay with an introduction stating the topic, a body that accomplishes the task, and a summarizing conclusion.

*Hint:* You may choose belief systems from among the world's major religions that are dominant in different world regions.

# DOCUMENT-BASED ESSAY QUESTIONS

Directions: The following questions are based on the accompanying documents. Some of the documents have been edited for the purpose of this assignment.

Write a well-organized essay with an introduction stating a thesis, a body of several paragraphs that accomplishes the task, and a summarizing conclusion. Use evidence from all of the documents to support the position you take in your thesis. Do not simply repeat the contents of the document; explain things in your words and relate the information to your thesis. Using your knowledge of social studies, include related information that is not included in the documents.

## Document-Based Essay #1

Historical Context: The physical geography of Latin America has influenced its economic and cultural development. Topography, natural resources, climatic conditions, and water bodies have determined how Latin America has developed.

Question: Discuss how the physical geography of Latin America has determined its economic and cultural development. Select any two Latin American nations to demonstrate the relationships between physical geography and a nation's development.

Part A: Summarize the main idea expressed or illustrated in each document.

Part B: Respond in an essay. Your essay should be based on a thesis statement. You should explain how the different aspects of a nation's physical geography have influenced its development.

Use all of the documents or illustrations in your essay.

## DOCUMENT 1  COUNTRIES AND TERRITORIES OF SOUTH AMERICA, CENTRAL AMERICA, AND THE CARIBBEAN

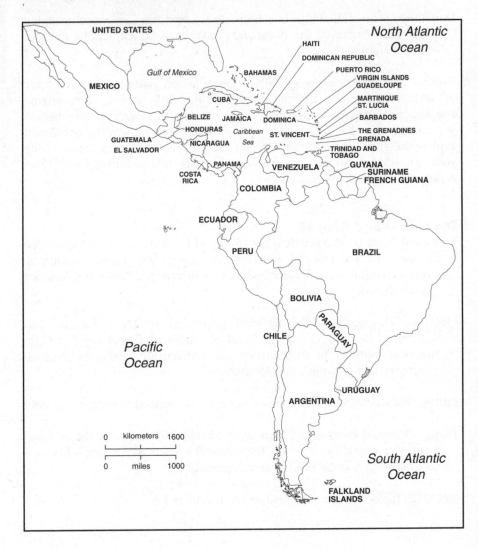

**DOCUMENT 2 WHERE LATIN AMERICANS LIVE**

> *Hint to the Student:*
> This map shows areas of population concentration in
> Latin America.

**POPULATION DISTRIBUTION IN SOUTHERN AMERICA**

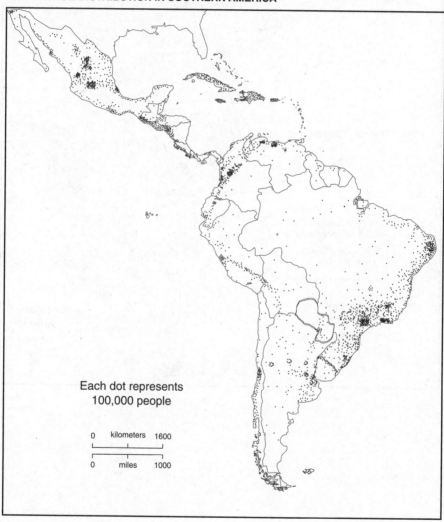

Each dot represents
100,000 people

| 0 | kilometers | 1600 |

| 0 | miles | 1000 |

## DOCUMENT 3  THE NATURAL SETTING OF SOUTH AMERICA, CENTRAL AMERICA, AND THE CARIBBEAN

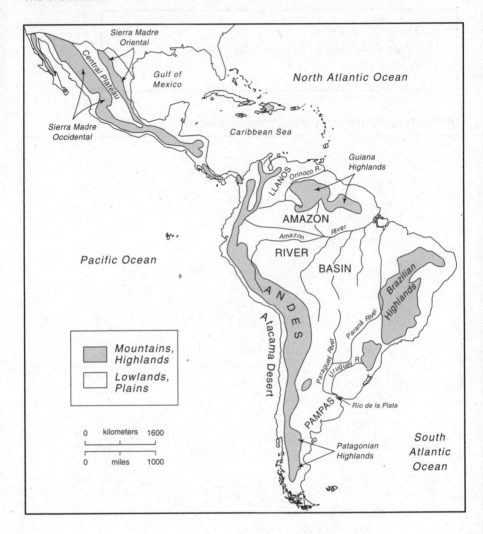

**DOCUMENT 4  CLIMATE OF LATIN AMERICA**

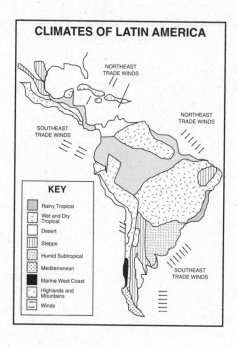

**DOCUMENT 5  CURRENTS OF LATIN AMERICA**

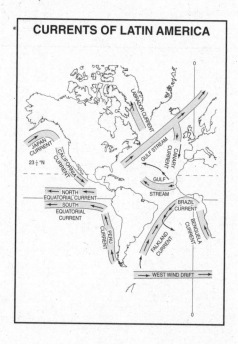

## DOCUMENT 6 TOPOGRAPHICAL AREAS IN LATIN AMERICA AND THE CARIBBEAN

ELEVATIONS

KEY

- Deserts
- Forests
- Hills
- Mountains/Tundra
- Plains
- Plateaus
- Rain Forests/Jungles

# DOCUMENT 7 NATURAL RESOURCES OF LATIN AMERICA AND THE CARIBBEAN

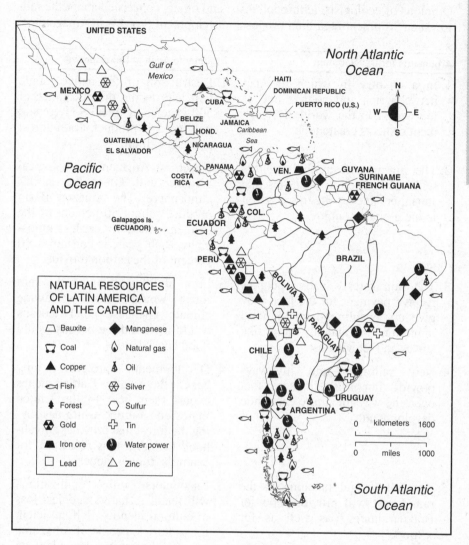

NATURAL RESOURCES OF LATIN AMERICA AND THE CARIBBEAN

| Symbol | Resource | Symbol | Resource |
|--------|----------|--------|----------|
| Bauxite | | Manganese | |
| Coal | | Natural gas | |
| Copper | | Oil | |
| Fish | | Silver | |
| Forest | | Sulfur | |
| Gold | | Tin | |
| Iron ore | | Water power | |
| Lead | | Zinc | |

## DOCUMENT 8  DEVELOPMENT PROJECTS IN AMAZONIA

Opinions of ecologists, anthropologists, and others concerned about the rain forest environment regarding proposed development projects in Amazonia

| Arguments for Development | Arguments Against Development |
| --- | --- |
| 1. In a country in which the gap between rich and poor is one of the widest in the world, development projects create jobs. | 1. Destruction of the native jungle will lead to the disappearance of 500 species of trees. Soil erosion will be a byproduct. Rain forest animals will die. |
| 2. The pig iron from the smelters will be exported to countries like Japan, enhancing Brazil's position in the global economy. | 2. Upsetting Amazonia's ecological balance will affect the earth's atmosphere. The Amazon Basin produces about 50 percent of the oxygen added to earth's atmosphere each year; it consumes 10 percent of the carbon dioxide. |
| 3. The rain forest's native peoples receive payment for the land they give up, enabling them to build modern homes and buy things like stoves and televisions. | 3. Loss of 20 percent of the rain forest would cause worldwide climate changes; polar icecaps would melt and the oceans would flood coastal cities. |
| 4. New railroads and highways provide important linkages that open the way for future economic development. | 4. Development projects only benefit the wealthy. Cattle ranches export their beef to the United States and Europe while destroying the forest that provides a livelihood to indigenous residents, for example, rubber tappers. |
| 5. Agriculture and ranching in the rain forest will provide food for Brazil's hungry as well as for export. | 5. Encounters with "civilization" will result in native peoples' loss of cultural identity. Self-sufficient for centuries, people of Amazonia are now becoming dependent on outside sources and on consumer goods, leaving them vulnerable to a culture incompatible with their own. |
| 6. Predictions about the complete destruction of the forests are exaggerated. The native jungle will renew itself no matter what human beings do to it. | |

**Document-Based Essay #2**

Historical Context: Photographs often reveal a great deal of information about the economic and cultural life of different people. In Africa traditional cultural patterns have been influenced by modern development in the 20th century.

Question: Discuss how the traditional cultural patterns or way of life of African peoples have changed because of modernizing developments that have taken place in Africa in the period following the establishment of nation states during the second part of the 20th century.

Part A: Summarize each of the photographic documents. Explain what you think the photographer is trying to show in each photo.

Part B: Discuss in an essay. Your essay should be based on a thesis statement. You should explain how the modernizing changes in Africa have effected traditional cultural patterns.

Use all of the photographic documents in your essay.

©Paul Almasy/CORBIS

**DOCUMENT 1  A STREET IN NAIROBI, KENYA.**

©Paul Almasy/CORBIS

**DOCUMENT 2  A VILLAGE IN THE CONGO.**

**DOCUMENT 3  A NEW SUPERMARKET IN BOTSWANA.**

©Liba Taylor/CORBIS

**DOCUMENT 4  FIELD HANDS ON A FARM IN KENYA.**

DOCUMENT 5  COLLEGE STUDENT AT THE UNIVERSITY OF NIGERIA.

DOCUMENT 6  A COUNTRY HOUSE OF A WEALTHY PLANTATION OWNER
IN SOUTH AFRICA.

**DOCUMENT 7  A BLACK HOME IN THE CAPE FLATS OUTSIDE CAPE TOWN.**

**DOCUMENT 8  THE MACHINERY OF MINING LOOMS NEAR THE CROWDED AFRICAN DWELLING AREAS OF THE COPPERBELT.**

**DOCUMENT 9  A STUDENT IN A BLACK SECONDARY SCHOOL.**

©Bettmann/CORBIS

**DOCUMENT 10  A MINING TOWN IN SOUTH AFRICA.**

# ERA I

# The Ancient World: Civilizations and Religion (4000 B.C.E.–500 C.E.)

# Part A: Early Peoples: Discovering the Human Past

When does human history begin? Fossil discoveries by paleontologists (scientists who study the earliest origins of the human race) like the Leakey family seem to indicate that there were hominids (humanlike) creatures in Africa as much as 5 million years ago and that humans may have developed there 1.75 million years ago. Basic technology—simple stone and wooden tools, animal skin clothing, the use of fire—may first have developed in Africa and then spread to other continents through migration. In fact by the end of the first period of human history, groups of *Homo sapiens* had probably spread across Europe, Africa, and Asia and trekked across to and peopled the Americas. Other evidence leads some scientists to speculate that the ancestors of modern humans evolved independently in several areas of Africa and Asia.

## Hunters and Gatherers: The Paleolithic Era

In looking into the development of human culture, anthropologists generally label the earliest period the Old Stone Age, lasting from roughly 400,000 B.C.E. to about 7000 B.C.E. This Paleolithic (from the Greek words for old and stone) Era featured simple tools, which the earliest humans chipped from various kinds of hard rock or fashioned from wood, plant fibers, and animal skin, hair, and bone.

Paleolithic peoples were hunters and gatherers, dependent upon resources and conditions provided by their environment. The basic economic decisions of what to use and produce, how to produce, and for whom to produce were functions of the plants, animals, and natural features available in the environmental setting. Survival of the group necessitated sharing the

**GEOGRAPHY**

**Human Systems**

**WORLD ISSUES**

Determination of Political and Economic Systems

products of its economic activities with all group members, answering the "for whom" question. The basic needs of food, clothing, and shelter determined the "what" and "how," drawing on the resource base, that is, the fund of materials and situations provided by their surroundings.

Their ability to work in organized social groups meant that early humans could cope with many different kinds of prey, with a variety of environmental conditions, and with numerous hunting, fishing, and gathering techniques. Most were probably nomadic, following the seasonal migrations of their quarry, and possessing an intricate knowledge of their targets' habits and environmental conditions. Kinship patterns seem to have been the basis of the social groupings that provided cooperative work and mutual protection. Extended families combined into clans and tribes of perhaps 30 to 50 members, with leadership probably based on physical prowess and knowledge of survival techniques. Gender specialization seems to have been the norm—males did the hunting and toolmaking, and women did the food gathering, utensil and fabric making, fire tending, and child rearing.

Archeological evidence points to the intellectual as well as the material achievements of these early humans. The ability to reason, remember, and communicate verbally enabled them to preserve knowledge and pass it on, as well as to speculate about spiritual matters and questions of the unknown. Burial sites with offerings suggest a belief in an afterlife, while rock and cave paintings and clay figurines indicate the concept of using magic in an attempt to control such factors as the abundance of food and the fertility of women.

Competition and hence fighting between groups for hunting/gathering grounds also seems to be characteristic of these earliest people, perhaps setting a pattern for what has become a constant factor in human relationships.

**GEOGRAPHY**

**Environment and Society**

GLOBAL CONCEPTS

**Identity**

CONCEPTS GLOBAL

## Development of Agriculture: The Neolithic Revolution

A series of ice ages created severe adversity for hunter–gatherer bands, as glaciers covered large areas of the northern hemisphere. Though nomadic paleolithic peoples had relied on agricultural products as well as animals, around 7000 B.C.E., some groups seem to have become sedentary, that is, they ceased wandering in search of sustenance. Domestication of both plants and animals created this possibility. People had learned to plant and cultivate seeds and harvest the food products of this activity. In a similar manner, they seized opportunities and devised ways of taming and controlling animals—sheep, goats, cattle, and pigs—for food, skins, wool and other products, and for use as beasts of burden.

This Neolithic (New Stone Age) Revolution, as anthropologists have called it, occurred in a number of places at roughly the same time. In the area now referred to as the Middle East, people raised barley, wheat, and legumes (lentils and peas) and herded sheep, goats, and pigs. West African farmers cultivated yams, millet, and sorghum. In the Americas, corn, squash, beans, potatoes, and other crops became the staples of agricultural production. China's northern areas became a center of other

GLOBAL CONCEPTS

**Technology**

CONCEPTS GLOBAL

**GEOGRAPHY**

**Places and Regions**

GLOBAL CONCEPTS

**Environment**

CONCEPTS GLOBAL

**GEOGRAPHY**

**Human Systems**

developments—besides field agriculture and animal husbandry, there have been finds of early forms of pottery and primitive bronze metallurgy. The permanence of a sedentary lifestyle required careful selection of a site upon which to settle. An adequate water supply, protection from natural disasters such as floods, fertile soil, abundant building materials for shelter; these factors were all essential to a successful permanent agricultural community.

## Surplus and Specialization

**WORLD ISSUES**

Determination of Political and Economic Systems

The potential for expansion of these sedentary villages lay in the amount of resources available, leading in some situations where resources were found in abundance to the production of a surplus. This increase in agricultural productivity meant that the carrying capacity of a given area of land was greater; it would support a larger human (and animal) population. This population increase was enhanced by a more abundant diet and gains in overall general health. This higher standard of living also brought about the threat of attack by other, less productive groups, necessitating protective measures such as the building of walls. The accomplishment of such tasks would require the organized effort of a significant labor force, an indication that these growing settlements were developing a more sophisticated level of social and political organization.

**GEOGRAPHY**

**Physical Settings**

GLOBAL CONCEPTS

**Technology**

CONCEPTS GLOBAL

The existence of an extra supply of food created the opportunity for greater variation in economic activity—specialization or division of labor. In nomadic hunter–gatherer groups, all able-bodied men hunted while women tended to camp life. In the earliest sedentary villages, agricultural tasks would have occupied everyone equally, with perhaps a gender specialization similar to their ancestral nomadic bands. But because agriculture and animal husbandry proved to be more productive, not everyone was needed for full-time cultivation.

GLOBAL CONCEPTS

**Identity**

CONCEPTS GLOBAL

Division of labor in turn led to great advancements in the quality and efficiency of tools, weapons, and utensils, as artisans could devote full-time to production and improvement. Hoes, rakes, and sickles for field use; baskets and pottery for food, oil, and beverage storage; woven textiles for clothing and decoration—all these products demonstrate an increasingly complex technology in the arts and crafts of neolithic peoples. Archeological finds also suggest a spiritual and mystical element in the thought processes of these peoples. Masks, jewelry, and intricately woven cloth may have served religious as well as decorative purposes.

Surplus and specialization generated yet another major consequence—greatly expanded trade and exchange between groups. Commerce between sedentary communities and nomadic groups stimulated cultural diffusion—the spread of ideas and techniques—and fostered further technological developments such as the use of the animal-drawn plow, the wheel, and the smelting of copper for more effective tools.

These neolithic economic patterns became the standard for many millennia. So-called traditional economies shared a number of common factors. Large populations involved in agricultural production supplemented by relatively small numbers of artisans and traders answered the basic economic questions of "what" and "how" guided by knowledge of which crops and livestock were best suited to local conditions. Increasingly, however, the "for whom to produce" issue was decided by an emerging leadership elite of kings, nobility, and priesthood.

Productive and occupational variety created another traditional aspect—the need and desire to exchange goods and services. Markets and merchants, including those involved in trading with other groups, often over long distances, met this demand. Yet another technological advance of the neolithic period set the stage for the next significant revolution in the development of human lifeways. Among the most agriculturally productive of environments were the great river plains of the temperate and subtropical regions. As societies grew in both population and social–political organization, they were able to harness the waters of these rivers to irrigate and thus cultivate larger tracts of land, promoting greater productivity, further increases in population, advances in the variety of goods, and a more abundant and comfortable lifestyle. The new forms of economic, social, and political structure emanating from these developments along the great rivers of South and East Asia and northeast Africa has been called by some scholars the urban and legal revolution.

**WORLD ISSUES**

Determination of Political and Economic Systems

**GEOGRAPHY**

**Human Systems**

GLOBAL CONCEPTS

**Environment**

CONCEPTS GLOBAL

# Part B: Riverine Civilizations: Cities, Kingdoms, and Legal Codes

**WORLD ISSUES**

Determination
of Political
and Economic
Systems

**GEOGRAPHY**

Places and
Regions

**WORLD ISSUES**

Population

**GEOGRAPHY**

Physical Settings

What is meant by the term civilization, and how do these civilizations differ from the human economic, social, and political forms that preceded them? Size and sophistication would seem to be the two most basic factors. In order to exercise a degree of control over such mighty rivers as the Nile in Egypt, the Tigris and Euphrates in Mesopotamia (present-day Iraq), the Indus in South Asia, and the Hwang Ho or Yellow in China, a large labor force and a high degree of organization and coordination were needed. Centralization of authority could provide this structure, resulting in the establishment of city-states and later kingdoms controlling large areas along the rivers.

It was irrigation, however, and its capacity to harness the waters of these great rivers that stimulated this process of centralization. A large, disciplined, and technically knowledgeable labor force was needed to build the dams, canals, reservoirs, and other devices essential to an efficient system for controlling flood waters and the soil-enriching silt they deposited.

Controlling and coordinating these activities and the larger populations that accompanied them required methods of communication and record-keeping, promoting the advent of writing and number systems. Calendars were developed for keeping track of seasonal cycles, especially the occurrence of floods. Grain and other food surpluses needed to be accounted for, and trading required some sort of monetary system. These developments, in turn, necessitated even greater growth in the size of human groupings and further specialization.

Leadership in the form of ruling individuals and groups took care of the need for control and coordination. Scribes, merchants, engineers, builders, carpenters, bricklayers, weavers, cartwrights, toolmakers, fishermen—the entire scope of goods and services providers flourished and came together in these ever-expanding human communities. This urbanization process set in motion a human tendency that has continued through subsequent historic periods and has greatly accelerated in recent centuries by yet another momentous development, the Industrial

Revolution. But humans do not live by economics alone. Like their paleolithic and neolithic forebears, the creatively thoughtful peoples of these riverine civilizations concerned themselves with the unknown and the supernatural. Speculation regarding questions about life after death, about the cause of natural phenomena, and perhaps most crucially about the nature of leadership encouraged the formulation of belief systems and the advent of yet another specialized occupation, that of the priest, interpreter of and communicator with the forces of the supernatural.

**GEOGRAPHY**

**Physical Settings**

Religious systems, with the society's ruler often serving as a god-king, provided yet another unifying factor for these nascent civilizations. A common set of values, a specified style of worship, temples as a focus of religious activities—all served to solidify not only the cultural consciousness of the society and its traditions but also the ruler's power and legitimacy. And it provided a rationale for a harmonious society, solidifying connections with the past and aiding in the shaping of the future.

The common value system, coupled with the need to manage economic affairs such as commerce and trade, social relationships among individuals and groups within society, and political processes led to the crystallization of legal codes. Rules and laws based on economic needs and practices and cooperative social behaviors were often supported by religious sanctions. These were spread by being written on papyrus (in Egypt), etched in clay tablets (in Mesopotamia), carved on stone columns (in South Asia), and perhaps even scratched on bones (in China) as ways of disseminating them to large populations and over the great distances covered by these "cradles of civilization."

GLOBAL
CONCEPTS

**Justice**

CONCEPTS
GLOBAL

# Part C: Cradles of Civilization: Ancient Societies

Though each of the four formative areas of human civilization shared most of the general attributes discussed in the previous section, each developed in a unique fashion, a function of its environmental situation. Far more archeological and historical evidence has been gathered regarding the two Middle Eastern civilizations than has come to light about those of South and East Asia. In fact, until the 1920s, the existence of an extensive civilization on the plain of the Indus River was not even suspected. Subsequent excavations there and increasing archeological activity in China have extended scholarly understanding of as well as speculation about these areas. Much more will undoubtedly be learned from further exploration and study.

The following chart depicts the uniquenesses and differences of each of the areas.

## CRADLES OF CIVILIZATION—A COMPARISON

|  | Egypt, The Valley of the Nile | Mesopotamia, Tigris and Euphrates | South Asia, The Plain of the Indus | North China, The Hwang Ho (Yellow) |
|---|---|---|---|---|
| **Environment and Its Impact** | Gentle predictable floods = positive, creative outlook | Tigris' violent flooding = pessimism, fear of disaster | Periodic flooding = renewal of fertile soil | Floods carrying loess = renewal of soil fertility |
|  | Arid climate = efficient food storage | Numerous tributaries = scattered city-states = disunity and warfare | Humid subtropical climate = difficulty storing food | Much mountainous and semidesert land = settlement only along rivers |
|  | Easily navigable river = political, cultural unity |  | Himalaya Mountains = shielded from winter cold | Violent flooding = dike-building for control |
|  | Deserts, cataracts = a degree of isolation | Areas of swamp and marsh = irrigation used for drainage | Monsoons and snowmelt = abundant water supply | Mountain, desert and jungle barriers = cultural isolation |
|  | Abundance of stone = permanent architecture | Lack of stone for building = reed and clay-brick structures | Passes in northwest = contact with Middle East |  |

| | Egypt, The Valley of the Nile | Mesopotamia, Tigris and Euphrates | South Asia, The Plain of the Indus | North China, The Hwang Ho (Yellow) |
|---|---|---|---|---|
| **Political Patterns** | God-king or Pharaoh as absolute ruler<br><br>Hereditary centralized monarchy<br><br>Long series of family dynasties | City-states with elected war chiefs evolving to kings<br><br>Series of empires, some formed by indigenous groups, some by invaders<br><br>Growth of legal codes | Centralized government evident in prominence of logically planned cities with public buildings and services | Small feudal kingdoms later unified by Zhou Dynasty<br><br>Highly centralized autocracy and unification under Ch'in<br><br>Dynastic Cycle and idea of mandate of heaven |
| **Social and Economic Patterns** | Pharaoh and royal family, high priests, palace officials<br><br>Relatively open society, skill + ambition = social mobility<br><br>Peasants = serfs, little land ownership; subject to draft for military and labor gangs | Nobility = king's family, high priests, royal officials<br><br>Clients = free citizens working for nobility<br><br>Commoners = free land-owning citizens<br><br>Slaves | Trade with Mesopotamia, South India, and Afghanistan<br><br>Royalty and nobility?<br><br>Religious priesthood?<br><br>Merchants and farmers?<br><br>(Minimal evidence = little definite knowledge) | King, aristocratic ruling class, and bureaucracy made up of warrior families<br><br>Peasant farmers (serfs) and slaves<br><br>Artisans/craft workers<br><br>Merchants |
| **Religious Patterns** | Pharaoh as deity in human form, proving that gods cared for people<br><br>Belief in afterlife, reflecting cyclical nature of seasons and floods<br><br>Great pyramids as symbol of eternal afterlife and Pharaoh's spiritual and temporal power<br><br>Concept of monotheism in (brief) cult of Sun god (Amon-Ra) | Hierarchy of greater and lesser deities according to function<br><br>Powerful and immortal deities, but humanlike in emotions and habits<br><br>Basis of later beliefs and tales—creation story, humans as images of gods, Garden of Eden, flood<br><br>Influential priesthood | Importance of fertility = worship of mother goddess<br><br>Clay tablet images of gods = prototypes of Hindu deities?<br><br>Clay animal figurines = great respect for livestock such as cows? | King worshiped as mediator between people and gods<br><br>Early worship of dead royalty set pattern for ancestor veneration<br><br>Confucianism = secular belief in ethical conduct and social harmony<br><br>Taoism = philosophy focusing on living in harmony with the laws of nature |

# Mesopotamia and Egypt: The Middle East

The area arching across today's Middle East up the plain of the Tigris and Euphrates rivers, along the east coast of the Mediterranean and then down the valley of the Nile River is referred to as the Fertile Crescent. It has the longest recorded history of any region on the globe due to the early emergence of the Mesopotamian and Egyptian civilizations. The agricultural productivity of these well-watered regions, their location at the crossroads of three continents and the nearness of both land and sea migration and trade routes has given them a central role in human history. In addition, the early development of writing systems, considerable cultural diffusion, and an arid climate conducive to the preservation of archeological evidence have given the modern world an extensive picture of what these early societies were like.

Peoples other than those of Egypt and Mesopotamia have influenced this history and have been affected by it. Some of these groups of diverse backgrounds can trace their roots to the area itself, while others migrated to the Middle East from elsewhere. There are many patterns and periods in Middle Eastern history, and often they overlap; that is, different patterns and movements frequently occurred at the same time in various parts of the area. The following list highlights the major contributors to the history of this region and to human culture.

GLOBAL CONCEPTS

**Environment**

CONCEPTS GLOBAL

GEOGRAPHY

**Places and Regions**

GEOGRAPHY

**Human Systems**

| Society | Area/Period | Achievements/Contributions |
|---|---|---|
| Sumerians | Southern Mesopotamia (3500–2300 B.C.E.) | City-states, mathematics (base 60 led to modern time and latitude systems), wheeled vehicles, ziggurats (temples), ideographic writing (cuneiform), schools |
| Egyptians | Nile Valley (Egypt) (3100–1200 B.C.E.) | Irrigation for control of river and expansion of cultivatable land, calendar, medicine, centralized hereditary monarchy, pictographic writing (hieroglyphics), pyramid tombs, and mummification |
| Babylonians | Mesopotamia (1900–1600 B.C.E.) | Hammurabi's law code, hereditary kingship, unification of entire Mesopotamian region |
| Hittites | Turkey and Syria (1800–1200 B.C.E.) | Iron metallurgy, political alliance with Egypt |
| Phoenicians | Present-day Lebanon (1400–800 B.C.E.) | Maritime navigation, phonetic alphabet, extensive sea-borne commerce |

| Society | Area/Period | Achievements/Contributions |
|---------|-------------|----------------------------|
| Assyrians | Northern Mesopotamia (900–612 B.C.E.) | Militaristic society, military engineers, siege machinery, coordinated military: infantry/archers/cavalry/chariots, empire arched from Mesopotamia to Egypt |
| Lydians | Turkey (ca. 700–550 B.C.E.) | Coining of money, monetary system |
| Hebrews/Jews/Israelites | Palestine (2000 B.C.E.–79 C.E.) | Monotheism, concept of a personal God, Ten Commandments, Old Testament |
| Chaldeans | Mesopotamia (612–539 B.C.E.) | Astronomy, moon phases = 4 week month, accurate solar year; astrology: the zodiac |
| Persians | Present-day Iran (1200–330 B.C.E.) | Extensive system of roads, unification of diverse peoples in large empire, period of peace and tolerance, enlightened rule |

**Judaism.** Among the smallest but most historically significant of these contributors to human culture were the Hebrews or Jews. Originally a loose confederation of nomadic tribes (called *habiru* by the early Egyptians and Mesopotamians), these people were the creators of a monotheistic religion based on the worship of the One God, Yahweh ("he who causes to be"). Though other societies often revered one particular deity as supreme, they generally had many others as well. Only the Hebrews came to see their Supreme Being as the only God, a god who had made a covenant or contract with them—Yahweh thought of them as his chosen people; they worshipped him alone.

Significant in the history of the Jews was their exile in Egypt (before 1000 B.C.E.), possibly due to a drought in their homeland of Palestine. After a period of enslavement, they escaped back to the "Promised Land" guaranteed them by their covenant with Yahweh. Political and religious differences split them into the northern Kingdom of Israel and the southern one of Judah (from which come the terms Judaism and Jews).

During the fifth and sixth centuries B.C.E., Jewish history and traditions were recorded in the Talmud and Torah—the latter became the basis of the Biblical Old Testament. Both the concept of monotheism and the idea of a legal code probably owe something to the influence of Mesopotamia, but it has been the Jews who refined and passed these notions on for them to become key ingredients in both Christianity and Islam. Indeed, much of the ethical-moral structure of Western culture is grounded in Judaism.

## The Indo-Europeans

GEOGRAPHY

**Environment and Society**

The originators of the various river valley civilizations such as the Sumerians, Egyptians, and Babylonians seem to have been indigenous to the immediate areas, but many of the other groups came from the outside. The prosperity and productivity of the river-based civilizations attracted nomadic peoples who were often quite proficient at warfare, having learned fighting techniques as a result of intense competition for the scarce resources, especially grazing lands, of less productive areas. These groups sometimes migrated into the riverine civilizations, to be absorbed, or occasionally to become influential enough to dominate the society already in place. More frequently the outsiders came as invaders and conquerors.

**GEOGRAPHY**

**Places and Regions**

Many of these newcomers were Indo-Europeans, peoples whose origins may have been in the great grasslands (steppes) of the middle of the Eurasian land mass. Scholars studying language patterns have discovered similarities among such diverse languages as English, Latin, Greek, Farsi (Persian), and Hindi/Urdu (the most widely spoken Indian tongue). Due perhaps to climatic changes or population pressures, these Indo-European groups began movements of massive scale into the extremities of Eurasia in the centuries between roughly 2000 and 1200 B.C.E. Among these migrants and frequent invaders were the Hittites and Persians of the Middle East, and the Aryans who moved into South Asia. Still later the ancestors of the Greeks and Romans, the Gauls and Celts, brought their languages and cultures to Southern and Western Europe.

## The Plain of the Indus: South Asia

**Early Civilizations.** Much less is known at present about the cultural patterns of this Cradle of Civilization than about those of the Middle East. Among the earliest peoples to settle in South Asia were the Dravidians, whose ancestors may have been a combination of peoples from the foothills to the west and north and others from central and southern India, with perhaps an infusion of migrants from further west. It is thought that in about 2500 B.C.E., in what is now Pakistan, the Dravidian culture developed, exemplified by the two largest settlements that have thus far been excavated—Mohenjo-Daro and Harappa. These major cities, along with dozens of other sites, demonstrate a considerable uniformity and were similar to other early river valley civilizations in the world.

**GEOGRAPHY**

**Physical Settings**

**WORLD ISSUES**

Determination of Political and Economic Systems

Analysis of the evidence gathered since the discovery of these sites in the 1920s—public buildings such as granaries and temples, extensive sewage systems, bathhouses, and marketplaces—would seem to indicate a considerable degree of governmental centralization. The people of this Indus culture had a writing system, often preserved on clay tablets, but scholars have not yet been able to decipher it. Other evidence of the sophistication of the culture comes from art—stone sculptures and clay tablets suggest an acute religious consciousness, with perhaps some ideas basic to Hinduism, the most widespread and longest-surviving of South Asian religions.

What led to the rapid decline of this culture around 1500 B.C.E.? The causes may have been natural—disease, climatic change—or a combination of natural and human factors. The incursions of the Indo-European Aryans across the mountain passes to the north certainly marks the beginning of a new phase of South Asian history. Contact between Dravidian and Aryan may at times have been violent; in other instances it was undoubtedly peaceful and cooperative. What is certain, however, is that the subsequent culture of the region demonstrates elements of both traditions.

Although present knowledge of Dravidian culture comes from archeological testimony, much of what is known of the Aryans is a product of oral and literary evidence contained in the oldest of Hindu sacred "scriptures," the Rigveda. This collection of hymns dedicated to their deities contains some indication that the Aryans at least thought of themselves as warriors and conquerors. Under the leadership of its chief or raja and with the guidance of its priests, each Aryan tribe used the advantage presented by the use of horses and bronze weapons to spread across and dominate much of the northern part of the South Asian subcontinent.

As in other areas where large-scale civilizations developed, centralization of political power evolved and a uniform social structure came about. Unlike other areas, however, the religious framework of this social and political structure became the basis of Hindu culture as it has evolved through more than three millennia. Thus the blend of Aryan and Dravidian cultures has fostered such major developments in South Asian life as the Sanskrit and Hindi/Urdu languages, the sharply delineated social hierarchy of caste, and the Hindu religion.

**Contact with the "West": Entering the Mainstream.** Despite the evidence of its religious uniqueness, society and culture in South Asia did not develop in isolation. The area's geographic "window on the west," which had provided commercial contacts with the civilizations of the Middle East, opened even wider near the end of the 6th century B.C.E. Persian

**Spatial Terms**

conquest of the Indus Plain introduced new political, economic, technological, and linguistic elements. Indian rulers adopted administrative policies copied from the Persian Empire, coinage of money spread from the Indus region to the plain of the Ganga, the Aramaic script of Persia was adapted to Indian languages, and innovative architectural techniques using stone would produce archeological remains useful to scholars of the modern age.

The relative peace of the Persian incursion was followed by the chaos and upheaval of the invasion of Alexander the Great, interjecting elements of the burgeoning Classical Greek culture. Thus southern Asia was drawn more comprehensively into the mainstream of civilization. The coalescing Hindu-Buddhist culture, along with expanded trade with both the Middle East and Southeast Asia, increased sophistication in urban life, and new political ideas set the stage for India's own Classical Age, exemplified by the Maurya and Gupta Empires.

## Along the Hwang Ho or Yellow River: Northern China

GLOBAL
CONCEPTS
**Culture**
CONCEPTS
GLOBAL

**Early Dynasties.** Chinese civilization originated in the Yellow River Valley about 4,000 years ago. According to legend, the Xia (Hsia) Dynasty ruled for about 500 years, from roughly 2000 to 1500 B.C.E. During this period the Chinese developed agriculture and a written language based on pictographic characters. By the time of the Shang Dynasty (1523–1028 B.C.E.), most Chinese were farmers, but there were also skilled craftspeople who produced bronze jewelry and weapons. The Zhou (Chou) Dynasty (1028–256 B.C.E.); the longest in Chinese history, followed the Shang. The Zhou kings ruled over a feudal system derived from a pattern of land grants from the king to relatives and supporters. The proliferation of political units stimulated the development of a class of capable civil servants who owed their positions at first to talent and merit and later to heredity. Such an aristocracy of bureaucrats was thus receptive to the new political ideas that were to follow. As the feudal states grew in power, the central power of the Zhou declined. The last 400 years of their rule was a period of conflict known as the time of warring states. Despite the turmoil of the period, China made great strides in technology. Iron tools and the iron-tipped plow were introduced, use of the horse as a beast of burden and instrument of warfare was refined, practical and ornamental bronzes were produced, irrigation canals were dug, and agriculture was improved.

**WORLD ISSUES**

War
and
Peace

**GEOGRAPHY**

**Physical Settings**

On another positive note, this era also has been called the Hundred Schools of Thought and led to the development of such philosophies as Confucianism, Taoism, and Legalism. These philosophical responses to political and social chaos attempted to prescribe some order to human relationships.

**The Ch'in: Centralization and the Idea of Empire.** The chaos of the warring states period was ended by Qin Shi Huangdi (Ch'in Shih-Huang-ti), the first emperor of China, who established the Qin (Ch'in) Dynasty (221–206 B.C.E.), the shortest but one of the most important dynasties in Chinese history. Its most obvious legacy is the name used by outsiders to refer to this most continuous of the world's cultures, China. The Chinese themselves refer to their society as Zhonngua, the Middle Kingdom.

The first Chinese empire was very absolutist and nearly totalitarian. Qin Shi Huangdi required that books supporting other philosophies be destroyed and reputedly had hundreds of scholars executed. He sent hundreds of thousands of laborers to work on the Great Wall, which ran approximately 2,000 miles across northern China. The wall was designed to repel the groups of nomadic invaders that then and throughout Chinese history have beleaguered the settled areas. The various legal systems of the different smaller states were replaced with imperial law; roads were built for armies to move on; canals were dug; and Chinese script (writing) as well as weights and measures were standardized.

Forced labor and harshness led to the downfall of the dynasty, but the Ch'in established the concept of a unified China under a strong centralized leadership accountable for the productive and beneficial functioning of society. When a ruler or dynasty did not fulfill the responsibility of providing a stable and well-ordered realm, the reign could be terminated by successful rebellion. The very success of a rebellion in overthrowing a dynasty was proof that it had lost the mandate of heaven, the support and approval of the gods. This notion and its practical application has proven to be the foundational principle of Chinese political and economic organization for over two millennia, leading to a long succession of dynasties with very few and brief periods of chaos and disorder.

GLOBAL CONCEPTS
**Diversity**
CONCEPTS GLOBAL

**GEOGRAPHY**

**Human Systems**

GLOBAL CONCEPTS
**Power**
CONCEPTS GLOBAL

**WORLD ISSUES**

Determination of Political and Economic Systems

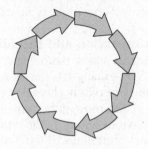

PROSPERITY & PEACE
New dynasty consolidates power
and restores stability, justifies claim
to mandate of heaven

RESTORATION
&
RENEWAL
Victors gain power,
establish new dynasty,
claim to have
mandate of heaven

DISORDER
&
DECLINE
Weak, corrupt
rulers raise taxes,
fail to provide
services, prevent
invasions; famines,
disasters occur;
mandate of heaven
is lost

REBELLION & CIVIL WAR
Instability, peasant uprisings, chaos,
economic hardship, lack of security

**THE DYNASTIC CYCLE**

**MAJOR CHINESE DYNASTIES**

| Dynasty | Achievements |
| --- | --- |
| Xia (ca. 2000–1500 B.C.E.) | Written language, pictographs<br>Development of agriculture: domestication of animals, cultivation of plants |
| Shang (ca. 1523–1028 B.C.E.) | Production of bronze jewelry, ritual vessels, and weapons<br>Sericulture (silk production) |
| Zhou (ca. 1028–256 B.C.E.) | Iron tools, iron plow<br>Fine bronzes<br>Irrigation canals dug<br>Confucianism, Taoism, Legalism, and numerous other philosophies develop |
| Qin (221–206 B.C.E.) | First empire, centralization of government<br>Great Wall begun, Canals and roads improved<br>Standardized writing system and system of weights and measures |
| Han (206 B.C.E.–220 C.E.) | Extended control to Central Asia<br>Established tribute system<br>Development of civil service exams<br>Paper, calendar, ceramics |

# Classical Civilizations: Empires and "Golden Ages"

The Intellectual and Philosophical Revolution, as it might be called, of the 6th century B.C.E. had profound effects for the entire Eurasian world. The secular political philosophies of China—Confucianism, Taoism, and Legalism—and the religiously focused belief systems of Southern Asia—Hinduism, Buddhism, and Jainism—provided the framework for the subsequent histories of those areas. A similar burst of human intellectual activity at about the same time stimulated significant cultural progress in the Mediterranean basin, producing the cultures of Greece and Rome. Several centuries later the rise of Christianity, rooted in the monotheistic ideas of Judaism, influenced and was influenced by the Greek and Roman civilizations. All these movements set the stage in or near all the cradles of civilization for the development of and domination by aggressive, sophisticated, and broadly influential cultures that have come to be identified as Classical Civilizations.

**Spatial Terms**

GLOBAL
CONCEPTS

**Change**

CONCEPTS
GLOBAL

## The Han Dynasty—Establishing the Structure of Chinese Culture

The abuses of the Qin emperor sparked a successful rebellion led by a peasant and minor government official Liu Pang, who founded the Han Dynasty. The centralized state begun during the Qin Dynasty was continued and expanded during the period of Han control (206 B.C.E.–220 C.E.). The Han rulers united the Chinese people and extended both the territory and the influence of the empire into central Asia and Tibet. Parts of Korea and Vietnam came under Chinese influence. The structure of government, which continued to exist in China until 1912, was established. China was divided into administrative units, with governors responsible to the emperor. The strict Legalist rule of the Qin period was relaxed, and Confucianism became the official state philosophy. A civil service examination system was established. To serve in government, an individual had to be trained in Confucian ideas and pass a series of civil service exams based on them. Education became important, and scholars became highly respected. Major cultural achievements were made during the Han Dynasty. The Chinese learned to make paper, invented a calendar, improved pottery making, and began the production of ceramics. At the same time, Chinese culture developed an element of stability and resistance to change based on Taoist beliefs. Of particular influence was the notion of a natural order of existence, which dictated that humans should do little to cause change. The importation of Buddhist ideas from India added an element of optimism for the future to China's complex philosophical mixture of ideas. Establishment of a solid family structure and a hierarchy of social classes based on occupation also contributed to what would become a stable and long-lasting society. (See pages 72–78 for background information on traditional Chinese belief systems and social structure.)

**The Tribute System.** As the Han emperors extended China's territory and control, contact with other peoples increased. As the preeminent East Asian power, the Chinese considered others to be barbarians who needed to acknowledge their inferior status by offering tribute. Nations that participated in the tribute system recognized China as their superior, and the relationship between China and these nations was much like any one of the five reciprocal relationships of Confucius. The tribute nations brought tribute (or gifts) to the Chinese emperor once a year, and in return the emperor promised protection in case of outside attacks. The Chinese emperor was regarded as the head of a family of nations, and his subordinates owed him respect and obedience. Any nation not willing to accept subordinate (or inferior) status would have no official way of dealing with the Chinese. In the eyes of the Chinese, they would forever remain barbarians.

GLOBAL
CONCEPTS
**Political Systems**
CONCEPTS
GLOBAL

**GEOGRAPHY**

**Physical Settings**

The extension of Han power brought with it a parallel expansion of China's trade relationships and an increasing diffusion of Chinese culture into other areas. Merchants established trading stations in Southeast Asia and opened routes along the great rivers of that area to the Bay of Bengal. Other contacts with Indian culture came via relationships with the Indianized state of Funan in Cambodia and southern Vietnam. Conquest of Korea gave the Han control of trade with Japan, and the Silk Road across the interior of Asia to Persia eventually brought the two greatest empires of the time, the Han and the Roman, into direct commercial contact.

GLOBAL
CONCEPTS
**Citizenship**
CONCEPTS
GLOBAL

Fundamental to the success of Chinese culture has been the role of the peasant. Backbone of the agricultural work force and basic unit of the labor forces that built walls, canals, temples, roads, and palaces, as well as key ingredient in the overthrow of corrupt and incompetent dynasties, China's peasantry has, from Han times, preserved the Confucian ethic of morality, order, harmony, and acceptance of one's role and responsibility in the social hierarchy.

By the end of the Han Dynasty (ca. 220 B.C.E.), then, Chinese culture had solidified those elements that would characterize the society right down to the 20th century. A sophisticated agricultural technology proved capable of sustaining an ever-increasing population. Prosperity and growth produced a vibrancy in the intellectual realms. Confucianism provided a stable and consistent social and political ethic grounded in secular rather than religious values. Through internal upheaval and chaos, and the depredations of numerous conquests by outsiders, the basic Chinese cultural heritage remained intact.

GLOBAL
CONCEPTS

**Identity**

CONCEPTS
GLOBAL

### *Classical Civilizations of the Mediterranean: Greece and Rome*

**GEOGRAPHY**

**Human Systems**

The time period when the civilizations of Greece and Rome were at their height is called both the classical period and the Age of Antiquity. For ancient Greece this period was from 750 to 150 B.C.E. For Rome it was from 500 B.C.E. to 200 C.E., even though the Roman Empire lasted until 476 C.E.

**Greece.** The Greeks were the first people of Western Europe to develop an extensive urban culture. This was accomplished even though Greece's geography made unity very difficult. Because of the many mountains in the Greek Peninsula, the Greek people were isolated from one another and formed individual city-states. Each city-state (polis, root of the word politics) was a small governmental unit organized around an urban center. Of the hundreds of these city-states dotting the Greek mainland and islands, the most famous were Athens and Sparta. There were major political, economic, and cultural differences between these two city-states. Sparta developed as a militaristic city-state. It emphasized military strength and rule by just a few people—the landowners and nobility. The majority of Spartans, including the slaves, or helots, had no voice in the government. Sparta could also be called an aristocracy because it was ruled by a small number of people. A Spartan citizen's first loyalty and duty was to the state. The political system did not promote individual freedom or progress in the arts and sciences, but it did establish some patterns that appeared later in European history. The elitism of the Spartan autocrats (dictatorial rulers) and the militaristic nature of the society has found successors even in the totalitarian states of the 20th century.

GLOBAL
CONCEPTS

**Environment**

CONCEPTS
GLOBAL

GLOBAL
CONCEPTS

**Political Systems**

CONCEPTS
GLOBAL

Athens eventually developed into a democratic city-state and had a lasting influence on the history of both Western Europe and the United States. By 450 B.C.E. Athens had developed the world's first democracy, that is, a system in which citizens take part and have a voice in their government. Because Athenian citizens voted directly for or against the laws, this system is called a direct democracy. However, there were limi-

GLOBAL
CONCEPTS

**Citizenship**

CONCEPTS
GLOBAL

tations in Athenian democracy. Women, for example, could not vote for officeholders, and only Athenian-born citizens could participate in government. Athenian democratic ideals were expressed in the famous Funeral Oration of Pericles. During the years of Pericles's leadership in the 5th century B.C.E. (461–429 B.C.E.), Athens made great progress in democracy as well as in the arts and sciences. Consequently, this period, called the Age of Pericles, also became known as the Golden Age of Athens. Historians refer to this long era of Greek accomplishments as the Hellenic Period (750–336 B.C.E.).

**Achievements of the Hellenic Greeks.** The Greeks left many legacies that have had a great impact on civilizations that followed:

1. *Philosophy.* The ancient Greeks believed in the ideal of the well-rounded person, that is, one who was intelligent, thoughtful, asked questions, and had a "sound mind in a sound body." According to the famous Greek philosopher Socrates, one should "know thyself." He also said, "The unexamined life is not worth living." Plato, his most famous student, wrote *The Dialogues.* One of these dialogues, called *The Republic*, contains Plato's idea that the ideal government would be one run by kings who were also philosophers. Plato's most famous student was Aristotle, whose thoughts on reason, logic, science, ethics, and government are found in his extensive writings, such as the *Nicomachean Ethics* and *Politics.*

2. *Literature.* Drama was the most outstanding Greek contribution in literature. The Greeks invented tragedy and comedy. Some famous Greek literary figures were Homer (*The Iliad* and *The Odyssey*), Sophocles (*Oedipus Rex*), and Aristophanes (*Lysistrata*). Also notable were the poet Pindar and the historians Herodotus and Thucydides.

3. *Mathematics and science.* Noteworthy achievements were made by Pythagoras (geometry), Hippocrates (medicine), and Democritus (matter composed of atoms).

4. *Architecture and sculpture.* The Parthenon was a temple built on a hill called the Acropolis. As with other Greek buildings, the Parthenon combined balance and symmetry and the use of tall, graceful columns. Many buildings throughout the Western world have imitated Greek architecture. The three basic styles of Greek columns or pillars are called Doric, Ionic, and Corinthian. Greek sculpture displayed dignity, realism, and simplicity, and it idealized the human form.

5. *The Olympic games.* These major athletic events were held in honor of the god Zeus, and they are the basis of the modern-day Olympics.

**Military Conflicts.** Although the Greek city-states often quarreled among themselves, they were able to unite against the Persians. In the Persian Wars (500–479 B.C.E.), the Greeks were able to stop the westward expansion of the Persian Empire. Important Greek victories were at the battles of Marathon and Thermopylae.

The Peloponnesian War (431–404 B.C.E.) was a conflict between Athens and Sparta. Sparta was victorious and brought Athens under its control but was unable to unite all the Greek city-states. This long and bitter conflict weakened both sides and left peninsular Greece open to conquest by an outsider.

Eventually, most of the Greek city-states were united under the control of King Philip of Macedon (a region to the north) in 338 B.C.E. When he died, his title, power, and lands were passed on to his son Alexander.

**Alexander's Empire.** Alexander the Great built an empire that extended as far south as Egypt and as far east as India. His conquests were made between 336 and 323 B.C.E. and resulted in the largest world empire up to that time. Alexander, who had been taught by Aristotle, was an admirer of the culture of Greece, and he spread Greek culture wherever he went. The mixture of Greek culture with the cultures of conquered areas—Egypt, the Middle East, and South Asia—became known as Hellenism. This period of cultural mixing and cultural diffusion lasted beyond Alexander's death in 323 B.C.E. and is referred to as the Hellenistic period. When Alexander died, his empire was divided into three parts, each part ruled by one of his generals. In less than 200 years, these three parts were once again united under the rule of the Roman Empire. Important cultural achievements during the Hellenistic period (336–150 B.C.E.) included:

1. *Philosophy.* During this period, philosophers developed new and different ideas about life. Diogenes founded the philosophical school of cynics. The idea of cynicism included criticism of materialism and social conventions and a distrust of human virtue. Zeno founded stoicism, advocating freedom from passions and desires and detachment from the outside world. Epicurus founded epicureanism, advocating the search for pleasure and happiness while maintaining a sense of moderation.

2. *Mathematics and Science.* The leading figures were Aristarchus (astronomy), Euclid (geometry), Archimedes (physics), and Eratosthenes (geography).

**Rome.** By 500 B.C.E. the Latin peoples of central Italy, also known as Romans, had created a republic. In a republic, citizens par-

GEOGRAPHY

Physical Settings

WORLD ISSUES

War
and
Peace

GEOGRAPHY

Spatial Terms

GLOBAL
CONCEPTS
**Diversity**
CONCEPTS
GLOBAL

GLOBAL
CONCEPTS
**Culture**
CONCEPTS
GLOBAL

ticipate in government by electing the rulers who represent them. The early Roman Republic was controlled by a few nobles, the patricians, and was thus actually an aristocracy. Over the next 200 years, however, important political gains were made by the plebeians—the farmers and the workers—who won the right to become members of the government assembly and to vote for tribunes. The tribunes could take action against the patrician-controlled consuls and the Senate. Plebeian gains also included the codification (writing down) of Roman law into the Twelve Tables, which enabled all to know what the laws were. Roman law established forms of justice and protection of human rights and property that have influenced legal systems throughout the Western world. In its period as a republic, Rome made progress as a democracy.

## The Roman Republic Becomes an Empire (340–27 B.C.E.).

After conquering and uniting the Italian Peninsula, Rome took control of the lands bordering the western Mediterranean Sea. These lands came under Rome's control after its success in the Punic Wars (264–146 B.C.E.) against Carthage, a rival city located in North Africa. Roman forces next turned their attention to the eastern Mediterranean area and conquered the Greek lands that had once been part of Alexander's empire (Greece, Egypt, the Middle East). The Mediterranean had become a Roman lake. The Romans admired the Hellenistic culture of the Greeks, and it is said that even though Roman force conquered Greece, Greek culture conquered Rome.

Under Julius Caesar, Roman legions conquered most of central and western Europe. Rome now held land on three continents, and by 50 B.C.E. it had become the largest empire known to the world. However, during this period of conquest, many changes took place in Rome. The Roman army changed from a civilian force to a selectively trained group of professional soldiers. As a result, soldiers were more loyal to their individual generals than to the republican government elected in Rome. As the military commanders gained more power, they fought among themselves in civil wars for control of Rome, and the republic was changed into a dictatorship. In 46 B.C.E. Julius Caesar became a dictator. He was succeeded by three generals after his death. Among these was Octavian, who became the first emperor of Rome when he took the title Caesar Augustus and established the Roman Empire. He ruled from 27 B.C.E. to 14 C.E. The so-called Augustan Age, which began with Octavian, was the start of 200 years of stability, peace, and progress in the Roman Empire, a period known as the Pax Romana, or Roman Peace (27 B.C.E.–180 C.E.).

**Christianity.** If Greece and Rome were two of the pillars provided to Western civilization from the classical period, a third was provided by new religious movement, Christianity. Christianity began during the Roman period with the birth of Jesus. It started as a reform movement among Jews and gained converts under the leadership of Paul, a Hellenized Jew. Christianity spread throughout the Middle East and other parts of the Roman Empire, although its followers were persecuted by Rome's emperors.

By 313 C.E. Christianity had become so widespread that the Emperor Constantine issued the Edict of Milan, which granted freedom of worship to all Christians in the empire—in both the western part, ruled from Rome, and the eastern part, ruled from the city of Byzantium on the Bosporus. With the decline of the western part of the Roman Empire, the Emperor Constantine moved to Byzantium, where he built a larger city, known as Constantinople (now Istanbul), in Turkey. Constantinople became the capital of the Eastern Roman Empire, also known as the Byzantine Empire.

**GEOGRAPHY**

**Places and Regions**

The Byzantine Empire was at its height from 527 to 565 C.E., under the Emperor Justinian and his wife Theodora. It included present-day Greece, Turkey, Israel, Egypt, Jordan, and Syria. The Justinian Code set up a legal system based on Roman laws. The beautiful church Hagia Sophia was built under Justinian. Christians in the empire called their church Eastern Orthodox to distinguish it from the Catholic Church in Rome. This Eastern Roman Empire outlasted the original centered in Rome; in the years after 600, it declined due to attacks from many outsiders.

**WORLD ISSUES**

War

and

Peace

**The Roman Empire Declines and Falls (180–476 C.E.).** During these years, the Roman Empire slowly declined for several reasons:

1. *Division of the empire.* The Emperor Constantine moved from Rome and made Constantinople (now Istanbul) his capital in the 4th century. This move split the empire into two parts— the western part, with its capital remaining at Rome, and the eastern part, or the Byzantine Empire, headed by Constantine.

2. *Political weaknesses.* The government in Rome became corrupt and because of the size of the empire was unable to keep control over all the territory under its rule.

3. *Economic problems.* The rulers wasted money, and heavy taxation led to anger among the people. A trade imbalance caused by importing many goods lowered the value of Rome's money.

4. *Social factors.* A decline in morality and patriotism was widespread. A rigid class system developed. Many slaves and non-Romans who lived in the major cities were badly treated.

5. *Invasions.* Beginning in the 3rd century, Germanic tribes invaded Roman lands and eventually were able to defeat Roman armies. In 476, Rome itself was conquered. (The Eastern Roman Empire, however, survived beyond 476.)

6. *Impact of Christianity.* The teachings of Christianity conflicted with the dictatorial policies of the emperors.

**Achievements of the Ancient Romans.** The Romans made many achievements in the arts and sciences and had a lasting impact on the Western world.

1. *Law.* Roman law was codified in the Twelve Tables. Over the years, many new statutes were added, and Roman law became the basis of the legal systems of Western Europe and South America.

2. *Language.* Latin was the basis for Romance languages, such as Spanish, French, and Italian. Many English words also come from Latin.

3. *Literature.* The speeches of Cicero and the works of Vergil *(The Aeneid)* and Horace are well known. The historians Livy, Plutarch, and Tacitus are still studied today.

4. *Architecture.* Roman-built roads, aqueducts, and buildings were found all over the empire and helped unite the territories. Some structures, such as the Colosseum in Rome, still stand. The Romans used the arch and were the first to use concrete as a building material.

5. *Government administration.* A good civil service of government officials helped to run the far-flung empire. Under the Pax Romana and a strong central government, unity and peace were brought to many areas of Europe. However, when the empire collapsed, disunity and disorder were common in the former Roman lands.

Greece and Rome bequeathed to the world and particularly Europe a number of enduring legacies, particularly those cited above. Their cultures became the model that future European rulers, writers, and scholars looked back to from the Holy Roman emperors of the 8th and 9th centuries, to the artists (Michelangelo), scientists (Leonardo da Vinci), and playwrights (William Shakespeare) of the Renaissance, and the philosophers and politicians of the Enlightenment (Thomas Jefferson).

GLOBAL CONCEPTS

Culture

CONCEPTS GLOBAL

GEOGRAPHY

Physical Settings

WORLD ISSUES

Determination of Political and Economic Systems

### South Asia's Golden Ages: Religion and Empire

Two interactive factors seem to have stimulated the dynastic empires that emerged in South Asia between the 4th century B.C.E. and the 4th century C.E. Most of the basic standards, practices, and customs, grounded in the religious structure, were in place by this time. The added impetus of extensive external military, political, and commercial contacts during this period

**Olmec Culture.** This early society developed in Central America along the Gulf of Mexico from about 1500 to 600 B.C.E. The Olmecs were an agricultural society capable of developing raised land platforms to plant in swamp areas. They were accomplished artists and traders who built what are believed to be some of the first ceremonial centers in Central America. The Olmecs were probably the forerunners to other civilizations that later developed. The mystery of exactly who the Olmec were and why they disappeared has not been completely explained.

**The Mayan Civilization.** Remains of this early culture have been found in what is today the Yucatán Peninsula of Mexico and Central America. By the 2nd century B.C.E., groups of Mayan clans were living in sophisticated communities. During the classic period of their history (300–900 C.E.), a large number of rival city-states existed. They were ruled by nobles and a priestly class. Warriors, farmers, merchants, and slaves made up the vast majority of the highly rigid, stratified Mayan social structure.

The Mayans made great accomplishments in science, especially in astronomy and mathematics—a system using twenty as a base rather than ten. The Mayan calendar was very accurate with eighteen months of twenty days each and a five-day month, adding up to 365 days, and Mayan buildings rival those of other ancient peoples. Religion dominated Mayan life.

During the classic period, the Mayan city-states engaged in ruinous wars, which led to the destruction and abandonment of the centers that had developed in the heavily forested areas of the Peten jungle in present-day northern Guatemala and Chiapas, Mexico. These bloody wars among competing dynasties devastated Mayan life. By 900 C.E. the Mayans had moved north to the Yucatan Peninsula and south to the Guatamalan highlands. Although new settlements were established after 1000 C.E., they did not reach the level of the earlier cities, and Mayan civilization came to be dominated by more militant societies.

### *Early Europeans: Celts and Gauls*

As first the Greek and then the Roman classical civilizations rose, prospered, and then declined, another culturally influential society flourished to the north of them. From roughly 800 B.C.E. to the middle of the 1st century C.E., the Celts (or Gauls as Julius Caesar called them) dominated Europe from the Balkans to Ireland and from southern Scandinavia to the northern Iberian Peninsula. Groups of proudly independent tribes who often fought one another as fiercely as they battled outsiders, the Celts were known to the Greeks and Romans as warriors and mercenaries.

GLOBAL CONCEPTS
Environment
CONCEPTS GLOBAL

**GEOGRAPHY**

Environment and Society

GLOBAL CONCEPTS
Political Systems
CONCEPTS GLOBAL

**GEOGRAPHY**

Places and Regions

GLOBAL CONCEPTS
Culture
CONCEPTS GLOBAL

GLOBAL CONCEPTS
Diversity
CONCEPTS GLOBAL

**GEOGRAPHY**

Places and Regions

Though a few tribes lived in fortified settlements, most were seminomadic farmers, combining cattle herding with small-scale agriculture supplemented by hunting. Applying new technologies to their farming, they utilized iron plows, created wheeled cultivators, and pioneered the use of fertilizer. They were also miners of salt, a valued item of trade, and their merchants trafficked in metals (iron, copper, and tin) and slaves. Celtic women seem to have been equal to men in many ways, even acting as warriors.

In religion, different tribes seem to have had their own gods and cult figures. As nomads, the Celts built no centers of worship—groves of trees, springs, and other natural features were set aside as sanctuaries. Among the most important individuals in the society were the priests or Druids. A long training process prepared them to become the all-round intellectuals of Celtic culture—seers, teachers, judges, and historians as well as worship leaders.

By 600 B.C.E., the Celts were trading with Greek merchants in southern France, and in the 3rd century B.C.E. briefly invaded Greece itself. Some groups crossed the Alps and raided northern Italy around 400 B.C.E. and eventually settled into an agricultural lifestyle there. These contacts resulted not only in trade, but in a stimulation of the Celtic art style. Based on simple shapes woven into complicated geometric designs, this free-flowing art used stylized animal figures and foliage motifs to decorate armor, coins, and pottery.

Celtic traders, soldiers, and craftsmen crossed to Britain and Ireland where they established towns and where their culture and traditions would outlast those on the continent, which were ultimately subjugated by the Romans. It was the Romans who distinguished between the Gauls, those Celts whom they conquered in France, and the Germans whom they did not, based on Julius Caesar's arbitrary division. The Celtic legacy can be found in many ways in modern Europe. Celtic languages are still spoken along the western fringes from Galicia in Spain and Brittany in France to Wales, Ireland, and Scotland in the British Isles. Many place names are derived from the Celts as well, some indicating the former location of a fort or dun—Verdun in France, Dundee in Scotland. Others were named for tribes such as the Parisii (Paris) or the Carnutes (Chartres).

### Early African Civilizations

Early societies other than the Egyptian civilization also developed in Africa. The production of iron tools and weapons made possible the increase of food production needed for the growing

African population. African Iron Age technology began in the East Africa kingdom of Kush in about 500 B.C.E. The technology of iron production may have been introduced to Kush by Phoenician traders or Assyrian conquerors from the Middle East. Iron making first appeared in West Africa among the Nok peoples of northern Nigeria about 300 B.C.E. It is believed that Iron Age technology spread southward throughout Africa with the migrations of the Bantu peoples about 100 C.E.

Various groups of Africans traded with one another. Eventually market towns emerged. There was trade with places as distant as India, Rome, Southeast Asia, and China. The trade with Southeast Asia had a long-lasting effect in that the cultivation of certain Southeast Asian crops (rice, yams, bananas, sugarcane) were brought to Africa.

**Iron Age Empires.** Two major urban cultures that developed in northeastern Africa were Kush and Axum. Kush civilization developed as early as 2000 B.C.E. At times, Kush was a province of Egypt. Consequently, Egyptian civilization influenced Kush. For example, in the Kush capital of Napata, there was a religious center dedicated to an Egyptian god. About 700 B.C.E. Kush invaded and conquered Upper (southern) Egypt, and eventually the Kush kings ruled as pharaohs over an empire stretching from the Mediterranean to modern Ethiopia. The Kushites were driven out of Egypt by the Assyrians in about 600 B.C.E., and the Kush capital was moved from Napata to Meroë in about 540 B.C.E. The reasons for this move were probably economic. The wealth of Kush was based on the trade of much sought-after African goods, such as ivory, gold, and ebony, with areas to the north and east. As Kush declined, it was eventually succeeded by Axum in about 350 C.E.

Axum originated in the coastal region of modern-day Eritrea about 300 B.C.E. and evolved into the modern Ethiopian state. The Axumites were Semitic, and they developed a written language of their own. The wealth of Axum was based on the control of northeast African and Red Sea trade routes, which brought them into contact with both the Mediterranean and Arabian worlds. The capital of Axum, Adulis, was a cosmopolitan area with people from Greece, Egypt, Rome, Persia, and India. Iron was traded to other Africans, and the goods received in exchange (ivory, gold, slaves) were in turn traded with Greece, Egypt, Arabia, and other countries.

Axum extended its control over Meroë in about 350 C.E. and also conquered areas on the Arabian Peninsula. Axum adopted Coptic Christianity in about 100 C.E. Persia invaded the Arabian

GLOBAL CONCEPTS
Technology
CONCEPTS GLOBAL

GEOGRAPHY
Places and Regions

GLOBAL CONCEPTS
Change
CONCEPTS GLOBAL

GEOGRAPHY
Physical Settings

GLOBAL CONCEPTS
Interdependence
CONCEPTS GLOBAL

provinces of Axum in the late 6th century, gaining control of some of Axum's more important trade routes, and the power of Axum began to decline. Muslim invasions in the 7th and 8th centuries also lessened the trading power of Axum, but the kingdom continued and eventually extended its borders to those of present-day Ethiopia and Eritrea.

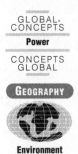

**The Earliest Trading Kingdom.** In West Africa the kingdom of Ghana developed along the Niger River around 300 C.E., becoming powerful for several reasons. First, it sat astride the western trans-Saharan trade route. Second, it was located between the salt mines to the north and the gold mines to the south. Third, the fertile plain of the Niger was conducive to agriculture. Fourth, strong central government developed. Fifth, its craftsmen were skilled in the smelting of iron. Sixth, population increase enabled Ghana's rulers to maintain a large army. Perhaps most crucial, however, was the advent of the use of the camel for long journeys across the desert, journeys that could not be undertaken by other beasts of burden.

The people to the north wanted gold, and the people to the south who had the gold needed salt from the people in the north. Their trade routes passed through Ghana, and the king taxed the trade in both directions and became very wealthy. He also claimed title to all gold in the kingdom and controlled the amount of gold on the market. The tax money was used to support the government and army. Iron tools made the farmers of Ghana more efficient, and iron weapons made it possible for them to subdue enemies and expand territory. Ghana's preeminence in the trans-Saharan trade lasted for nearly a thousand years and established a pattern that would later be used by other kingdoms.

### Early Cultures of East Asia

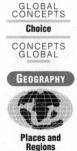

As one of the four early centers of civilization, China exerted a major influence on neighboring regions, especially Korea, Japan, and Southeast Asia. The first contacts between the Japanese and Chinese took place through Korea. Chinese civilization was much more sophisticated than that of the Japanese, and some powerful Japanese determined that elements of Chinese civilization should be introduced in Japan. By the 10th century, Japan had been transformed, but it was not just an imitation of China. Chinese culture was adapted to suit Japanese needs.

**Japan's Early History.** One of the major sources of information on early Japanese history is contained in the chronicles of Chinese and Korean visitors to Japan as early as the 3rd century

C.E. Another source of information is found in archeological discoveries, indicating that Stone Age people lived in Japan perhaps as long as 200,000 years ago. The third major source of information is contained in the myths, legends, and traditions of the Japanese, which were first written down in the 8th century C.E. in the Kojiki (Record of Ancient Matters) in 712 and the Nihongi (Chronicles of Japan) in 720.

The Jomon culture in Japan dates from about 3000 to 300 B.C.E. The people of this culture maintained themselves by hunting and gathering and represent Stone Age culture in Japan. From 300 B.C.E. to 300 C.E. a new wave of migrants from the mainland introduced wet-rice cultivation, bronze working, and finally iron working. This new culture was called Yayoi.

GLOBAL
CONCEPTS

Culture

CONCEPTS
GLOBAL

The Tomb Period (300–650 C.E.), so called because of burial mounds or tombs created during this period, was the most advanced culture of prehistoric Japan. During the Tomb Period, references to Japan show up in Chinese chronicles and indicate that Japan was organized along clan lines. Toward the end of the Tomb Period, the Yamato clan gained ascendancy and became the most powerful of the warring clans in Japan. Much of Japan's subsequent history was characterized by such political competition.

**Southeast Asia.** Little is known about the earliest inhabitants of Southeast Asia, since the humid tropical climate is not conducive to the preservation of archeological and anthropological evidence. They were most likely people who grew rice and worked with bronze. Migrations from the Indian subcontinent and China added to the native populations. (To this day, China refers to the entire region as *nanyang*, lands of the southern ocean.) The Indian cultural diffusion included its ancient language, Sanskrit, as well as the spread of Hinduism, Buddhism, and Islam. Chinese influence was seen in the adoption of the Confucian cultural patterns and in the racial similarities between ethnic Malays and Chinese. China also controlled Vietnam for almost 1,000 years, up until 939 C.E. In other parts of Southeast Asia, several kingdoms emerged and grew into large empires. The Funan Empire, 100 C.E., located in Cambodia and southeast Vietnam, controlled seaborne trade routes between India and China. Later trading empires followed similar patterns.

GEOGRAPHY

Places and
Regions

By the 5th century C.E., human culture had settled into a pattern that had grown out of the agricultural and urban/legal revolutions and would prevail until the religious/philosophical, scientific/technological, and commercial/financial upheavals of a millennium later.

# REVIEW QUESTIONS

*Multiple Choice.* Select the letter of the answer that correctly completes the statement.

1. In the Middle East during neolithic times, the development of farming brought about
   A. the establishment of permanent settlements
   B. a return to a nomadic lifestyle
   C. rise of hunting as an important occupation
   D. a decline in food production

2. Which evidence from an early culture would most strongly support the hypothesis that the culture had a sophisticated level of civilization?
   A. trade and tax records
   B. religious statues
   C. glazed pottery
   D. iron weapons

3. The transition of human economic activity from hunting and gathering to farming and herding is referred to as the
   A. Revolution of Rising Expectations
   B. Neolithic Revolution
   C. Industrial Revolution
   D. Revolution of Food Production

4. In the ancient kingdom of Babylon and in the Roman Republic, an important feature of life was the development of
   A. codified laws
   B. social and political equality
   C. a monotheistic religion
   D. agricultural communes

5. Which was true of food-gathering societies in prehistoric times?
   A. Society was highly urbanized.
   B. The population tended to be small.
   C. The concept of private property was important.
   D. They had written languages.

6. A major result of the development of civilization in ancient Egypt was the
   A. conquest and settlement of Western Europe by the Egyptian Empire
   B. establishment of a democratic system of government in Egypt
   C. establishment of trade routes between Egypt and other kingdoms
   D. decline of agriculture as an important occupation in Egypt

7. The river valleys of the Tigris-Euphrates, the Nile, and the Indus were centers of civilization because they
   A. had rich deposits of iron ore and coal
   B. were isolated from other cultural influences
   C. were easily defended from invasion
   D. provided a means of transportation and irrigation

8. One way in which the cultures of the Maya, the Gupta, and Ghana were similar is that they
   A. were destroyed by military forces of European civilizations
   B. developed great civilizations without major influence from Western Europe
   C. depended on trade with European nations to remain economically powerful
   D. were made up of nomadic groups of skilled herdsmen

Base your answer to the next question on the following quote:

**"... for the administration is in the hands of the many and not of the few ... an Athenian citizen does not neglect the state because he takes care of his own household.... We alone regard a man who takes no interest in public affairs, not as a harmless but as a useless character...."** Pericles, 431 B.C.E.

9. Which type of political system does this quotation suggest that people of ancient Athens valued?
   A. monarchy
   B. aristocracy
   C. democracy
   D. autocracy

10. Which statement best explains the Golden Ages of the Gupta Empire of India, Hellenic Greece, and the Han Dynasty?
    A. The winning of a war often inspires scientific and artistic achievement.
    B. A combination of wealth and a time of relative peace often leads to cultural achievement.
    C. A dictatorship usually encourages cultural growth and development.
    D. Periods of censorship are needed for a nation to achieve cultural and scientific greatness.

# THEMATIC ESSAYS

## Essay #1: The Development of Civilizations

Civilizations develop where geography and climate present humans with conditions in which they can live together in large cooperative groups.

**Task:**

1. Define the term "civilization."
2. Select two different early civilizations and demonstrate how each developed in a unique way based on its geography and climate.

**Directions:** Write a well-organized essay with an introduction stating the topic, a body that accomplishes the task, and a summarizing conclusion.

*Hint:* You may choose any two civilizations that flourished between 3000 B.C.E. and the 6th century C.E., including those based in river valleys, those located on larger bodies of water, and those that developed on plains or plateaus.

## Essay #2 Theme: The Movement of People and Products

Movement of people and products has been a factor in the development of human societies.

**Task:**

1. Define the terms "trade" and "migration."
2. Select one example of a trade pattern and one example of a human migration. For each, discuss the impact it had on the societies it influenced.

**Directions:** Write a well-organized essay with an introduction stating the topic, a body that accomplishes the task, and a summarizing conclusion.

*Hint:* You may choose any trade pattern and migration pattern that developed between 3000 B.C.E. and the 6th century C.E., including those using bodies of water or those that crossed plains, plateaus, or mountains.

# DOCUMENT-BASED ESSAY QUESTION

**Directions:** The following question is based on the accompanying documents (Documents 1–9). Some of the documents have been edited for the purpose of this assignment.

Write a well-organized essay with an introduction stating a thesis, a body of several paragraphs that accomplishes the task, and a summarizing conclusion. Use all of the documents and analyze each one. Use evidence from the documents to support the position you take in your thesis. Do not simply repeat the contents of the document; explain things in your words and relate the information to your thesis. Using your knowledge of the social studies, include related information that is not included in the documents.

**Historical Context:** Many historians have noted that during the 5th century A.D., Roman civilization was in decline. Their explanations for the principle causes of this decline often differ.

**Question:** Discuss the causes of the decline of Roman civilization.

**Part A:** Summarize the main idea stated or illustrated in each of the documents (Documents 1–9) as that idea related to the decline of Roman civilization.

**Part B:** Respond in an essay. Your essay should be based on a thesis statement—your viewpoint regarding the decline of Roman civilization. In your essay you should use information from all the documents as evidence. Present the evidence and analyze it from the point of view of your thesis. Support your thesis with related information based on your knowledge of the social studies.

## DOCUMENT 1

As the happiness of a *future* life is the great object of religion, we may hear without surprise or scandal that the introduction, or at least the abuse, of Christianity, had some influence on the decline and fall of the Roman Empire. The clergy successfully preached the doctrines of patience and pusillanimity (faintheartedness); the active virtues of society were discouraged; and the last remains of military spirit were buried in the cloister (religious retreats for monks and nuns) . . .
    —Edward Gibbon (1898), *The Decline and Fall of the Roman Empire*

In what way did the spread of Christianity contribute to Rome's decline?

_____

_____

_____

## DOCUMENT 2

We may say, then, that there is one prominent feature. . . . It is a gradual absorption of the higher classes by the lower, accompanied by a gradual leveling down of standards. . . . The main problem, therefore, which we have to solve is this. Why was the city civilization of . . . (Rome) unable to assimilate the masses, why did it remain a civilization of the élite . . . ?
    —Michael Rostovstzeff (1957), *The Social and Economic History of the Roman Empire*

Describe the social problem cited in this passage.

_____

_____

_____

_____

_____

## DOCUMENT 3

There were land taxes, property taxes, occupation taxes, poll taxes. It has been said of this period that "the penalty of wealth seemed to be ruin." The heart was then out of enterprising men. Finally the burden became so intolerable that . . . tenants fled from their farms and business men and workmen from their occupations.
    —Henry J. Hall (1947), *The New Deal in Old Rome*

Describe the economic problem cited in this passage.

_____

_____

_____

## DOCUMENT 4

Indeed, we are inclined to believe that it would be impossible to maintain permanently a political and social organization of the type and magnitude of Rome in the face of complete lack of modern sanitary knowledge. A concentration of large populations in cities, free communication with many other parts of the world, constant and extensive military activity involving the mobilization of armies in camps, and the movement of large forces back and forth from all corners of the world—these alone are conditions which inevitably determine the outbreak of epidemic disease.

—Hans Zinsser (1934), *Rats, Lice, and History*

What factors might have led to disease contributing to the decline of Rome?

_____

_____

_____

## DOCUMENT 5

. . . (T)he overwhelming majority of the population had been systematically excluded from political rights and political responsibilities. They could not organize to protect themselves; they could not serve in the army even if they had so desired. Their economic plight was hopeless. Most of them were serfs bound eternally to the soil, and the small urban group saw their cities slipping into uninterrupted decline.

—Joseph R. Strayer, H. W. Gatzke, and H. H. Harbison (1961),
*The Course of Civilization*

How did political issues affect the majority of Romans?

_____

_____

_____

**DOCUMENT 6**

. . . the evidence indicates that . . . (the city workers and peasants) did not share in the prosperity of the early empire and certainly got more than their share of distress in hard times. The immediate source and sign of evil was the institution of slavery. The abundance of slaves led to the growth of the *latifundia*, the great estates that . . . came to dominate agriculture and ruin the free peasantry. Unable to compete with these capitalistic enterprises, the peasants either became *coloni* of the large landowners or drifted to the cities, to aggravate the chronic unemployment there; the workers of the empire had to support a large class of the idle poor as well as the idle rich. The abundance of slaves likewise kept wages low. . . . the masses lived in more or less poverty . . .

—Herbert J. Muller (1952), *Uses of the Past*

What impact did slavery have on the Roman economy?

_____

_____

_____

**DOCUMENT 7**

**ALARIC, CHIEF OF THE VISIGOTHS,
AFTER HIS CONQUEST OF ROME, 410 c.e.**

What was the impact of groups like the Visigoths?

_____

_____

_____

**DOCUMENT 8**

The fact that Rutilius Namatianus, early in the 5th century, considered it as worthy of special comment that the bridges were still down and the posting-inns were deserted in Italy after the sack of Rome by Alaric suggests that, to his Gallic correspondent, such a failure in the system would still have seemed unusual in 417 C.E.

—Logan Thompson (1997), "Roman Roads," *History Today*, Vol. 47

Why would it seem unusual for bridges to "still be down" and "inns to still be deserted" at this time?

_____

_____

_____

**DOCUMENT 9**

September 20, 451. Roman soldiers routed Attila the Hun on this day in 451, sending him and his confederation of Goths and other northern tribes into a rare and unaccustomed defeat. The decisive loss was one of the few setbacks for the savage military leader who had by that time conquered all the countries between the Black Sea and the Mediterranean and severely weakened the Roman Empire. He was fearfully known as the "Scourge of God."

Does it seem unusual for the Roman army to achieve such a victory at this point in history? Why?

_____

_____

_____

## DOCUMENT-BASED QUESTIONS:
## SKILL-BUILDING EXERCISES

### DOCUMENT

Selections from *Hammurabi's Code of Laws*.

27. If a chieftain or man be caught in the misfortune of the king (captured in battle), and if his fields and garden be given to another and he take possession, if he return and reaches his place, his field and garden shall be returned to him, he shall take it over again.

102. If a merchant entrust money to an agent (broker) for some investment, and the broker suffer a loss in the place to which he goes, he shall make good the capital to the merchant.

117. If any one fail to meet a claim for debt, and sell himself, his wife, his son, and daughter for money or give them away to forced labor: they shall work for three years in the house of the man who bought them, or the proprietor, and in the fourth year they shall be set free.

What are some of the ways in which this law code protected the citizens of Babylon?

_____

_____

_____

### DOCUMENT

**From the Epic of Gilgamesh, a legendary Mesopotamian chronicle.**

**In his grief the hero Gilgamesh laments to Siduri, the wine-making woman:**
Enkidu my brother whom I loved, the end of mortality has overtaken him.
I wept for him seven days and nights till the worm fastened on him.
Because of my brother I am afraid of death,
Because of my brother I stray through the wilderness and cannot rest.

**And she replies:**
'Gilgamesh, where are you hurrying to?
You will never find the life for which you are looking.
When the gods created man they allotted to him death,
but life they retained in their own keeping.

As for you, Gilgamesh, fill your belly with good things;
day and night, night and day, dance and be merry, feast and rejoice.
Let your clothes be fresh, bathe yourself in water,
cherish the little child that holds your hand,
and make your wife happy in your embrace;
for this too is the lot of man.'

What advice does Siduri give to Gilgamesh?

_____

_____

_____

**DOCUMENT**

**CLAY SEAL, A PRODUCT OF THE INDUS VALLEY CULTURE
CA. 2600–1900 B.C.E.**

What conclusions can you draw or inferences can you make about the Indus
Valley culture from examining this seal?

_____

_____

_____

## DOCUMENT

### A Brief Timeline of the Celtic People

| | | |
|---|---|---|
| * | 900 B.C.E. | Gaelic-speaking people in England |
| * | 600 B.C.E. | Gaelic-speaking Celts from Spain arrive in Ireland |
| * | 500 B.C.E. | Brythonic Celts reach Britain |
| * | 400 B.C.E. | Celts invade Italy |
| * | 390 B.C.E. | First encounter with the Romans |
| * | 387 B.C.E. | Celtic Gauls defeat Rome at Alia |
| * | 387 B.C.E. | Brennus' sack of Rome |
| * | 335 B.C.E. | Alexander the Great encounters Celts on the Danube |
| * | 279 B.C.E. | Celts invade Greece |
| * | 225 B.C.E. | Celts advance on Rome again |
| * | 113 B.C.E. | War between Rome and Celtiberians |
| * | 61 B.C.E. | Caesar conquers Brigantium, breaks Celtiberian resistance |
| * | 58 B.C.E. | Caesar arrives in Gaul |
| * | 55 B.C.E. | Caesar crosses the Channel for first time |
| * | 54 B.C.E. | Caesar defeats King Casivellaunus. Death of Dumnorix |
| * | 51 B.C.E. | Caesar pacifies Gaul |
| * | 40 C.E. | Caligula's attempt to conquer Britain |
| * | 61 C.E. | Suetonius Paulinus defeats Iceni (Boudiccea's Rebellion) |
| * | 122 C.E. | Hadrian's Wall erected |
| * | 286 C.E. | Bacaudae rebel in Northern Gaul |
| * | 360 C.E. | St. Martin founds first Gallic monastery near Tours |
| * | 410 C.E. | Emperor Honorius tells the British they're on their own |
| * | 417 C.E. | Constantius' legions defeat Saxons in Hallelujah Battle |
| * | 431 C.E. | Pope Celestine sends Palladius to Ireland |
| * | 450 C.E. | Saxon incursion stemmed by King Arthur in 12 battles |
| * | 450 C.E. | Capitol of Kings of Ulster (Northern Ireland) destroyed |
| * | 450 C.E. | The Uí Néill and Eóganachta form an alliance in Ireland |
| * | 500 C.E. | St. Patrick comes to Ireland |
| * | 663 C.E. | Council of Whitby decides for Roman over Celtic Church |

What geographic areas seem to have been influenced by the Celts? What impact does religion seem to have had on later Celtic culture?

_____

_____

_____

**DOCUMENT**

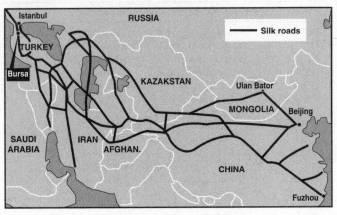

**MAP OF THE SILK ROAD**

Discuss the importance of the Silk Road in promoting commerce and communication in the ancient world.

_____

_____

_____

**DOCUMENT**

Apollo was the son of Zeus, king of the Greek gods. He has been called "the most Greek of all the gods." He is a beautiful figure in Greek poetry, the master musician who delights Olympus as he plays on his golden lyre; the lord too of the silver bow, the Archer-god, far-shooting; the Healer, as well, who first taught men the healing art. Even more than of these good and lovely endowments, he is the god of Light, in whom is no darkness at all, and so he is the god of Truth. No false word ever fell from his lips. And he rides across the sky in his chariot, the Sun.

What inferences can you make about the values of Greek culture from this picture and description of Apollo?

_____

_____

_____

**DOCUMENT**

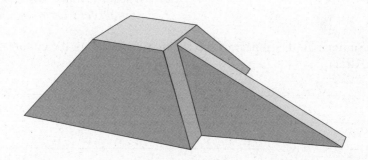

A major problem facing the builders of the Ancient Egyptian Pyramids, was that of getting the large stone blocks to the height they required. The method shown (above), is the only one proven to have been used. The ramps were built on inclined planes of mud brick and rubble. They then dragged the blocks on sledges to the needed height. As the pyramid grew taller, the ramp had to be extended in length, and its base was widened, else it would collapse. It is likely that for the construction of each pyramid, several ramps were probably used.

What would have been the role of human labor in the building of the pyramids?

_____

_____

_____

**DOCUMENT**

**Bantu migrations.** Bantu is a family of languages that are closely related and represent the largest linguistic family of African languages. Bantu speaking people migrated out of north-central Africa in the last century B.C.E. and these migrations continued all throughout the first millenium C.E. They migrated south into the rain forest regions around the Congo and east into the East African highlands. Wherever they migrated, languages mixed with and replaced indigenous languages. . . . Further migrations in the first millenium then displaced the earlier Bantu immigrants, who pushed farther east and south. These Bantu immigrants would eventually found the civilization of the Mwenumatapa, or "Great Zimbabwe." The Bantu spread iron-smelting techniques across Africa, and were responsible for diffusing agriculture, particularly high-yield crops such as yams, bananas, and plantains. The spread of agriculture led to the explosive growth of village life all throughout Africa.

—Richard Hooker World Civilizations:
*An Internet Classroom and Anthology*

Summarize the impact of the Bantu migrations on the cultures of Southern Africa.

_____

_____

_____

**DOCUMENT**
# Legal Status (of Women) in the Roman World

**The Twelve Tables (excerpts). Rome, 450 B.C.E. (traditional date). (*FIRA*2, VOL. 1, P. 23. Tr. *ARS*. L)**

These laws, the basis of Roman civil law, have their origins in what the Romans called *mos maiorum*, the tradition of their ancestors. The codification and publication of the ancestral laws on twelve bronze tablets in the Roman Forum represented a victory for the plebeian class, which hitherto had been subject to prejudiced legal interpretations by the patricians. Though some of the laws became outdated, the code was never abolished.

**Table IV. Paternal power**
3. To repudiate his wife, her husband shall order her . . . to have her own property for herself, shall take the keys, shall expel her.

**Table V. Inheritance and guardianship**
1. . . . Women, even though they are of full age, because of their levity of mind shall be under guardianship

4. If anyone who has no direct heir dies intestate, the nearest male (heir) shall have the estate;

5. If there is not a male (heir), the male clansmen shall have the estate.

**Table X. Sacred law**
4. Woman shall not tear their cheeks or shall not make a sorrowful outcry on account of a funeral.

—Mary R. Lefkowitz and Maureen B. Fant (1992),
*Women's Life in Greece and Rome.*
*A Source Book in Translation*

What conclusions can you draw regarding the status of women in ancient Rome?

_____

_____

_____

**DOCUMENT**
**AN ILLUSTRATION OF JERUSALEM AS IT APPEARED IN 66 C.E.**
**THE NORTHERN GATE WITH THE ROMAN FORT.**

What might this picture tell you about the Roman occupation of Jerusalem in the 1st century C.E.?

_____

_____

_____

_____

_____

# ERA II

# Expanding Zones of Exchange and Encounter (500–1200)

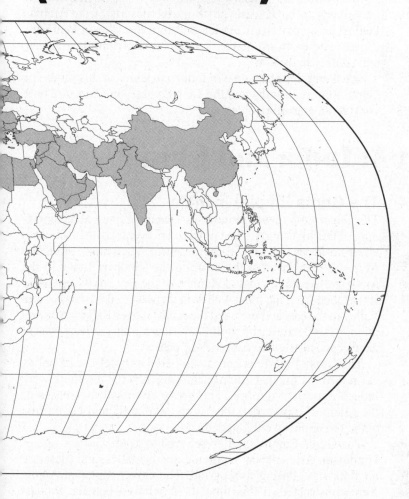

## Introduction

The 4th and 5th centuries probably represent the dividing line between ancient civilization and medieval history. This was an age of change and transition in the world, from the Classical Civilizations with their emphasis on the human ability to reason, to the Church's emphasis on moral and spiritual beliefs.

**GEOGRAPHY**

**Places and Regions**

The Germanic invasions of the 4th and 5th centuries led to the end of the Western Roman Empire, and various Germanic kingdoms were established in what had been the Western Empire. The Eastern Empire, the Byzantine, remained vibrant, and had a strong impact on the development of Russia and Eastern Europe.

Meanwhile the Muslim Empire was rising in the Middle East, ready to burst westward from the deserts of the Arabian Peninsula, across North Africa and into the Iberian Peninsula (Spain) and eastward across Persia and into central, southern, and southeastern Asia.

Great empires also arose in India and China at this time. The Gupta Empire in India and the Tang Dynasty in China are both considered eras of a golden age.

# Part A: India and China

## The Gupta Empire in India

The Gupta Empire was founded by Chandragupta I at the beginning of the 4th century. The Gupta rulers eventually consolidated all of northern India under their control. The empire stretched from the Himalayas in the north to the Vindhya Range in the south and eventually included much of the Deccan Plateau also. It stretched from the Indus Valley in the west to the Brahmaputra Valley in the east and included the great Ganges River valley and plain. After centuries of conflict, northern India, at least, was to experience nearly two centuries of peace.

**GEOGRAPHY**

**Places and Regions**

The Gupta Empire is not remembered as much for its political reform as for its cultural achievements, though there were indeed important reforms. The heavy taxes and the abuses of the rulers who preceded them were abolished, and Gupta rule tended to be fairly enlightened.

**GEOGRAPHY**

**Physical Settings**

The Gupta Empire is often referred to as the Golden Age of Hinduism. Art, science, medicine, mathematics, and literature all flourished during this period. The cave temples at Ajanta were constructed at this time. It is believed that the Indians developed the numbers we know as Arabic numerals and that their use spread through trade. They developed the concept of zero and determined the value of π. Doctors were performing plastic surgery. The "Iron Pillar" at Delhi was constructed, and to this day has not rusted. Kalidasa, the "Indian Shakespeare," wrote *Sakuntala*, his most famous play, and the poem, "The Cloud Messenger." Sanskrit, the language of the Aryan invaders, was developed and used in writing literature. Universities with free board and tuition were established.

There was a revival of Hindu religious beliefs and the power of the Brahmans. Caste lines were reinforced. The influence of Indian civilization was spread by traders and missionaries to Burma, Thailand, Indochina, and Indonesia.

## The Tang and Song Dynasties

The fall of the Han Dynasty began another period of conflict in China, but the country was united again by the Tang Dynasty (618–907). Tang rulers expanded their control to include nearly all of modern-day China. The empire stretched from the northeastern territories south of the Great Wall to the deserts of central Asia and southward into northern Vietnam. The Tang rulers established a strong central government. The emperors created a council of ministers to act as advisers and sent inspectors into the provinces to check on and keep the provincial governors under control. They promoted trade; as a result, China became one of the richest and most powerful political units in the world. The arts flourished. China's greatest poets, Lipo and Tufu, lived during the Tang Dynasty. Buddhism flourished. Chinese Buddhists invented movable block printing about 800 years before Gutenberg in Europe. The first great encyclopedia was produced in 801. The world's first printed book, the Buddhist *Diamond Sutra*, was produced by Wang Chieh in 868. Porcelain was first made ca. 900. Because of the great achievements of the Tang Dynasty, it is often referred to as China's golden age. During this time period, the Japanese modeled their capital city after the Chinese capital of Chang-an and organized Japanese society after the Chinese example. A central government and imperial bureaucracy much like that of China was created.

The next great dynasty, the Song (Sung), lasted from 960 to 1279, and this period is also considered a golden age. Chinese culture and trade continued to flourish. The Chinese invented the compass, improved ceramic techniques, developed gunpowder, began the use of paper money in trade, and produced some of China's greatest landscape paintings. The Song were defeated by the Mongols in 1279.

**GEOGRAPHY**

**Places and Regions**

# Part B: Islamic Civilization—"Golden Age" and the Rise and Spread of Islam (622–1453)

**GEOGRAPHY**

Places and Regions

Islam became a powerful force in the Arabian Peninsula during Muhammad's life and after his death in 632. During the next 100 years Islam spread from the Arabian Peninsula westward to North Africa and Spain, as well as to other parts of the Middle East. In later years it was brought to Asia and Africa, south of the Sahara, and by the last half of the 20th century, Islam was a major religion in many nations of Africa (for example, Morocco, Nigeria) and Asia (for example, Bangladesh, Indonesia). There is also a large Muslim community in the Philippines.

**GEOGRAPHY**

Places and Regions

Upon Muhammad's death, Muslims chose a leader who was called caliph. The first caliph was Abu Bakr, the father of Muhammad's wife, Aisha. After his death, control of the caliphate (the Muslim-dominated lands in the Arabian Peninsula and those to the immediate west and north) passed eventually to the Umayyad clan. Under the Caliph Muswiyah, the Umayyads made Damascus the Muslim capital in 661. However, Umayyad leadership was opposed by the followers of Ali (the husband of Fatimah, Muhammad's daughter), who served as caliph from 656 until he was assassinated in 661. Ali's followers eventually formed the Shi'ite branch of Muslims, in opposition to the Sunni branch of Muslims.

Shi'ite Muslims drew up their own ideas about Islam. One was that the correct interpreters of the Quran were the descendants of Ali, especially twelve leaders known as imams. They believe that the twelfth imam, who disappeared about 1,000 years ago, will reappear as the mahdi and save the world. Shi'ite Muslims (from the Arabic phrase *Shi'a Ali,* the party of Ali) currently make up 10 percent of the world's approximately 900 million Muslims. The largest group of Shi'ites is in Iran. Ninety percent of the world's Muslims are Sunnis (from the Arabic word *sunna,* customs), who accept individuals other than Ali's descendants as the true successors to Muhammad. The schism (division, split) into two Muslim branches or sects, which began in the late 600s after Ali's assassination, continues with the growth of many subsects and small groups.

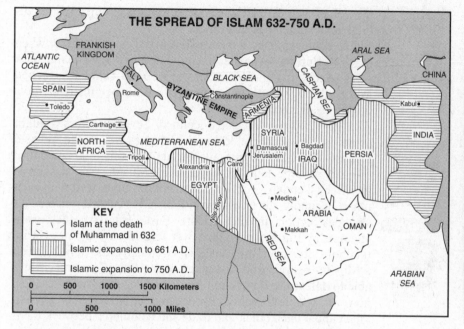

THE SPREAD OF ISLAM 632-750 A.D.

KEY

Islam at the death of Muhammad in 632

Islamic expansion to 661 A.D.

Islamic expansion to 750 A.D.

| 0 | 500 | 1000 | 1500 Kilometers |

| 0 | 500 | 1000 Miles |

The Umayyad Dynasty lasted from 638 to 750. During that time, its conquests spread Islam throughout three continents.

1. In North Africa and Western Europe (Portugal, Spain, and France) until the Muslims were defeated by Charles Martel in 732 at Tours (in France).

**GEOGRAPHY**

**Places and Regions**

2. In Southwest Asia (in Jerusalem, the Umayyads built a mosque over a holy site).

There were many reasons for the successful territorial expansion of the Umayyads and the spread of Islam. One important reason was the Islamic idea that it was necessary to bring Islam to nonbelievers and that to die in a holy war (jihad) guaranteed a place in heaven. Another reason was that the Umayyads were skilled warriors, and they hoped to gain wealth and fertile lands—a contrast to their harsh life in a desert region. In addition, many conquered peoples were willing to convert to Islam, while others were forced to convert. Finally, the conquered Jews and Christians were treated tolerantly (as dhimmis—"people of the book") because some of their ways were similar to those of Muslims.

**GEOGRAPHY**

**Environment and Society**

The Abbasids, another group of Muslims, defeated the Umayyads and created a dynasty that lasted from 750 to 1250. Under the Caliph Mansur, Baghdad became the capital of the new caliphate. The period of the Abbasid caliphate is known as

277

the golden age of Islam because of the many outstanding cultural achievements at this time.

The achievements in the Muslim world came at a time when much of Europe was experiencing a period known as the Dark Ages. Accomplishments under the Abbasid caliphate reached Europe through trade and commerce and shaped many features of European culture.

**GEOGRAPHY**

**Spatial Terms**

**GEOGRAPHY**

**Environment and Society**

After 1200 the Abbasids declined. Several factors brought about the end of the golden age of Islam as well as the Abbasid Dynasty. First, it was difficult for the Abbasids to keep control over such a large area. Moreover, many Muslim groups, such as the Arabs, Persians, and Turks, did not get along well with each other. Secondly, the Crusades (1095–1291) caused much death and destruction in the Middle East. The Crusades were attempts by Europeans to take over Jerusalem and other Christian holy sites from the Muslims. Eventually, the Seljuk Turks, a Muslim people who had taken over Abbasid territory, were able to defeat the European forces. As a result of the Crusades, however, people from both Europe and the Middle East learned much about each other, and trade and commerce between them increased. This process of cultural diffusion enabled Europe to benefit from the Muslim cultural and scientific advances. Finally, the Abbasids were unable to beat back attacks on their lands by the Turks and the Mongols.

### THE GOLDEN AGE OF ISLAM

| Subject | Achievement |
| --- | --- |
| Science | Manufacture of glass, chemical compounds, laboratory equipment; books on chemistry and optics |
| Scholarship | Works of Greeks, Persians, and Indians translated into Arabic; House of Learning in Baghdad |
| Mathematics | Algebra; number system adopted from India and eventually transmitted to Europe as Arabic numerals; same for a decimal system and the concept of zero; a system to calculate square and cube roots of numbers. |
| Astronomy | Observatories; calculation of distances in space; use of the astrolabe in navigation; estimating the earth's circumference and acknowledging it is shaped like a sphere |
| Medicine | Advances in surgery and anesthetics; pharmacies; diagnosis and treatment of diseases such as smallpox and measles; medical encyclopedias, hospitals; examinations for physicians |
| Literature | *The Arabian Nights;* poems of Omar Khayyam; histories written by travelers such as Ibn-Khaldun |
| Art and architecture | Mosques with elaborate details of trees, flowers, geometric designs, and writing from the Quran; illuminated manuscripts; colorful carpets and textiles |

278

# Part C: Medieval Europe

## The Middle Ages (500–1500)

The time between the fall of the Roman Empire and the start of the modern era is known as the Middle Ages, or the medieval period. The first 500 years of this period is sometimes called the Dark Ages, due to the disruptive economic and social conditions as well as the absence of a strong and stable central government. During this time, Europe experienced many invasions. The first group of invaders were the Germanic tribes, some of whom eventually settled down and formed kingdoms. Later invaders included the Norse, the Magyars, and the Muslims. These invasions ended about the year 1000. Political power was decentralized, that is, it was held by several small, weak groups throughout Europe. Among these were the Franks (in Gaul, or France), the Ostrogoths (in Italy), the Visigoths (in Spain), and the Angles and Saxons (in England). People felt more loyalty to a local ruler in a small territory than to a larger political unit. The protection given by a local ruler, or lord, to people who performed services for him in return was the basis of feudalism, which developed in the 800s. This was the form of government prevalent in Europe until the 1400s.

**GEOGRAPHY**

Human Systems

**Charlemagne and the Holy Roman Empire.**  One group of Germans, the Franks, were able to create a strong kingdom by the 5th century. The kingdom of the Franks grew in power during the early Middle Ages. Under Charles Martel, the Franks stopped the advance of Muslim forces in 732 at the Battle of Tours in France. Martel's grandson was Charlemagne (768–814), who became the most important ruler in medieval Europe.

Charlemagne conquered and united lands in central and western Europe, some of which had been part of the Roman Empire. These included parts of present-day Italy, Spain, France, Germany, the Czech Republic, Slovakia, Austria, Belgium, and Holland. For these efforts and for spreading Christianity, Charlemagne was crowned as the first Holy Roman Emperor by Pope Leo III in 800. Charlemagne's empire became known as the Holy Roman Empire.

**GEOGRAPHY**

Places and Regions

Charlemagne built schools and was able to run his empire's provinces with the help of the *missi dominici*, appointed officials who traveled in the provinces and kept Charlemagne informed about various nobles. Consequently, under Charlemagne's rule, a rare example of a stable, centralized government existed in the Middle Ages. After his death, however, the empire was divided, and his successors were not able to maintain order and stability.

**Feudalism.** Feudalism developed in Europe in response to the breakdown in central authority in the Frankish empire following Charlemagne's death and also because of the instability and chaos caused by the numerous invasions in the 9th and 10th centuries, especially those of the dreaded Vikings or Norse. Feudalism began in France in the late 9th century and spread throughout much of Europe. It was a way of life that involved agreements, promises, and exchanges between different groups of people to help them live together. It involved social, economic, and political relationships.

1. *Social.* A strict class system existed, based on land and military power. Each class had specific rights as well as responsibilities and obligations to the other classes. The classes were serfs, knights, and landowning nobles and lords. A code of chivalry set rules of behavior that everyone followed, especially the knights and lords.

2. *Economic.* Serfs worked the land on a manor (a large estate held by a lord) and supplied food to the landowner, who promised protection and shelter in return. The landowner in turn also promised to fight for a higher noble, such as an overlord or a king, who gave him a piece of land in return. In this relationship, the landowner owed loyalty, or fealty, to the king and became a vassal of the king. In this manorial system, each manor supported itself economically and was self-sufficient. The three-field system was used for growing food.

3. *Political.* The serfs were bound to the land and had no say in political matters. The king's power rested on his relationship with his vassals. By receiving a fief (a grant of land) from the king (as suzerain), in a ceremony called investiture, the vassals came under the king's protection and in return owed homage, promising allegiance and military service. Although a vassal, the landowning noble exercised great political power in his area because he passed laws, levied taxes, and acted as a judge.

**The Role of the Roman Catholic Church.** The Christian or Roman Catholic Church was the most powerful and influential institution in Europe in the Middle Ages. It was the only institution able to provide some order amid the chaos in Europe. The Roman Catholic Church was a major force in the lives of people, providing education, the means to salvation, and many services usually provided by governments.

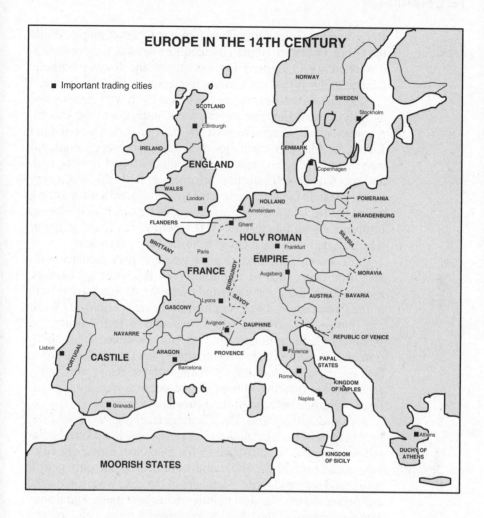

## EUROPE IN THE 14TH CENTURY

■ Important trading cities

NORWAY

SWEDEN

Stockholm

SCOTLAND

Edinburgh

IRELAND

DENMARK

Copenhagen

ENGLAND

WALES

London

HOLLAND

Amsterdam

POMERANIA

BRANDENBURG

FLANDERS

Ghent

BRITTANY

Paris

HOLY ROMAN

Frankfurt

SILESIA

FRANCE

EMPIRE

Augsberg

MORAVIA

GASCONY

Lyons

SAVOY

BURGUNDY

AUSTRIA

BAVARIA

Avignon

DAUPHINE

REPUBLIC OF VENICE

NAVARRE

PORTUGAL

Lisbon

CASTILE

ARAGON

Barcelona

PROVENCE

Florence

PAPAL
STATES

Rome

KINGDOM
OF NAPLES

Naples

Granada

Athens

DUCHY OF
ATHENS

KINGDOM
OF SICILY

MOORISH STATES

Although early Christians were persecuted in the Roman Empire for almost 300 years after the crucifixion of Jesus, Christianity continued to gain converts and to grow in power. Christianity was spread through the efforts of St. Paul and other followers of Jesus. In 313 the Edict of Milan, under the Emperor Constantine, permitted religious freedom for Christians. In 392 the Emperor Theodosius made Christianity the official state religion of the empire. By this time the Roman Empire had split into an eastern part centered in Constantinople and a western part centered in Rome. Different views on religious authority and teachings developed between the church in Rome (headed by the Pope) and the church in Constantinople (headed by the Patriarch). Eventually, these differences led to an official division of the Christian Church in 1054 into the Roman Catholic Church in

**GEOGRAPHY**

**Places and Regions**

Rome and the Greek Orthodox Church in Constantinople. While the Greek Orthodox Church divided into several Eastern Orthodox churches in Eastern Europe, it was the Roman Catholic Church that was to exert a strong influence in Western Europe.

1. *Political.* Besides having the power to crown Charlemagne as Holy Roman Emperor in 800, the Church could use excommunication as a weapon against any ruler or person who did not follow the Church's teachings. A person who was excommunicated was no longer considered a member of the Christian faith and was thus denied salvation. In an era of faith, this was a very strong threat. In the 13th century, the Church created a special court, called the Holy Inquisition, to investigate anyone who disobeyed or disagreed with its teachings. If a person was found guilty as a heretic, that individual could be tortured or put to death.

2. *Economic.* The Church grew wealthy from its many lands and from taxes such as the tithe. With this wealth, convents, monasteries, and great cathedrals were built. Many were built in the Gothic style. The Church's role in the economy of Western Europe was so great that it was able to forbid usury, the practice of lending money with interest. However, the prohibition on interest was only for Christians; Jews were permitted to become moneylenders and to charge interest. As a result, many Jews created banking houses. Some became wealthy but suffered prejudice because of their financial activities.

3. *Social and cultural.* The Church's teachings were the rules by which most people led their lives. Bishops, priests, and other religious figures were looked to for guidance, especially since they could explain the Bible and were usually the only people who could read and write. Members of the clergy were educated and preserved the classical culture of ancient Greece and Rome. Many members of the clergy encouraged writers, painters, and sculptors to produce works with religious themes. The Church was a stabilizing and unifying influence at a time when Western Europe was going through a period of disorder and confusion.

Since the Jews of Western Europe did not follow Church teachings, they were often the target of prejudice, persecution, and expulsion. Moreover, laws that restricted where Jews could worship and live (ghettos were the result) were frequent (as were forced conversions). These anti-Jewish actions are examples of anti-Semitism.

**The Crusades.** These were attempts by the Christians of Western Europe to regain control of Jerusalem and other parts of the Holy Land from the Muslims. These holy wars lasted for approximately 200 years. There were eight Crusades. The first

Crusaders leave to fight in the Middle East.

Crusade came in response to a request from Pope Urban II in 1095 and was successful. Other Crusades and fighting between Christians and Muslims continued until 1291, with the Muslims finally emerging victorious. Muslims kept control of the Holy Land until World War I.

Besides hoping to regain the Holy Land in the Crusades, the Church had other goals. It wanted to increase its power and wealth and unite the Western (Roman) and Eastern (Byzantine) branches of Christianity. Although the Crusades failed to achieve these goals, they had important results for European history.

1. *Political.* European kings gained more power, especially since many feudal lords were killed while fighting in the Crusades. Other lords sold their lands to get money to go on the Crusades. As kings increased their power, they eventually were able to create nation-states, which they ruled.

2. *Economic.* Trade and commerce increased, especially in towns and port cities used by the Crusaders. Goods from the Middle East, such as spices, pepper, and carpets, began to appear throughout Europe. Feudalism was weakened, as many serfs joined armies or left their manors to settle in the cities that began to grow because of increased trade.

GEOGRAPHY

Human Systems

3. *Social and cultural.* Europeans learned much from the more advanced culture of the Muslim world at the time of the Crusades. Developments from the golden age of Islam made their way into Europe. These developments were in such fields as mathematics, science, art, and literature. The Europeans also discovered many

Greek and Roman writings that had been lost to them but preserved by Muslim scholars. Classical civilization was reintroduced. The new ideas and new goods brought to Europe because of the Crusades were factors that slowly helped to bring an end to the Middle Ages and led to the period we call modern history. Other factors that brought on this change from medieval to modern times included: the growth of towns and a merchant middle class (the bourgeoisie); increased use of gunpowder and more effective weapons; renewed interest in learning, both about humans and about the world they lived in; increased contact with people outside of Europe; and the rise of nation-states.

# Part D: The Byzantine Empire

The Byzantine Empire was at its height from 527 to 565, under the Emperor Justinian and his wife Theodora. It included present-day Greece, Turkey, Israel, Egypt, Jordan, and Syria. The Justinian Code set up a legal system based on Roman laws. The beautiful church Hagia Sophia, or the "Holy Wisdom," was built under Justinian. Christians in the empire called their church Eastern Orthodox to distinguish it from the Catholic Church in Rome. In the years after 600, the Byzantine Empire declined as it was subject to attacks from many outsiders. In 1453 the Ottoman Turks, who were Muslims, captured Constantinople and ended Christian dominance in the eastern Mediterranean.

## Conversion to Christianity and the Byzantine Commonwealth (863–1453)

The conversion of the peoples of Eastern Europe to Orthodox Christianity and the adoption of elements of Byzantine culture created a sense of religious and cultural unity throughout the entire region. These factors gave the people of Eastern Europe a new identity. The work of two Byzantine missionaries, Cyril (826–869) and Methodius (815–885), was instrumental in the conversion of the Slavs. Preaching and conducting worship in the vernacular (the common spoken language), the brothers Cyril and Methodius were very successful in converting tribes of Slavs in Moravia (present-day Czech Republic). Cyril created an alphabet (Cyrillic), based on Greek and Coptic letters (language of Christian Egypt letters and grammar for the spoken Slavic language). This evolved into Church Slavonic, the liturgical language that unified early Slavic literature and culture. While the mission of Cyril and Methodius was confined to Moravia, their followers soon converted both Slavic and non-Slavic nations throughout Eastern Europe: Bulgaria, in 865; Serbia, in 874; Romania, in 900; Rus'/Ukraine, in 988. Poland and Hungary were converted by German missionaries and came under the influence of the Roman Catholic Church.

By the year 1000, the Byzantine Empire and its Orthodox satellites (including Hungary) formed the Byzantine Commonwealth, an alliance to promote trade and economic expansion in Eastern Europe as well as to provide a common defense against the Arabs, Turks, and Germans. It was also a political triumph for the Greek East over the Latin West in developing Eastern Europe as a sphere of influence. Poland joined forces

**GEOGRAPHY**

Places and Regions

**GEOGRAPHY**

Human Systems

with the Baltic peoples, particularly the Lithuanians, and became a Roman Catholic rival to the nations of the Byzantine Commonwealth, especially the Russians.

## Turkish Domination (1453–1821)

Despite the establishment of the Byzantine Commonwealth, by 1450 the Ottoman Turks had captured much of the Byzantine Empire and Eastern Europe. The behavior of the Latin West, especially the Crusaders, created suspicion and hatred of both the Papacy and Western Europe among Greeks and Slavs.

*Multiple Choice.* Select the letter of the answer that correctly completes the statement.

1. The Gupta Empire was considered a golden age for all of the following reasons *except*
   A. Arabic numerals were developed
   B. the iron pillar was constructed
   C. Indian rule was extended into southern China
   D. Indian doctors performed plastic surgery

2. Sunni and Shi'ite Muslims disagreed over
   A. the validity of the Quran
   B. the extent of the Muslim Empire
   C. who should be able to claim the title of caliph
   D. the destruction of idols in newly gained territories

3. All of the following are reasons for the successful expansion of the Ummayads and Islam *except*
   A. the concept of jihad promised a place in heaven to those who died in holy war
   B. Muslims believed it was necessary to bring Islam to nonbelievers
   C. Christians and Jews were treated as the "people of the book"
   D. the surrounding areas had not yet developed any form of central government

4. All of the following are true of the Crusades *except* that they
   A. led to greater power in the hands of kings
   B. increased trade and commerce between Europe and the Middle East
   C. weakened the system of feudalism
   D. caused a decline of interest in learning

5. All the following were achievements of the golden age of Islam *except*
   A. the preservation of Greek and Roman writings
   B. the manufacture of glass
   C. the diagnosis and treatment of smallpox
   D. the development of Roman numerals

6. All of the following are true of the Dark Ages *except*
   A. Europe experienced a series of invasions by Germanic tribes and others
   B. centralized political control was prevalent
   C. the state of learning declined
   D. many different dialects developed

7. Charlemagne's achievements included all of the following *except*
   A. the spread of Christianity
   B. the extension of his empire to the Far East
   C. the creation of a stable, centralized government
   D. the establishment of monastery schools

8. All of the following are true of feudalism *except* that it
   A. developed in Europe at the fall of the Roman Empire
   B. involved a strict class system
   C. included a code of chivalry
   D. was a time during which serfs were bound to the land

9. The most powerful and influential institution during the Middle Ages in Europe was the
   A. mosque
   B. family
   C. Catholic Church
   D. clan

10. The Holy Inquisition investigated
    A. heresy
    B. civil wrongs
    C. criminal charges
    D. political corruption

**Essay #1 Theme:** Achievements of Empires
The achievements of civilizations have had an impact on diverse areas of the world.

**Task:**
1. Describe achievements of three empires in Asia and the Middle East.
2. Describe the impact of three of the achievements of Asian and Middle Eastern empires on European civilization.

**Directions:** Write a well-organized essay with an introduction stating the topic, a body that accomplishes the task, and a summarizing conclusion.

*Hint:* You may choose the Tang Dynasty, the Song Dynasty, the Gupta Dynasty, the Byzantine Empire, the Ummayads, etc.

**Essay #2 Theme:** Feudalism
Feudalism affected the lives of Japanese, Europeans, and Chinese.

**Task:**
1. Define the term "feudalism."
2. Choose two feudal systems and describe the economic, social, and political impact on the lives of the people under each of those systems.

**Directions:** Write a well-organized essay with an introduction stating the topic, a body that accomplishes the task, and a summarizing conclusion.

*Hint:* You may use the Tokugawa period in Japan, the Zhou Dynasty in China, the Middle Ages in Europe.

# DOCUMENT-BASED ESSAY QUESTION

**Directions:** The following question is based on the accompanying documents (Documents 1–5). Some of the documents have been edited for the purpose of this assignment.

Write a well-organized essay with an introduction stating a thesis, a body of several paragraphs that accomplishes the task, and a summarizing conclusion. Use all the documents and analyze each one. Use evidence from the documents to support the position you take in your thesis. Do not simply repeat the contents of the document; explain things in your words and relate the information in your thesis. Using your knowledge of the social studies, include related information that is not included in the documents.

**Historical Context:** After the death of Charlemagne, as central power deteriorated, a new system of politics and economics evolved, with a new system of loyalties.

**Question:** Discuss the political, economic, and social aspects of feudalism.

**Part A:** Summarize the main idea stated in each of the documents as that idea relates to the development of feudalism.

**Part B:** Respond in an essay. Your essay should be based on a thesis statement—your viewpoint regarding feudalism as a social, economic, and political system. In your essay you should use information from all of the documents as evidence. Present the evidence and analyze it from the point of view of your thesis. Support your thesis with related information based on your knowledge of the social studies.

## DOCUMENT 1

"36. Our woods and forests shall be well taken care of and where there shall be a place for a clearing let it be cleared. Our stewards shall not allow the fields to become woods and where there ought to be woods they shall not allow anyone to cut too much or damage them. And they shall look carefully after our wild beasts in the forests and also take care of the goshawks and sparrowhawks reserved for our use. They shall collect dilligently our tax for the use of our forests and if our stewards or our mayors or their men put their pigs for fattening in our forests they shall be the first to pay the tenth of them to give a good example so that thereafter the other men will pay the tenth in full."

—Louis the Pious—a list of instructions for the use of stewards on royal properties

## DOCUMENT 2

"And no one shall buy honey, fat, salt herrings, or any kind of oil, or millstones, or fresh hides, or any kind of fresh skins, unless he is a gildsman; nor keep a tavern for wine, nor sell cloth at retail, if he is not a gildsman; and whoever shall do this and be convicted, shall forfeit all to the king."

—Ordinances of the Guild Merchant of Southampton

## DOCUMENT 3

"52. If anyone has been dispossessed or removed by us, without the legal judgment of his peers, from his lands, castles, franchises, or from his right, we will immediately restore them to him; and if a dispute arise over this, then let it be decided by the five and twenty barons of whom mention is made below in the clause for securing the peace. . . ."

—Magna Carta

**DOCUMENT 4**

"The King to the Sheriff of Kent. . . . That every man and woman of our kingdom of England of whatever condition, free or bond, ablebodied, and within the age of sixty years, not living by trade or practicing a certain craft, or having his of his own by which he may live, or his own land in the tillage of which he may occupy himself, and not serving another, if, his station considered, he be needed to serve in appropriate service, he shall be bound to serve him who so requires him."

—An Ordinance Concerning Laborers and Servants

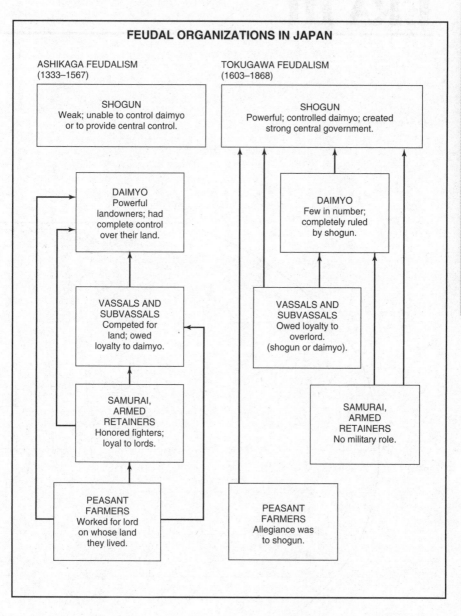

**FEUDAL ORGANIZATIONS IN JAPAN**

ASHIKAGA FEUDALISM
(1333–1567)

TOKUGAWA FEUDALISM
(1603–1868)

SHOGUN
Weak; unable to control daimyo
or to provide central control.

SHOGUN
Powerful; controlled daimyo; created
strong central government.

DAIMYO
Powerful
landowners; had
complete control
over their land.

DAIMYO
Few in number;
completely ruled
by shogun.

VASSALS AND
SUBVASSALS
Competed for
land; owed
loyalty to daimyo.

VASSALS AND
SUBVASSALS
Owed loyalty to
overlord.
(shogun or daimyo).

SAMURAI,
ARMED
RETAINERS
Honored fighters;
loyal to lords.

SAMURAI,
ARMED
RETAINERS
No military role.

PEASANT
FARMERS
Worked for lord
on whose land
they lived.

PEASANT
FARMERS
Allegiance was
to shogun.

# ERA III

# Global Interactions (1200–1650)

# Part A: The Renaissance

The Renaissance refers to the period between 1400 and 1700 when there was a great rebirth of cultural and scholarly activity in Western Europe. This activity began with a revival of interest in the cultures of ancient Greece and Rome. These classical cultures had stressed human endeavor and human conduct, and the Renaissance was marked by a return to the concerns of individual humans and their lives. The Renaissance had other characteristics.

1. An emphasis on the individual as a reasoning, thinking, and questioning person. Human beings were seen as the center of all things, as was life here on earth. These were secular, or worldly, concerns. (This was in direct contrast to the Middle Ages, when there was concern with matters of religion, authority, and tradition. Salvation and the hereafter were emphasized.)

2. Humanism was an important influence in the arts and sciences. This meant that paintings of people were more realistic and "human" than in the Middle Ages. Writers wrote about simple, everyday events. Much writing was done in the vernacular languages—that is, in everyday speech in national languages, such as Italian, that were commonly spoken—rather than in Latin, the language used chiefly by church officials and educated people. Scientists questioned traditional ideas about humans and the universe. They used reason and experimentation to try to understand those things that had previously been accepted on faith or because of religious beliefs. Their advances eventually became known as the Scientific Revolution.

3. The Renaissance began in Italy and was supported by wealthy families who were patrons of the arts. The Medicis in Florence were one such family.

4. The Renaissance gradually spread to other parts of Europe, northward to Holland, Germany, France, and England, and to Spain.

The characteristics described above can be seen in the achievements of several famous people in the fields of art, literature, and science presented in the table.

## RENAISSANCE ACHIEVEMENTS

| Field | Name | Nationality | Achievement |
|---|---|---|---|
| Art | da Vinci | Italian | *The Last Supper; Mona Lisa* |
| | Michelangelo | Italian | Sistine Chapel; *Piéta; David* |
| | Titian | Spanish | *Assumption of the Virgin* |
| | El Greco | Spanish | *Views of Toledo* |
| | Rembrandt | Dutch | *The Night Watch; The Anatomy Lesson* |
| Literature | Dante | Italian | *The Divine Comedy* |
| | Chaucer | English | *Canterbury Tales* |
| | Erasmus | Dutch | *In Praise of Folly* |
| | Shakespeare | English | *Macbeth; Julius Caesar; Hamlet* |
| | Rabelais | French | *Gargantua and Pantagruel* |
| | Machiavelli | Italian | *The Prince* |
| | Cervantes | Spanish | *Don Quixote* |
| Science | Copernicus | Polish | "The sun is the center of the universe." |
| | Galileo | Italian | Telescope; law of falling bodies |
| | Gutenberg | German | Printing press |
| | Harvey | English | Circulation of blood in the body |
| | Leeuwenhoek | Dutch | The microscope |
| | Newton | English | Laws of motion and gravity |

# Part B: The Reformation

## The Reformation and Counter-Reformation

The Reformation, which is also called the Protestant Reformation, was a movement to reform or change certain ideas and practices of the Roman Catholic Church. It began in 1517 when Martin Luther, a German priest, placed his Ninety-Five Theses, or statements, on a church door in Wittenburg, Germany. In this document Luther protested against certain Church practices and also stated his own religious beliefs, which differed from those of the Roman Catholic Church.

1. Luther protested certain Church practices, such as the sale of indulgences (paying money for Church pardons), simony (selling of Church offices), and nepotism (giving Church positions to relatives). He also protested against the worldly and materialistic life led by some Church officials and against the power of the Pope to do certain things. Luther saw these practices as Church abuses.

2. Luther believed that the Bible and not the Pope was the final authority on religious matters. He wanted the Bible to be translated into German so that each person could read it and interpret it for himself or herself. Luther believed that salvation was achieved through faith alone, not through both faith and good works as the Church claimed. Faith was a free gift given to humans through God's grace, and it was God's mercy that permitted humans to be saved.

**Factors That Led to the Reformation.** Luther's protests against Church practices and beliefs about salvation were shared by many people, especially in northern Europe. Other factors that caused the Reformation were:

1. *Economic.* Some rulers were upset about the economic power and wealth of the Church. This power and wealth came from taxes imposed by the Church as well as from the vast amounts of land that it owned. These rulers hoped to obtain this wealth for themselves and their subjects.

2. *Political.* Many felt that the Pope had too much power over political and other secular, or nonreligious, matters. Many rulers challenged the Pope's claim to being supreme in secular as well as religious affairs. They resisted the Church's claim to having power over them and other civil officials and to its interference in political matters concerning their nation.

3. *Renaissance thought.* The Renaissance emphasized the ability of humans to think and reason for themselves. Along with this came the questioning of traditional authority. In this atmosphere, many people during the Renaissance began to disagree with certain Church practices and ideas.

4. *Previous Church problems and reform attempts.* Even before Luther, there had been problems within the Church, such as the Babylonian Captivity of 1309–1377, when the Popes lived in France and were under the control of the king of France, and the Great Schism of 1378–1417, when two Popes competed for control of the Church. Other reformers had attacked some of the same practices that Luther protested against. These included John Wycliffe (England), John Hus (Bohemia), and Desiderius Erasmus (Holland).

**Immediate Impact of Luther's Actions.** Luther established the Lutheran Church in Germany. Lutheranism was the first of the new Protestant religions. It was accepted as a new religion in northern Germany as well as in most of Scandinavia (Norway and Sweden). Other Protestant religions also began as the result of activities of additional reformers who challenged the Catholic Church, such as Ulrich Zwingli in Switzerland, John Knox in Scotland, and John Calvin, whose ideas, especially that of predestination, won acceptance in Switzerland, Scotland, Holland, England, and parts of France. (According to predestination, God chose certain people, called the elect, to be saved, while those who had not been chosen could never achieve salvation, no matter what they did on earth.)

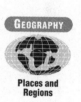

**GEOGRAPHY**

Places and Regions

The Protestant Reformation also spread to England, where King Henry VIII broke with the Church because of marriage problems. He defied the authority of the Pope and divorced Catherine of Aragon. During his rule, Parliament passed the Act of Supremacy in 1534, which made the Anglican Church of England independent from the Pope, with the king as its head. Afterwards, Henry took over some Church lands.

**GEOGRAPHY**

Places and Regions

Luther's ideas as well as those of other reformers throughout Europe were spread more easily due to the printing press, which was invented in Germany in 1450.

**The Reaction of the Catholic Church.** While the Protestant Reformation was underway, the Roman Catholic Church acted to maintain its power and to reform itself. This movement to revise the spiritual mission of the Catholic Church and to stop the spread of Protestantism was called the Counter-Reformation. Among the actions it carried out were:

1. Luther was excommunicated.

2. At the Council of Trent (1545–1563), the Church upheld its traditional beliefs and practices, including the supreme power of the Pope over the Church and the necessity of both faith and good works for salvation. It also corrected some abuses, banning the sale of indulgences and forbidding simony. It also drew up the Index. This was a list of books that Catholics were not allowed to read because they contained heretical ideas.

3. The Inquisition, or the Church courts established during the Middle Ages, took measures against heretics. The Inquisition was very effective in southern Europe, especially in Italy and Spain.

4. The Jesuit order was founded in 1534 by Ignatius Loyola and known officially as the Society of Jesus. The Jesuits helped to defend and preserve Catholic teachings.

**Results of the Reformation.** The Reformation shattered the religious unity of Western Europe and led to the development of Protestant religions. By 1600 almost all of Western Europe was divided into Protestants and Catholics, with each group hostile to the other. In the 1600s these feelings erupted into wars. Several religious wars were fought, the most serious of which was the Thirty Years War (1618–1648).

The monarchs of the European nations and local civil officials, especially in central and northern Europe, gained in power and wealth as the strength of the Catholic Church declined. They were able to take over Church lands and taxes.

Progress was made in education and literacy, especially because of the greater interest in reading the Bible.

At first, because of the growing competition between Protestants and Catholics, religious intolerance grew.

# Part C: Global Interactions in Asia—Japan

## IMPORTANT DATES IN JAPANESE HISTORY

| | |
|---|---|
| 3000–300 B.C.E. | Jomon culture |
| 300 B.C.E.–250 C.E. | Legendary period |
| 250 B.C.E.–250 C.E. | Yayoi culture |
| 250–645 | Tomb culture |
| 552 | Introduction of Buddhism to Japan |
| 604 | Shotoku Taishi's *Seventeen Article Constitution* |
| 645 | Taika Reforms |
| 702 | Taiho Code |
| 710–784 | Nara period |
| 794–1185 | Heian period |
| 858–1156 | Fujiwara period |
| 1192–1333 | Kamakura (or Minamoto shogunate) period |
| 1274, 1281 | Mongol invasions |
| 1338–1568 | Ashikaga (shogunate) period |
| 1549 | Arrival of Francis Xavier and Christianity |
| 1603–1868 | Tokugawa (shogunate) period |
| 1868–1912 | Meiji Restoration |

## The Feudal Period (1185–1600)

During Japan's feudal period, power rested in the hands of a military ruler rather than in those of the emperor. Feudalism was a political, economic, and social system based on land rights and individualized bonds of loyalty.

In the period from 794 to 1185, called the Heian period, a single family, the Fujiwara, came to dominate the imperial court and government by marrying their daughters to the emperors. During this period the power of the central government declined, allowing clans in the countryside to claim land belonging to the emperor. As a result, the economic strength of the imperial government decreased, as did its ability to protect the outlying regions of the empire. The noble families in the countryside became more powerful, as peasants who could not protect themselves from roving bands of robbers and the Ainu gave up their land, which became part of the noble's estate. In return, the peasant was entitled to the protection of the noble and his samurai (warriors on horseback). The daimyo (the more powerful lords) built palaces, collected taxes from the peasants, and increased the size of their military. The military and the peasants built up a loyalty system to the daimyo, who protected

301

and employed them. The daimyo and the samurai became the real rulers of Japan. A feudal system similar to Europe's during the Middle Ages was the result. The daimyo controlled their own land, collected taxes, created armies, built castle headquarters, and through the peasants encouraged economic self-sufficiency. This feudal system lasted for approximately 500 years.

As the power of the Fujiwara declined, two daimyo families, the Taira and the Minamoto, struggled for power. The Minamoto, under the leadership of Yoritomo, won this struggle. Yoritomo forced the emperor to grant him the title of shogun (military ruler or general), and the daimyo and samurai gained control of Japanese government, which would last until the Tokugawa shogunate. The shoguns were the real heads of government until the Meiji Restoration in 1867, although the imperial family continued to occupy the throne. The imperial family was used to legitimize the power of the shoguns by the granting of the shogun title.

WORLD ISSUES

Determination
of Political
and Economic
Systems

## Bushido

During the feudal period a warrior code developed, which drew on the military discipline of the samurai, Confucian ethics, Shinto, and Zen Buddhism. Bushido (the way of the warrior) was a code of conduct that stressed the importance of superior-inferior relationships and the unswerving loyalty of the samurai to their lords and through them, to the lord's superiors, including the emperor. Family loyalty was important, though it was expected that a loyal samurai would sacrifice his family for the good of his lord. The samurai subordinated individual desires for the good of the group or society. Self-discipline and self-control were stressed, as was complete indifference to death. It was considered glorious to die in battle and absolutely unacceptable to surrender. To avoid surrender or capture, a samurai was expected to commit harakiri or seppuku (ritual suicide involving disembowelment). Samurai also committed suicide in this way to atone for behavior unworthy of a samurai, for example, disloyalty to a feudal lord, if that disloyalty was discovered. According to the code of bushido, a samurai must be brave, honorable, loyal to lord and emperor, and able to subordinate his emotions.

GLOBAL
CONCEPTS

Identity

CONCEPTS
GLOBAL

## Mongol Invasion

In 1270 Kublai Khan demanded that the Japanese pay tribute, but the Minamoto shogun refused. The Khan sent a Mongol force of 40,000 to Kyushu in 1274. The Japanese samurai were no match for the Mongol force, but they received assistance in

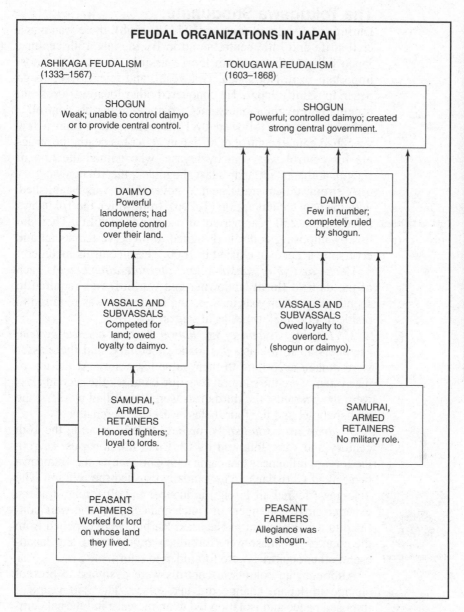

**FEUDAL ORGANIZATIONS IN JAPAN**

**ASHIKAGA FEUDALISM**
**(1333–1567)**

**SHOGUN**
Weak; unable to control daimyo
or to provide central control.

**DAIMYO**
Powerful
landowners; had
complete control
over their land.

**VASSALS AND
SUBVASSALS**
Competed for
land; owed
loyalty to daimyo.

**SAMURAI,
ARMED
RETAINERS**
Honored fighters;
loyal to lords.

**PEASANT
FARMERS**
Worked for lord
on whose land
they lived.

**TOKUGAWA FEUDALISM**
**(1603–1868)**

**SHOGUN**
Powerful; controlled daimyo; created
strong central government.

**DAIMYO**
Few in number;
completely ruled
by shogun.

**VASSALS AND
SUBVASSALS**
Owed loyalty to
overlord.
(shogun or daimyo).

**SAMURAI,
ARMED
RETAINERS**
No military role.

**PEASANT
FARMERS**
Allegiance was
to shogun.

the form of a typhoon, which destroyed much of the Mongol
fleet. The Mongols were forced to abandon their invasion. To
the Japanese, the typhoons were divine winds, kamikaze (*kami*-
gods; *kaze*-winds) sent by the gods to protect Japan. A similar
storm destroyed much of the Mongol fleet when they attempted
a second invasion in 1281.

**GEOGRAPHY**

**Environment
and Society**

303

# The Tokugawa Shogunate

During the Ashikaga shogunate (1338–1568), there was much civil strife and little central control. By the late 15th century, Japan fell into the hands of local warlords. Three of the most important were Nobunaga, Hideyoshi, and Ieyasu. Nobunaga began to reunify Japan. He conquered other local warlords and eventually brought about twenty provinces under his control.

Nobunaga was followed by Hideyoshi, who within a few years had gained control of all Japan. After his death, the struggle for control was won by Ieyasu, who gained the title of shogun and created Japan's last shogunate, the Tokugawa.

GLOBAL CONCEPTS

**Political Systems**

CONCEPTS GLOBAL

A strong bureaucratic central government was established, with the new capital at Edo (Tokyo), from which the Tokugawa ruled over a 250-year period of peace and stability. They did this by imposing controls designed to preserve the social and economic order as it existed in 1600. These controls included:

1. *The system of sankin-kotai (alternate attendance).* Each of the daimyo (local landowner and warlord) was required to spend every other year in Edo, and his family was required to reside in Edo at all times as hostages.

2. *The class system of the nation became a caste system.* Membership in a class was made hereditary, and the classes were ranked according to their value to society. At the top of the system were the samurai (warrior-knights); the second class were the peasants; the third class were the skilled workers, the craftspeople; and the fourth class were the merchants.

3. *Japan was isolated.* Portuguese traders came in the 16th century and were followed by Christian missionaries. Fearing the foreign influences that came with Christianity, the Tokugawa persecuted Christians and eventually crushed the religion. The Tokugawa feared all foreign influence, and all foreign traders, except a small contingent of Dutch and Chinese who were confined to a small island in Nagasaki Harbor, were expelled from the country. Japanese were forbidden to go abroad, and Japanese in other countries were forbidden to return.

**GEOGRAPHY**

**Physical Settings**

Although the Tokugawa controls were designed to prevent change in Japan, change did take place. The 250 years of imposed peace and isolation led to an increase in internal commerce, the development of cities, and the strengthening of the economic power of merchants. Most of the samurai, with no wars to fight, fell on hard times and often married daughters of merchants to improve their fortunes. Many of the samurai became scholars and teachers, and the literacy rate increased considerably. During their long period of isolation, the Japanese developed a strong feeling of their own uniqueness.

GLOBAL CONCEPTS

**Identity**

CONCEPTS GLOBAL

*Multiple Choice.* Select the letter of the answer that correctly completes the statement.

1. The Renaissance was all of the following *except*
   A. a revival of learning
   B. a time of emphasis on the individual
   C. a movement that began in northern Europe
   D. an era during which the Church regained influence over daily life

2. All of the following were Renaissance artists *except*
   A. Picasso
   B. Michelangelo
   C. El Greco
   D. Leonardo da Vinci

3. The Reformation was a movement to
   A. reorganize government control in northern Europe
   B. reform the practices of the Roman Catholic Church
   C. destroy the feudal system in France
   D. increase the power of the Pope

4. In the Ninety-Five Theses, Martin Luther protested all of the following *except*
   A. the sale of indulgences
   B. the translation of the Bible into German
   C. simony
   D. nepotism

5. The new Protestant religions included all of the following *except*
   A. Presbyterian
   B. Lutheran
   C. Methodist
   D. Russian Orthodox

6. All of the following were leaders of the Protestant Reformation *except*
   A. Martin Luther
   B. John Calvin
   C. Catherine of Aragon
   D. Ulrich Zwingli

7. All of the following are true of the Act of Supremacy *except*
   A. made the Anglican Church of England independent from the Pope
   B. made the King of England head of the Anglican Church
   C. was passed by Parliament in 1534
   D. created an English Papacy

8. The Counter-Reformation did all of the following *except* that it
   A. led to the excommunication of Martin Luther
   B. reaffirmed the supremacy of the Pope
   C. led to the founding of the Society of Jesus (Jesuits)
   D. destroyed the Protestant movement

9. Under the Japanese feudal system, real power in Japan was held by
   A. the emperor
   B. a series of petty kingdoms
   C. the daimyo and samurai
   D. the peasant class

10. All of the following are true of the Tokugawa shogunate *except* that it
    A. was centered at Edo
    B. created a strong central government
    C. isolated Japan from the west
    D. was a period of great internal strife

**Essay #1 Theme:** The Renaissance
The Renaissance was a time of major change in European society.

**Task:**
1. Describe the changes that took place in Europe during the Renaissance.
2. Describe the causes of the Renaissance in Europe.

**Directions:** Write a well-organized essay with an introduction stating the topic, a body that accomplishes the task, and a summarizing conclusion.

*Hint:* You may wish to consider scholarship, the arts, science, literature, religion, etc.


**Essay #2 Theme:** Reformation
There were many causes of the Protestant Reformation.

**Task:**
1. Describe the causes of the Protestant Reformation.
2. Describe the changes brought about by the Protestant Reformation.

**Directions:** Write a well-organized essay with an introduction stating the topic, a body that accomplishes the task, and a summarizing conclusion.

*Hint:* You may wish to consider the Ninety-Five Theses, John Calvin, John Knox, the Inquisition, etc.

## DOCUMENT-BASED ESSAY QUESTION

**Directions:** The following question is based on the accompanying documents (Documents 1–5). Some of the documents have been edited for the purpose of this assignment.

Write a well-organized essay with an introduction stating a thesis, a body of several paragraphs that accomplishes the task, and a summarizing conclusion. Use all the documents and analyze each one. Use evidence from the documents to support the position you take in your thesis. Do not simply repeat the contents of the document; explain things in your words and relate the information in your thesis. Using your knowledge of the social studies, include related information that is not included in the documents.

**Historical Context:** The Reformation was a reaction of humanist thinkers to the strict control of the Roman Catholic Church, and the Counter-Reformation was a reaction to that.

**Question:** Discuss the beliefs of Reformation-minded thinkers and explain how those thinkers caused a reaction on the part of the Roman Catholic Church.

**Part A:** Summarize the main idea stated in each of the documents as that idea related to the Reformation or the Counter-Reformation.

**Part B:** Respond in an essay. Your essay should be based on a thesis statement—your viewpoint regarding the causes of the Reformation and the reaction it caused in the Roman Catholic Church. In your essay you should use information from all of the documents as evidence. Present the evidence and analyze it from the point of view of your thesis. Support your thesis with related information based on your knowledge of the social studies.

### DOCUMENT 1

"And, in this way, every Christian is expected to believe .explicitly and implicitly all the truth which the Holy Spirit has put in Scripture, and in this way a man is not bound to believe the sayings of the saints which are apart from Scripture, nor should he believe papal bulls, except in so far as they speak out of Scripture, or in so far as what they say is founded in Scripture simply. But a man may believe bulls as probable, for both the pope and his curia make mistakes from ignorance of the truth. And, with reference to this ignorance, it can be substantiated that the pope makes mistakes and may be deceived."

—John Hus, *The Church*

## DOCUMENT 2

"And to put the matter even more plainly; if a little company of pious Christian laymen were taken prisoner and carried away to a desert, and had not among them a priest consecrated by a bishop, and were they to agree to elect one of them, married or unmarried, and were to order him to baptize, to celebrate the mass, to absolve and to preach; this man would as truly be a priest, as if all the bishops and all the Popes had consecrated him. That is why in case of necessity every man can baptize and absolve, which would not be possible if we were not all priests."

—Martin Luther, *Address to the Christian Nobility of the German Nation*

## DOCUMENT 3

"Predestination we call the eternal decree of God, by which he has determined in himself, what he would have to become of every individual of mankind. For they are not all created with a similar destiny; but eternal life is foreordained for some, and eternal damnation for others. Every man, therefore, being created for one or the other of these ends, we say, he is predestinated either to life or to death."

—John Calvin, *Institutes of the Christian Religion*

## DOCUMENT 4

"Rules for Thinking with the Church

1. Laying aside all private judgment, we ought to keep our minds prepared and ready to obey in all things the true Spouse of Christ our Lord, which is our Holy Mother, the Hierarchical Church.
XV. We ought not habitually to speak much of Predestination; but if sometimes mention be made of it in any way, we must so speak that the common people may not fall into error, as happens sometimes when they say: 'It is already fixed whether I am to be saved or damned, and there cannot be any other result whether I do good or ill; and, becoming slothful in consequence, they neglect works conducive to their salvation, and to the spiritual profit of their souls.'"

—Ignatius of Loyola, *Spiritual Exercises*

## DOCUMENT 5

"Catholics . . . Recall how you have treated the Evangelicals. You have pursued and imprisoned them and left them to be consumed of lice and rot in foul dungeons in hideous darkness and the shadow of death, and then you have roasted them alive at a slow fire to prolong their torture. And for what crime? Because they did not believe in the pope, the mass, purgatory, and other things which are so far from being based on Scripture that even the very names are not to be found there."

—Sebastian Castellioi, *Concerning Heretics*

# ERA IV

# The First Global Age (1450–1770)

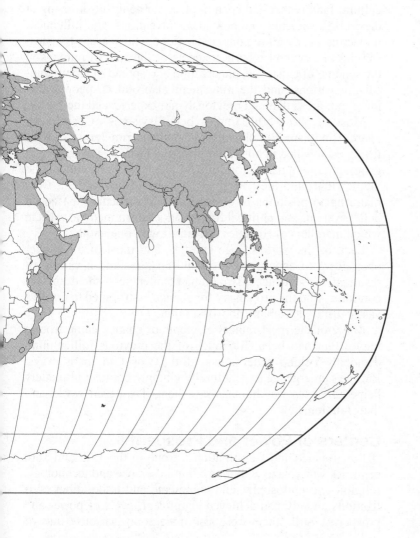

# Part A: Continuity and Change: Established Structures, New Ideas

The world of the 15th century was one of many contrasts. Perhaps the most overarching of these was the contrast between cultural factors that had been in place for centuries in many of the world's societies and new ideas, inventions, and influences impacting nearly all regions of the globe. The age saw the blossoming of new and reborn concepts of the role of humans in the scheme of existence, the creation and spread of technological innovations, and the movement of products, people, and ideas into areas that had previously not experienced them.

Most of the world's major belief systems—Christianity, Islam, Hinduism, Buddhism, and Confucianism/Taoism—were firmly established in both their principal ideas and in particular geographic regions. Major political ideologies, absolutism and divine right, and their resultant systems of government were maturing to positions of strength. Social structures based on belief systems and political frameworks determined the ways in which members of societies interacted with one another.

Each of the world's large cultures, and most of its smaller ones, were to experience profound changes and a variety of resultant consequences. Two human tendencies—the desire for continuity and the propensity for change—struggled to create a vastly different human and world order.

Many of the most radical elements of change came from a region that had been, for much of the previous millennium, decidedly behind other areas of the world in many ways. Europe's emergence as a culturally vibrant continent ultimately helped alter the way humans saw themselves, their world, and their relationships.

## Centers of Power and Prosperity

If Renaissance and Reformation Europe in the 15th and 16th centuries was ablaze with innovation in science and technology, religion and philosophy, and commerce and trade, other civilizations already had achieved significant levels of power and prosperity. Still others were also undergoing various kinds of rebirth in their own ways. The venerable culture of China had seen the restoration of native (as opposed to conquerors') rule in the form of the Ming Dynasty (1368–1644), which presided over an agricultural and commercial revival. Between 1399 and 1453, the Ottoman Turks of Asia Minor established an empire that would dominate the Middle East for centuries to come. In western Africa, the successive trading empires of Mali and Songhai wielded great power and reached high levels of affluence and accomplishment controlling trans-Saharan commerce between the 13th and 16th centuries. A new power rose in South Asia early in the 1500s—Mughals (Moguls/Moghuls), Muslim invaders from Central Asia, established a dynasty that conquered and controlled most of the subcontinent until 1739. Even in the Americas, geographically isolated from the other continents, the Aztec and Incan empires reached high levels of societal sophistication. The resources, wealth, and accomplishments of these empires stimulated and attracted Europeans eager for profit and products.

**GEOGRAPHY**

Places and Regions

# Part B: Amerindian Civilizations/MesoAmerican Societies

Several very sophisticated societies had developed in Central America during the centuries between 300 and 1400 C.E. The heirs to those cultures were flourishing in the 15th century and were about to encounter the wider world for the first time.

## The Aztec Empire

GLOBAL
CONCEPTS
**Political Systems**
CONCEPTS
GLOBAL

The Aztecs were a warrior people with a rigid social structure who rose to the leadership of an alliance of city-states in the 1400s. The Aztec capital was Tenochtitlán, an island city in Lake Texcoco, the site of present-day Mexico City. The Aztec Empire was ruled by a warrior king, who was supported by a warrior class and a priestly class, which controlled the Aztec religious ceremonies. The Aztecs had, as did other MesoAmerican peoples, a polytheistic religion. Of particular importance was their god of war, Huitzilopochtli, who could only be worshiped properly through human sacrifice and the offering of blood. The Aztecs believed that their gods had great powers and required human sacrifice in ceremonies designed to win their favor in battle.

**GEOGRAPHY**

**Physical Settings**

War was the policy of the Aztec Empire toward all peoples who did not accept a tributary status, which included the supplying of slaves for sacrifice. Although the Aztec Empire was expanding in the early 1500s, the Aztecs could not conquer all their enemies in central Mexico. The Aztec Empire was the center of MesoAmerican civilization prior to the arrival of the Spaniards.

The Spanish conquistador (conqueror) Hernan de Cortés relied heavily on the military support of the Aztecs' enemies, particularly the Tlaxcalans, in his conquest of the empire in the 1520s. Trade played an important role in the Aztec Empire. Farming was also of great importance. Corn, beans, squash, and peppers were the main staples. Landownership was controlled by the government. Land was given to families headed by male warriors and could be handed down.

The Aztecs were a literate people who spoke a language called Na'nhautl. The Aztecs were adept at making parchment paper and excelled in gold and silver metallurgy. To measure time, they adopted the Mayan calendar. They were skilled engineers and architects.

## The Incas

The Incas ruled a highly regimented empire that included much of the Andean region of South America, stretching from southern Colombia through Ecuador, Bolivia, Peru, into northern Chile and northwestern Argentina. Beginning in the 13th century, the Incas began to expand and conquer other peoples, including other advanced civilizations such as the Tihuanaco and the Chimu. The acceptance of Incan rule meant that a conquered people could retain its own rulers.

**GEOGRAPHY**

**Places and Regions**

Religion played a crucial role in Incan life. The term Inca refers to the ruler of the empire and his extended family, which numbered in the thousands. The Inca was believed to be a descendent of the sun god, Inti, and was worshiped like a living god. The Incas sought through their worship to influence their gods to help them, and a large group of priests regulated the ceremonial life of the empire. Offerings of food, animals, and at times human sacrifice were made to the gods.

**GEOGRAPHY**

**Physical Settings**

Land was not privately owned. It was given by the Inca to the tribe and distributed. The land was subdivided into four parts: one section was given to the farmers; a second was set aside for the sun and the crops given to the priests of the temples; a third went to the emperor, who used the crops for the government officials, the military, and his personal household; and the last section was farmed for those who could not provide for themselves. Potatoes, cotton, maize, beans, squash, and tomatoes were the principal crops.

GLOBAL
CONCEPTS

**Choice**

CONCEPTS
GLOBAL

The Incas excelled in engineering and architecture. Remnants of the Incan road system, bridges, and building construction can still be found throughout the Andean region. Cuzco, located in the highlands of Peru, was their major capital. The official language of the Inca Empire was Quechua, but the Incas allowed subject peoples to use their own languages. They had no written language and therefore kept no written records or books. Instead they used a quipu, which was a main string with small colored strings attached and tied into knots to record knowledge. The Incas were skillful artisans who excelled in metalwork, pottery, and textiles. Cotton and the wool from the llama, alpaca, vicunya, and guanaco were used for clothing. The Incas were particularly adept in the use of gold and silver for fine jewelry and other ornaments. In the 1530s the Spanish conquistadors, led by Pizarro, ended the reign of the Incas and destroyed their civilization.

GLOBAL
CONCEPTS

**Culture**

CONCEPTS
GLOBAL

Thus the arrival of Europeans in the 16th century spelled the end of the independent development of societies in the Americas. Conquest and especially newly introduced diseases destroyed what had been a long series of sophisticated and highly accomplished civilizations.

# Part C: Trading Kingdoms of West Africa

## Mali

The West African trading empire of Mali originated in 1200, replacing the kingdom of Ghana. Its power was based on the use of iron, its wealthy farming region, its control of the trans-Saharan trade routes, and the salt and gold mines. Like Ghana, Mali taxed all goods transported through the kingdom and became extremely prosperous. Income from taxes was used to support the government and military and to build enormous mosques and palaces. Timbuktu became an important center of Arabic and Islamic learning. Mali was a Muslim kingdom, and its most famous ruler, Mansa Musa, on his pilgrimage to Makkah scattered so much gold in North Africa that it took years for the gold market to recover. In the early 15th century, people from the north and south attacked, and people within the kingdom revolted. Mali went into a state of decline, from which it did not recover.

**GEOGRAPHY**

**Human Systems**

GLOBAL CONCEPTS

**Power**

CONCEPTS GLOBAL

## Songhai

This Muslim kingdom began to expand into an empire in the 15th century under Sunni Ali. The empire of Songhai was greater in extent than either Ghana or Mali (at its height it contained an area about equal to the continental United States) and also controlled the trans-Saharan trade routes and sources of gold and salt. Both imports and exports were taxed. Cities grew up around commercial and religious centers. In the late 16th century, Songhai was invaded by armies from Morocco equipped with guns and cannons. The spears and arrows of the larger Songhai army were no match for them, and the Songhai were defeated. The Songhai Empire disappeared.

The kingdom of Kongo originated in Central Africa in the coastal region in the late 14th century. Trade and agriculture were the basis of Kongo's economy. The king was considered divine and absolute. The Portuguese appeared in Kongo in 1482 and were interested in obtaining slaves. The divisions caused by disagreements over European influence and the sale of the Kongolese as slaves caused serious problems, and the kingdom disintegrated. Arab and European interest in African trade goods and particularly slaves seriously disrupted the political and economic stability of the continent south of the Sahara.

# Part D: The Middle East and Southwest Asia

## The Ottoman Empire

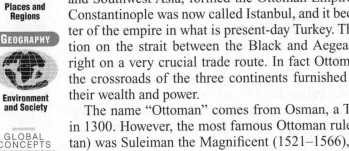

The Ottomans were one of several Turkish peoples who eventually took over the territory once held by the other Muslim kingdoms in the Middle East. They also captured Constantinople in 1453, thereby ending the Byzantine Empire. All this territory, which consisted of land in North Africa, southeastern Europe, and Southwest Asia, formed the Ottoman Empire. The city of Constantinople was now called Istanbul, and it became the center of the empire in what is present-day Turkey. The city's location on the strait between the Black and Aegean Seas put it right on a very crucial trade route. In fact Ottoman control of the crossroads of the three continents furnished the basis for their wealth and power.

The name "Ottoman" comes from Osman, a Turkish leader in 1300. However, the most famous Ottoman ruler (called sultan) was Suleiman the Magnificent (1521–1566), under whom the empire reached the height of its power. He was also called "Suleiman the Lawgiver" because of many legal, educational, and military changes he made. For a time, the empire was well organized, functioning basically as a conquering army constantly at war.

The Ottoman Turks developed an efficient set of administrators, similar to a civil service, to help run the vast territory in the empire. The attempt by the Ottoman Turks to expand their empire farther into Europe was finally stopped at the Battle of Vienna in 1683. Many historians trace the beginnings of the empire's decline to this failed siege of a major European capital.

## Persia Under the Safavid Dynasty

Early in the 16th century, a new dynasty arose in the geographically key region south of the Caspian Sea. Since the time of the ancient Persians and Parthians, much east-west trade had passed through this area. Control of the trade conveyed power and influence to these new Persians, the Safavids. The leaders of this powerful Muslim state embraced the Shi'ite version of Islam based on the leadership of those claiming direct descent from the Prophet Muhammad. The Safavid Empire was a theocracy, its laws and leadership based on the Quran. It reached its peak of power under Shah Abbas (1587–1629), a military conqueror who also vigorously supported trade and commerce and was a lavish patron of the arts. The majestic Safavid capital of Isfahan, with its bustling markets, extensive textile industry, and beautiful public buildings was the center of this trade and artistic achievement.

# Part E: South Asia

## Muslims and Mughals in India

**GEOGRAPHY**

**Human Systems**

In South Asia as in other regions adjacent to the Middle East, the expansion of Islam had a profound impact on political events and social relationships. First traders, then Muslim invaders brought the new monotheistic faith to the subcontinent. Based on control of key trade routes and reaping the rewards of the agriculturally productive northern river plains, a series of Muslim empires dominated the subcontinent for centuries.

**GLOBAL CONCEPTS**

**Power**

**CONCEPTS GLOBAL**

**GEOGRAPHY**

**Spatial Terms**

**The Delhi Sultanate (1206–1526).** The thirty-four different kings (sultans) who ruled during the history of this kingdom, or sultanate, held power in northern and central India. However, the earliest Muslim takeover in the subcontinent began in the 8th century with the conquest of part of what is now Pakistan. Muslim invaders, such as Mahmud of Ghazni, continued to come from the west (Afghanistan), to spread Islam, and gain more territory. Their successors established the Delhi sultanate. During the last years of the sultanate, the south of India was exposed to European contact and settlement. Vasco da Gama of Portugal landed in 1498 in Calicut. Soon thereafter, Spanish, French, Dutch, and English traders began to appear and established trading posts.

**Islam as a Major Religion in South Asia.** The history of Hindu–Muslim relations in South Asia has been at times peaceful and at times violent. The term communalism describes those instances when serious tensions have arisen between the two groups. Respect by each group for the other begins with an appreciation of basic beliefs, practices, and differences. It also includes shared concepts. A comparison of these concepts appears in the table below.

|  | Hinduism | Islam |
|---|---|---|
| Holy sites | Benares (Varanasi)<br>Ganges River | Makkah, Medina,<br>Jerusalem |
| Art | Carved images of deities,<br>ornate and decorative | Images of Muhammad,<br>Allah, people, animals<br>forbidden; calligraphic<br>verses from Quran |
| Holy books | Vedas, Upanishads,<br>Ramayana, Mahabharata | Quran (Koran) |

|               | Hinduism                                          | Islam                                                         |
| ------------- | ------------------------------------------------- | ------------------------------------------------------------ |
| Dietary taboos | Beef                                             | Pork                                                         |
| Obligations   | Dharma                                            | Five Pillars                                                 |
| Deity beliefs | Belief in different gods is acceptable            | Monotheistic                                                 |
| Life after death | Reincarnation, moksha, depending on karma      | Paradise for true believers and those who act righteously    |
| Divisions     | Stratification/hierarchy based on caste           | Equality of all before Allah; schism between Sunni and Shi'ite sects |
| Attitude on life | Ahimsa—doctrine of nonviolence                 | Jihad—concept of holy wars                                   |
| Political attitudes | Separation between civil and religious authority | Theocratic—Quran as basis for legal system            |

**The Mughal (Mogul) Dynasty (1526–1760).** This dynasty emerged as a result of military victories by Babur over the Delhi sultan. Babur was a Turkish-Mongol prince, a Muslim, a descendant of Genghis Khan, and originally from Central Asia. As had been the case with earlier Islamic invasions, this one came from Afghanistan. Babur, in fact, hated the heat and dust of India, and after capturing Delhi in 1526 and consolidating his control in the north, he retired to the cool mountains of Kashmir.

**Places and Regions**

Babur's grandson, Akbar (1556–1605), built the Mughal Empire into a military and economic power admired around the world for its productivity and grandeur. As a conqueror, Akbar greatly expanded Mughal territorial control. Even so, he became a very popular ruler, particularly because he won the respect of his Hindu subjects. His reign featured toleration of other religions, and he employed many Hindus in his government.

GLOBAL CONCEPTS

**Empathy**

CONCEPTS GLOBAL

Akbar's long period as emperor was also known for political stability and cultural achievements. Government administration was carried out by an efficient bureaucracy made up of both Muslims and Hindus. Though his government established both a department of finance (diwan) and a royal mint, the central government left village level government to local communities.

**Physical Settings**

This greatest of the Mughal emperors was a philosopher and intellectual as well—he might even be called a "Renaissance Man," so wide-ranging were his interests and capabilities. Perhaps the most radical of his actions as emperor was the attempt to heal the division between Muslim and Hindu. He abolished the pilgrim tax on those visiting holy places and the jizya or tax on non-Muslims. Akbar himself, though a Muslim, had several Hindu wives and created a "universal religion" combining Jain and Zoroastrian ideas as well as Muslim and Hindu ones. His openness on religious issues ultimately backfired, however, provoking rebellions by dissatisfied Muslims, and misunderstanding and rejection by almost all religious groups.

Akbar was a lavish patron of the arts, especially painting and "illuminated" books, those filled with elaborate illustrations. His architects built magnificent palaces and mosques, greatly expanding the ancient cities of Delhi and Agra. At one point he even had an entire new capital city constructed some twenty miles from Agra. His occupation of it lasted only some thirteen years, however, perhaps because of a water supply inadequate to the large population needed to run such a huge imperial administration. It was during Akbar's reign that European traders became prominent in commerce between South Asia and the West.

One of Akbar's successors was his grandson, Shah Jahan (1628–1658). He continued many of Akbar's policies, expanding the empire to the south, and building his own magnificent capital at Delhi. This city's location linked the plains of the Indus and Ganges rivers. With its wide avenues, its magnificent Jama Masjid (Great Mosque) and imposing Red Fort, the Mughal capital became one of the most splendid urban centers of the Muslim world. Shah Jahan employed 20,000 workers and spent nearly twenty years in the construction of the Taj Mahal. This great building was a memorial to his wife, Mumtaz Mahal.

Another Mughal ruler was Aurangzeb (1658–1707), who was a harsh and unpopular leader. A very strict Muslim who wanted to spread Islam, he carried out policies that angered Hindus, Sikhs, and other groups. This was one factor leading to the breakdown of the Mughal Empire. Other factors included corrupt administration, wasteful spending of money, and excessive military campaigns. Although the empire did not end until 1857, the Mughal rulers after Aurangzeb had very little influence in India. The weakness and disunity of the Mughals was one reason Britain was able to gain control in India.

# Part F: East Asia

## China: Insiders and Invaders

**The Ming Dynasty.** In 1368 the Mongols were replaced by the Ming Dynasty (1368–1644). The Ming Dynasty is most famous for the production of fine porcelain and for the sea voyages carried out during the early part of the Ming period. China sent ships to South and Southeast Asia and briefly carried on limited trade with areas as far away as the Red Sea and East Africa. Beautiful palaces were constructed in Beijing, including the Imperial City with the residence of the emperor, the Forbidden City, at its center.

**GEOGRAPHY**

**Spatial Terms**

The most significant achievement of the Ming, however, was an agricultural revolution that increased food production and resulted in a population explosion. Fast-growing varieties of rice allowed two harvests, terracing and new irrigation techniques extended the area of cultivatable land, and tax breaks promoted resettlement of land abandoned in earlier times of strife. Urban centers grew around local and regional markets, and the raising of export crops like silk and cotton enhanced trade. The Ming administration introduced mandatory service by citizens to the state and created a two-million-man standing army for defense and domestic control.

**WORLD ISSUES**

Population

**GEOGRAPHY**

**Environment and Society**

GLOBAL
CONCEPTS

**Citizenship**

CONCEPTS
GLOBAL

By the middle of the 1400s, though, the Ming had turned their attention inward. Internal wars, threats from the Mongols to the north, and a failed attempt to annex Vietnam supplanted trade as the most important concern. Weak emperors and a conservative bureaucracy increased the trend toward isolation. The first Europeans to arrive were the Portuguese, who founded a colony at Macau in 1557. Soon they, the Dutch, and the Japanese controlled China's seaborne trade.

**GEOGRAPHY**

**Places and Regions**

**The Qing or Manchu Dynasty.** To repel Mongol invasions, the Ming called on the Manchu, a people to the northeast, for assistance. However, the Manchus gradually conquered China and established the second foreign-ruled dynasty, the Qing (Ch'ing) (1644–1912).

The Manchus ruled an empire in which they were greatly outnumbered by the Chinese people they ruled. To facilitate their rule, they distanced themselves from the Chinese. Chinese were forbidden to emigrate to Manchuria in the northeast, Manchus and Chinese were not allowed to intermarry, and the Manchus retained their own language. Most of the key positions in government and the military were held by Manchus.

GLOBAL
CONCEPTS

**Power**

CONCEPTS
GLOBAL

# Part G: Europe: The Quest for Products and Profits

## SECTION 1: THE AGE OF EXPLORATION

**WORLD ISSUES**

World
Trade and
Finance

**GEOGRAPHY**

**Spatial Terms**

From the late 1400s to about 1750, the economic life of Western Europe changed greatly. This transformation was caused by an explosion of trade. In time, the search for trade and for alternate routes to Asian markets caused explorers to sail across the oceans, and the Europeans encountered lands that previously had been unknown to them. Spain and Portugal opened up the Age of Exploration and colonization as they ventured overseas to find new trade routes and markets. The first voyages explored the coast of Africa, and eventually Vasco da Gama of Portugal sailed around the Cape of Good Hope to India. Christopher Columbus, explorer for Spain, was the first to sail westward, reaching the Americas in 1492. These overseas explorations continued for a period of about 250 years, ending European isolation and eventually leading to European global domination.

**Reasons for the Age of Exploration.** There were many reasons why the nations of Western Europe undertook these voyages. These included:

1. The Renaissance spirit of inquiry and curiosity, which aroused interest in other parts of the world.

2. Scientific advances in navigational instruments and improved sailing vessels that made such voyages possible.

GLOBAL
CONCEPTS

**Technology**

CONCEPTS
GLOBAL

3. Interest in finding new routes to South and East Asia, stirred by the Crusades and the stories of Marco Polo. The Europeans wanted the products of the Asians, such as spices, but they had to pay high prices for them because the Arabs, the Ottomans, and Italian city-states controlled the routes to the east.

4. The desire for land and resources by the new nation-states of Europe.

5. Many adventurers were stirred by the lust for gold, a desire for glory, and faith in God. Many Europeans who ventured overseas went in search of riches and fame, whereas others wanted to spread their religion.

The major explorers and their achievements are presented in the following table.

**EXPLORERS AND THEIR ACHIEVEMENTS**

| Name | Nation | Achievement/Area of Exploration |
|------|--------|--------------------------------|
| Christopher Columbus | Spain | Americas; the "New World" |
| Bartolomeo Diaz | Portugal | East coast of Africa to Cape of Good Hope |
| Vasco da Gama | Portugal | East and west coasts of Africa; India |
| Pedro Cabral | Portugal | Brazil |
| Ferdinand Magellan | Spain | Philippines; one of his ships circumnavigated the globe, proving that the earth was round |
| Hernan de Cortés | Spain | Conquered Mexico |
| Juan Pizarro | Spain | Conquered Peru |
| Jacques Cartier | France | St. Lawrence River |
| Giovanni Verrazano | France | East coast of North America |
| Samuel de Champlain | France | Canada |
| John Cabot | England | Northeast coast of North America; Labrador |
| Sir Francis Drake | England | Circumnavigation of the world |
| Henry Hudson | Holland | New York |

**Results of the Age of Exploration.** The European voyages had many far-reaching effects. One was the establishment of colonial empires. Spain colonized Central and South America, while England colonized part of North America. Other Western European nations also established colonies. Eventually the rivalry among European nations for control of colonies and for sea routes led to wars. These included the French and Indian War between England and France in North America (1756–1763) and the defeat of the Spanish Armada by England in 1588. As the Europeans colonized overseas areas, they came to dominate native peoples. Also, colonies enabled the nations of Western Europe to acquire sources of raw materials, which they turned into manufactured goods. This made them rich. Finally, the Age of Exploration was made possible by the start of a commercial revolution that was further expanded by the encounter with a wider world.

GEOGRAPHY

Spatial Terms

GEOGRAPHY

Physical Settings

GLOBAL CONCEPTS

Interdependence

CONCEPTS GLOBAL

# SECTION 2: THE COMMERCIAL REVOLUTION

The term commercial revolution refers to the changes in trade and business practices that began in the 1400s and continued throughout the Age of Exploration. They were to transform the economies of Europe. This was not a revolution in the way goods were manufactured but in the way goods were bought and sold. It took place over three centuries. The changes included:

1. The growth of trade within Western Europe. Also, trade became more worldwide, and goods were traded between Europe and Asia and the Americas.

2. The growth of capitalism as an economic system. Under this system, property is privately owned and capital (money) is used to make a profit. A new type of business called a joint stock company was formed to undertake risky ventures that required large amounts of capital, such as traveling overseas and establishing colonies. Joint stock companies, such as the Dutch East India Company, were privately owned and sold stock to investors who were willing to risk their money in the hope of making a profit. Capitalism also came to be known as the free-enterprise system. To meet the needs of this system, a banking system arose. These developments eventually led to the concept of a market economy.

3. The Atlantic Ocean as the center of economic activity, replacing the Mediterranean Sea. Also, the nations located on the Atlantic Ocean became wealthier and more powerful than the other nations of Europe.

4. The development of mercantilism, or the economic theory that claimed it was important for a nation to acquire overseas colonies because they could provide gold, silver, and raw materials that would make that nation wealthy and more powerful. The raw materials obtained from the colonies were used to make manufactured goods, which could be sold at high prices in the colonies. At the same time the wealth acquired could be used to expand and maintain large naval forces and armies. Mercantilists also said that a nation should export more than it imports, thereby achieving a favorable balance of trade. This would result in a nation's becoming highly self-sufficient.

5. The increase in manufactured goods, which spurred an increased demand for these goods by consumers.

**Effects of the Commercial Revolution.** Because of the commercial revolution, the power of several European nation-states and their absolute monarchs increased. Trade and overseas empires made nations such as England, Spain, and France wealthy and powerful. Also, population shifts occurred. Many Africans were brought as slaves to work in the Americas. Many Europeans left their homelands to settle in the colonies. As a result, European culture was spread to areas around the world. Finally, a new production system, the domestic system, was developed in Europe. Under this system, goods were produced in the home rather than in a shop. Although the domestic system was used mainly to produce wool, other items such as buttons and gloves were also made this way. It enabled merchants to increase production. In time, it would be replaced by the factory system.

GLOBAL CONCEPTS

**Power**

CONCEPTS GLOBAL

**GEOGRAPHY**

Spatial Terms

**WORLD ISSUES**

| Human |
| Rights |

**WORLD ISSUES**

| Economic |
| Development |

# SECTION 3: EUROPE ENCOUNTERS THE PEOPLES OF AFRICA, ASIA, AND THE AMERICAS

**GEOGRAPHY**

**Physical Settings**

In the late 15th century, the European nations became rivals for the rich trade of the Indies and other parts of Asia. European monarchs granted monopolies on trade to chartered companies such as the British East Africa Company, Dutch East Indies Company, and French East India Company. The trading companies established trading posts and stopovers (way stations) along the coast of Africa, which were located on the route to Asia. Until the 19th century, the European presence was limited to the coastal areas and the trade in gold, ivory, and slaves.

Of greatest significance was what historians have labeled the Columbian Exchange, the transfer of agricultural products, livestock, and diseases between the Americas and the rest of the world. Until Christopher Columbus' voyages in the 1490s, North and South America had for millennia been almost completely isolated from contact with Europe, Asia, and Africa.

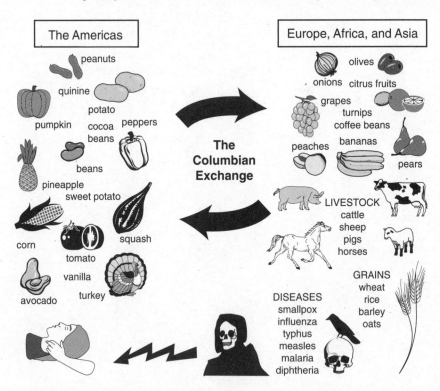

Consequently, its people and their products had evolved in quite different directions. As extensive trade and migration followed in the 17th century, the results proved disastrous for the peoples of the Americas, and beneficial to Europeans.

Diseases previously unknown in the New World, such as smallpox and measles, devastated entire Native American populations. At the same time, food products such as potatoes and corn became staples of the European diet, enhancing health and nutrition. This, in turn, contributed significantly to population increase in Europe and elsewhere. The economic effects of these results were felt in Africa as well; increased demand for American agricultural products and a decreased Native American labor supply led to the development of the slave trade.

### Spain: Acquisition of a Colonial Empire

The Spanish and Portuguese were the first to explore and trade extensively in the Americas, Africa, and Asia, aided by their geographic location. Both made vast claims in the Americas and carved out colonial empires there. In addition, Spain gained control of the Philippines and the Portuguese dominated trade in Southeast Asia from a series of coastal trade centers. In 1494, in the Treaty of Tordesillas, Spain obtained all the Americas except for what is today Brazil, which went to Portugal.

**Colonialism.** As the Spanish empire in the New World was established, the Native American civilizations located in the colonized areas were for the most part destroyed by superior military forces and diseases. Forced labor on the encomienda (large plantations) and in the mita system (work on roads, churches, and public buildings or in mines and textile mills) were other factors contributing to the destruction of Native American cultures and peoples.

The Spaniards brought the characteristics of their society to their New World empire. Spain imposed a political, religious, and linguistic unity on its colonial empire. The Spanish colonial organization penetrated wherever wealth could be found and Roman Catholicism could be preached.

The growing scarcity of Native American labor led to the importation of African slaves to the Americas for use on plantations, in the mines, and for other purposes. Efforts by a few Roman Catholic clergymen to protect the Native Americans from abuses of their human rights were largely ignored in a colonial economy, which operated on the principles of the mercantilist system. Bishop Bartolomé de Las Casas sought to enlist the Spanish crown in the protection of the Native Americans,

GEOGRAPHY

Environment and Society

WORLD ISSUES

Population

GLOBAL CONCEPTS

Environment

CONCEPTS GLOBAL

GEOGRAPHY

Places and Regions

GEOGRAPHY

Human Systems

GEOGRAPHY

Physical Settings

but his efforts failed. The *latifundia* (the *hacienda* and plantations), which were large, self-sufficient forms of landownership, predominated. These landholdings were characterized by unproductive use of land, dependent labor, a low level of technology, and little capital investment.

**Colonial Social Structure and Politics.** The Spanish colonial organization was based on a hierarchical structure, which placed the Spanish at the top of colonial society. This privileged class of Spanish elite, *peninsulares* (Spanish-born nobles), and *creoles* (their American-born children) dominated the colonial economy. They acquired vast areas of land; profits from these enriched the peninsulares, and taxes on them enhanced the royal treasury of Spain. Next were the *mestizos* (peoples of mixed Caucasian and Native American ancestry) followed by mulattos (Caucasian and African ancestry), African slaves, and Native Americans. The Spanish Roman Catholic Church helped in the subjugation and control of the Native American population and the ordering of colonial society. The hierarchical Roman Catholic Church was a large landholder throughout the Spanish colonies in the Americas. Both the regular hierarchy and the religious orders (the Jesuits, Franciscans, and Dominicans) took responsibility for the education of the Native American populations. The Jesuit order played a particularly important mission role in protecting the Native American populations. Jesuit interference with the Spanish colonists' exploitation of the Native American population led to their expulsion from Portuguese America (1759) and Spanish America (1767).

GLOBAL CONCEPTS
Diversity
CONCEPTS GLOBAL

The Spanish empire was controlled by the crown through the royal Council of the Indies. Spanish territory in the New World was divided into viceroyalties headed by appointed governors, called viceroys. The governor was assisted by an administrative and judicial tribunal called the *audiencia*. Numerous other officials were appointed by the crown. The viceroyalties of New Spain, Peru, New Granada, and La Plata were the four major territorial units of the Spanish colonial empire by 1800.

GLOBAL CONCEPTS
Political Systems
CONCEPTS GLOBAL

### The Portuguese Empire in America

The Portuguese empire began to take shape in the 1400s due to the voyages of exploration sponsored by Prince Henry the Navigator. Credit for the discovery of Brazil is given to Pedro Cabral, who claimed the territory for the king of Portugal in 1500. Portugal's primary colonial interests were in Africa and Asia. This situation changed in the 1600s due to Portugal's loss of most of its colonies in Asia, the growing value of Brazil's

GEOGRAPHY

Places and Regions

sugarcane production, and the discovery of gold and diamonds. Portugal had less of a dominating presence in Brazil than the Spanish had in their Latin American empire. The Portuguese did not settle in large numbers in Brazil, and because men greatly outnumbered women, the population increase resulted primarily from intermarriage. Class lines were more economic than racial in Brazil because of this intermixture of Portuguese, Native Americans, and Africans.

The Tupi-Guarani, an Amerindian grouping of tribes who spoke dialects of the Tupian language, inhabited the Brazilian coastline when the Portuguese arrived to trade and settle in the 1500s. The Tupian peoples survived on subsistence hunting and fishing and the cultivation of manioc, sweet potatoes, and beans. They were fierce and warlike, but contact with the Europeans eventually proved fatal due to disease, warfare, and attempted enslavement for labor.

The growing need for a reliable source of labor on the sugarcane plantations led to the importation of large numbers of Africans as slaves starting in the mid-1500s. Because the Roman Catholic Church did not play as wide a role in Brazil as in Spanish territory, the African slaves were able to retain some of their religious and cultural beliefs. These blended with Christian and Native American concepts and emerged as Candomble, an Africanized ritualistic and formalized cult that existed beneath the façade of the Roman Catholic Church.

The Portuguese penetrated deeply into the interior of the South American continent. *Bandeiras*, quasi-Euro-Amerindian military expeditions in search of Indian slaves and precious mineral wealth, pushed Portuguese claims to the Andes Mountains.

## The Dutch, French, and English in the Americas
In the second half of the 16th century, the Dutch, French, and English sought to establish colonies in the Americas. They took possession of territory primarily in the Caribbean region and along the northeastern coast of South America.

Starting in the 1580s, the Dutch attempted to gain control of northeastern Brazil. The profitable sugar-cane industry was a target of growing Dutch sea power, financial strength, and technical and business expertise. The Dutch presence in the sugar-producing areas south of the Amazon River lasted until the 1640s, when Portugal reestablished its independence from Spain, which enabled the Portuguese to drive out the Dutch. The Dutch were able to hold onto Dutch Guiana (present-day Surinam), and they retained a number of islands in the Caribbean. Their brief tenure as colonizers of New York was ended by the British in 1624.

**WORLD ISSUES**

Population

**GEOGRAPHY**

Environment
and Society

GLOBAL
CONCEPTS

Identity

CONCEPTS
GLOBAL

GLOBAL
CONCEPTS

Diversity

CONCEPTS
GLOBAL

**Places and Regions**

**Human Systems**

During the 1500s, besides laying claims to parts of North America (Canada), the French sought to establish a presence in the Caribbean and South America. Attempts to gain a foothold in Brazil were defeated by the Portuguese in the mid-1500s. Settlements on the north coast of South America in French Guiana began in 1604. Control of this territory shifted back and forth among the French, Dutch, Portuguese, and British. Martinique and Guadeloupe in the French West Indies were settled and colonized beginning in 1635 and became valuable sugar producers. Haiti was ceded by Spain to France in 1697. This western region of the island of Hispaniola became France's most prosperous colony in the Americas. The establishment of a plantation economy, based on slave labor and restrictive mercantilist trade policies, was promoted by the French crown.

Besides the settlements along the eastern coast of North America, the British were also able to establish themselves throughout the Caribbean. Jamaica, Barbados, and Trinidad-Tobago were their principal possessions in what became the British West Indies in the late 1600s. As elsewhere in the Caribbean, large numbers of African slaves were brought in to provide labor for the sugar-cane plantations in the British West Indies. The first English settlements of South America, in present-day Guyana, began in the 1600s.

**WORLD ISSUES**

Economic Development

**GEOGRAPHY**

**Physical Settings**

The English, French, and Dutch colonies in the Caribbean basin all developed a highly profitable sugar-cane-plantation economy, utilizing imported African slave labor. The colonies were controlled by trading policies that favored the "mother" country. The European colonial powers exploited the resources of the Caribbean Islands to further their own economic development.

## Movement Toward Independence in Latin America in the 1770s

GLOBAL CONCEPTS

**Change**

CONCEPTS GLOBAL

**WORLD ISSUES**

Determination of Political and Economic Systems

The 1700s was a period of great political, social, and economic change for the European powers. Britain's thirteen colonies in North America won their independence as a result of the American Revolution. In the late 1700s the French Revolution shook the stability of Europe. The writings of the Enlightenment, expressed in the works of Locke, Rousseau, Voltaire, Montesquieu, and others, led to the spread of revolutionary ideas in Europe and the Americas. In the 1700s Spain sought to reform its American empire. New viceroyalties were created, and an intendancy system was introduced to increase revenues and improve the colonial administration. A Spanish officer appointed by the crown, an *intendente*, had complete control in matters of justice, war, fiscal problems, and general public administration over a given area. Despite these reforms, the foreign policy of Spain's Bourbon monarchy, which allied the nation with France, led to a series of military engagements that greatly weakened the Spanish empire. Spain's economic situation and military power continued to decline into the 1790s.

## *Slavery and the Slave Trade in Africa*

Slavery has existed in the world since the development of civilization. It existed in ancient Greece, Rome, and China as well as Africa long before the arrival of the Europeans. However, slavery in Africa was quite different from the slavery that developed later, especially in the Americas. Slaves were captives taken in warfare or criminals and debtors. Slavery was not necessarily hereditary, and it was not seen as total ownership of another human being. Slaves had certain rights and might even be allowed to purchase freedom and own property. The slave trade also existed in Africa before the Europeans arrived. Arabs captured slaves or took them in exchange for other goods and sold them in India, Egypt, Persia, and other places.

The first African slaves to be transported to Europe were taken by the Portuguese in the 15th century. There was no great need for slaves in Europe, however, and they did not become an important item of trade until after the development of plantation agriculture in the Caribbean and North America. In order to raise sugar and tobacco on large plantations, many workers were needed. The native peoples of America did not survive the labor. Indentured servants eventually gained their freedom. Africans, accustomed to hard labor in the tropics, seemed a suitable replacement, and the slave trade increased greatly by the mid-16th century. The Europeans were involved in the highly destructive slave trade from the 16th to the 19th centuries, and their primary interest in Africa was in acquiring slaves.

A triangular trade developed. Cheap European goods, usually cloth and trinkets, were shipped from Europe to Africa (the outward passage), where they were traded for African captives. The Africans were transported to the Americas (the middle passage), where they were traded for sugar and tobacco. These were transported back to Europe (the inward passage), where they could be sold for considerable profit. The profits from this triangular trade in large part provided the capital investment that made the Industrial Revolution in England and America possible. For the most part, the Europeans did not go into the interior and take their own captives. They established stockades (slave factories) in the coastal regions and purchased captives

GLOBAL CONCEPTS
**Human Rights**
CONCEPTS GLOBAL

**GEOGRAPHY**
Environment and Society

GLOBAL CONCEPTS
**Interdependence**
CONCEPTS GLOBAL

**GEOGRAPHY**

Spatial Terms

from the Africans or from Arab slave raiders. However, to provide the vast numbers of captives the slave traders demanded, it became necessary to raid other villages and groups, and this required guns. As a result, one of the most important articles of trade to the Africans became guns.

**•Effects of the Slave Trade.** African societies suffered profound negative effects as a result of this buying and selling of human beings as chattel.

1. *Depopulation.* An estimate of the number of Africans lost to the slave trade probably approaches 50 million. Many were killed in tribal warfare. Many died of disease in overpacked slave ships.

2. *Increased tribal warfare.* Villages and crops were destroyed in the warfare to provide captives for the slave trade. Bitterness among Africans themselves developed that still affects relations between ethnic groups in the modern African nations.

3. *Insecurity and fear.* Africans fearing the slave raids sometimes abandoned their villages and moved farther into the interior. Others lived in a constant state of fear, more interested in avoiding capture than in the development of their own society. Arts and crafts declined.

4. *Economic disruption and decay.* Some African states abandoned their traditional ways of making a living and took part in the slave trade. While the slave trade lasted, they were wealthy and powerful, but when it ended, their economies were ruined and the states disappeared. Benin is an example.

5. *The trans-Saharan trade was destroyed.* Because of the huge profits in the slave trade, the trans-Saharan routes of trade lost importance, and the kingdoms in the interior of West Africa declined.

6. *Racism.* To justify the slave trade, those involved nurtured the belief that black Africans, because of their color, were inferior. This belief was accepted by Europeans and Americans, who knew nothing of Africa and its cultures. The resulting prejudice and bias were later used to excuse the imperialist expansion of European nations into African territories.

## The British in South Asia: Roots of the Raj (1600–1757)

The British involvement in India, an example of imperialism, grew from economic contact to direct political control. Britain was able to outmaneuver its European rivals, especially the French, build alliances with some Indian rulers, and inflict military defeat on other rulers.

**The British East India Company.** Granted a charter from Queen Elizabeth I in 1600, the British East India Company received permission from the Mughals to trade in India as early as 1613. From this time until 1858, the company exercised powers usually associated with a government. It had, for example, its own private army. One of its employees, Robert Clive, led military forces to victories over both French and native Indian armies. As a result of the most important of these victories, at Plassey in 1757, the British became the dominant economic and unofficial political power in the subcontinent.

## The Early Colonial Period in Southeast Asia (1500–1700)

When the Portuguese took control of the Strait of Malacca in 1511 and the Spanish landed at Cebu Island (part of the present-day Philippines) in 1521, the period of European colonialism began. Eventually, other nations—England, France, and the Netherlands in particular—established colonies in Southeast Asia. With the exception of the present-day nation of Thailand (formerly Siam), every part of the region was colonized at one point in its history.

What were the main reasons for colonialism? European nations were interested in the spices from the region. The aim of Christopher Columbus in 1492 was to reach the "spice islands" in the "Indies." In later years, European interest in the area was focused on its mineral deposits, its agricultural products, and political control of territory.

From the pioneering voyage of Vasco de Gama (1497–1499), the Portuguese enjoyed primacy of position in the lucrative spice trade between the East Indies to Europe as well as trade with India and coastal Africa. Their string of ports controlled key navigation routes—the Cape of Good Hope at the tip of Africa, key harbors on the Indian coast, and the vital Strait of Malacca, the western entryway to the waters of South and East Asia. Spanish conquest of the Philippines (1564–1571) gave them control of the trans-Pacific trade. Each year the "Manila Galleons" followed the prevailing winds from the Asian islands to Mexico and back carrying tons of gold, silver, and fine Chinese silk, in great demand by the aristocracy of Europe. A highly profitable 1599 Dutch trading expedition to the Indies led, in 1602, to the formation of the Dutch East India Company. Their fleets sailed directly across the Indian Ocean, bypassing Portuguese coastal trading stations. By the 1620s, the Dutch had gained control of the Cape of Good Hope at the southern tip of Africa and the island of Ceylon (Sri Lanka) southeast of India

GLOBAL CONCEPTS
**Power**
CONCEPTS GLOBAL

**WORLD ISSUES**
Determination of Political and Economic Systems

GLOBAL CONCEPTS
**Power**
CONCEPTS GLOBAL

**GEOGRAPHY**

**Places and Regions**

GLOBAL
CONCEPTS
**Power**

CONCEPTS
GLOBAL

and had wrested dominance of the spice trade from the Portuguese. They negotiated lucrative commercial concessions from East Indian rulers in exchange for aid in local disputes, and the Dutch supported them against the Portuguese. Other mutual aid agreements, annexations, and military conquest made the Dutch masters of the vast archipelago of resource-rich islands between the Asian mainland and Australia, a mastery they maintained until the middle of the 20th century.

# Part H: The Rise of Nation-States: Royal Power and Absolutism

Besides the profound cultural (Renaissance), religious (Reformation), and economic (commercial revolution and exploration) changes that took place in Europe between the late 1400s and early 1700s, a series of great political changes also took place. The changes involved the creation of nation-states with strong monarchs and centralized governments in England, France, and Spain. The term nation-state refers to a specific area of land with fixed boundaries, united under the rule of a central government. The people in a nation-state are usually united by many common factors, such as language, religion, race, and culture.

GLOBAL CONCEPTS
**Change**
CONCEPTS GLOBAL

**Physical Settings**

The growth of nation-states in Western Europe began as feudalism declined. England and France had developed into highly centralized nation-states by 1500. Spain, only recently unified politically, rapidly and aggressively consolidated royal power, using the influence of the Catholic Church. Their governments were under the leadership of strong rulers, who often reigned as absolute monarchs, that is, the king or queen had complete or absolute rule over the nation and its subjects. Such monarchs are also called autocrats, and their governments are referred to as autocracies.

GLOBAL CONCEPTS
**Political Systems**
CONCEPTS GLOBAL

In Central and Eastern Europe, ethnic and cultural diversity impeded the development of nation-states based on commonalities of language and tradition. The shifting boundaries of the Holy Roman Empire and the widespread holdings of the Habsburg dynasty created more loosely knit political units resistant to centralization. In addition, the power of the landowning nobility in these areas had been reasserted at the expense of both monarchs and the urban middle class. Unlike the west where the peasantry had maintained the social and economic gains of the late Middle Ages, eastern peasants succumbed to the concerted efforts of landowners to reestablish serfdom.

GLOBAL CONCEPTS
**Diversity**
CONCEPTS GLOBAL

# Spanish Unification and the "Golden Century"

**Places and Regions**

**Unification and Inquisition.** Events on the Iberian Peninsula in the late 15th century stimulated the Spanish in their efforts to develop politically and economically. The area was a patchwork of separate kingdoms, disunited, and extremely diverse in language, culture, and religion. Once dominated by Muslims, conquerors of the area in the 8th century, the Catholic rulers of the north had since been engaged in a *reconquista*, a campaign to reconquer the peninsula for Christianity.

Two factors ultimately crowned the success of this campaign. In 1469, the marriage of King Ferdinand of Aragon and Queen Isabella of Castile united the two dominant kingdoms and created a loose confederation of all the Christian areas except Portugal—conflict elsewhere enabled it to maintain its independence and even expand. When the Pope (a Spaniard himself) granted "Their Catholic Majesties" great power in religious decisions, the stage was set to turn Spain into a rigid Catholic society.

GLOBAL
CONCEPTS

**Power**

CONCEPTS
GLOBAL

This "purification" had two thrusts. Spain had not expelled its Jews in medieval fits of anti-semitism as had England and France; in fact many Jews and former Jews had attained positions of power and wealth. Now, however, religious orthodoxy required their conversion or expulsion. The Inquisition, a ruthless campaign of force and torture, accomplished this. In 1492, Spanish armies conquered the last Muslim kingdom, and through force, terror, and religious dogmatism, Spain was united and on the verge of an era of great power and glory.

Another royal marriage raised Spanish royal power to new heights; the daughter of Ferdinand and Isabella wed the heir to the throne of the Holy Roman Empire, which dominated Central Europe from the North Sea to the Mediterranean. Their son, the Holy Roman Emperor Charles V, ruled directly over a vast empire that included the Netherlands, Southern Italy, and Spain, and all its colonial possessions in Asia and the Americas as well as the Holy Roman Empire itself. Charles was more a Northerner than a Spaniard, using the vast revenues of the colonies to combat the spread of Protestantism in northern Germany. Thus for the first half of the 16th century, Spain became deeply enmeshed in the international political and religious affairs of Europe.

**Places and Regions**

Upon his abdication in 1556, Charles divided his realm between his younger brother, Ferdinand, and his son, Philip. Spain, its colonies, and the lands in Italy and the Netherlands went to the devoutly Catholic Philip II. In the tradition of the reconquista and his father, Philip, too, responded to the call of the Pope and expended great finances and energy against the enemies of Catholicism, renewing the Inquisition and brutally opposing a Protestant and middle class rebellion in the Netherlands. His merchant galleons dominated trade on the high seas, and his navy decisively helped blunt the thrust of the Ottoman Empire in the eastern Mediterranean at the Battle of Lepanto in 1571.

Spain under Philip and his predecessors and heirs used its wealth to patronize a flowering in art and literature as well. Miguel de Cervantes' *Don Quixote* is regarded by some as the birth of the modern novel, and the paintings of Diego Velasquez glorified the power of the Spanish royal family. El Greco's austere and supernatural works depicted the deep and abiding Catholicism of Spain and its ascetic monarch.

GLOBAL
CONCEPTS
**Culture**
CONCEPTS
GLOBAL

It was ultimately Philip's boundless and dogmatic faith that contributed in a major way to the eclipse of Spain's dominance. In 1588 he launched the Grand Armada in an attempt to curb the power of the Protestant Queen Elizabeth of England as she had provided support for the Dutch. The defeat of this huge fleet by the English navy and unfavorable weather conditions was added to growing financial difficulties. High taxes, a lack of business investments, and huge loans used to finance religious wars contributed to Spain's decline as the preeminent European power after Philip's death in 1588.

## England—Absolutism with Limits

William the Conqueror, the Duke of Normandy in France, crossed the English Channel with his Norman army and invaded England. After his victory in the Battle of Hastings in 1066, he was crowned king of England, and he ruled as a strong monarch. To determine the population and wealth of England, he carried out a survey. The result was a list of all the property in England called the Domesday Book. William introduced feudalism in England, but he made all the feudal lords and knights take the Salisbury Oath in which they promised allegiance to him. William's successors gained additional strength, uniting England under their control. At the same time, however, the other great feudal aristocrats and the urban merchants used their influence to preserve or gain a share in government. The Magna Carta of 1215 guaranteed rights to the nobility, which were later extended to other groups. In 1295, Edward I, in need of tax revenue to finance a war in France, called nobles and merchants together to ask their support. This Model Parliament established a pattern of representative government in which the ruler shared authority.

**GEOGRAPHY**

**Physical Settings**

**WORLD ISSUES**

Determination
of Political
and Economic
Systems

The Hundred Years War (1337–1453) fought between England and France, increased royal power and English unity. Although the British lost their territories in France, they increased their feelings of loyalty to their kings and their homeland. During the period of Tudor rule (1485–1603), two monarchs became very popular as they expanded royal power and the nation's prosperity. Henry VIII (1509–1547) defied the pope and helped establish the Anglican Church. His daughter, Queen Elizabeth I (1558–1603), defeated the Spanish Armada and encouraged the growth of the British navy and overseas exploration.

Although the Tudor monarchs were powerful, they could not be called absolute rulers. Limitations on their power had been set by the Magna Carta and the British Parliament. However, in the 17th century, the Stuart rulers who succeeded the Tudors attempted to assert absolute authority and disregarded the traditional limitations on a monarch's powers.

## France—"L'étât C'est Moi" (The King Is the State)

After the Hundred Years War, royal power in France became more centralized. Louis XI (1461–1483) increased his power by decreasing the power of the feudal lords, taking their lands and thereby laying the foundation for a strong monarchy. The rulers of France in the 1500s continued to centralize authority in the crown. Henry IV (1589–1610), the first Bourbon ruler, ended the religious strife and civil wars between French Protestants and Catholics. A Protestant, he adopted Catholicism to avoid bloodshed and issued the Edict of Nantes in 1598, which granted a measure of religious freedom to French Protestants, who were called Huguenots. Henry and other members of the Bourbon family ruled France until the Revolution of 1789.

Louis XIII, Henry's son, made Cardinal Richelieu his adviser and chief minister. From 1624 to 1642, Richelieu laid the foundations for a strong French monarchy by weakening the nobles and increasing taxes, which added to royal wealth. Richelieu made the monarchy absolute within France, and his foreign policy made France the strongest power in Europe.

By the mid-1600s King Louis XIV (1643–1715), who was known as the Sun King, ruled as an absolute monarch. Examples of his form of absolutism were:

1. He believed in the divine right theory of government, which held that a monarch's power came from God and that the monarch was accountable not to the people he ruled but only to God.

GLOBAL CONCEPTS
Power
CONCEPTS GLOBAL

GLOBAL CONCEPTS
Power
CONCEPTS GLOBAL

2. He used his wealth for his own benefit rather than for the people. The great palace at Versailles, near Paris, was built at his direction. The construction of the palace seemed to support his statement: "L'étât, c'est moi" (I am the state). '

3. He never summoned the Estates-General, a law-making body, to meet.

4. He led France into many wars, hoping to gain territory. Few of these were successful, and their major result was to increase the dissatisfaction of the French people because of many deaths and high taxes.

5. His control over the French economy was aided by the actions of his finance minister, Jean Colbert.

6. He promoted artistic and musical works to glorify his rule, and he made France the cultural center of Europe. These activities also increased the spirit of French nationalism.

7. He revoked the Edict of Nantes, which was a blow to religious freedom and forced many Huguenots to leave France.

The absolutism in England and France eventually sparked strong political reactions and resulted in important democratic developments.

GEOGRAPHY

Physical Settings

WORLD ISSUES

Determination
of Political
and Economic
Systems

## England—Stuart Absolutism and Its Downfall in the 17th Century

Following Queen Elizabeth I were the rulers of the Stuart Dynasty (1603–1649), James I and Charles I. They ruled as absolute monarchs, believing they should have no limits set on their power. The Stuart rulers did not respect previous democratic traditions and preferred to rule by divine right. They came into conflict with Parliament because they disregarded it in raising money, imprisoned people unfairly, and persecuted Puritans (English Protestants who wanted a simple "pure" style of Christianity). However, the underlying conflict was the question of where power would be centered—in the monarchy or in the Parliament. In 1628, in exchange for its granting more revenues, Parliament made Charles I agree to the Petition of Right (see chart on the development of democracy, page 342), which limited the power of the monarch. As soon as he received the money, Charles dissolved Parliament and ruled for eleven years (1629–1640) without Parliament. Ignoring the Petition of Right, Charles appointed special royal courts, such as the Court of Star Chamber, to try individuals who disagreed with him, particularly Puritans. These royal courts ignored the traditional common law.

In 1640, when Scottish rebels invaded England, Charles was forced to call Parliament into session. Led by Puritans, this Parliament, which sat from 1640 to 1660, is known as the Long

GLOBAL
CONCEPTS
**Power**
CONCEPTS
GLOBAL

GEOGRAPHY

Physical Settings

WORLD ISSUES

Human
Rights

Parliament, and it changed English history by limiting the absolute powers of the monarchy. In 1641 Parliament denied Charles's request for money to raise an army to fight the Irish rebellion. In response, Charles led troops into the House of Commons to arrest some of its Puritan members. The attempt by Charles to arrest members of Parliament sparked the beginning of a civil war, as Parliament soon raised an army to fight the king.

### DEVELOPMENT OF DEMOCRACY IN ENGLAND

| Democratic Achievements | Their Importance |
| --- | --- |
| Petition of Right, 1628 | Parliament's consent needed for taxes; the king could not imprison someone without a trial or quarter soldiers in someone's home without permission. |
| Habeas Corpus Act, 1679 | An arrested person has the right to know the charges against him, to be brought before a judge, and to be given a fair and impartial chance to defend himself. |
| Bill of Rights, 1689 | Strictly limited the power of the monarch in such matters as levying taxes, maintaining an army, and interfering in the affairs of Parliament; basic civil liberties are guaranteed to the people, such as a speedy trial and protection from cruel and unusual punishment and from excessive fines and bail. |
| Toleration Act, 1689 | Freedom of worship permitted for all Protestant religions. |
| Political parties | Two political groups arose in Parliament, each having members with common backgrounds, interests, and goals. They competed peacefully with each other for control of Parliament and became known as political parties. They were the Tories (later called Conservatives) and Whigs (later called Liberals). Political parties are an example of freedom of expression and give voters a chance to choose between different candidates and policies. |
| Cabinet system | The Cabinet consisted of members of Parliament who became advisers, or ministers, to William and Mary. These ministers eventually came from the majority party, with the leader becoming the prime minister. Over the years, their power increased because they were chosen from the elected officials in Parliament. The monarch became just a figurehead—a symbol of the nation, with the power to reign but not to rule. |

**The English Civil War (1642–1645).** This conflict, which lasted from 1642 to 1645, was between the supporters of King Charles, called the Cavaliers, and the supporters of Parliament, called the Roundheads. The Parliamentary forces emerged victorious under the leadership of Oliver Cromwell, a Puritan.

**The Puritan Revolution (1642–1660).** This period included the Civil War and the rule by Oliver Cromwell, which began in 1649. Under Cromwell's leadership, the Parliament voted to abolish the monarchy, and Charles I was tried and beheaded in 1649. England was now a republic or, as it called itself, a commonwealth. However, in 1653, supported by his army, Cromwell took the title of Lord Protector and ruled as a military dictator. His dictatorial policies, which included religious intolerance, strict moral codes, and violence against the Irish, caused resentment. Soon after his death, Parliament invited Charles II, the exiled son of Charles I, to take the throne.

**The Stuart Restoration (1660–1688).** Aware of English democratic traditions and the fate of his father, Charles II was careful not to anger Parliament. He acknowledged the rights of the people established by the Magna Carta and the Petition of Right. In 1679, he agreed to the Habeas Corpus Act. (See the chart on the development of democracy, page 342.) On his death in 1685, his brother James II became king. James angered Parliament because of his pro-Catholic actions and his claim to divine right rule. Parliament invited James's older daughter, Mary, and her husband, William of Orange, a Dutch prince who was Protestant, to take the throne.

**The Glorious Revolution (1688–1689).** William and Mary accepted Parliament's offer and arrived in England with an army. They were proclaimed king and queen, as James II fled to France. As a result of this bloodless revolution, which is known as the Glorious Revolution, Parliament gained in power and prestige. To protect its newly won supremacy over the monarchy, Parliament passed a Bill of Rights that was signed by William and Mary in 1689. (See the chart on the development of democracy, page 342.) With the support of an army supplied by the Catholic king of France, James invaded Ireland, hoping to regain the English throne. A force under William defeated this "Jacobite" army at the Battle of the Boyne, ending the threat of the English crown reverting to Catholicism. Thus, by the end of the 17th century, England had become a limited, or constitutional, monarchy, the first in Europe. All the major decisions were

WORLD ISSUES

Human
Rights

GLOBAL
CONCEPTS

Change

CONCEPTS
GLOBAL

WORLD ISSUES

Determination
of Political
and Economic
Systems

made by Parliament, and the ruler's actions were limited by Parliament. Key steps in this development as well as other democratic advances up to the year 1800 are in the chart entitled "Development of Democracy in England," page 342.

**Impact of the Growth of Democracy in England.** The growth of democracy in England had worldwide influence.

1. The democratic advances in England influenced political revolutions in the British colonies in North America (1776) and in France (1789). These ideas also influenced the emergence of some democratic nations from imperialism in the 20th century (India, 1947). A major factor in the American Revolution was the emphasis by colonists on their rights as English subjects. Indeed, many democratic ideas and practices developed in England were included in American documents, such as the original Constitution and the first ten amendments, called the Bill of Rights.

2. The writings of John Locke, a 17th-century English philosopher, were a source of democratic ideas. They influenced the American colonists and had a direct impact on the writing of the American Declaration of Independence. Locke's ideas also influenced the leaders of the French Revolution. Locke believed that governments get their power from the consent of the governed (the people) and that the people have the right to change the government when the government abuses its power. For Locke, the chief purpose of any government was to protect the rights of the people. His idea of a social contract concerned an exchange of rights and responsibilities between a government and its citizens. Locke's chief work was *Two Treatises on Civil Government*.

GLOBAL CONCEPTS

**Political Systems**

CONCEPTS GLOBAL

## Middle Class Democracy: The Netherlands (1520–1600)

**WORLD ISSUES**

Determination of Political and Economic Systems

**GEOGRAPHY**

**Places and Regions**

The Netherlands, focal point of Europe's commercial revolution and center of its trade patterns, rejected absolutism completely. Back to the days of the Hanseatic League, each of the seventeen provinces of this area had acquired and preserved a degree of independence from monarchs and even their representative body, the Estates-General. Textiles, shipping, and banking provided the financial power behind these "liberties," and the work ethic of the merchant class furnished the motivation.

A new factor was added early in the 16th century: The rise of Protestantism, especially the reformed or Calvinist version. This set of beliefs appealed to the region's dominant middle class, already predisposed to supporting the idea that effort and hard work were the source of their God-given success. Added to the growing disgust with corruption and abuse of power in the Catholic Church, these factors created a situation ripe for revolution.

It came with the accession of Philip II of Spain to the Habsburg throne in 1556—his dominions included the Netherlands. A devout and some would say dogmatic Roman Catholic, Philip was determined to eradicate Protestantism and raise taxes for governing the provinces. In response, working class Protestants rampaged through Catholic churches, destroying statues, images, stained glass windows—anything that represented the idolatry of the "unpurified" church. Born of the same Puritanism that would later spark the revolution in England, these actions prompted Philip to attempt a military solution. Over a decade of fierce and brutal conflict resulted in a partition of the Low Countries. The southern region had remained in Spanish hands and therefore Catholic—this area became Belgium.

The northern provinces, however, resisted successfully and in 1581 declared their independence, forming the United Provinces of the Netherlands. With continued resistance and an alliance with England, the United Provinces gained recognition of their status from the Spanish crown in 1609. Even so, it was not until the Peace of Westphalia (1648), ending the Thirty Years War, that Dutch independence was confirmed.

Dutch political and economic success was grounded in hardheaded practicality and a fierce sense of independence. The government of the United Provinces was unique in Europe, a republic dominated by prosperous middle class merchants who valued thrift, diligence, and simplicity. It was unique, too, because toleration became a cornerstone of Dutch political and economic practice. In a practical sense, toleration attracted investors of all faiths and backgrounds, and the Netherlands profited greatly from this. They also benefited greatly from dominating trade from a neutral status when other European powers were expending finances and resources for warfare on the continent and in overseas colonies.

**GEOGRAPHY**

**Places and Regions**

**WORLD ISSUES**

Determination of Political and Economic Systems

## German Absolutism: Austria and Prussia (1600–1740)

Even though absolutism developed later in Eastern Europe, it proved more enduring, resisting democratic and Enlightenment ideas more rigorously right down to the First World War. German autocracy was derived from a combination of factors unique to the region:

1. Pressure from invaders. Even though the Austrian Habsburgs successfully resisted the Ottoman attacks on Vienna in

1529 and 1683, a constant state of military readiness created a need for unity and support.

2. Constant agitation by and competition from minority ethnic groups.

3. Political competition and warfare among the numerous rulers and political units left over from the feudal period.

4. The Thirty Years War, pitting Protestant rulers against Catholic ones in the German states and weakening the aristocratic soldier classes and the representative groups (Estates) through which they had exercised some limitations on monarchs, increasing royal power.

5. Canny rulers gaining the support of landowning groups, by allowing the reimposition of serfdom.

Thus rulers acquired three advantages in their quest to establish absolute monarchies—the power of taxation without aristocratic consent, the command of large standing armies, and the power to conduct diplomatic affairs with other nations based on their own decisions.

**Austria and the Habsburg Dynasty.** Weakened by the religious strife in the north during the early 17th century, Austrian rulers of the Holy Roman Empire focused on their lands to the east and south. Ferdinand II (1619–1637) put down a revolt in Bohemia by Czech nobles, redistributed their land, and stamped out Protestantism in the area. Ferdinand III centralized government administration in Austria itself and created a standing army for both defense and domestic control. When the Ottoman siege of Vienna failed in 1683, the Habsburgs, with Russian and other allies, pushed the Turks back and by 1699 controlled Hungary and a large part of Romania.

Complete autocratic centralization was never possible, however, in part because of the vigorous independence of the Hungarian nobility and the lack of a unifying language and culture. Charles VI attempted to guarantee the unity of the three Habsburg realms (Bohemia, Austria, and Hungary) proclaiming in the Pragmatic Sanction (1713) that they should never be divided. The Estates of the three areas, particularly Hungary, continued to strive for influence and resist the power of the crown.

**Hohenzollerns and the Ascendance of Prussia.** How did a small, landlocked, and relatively unproductive north German kingdom become the core of a militant and powerful empire? The tiny state of Brandenburg, overrun by Swedish and Habsburg armies during the Thirty Years War, and Prussia, tributary state to the King of Poland, were united in 1618 by the Hohen-zollern rulers. Formerly a bit player on the stage of the Holy Roman Empire, this dynasty's fortunes changed with the accession to the throne in 1640 of Frederick William, who came to be known as the Great Elector. Taking advantage of an aristocracy weakened by religious wars, and supported by a population tired of the depredations of the marauding armies of Sweden and Poland, he established a standing army and exacted taxes to pay for it.

By his death in 1688, Frederick William had consolidated his widely separated lands into a viable, but still small and weak German-speaking kingdom. It was left to his near-namesake, King Frederick William I (1713–1740) to imbue this new nation-state with an element of his own concept of political power as a function of military might. His strong centralized bureaucracy, coupled with the size and strength of his army precluded significant opposition. He overcame opposition from the great landowning aristocracy of Prussia, the Junkers, by co-opting them into the officer corps, giving them military as well as economic power over other groups in the society. By 1740, Prussia, which ranked twelfth in population, had Europe's fourth largest army—only those of France, Austria, and Russia were larger.

The "Sparta of the North," as some historians have called it, became a militaristic society where obedience became the primary virtue of the ordinary citizen as well as of the officer or soldier. The precision, skill, and discipline of the Prussian military became the envy of others, and for the next two centuries Prussian arms nearly always prevailed when put to the test of battle.

## Absolutism and Autocracy in Russia

The vast northern forests and southern steppes (grasslands) of Eastern Europe had for centuries been the home of people of Slavic cultural background. Invasions by Vikings from the north and conquest by Mongols from the east had seen the rise and then destruction of a kingdom at Kiev (in the modern Ukraine). But Mongol rule had unified the diverse Slavic peoples of the area administratively and in eventual militant opposition to their Asian overlords.

**The Rise of Moscow (1450–1685).** The princes of Moscow emerged from a period of war and political maneuvering to claim preeminent power. When the Byzantine Empire fell to

GEOGRAPHY

Physical Settings

GLOBAL CONCEPTS

Power

CONCEPTS GLOBAL

GLOBAL CONCEPTS

Environment

CONCEPTS GLOBAL

GEOGRAPHY

Use of Geography

the Ottoman Turks in 1453 with the capture of Constantinople, Prince Ivan III declared Moscow to be the "Third Rome," or the center of the Eastern Orthodox Church. (Constantinople had taken the title of "Second Rome" after the original capital of the Roman Empire was overrun by Germanic tribes in 476.) Moscow's position as the new headquarters of the Church after the fall of Kiev contributed greatly to its rise to prominence. The support of the Russian Patriarch enhanced Moscow's image as the leading city of Russia. In 1462 Ivan married Sophia Paleologos, niece of the last Byzantine emperor, and adopted her family's symbol (the double-headed eagle), declaring himself tsar (czar), or "Caesar" (emperor), of all the Russias. From Ivan III's reign (1462–1505) until the fall of the monarchy in 1917, Russia's tsars considered themselves the defenders of the Orthodox Church.

GLOBAL
CONCEPTS
**Power**
CONCEPTS
GLOBAL

Under Tsar Ivan IV (1533–1584), often referred to as "the Terrible," Russia's government became centralized. Often using brutal and ruthless force, Ivan ended the independent authority of local princes and boyars (nobles), making the aristocracy subservient to an autocratic central monarchy. He also created a new service nobility that was loyal only to the tsar. By the year of his death, Ivan had extended Moscow's control over most of Russian land formerly controlled by the Mongols.

Ivan's weak successor, Theodor, died without an heir in 1598, ending the dynasty known as the House of Rurik and beginning a period of anarchy known as the time of troubles. This ended in 1613 with the selection by the Zemskii Sobor (Council of Nobles) of a new tsar, Mikhail (or Michael) Romanov, and the establishment of a new dynasty. Under the early Romanovs, the power of the monarchy grew even stronger, while Russia's borders (particularly in Ukraine) were expanded.

### Peter the Great and Westernization (1685–1725).

GLOBAL
CONCEPTS
**Change**
CONCEPTS
GLOBAL

**Use of Geography**

Under Piotr, or Peter I, usually referred to as "the Great," Russia underwent important changes. Following a policy of Westernization in order to modernize his nation, Peter forced the nobility and upper classes to imitate their counterparts in Western Europe socially and culturally. A Western European-style bourgeoisie (urban middle class) was also created. An enormous civil service and government bureaucracy that drew from both the upper and middle classes was established. Peter encouraged the development of new industries and the importation of Westerners to train Russians. A new capital city, St. Petersburg, was built on the Baltic Sea. Known as the "Window to the West," St. Petersburg was modeled after Western European cities. The Patriarchate was abolished and replaced with the Synod (Council) of Bishops under the control of a Procurator (one of the tsar's ministers). The education system, once administered by the Church, was also taken over by the state. The army was modernized, the latest weapons technology imported, and a navy was created. Under Peter, Russia expanded westward to the Baltic and southeast to the Black Sea. For the first time in history, the nation of Russia was no longer landlocked, although both water routes were limited. Even though most of the population were peasants and remained unaffected by the Petrine Reforms, Russia was transformed into a modern world power.

# REVIEW QUESTIONS

*Multiple Choice.* Select the letter of the answer that correctly completes the statement.

Base your answer to the next question on the following quote:

**"His subjects had no redress against the injuries he did them, for in theory he was answerable for his acts to God alone."**

1. The quotation best describes which type of government?
   A. limited monarchy
   B. direct democracy
   C. absolute monarchy
   D. oligarchy

2. Which was an important result of the commercial revolution in Europe?
   A. domination of European trade by Italian city-states
   B. emergence of the peasant class into positions of political and social power
   C. rise in the political and economic importance of the middle class
   D. support of free public education

Base your answer to the next question on the following quote:

**"Yesterday, your Ambassador petitioned my Ministers regarding your trade with China. . . . Our Celestial Empire possesses all things in great abundance and lacks no product within its own borders. There is, therefore, no need to import any product manufactured by outside barbarians in exchange for our own goods."**
   —Emperor Ch'ien Lung of China to King George of England

3. In the view of the Emperor, which foreign policy action was in the best interest of China?
   A. maintaining economic isolation
   B. expanding foreign trade
   C. increasing international interdependence
   D. developing into a colonial power

4. The concept of mercantilism is best illustrated by the
   A. political structure of China during the Ming Dynasty
   B. social kinship system of the people of the Songhai Empire
   C. military strategies of the armies of Prussia
   D. economic relationship between Spain and its Latin American colonies

5. West African kingdoms, such as Mali and Songhai, based their economic systems primarily on
   A. exporting slaves
   B. agriculture and trade
   C. commercial fishing
   D. hunting and gathering

6. Peter the Great changed Russia by
   A. abolishing all social class distinctions
   B. becoming a constitutional monarch
   C. preventing wars with neighboring nations
   D. introducing Western ideas and customs

7. Which effect did the Mughals have on India during their rule?
   A. Parliamentary republics were established.
   B. India became unified under one language.
   C. Muslim culture dominated in parts of India.
   D. Hinduism became the dominant religion in northern India.

8. The Magna Carta and English Bill of Rights are documents that
   A. limited the power of the monarch
   B. established England as an independent state
   C. intensified the conflict between church and state
   D. decreased the wealth of the nobles

9. Which is an accurate statement about the history of slavery in Africa?
   A. African kingdoms had abolished slavery but the Europeans reintroduced it.
   B. Slave trading affected east Africa but not west Africa.
   C. The European slave trade destroyed the stability of many African societies.
   D. Only Europeans engaged in slave trade.

10. A problem faced by the rulers of the Austro-Hungarian Ottoman Empires was the
   A. effect of urbanization of a rural population
   B. monopoly of the traditional church
   C. inability to produce modern weapons
   D. tensions among many different groups

# THEMATIC ESSAYS

### Essay #1 Theme: The Rise of Absolute Monarchies
Absolute monarchies were based on the idea that human political and social leadership was based on "divine right" or the "mandate of heaven."

**Task:**
1. Define the idea of absolute monarchy.
2. Select two different monarchs and, for each, demonstrate the extent to which he or she was able to exert absolute power.

**Directions:** Write a well-organized essay with an introduction stating the topic, a body that accomplishes the task, and a summarizing conclusion.

*Hint:* You may choose any two monarchs, including, but not limited to those from Western Europe (England, France and Spain) or Eastern Europe (Russia, Prussia, Austria-Hungary), the Middle East (Ottomans, Safavids), South Asia (Mughals), or East Asia (Ming, Manchus).

### Essay #2 Theme: The Growth of Multiregional Empires
Empires develop when a society's economic and political power enable it to expand its control over large areas of land and diverse groups of people.

**Task:**
1. Define the term "empire."
2. Select two empires that flourished during the period 1450–1770 C.E. and discuss the impact of each on EITHER:
   - the society that created that empire;
     OR
   - the societies that were conquered/controlled by that empire.

**Directions:** Write a well-organized essay with an introduction stating the topic, a body that accomplishes the task, and a summarizing conclusion.

*Hint:* You may choose any two empires, including any from Western Europe, Eastern Europe, the Middle East, South Asia, or East Asia.

## DOCUMENT-BASED QUESTIONS:
## SKILL-BUILDING EXERCISES

**DOCUMENT**

Serenity pervades a Chinese garden of the Ming Dynasty (1368–1644), for this is a place of retreat from the doings of humankind. It is where the functionary of the kingdom could indulge his "longing for mountains and waters" without turning his back on his unrelenting obligations to state and family.

Originally designed by Taoist poets, classical gardens were meant to create an atmosphere of tranquility for contemplation and inspiration. A Chinese calligraphic inscription above the entrance to the garden (not shown) means "Garden of Ease."

What conclusion can you draw about the role of nature in the culture of Ming China?

_____

_____

_____

**DOCUMENT**

**DUTCH MERCHANTS GREET THE FIRST SHIP TO ARRIVE IN AMSTERDAM CARRYING SPICES FROM THE EAST INDIES (17TH CENTURY)**

What relationship might this event have to Europe's commercial revolution?

_____

_____

_____

**DOCUMENT**

## The Petition of Right 1628

"The Petition exhibited to his Majesty by the Lords . . ., and Commons, in this present Parliament assembled, concerning divers Rights and Liberties of the Subjects, . . .

To the King's Most Excellent Majesty (Charles I),

Article X. (We) do therefore humbly pray your most excellent Majesty, that no man hereafter be compelled to make or yield any gift, loan, benevolence, tax, or such like charge, without common consent by act of parliament; and that none be called to make answer, or take such oath, or to give attendance, or be confined, or otherwise molested or disquieted concerning the same or for refusal thereof; and that no freeman, in any such manner as is before mentioned, be imprisoned or detained;"

Discuss this document as a step in the development of English democracy.

_____

_____

_____

**DOCUMENT**

In *Two Treatises of Government* John Locke (English political philosopher 1632–1704) said that the state exists to preserve the natural rights of its citizens. Therefore, he said that if a government fails in that task, citizens should rebel against it. Locke thought that the state of nature (anarchy) was a happy and tolerant state. Perhaps most importantly, Locke introduced the system of *checks and balances*, which was later the foundation on which the U.S. government was founded.

How do Locke's ideas differ from those of the absolute ruler of his time?

_____

_____

_____

**DOCUMENT**

**Concerning cruelty and clemency, (kindness) and whether it is better to be loved than feared**

"Coming now to other qualities . . . , I say that every prince ought to desire to be considered clement (kind) and not cruel. Nevertheless he ought to take care not to misuse this clemency (kindness). (A) prince, so long as he keeps his subjects united and loyal, ought not to mind the reproach of cruelty; because with a few examples he will be more merciful than those who, through too much mercy, allow disorders to arise . . ."
—Nicolo Machiavelli (1513), *The Prince*

What might Machiavelli's views be regarding the idea of democracy?

_____

_____

_____

**DOCUMENT**

"Three hundred years ago Peter I of Russia made a visit to London. . . . Always eager to learn about Western ways, especially those that might help modernize Russia, the young Czar found much in England to admire. . . . "The English island is the best and most beautiful in the world" (Massie, p. 216). . .

Although he disliked the idea that anyone would be able to oppose a monarch, he professed to admire the candor displayed in Parliament; he is quoted as saying, however sincerely, " . . . it is good to hear subjects speaking truthfully and openly with their king. This is what we must learn from the English!" (Massie, p. 214)

355

When Peter returned to Russia, he was accompanied by dozens of Englishmen: most notably, engineers and mathematicians, as well as barbers who would soon be busy shaving the beards off of Russian nobles at the orders of the Czar!

Two other changes affected the lives of many more people. Peter reformed Russian coinage according to the English model, and he authorized an English tobacco concession in Russia, thereby increasing the market for tobacco—as well as the demand for slaves to work in the tobacco colonies of Maryland, Virginia, and North Carolina."

—Robert K. Massie (1980), *Peter the Great*

How did Peter the Great's visit to England affect both his own people and those of other parts of the world?

_____

_____

_____

## DOCUMENT

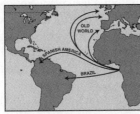

1451 to 1600

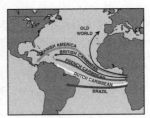

1601 to 1700

1701 to 1810

## THE TRANSATLANTIC SLAVE TRADE

Discuss the impact that this development would have had on Western Africa.

_____

_____

_____

**DOCUMENT**

During this same time, (Cortés) commanded that Motecuhzoma and Itzcohuatzin, the military chief of Tlatelolco, be made prisoners. The Spaniards hanged a chief from Acolhuacan . . . . They also murdered the king of Nauhtla, Cohualpopocatzin, by wounding him with arrows and then burning him alive.

The Spaniards attacked the musicians first, slashing at their hands and faces until they had killed all of them. The singers—and even the spectators—were also killed. This slaughter in the Sacred Patio went on for three hours. Then the Spaniards burst into the rooms of the temple to kill the others: those who were carrying water, or bringing fodder for the horses, or grinding meal, or sweeping, or standing watch over this work.

The king Motecuhzoma, . . . protested: "Our lords, that is enough! What are you doing? These people are not carrying (weapons). They are completely unarmed!"

—Miguel Leon-Portilla, ed. (1962), *The Broken Spears:*
*The Aztec Account of the Conquest of Mexico*

How might this account differ from one written by Cortes?

_____

_____

_____

**DOCUMENT**

**Sidi Ali Reis (Ottoman Turkish Admiral): *Mirat ul Memalik (The Mirror of Countries)*, 1557 C.E.**

(A)fter a journey of 20 days . . . in the capital of India, called Delhi. As soon as Humayun heard of our arrival he sent the Khanikhanan (Prime Minister) and other superior officers with 400 elephants and some thousand men to meet us, and, out of respect and regard for our glorious Padishah (Sultan of the Ottoman Empire), we were accorded a brilliant reception. That same day the Khanikhanan prepared a great banquet in our honor; and as it is the custom in India to give audience in the evening, I was that night introduced with much pomp and ceremony into the Imperial hall.

**Letter to James I, King of England, from The Great Mughal Jahangir: 1617**

For confirmation of our love and friendship, I desire your Majesty to command your merchants to bring in their ships of all sorts of rarities and rich goods fit for my palace; and that you be pleased to send me your royal letters by every opportunity, that I may rejoice in your health and prosperous affairs; that our friendship may be interchanged and eternal.

357

What information in these passages might stimulate European interest in India?

_____

_____

_____

## DOCUMENT

### A Timeline of the Ottoman Empire: 1243–1924

| | |
|---|---|
| ca. 1243 | Turkish nomads settle in Asia Minor. |
| 1299–1326 | Osman I declares himself sultan and establishes the Ottoman Empire. |
| 1355 | Ottomans and Serbs attack Constantinople. |
| 1389 | Ottomans defeat Serbs at Kosovo. |
| 1451–1481 | Mohammed the Conqueror. |
| 1453 | Constantinople is conquered. |
| 1520–1566 | Suleiman II the Magnificent. |
| 1526 | Battle of Mohacs. |
| 1529 | First siege of Vienna. |
| 1571 | The Battle of Lepanto. |
| 1641–1687 | Reign of Mohammad IV. |
| 1683 | Second siege of Vienna. |
| 1703–1730 | Cultural revival under Ahmed III. |
| 1774 | Treaty of Kucuk Kaynarca. |
| 1798–1799 | Napoleon attempts to conquer Egypt. |
| 1822–1830 | Greek War of Independence. |
| 1829 | Treaty of Adrinople. |
| 1853–1856 | The Crimean War involving Russia and Britain. |
| 1876 | The Ottoman Constitution is proclaimed. |
| 1908 | The Committee of Union and Progress (The Young Turks) is formed. The Ottoman Constitution is restored. |
| 1912–1913 | The First and Second Balkan Wars. |
| 1914 | The Empire enters World War I as one of the Central Powers. |
| 1915 | The Armenian Massacre. |
| 1919–1924 | End of the Ottoman Empire. |

"The Ottoman state was (based) upon, committed to and organized for conquest. . . . An end to significant and sustained conquest rocked the entire structure. . . ."

—N. Itkowitz (1980), *Ottoman Empire and Islamic Tradition*

What evidence in the timeline supports the quotation?

_____

_____

_____

# DOCUMENT-BASED ESSAY QUESTION

**Directions:** The following question is based on the accompanying documents (Documents 1–9). Some of the documents have been edited for the purpose of this assignment.

Write a well-organized essay with an introduction stating a thesis, a body of several paragraphs that accomplishes the task, and a summarizing conclusion. Use all the documents and analyze each one. Use evidence from the documents to support the position you take in your thesis. Do not simply repeat the contents of the document; explain things in your words and relate the information in your thesis. Using your knowledge of the social studies, include related information that is not included in the documents.

**Historical Context:** During the "Age of Absolutism" the predominant political idea among rulers was that of "divine right" or the "mandate of heaven."

**Question:** Discuss the ways in which rulers justified this concept.

**Part A:** Summarize the main supporting idea stated or illustrated in each of the accompanying documents (Documents 1–9).

**Part B:** Respond in an essay. Your essay should be based on a thesis statement—your viewpoint regarding the ways in which absolute rulers justified their power. In your essay you should use information from all of the documents as evidence. Present the evidence and analyze it from the point of view of your thesis. Support your thesis with related information based on your knowledge of the social studies.

**DOCUMENT 1**

**LOUIS XIV IN HIS YOUTH AS THE RADIANT SUN KING, DRIVING THE CHARIOT OF APOLLO (GREEK GOD OF THE SUN) ACROSS THE HEAVENS**

How does this painting reflect the concept of "Divine Right"?

_____

_____

_____

**DOCUMENT 2**

**From Catherine II (The Great), *Proposals for a New Law Code***

The Sovereign is absolute; for there is no other Authority but that which centers in his single Person, that can act with a Vigour proportionate to the Extent of such a vast Dominion. A Society of Citizens, as well as every Thing else, requires a certain fixed Order: There ought to be *some to govern*, and *others to obey.* . . .

According to Catherine the Great, what is the importance of an absolute ruler?

_____

_____

_____

## DOCUMENT 3

We have already seen that all power is of God. The ruler, adds St. Paul, "is the minister of God to thee for good. . . . Rulers then act as the ministers of God and as his lieutenants on earth. It is through them that God exercised his empire. . . . Consequently, as we have seen, the royal throne is not the throne of a man, but the throne of God himself." The Lord "hath chosen Solomon my son to sit upon the throne of the kingdom of the Lord over Israel." . . . St. Peter unites these two duties when he says, "Fear God. Honour the king."

—Jacques-Benigne Bossuet (1709), *Politique tiree des propres paroles de l'Ecriture sainte* in J. H. Robinson

What authority does Bossuet cite as justification for absolutism?

_____

_____

_____

## DOCUMENT 4

And as ye see it manifest that the King is overlord of the whole land, so is he master over every person . . . having power over the life and death of every one of them. For although a just prince will not take the life of any of his subjects without a clear law, yet the same laws whereby he taketh them are made by himself or his predecessors, and so the power flows always from himself . . . .

—James I, "True Law of Free Monarchies"

According to King James I, what is the role and function of a ruler?

_____

_____

_____

## DOCUMENT 5

The king's great qualities shone more brilliantly by reason of an exterior so unique and incomparable as to lend infinite distinction to his slightest actions; the very figure of a hero, with a natural but most imposing majesty that appeared even in his most insignificant gestures and movements, . . . proportions such as a sculptor would choose to model; a perfect countenance and the grandest air ever (given) to man; all these advantages enhanced by a natural grace which enveloped all his actions with a singular charm which has never perhaps been equaled. He was as dignified and majestic in his dressing gown as when dressed in robes of state, or on horseback at the head of his troops.

—Saint-Simon (1746), "Portrait of Louis XIV"

In what way does this passage support the concept of absolutism?

_____

_____

_____

**DOCUMENT 6**

**SULEIMAN "THE MAGNIFICENT" OR "THE LAWGIVER" (KANUNI)
SULTAN OF THE OTTOMAN EMPIRE (1520–1556)**

Suleiman had many titles; in inscriptions he calls himself: "Slave of God, powerful with the power of God, deputy of God on earth, obeying the commands of the Qur'an and enforcing them throughout the world, master of all lands, the shadow of God over all nations . . ."

How did Suleiman define his role in relation to God and humans?

_____

_____

_____

**DOCUMENT 7**

## AKBAR (THE GREAT) MUGHAL EMPEROR OF INDIA (1556–1605)

The majority of Islamic scholars . . . concluded that the monarch was divinely appointed by God to serve humanity. . . . In particular, they subscribed to the notion that God had created a Divine Light that is passed down in an individual from generation to generation; this individual is known as the **Imam**. The central theorist of Akbar's reign was Abu'l Faz'l. . . . He believed that the Imamate existed in the world in the form of just rulers. The Imam, in the form of a just ruler, had secret knowledge of God, was free from sin, and was primarily responsible for the spiritual guidance of humanity.

—Richard Hooker, *World Civilizations An
Internet Classroom and Anthology*

What was the relationship between God and the ruler, according to Abu'l Faz'l?

_____

_____

_____

## DOCUMENT 8

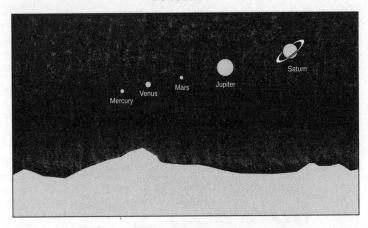

The five visible planets—Saturn, Venus, Mercury, Mars, and Jupiter—were believed to be the ministers of Shangdi, the Lord on High. Their conjunction in the predawn sky of February 1953 B.C.E. was thought to indicate Shangdi's conferral of the right to rule on the Xia Dynasty.

—"The Mandate of Heaven," by David W. Pankenier, *Archaeology Abstracts* Volume 51, Number 2, March/April 1998.

How did the early Chinese explain the ruler's right to his position of authority?

_____

_____

_____

## DOCUMENT 9

The (new dynasty) developed a political theory to justify their conquest and their usurpation of the emperorship in a doctrine called **t'ien ming**, or the "mandate" or "decree of Heaven." In its early form, this political theory asserted that Heaven, *Tien*, was primarily interested in the welfare of human beings. For this reason it has established governors and rulers who assume the responsibility for the welfare of their people. It mandates that certain people be in charge; while they rule justly, fairly, and wisely, Heaven maintains that certain rulers or dynasties remain in power. . . . This Mandate is not equivalent to fate or destiny, it is more of an imperative. Humans are free to rule unjustly, they are free to harm the people they rule over; their rule, however, will come to a swift end as Heaven passes on its mandate to another family.

—Richard Hooker, *World Civilizations An Internet Classroom and Anthology*

What is Heaven's primary reason for giving its mandate to rulers?

_____

_____

_____

# ERA V

# An Age of Revolutions (1750–1918)

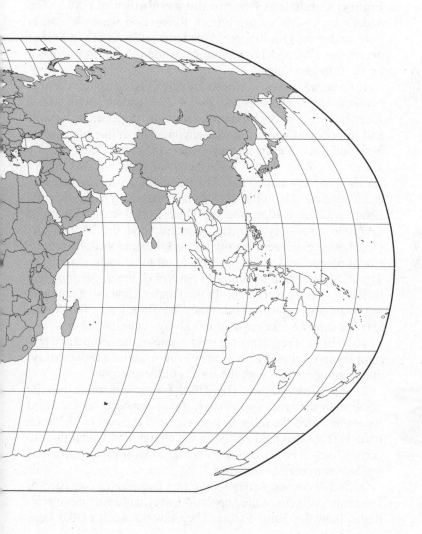

# Part A: The French Revolution, the Enlightenment, and the Napoleonic Era

## The French Revolution

**France: Conditions Prior to the Revolution of 1789.** The underlying causes of the French Revolution were the conditions under the Old Régime. This term refers to life in France during the 17th and 18th centuries, while the nation was ruled by the Bourbon kings.

GLOBAL
CONCEPTS
**Human Rights**
CONCEPTS
GLOBAL

1. *Political causes.* The absolute rule of King Louis XIV was continued by King Louis XVI (1774–1792) and his wife, Marie Antoinette. Louis XVI did not permit any criticism of himself and imprisoned without a trial anyone who spoke out against his policies. Imprisonment was often carried out by *lettres de cachet*, letters with the royal seal. He was a poor leader and very unpopular. The population was divided into three classes. The First Estate was the clergy; the Second Estate was the nobles; and the Third Estate was made up of everyone else—city workers, peasants, and the bourgeoisie. (The bourgeoisie were mainly bankers, businesspeople, professional people, and others who made up the middle class.) The

GLOBAL
CONCEPTS
**Citizenship**
CONCEPTS
GLOBAL

Third Estate, which included 90 percent of the population, had little say in the government. In the Estates-General, a lawmaking body, each estate had one vote. The Third Estate felt powerless because the other two estates always voted together.

Most of the French people were aware of the democratic revolutions in England (17th century) and America (18th century) and were impressed with the results of these events.

**GEOGRAPHY**

**Human Systems**

2. *Economic causes.* The Third Estate was more heavily taxed than the other two estates. Taxes imposed on the Third Estate included the *taille* (a land tax) and the *corvée* (labor on roads). They also paid a tithe to the church and feudal dues to certain lords. The bourgeoisie were upset with strict restrictions on their commercial activities.

3. *Social causes.* Although the first two estates consisted of less than 5 percent of the population, they had many more privileges than the Third Estate. They owned much of the land,

were exempt from most taxes, and generally lived much better than members of the Third Estate.

4. *Influence of the Enlightenment.* The Enlightenment, also called the Age of Reason, was an intellectual movement in the 17th and 18th centuries. It was sparked by the scientific progress of the previous age (the Scientific Revolution). Educated Europeans had learned that natural laws governed the physical universe. They reasoned that similar laws must govern human society as well. If people were able to discover these laws, they might be used to construct a better government and more just societies. The thinkers, philosophers, and writers who examined the political and social problems of the time were known as Philosophes. They believed that everything, even government and religion, should be open to reason and criticism. They were convinced that through the use of reason, logic, and experience, people could improve their society—its laws, economy, and so on. The Philosophes claimed that humans had certain natural rights. Traditional royal and Church authority, particularly in France, were in conflict with these rights and had to undergo change. The most important French writers of the Enlightenment are listed in the chart below.

GLOBAL
CONCEPTS

**Change**

CONCEPTS
GLOBAL

## FRENCH WRITERS OF THE ENLIGHTENMENT

| Name | Major Work and Ideas |
| --- | --- |
| Montesquieu (1689–1755) | *The Spirit of the Laws.* There should be a separation of powers in government as well as a system of checks and balances. These features would prevent tyranny and absolutism. |
| Voltaire (1694–1778) | *Letters Concerning the English.* Written in support of the concepts of England's limited monarchy and its ideas on freedom of speech and religion. |
| Rousseau (1712–1778) | *The Social Contract.* Inequality among people can be ended by citizens coming together and agreeing to a general will. The general will is what the majority desires and should be carried out by the government. |
| Diderot (1713–1784) | *The Encyclopedia.* Absolutism and the injustices of the Old Regime were wrong. |

There were also other important Enlightenment writers. Adam Smith of England *(The Wealth of Nations)* said that people should be free to conduct business without government interference. This was the laissez-faire philosophy of economics. The American Thomas Paine *(Common Sense)* claimed that it was right and natural for the American colonists to revolt against England, a tyrannical government that was thousands of miles across the Atlantic Ocean. John Locke was also a major Enlightenment writer.

The Enlightenment's concern with natural rights and the use of reason, logic, and experience was seen in the field of science as well as in politics and economics. During the 16th and 17th centuries, the way the people of Europe viewed themselves and the universe underwent a dramatic transformation in what was called the Scientific Revolution. The discoveries of a succession of astronomers, physicists, and mathematicians undermined many ideas that had been accepted for centuries. A new system of ideas and theories was created, based on the direct observation of nature and a belief in the power of reason. The scientific method, based on carefully planned experiments, observation of results, and the formulation of general laws, was the basis of the Scientific Revolution. Scientists such as Isaac Newton (1642–1727) of England used the scientific method to investigate nature. Newton, the leading figure in the Scientific Revolution, put forth important theories about gravity and the movement of planets. His famous book was the *Principia Mathematica*.

**The French Revolution of 1789: Outbreak and Major Developments.** In 1789 King Louis XVI called the Estates-General into session because he needed money to solve France's financial problems. This was the first time this body had been summoned since 1614 (175 years before). When the Estates-General met, the Third Estate refused to accept the traditional method of voting—each estate met separately and had one vote—because it would be outvoted by the other two estates. It demanded that all three estates meet together and that each deputy have a vote. When the king refused, the Third Estate, on June 17, 1789, declared itself to be the National Assembly and in the Tennis Court Oath pledged to write a constitution for the nation. This declaration was the beginning of the French Revolution. On July 14, 1789, the revolution spread as a mob stormed and destroyed the Bastille—a prison that was a symbol of the Old Regime. The next day the king recognized the National Assembly. The National Assembly, which was made up of moderates, took power and began to carry out reforms. They passed the Declaration of the Rights of Man on August 27, 1789. This document was similar to the American Declaration of Independence and the English Bill of Rights. It stated the following democratic ideals:

1. The class structure and privileges connected with the three estates were ended, abolishing the remains of feudalism.

GLOBAL CONCEPTS
**Change**
CONCEPTS GLOBAL

GLOBAL CONCEPTS
**Justice**
CONCEPTS GLOBAL

2. All people were equal before the law and had certain basic freedoms, including freedom of religion, speech, and the press.

3. The spirit of Liberty, Equality, and Fraternity was to guide the nation. In 1790 the National Assembly abolished the special taxes and privileges of the Catholic Church in the Civil Constitution of the Clergy. It also granted freedom of worship, confiscated all Church land, and placed the Church under the government's control.

The French Constitution was written in 1791, and it created a limited, or constitutional, monarchy and established separate executive, legislative, and judicial branches of government.

However, King Louis's unsuccessful attempt to flee the country and war with Austria and Prussia enabled radicals, such as Robespierre, Danton, and Marat, to take over the Revolution. In 1792 delegates were elected by universal manhood suffrage to the National Convention, which took the place of the National Assembly and contained more radical members, such as the Jacobins. The first act of the National Convention was to declare France a republic. Louis XVI was brought to trial and executed in 1792.

The National Convention was soon taken over by extremist groups, who formed the Committee of Public Safety, which put the executive, legislative, and judicial powers of government in the hands of a small group of revolutionaries. The committee was given power to conduct the war with France's enemies and to enforce the ideals of the Revolution by all means possible. The leading figures were Danton and Robespierre, who began a Reign of Terror (1793–1794) in which they executed at the guillotine all enemies of the revolution, who were to them the nobles or anybody who spoke out against them.

GLOBAL
CONCEPTS

**Human Rights**

CONCEPTS
GLOBAL

Eventually, more moderate groups, anti-Jacobins, took over the National Convention. Danton and Robespierre were themselves sentenced to die by the guillotine in 1795. The Convention wrote a new constitution in 1795 that made France a republic. It established a five-member Directory government that ruled France until 1799, when it was replaced by the military dictatorship of Napoleon Bonaparte. (See The Rise and Fall of Napoleon, on the next page.) This return of government to moderate control is called the Thermidorian Reaction.

**Importance of the French Revolution.** The French Revolution had many important and long-lasting results. It brought about a basic change in the relationship between the government and the governed. Along with the revolutions in England and the United States, the French Revolution advanced democracy by recognizing the value and worth of the individual. Political power passed from an absolutist monarch who ruled by Divine Right and the nobles to the masses of people. A greater sense of nationalism and patriotism developed. Also, the remaining feudal features of French society were removed. The growing power of the bourgeoisie helped France to become a strong capitalist nation.

## The Rise and Fall of Napoleon (1799–1815)

Napoleon Bonaparte was an ambitious, brilliant military officer who won many victories in wars against France's enemies. In 1799 in a coup d'etat (a sudden takeover of a government), he came to power in France in a new government called the Consulate. The Directory had lost support because of worsening economic problems and its inability to defeat Russia and Austria in the war. The Consulate was headed by three consuls, with Napoleon as First Consul. The new government, France's fourth in ten years, was called a republic, but it was a military dictatorship under the control of Napoleon. He took the title of Emperor Napoleon I in 1804. The French people accepted his ruthless methods because they believed he would bring peace and stability to the nation.

At first, Napoleon was brilliantly successful in his war against France's European enemies. Under Napoleon's leadership, French forces won victories and took large amounts of land in Europe. By 1808 Napoleon dominated Europe, and he reorganized many parts of Europe, making members of his family rulers in Italy, Spain, and other places.

The Napoleonic Empire soon became too large to control, however, and in time Napoleon suffered severe military setbacks. His attempt to conquer Russia in 1812 failed due to the harsh winter conditions and the scorched-earth fighting tactics of the Russians. At the Battle of Waterloo in 1815, fought near Brussels in Belgium, Napoleon's forces were defeated by the combined forces of European nations led by the Duke of Wellington of Britain.

**Results of the Napoleonic Era.** Napoleon made many significant contributions to governing France. Both within France and in the areas he conquered, Napoleon sought to carry out the ideals of the French Revolution as he interpreted them. Indeed, he called himself a son of the Revolution and carried out the following reforms:

1. The Code Napoleon brought all the laws, regulations, and reforms of the revolution into a single system of law. Based on the belief that all people are equal before the law, the Napoleonic

GLOBAL
CONCEPTS

**Political Systems**

CONCEPTS
GLOBAL

**GEOGRAPHY**

**Use of Geography**

**WORLD ISSUES**

| War |
| and |
| Peace |

Code became the fundamental law of France and the parts of Europe governed by France.

2. The Concordat of 1801 provided for a peaceful relationship between the French government and the Catholic Church.

3. An efficient, centralized government was created in France, with specific power over the education and banking systems. Government officials were selected based on merit through an examination system, and a public school system was established.

4. Many European monarchs lost their thrones to Napoleon's armies. Peoples in these areas, such as Spain and Italy, learned of the ideals of the French Revolution. At first, some of these people welcomed Napoleon because they believed he had liberated them from foreign and unjust rule. Eventually, they turned against Napoleon's dictatorial rule and fought against him. However, as a result of Napoleon's conquests, the ideas of the French Revolution were spread throughout Europe. The ideals of social justice, liberty, and democracy became rallying cries for reformers. Combined with the rise of the spirit of nationalism, which was stirred by the struggle against Napoleon's armies, the dreams of liberty and equality made many national groups determined to gain self-government in the years after 1815.

GLOBAL CONCEPTS

Culture

CONCEPTS GLOBAL

GEOGRAPHY

Environment and Society

# Part B: Nationalism and Unification in Europe

## The Metternich Age and the Growth of Nationalism (1815–1871)

After Napoleon's defeat, five major European powers—England, Russia, Prussia, France, and Austria—met at the Congress of Vienna in 1814 and 1815 to draw up peace plans and settle a number of important territorial questions by redrawing the map of Europe. Under the leadership of Austria's Count Metternich, the Congress of Vienna sought to restore political life in Europe, including former rulers and boundaries, to what it had been prior to Napoleon and to maintain peace and stability. Such a policy of restoring past ways and turning the clock back is called reactionary. Metternich wanted to wipe out the ideas spread by the Napoleonic era and return to the old days of absolutism and special privilege. The decisions reached at the Congress of Vienna were based on three principles—legitimacy, the balance of power, and compensation. Legitimacy meant restoring the ruling families that reigned before the French Revolution to their thrones. Balance of power meant that no one nation should be strong enough to threaten the security of the others. To do this, shifts of territory were necessary. This involved compensation, or providing one state with territory to pay for territory taken away from that state.

Metternich opposed the French Revolution ideas of freedom and equality. He sought to maintain what had been the status quo prior to the French Revolution. During the Metternich age (1815–1848), there were challenges to the status quo. However, most attempts by European peoples against these reactionary policies in order to achieve national unity were put down by force. These attempts, which led to revolutions in 1830 and in 1848, were inspired by a nationalistic spirit, whereby a group of people, such as the Italians, Poles, or Germans, sought to create their own nation and establish self-government. Although most of these revolutions failed, two successful attempts were made in Belgium and Greece in 1830. The Quadruple Alliance, representing the four powers that had defeated Napoleon, did not want these revolutionary movements to succeed. From this alliance emerged the Concert of Europe. This was a form of international government, arranged by concert, or agreement, among its members. It wanted to keep the balance of power that the

GEOGRAPHY

**Environment and Society**

GLOBAL CONCEPTS

**Choice**

CONCEPTS GLOBAL

Congress of Vienna had set up. Although the Congress could not suppress nationalism permanently, it was able to postpone its success for a half century. The unification of Italy and of Germany in the later 1800s were the first breaks in the territorial settlements of 1815.

The spirit of nationalism influenced the political history of Europe from 1815 to 1914. Nationalism is the belief that a group of people who share a common culture, language, and historical tradition should have their own nation in a specific area of land. Once the people accomplish their nationalistic goals and form a nation-state, they can then make their own laws and are said to be sovereign and to have autonomy. Nationalism was the guiding force that led to the unification of both Italy and Germany in the late 19th century. The Italians, Poles, Hungarians, Turks, and others who were ruled by the large dynastic states that dominated Europe—the Austrian Empire, the Russian Empire, and the Ottoman Empire—all struggled to win freedom and form their own nation-states.

**Unification of Italy.** In 1815 there was no nation called Italy; Italy was really a geographic expression. The Italian Peninsula was divided among large and small states, such as the Lombardy province and the kingdom of Sardinia-Piedmont. Austria, which controlled the states in the northern part of the Italian Peninsula, was against any kind of unity. But by 1861 all the Italian states had become unified into a nation. Those most responsible for bringing unification about were:

1. *Cavour.* Considered the brain of unification, he was a successful diplomat who got France to help him fight the Austrians. He also expanded the power of Sardinia-Piedmont by adding to it other Italian states.

2. *Mazzini.* The soul of unification, he wrote and spoke eloquently about his desires for Italian unity. He was the founder of the Young Italy movement.

3. *Garibaldi.* The sword of unification, he conquered southern Italy and joined it to the state that Cavour had unified under the control of Sardinia-Piedmont in the north.

4. *King Victor Emmanuel.* Formerly the King of Sardinia-Piedmont, he became the ruler of a united Italy in March 1861.

**Unification of Germany.** In 1815 there was no nation called Germany. Instead, there were more than thirty independent German states that had their own traditions, laws, and economic regulations. The largest of these states, Prussia, located in northern Germany, led the movement for unification. The

GLOBAL
CONCEPTS

**Change**

CONCEPTS
GLOBAL

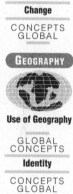

**GEOGRAPHY**

Use of Geography

GLOBAL
CONCEPTS

**Identity**

CONCEPTS
GLOBAL

**GEOGRAPHY**

Use of Geography

chief obstacle to Prussia's leadership was Austria. It sought to dominate German affairs and did not want to see the German states unified. But by 1871, under the leadership of Prussia's chief minister, Otto von Bismarck, Austria's power was weakened and the German states achieved unification.

Otto von Bismarck

**WORLD ISSUES**

War
and
Peace

**GEOGRAPHY**

**Use of Geography**

Following a policy of blood and iron, Bismarck used military means to achieve his goal of German unity under Prussia's leadership. Under this policy, Prussia won victories in the Danish War (1864), the Austro-Prussian War (or Seven Weeks' War, 1866), and the Franco-Prussian War (1870–1871). As a result of these wars, Prussia was able to gain land, such as Schleswig-Holstein from Denmark and Alsace-Lorraine from France, unite other German states with Prussia, and reduce the influence of Austria in German affairs. King William I of Prussia became the ruler of a united Germany in 1871 and was called emperor, or kaiser.

**Conclusion.** Nationalism can be positive (a force for good) or negative (a force for evil). The desire by Italians and Germans to form their own nations brought together people with common ties and histories. The wishes of a group of people to achieve sovereignty and self-determination are common themes throughout history and exist even in our own day. However, nationalistic desires can become so intense that hatred and unnecessary bloodshed can result. The reign of terror in France was one example; Bismarck's humiliation of France after the Franco-Prussian war was another. Intense nationalism can also be dangerous when it turns into chauvinism and excessive ethnocentrism. This occurs when a group of people claim to be superior to another group of people. Such claims have often led to prejudice and wars.

GLOBAL
CONCEPTS

**Identity**

CONCEPTS
GLOBAL

Era V **AN AGE OF REVOLUTIONS (1750–1918)**

# Part C: The Industrial Revolution

**World Issues**

Economic
Growth and
Development

A major upheaval in the way people live, work, and think began about 200 years ago and in many ways is still going on today. This change is called the Industrial Revolution, and it accomplished on a massive scale the replacement of human power and animal power with the power of machines. The Industrial Revolution began in England in the 1750s and involved vast changes in the production of goods. These changes were as follows:

1. From handmade goods to machine-made goods.

2. From production at home to production in factories (from the domestic system to the factory system).

3. From producing small amounts to producing large amounts (mass production).

GLOBAL
CONCEPTS

**Technology**

CONCEPTS
GLOBAL

4. The increased use of science and new forms of energy (steam power, for example) to speed up production and meet human needs. The use of science in these ways is referred to as technology.

**Causes and Preconditions in 18th-Century England.** The Industrial Revolution began in England because of a combination of fortunate conditions that existed at the time.

1. *Natural resources*. Britain was fortunate to have large amounts of coal and iron ore.

2. *Geography*. England had many good harbors, and coastal and river trade was well developed. England also had relatively good roads and numerous canals for the cheap transport of raw materials and finished goods.

3. *Investment capital*. Entrepreneurs and other private individuals had money that they, as capitalists, were willing to invest and risk in business ventures.

4. *Labor supply*. There were large numbers of skilled workers in the population.

5. *Increased demand*. There was a great demand for British products, both in the domestic market (within the nation) and in foreign markets.

6. *Transportation and colonial empire*. Britain had a good navy and had built up a shipping industry. Its expanding colonial empire furnished raw materials and markets for goods.

7. *Agricultural changes.* An agricultural revolution that occurred in the 1700s brought changes in farming that made the Industrial Revolution possible. These changes resulted in the production of more food and required fewer farmers to produce it. Many people left the farms and went to the cities to find work in factories.

8. *Role of government.* Britain had a stable government that had established a good banking system, promoted scientific experimentation, and passed laws to protect business.

9. *Inventions.* The changes in production came first in the cotton textile industry. Several inventors devised inventions that sped up and improved the manufacture of textiles.

### EUROPEAN INVENTORS OF THE INDUSTRIAL REVOLUTION

| Inventor | Invention and Its Importance |
| --- | --- |
| John Kay | Flying shuttle—speeded up the weaving process |
| James Hargreaves | Spinning jenny—could spin many threads at one time |
| Richard Arkwright | Water frame—used water power to increase spinning; first machine to replace human hand power with another power source |
| Edmund Cartwright | Power loom—used water power to make weaving faster |
| James Watt | Steam engine—use of steam as a source of power |
| George Stephenson | Steam locomotive—improved ground transportation |

The locomotive was developed during the Industrial Revolution.

**Responses to the Industrial Revolution.** The Industrial Revolution fundamentally changed the way people lived. Families moved to industrial cities by the millions to work in the new factories. The first years of adjustment to the new industrial society were a period of severe difficulty for workers. Men, women, and children worked long hours under deplorable conditions in factories. People were crowded into towns and cities that had made little provision for housing or for sanitation. With more people working in factories and living in cities, occupational, health, and housing problems developed. Moreover, even though they were becoming more populated than rural areas, cities had not gained political power. These problems associated with industrialization developed in Britain as well as in other areas of Europe where industrialization took place. In response to workers' protests and reformers' appeals, various reform measures were adopted. These reforms indicated that Europeans had begun to understand the changes in the working and living conditions of those who labored under the factory system. Reform measures in Britain were as follows:

1. *Social and economic reforms.* Harmful working conditions such as child labor, low wages, faulty ventilation, and dangerous equipment were brought to public attention by the Sadler Report on factories and the Ashley Report on mines. In time, members of Parliament became concerned about children as young as five or six working long hours in factories and mines and about the dangerous, unhealthful conditions for all workers in factories. Laws such as the Factory Act (1833) and the Mines Act (1842) were passed to improve conditions for workers. The need for workers to unite to protect and advance their interests led to the formation of labor unions.

2. *Political reforms.* The move to reduce property rights as the basis for suffrage (the right to vote) and to give cities more representation in Parliament led to the passage of the Reform Bill of 1832. This bill also did away with most "rotten boroughs" (areas that no longer had many people but had kept the same amount of representation in Parliament). The middle class, workers, and women were to benefit from the Reform Bill of 1832 and similar legislation passed in the 19th and early 20th centuries. By 1928, for example, Britain provided for universal suffrage. This meant that both women and men had the right to vote. The expansion of suffrage in Britain and other European countries was partially due to changes brought about by the Industrial Revolution.

**The Development of Socialism.** Political scientists and philosophers struggled with the problems presented by industrialization, seeking to discover how the political system should respond.

One of these solutions was socialism, which was a criticism of capitalism and called for a basic change in the economic system in order to correct these problems. Socialists maintained that it was necessary to transfer ownership of the means of production (factories, mines, railroads, land) from private individuals to the state. According to socialist theory, the government, as elected by the people, should own all the means of production and should also make all the key economic decisions. These decisions included: What should be produced? Who should produce it? What should the price be? and How should the product be distributed? This kind of planned, or command, economy is in contrast to a free-enterprise or market economy. In a market economy, according to capitalist principles, the key economic decisions are basically made by private individuals acting on their own.

One group of socialists wanted to create an ideal society, or a utopia. Utopian socialists believed that a socialist society would emerge peacefully and that even capitalists would be willing to help create it. Among the utopian socialists of the 19th century were a wealthy British manufacturer, Robert Owen, and a French philosopher, Charles Fourier.

In contrast to utopian socialists were those people who believed in a radically different type of socialism called scien-

**GEOGRAPHY**

Environment
and Society

Karl Marx

tific socialism or communism. That was a type of socialism based on what they believed were scientific ideas about the way society operates. The leading scientific socialist thinkers were Karl Marx and Friedrich Engels of Germany. Their ideas were contained in two books: *The Communist Manifesto* (1848) and *Das Kapital* (1867). Their major ideas came to be known as Marxism and included:

1. *Economic interpretation of history*. All history is determined by economic conditions. Whichever group or class controls the means of production will control the government.

2. *Class struggle*. In all societies throughout history, there have been struggles for power between two economic groups—the haves and the have nots. In industrial societies the struggle has taken place between the capitalists, or bourgeoisie, and the workers, or proletariat.

3. *Surplus value theory*. Surplus value was the difference between the price of a good and the wage paid to a worker. According to Marx, this difference was kept by the capitalists as their profit. For Marx, this was wrong, especially as he felt that workers were paid far too little in wages. Such abuse, or exploitation of workers, was unjust.

4. *Inevitability of socialism*. Eventually all these conditions would lead to depressions and poverty and would result in a violent overthrow by the workers of the government, primarily because the capitalists would not peacefully give up their economic and political power. This communist revolution would result in a dictatorship of the proletariat, a government that would be more just and would rule on behalf of the working class. The government would operate under the theory of socialism. Eventually, a classless society would emerge, and there would be no need for a government; the government would wither away.

**The Impact of Communism.** The history of communism since Marx put forth his ideas shows a wide difference between what Marx said and what has actually happened.

1. His prediction that communist revolutions would occur mostly in Western European industrialized societies was wrong. The first two communist revolutions took place in agricultural societies—Russia (1917) and China (1949).

2. Communism never won control in industrialized societies in Western Europe or in North America. Marx failed to see the growth of unions and their ability to work toward their goals in a free, democratic system. He also did not realize that the living conditions of the workers would improve in the 19th century and that workers would become part of the middle class.

3. As the 1990s began, it was clear that communist societies had failed to achieve their goals. Economic and political problems in Eastern Europe and the Soviet Union led to the collapse of communism in those areas (1989–1991). In addition, throughout this century, there have been constant attempts by people in these communist nations to leave, seeking a better life elsewhere, specifically in non-communist countries.

# Part D: Imperialism

Imperialism can be defined as the control by one nation over a weaker area or nation. This control has usually been both political and economic. Since the areas under control are called colonies, the practice of imperialism can be referred to as colonialism. There were two distinct periods of imperialism—the "old imperialism" (1500–1800) and the "new imperialism" (beginning in the 1880s). The old imperialism had the following characteristics: concerned with establishing trade routes and obtaining resources; carried on at first by private individuals and companies; took place mainly in the western hemisphere, the Americas. (See the section on Latin America.) The new imperialism had these general characteristics: concerned with establishing trade and markets, obtaining resources, and making large financial investments; carried on by governments as official policy; took place mainly in the eastern hemisphere, Africa, and Asia. There were many reasons for the new imperialism.

1. *Economic.* The increased supply of manufactured goods produced by the Industrial Revolution encouraged European nations to find new markets for these goods. Investors with surplus capital looked overseas to make investments that would bring them profits. The need for raw materials to produce more goods was another important consideration.

2. *Political.* Nations hoped to gain prestige and glory by expanding their power. These nationalistic desires sparked nations to achieve a balance of power with other nations that were also seeking to build colonial empires.

3. *Social.* European nations felt that they were superior to other global areas. They felt that they had both an obligation and a right to spread their culture and way of life into these areas. These feelings of ethnocentrism can be seen in Rudyard Kipling's poem *The White Man's Burden,* which concerns the obligation of carrying Western civilization to those considered less fortunate. These feelings were also the result of 19th-century notions of white racial superiority and the theory of social Darwinism. This was the belief that social progress depended on competition among human beings, resulting in the survival of the fittest.

**Forms of Imperialist Control.** Imperialism took many different forms in the 19th century.

**WORLD ISSUES**

World Trade and Finance

**GEOGRAPHY**

Use of Geography

GLOBAL CONCEPTS

**Interdependence**

CONCEPTS GLOBAL

**GEOGRAPHY**

Human Systems

1. *Sphere of influence.* A nation gained sole economic power in a region and had exclusive economic rights to trade, to invest, and to develop mines, railroads, or factories. It could not be interfered with by other nations. This form of imperialism was used in China, where each foreign nation—for example, Germany—had economic control in a specific area.

**GEOGRAPHY**

**Use of Geography**

2. *Concession.* In this form, a foreign nation obtained special privileges. An underdeveloped area gave permission to a technologically advanced nation to do something of economic value in the area. (For example, the Arabs let the British drill for oil and build a railroad in the Middle East.)

3. *Protectorate.* A colonial nation allowed the native ruler of an area to remain in office as a figurehead, while in reality the colonial power made all the major decisions (France in Tunisia). The former Eastern European satellite nations controlled by the former Soviet Union after World War II can be thought of as protectorates.

4. *Colony.* An imperialist nation takes total control over an area and makes it part of its empire. (France in Indochina, the Netherlands in Indonesia, Britain in India.)

**Colonial Policies.** The major imperialist nations followed different policies in ruling their empires. These policies influenced the patterns of independence that took place after 1945.

GLOBAL CONCEPTS

**Choice**

CONCEPTS GLOBAL

1. *England.* Its policy of indirect rule permitted local rulers to retain some power in an area. Nevertheless, because the British felt that their democratic values were superior and should be spread, they sought to educate selected Africans and Asians in English schools. It was hoped that these natives would plant British political and social ideals in their native lands. People who received such an education, such as Gandhi and Nehru in India, eventually led their people to independence in nonviolent ways, based on democratic ideas. Britain was never involved in harsh colonial wars for independence as were some of the other European nations.

2. *France.* Its policy of direct rule viewed colonies as if they were actually parts of France. Decisions for the colonies were made directly in Paris. Since the French language and culture were assumed to be preferable, all people were to learn them in colonized areas. These attitudes were the basis for France's claim to carry out a civilizing mission and to accomplish assimilation of native peoples. Since France viewed areas such as Algeria and Indochina as much a part of French territory as Paris, the French were unwilling to give in to demands for independence that grew

**GEOGRAPHY**

**Use of Geography**

after the end of World War II. Consequently, France fought bitter, unsuccessful colonial wars in these areas.

3. *Portugal.* Its policy of paternalism viewed colonies as though they were children, and Portugal did little to prepare its colonies for independence. As with France, it looked on its colonies as parts of Portugal. Consequently, it too was unwilling to grant independence to its colonies in Angola and Mozambique without military struggle.

4. *Belgium.* It followed policies of paternalism and exploitation in the Congo. Belgium did little to pave the way for independence and left the area amid much bloodshed in 1960. Consequently, this former colony had severe political problems in creating a stable government when it became independent.

**Independence and Decolonization.** During the period after World War II, independence came to almost all areas that had come under European imperialist control. This period of decolonization saw the emergence of over fifty new nations. The end of imperialism after 1945 was a result of many factors: nationalist movements in the colonies grew powerful, gaining support from native people as well as from some people in the imperialist nations; the Western European nations were weary after fighting World War II; the creation of the United Nations was linked to global concern for human rights and recognition of the need for people to achieve self-determination.

Although decolonization was achieved in both peaceful and violent ways, many former colonies retain ties today to their former foreign rulers. Many of Britain's colonies, after independence, voluntarily chose membership in the British Commonwealth of Nations. The organization meets to discuss matters of mutual interest and provides certain economic privileges for members. Although it no longer exists, the French Community was an organization similar to the British Commonwealth. It included France and several of its former colonies. France's interest in its former colonies can be seen in its giving economic aid and in providing military support when requested. For example, in recent years, French forces were sent to the African nations of Chad and Gabon to put down armed opposition to the governments there.

**Evaluation of Imperialism.** European imperialism had both positive and negative consequences, as summarized in the following table.

GLOBAL
CONCEPTS
**Change**
CONCEPTS
GLOBAL

**GEOGRAPHY**

**Use of Geography**

**WORLD ISSUES**

Human
Rights

## EUROPEAN IMPERIALISM

| Consequence | Positive | Negative |
|---|---|---|
| Political | Brought stability and unification; training for independence; promoted the nation-state idea | Colonial wars; discrimination; drew boundaries without consulting native peoples |
| Economic | Introduced modernization; improved means of transportation and communication; created industries; taught new skills; improved the standard of living; provided employment | Took wealth away from colony; treated workers badly; did not provide for advancement or mangement by colonized people; destroyed traditional industries and patterns of trade |
| Social | Introduced Christianity and other aspects of Western culture; built schools and hospitals; modern medicine | Looked down on native cultures; promoted racism and cultural inferiority; introduced Western vices and diseases |

# SECTION 1: SOUTH ASIA

## The British Raj (Rule) (1760–1947)

**WORLD ISSUES**

Determination of Political and Economic Systems

The British involvement in India, an example of imperialism, grew from economic contact to direct political control. Britain was able to outmaneuver its European rivals, build alliances with some Indian rulers of small areas, and inflict military defeat on other rulers.

**The British East India Company.** Granted a charter from Queen Elizabeth I in 1600, the British East India Company received permission from the Mughals to trade in India as early as 1613. From this time until 1858, the company exercised powers usually associated with a government. It had, for example, its own private army. One of its employees, Robert Clive, led military forces to victories over both French and native Indian armies. As a result of the most important of these victories, at Plassey in 1757, the British became the dominant economic and unofficial political power in the subcontinent.

**The Sepoy Mutiny and Direct Rule by Britain.** The Sepoy Mutiny of 1857 was fought against the British for both religious and political reasons. It began when Indians in the British army (sepoys) suspected that the grease used on bullet cartridges came from cows and pigs. If so, to bite into these cartridges would have violated Hindu and Muslim beliefs. These suspicions led to a rebellion that gradually spread beyond the military and became an anti-Western movement. (In fact, some Indian historians view the Sepoy Mutiny as a war of independence.) Eventually it was severely crushed. Nevertheless, the East India Company was abolished and replaced as a governing body by the British Crown. In 1876 Queen Victoria was proclaimed Empress of India. What was now called the Crown Colony of India actually included present-day Pakistan, India, and Bangladesh.

GLOBAL CONCEPTS

**Human Rights**

CONCEPTS GLOBAL

Rule by Britain brought some benefits to the colonized people, such as improved transportation and communication, health services, education, and political unity. However, colonial rule was more beneficial for the British, allowing them to exploit Indian resources and provide employment for many English people. In addition, Indians felt that their cultural values, beliefs, and practices were threatened because they clashed with those of the British. British ethnocentrism stirred bad feelings.

**Growth of an Indian Nationalist Movement.** The movement for Indian independence grew from distrust of British economic, cultural, and political practices. In addition, Indians felt it was wrong for Britain to preach democratic ideals while denying Indians democratic rights, such as the right of self-determination. The Sepoy Mutiny could be viewed as the first major step in an Indian nationalist movement. Other important developments included:

1. In 1885 the Indian National Congress was founded, initially to promote a gradual relaxation of British economic and political control. It eventually became known as the Congress Party. In the 20th century, leading political figures associated with the Congress Party were Mohandas Gandhi, Jawaharlal Nehru, and Indira Gandhi.

2. In 1906 the Muslim League was created by those Muslims who feared that the Congress Party was becoming too strongly dominated by Hindus. One of its founders was Mohammed Ali Jinnah.

3. From 1914 to 1918 British participation in World War I adversely affected Britain in the colony of India. Indian soldiers fought in Europe and gained military distinction. However, they soon began to question for whose interests they were really fighting. Also, they came to realize that the terrible tragedies associated with the war cast doubt on the British claim of the superiority of European culture and civilization.

4. In 1919 the Amritsar Massacre occurred when British troops fired on unarmed Indians attending a political rally. The death of hundreds of people in this town in the Punjab infuriated Indians.

5. In 1921 the Montagu-Chelmsford Reforms provided for a limited amount of self-government. This included a two-house legislature with limited powers that would have more members elected by Indians than appointed by the British.

6. In 1935 the Government of India Act extended the policy of limited self-government by letting Indian provinces have more control over their own affairs. It was intended to set the groundwork for India to become a self-governing dominion within the British Empire, like Canada.

7. Gandhi's nonviolent movement. Known as Mahatma ("the great soul"), Mohandas K. Gandhi organized boycotts and other nonviolent activities, such as a march to the sea to protest a salt tax, in an attempt to shame the British and achieve swaraj (self-rule). Gandhi also went on frequent hunger strikes. His nonviolent actions stemmed from the Hindu idea of "ahimsa." His tactics were described as examples of passive resistance and civil disobedience.

**World War II, Partition, and Independence.** With the end of World War II in 1945, Britain moved to seek a peaceful transition for Indian independence. Britain was exhausted after the war and did not want to spend the money or use the personnel needed to maintain the colony. It also wanted to adhere to the principles of the United Nations charter concerning self-determination for all people. However, even though the British had hoped to leave behind them one united country, there was much tension between Hindus and Muslims. The Congress Party, led by Jawaharlal Nehru, and the Muslim League, led by Mohammed Ali Jinnah, were unable to resolve all their differences. These differences led to much bloodshed and threatened to bring on a civil war if no agreement was reached on a partition plan. Eventually, on August 15, 1947, independence came with the creation of two independent nations, India and Pakistan, formed by a partition of the subcontinent.

GLOBAL
CONCEPTS

**Change**

CONCEPTS
GLOBAL

Era V **AN AGE OF REVOLUTIONS (1750–1918)**

# SECTION 2: CHINA

## China's Relationships with the West

Westerners became interested in opening relations with China for a number of reasons. Western missionaries wished to convert the Chinese to Christianity. Western traders were interested in obtaining Chinese silks, tea, ceramics, spices, and other luxury goods and in selling Western goods to the Chinese. In the 19th century, during the period of European imperialism, the Europeans sought to conquer Chinese territory and exploit its resources.

Chinese interest in Christianity and foreign trade was limited, however. The government, in an effort to limit foreign influence, restricted the activities of the missionaries. European trade with China was restricted to the port of Guangzhou (Canton) in 1757, and severe restrictions were placed on that trade. Foreign relations with the Chinese could only be conducted through the tributary system. The Chinese considered themselves superior to all other nations, and all non-Chinese were considered "barbarians."

## The Tribute System and Trade

The Chinese applied the idea of the tribute system to trade with the Europeans. As long as trade didn't interfere with the Chinese way of life and economy, and as long as the Westerners "knew their place," the Chinese would allow trade, but they

**GEOGRAPHY**

**Use of Geography**

believed they controlled that trade. The Europeans sought trade, not the Chinese. The Chinese believed that they produced everything they needed, and they saw trade as a favor extended to the Europeans. They were willing to sell to the Europeans, because they could understand that Europeans would want fine Chinese products. However, they did not believe that there was anything they might want from the Europeans. They did not wish to purchase European products, and the Europeans must therefore accept all the Chinese restrictions on trade or no trade would be allowed.

## The West Carves Up China in the 19th Century

**GEOGRAPHY**

**Human Systems**

The Chinese enjoyed a favorable balance of trade with the Europeans for many years. However, in opium, the Europeans finally found a product that turned the balance of trade in their favor. By 1839 the British were making enormous profits from the opium trade, and the Chinese government took steps to end the trade. British opium was confiscated and destroyed, and the British were informed they could no longer trade with China. In 1840 the British sent warships to China and the Opium War began. In 1842 the Chinese were defeated because of the superior technology of the West.

The treaty ending the war, the Treaty of Nanjing (Nanking) (1842), was the first of the unequal treaties forced upon China. The Chinese were forced to open five ports to trade; Hong Kong was ceded to the British; China was to pay a $21 million indemnity to Britain; foreign merchants were to be allowed to reside in the treaty ports; and the Chinese were not allowed to set tariffs (taxes on imports) in the treaty ports. Other nations, including the United States, Germany, Russia, and France,

**WORLD ISSUES**

War
and
Peace

---

**Causes of the Opium War**

**Background Causes**

**Chinese:**

1. British imported opium from India into China; addiction became a problem in China, upsetting society.
2. As demand for opium increased, silver was drained from China to pay for it, upsetting the economy and resulting in an unfavorable balance of trade.
3. Chinese law made opium trade illegal, British continued the trade.

**British:**

1. British resented being treated as inferiors under the tribute system.
2. Chinese put such a high tariff on British products most Chinese couldn't buy them.
3. British resented being restricted to Canton.
4. Chinese refused to import British textiles, one of Britain's most important industries.
5. Chinese law was applied to British citizens in China, and Chinese law was harsh.
6. British wanted free trade but did not want to trade through guilds or trade associations called cohongs, which was required in China.

**Immediate Cause**

Chinese officials burned British opium.

---

quickly followed suit, and China was forced to agree to more demands. Western diplomats were allowed to live in Beijing (Peking), Christian missionaries were able to establish churches, foreign powers were granted concessions in Chinese ports, and foreigners gained the right of extraterritoriality.

Furthermore, China was carved into spheres of influence, areas of China where only one imperialist Western power was allowed to dominate, with exclusive rights to trade. In 1894 China and Japan went to war over their interests in Korea, a Chinese tributary state. The Japanese, who had instituted rapid industrialization and militarization in the 1860s to prevent Western nations from carving up Japan, defeated China. China was forced to cede Taiwan and the Pescadores Islands to Japan, and Chinese influence in Korea was ended. Within a few years, Japan annexed Korea. China was being whittled away, but the Chinese, because of their lack of technological progress, were powerless to stop it. To prevent its exclusion from the China trade, in 1899 the United States encouraged Western nations to adopt the Open Door Policy: all nations would have equal trading rights in China and would recognize the territorial integrity of China.

**WORLD ISSUES**

Economic
Growth and
Development

---

### Treaty of Nanjing (Nanking):
### The First Unequal Treaty

**Britain Gained:**

1. Payment for the opium
2. Control of Hong Kong
3. Freedom to trade in five cities
4. Abolition of the tariff on British goods or the right to set the tariff low
5. Extraterritoriality
6. Most-favored nation clause

**China Lost:**

1. The right to control the British in China
2. Control over parts of Chinese territory and the Chinese people in it
3. The right to control their own infant industries with the tariff
4. Control of trade
5. Prestige—they were defeated by the "barbarians" and couldn't compete with them

## Chinese Response to Foreign Imperialism

Although the scholar-bureaucrats of China were resistant to change, some attempts at reform were made. The tributary system was replaced by a government office to deal with foreign representatives as diplomatic equals. Those in the government who favored reform wished to adopt Western technology without making any major changes in China's government or society. These reformers believed that the Chinese had been defeated only because of the superior armaments of the West. Western experts were employed to create and train a modern army and navy. A small effort was also made at industrialization. Coal mines were opened, arsenals and dockyards were built, and railroads and telegraph lines were constructed.

The real power in China between 1861 and 1908 was the Empress Dowager Cixi (Tzu-hsi), who ruled as regent for her son and then her nephew. In 1898 Guang-Xu (Kuang Hsu) took control of the government from his aunt and issued daily edicts calling for reforms. This period was called the Hundred Days Reform. Guang-Xu's edicts called for changes in government, in education, foreign policy, agriculture, technology, and the military. These reforms threatened the interests of Confucian scholars, government officials, Cixi, and also foreign interests in China. Cixi regained control of the government within three months and ended the reform movement. In 1900 anti-foreigner Chinese called "Boxers," with the secret support of the Empress Dowager, attacked the foreign delegations in Beijing, hoping to expel the foreigners (Westerners) from China. The Boxers were defeated by combined foreign forces after 55 days.

## Overthrow of the Emperor (1911–1912)

Revolts against the Manchu Qing (Ch'ing) Dynasty began in the late 1700s. However, most of the rebellions were limited and easy to suppress. One of the strongest uprisings against the Manchu was the Taiping Rebellion, which spread across southern and central China from 1850 to 1864.

A successful rebellion against the Manchus began on October 10, 1911. The revolutionaries declared a republic and elected Sun Yat-sen as the provisional president. His program for China was known as the Three Principles of the People, and the party to carry it out was the Kuomintang, the National People's Party, or the Nationalist Party.

GLOBAL
CONCEPTS
**Change**
CONCEPTS
GLOBAL

## Three Principles of the People

1. Nationalism meant both restoring the pride of the Chinese people and Chinese rule and removing the foreigners, their concessions, and their spheres of influence.

2. Democracy meant popular sovereignty, but it was to be approached in three stages: first, a military government to remove the Manchu Dynasty and defeat the Westerners; second, rule of the Kuomintang; and third, constitutional government, with popularly elected executive, judicial, and legislative branches called yuans.

3. Livelihood meant a program of land reform, the redistribution of land to the peasants, and the elimination of the system of tenant farming. The government was to control transportation, communication, and heavy industry.

The Manchus turned to Yuan Shih-kai (a former general in the Manchu army) to defeat the revolution. Instead, Yuan reached an agreement with the revolutionaries and used his power to force the abdication of the Manchu emperor. In return, Sun Yat-sen resigned as president of the republic and was replaced by Yuan. Yuan became a military dictator and eliminated the democratic reforms instituted by Sun and the Kuomintang. Sun and his followers tried to overthrow him, but Sun was forced into exile. Yuan died in 1916, and Sun returned to China. However, warlords who had been building up their own power in the provinces began to struggle against each other to gain control of the country. China fell into a decade of total chaos, with warlords fighting each other.

# SECTION 3: JAPAN

## Americans Arrive in Japan

On July 14, 1853, Commodore Matthew Perry, in command of four U.S. ships, sailed into Tokyo Bay. The Japanese had never seen steamships before and were astonished at the fire power of the warships. Perry carried with him a letter from U.S. President Millard Fillmore, demanding that Japan open its ports to American trade and ships, and that the government guarantee fair treatment of American sailors (shipwrecked sailors were badly treated).

The Japanese were opposed to the American demands, but the government of the shogun realized that the Japanese could not defend themselves against American technology. In 1854 the shogun's government signed a treaty opening two Japanese ports to American ships to take on supplies, and an American consulate was opened. Within four years, the United States had been granted full trade rights in several other ports, extraterritoriality, and limitations on the Japanese right to impose tariffs on American goods. Soon the European powers were demanding the same rights. The Japanese believed that Japan would be cut up into spheres of influence, as China had been, unless they took steps to prevent it.

**GEOGRAPHY**

Use of Geography

GLOBAL
CONCEPTS

**Change**

CONCEPTS
GLOBAL

Era V **AN AGE OF REVOLUTIONS (1750–1918)**

## Meiji Restoration (1868–1912)

Many Japanese blamed the shogunate for failing to defend Japan against foreign interference and believed that the Tokugawa could not resist the foreigners. In 1868 samurai forces overthrew the shogunate and restored the emperor's rule. This so-called Meiji Restoration brought to the throne Emperor Matshuhito, who was only fifteen years old.

## Changes by 1912

The Japanese who led the overthrow of the shogun and the restoration of the emperor believed that the only way to remove the threat of the Western powers was a rapid program of modernization to enable Japan to compete with the West. Japan already had a high literacy rate, a high degree of urbanization, a large pool of skilled labor, and channels for mass training of citizens. What stood in the way of full-scale modernization was the feudal system, which the leaders of the restoration set about to destroy.

The daimyo (feudal lords) were persuaded to give up their estates, and Japan was divided into prefectures under the direct control of the government in Tokyo (the new name for Edo). Class divisions and restrictions were abolished, and equality of all people was declared. The samurai lost all their special privileges, and universal military service was adopted. An education system was established.

The leaders of the restoration created a highly centralized bureaucratic government, which was an oligarchy (a small group controlling the government and allowing little opposition). In 1889 the Japanese were presented with a written constitution, a "gift from the emperor." The new constitution established a two-house legislature, called the Diet. This was a severely limited democracy, and the small elite group who took control of the government in 1868 remained in control. The Western powers recognized Japan's efforts to provide at least a limited democracy.

A program of rapid modernization was begun. The government constructed railroads, highways, and telegraph lines and also built industries—textile mills, armaments factories, shipbuilding facilities—and opened mines. Later these industries were sold to private enterprise, thereby sponsoring the development of the zaibatsu (Japanese industrial monopolies that controlled all aspects of an industry). Japanese students were sent to Western nations to study, and Western advisers were employed. Western experts were hired to assist the Japanese in developing a modern army and navy. By the close of the 19th century, the foundations of a truly modern state had been laid.

## Japanese Expansion Prior to World War II

Japanese aggression against weaker neighbors resulted from its need to acquire raw materials for its industrialization. Such aggression was modeled after imperialist actions of the Western powers in the late 19th and early 20th centuries. By the late 19th century, Japan's rulers were concerned that Korea, "a dagger pointed at the heart of Japan," would fall into the hands of an imperialist Western power because the Manchu Dynasty in China could not defend it. This led to the Sino-Japanese War (Sino means Chinese) of 1894 to 1895, which was won by Japan. The Treaty of Shimonoseki granted Japan control of Taiwan, the Pescadores, and China's Liaotung Peninsula, plus an indemnity of several hundred million dollars and trade concessions in China. Korea was declared to be independent of China, and Japan began to seek control of the region.

Japan's chief rival in Korea was Russia, and the Japanese launched an attack in 1904 against the Russian fleet based at Port Arthur, beginning the Russo-Japanese War. The Russians were driven out of Korea and southern Manchuria, and Japan captured Port Arthur. In 1905 U.S. President Theodore Roosevelt negotiated peace between the two belligerents. The Treaty of Portsmouth gave Russia's lease on Port Arthur and its concessions in southern Manchuria to Japan. By 1910 Korea had been annexed by Japan.

**WORLD ISSUES**

Determination
of Political
and Economic
Systems

**WORLD ISSUES**

Economic
Growth and
Development

**WORLD ISSUES**

War
and
Peace

**GEOGRAPHY**

Use of Geography

# SECTION 4: AFRICA

## European Imperialism in Africa

In the late 19th century, the Europeans began to explore the interior of Africa and to expand their control. This imperialist expansion was made possible by their technological superiority. As the Europeans expanded in Africa, they dominated the African people as well as their territory. They used the excuse of "the white man's burden," a legacy of the slave trade, to justify this expansion, claiming that it was their duty to bring civilization, progress, and Christianity to the less developed regions of the world. In reality, their major goal was to accumulate profit and power. This period of European imperialism was influenced by industrial capitalism and the increasing demands for raw materials for European factories and for markets for European manufactured goods. The Europeans needed African resources—mineral, land, forest products. They also desired greater power and prestige. The more territory they controlled, the more powerful and important they became, and European nations became rivals for African territory.

The Africans resisted the intrusion of Europeans and felt they were defending themselves against invasion. The Zulu fought the British and Boers in South Africa. The Sudanese fought the British. The Mandingo fought the French in West Africa. The Germans were forced to fight in East Africa. The Africans fought conventionally and also used guerrilla tactics, but their weapons were no match for those of the Europeans. Some of the African peoples used passive resistance. The Bushmen and Hottentots in South Africa simply disappeared into the bush.

In 1875, European holdings in Africa were fairly small, but by 1914 all of Africa except Ethiopia and Liberia were under European control. The scramble for Africa began after King Leopold of Belgium announced he was taking control of the vast Congo Free State in Central Africa in 1879. In 1885, at the Berlin Conference, the European nations reached agreement on how Africa should be divided into colonial territories.

Some Africans served as mercenaries in the European armies or worked with the colonial governments. The British used a colonial policy known as indirect rule. They left tribal leaders in charge, but the Africans were actually puppet rulers who followed directions from the British colonial administrators.

The French practiced a policy of assimilation. Their hope was to make the Africans "French" by changing their culture

GLOBAL
CONCEPTS
**Power**
CONCEPTS
GLOBAL

**GEOGRAPHY**

**Use of Geography**

GLOBAL
CONCEPTS
**Political Systems**
CONCEPTS
GLOBAL

GLOBAL
CONCEPTS

**Change**

CONCEPTS
GLOBAL

GEOGRAPHY

**Human Systems**

and traditions. The French ruled more directly than the British and removed the traditional rulers.

The Belgians used a policy of paternalism, treating the indigenous peoples as children who needed to be cared and provided for.

The Portuguese at first believed the Africans needed to be taught discipline and obedience. In the 20th century, however, this attitude changed, and they adopted a policy of assimilation intended to eventually make the Africans citizens of Portugal.

German rule in Africa was different in different colonies. In some they used forced labor. In others they tried the indirect rule approach.

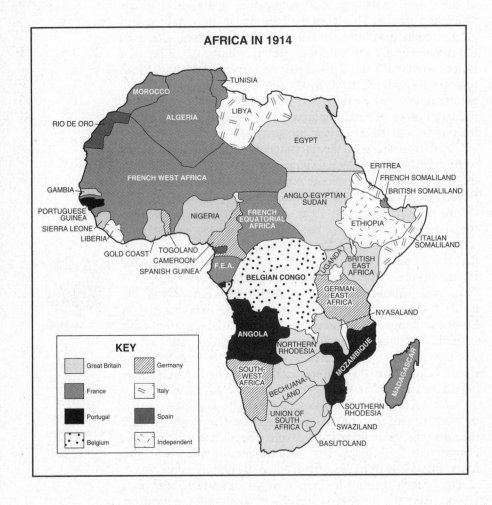

AFRICA IN 1914

KEY

| | |
|---|---|
| Great Britain | Germany |
| France | Italy |
| Portugal | Spain |
| Belgium | Independent |

# Effects of European Rule on Africa

1. *Establishment of boundaries.* When the Europeans divided Africa, they drew up boundaries that had nothing to do with physical features or ethnic boundaries. As a result, ethnic groups found their territories divided among more than one colony; some were within boundaries with traditional enemies. Because the colonies were granted independence based on the European-drawn boundaries, the problems created by dividing ethnic territories or expecting enemies to coexist remain in modern Africa.

2. *Changes in agriculture.* To provide raw materials for their industries, the Europeans encouraged the development of plantations and the cultivation of cash crops such as cocoa, cotton, coffee, peanuts, and palm oil. Many Africans concentrated on the cultivation of these cash crops, and they had to import food crops to feed themselves. In areas of heavy European settlement, such as South Africa and the Kenya highlands, the best farmland was reserved for Europeans.

3. *Transition from barter to money economy.* Taxes such as the head tax or the hut tax had to be paid in cash. To pay the tax, many Africans were forced to work for Europeans. They had to move to the city, sometimes with their families, sometimes leaving the family in the countryside to work the land, thereby destabilizing the family system. In addition, the money economy created greater disparities in wealth. Some Africans accumulated capital, while others did not. As a result, social tension was created between the haves and the have nots.

4. *Changes in the landholding system.* Europeans introduced the idea of individual ownership of land. This weakened tribal ties and also meant that for some, there was no land, thus destroying the Africans' traditional way of making a living.

5. *Exploitation of resources.* The Europeans needed raw materials for their factories, so they developed the resources of Africa by opening mines and plantations. The benefits of this development went to the Europeans, not the Africans.

6. *Improved transportation and communications.* In order to exploit the resources of Africa, the Europeans had to build railroads and communications systems. These improvements benefited the Africans by assisting in the development of national unity and opening remote regions of the interior to economic development. However, they also accelerated the migration of African labor to areas where work could be found, further weakening tribal and family ties.

7. *New legal and judicial systems.* The European nations introduced their own ideas of law and justice in the colonies.

GLOBAL CONCEPTS

**Identity**

CONCEPTS GLOBAL

**GEOGRAPHY**

**Human Systems**

**WORLD ISSUES**

Determination of Political and Economic Systems

**GEOGRAPHY**

**Environment and Society**

**GEOGRAPHY**

**Human Systems**

Era V **AN AGE OF REVOLUTIONS (1750–1918)**

Secular law and religious law were separated, while traditional law was changed or abolished, again weakening group ties and eroding traditional authority systems.

8. *Education.* Although education was not freely available to all Africans, some education was provided. Through European education, Africans learned of democracy and natural human rights and again began to reject traditional authority systems. Traditional African culture was downgraded and European culture upheld as the example of how things should be. Educated Africans became the core of the nationalist movements in Africa and led the struggle for political independence from colonial domination.

9. *Preventive medicine and improved nutrition.* Because of Western medicines and medical practices, the infant mortality rate and overall death rate dropped dramatically. As a result, Africa has the most rapidly increasing population growth rate (about 3 percent) of any of the continents.

# Part E: Global Changes and Revolutions (1750–1914)

## SECTION 1: RUSSIA

### Expansion and Modernization Under the Tsars (1725–1905)

Under the tsars and tsaritsas who succeeded Peter I, Russia continued to expand its empire and its involvement with Western Europe. During the reign of Ekaterina or Catherine II (1762–1796), usually referred to as "the Great," Russia regained the parts of Ukraine and Belarussia lost under the last Rurik tsars, as well as Lithuania. In the southeast, the last of the Tartar tribes were defeated, thus gaining the entire Crimea and much of the northern coast of the Black Sea at the expense of the Ottoman Turks. This began a traditional policy that was pursued by the Soviet government as well as the later tsars—to gain Constantinople (modern-day Istanbul) and the straits that connect the Black Sea with the Aegean and the Mediterranean (the Dardanelles) in order to have access to major trade routes. In addition, much of Siberia was explored and settled by Russians.

Tsar Alexander I (1801–1825) was credited as the monarch who defeated Napoleon. This victory was due to the "Scorched Earth" policy (retreating and burning anything that could not be taken rather than leaving it for the enemy) that the Russians adopted in response to Napoleon's invasion. A lack of supplies and the severely cold winter devastated the French army. Thousands died during the chaotic retreat. At the Congress of Vienna, Russia acquired most of Poland. Alexander also gained Finland from Sweden in 1809.

Under the strong autocratic rule of Nikolai or Nicholas I (1825–1855), Russia was unsuccessful in further expansion. Greatly shaken by the Decembrist Revolt of 1825 (in which officers favoring democratic reforms tried to overthrow Nicholas), the tsar fought any movement for change. Fearing that reform would undermine his authority, Nicholas followed repressive policies at home and abroad (he earned the title "Policeman of Europe"). Yet, Russia's defeat in the Crimean War (1854–1856) revealed the need for both reform and modernization.

GLOBAL
CONCEPTS

**Empathy**

CONCEPTS
GLOBAL

**WORLD ISSUES**

War

and

Peace

**GEOGRAPHY**

**Use of Geography**

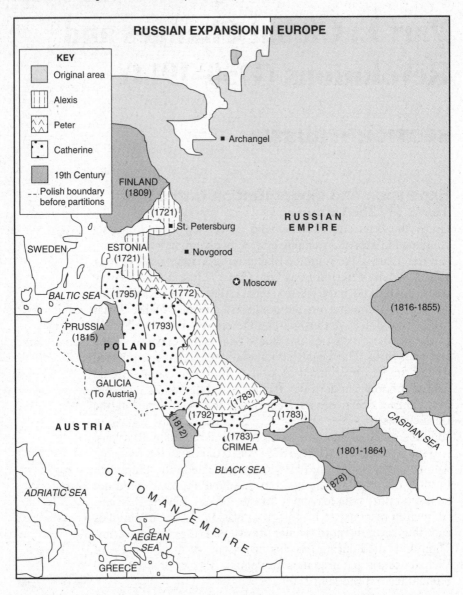

## RUSSIAN EXPANSION IN EUROPE

**KEY**

Original area

Alexis

Peter

Catherine

19th Century

Polish boundary
before partitions

Archangel

FINLAND
(1809)

(1721)

St. Petersburg

RUSSIAN
EMPIRE

SWEDEN

ESTONIA
(1721)

Novgorod

BALTIC SEA

(1795)

(1772)

Moscow

(1816-1855)

PRUSSIA
(1815)

(1793)

POLAND

CASPIAN SEA

GALICIA
(To Austria)

(1783)

(1792)

(1783)

AUSTRIA

(1812)

(1783)
CRIMEA

(1801-1864)

ADRIATIC SEA

OTTOMAN EMPIRE

BLACK SEA

(1878)

AEGEAN
SEA

GREECE

Alexander II (1855–1881), the son of Nicholas I, made many of the necessary changes that his father would not. Known as the "Tsar Liberator," Alexander ended the institution of serfdom (peasants were bound to the land they farmed and were therefore controlled by the landowner), which held back the expansion of Russian agriculture and promoted many abuses and social evils. Industrialization was also started in order to make Russia competitive with other European nations. Finally, Alexander

Tsar Nicholas I

Tsar Alexander II

instituted reforms in government, education, and the military that ended many abuses and cruelties and modernized the Russian system. Despite the many changes made by Alexander II, new problems were created by the reforms themselves.

1. The liberation of the serfs created many small farmers who could not pay off their debts. This resulted in mass foreclosures and enormous migrations of unskilled workers to the cities.

2. The abundance of unskilled labor gave factory owners the opportunity to exploit the workers, or proletariat.

3. Widespread exploitation of workers resulted in poverty, slums, and unsafe working conditions in Russian cities and industrial centers.

4. The exploited workers became strong supporters of revolutionary ideas and parties, particularly the Socialists, Communists, and Anarchists. The assassination of Alexander II in 1881 resulted in the end of reform and a renewal of repression.

Alexander III (1881–1894) reacted to his father's murder by enforcing strict control over his subjects. Reinstituting a policy of Russification (forcing Russian language, culture, and religion on all peoples in the Russian Empire), Alexander created resentment and revolutionary feelings.

# SECTION 2: OTTOMAN EMPIRE (1453–1918)

During the 1800s, the Ottoman Empire began to decline. Reasons for its decline included corruption and inefficiency on the part of the rulers as well as their inability to hold together so many different peoples. Many of the subject people wished to break free from Ottoman control. Several short wars with other nations weakened Ottoman rule and caused a loss of territory. Finally, the Ottomans failed to modernize and keep up with the growth in industry, technology, learning, science, weapons, and trade that was occurring in Western Europe. As a result, the declining empire became known as "the Sick Man of Europe."

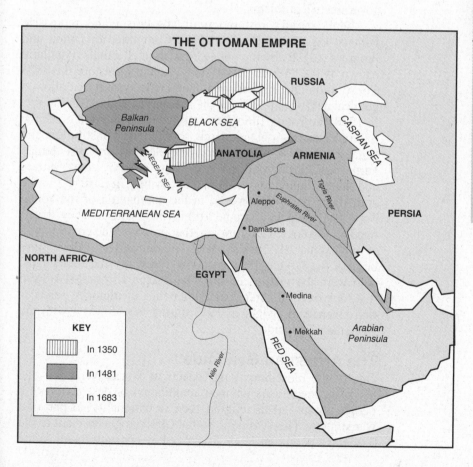

THE OTTOMAN EMPIRE

RUSSIA
Balkan Peninsula
BLACK SEA
CASPIAN SEA
AEGEAN SEA
ANATOLIA
ARMENIA
Tigris River
Aleppo
Euphrates River
MEDITERRANEAN SEA
PERSIA
Damascus
NORTH AFRICA
EGYPT
Medina
KEY
Mekkah
Arabian Peninsula
In 1350
RED SEA
In 1481
Nile River
In 1683

# THE GROWTH OF TURKISH NATIONALISM (1876–1912)

By the mid-1870s the weaknesses in the Ottoman system had made it clear that reform was needed if the Turkish empire were to continue to exist. Under the influence of young Turkish intellectuals who had been educated in Western Europe, the Ottoman government allowed the creation of a constitution in 1876. Supported by the leaders of the non-Turkish minority groups as well, the reformers proposed the transformation of the empire into a constitutional monarchy with a freely elected assembly in which all groups would be proportionately represented. Sultan Abdul Hamid II (r. 1876–1909) responded by revoking the constitution and beginning a period of political repression in 1878. He ordered the massacre of over 200,000 Armenians, claiming this large Christian minority was responsible for revolutionary activity. This began a tradition in the Ottoman Empire of "scapegoating" or blaming others for a government's problems.

Abdul Hamid's restoration of absolutism and repressive policies led to the creation of the Committee of Union and Progress (C.U.P.) by the young Turkish intellectuals. Popularly known as the "Young Turks," they wanted to restore the 1876 Constitution and implement a democratic system that allowed political representation for all the nations in the Ottoman Empire. In 1908, the Young Turks led a military takeover that made the Sultan a constitutional monarch, restored the Constitution, and began preparations for the first free elections for an Ottoman Parliament. Strong opposition to the reforms by conservatives and the continued loss of Ottoman territory in Eastern Europe and Africa resulted however, in the domination of the Young Turk leadership by extreme Turkish nationalists. They developed an ideology, Pan-Turkism, that proposed the creation of a strong exclusively Turkish state. The minorities of the empire became the targets of persecution, especially the Armenians, who were the victims of further massacres from 1894–1896 that took over 300,000 lives. This policy of minority persecution reached its height in 1915 during World War I with the Armenian Genocide.

## The Armenian Genocide

One of the most horrifying aspects of World War I was the use of genocide (the planned annihilation or destruction of a people because of its religion, race, or nationality) as part of a war strategy. This was done by the Ottoman government to the Armenian people in 1915. Frustrated by constant losses in the war, the Ottoman leadership made the Armenians "scapegoats" and claimed they were responsible for the Empire's poor military performance. The leaders of the government, a group of army officers known as the Young Turks, adopted this policy as a means of shifting the population's anger and dissatisfaction with the war effort away from themselves. Accusing Armenians of working with the Allies against the Ottoman Empire, the government began a systematic extermination of them on April 24, 1915. Armenian men were rounded up and massacred while the women and children were taken on death marches into the desert. Armenia's political and religious leaders were publicly executed. Armenian churches and institutions were destroyed and their confiscated homes given to Turkish people. Some Armenians were able to escape into Russia or Syria, but the majority were slaughtered. Out of a population of only three million, almost two million were massacred. The surviving Armenians established a republic in the Soviet Union after the war. The Young Turk leaders, who had fled Ottoman Turkey after the defeat of the Central Powers, were found guilty of war crimes by an Ottoman military court, but were never punished. After the modern nation of Turkey was established in 1922, the new government under Mustafa Kemal (later known as "Ataturk") denied the Armenian Genocide ever occurred. This policy of official denial has been continued by successive Turkish governments until the present day.

## THE GREEK WAR OF INDEPENDENCE (1821–1832)

The first people in the Ottoman Empire to rebel against Turkish rule were the Greeks. In 1821, they rose up inspired by a new sense of nationhood led by young Greeks who had been educated in Western Europe and exposed to the concepts of nationalism and democracy. Using the slogan "Freedom or Death" to rally the population, they were supported by the clergy of the Greek Orthodox Church and foreigners who were **philhellenes** or "friends of Greece," such as the English poet Lord Byron. Unsuccessful at first, they soon gained support by the British, French, and Russians who were hoping to gain influence in the region. Both Austria and Prussia opposed their support as they feared it would encourage the other Eastern Europeans to demand independence as well. This produced a conflict of interests that permanently ended the agreements made by the Great Powers at the Congress of Vienna to oppose revolution. The Greek cause also had support from famous writers, artists, and composers throughout Western Europe. By 1832, parts of

Greece had been freed from Ottoman control and formed the modern Greek state.

## Independence and Pan-Slavism (1821–1914)

The Greek struggle for independence in 1821 touched off a movement throughout Eastern Europe to end Turkish domination in that region. As revolutions broke out in each country, the rivalry between Russia and Austria intensified. The other major European powers became involved, trying to maintain the balance of power. In 1683 the Habsburgs defeated the Turks and captured Hungary. In 1815 Russia and Austria divided Poland at the Congress of Vienna after the Napoleonic Wars. By 1900, Austria had also gained Bohemia (modern-day Czech Republic) and Croatia. Both Russia and Austria had great interest, therefore, in the shape of the new independent Eastern European states.

GLOBAL
CONCEPTS

**Change**

CONCEPTS
GLOBAL

GEOGRAPHY

Use of Geography

Throughout the 19th century, Russia financed and supported wars for independence in Greece, Serbia Montenegro, Bulgaria, and Romania. Developing the concept of Pan-Slavism (political, religious, and cultural unity of all Slavs and/or Orthodox Christians), Russian tsars came into conflict with the British, Germans, and French, as well as the Austrians and Turks. Territorial gains made by the Eastern European nations from the Ottomans in the Second Russo-Turkish War (1877–1878) and the Balkan Wars (1912–1913) were limited by the rest of the Great Powers, who feared Russia's growing influence in the region. The modern nation of Albania was created in 1913, as a compromise between Russia and the other Western powers concerning Serbian expansion. By 1914 tensions had grown so great in Eastern Europe, especially in the Balkans, that it was called the "Tinderbox of Europe." The incident that set off World War I, the assassination of the Austrian Archduke Franz Ferdinand by a Serbian nationalist, was one further example of how explosive the tension of Eastern Europe had become.

# SECTION 3: LATIN AMERICA

## Establishment of Political Independence in Latin America

The 1700s was a period of great political, social, and economic change for the European powers. Britain's thirteen colonies in North America won their independence as a result of the American Revolution. In the late 1700s the French Revolution shook the stability of Europe. The writings of the Enlightenment, expressed in the works of Locke, Rousseau, Voltaire, Montesquieu, and others, led to the spread of revolutionary ideas in Europe and the Americas. In the 1700s Spain sought to reform its American empire. New viceroyalties were created, and an intendancy system was introduced to increase revenues and improve the colonial administration. A Spanish officer appointed by the crown, an *intendente*, had complete control in matters of justice, war, fiscal problems and general public administration over a given area. Despite these reforms, the foreign policy of Spain's Bourbon monarchy, which allied the nation with France, led to a series of military engagements that greatly weakened the Spanish empire. Spain's economic situation and military power continued to decline into the 1790s.

The Napoleonic era that followed the French Revolution caused dislocations that eventually led to a period of Latin American revolutions from 1808 to 1826. Despite the distance and isolation of Spain's colonies from Europe, the political ideas of the Enlightenment and the American and French revolutions affected the people in the Spanish colonies. The English, Dutch, French, and Americans increasingly traded with Spain's American empire. Moreover, some of the creole elite in the Spanish colonies, such as the Venezuelan Francisco Miranda, promoted the independence of Spanish America.

Napoleon's armies invaded Spain and Portugal in 1806 to 1807. The capture and exile of the Spanish royal family to France and the placement of Joseph Bonaparte on the Spanish throne broke the bond that tied Spanish America to Spain. A movement that began as a rejection of French control ended as a series for wars of independence against Spain.

The liberators, Simón Bolívar and José San Martín, and their supporters raised armies to drive the Spanish out of South America. In Mexico the leadership of Fathers Hidalgo and Morelos and other revolutionaries led to the eventual success of Agustín de Iturbide, who established Mexican independence in 1821.

Creole nationalism was too strong to overcome, and with the help of the mestizo population, the Spanish were driven out.

## Case Study in Independence: Haiti

The movement toward Haitian independence was sparked by the French Revolution. Throughout the 1790s, the former slaves, first led by Toussaint l'Ouverture, increasingly sought to drive out the white slave owners. Despite a major attempt by Napoleon to restore French authority in 1802, independence was inevitable. In 1804 Jean-Jacques Dessalines, an ex-slave, was able to drive out the French, and Haiti became the second nation in the western hemisphere to win complete independence.

## Case Study in Independence: Mexico

In 1810 Miguel Hidalgo, a priest, joined with other creole plotters, most notably Ignacio de Allende, and issued the famous Grito de Dolores. This symbol raised the cry of rebellion against the Spanish government in New Spain. The first phase of the struggle for independence ended with the royalists' defeating the insurgents and executing many of the leaders of the rebellion. Despite this setback, one of Hidalgo's lieutenants, Jose Morelos, called together a congress, which wrote a constitution and declared independence. Morelos was captured and executed in 1815. However, independence was finally secured in 1821 when Agustín de Iturbide, a creole military officer who had helped defeat the earlier rebellions, negotiated with Vincente Guerrero, by then the principal insurgent leader, to form the Plan of Iguala, which called for independence under a monarchy. Iturbide forced the Spanish out and briefly ruled Mexico as emperor.

### LATIN AMERICAN INDEPENDENCE MOVEMENTS TO 1828

| Country | Year of Independence | Independence Movement Leaders |
|---|---|---|
| Haiti | 1803–1804 | Toussaint l'Ouverture |
| Mexico | 1821 | Father Miguel Hidalgo |
| | | José Morelos |
| | | Agustín de Iturbide |
| Colombia | 1819 | Simón Bolívar |
| Venezuela | 1821 | Francisco de Miranda |
| | | Simón Bolívar |
| Ecuador | 1822 | José de Sucre |
| | | Simón Bolívar |
| Argentina | 1816 | José de San Martin |
| Chile | 1818 | José de San Martin |
| | | Bernardo O'Higgins |
| Peru | 1824 | José de Sucre |
| | | Simón Bolívar |

| Country | Year of Independence | Independence Movement Leaders |
|---|---|---|
| Bolivia | 1825 | Simón Bolívar |
| Uruguay | 1814, 1828 | José Artigas |
| Brazil | 1822 | José Bonifacio |
| | | Emperor Dom Pedro |
| Paraguay | 1811 | Fulgencio Yegros |
| Central American Republics | 1812–1825 | José Delgado |
| | | José del Valle |

## Case Studies: Argentina, Chile, and the Role of José de San Martin

In 1810 a revolutionary regime in Buenos Aires declared independence. José de San Martín, the real architect of independence, had liberated the future Argentina by 1816. He crossed the Andes Mountains with an army in 1817 and helped Bernardo O'Higgins drive the Spanish army out of Chile the following year. San Martin was also involved in the liberation of Peru, but he left the final military struggle in that country after an historic meeting with Simón Bolívar, the Liberator.

## Case Study: The Andean Region and the Role of Simón Bolívar, "the Liberator"

Simón Bolívar, by birth a member of the creole landowning elite, supported the growing independence movement. Between 1810 and 1821, the Liberator was involved in wars to free the future nations of Venezuela, Colombia, Ecuador, Bolivia, and Peru. He was made the first constitutional president of Gran Colombia in 1821. With the help of Francisco Santander and Antonio José de Sucre, Bolívar defeated the Spanish royalist forces by 1826, and they withdrew from Peru.

## Case Study: Brazil

Napoleon's invasion of Portugal resulted in the royal family leaving for Brazil. Joao VI became king of Portugal, Brazil, and the Algarve in 1816. Joao helped the British commercial interests by opening the Brazilian ports to trade with friendly nations. This measure also resulted in promoting Brazil's economic autonomy. However, in 1821 political events in Portugal caused Joao to return there. He left behind his son, Pedro I, as regent of Brazil. In 1822, Pedro issued his famous "I am staying" statement after the Portuguese parliament ordered him to return to Portugal. Later that year, independence was declared. In contrast to Spanish America, Brazilian independence was achieved peacefully. Pedro I was declared emperor of Brazil in 1822.

## Case Study: The Caribbean

The one area where Spain retained its colonies was in the Caribbean. Cuba and Puerto Rico remained possessions of Spain until the Spanish-American War in 1898. The sugar-plantation owners dominated the economies of these two Greater Antilles islands, and slavery was the main source of labor, particularly in Cuba. The cooperation of Spanish and creole landowners, merchants, and government officials prevented an independence movement from developing on these islands.

In the British, French, and Dutch Caribbean colonies, with the exception of Haiti, independence has been attained more recently, if at all. Many of the British-held islands did not achieve independence until the post-World War II period. Some islands have remained attached to Great Britain. The French-speaking islands were made overseas departments, which gave them the privilege of representation in the nation's politics and the right of French citizenship. However, the real political power remained in France.

## Early Attempts at Unification Fail

The initial attempts at unification of the newly independent states did not last, mainly because nationalistic feelings in the Latin American countries led to political fragmentation. The political union of present-day Colombia, Venezuela, Ecuador, and Panama in Gran Colombia was established in 1819 through the efforts of Simón Bolívar, Francisco Santander, and others. At the Congress of Cucuta in 1821, a constitution was adopted. Bolívar and Santander were elected the first president and vice president for all of Colombia. Santander remained to direct the government after Bolívar went off to liberate Peru. The central government promoted a program of liberal reform. However, attempts by the landed elite to safeguard their local authority and autonomy in Venezuela and Ecuador led in 1826 to an open revolt that broke out in Venezuela. The return of Bolívar temporarily brought unity and peace. However, a brief war soon began between Peru and Gran Colombia in 1828, and this caused the local landed elite to renew their struggle for a political entity that would be more easily influenced and run in their interests. In 1830 first Venezuela and then Ecuador formally seceded. The remaining part of Gran Colombia became the Republic of New Granada.

The Federation of Central America was created when the five provinces—Guatemala, El Salvador, Honduras, Nicaragua, and Costa Rica—declared independence in 1821 and joined the

Mexican Empire under Iturbide. They drafted a constitution and adopted a republican form of government. The new government immediately had political difficulties, and in 1823 the five provinces left the federation and became independent states. By the 1840s the federation had ceased to exist.

## Sources of Stability and Power: The Landed Elite, the Military, and the Roman Catholic Church

The failure of unification in South America and in Central America was a result of the concentration of power in the hands of the creole landed elite in the independent nations of Latin America. The large landowners gained enormous power in their local areas and were unwilling to surrender it to a strong central government. The creole aristocracy, who owned large estates called latifundio, replaced the Spanish officials and peninsulars. They were unwilling to share political power, and the large landowners became a conservative force that sought to maintain stability and their traditional local powers. Instead of unity, Latin America fell victim to frequent disputes concerning ownership of land within each nation and along border areas. These problems have continued to our present day.

The role of the military also proved to be a continuing problem in Latin America. In the early years, military leaders were called on to maintain law and order and act as a stabilizing influence. The military shared a common goal with the landed elite, which was to preserve the status quo. In some countries, the military was the only organized force that could prevent chaos after the wars of national independence.

The rebellions that frequently broke out in the Spanish-speaking republics in the 1800s led the armed forces of many nations to control their countries for long periods. The rise of the military dictator, the caudillo, became a tradition in many countries. José Antonio Paez of Venezuela and Andres Santa Cruz of Bolivia are early examples of caudillos in their nations. Venezuela suffered fifty revolutions and Bolivia sixty revolutions by 1900.

Military figures continued to gain and hold onto power in the 20th century. The military continues to see itself as the preserver of stability and tradition. Today, a military coup d'état is justified to prevent the possibility of a communist takeover and social disintegration. This was the case in Chile when General Augusto Pinochet seized power in 1973.

After the wars of independence, the Roman Catholic Church remained a key institution throughout Latin America. Until recently, the Church often supported the landed elite and military in their efforts to preserve tradition and social order and showed little concern for social problems. However, in recent years the role of the Church in some Latin American nations has changed, as the clergy has taken a more active role in causes concerning human rights. Some members of the clergy have supported the ideas of the liberation theology, a church of the people and even rebellions against the government in power. The struggle within the Church between conservatives, who believe that the clergy should continue its traditional historic role, and radicals, who want the clergy to play a more social and political role, continues. In addition, the Roman Catholic Church is also under pressure due to inroads made by Protestant denominations, particularly the evangelical movements that stress the importance of reconciliation and personal experience with God.

## Political Evolution Since Independence

In Latin America, a concept of citizenship was slow to develop after independence. There also were difficulties in attempting to institute a republican form of government. Political participation was open primarily to the wealthy members of society. The landed elite consolidated their hold on the executive and legislative branches of government. In theory, some democratic traditions were established in many Latin American countries in the 19th century. For example, constitutions were written, elected legislative bodies were provided for, and judicial systems were created. However, in practice, the *caudillo* acted as a dictator and often ignored the democratic features of government.

## Mexico

In the late 1820s a military caudillo, Antonio Santa Anna, rose to power. He dominated Mexican politics to the mid-1850s and supported a conservative and centralist concept of government. Unfortunately, Santa Anna resorted to dictatorial rule and corrupt policies that had disastrous consequences. Mexico, under Santa Anna's leadership, fell victim to U.S. expansionism. The successful rebellion led by Americans in Texas in the 1830s and the Mexican War in the 1840s led to a loss of over 40 percent of Mexico's territory.

After Santa Anna's exile in 1855, Benito Juárez tried to rule Mexico under more democratic ideals. In the mid-1870s, Porfirio Diaz, a soldier and protégé of Juárez, was elected president and held political power until the Mexican Revolution of 1911. During Díaz's rule, Mexico was transformed into a politically stable and economically progressive nation, but at the expense of political freedom and democratic government. Foreign investment was encouraged in railroads, oil, and mining. Díaz's political power was based on the use of a repressive police force, the *rurales*, to control his opponents. The peasants continued to live under terrible conditions, and the urban labor movement was suppressed. Díaz was supported by the elite hacienda owners, the Roman Catholic Church, and the military.

# REVIEW QUESTIONS

*Multiple Choice.* Select the letter of the answer that correctly completes the statement.

1. The ideas of the European Enlightenment encouraged revolution in
   A. Europe and Asia
   B. Europe and its colonies
   C. Europe and the Middle East
   D. Europe and Africa

2. The revolutions of the 19th century were similar in that they were all
   A. inspired by the French Revolution of 1789
   B. the result of the development of nationalism
   C. inspired by European ideas or events
   D. the result of industrialization

3. Which of the following groups consists of revolutionary leaders only?
   A. Toussaint l'Overture, Maximillian Robespierre, Klemens von Metternich
   B. Simon Bolivar, Sun Yat Sen, Friedrich Engels
   C. Guiseppe Mazzini, Napoleon Bonaparte, Otto von Bismarck
   D. Fr. Miguel Hidalgo, Karl Marx, Emperor Matshuhito

4. Which of the following was not nationalist in origin?
   A. Greek War of Independence (1821)
   B. Meiji Restoration (1868)
   C. Boxer Rebellion (1900)
   D. Industrial Revolution (early 1800s)

5. Which of the following revolutions did not replace a monarchy with a democracy?
   A. France (1789)
   B. Colombia (1821)
   C. Japan (1868)
   D. China (1911)

6. The only African nations to avoid European imperialism in the 19th century were
   A. Congo Free State and Sierra Leone
   B. Union of South Africa and Angola
   C. Ethiopia and Liberia
   D. Orange Free State and Transvaal

7. Which of the following did not occur during the 19th century?
   A. Industrial Revolution in Western Europe
   B. Division of China into "protectorates"
   C. European imperialism of Latin America
   D. Rise of nationalism in Eastern Europe

8. Which of the following leaders encouraged 19th-century imperialism?
   A. King Louis XVIII of France
   B. King Leopold of Belgium
   C. Dr. Sun Yat Sen
   D. Mohandas K. Gandhi

9. The region least affected by 19th-century imperialism was
   A. Asia
   B. Africa
   C. Middle East
   D. Latin America

10. Which was the only non-European nation to practice imperialism in the 19th century?
    A. India
    B. Ethiopia
    C. Japan
    D. Brazil

# THEMATIC ESSAYS

## Essay #1 Theme: Revolution

Throughout the period of 1750–1914 revolutions erupted throughout the world. Some were the result of political, economic, or social dissatisfaction within a nation, whereas others were in response to foreign domination.

**Task:**
1. Define the term "revolution."
2. Select one nation that you have studied and give one specific historical example showing why revolution developed in that nation.
3. Assess whether or not the revolution was successful and whether it was either positive or negative for that nation.

## Essay #2 Theme: Imperialism

The Industrial Revolution in Western Europe during the 19th century led to shortages of much needed natural resources and raw materials. This resulted in these nations imperializing nonindustrialized regions of the world.

**Task:**
1. Define the term "imperialism."
2. Select one nation you have studied that either practiced imperialism or was imperialized and give one specific example showing how imperialism affected that nation.
3. Assess whether imperialism was either positive or negative for that nation.

## DOCUMENT-BASED ESSAY QUESTIONS

**Essay #1**
This task is based on the accompanying documents (Documents 1–4). Some of these documents have been edited for the purposes of this task. The essay is designed to test your ability to work with historical documents. As you analyze the documents, take into account both the source of each document and the author's point of view.

**Historical Context:** The 19th and early 20th centuries saw the growth of nationalism. The documents relate the nationalistic beliefs of four leaders of different nations during this period.

**Task:**
Analyze the statements of each leader in order to understand how nationalism influenced the historical events of that nation.

**Part A:** The documents below relate the nationalistic ideas of four leaders during the 19th and early 20th centuries. Examine each document carefully and then answer the question that follows it.

**Part B:** Write a well-organized essay that includes an introduction with a thesis statement, several paragraphs explaining the thesis, and a conclusion. Use evidence from the documents to support your position. Do not simply repeat the contents of the documents. You should also include specific related outside information based on your study of history.

### DOCUMENT 1

"Soldiers of France! . . . All of you are consumed with a desire to extend the glory of the French people; all of you long to humiliate those arrogant kings who dare to contemplate placing us in chains; all of you desire to dictate a glorious peace, one which will repay the Patrie (Nation) for the immense sacrifices it has made."

—Napoleon Bonaparte (1796), *The Corsican:*
*A Diary of Napoleon Bonaparte's Life*

According to the reading, how does Napoleon Bonaparte appeal to nationalism in order to encourage support for his military conquests?

_____

_____

_____

## DOCUMENT 2

"Young Italy is a brotherhood of Italians who believe . . . that Italy is destined to become one nation. . . . They join this association in the firm intent of consecrating both thought and action to the great aim of reconstituting Italy as one independent sovereign nation of free men and equals. . . . The means by which Young Italy proposes to reach its aim are education and insurrection, to be adopted simultaneously, and made to harmonize with each other."

—Giuseppe Mazzini (1831),
*Young Italy*

According to the text, how did nationalism influence the vision Italian leaders had of their country after independence?

_____

_____

_____

## DOCUMENT 3

"We are not Europeans; we are not Indians; we are a mixed species of aborigines and Spaniards. Americans by birth and Europeans by law, we find ourselves engaged in a dual conflict: we are disputing with the natives for titles of ownership, and at the same time we are struggling to maintain ourselves in the country that gave us birth against the opposition of foreigners. . . for we, having been placed in state lower than slavery, have been robbed not only of our freedom, but also of our rights."

—Simón Bolívar (1819), Address to
the Congress of Angostura

According to the text, in what ways was national identity even more difficult for the peoples of Latin America than those of Europe?

_____

_____

_____

## DOCUMENT 4

"People all over the world refer to Japan as the Land of the Gods and call us descendants of the gods. Indeed, it exactly as they say: our country, as a special mark of favor from the heavenly gods, was begotten by them, and thus there is an immense difference between Japan and all other countries . . . . Ours is a splendid and blessed country . . . and we, down to the humblest man and woman, are the descendants of the gods."

—Hirata Atsutane (19th-century writer)

According to the reading, how did traditional national beliefs prepare Japan to be an imperialist power?

_____

_____

_____

**Essay #2**

This task is based on the accompanying documents (Documents 1–4). Some of these documents have been edited for the purposes of this task. The essay is designed to test your ability to work with historical documents. As you analyze the documents, take into account both the source of each document and the author's point of view.

**Historical Context:** The industrialization of Western Europe in the 19th century created a need for raw materials and natural resources. This led many Western European nations to imperialize non-European nations that possessed these resources. The documents relate different opinions on 19th-century imperialism by both Europeans and non-Europeans.

**Task:** Analyze the opinions on 19th-century imperialism in order to evaluate its effects on both the Europeans and the peoples they imperialized.

**Part A:** These documents relate the opinions of both Europeans and imperialized peoples on 19th-century imperialism. Examine each document carefully and then answer the question that follows it.

**Part B:** Write a well-organized essay that includes an introduction with a thesis statement, several paragraphs explaining the thesis, and a conclusion. Use evidence from the documents to support your position. Do not simply repeat the contents of the documents. You should also include specific related outside information based on your study of history.

### DOCUMENT 1

"We now feel that British rule over these territories . . . has brought security, peace and comparative prosperity to countries that never knew these blessings before. In carrying out this work of civilization, we are fulfilling what I believe to be our national mission. . . . You cannot destroy the practices of barbarism, of slavery, of superstition, which for centuries have desolated the interior of Africa, without the use of force; . . . we may be rest assured that for every life lost, a hundred will be gained, and the cause of civilization and prosperity of the people will in the long run be eminently advanced."

—Joseph Chamberlain (1897),
*Foreign and Colonial Speeches*

According to the text, how does Chamberlain justify British colonialism in Africa?

_____

_____

_____

### DOCUMENT 2

"History shows one way, and one way only, in which a high state of civilization has been produced, namely the struggle of race with race, and the survival of the physically and mentally fitter race. . . . The great function of science is to show us . . . how the nation is a vast organism subject . . . to the great forces of evolution. . . . Is it not a fact that our strength depends . . . upon our colonies, and that are colonies have been won by the ejection of inferior races? . . . This struggle of . . . nation with nation, may have its mournful side; but we see as a result of it the gradual progress of mankind to higher intellectual and physical efficiency."

—Karl Pearson (1900), "National Life
From the Standpoint of Science"

According to the reading, how does Pearson use Darwin's theories to justify European imperialism?

_____

_____

_____

### DOCUMENT 3

"Decades of imperialism have been prolific in wars; most of these wars have been directly motivated by aggression of white races upon 'lower races' and have resulted in the forcible seizure of territory. . . . Imperialism is only in the interests of competing groups of businessmen . . . that these groups . . . use public resources to push their private businesses, and spend the blood and money of the people in a vast and disastrous military game. . . . Nowhere under such conditions is the theory of white government as a trust for civilization made valid. . . . This failure to justify by results the forcible rule over alien peoples . . . is inherent in the nature of such domination."

—John Atkinson Hobson (1902), *Imperialism*

According to the text, why does Hobson reject the nationalistic and scientific arguments for European imperialism?

_____

_____

_____

## DOCUMENT 4

"It was not that Masoudi was any the less convinced about the desirability of many of the things the White Man had to offer. Their clothes were far superior, even if . . . they were the real reason why his villagers had to plant that ridiculous cotton which everyone knew ruined the soil. The oil lanterns and bicycle were also good things, and so was the hospital in Matadi. . . . But what Masoudi could never understand was why the White Man expected him and the others to change their beliefs, to abandon the ways of the ancestors. . . . Did the Black Man expect the White Man to change his beliefs, to abandon his traditions?"

—Colin M. Turnbull, *The Lonely African*

According to the reading, why did the imperialized peoples become resentful of European domination?

_____

_____

_____

# ERA VI

# A Half-Century of Crisis and Achievement (1900–1945)

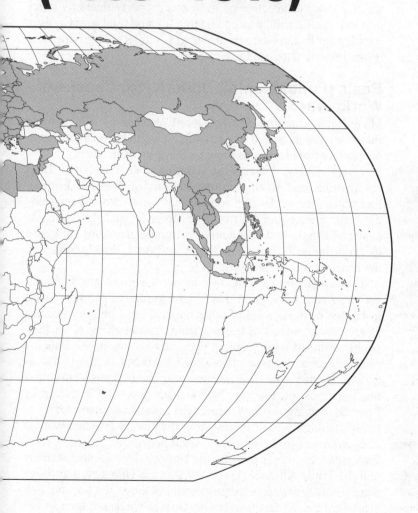

# Part A: World War I

The Congress of Vienna laid the foundation for a century of peace in Europe, broken only by a few brief and local wars (Franco-Prussian, Russo-Turkish, and Crimean). Beginning about 1870, a series of forces combined to move Europe toward war. These forces included a growing spirit of nationalism, increasingly dangerous colonial conflicts, a complex system of entangling alliances, and a rising tide of militarism.

Between 1914 and 1918 war swept across Europe. This war was far more destructive of lives and property than any other previous conflict and was considered the first total war. Civilian populations became targets along with soldiers. Terrifying new weapons were used for the first time.

## Basic (Fundamental, Underlying) Causes of World War I

Many factors contributed to the start of World War I. All the major European powers shared some blame, although historians disagree on whether one nation was more to blame than the others.

**GEOGRAPHY**

**Human Systems**

1. *Imperialism.* The desire to control other areas led to sharp competition and rivalry among nations of Western Europe. Examples include: Britain and Germany in Africa and the Middle East; France and Germany in Morocco; and Austria-Hungary and Russia in the Balkans. As European nations struggled to claim more territories in Africa and Asia, they approached the brink of war several times.

**GEOGRAPHY**

**Places and Regions**

GLOBAL CONCEPTS

**Identity**

CONCEPTS GLOBAL

2. *Nationalism.* Strong ties to one's nation and/or ethnic group stirred strong emotions. Many groups of people wanted to be free of the control of other nations. For example, Bosnia-Herzegovina wanted to be free from Austria-Hungary so they could be united with Serbia. Other nationalities in the Balkans also wished to be free of control by Austria or the Ottoman Empire and to create their own nations. The Balkans were called the tinderbox of Europe. Nationalism was also a factor in France's wanting *revanche* (revenge) against Germany for Germany's taking Alsace-Lorraine after the Franco-Prussian War.

**GEOGRAPHY**

**Physical Settings**

3. *Alliances and the lack of world peacekeeping machinery.* Two alliances, the Triple Entente (France, Russia, and Britain) and the Triple Alliance (Germany, Austria-Hungary, and Italy) were formed for defensive purposes, but they soon became two armed camps. At this time no organization existed, such as the

EUROPE IN 1914

**KEY**

Allied powers

Central powers

Neutral countries

United Nations, to foster world peace or to help settle disputes among the major powers.

4. *Militarism*. As the alliance system divided Europe into two opposing camps, each nation began to increase its military strength. The growth of armies and navies, as well as the development of weaponry, added to the mood of belligerence (warlike attitude) and a tendency to settle disputes by fighting. Manufacturers of arms increased production, as governments sought to build up their military strength. Economic rivalry between Germany and Britain poisoned relations between the two nations. Germany's growing navy was seen by Britain as a threat to its security.

## Immediate Cause of the War

The spark that set off World War I was the assassination of the Austrian Archduke Francis Ferdinand in June 1914 in the town of Sarajevo. The assassin was a Serbian nationalist, Gavrilo Princip, who wanted to free Bosnia-Herzegovina from the Austro-Hungarian Empire and unite them with Serbia.

## Developments in the War

Austria, backed up by Germany and glad to receive Germany's blank check, threatened Serbia. This angered Russia, causing it to get its armed forces ready for war. Because of the alliance system, country after country was drawn into the conflict and all the major powers were soon fighting each other. A local, regional crisis thus became the spark of a major war. The war, known as the Great War at first, turned into the most violent European conflict since the Napoleonic Wars, almost 100 years before. With neither side able to win, the armies faced one another from trenches. The war was a stalemate until 1917, when the United States entered the war on the side of the Triple Entente nations, or the Allies (Britain, France, and Russia). This helped to bring victory against the Central Powers (Germany, Austria-Hungary, Italy, and Turkey—a late entrant into the war). The war ended in November 1918, having lasted over four years.

## Results of World War I

The war changed the course of the world's history, causing economic chaos and radical social changes in many countries. Some of the most powerful nations in Europe lost their influence and began to decline. Many monarchs lost their thrones. A communist government came to power in Russia, and the seeds of a second great conflict (World War II) were sown when World War I ended and the peace treaty was drawn up.

GLOBAL
CONCEPTS
**Change**
CONCEPTS
GLOBAL

1. *Economic.* The war was very costly to the participants. The losers became debtor nations. Many economic problems arising from the war were partly responsible for the worldwide depression that began in 1929.

2. *Social.* Millions were killed and wounded from the fighting. More than 8 million soldiers died, and almost as many civilians were killed. Several deadly weapons were used for the first time in warfare—gas, tanks, airplanes, submarines, and the machine gun. Most Europeans failed to understand the destructive power of these weapons and how horrible modern warfare had become.

3. *Political.* The League of Nations was formed in an effort to secure world peace. The political problems and hatreds that emerged in some nations provided a basis for the rise of dictatorships later in Germany and in Italy.

### MAJOR TERRITORIAL CHANGES AFTER WORLD WAR I

| Changes | Taken From |
| --- | --- |
| 1. Poland recreated, with a corridor to the sea | Germany and German-conquered area of Russia |
| 2. Romania enlarged | Austria-Hungary |
| 3. Yugoslavia and Czechoslovakia created as new nations | Austria-Hungary |
| 4. Austria and Hungary become separate nations | Austria-Hungary |

| WORLD ISSUES | MAJOR TERRITORIAL CHANGES AFTER WORLD WAR I (cont'd) | |
|---|---|---|
| War | **Changes** | **Taken From** |
| and | 5. Finland, Estonia, Latvia, and | Russia |
| Peace | Lithuania created | |
| | 6. Alsace-Lorraine to France | Germany |
| | 7. Syria, Lebanon, and Palestine | Turkey |
| | became mandates | |

## The Versailles Treaty (1919)

The Versailles Treaty officially ended World War I. It was drawn up at the Paris Peace Conference by David Lloyd George (Britain), Georges Clemenceau (France), Vittorio Orlando (Italy), and Woodrow Wilson (United States). It forced Germany to accept "war guilt" and stripped Germany and Austria-Hungary of much territory. Germany was also forced to pay huge amounts of money to the victors as reparations. It was prohibited from uniting with Austria and required to limit its armed forces (demilitarization). This *diktat* (dictated peace), as it was called by Germany, caused much resentment in that country and was later used by Hitler as propaganda in his rise to power in the 1930s. The treaty also created the League of Nations. The League was one of the Fourteen Points that America's Wilson had asked for in an attempt to prevent future wars. The U.S. Senate refused to ratify (approve) the Versailles Treaty. Therefore, the United States did not become a member of the league. For this reason, as well as the fact that it had no enforcement powers, the league was seen as a weak organization.

# Part B: The Rise of the Modern Totalitarian State

Totalitarianism is a political philosophy that emerged in the 20th century. Totalitarianism describes governments in which one political party monopolizes all power and exercises complete authority over the people and their activities. It involves total control of all aspects of an individual's life by the government, with both civil and political rights being curtailed. Although various forms of totalitarianism exist in parts of the world today, its earliest examples were in three European nations during the 20-year period following World War I. These nations were the Soviet Union (under communism), Italy (under fascism), and Germany (under Nazism). Totalitarian societies look down on individual human rights and civil liberties. The values of democracy are not found in such societies. Totalitarian states emphasize: (1) glorification of the whole community (that is, the state); (2) authoritarian rule by a dictator or by selected members of the one political party allowed to exist; (3) control of the individual citizen's life; (4) belief in the idea that the individual should benefit the state and exists solely to serve the state's interests. In Western Europe, these features of totalitarianism were most characteristic of Germany under the control of Adolf Hitler and the Nazi Party, from 1933 to 1945. This government, known as the Third Reich, arose after the period of the Weimar Republic.

**WORLD ISSUES**

Determination
of Political
and Economic
Systems

# SECTION 1: GERMANY

## Germany Under the Weimar Republic (1919–1933)

The Weimar Republic was the name of the German government that came to power after World War I. It was a democratic government, with a constitution that was drawn up in the city of Weimar. However, this experiment with democracy in Germany faced many problems, including economic chaos and street violence. It was not successful for a number of reasons.

**GEOGRAPHY**

**Spatial Terms**

**WORLD ISSUES**

Hunger
and
Poverty

1. In the early 1920s the Weimar government printed paper money with little to back it, resulting in severe inflation. This devastated the German economy and resulted in severe unemployment and street violence.

2. When Germany was unable to meet its reparations payments in 1923, France sent troops to occupy the Ruhr Valley, Germany's chief industrial area.

3. There was terrible unemployment in Germany in the early 1920s and again in the 1930s.

4. The German economy was restored after 1923 and conditions improved. However, in 1929 a worldwide depression that threatened the stability of democratic governments everywhere brought much suffering to Germany. Unemployment rose to 6 million in 1932, and Germans lost faith in their political leaders. This further fueled the bad feelings that had been caused by the Versailles Treaty.

5. The government was unstable because no single party was able to achieve a majority in the Reichstag, the more powerful of the two legislative houses created by the Weimar constitution. As a result, German political leaders seemed helpless to deal with the severe economic problems.

These problems led many Germans to conclude that democracy was ill suited to their nation and that autocracy was preferable, especially since it had brought Germany political unification, economic growth, and respect as an international power. A strong democratic tradition did not exist in German history.

## The Role of Adolf Hitler

Hitler was born in Austria and served in the German army during World War I. He joined the Nazi Party (National Socialist German Workers Party). He spoke out against the Weimar government and was arrested for his role in the Munich Putsch of 1923, an unsuccessful attempt to overthrow the government.

While imprisoned, he wrote the book *Mein Kampf* (My Struggle) that contained his ideas for a stronger and more powerful German nation. It also revealed his racist beliefs concerning the alleged superiority of Aryans as a "master race" and the need to eliminate all groups he considered inferior, such as Jews, Slavs, Gypsies, and blacks. Hitler was a stirring and charismatic speaker when addressing large crowds, thereby attracting many people to the Nazi Party.

## Rise of the Nazis to Power

In addition to the problems of the Weimar government and the powerful role played by Hitler, a number of other factors led to the rise of the Nazis in Germany:

1. *Economic problems*. The Nazis offered simple explanations for both the causes of Germany's economic problems and its cures. These problems, as described above, affected millions of Germans. The reparations demanded by the Versailles Treaty were condemned as unjust and blamed for causing the economic crisis.

2. *Patriotic appeals*. The Nazi program stirred German nationalism. It called for:
- a large increase in the armed forces;
- the expansion of the German fatherland to include territory in Europe where people of German descent lived (Austria, parts of Poland, and Czechoslovakia);
- control over educational and cultural institutions to teach Nazi principles of racism and physical fitness for the glory of the state;
- ignoring the Versailles Treaty and refusing to accept the war-guilt clause;
- regaining land that Germany had held in Europe and its overseas colonies prior to World War I;
- the use of violence as a legitimate means to achieve domestic and international goals;
- the importance of looking back to and glorifying the mythical German race (the so-called *Volk*) as the source of all strength and power.

The Nazis also claimed that Nordic Germans were destined to rule the world and to eliminate undesirable peoples. They blamed the Weimar government for accepting the Versailles Treaty and said it had been forced to do so by Jews, communists, and others. Finally, the Nazis claimed that German forces had not been defeated in World War I but had been stabbed in the back.

3. *Anti-Semitism*. Prejudice toward Jews had existed in Germany for hundreds of years, resulting in exile, loss of life and property, and hatred. However, Hitler's prejudice against Jews

**GEOGRAPHY**

**Places and Regions**

**WORLD ISSUES**

Terrorism

was fanatical; he used Jews as scapegoats and blamed them for his own personal failures and also for Germany's problems. These false notions became persuasive parts of Nazi propaganda, especially when they were blended with Hitler's master race theories. Hitler claimed that the Aryans (Germans) were a master race who were naturally entitled to control and rule peoples of less "pure" blood, such as Slavs and Jews. (The Holocaust, in which 6 million Jews were systematically murdered after Hitler came to power, was the tragic consequence of these misguided notions.)

WORLD ISSUES

Human
Rights

4. *Fear of communism and of Soviet Russia.* The Nazis played upon these fears with much success and portrayed themselves as the only ones capable of protecting Germany from foreign beliefs and potential aggressors. In this way, they were able to win the support of large segments of the German population, such as bankers and industrialists.

5. *Use of private, illegal armed groups.* Many of Hitler's followers were organized into private armies. One such group was the Storm Troopers (S.A.), or Brown Shirts, who used scare tactics and violence to terrorize Jews and opponents of the Nazis.

6. *Lack of meaningful opposition.* Few strong voices inside Germany spoke out against the Nazis. Many Germans came to gradually support Hitler, while others were apathetic. Others feared speaking against him, and many who did were intimidated. Internationally, there was little awareness of or concern about the Nazi movement.

GLOBAL
CONCEPTS

Power

CONCEPTS
GLOBAL

**The Nazis Come to Power.** The formal takeover of Germany by the Nazis took place in January 1933 when the president of the Weimar Republic, Paul von Hindenburg, appointed Hitler as chancellor. By this time, the Nazis had become the largest political party in Germany, and they formed the single largest block in the Reichstag, the German parliament. Yet they had never won a clear majority in any national election. (In 1932, for example, they won slightly less than 40 percent of the seats in the Reichstag.) Although Hitler promised to preserve the Weimar constitution, he soon carried out policies that destroyed the democracy that had existed under the Weimar Republic. The result was a totalitarian dictatorship that eventually brought about World War II and brought devastation to Germany and to most of Europe. Hitler's distorted ideas, along with his antidemocratic beliefs and tactics, unfortunately found a receptive audience in post-World War I Germany. He was called *der Führer*, or leader.

GLOBAL
CONCEPTS

Political Systems

CONCEPTS
GLOBAL

# SECTION 2: ITALY

## Italy Under a Fascist Government (1922–1943)

Italy experienced totalitarian rule under a fascist government headed by Benito Mussolini. The word "fascist" comes from the word "fasces," an axe-like weapon that was a symbol of the ancient Roman Empire. Mussolini wanted Italians to feel a strong sense of nationalism and to remember the glory of the Roman Empire. Mussolini and his Black Shirt followers came to power for some of the same reasons that led to the rise of the Nazis in Germany.

1. *Economic.* The costs of World War I had been staggering. After the war, there was high unemployment, strikes, and severe inflation.

2. *Political.* The weak and divided government of King Victor Emmanuel III was unable to provide leadership or to inspire confidence in its ability to solve the postwar crisis. Also, there was no strong democratic tradition in Italy. Moreover, the fear of communism and a communist-led revolution was seized upon by Mussolini, who promised to defend Italy and thereby won followers.

3. *Social.* Italy was suffering from low morale, and was saddened by the many deaths in World War I. Mussolini promised the Italian people security, order, and economic progress in exchange for their liberties and freedom.

**Mussolini in Power.** As a result of his famous March on Rome in 1922 supposedly to save Italy from a communist revolution, Mussolini came to power. Neither the king nor the army opposed him. He soon established a police state, destroying civil liberties and demanding that people recognize him as Il Duce, the leader. Mussolini reorganized the economy of Italy, establishing fascist-controlled associations in all industries, and Italy was run as a corporate state.

GLOBAL CONCEPTS

**Identity**

CONCEPTS GLOBAL

GLOBAL CONCEPTS

**Power**

CONCEPTS GLOBAL

# SECTION 3: RUSSIA

## The Russian Revolution (1905–1917)

During the reign of Nicholas II (1894–1917), Russia made its greatest strides toward reform, modernization, and, ironically, revolution. From 1894 to 1905, Nicholas followed his father's (Alexander III) policies in opposing reform. Despite great gains made in the industrialization program under the direction of Finance Minister Sergei Witte, the conditions in urban slums and factories were still terrible. After the embarrassing defeat in the Russo-Japanese War (1904–1905) and the massacre of peaceful demonstraters in St. Petersburg in January of 1905, known as *Bloody Sunday*, uprisings broke out in every major Russian city and industrial center. Known as the 1905 Revolution, this series of revolts frightened the government into making reforms, most notably the creation of the *Duma*, or parliament. While Russia technically became a constitutional democracy, the Duma was little more than an advisory body that could be dissolved by the tsar at will.

Tsar Nicholas II

436

In 1906 the monarchy instituted its own reforms in order to restore public confidence. Under the guidance of Prime Minister Piotr Stolypin, a program of industrial expansion, foreign investment, and land reform was instituted.

In 1914 Russia entered World War I (1914–1918), a conflict that it was neither militarily nor economically ready to fight. For three years the Russians suffered defeats by the technologically superior German forces. (See "World War I," page 426.) Enormous casualties and government inefficiency led to widespread dissatisfaction with the conduct of the war. Scandal within the royal family also hurt the prestige of the monarchy. Tsaritsa Aleksandra had fallen under the influence of a fraudulent "holy man," Grigorii Efimovich Rasputin, who was able to control the Tsarevitch (Prince) Alexei's hemophilia (probably through hypnosis).

While the tsar was away at the front running the war, Rasputin exercised a destructive domination over the German-born tsaritsa, who was already suspected by many of being a spy. His interference produced corruption and even greater inefficiency. By February 1917, food shortages and an outbreak of strikes and riots led to the collapse of the tsar's authority in St. Petersburg and other cities. Nicholas II was forced to abdicate, and a provisional (temporary) democratic government was formed by the Duma, headed first by Prince Georgii L'vov and later by Aleksandr Kerenskii.

The provisional government attempted to make Russia a democracy by instituting political reforms. By October of 1917, however, the provisional government had been overthrown by force and the Bolshevik (Communist) Party had taken power. There were a number of reasons for this:

GLOBAL CONCEPTS
**Change**
CONCEPTS GLOBAL

1. Kerenskii's decision to continue fighting the war was very unpopular.

2. Russia did not have a democratic tradition. Most of the provisional government's goals were not understood and appeared to be irrelevant to the majority of the population.

3. The war continued to create shortages and strain the economy. Conditions in the cities did not improve, and unrest began again.

4. The Bolsheviks capitalized on the unpopularity of the war. They undermined support for the provisional government through antiwar propaganda.

5. The monarchy had held the Russian Empire together. With the traditional symbol of unity (the tsar) gone, the provisional government could provide no equivalent institution.

6. Kerenskii was experimenting with democracy in a nation with no democratic heritage during a war, a time when most democracies temporarily suspend civil liberties.

7. The war wasted the best troops the provisional government had. The regiments that remained to protect the provisional government were poorly trained and unreliable.

8. The Bolshevik leader Lenin promised "bread, peace, and land" as well as a "workers' state," promises that were better understood than the democratic principles put forth by the provisional government.

9. The Bolsheviks influenced the soviets, or local committees, that represented workers, soldiers, and farmers. Closely linked throughout Russia, they became influential, especially in the cities.

**Lenin (1917–1924).** Born Vladimir lllich Ulianov, Lenin founded the Bolshevik, or "Majority," Party at a 1903 Socialist Party Conference in London. While the Bolsheviks were never a majority, they were "professional revolutionaries" who ruthlessly pursued power, using any means necessary in order to succeed. The other Russian Socialists, the Mensheviks, or "Minority," favored gradual, peaceful change, without the violence and terror advocated by the Bolsheviks.

When the Bolsheviks seized power in 1917, Lenin immediately made peace with Germany and took Russia out of the war. Giving away sizable parts of Russia in a peace agreement (Treaty of Brest-Litovsk) and having no widespread support, the Bolsheviks soon faced strong opposition throughout Russia. A civil war followed (1918–1921) in which the Bolsheviks, or Reds, fought the combined forces of anti-Bolshevik groups, or Whites. The dependence of the White army on foreign nations for military supplies as well as the disunity among its leadership eventually led to a Bolshevik victory.

Once the Bolsheviks were firmly in power, Lenin realized that Russia was not ready to become a communist state. In the new political order, the Communist Party would run the state until such time as society could be transformed into a pure communist state. The central government planned and controlled all aspects of political, social, and economic life through a series of party organs. Facing great opposition, especially from the peasants, Lenin tried to ease the population into communism by instituting the N.E.P. (New Economic Program) in 1921. This policy combined features of both capitalism and socialism by allowing private enterprise on a small scale while the state retained control of large industries. Under the N.E.P. (1921–1928), the Soviet economy experienced only limited growth.

**WORLD ISSUES**

Determination
of Political
and Economic
Systems

When Lenin died in 1924, a struggle for power developed between Leon Trotskii, Lenin's chosen successor, and Joseph Dzhugashvili, known as Stalin ("Man of Steel"), who was Communist Party Secretary. By 1925 Stalin had gained control and removed Trotskii from all official positions. In 1929 Trotskii was deported as Stalin began to remove all possible opposition and rivals (Trotskii was assassinated by Stalin's agents in Mexico in 1937).

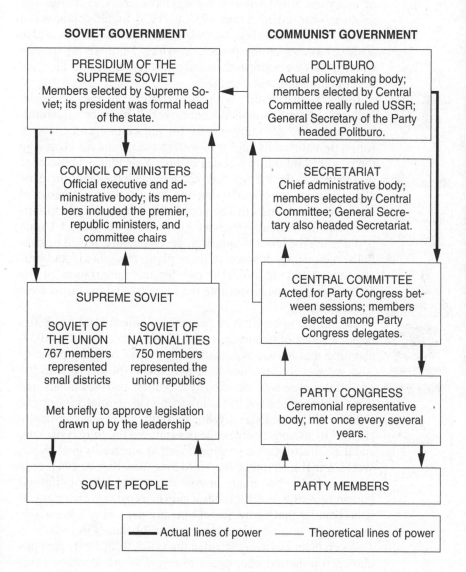

**SOVIET GOVERNMENT**          **COMMUNIST GOVERNMENT**

PRESIDIUM OF THE SUPREME SOVIET
Members elected by Supreme Soviet; its president was formal head of the state.

POLITBURO
Actual policymaking body; members elected by Central Committee really ruled USSR; General Secretary of the Party headed Politburo.

COUNCIL OF MINISTERS
Official executive and administrative body; its members included the premier, republic ministers, and committee chairs

SECRETARIAT
Chief administrative body; members elected by Central Committee; General Secretary also headed Secretariat.

SUPREME SOVIET

SOVIET OF THE UNION
767 members represented small districts

SOVIET OF NATIONALITIES
750 members represented the union republics

Met briefly to approve legislation drawn up by the leadership

CENTRAL COMMITTEE
Acted for Party Congress between sessions; members elected among Party Congress delegates.

PARTY CONGRESS
Ceremonial representative body; met once every several years.

SOVIET PEOPLE          PARTY MEMBERS

── Actual lines of power     ── Theoretical lines of power

**Stalin (1925–1953).** Stalin's rule proved to be one of the most brutal and ruthless dictatorships in modern history. From his consolidation of complete power in 1929 until his death in 1953, he was responsible for millions of deaths, starting with the elimination of all possible rivals. Stalin created his own secret police, which spied on, arrested, tortured, and executed

party members, government officials, artists, writers, clergy, workers, and peasants he suspected of not supporting his policies. In time, his fears became paranoia (fear and suspicion of everyone, often without cause), and even close friends and relatives were killed. From 1935 to 1936 Stalin conducted a series of show trials (hearings where the verdicts were decided in advance) known as the purges, in which hundreds of leading Communists were arrested, forced to confess to crimes they had never committed, and executed.

In 1928, dissatisfied with the slow growth rate of Soviet industry, Stalin abandoned Lenin's N.E.P. in favor of centralized economic planning. Goals for agriculture and industry (often unrealistically high), as well as the means for achieving them, were laid out in a series of Five-Year Plans. These were

designed to make the U.S.S.R. catch up with the other industrialized nations by emphasizing the industrial development of steel, iron, coal, and oil. The population was expected to sacrifice and do without consumer goods until the Soviet Union could reach the level of industrial development attained by capitalist nations. Opposition to these plans was quickly and brutally put down. In order to pay for the importation of the technology needed to institute the Five-Year Plans, farms were

collectivized.

To end the opposition of peasants to collectivization, Stalin began a series of genocides (mass killings) from 1932 to 1937, claiming that he was eliminating the *kulaks* (wealthy peasants who supposedly exploited their neighbors). In fact, few of the 14.5 million peasants who died by execution, perished in Siberian labor camps, or starved in Stalin's man-made famine in Ukraine (1932–1933) were kulaks. While outright opposition was finally crushed by these genocides, the peasants did not fully cooperate, and the collectivization program failed to achieve its goal. When World War II interrupted the Third Five-Year Plan in 1941, only heavy industry had made any progress. The loss of life and human suffering that this modest gain had cost was enormous. It is no wonder that many Soviet citizens, especially Ukrainians, first saw the invading German armies as liberators in 1941.

When Nazi Germany invaded the U.S.S.R. in 1941, the population was forced once again to resort to the scorched earth policy used so effectively against Napoleon. By 1944 overextension of supply lines, the harsh Russian climate, and stiff military resistance by the Russians, despite heavy losses, had worn down the German forces. By 1945 the Soviet army had pushed the Nazis out of Russia and Eastern Europe into Germany and occupied the eastern portion of that nation. Despite an agreement made with the Allies earlier that year (the Yalta Conference) that the U.S.S.R. would only occupy Eastern Europe

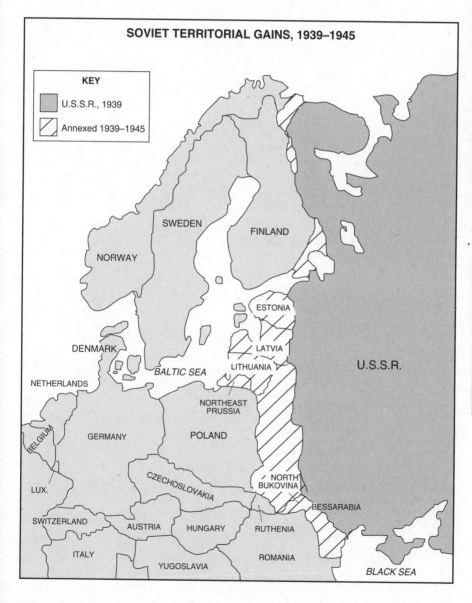

## SOVIET TERRITORIAL GAINS, 1939–1945

**KEY**

U.S.S.R., 1939

Annexed 1939–1945

NORWAY · SWEDEN · FINLAND · DENMARK · NETHERLANDS · BELGIUM · LUX. · SWITZERLAND · ITALY · GERMANY · NORTHEAST PRUSSIA · POLAND · CZECHOSLOVAKIA · AUSTRIA · HUNGARY · YUGOSLAVIA · ESTONIA · LATVIA · LITHUANIA · BALTIC SEA · NORTH BUKOVINA · RUTHENIA · ROMANIA · BESSARABIA · U.S.S.R. · BLACK SEA

temporarily, Soviet forces remained. Instead of holding free elections for self-determination in each Eastern European nation, Stalin placed puppet communist governments throughout Eastern Europe. These countries became satellites, controlled by the Soviet government. By Stalin's death in 1953, Eastern and Western Europe were divided by ideological differences and mutual fear. This last legacy of Stalin became known as the Iron Curtain.

# Part C: World War II

Although the war started in Europe, it soon became a global conflict that dwarfed all previous wars in geographical extent and in human and material losses suffered. Fighting took place on three continents—Europe, Africa, and Asia—and on the seas, lands, and oceans around the globe. More nations (over fifty) were belligerents (fighters in the war) than in any war in history. The chief antagonists on the Allied side were Great Britain, France, the United States, the Soviet Union, and China. On the opposing side were Germany, Italy, and Japan, the so-called Axis powers.

**WORLD ISSUES**

War
and
Peace

## Causes

Many of the causes of World War II were similar to those that brought on the first world war. After World War I, many nations hoped to prevent another war by establishing what could be called a house of peace. The foundations of this house included: the Versailles Treaty, the League of Nations, disarmament conferences (held in Washington, D.C., and in London), and the Kellogg-Briand Pact, which attempted to outlaw war. Unfortunately, the house of peace crumbled for a number of reasons, most of them due to the actions of the Axis powers (Germany, Italy, and Japan). The basic causes of the war were:

1. *Militarism.* Large amounts of money were spent on weapons. Military strength was seen as a source of national pride. The leaders of the Axis nations were always seen in military dress.

2. *Nationalism and racism.* The Axis nations saw themselves as superior to others and with the right therefore to extend their culture and their borders (the German "master race" theory, the Italian wish to revive the ancient Roman Empire, the Japanese pride based on Shinto teachings and the necessity to establish a new order in Asia).

3. *Imperialism.* The Axis nations sought to take over other lands for political, racist, and economic reasons. Japan moved into China (1931, 1937); Italy conquered Ethiopia (1938); and Germany annexed Austria (the *Anschluss*, or union) and Czechoslovakia (1938, 1939).

**GEOGRAPHY**

**Spatial Terms**

4. *Failure of collective security.* The democratic nations of Europe and the United States did little to curb the aggressive policies of Germany, Italy, and Japan. The League of Nations condemned some of these aggressive moves but was unable to take any other action.

5. *Appeasement.* To give in to a potential aggressor, hoping that the aggressor will be content and not commit any further harmful acts is called appeasement. It later came to mean the policy of accepting territorial aggression against small nations in the hope of avoiding a general war. This policy was followed by the British prime minister, Neville Chamberlain, at the Munich Conference in 1938. Here, he agreed to accept German annexation of the Sudetenland portion of Czechoslovakia in return for Hitler's guarantee of independence for the rest of Czechoslovakia. The policy proved to be a failure when Hitler later sent the German army to occupy all of Czechoslovakia in violation of the Munich Agreement.

## The Start of the War

The German attack on Poland in September 1939 was the actual start of the war. Britain and France finally realized that they would have to use military force to stop Hitler's aggression and threat to conquer all of Europe. Just prior to its attack on Poland, Germany signed a nonaggression pact with the Soviet Union. Under this agreement, Russia would take over eastern Poland and the Baltic states of Estonia, Latvia, and Lithuania and would not contest Hitler's attempt to take over western Poland. Also, Russia and Germany promised not to fight each other.

GLOBAL CONCEPTS
**Power**

CONCEPTS GLOBAL

## Developments in the War

Using blitzkreig warfare ("lightning war"), Germany overran most of Europe, except for England, by 1941. In June of that year, Germany broke its promise not to attack Russia and invaded that nation. The Russians suffered great losses and were driven back to the outskirts of Moscow, Leningrad, and the Volga River, where they held and gradually began to turn the tide. Also, in 1941 the United States entered the war after its navy was attacked by Japan at Pearl Harbor, Hawaii. The nations now fighting the Axis powers were known as the Allies (United States, Britain, France, Soviet Union). With the invasion of Normandy in western France on June 6, 1944 ("D-Day"), Allied forces began to retake German-held lands and pushed the Germans eastward. Russian forces entered the German-held Eastern European nations and pushed the Germans westward. On May 8, 1945 ("V-E Day"), Germany surrendered. In Asia, by 1941 Japan had conquered large areas of East and Southeast Asia. These Pacific areas were slowly retaken by U.S. forces between 1942 and 1945. In August 1945 the United States dropped two atomic bombs on the Japanese cities of Hiroshima and Nagasaki. On September 2, 1945 ("V-J Day"), Japan surrendered.

# TERRITORIAL CHANGES IN EUROPE 1945–1948

Leningrad

NORWAY

0      300 miles

0      300 km

ESTONIA

SWEDEN

LATVIA

DENMARK

*NORTH SEA*

*BALTIC SEA*

LITHUANIA

ODER-NEISSE LINE

E. PRUSSIA

Stettin

*U.S.*

(TO POLAND)

Berlin

*BR. ZONE*

NETH.

Warsaw

U.S.S.R.

BELG.

*SOV. ZONE*

GERMANY

POLAND

(TO U.S.S.R.)

LUX.

Prague

Nuremberg

CZECHOSLOVAKIA

*U.S. ZONE*

*SOV. ZONE*

(TO CZECH.)

FRANCE

*FR. ZONE*

AUSTRIA

Vienna

SWITZ.

*FR. ZONE*

*U.S. ZONE*

*BR. ZONE*

HUNGARY

ROMANIA

Budapest

Trieste

(TO FRANCE)

(TO YUGOSLAVIA 1954)

Bucharest

Belgrade

(TO BULGARIA)

ITALY

YUGOSLAVIA

BULGARIA

*ADRIATIC SEA*

CORSICA

Rome

SARDINIA

ALBANIA

GREECE

DODECANESE ISLANDS
(TO GREECE)

*MEDITERRANEAN SEA*

## KEY

Territorial changes after World War II

Soviet occupation zones

Occupation zones of Western powers

- - - International boundaries after World War II

## The Holocaust

This word refers to the intentional persecution and systematic murder of European Jews by the Germans from 1933 to 1945. Six million Jews were exterminated, mostly in concentration and death camps such as Auschwitz, Dachau, and Treblinka. The planned extermination of a group of people because of their religion, race, or ethnicity is called genocide. The genocidal tactics of the Nazis were a horrible extension of Hitler's anti-Semitic attitudes. The Nazi plan to kill all Jews was known as "the final solution." The world stood by and did nothing while these tactics such as gas chambers, ovens, medical experiments, and firing squads were being used. There were scattered instances of Jewish armed resistance, such as in the Warsaw Ghetto Uprising in 1943 and the destruction of a crematorium in Auschwitz in 1944. After the war, at the Nuremberg War Crimes Trials, several Nazis were found guilty of genocide and of crimes against humanity.

In addition to Jews, other groups of people labeled "inferior" by the Nazis were also sent to the concentration camps. These included homosexuals, Jehovah's Witnesses, Gypsies, Slavs, and mentally retarded people.

## Results of World War II

The world of 1945 bore little resemblance to the world of the 1930s. Europe was shattered and lay in ruins, its people facing an uncertain future.

1. *Political.* The United States and the Soviet Union became the two leading superpowers and eventually clashed on many issues in what became known as the Cold War. Germany was divided into four zones of occupation—American, British, French, and Soviet. Poland's boundaries with the Soviet Union were changed, moving futher westward. The Soviets established a sphere of influence, as an imperialist power, in many Eastern European nations. Some Soviet activities were in violation of the Yalta agreements of 1945. Britain and France lost some of their status as world powers; nationalistic movements in their colonies were to lead to a loss of their empires. The Allies helped to create the United Nations.

2. *Economic.* The war proved to be the most costly ever fought. The loss of life and property in World War II far surpassed that of any previous conflict. The economies of many European nations were destroyed. Communism spread into the nations of Eastern Europe.

3. *Social.* More people, soldiers and civilians, were killed than in any other war. Much of this was due to new highly destructive weapons, as well as to the racist policies of the Axis powers. At war's end, millions of people had become refugees and displaced persons.

4. *Scientific.* The Atomic Age had begun with the dropping of atomic bombs on Hiroshima and Nagasaki.

*Multiple Choice.* Select the letter of the answer that correctly completes the statement.

1. Stalin, Hitler, and Mussolini were similar in that they
   A. belonged to the same political party
   B. permitted many political parties to exist
   C. permitted only one political party to exist
   D. favored both the Democratic and Republican political parties

2. What was true of both the Paris Peace Conference (1919) and the Yalta Conference (1945)?
   A. Russia was represented by Stalin.
   B. Treaties were signed.
   C. England had a delegate.
   D. World wars had just ended.

3. Winston Churchill was most concerned about his nation's
   A. struggle against Germany
   B. agricultural production
   C. economic competition with the United States
   D. construction of a tunnel under the English Channel

4. The technology developed in World War I resulted in
   A. a smaller number of refugees during the war
   B. smaller nations becoming part of larger empires after the war
   C. increased military casualties in battles fought during the war
   D. a reduction in transportation improvements after the war

5. Which was one part of "the final solution"?
   A. attack in Pearl Harbor
   B. blitzkrieg over Poland
   C. killings at Auschwitz
   D. bombings of Hiroshima and Nagasaki

6. "Weimar Republic to institute changes in Germany."
   "Provisional government stirs Russian hopes."

   These headlines reflected attempts to establish a
   A. monarchy
   B. dictatorship
   C. democracy
   D. colony

7. "Italy conquers Ethiopia"
   "Japan seizes Manchuria"

   Both headlines best reflect the concept of
   A. imperialism
   B. nationalism
   C. totalitarianism
   D. isolationism

8. The failure of collective security in the 1930s was interpreted as a sign of
   A. racism
   B. appeasement
   C. alliance building
   D. militarism

9. The Russian Duma and the German Reichstag exercised power that was
   A. authoritarian
   B. legislative
   C. executive
   D. judicial

10. Which pair favored collectivization and an end to private property?
    A. Lenin and Stalin
    B. Hitler and Mussolini
    C. Churchill and Roosevelt
    D. von Hindenburg and Nicholas II

**Essay #1 Theme: Conflict**
At various times in global history, nations have acted in ways that caused armed conflict with other nations.

**Task:**
1. Choose two nations from your study of global history and geography.
2. For *each* nation:
   - Describe one action it took that caused armed conflict with another nation.
   - Explain why it took this action.
   - Evaluate whether it would take this action today.

You may use any example from your study of global history and geography. Some suggestions you might wish to consider include: Germany in the 20th century, Italy in the 20th century, Japan in the 20th century.

*Hint:* You are not limited to these suggestions.

**Essay #2 Theme: Change**
Throughout history, changes of government in a nation have frequently occurred. These changes have at times been led by a single group or political party.

**Task:**
1. Select two nations from your study of global history and geography.
2. For *each* nation:
   - Name the group or political party, and its leader, that caused a change in government.
   - Describe how the group or political party was able to bring about the change.
   - Analyze one reason why the group or political party was successful in bringing about the change.

You may use any example from your study of global history and geography. Some suggestions you may wish to consider include: Russia in the 20th century, Germany in the 20th century, Italy in the 20th century.

*Hint:* You are not limited to these suggestions, but you cannot use the United States in your answer.

# DOCUMENT-BASED ESSAY QUESTIONS

**Essay #1**
This task is based upon the accompanying documents (1–6). Some of these documents have been edited for the purposes of this task. This task is designed to test your ability to work with historical documents. As you analyze the documents, take into account both the source of each document and the author's point of view.

**Directions:** Read the documents in Part A and answer the questions after each document. Then read the directions for Part B and write your essay.

**Historical Context:** Throughout history, societies have held different viewpoints on governmental decision-making, power, and the role of the citizen. These viewpoints can range from absolute control to democracy.

**Task:**
Using information from the documents and your knowledge of global history and geography, write an essay in which you
• Compare and contrast the different viewpoints societies have held about the process of governmental decision-making and about the role of citizens in the political decision-making process
• Discuss the advantages and disadvantages of a political system that is under absolute power or is a democracy.

### Part A
### Short Answer

**Directions:** Analyze the documents and answer the questions that follow each document in the space provided.

#### DOCUMENT 1
"We are a democracy because the power to make the laws is given to the many rather than the few. But while the law gives equal justice to everyone, it has not failed to reward excellence. While every citizen has an equal opportunity to serve the public, we reward our most distinguished [best] citizens by asking them to make our political decisions. Nor do we discriminate against the poor. A man serves his country no matter how low his position on the social scale.

An Athenian citizen does not put his private affairs before the affairs of the state; even our merchants and businessmen know something about politics. We alone believe that a man who takes no interest in public affairs is more than harmless—he is useless."

—"Pericles' Funeral Oration"
Athens, 5th century B.C.

450

According to Pericles, what is the responsibility of a citizen in a democracy?

_____

_____

_____

### DOCUMENT 2

"The one means that wins the easiest victory over reason: terror and force"

"A majority can never replace one man . . . Just as a hundred fools do not make one wise man, an heroic decision is not likely to come from a hundred cowards."

"In the size of the lie there is always contained a certain factor of credibility, since the great masses of the people . . . will more easily fall victims to a great lie than to a small one."

—Adolf Hitler, *Mein Kampf*
Germany, 1924

Is Hitler willing to let ordinary citizens have a role in political decision making? Explain.

_____

_____

_____

### DOCUMENT 3

"The State of Israel will be open for Jewish immigration and for the ingathering of the exiles; it will foster the development of the country for the benefit of all inhabitants; it will be based on freedom, justice, and peace as envisaged by the Prophets of Israel; it will ensure complete equality of social and political rights to all its inhabitants irrespective of religion, race, or sex; it will guarantee freedom of religion, conscience, language, education, and culture; it will safeguard the Holy Places of all religions; and it will be faithful to the principles of the Charter of the United Nations."

—Declaration of the Establishment
of the State of Israel, 1948

Why can Israel be called a democracy?

_____

_____

_____

**DOCUMENT 4**

"After socialism, Fascism combats the whole complex system of democratic ideology [theory], and repudiates [denies] it, whether in its theoretical premises [basis] or in its practical application. Fascism denies that the majority, by the simple fact that it is a majority, can direct human society; it denies that numbers alone can govern by means of a periodical consultation [elections], and it affirms the . . . beneficial, and fruitful [useful] inequality of mankind, which can never be permanently leveled through . . . universal suffrage."

—Benito Mussolini, 1932

What was the basis of Mussolini's arguments against democracy?

_____

_____

_____

**DOCUMENT 5**

". . . Whereas . . . King James II, . . . did attempt to undermine . . . the laws and liberties of this kingdom . . . Therefore, the Parliament declares:
  1. That the King's supposed power of suspending laws without the consent of Parliament is illegal.
  4. That the levying of taxes for the use of the King without the consent of Parliament is illegal.
  8. That the King should not interfere with the election of members of Parliament.
  13. And that to redress grievances and amend, strengthen, and preserve the laws, Parliament ought to be held [meet] frequently."

—English Bill of Rights

How did the English Bill of Rights change government decision making?

_____

_____

_____

**DOCUMENT 6**

*"But what happens when the sun sets?"*

Based on this illustration, who controlled the government of France from the mid-1600s to the early 1700s?

_____

_____

_____

## Part B
## Essay

**Directions:**
• Write a well-organized essay that includes an introduction, several paragraphs, and a conclusion.
• Use evidence from the documents to support your response.
• Do not simply repeat the contents of the documents.
• Include specific related outside information.

**Historical context:**
Throughout history, societies have held different viewpoints on governmental decision making and the role of citizens in this decision-making process. The decision making process can range from absolute control to democracy.

**Task:**

Using information from the documents and your knowledge of global history and geography, write an essay in which you

- Compare and contrast the different viewpoints societies have held about the process of governmental decision-making and about the role of citizens in the political decision-making process.
- Discuss the advantages and disadvantages of a political system that is under the absolute control of a single individual or a few individuals, or a political system that is a democracy.

Be sure to include specific historical details. You must also include additional information from your knowledge of global history and geography.

**Essay #2**

This task is based upon the accompanying documents (1–5). Some of these documents have been edited for the purposes of this task. This task is designed to test your ability to work with historical documents. As you analyze the documents, take into account both the source of each document and the author's point of view.

**Directions:** Read the documents in Part A and answer the questions after each document. Then read the directions for Part B and write your essay.

**Historical Context:** Throughout history, nations have gone to war for various reasons. The reasons can be categorized as political, economic, or social (cultural).

**Task:**

Using information from the documents and your knowledge of global history and geography, write an essay in which you
• Compare and contrast the different reasons why nations have gone to war.
• Evaluate why nations go to war.

### Part A
### Short Answer

**Directions:** Analyze the documents and answer the questions that follow each document in the space provided.

#### DOCUMENT 1

"The history of recent years, and in particular the painful events of the 28th June last, have shown the existence of a subversive movement with the object of detaching a part of the territories of Austria-Hungary from the Monarchy. The movement which had its birth under the eye of the Serbian government has gone so far as to make itself manifest on both sides of the Serbian frontier in the shape of acts of terrorism and a series of outrages and murders."

—Austrian ultimatum to Serbia
July 23, 1914

Why is Austria-Hungary so angry with Serbia?

_____

_____

_____

## DOCUMENT 2

"Our general purpose is to redeem Europe from the perpetually recurring fear of German aggression and to enable the peoples of Europe to preserve their independence and their liberties. No threats will deter us or our French allies from this purpose."

—Neville Chamberlain,
British Prime Minister, 1939

Why is Chamberlain willing to go to war against Germany?

_____

_____

_____

## DOCUMENT 3

"I am not now thinking of the loss of property involved . . . but only of the wanton and wholesale destruction of the lives of non-combatants, men, women and children engaged in pursuits which have always, even in the darkest periods of history, been deemed innocent and legitimate. Property can be paid for; the lives of innocent people cannot be. The present German submarine warfare against commerce is a warfare against mankind. There is one choice we cannot make . . . we will not choose the path of submission and suffer the most sacred rights of our nation and our people to be ignored or violated. The wrongs against which we now array ourselves are no common wrongs: they cut to the very roots of human life."

—Woodrow Wilson, Address to
Congress Recommending War,
April, 1917

Why is Woodrow Wilson asking for a declaration of war from Congress?

_____

_____

_____

## DOCUMENT 4

"The greatest single underlying cause of the War was the system of secret alliances . . . It gradually divided Europe into two hostile groups of Powers who were increasingly suspicious of one another and who steadily built up greater and greater armies and navies."

Sidney Fay, "The Origins of
The World War," 1928

What does Sidney Fay think was the main reason for the outbreak of war in Europe?

_____

_____

_____

### DOCUMENT 5

"A government should not mobilize an army out of anger, military leaders should not provoke a war out of wrath. Act when it is beneficial, desist when it is not. Anger can revert to joy, wrath can revert to delight, but a nation destroyed cannot be restored to existence, and the dead cannot be restored to life."

—Sun Tzu, The Art of War, 300 B.C.E.

Does Sun Tzu think it is good to begin a war because of anger? Explain.

_____

_____

_____

## Part B
## Essay

**Directions:**
- Write a well-organized essay that includes an introduction, several paragraphs, and a conclusion.
- Use evidence from the documents to support your response.
- Do not simply repeat the contents of the documents.
- Include specific related outside information.

**Historical context:**
Throughout history, nations have gone to war for various reasons. The reasons can be characterized as political, economic, or social (cultural).

**Task:**
Using information from the documents and your knowledge of global history and geography, write an essay in which you
- Compare and contrast the different viewpoints about why nations go to war.
- Make a ranking list of the three major reasons why nations go to war. Explain the reasons for your choices and explain whether each reason for war is political, economic, or social.

**Be sure to include specific historical details. You must also include additional information from your knowledge of global history and geography.**

# ERA VII

# The World
# Since 1945

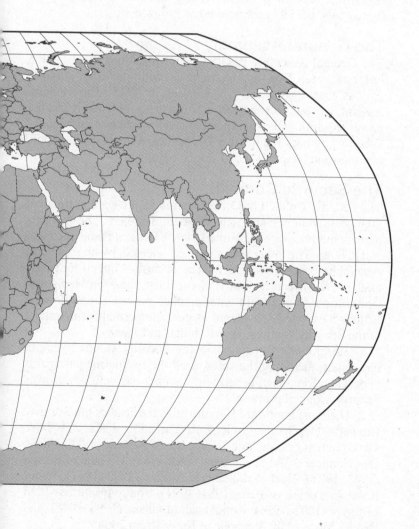

# Part A: The United Nations

The United Nations was created in 1945. Its founders included the United States and the other World War II Allies. They hoped to make the UN a more effective international peace-keeping organization than the League of Nations had been. The UN Charter listed the organization's goals: to maintain peace and prevent war; to fight against hunger, disease, and ignorance; to improve social and economic conditions; and to build friendship and cooperation among nations. To accomplish these goals, the UN is structured as follows:

## The General Assembly

The General Assembly has 193 member nations. Each nation has one vote. This figure contrasts with the fifty member nations that signed the UN Charter in 1945. The General Assembly meets to consider international problems. It has the power to admit and expel members and to make recommendations to members and to other UN bodies. A decision on important questions requires a two-thirds majority.

## The Security Council

The Security Council has fifteen members. Five are permanent members, while ten are nonpermanent members. The five permanent members are the United States, Britain, France, Russia, and China. The other members are elected by the General Assembly for a two-year term. The Security Council functions as the UN's executive body; it can investigate problems and take action to maintain international peace. The following nations have been considered as possible permanent members of the Security Council: Brazil, India, and Japan.

1. Resolutions for action in the Security Council require nine votes, including the votes of all the five permanent members. Therefore, each permanent member has veto power over Security Council proposals.

2. The most important UN official is the head of the Security Council—the Secretary-General. The individuals who have served in that post include Trygve Lie of Norway (1946–1953), Dag Hammarskjöld of Sweden (1953–1961), U Thant of Burma (1961–1971), Kurt Waldheim of Austria (1972–1981), Javier Perez de Cuellar of Peru (1981–1991), Boutros Boutros-Ghali of Egypt (1992–1996), Kofi Annan of Ghana (1996–2006), and Ban Ki-Moon of the Republic of Korea (from 2006).

## Specialized Agencies

The United Nations oversees a number of specialized agencies that administer specific social and economic programs. Among these organizations is UNESCO (United Nations Educational, Scientific and Cultural Organization) whose "mission is to contribute to the building of peace, the eradication of poverty, sustainable development and intercultural dialogue through education, the sciences, culture, communication and information." The World Health Organization (WHO) is "responsible for providing leadership on global health matters and providing technical support to countries (by) monitoring and assessing health trends." "Raise levels of nutrition, improve agricultural productivity, better the lives of rural populations and contribute to the growth of the world economy"—this is the mandate of the Food and Agricultural Organization of the UN. Altogether about two dozen other groups promote progress in such areas as the status of women, banking, labor, trade, weather, tourism, and atomic energy.

**GEOGRAPHY**

Places and Regions

## Activities and Challenges

The UN has generally been more successful in dealing with social and economic issues than with political ones. Examples can be seen in its virtual elimination of smallpox and in the reduction of other diseases through the effort of WHO. On the other hand, there has been frustration with the lack of success in dealing with the AIDS epidemic, especially in African nations. FAO programs have succeeded in handling some famine situations around the world, but North Korea's adamant, self-imposed political isolation has prevented the UN from helping with that country's ongoing food crisis. UNESCO and WHO have promoted a worldwide focus on women's equality and health issues, improving conditions in a number of regions. Under UN sponsorship, the Kyoto Protocol set standards for environmental protection in spite of the lack of support from some critical highly industrialized nations including the United States.

Since 1946 the UN International Court of Justice has delivered dozens of judgments on disputes concerning land frontiers and maritime boundaries, territorial sovereignty, the nonuse of force, noninterference in the internal affairs of states, diplomatic relations, hostage taking, the right of asylum, nationality, guardianship, rights of passage, and economic rights.

In the political arena, the United Nations has had limited success, although it did provide a forum for ongoing diplomacy in diffusing potentially dangerous situations during the Cold War period. Peacekeeping forces have served in numerous contentious areas: Cyprus during Greek-Turkish disputes, several areas in the Middle East including Lebanon, the Indian-Pakistani quarrel over Kashmir, newly independent East Timor after the attempted Indonesian takeover of that former Portuguese colony, and in Bosnia and Kosovo following the breakup of the former Yugoslavia. However, the UN was faulted for failing to prevent ethnic cleansing, especially the mass killings at Srebenica. UN peacekeeping and humanitarian aid efforts in Somalia, Rwanda, and Haiti have also been criticized for their lack of success.

Peacekeeping efforts benefit from substantial investment, including the involvement of 120,000 personnel working in fifteen countries. These efforts generally have admirable goals, but can be thwarted by the nations where conflicts occur. UN membership is balanced with national sovereignty; in nations such as Sudan, Chad, Cote d'Ivoire, and the Democratic Republic of the Congo host governments have rejected or limited UN attempts to protect civilian populations.

In the area of nuclear nonproliferation, the UN has achieved some modest results but has also failed to deal effectively with the ambitions of Iran and North Korea and the perceived instability of a nuclear-armed Pakistan. At the same time, its resolutions regarding international terrorism did enlist near-unanimous support of the membership in the wake of the September 11, 2001, destruction of the World Trade Center in New York and subsequent terrorist attacks elsewhere.

In the Middle East, the United Nations has been consistently criticized for its lack of success in dealing with Arab-Israeli relationships, in spite of the passage of numerous resolutions. When the UN's recognition established the legitimacy of Israel at its birth in 1948, it also created the basis for a "two-state" solution to the Arab-Jewish question as it existed at the time. In the ongoing attempt to increase recognition of Arab claims, a campaign led by Palestinian National Authority President Mahmoud Abbas has pressed the UN to once again consider Palestine's application for membership. In spite of nominal support from some influential European nations, the issue seemed to have little chance of success in the short run, given opposition by influential Security Council members.

A scandal allegedly involving individuals close to a former UN secretary general arose in relation to Iraqi oil exports before the fall of the Saddam Hussein regime. Charges included the misuse of funds, illegal kickbacks, bribery, and corruption. Perhaps because it is seen as an agent of modernization and "westernization," the UN has become a target of Islamist terrorist attacks in Iraq, Nigeria, Algeria, Afghanistan, and Somalia.

During the nearly seven decades since its birth, perhaps the UN's greatest accomplishments have been creation of the Universal Declaration of Human Rights, the relatively rapid phasing out of colonialism with surprisingly little bloodshed, and the enlistment and retention of a virtually universal membership.

South Sudan became the UN's 193rd member after a UN-administered referendum helped it become independent. Looking to the future and its potential to improve conditions in war-torn, ethnically fractious, poverty-stricken, and famine-riddled nations like Sudan, the UN in 2000 adopted a set of Millennium Development Goals. These goals have targeted poverty and hunger, universal education, gender equality, maternal and child health, AIDS/HIV, environmental sustainability, and global partnerships as focal areas for emphasis. A "global action plan" resolution passed in 2011 reiterated the organization's commitment, engaged world leaders and nations, gained support of private groups, and gained pledges of $40 billion in the campaign to achieve measurable results by 2015 and beyond.

# Part B: Western Europe and the Cold War

## The Cold War and the Era of the Superpowers

The period after World War II (the postwar period) was marked by the dominance of two superpowers—the United States and the former Soviet Union. Each nation had different philosophies about politics, economics, and human rights. Each thought it was superior to the other. The two nations engaged in a cold war, which was not a shooting war but a war of words and propaganda; it also involved competition in science, weapons, and seeking friends among the new emerging nations in Africa and Asia. Western European nations sided with the United States in what was called the free world. The Soviet Union occupied the Eastern European nations and, with them, formed the communist bloc. As the 1990s began, however, the Cold War came to an end, seen in the peaceful overthrow of communist governments in Eastern European nations such as Poland and Czechoslovakia. But the most striking event marking the end of the Cold War and the decline of communism occurred on December 8, 1991, when the leaders of Russia and other Soviet republics announced that the Soviet Union no longer existed. Taking its place would be several independent nations, for example, Russia, Ukraine, and Belarus, that would be members of the Commonwealth of Independent States. The Cold War era, from 1945 to 1991, was distinguished by certain key events in Western Europe.

## NATO

NATO, the North Atlantic Treaty Organization, was formed in 1949. It was a defensive alliance consisting of the United States, Canada, and ten Western European nations. The twelve founding members expanded to sixteen member states during the Cold War. After the fall of communism in Eastern Europe, ten former Eastern Bloc nations joined NATO from 1999 to 2004. By 2005, NATO had twenty-six member nations. Its formation was part of the U.S. policy of containment, through which the United States and its European allies hoped to prevent the spread of communism by the threat of military power. Two important parts of the containment policy in 1947 were the Marshall Plan (to provide economic aid) and the Truman Doctrine (to provide military aid to prevent a communist takeover in Greece and Turkey). To counter NATO, the Soviet Union and its allies formed the seven-member Warsaw Pact in 1955.

However, in March 1991 the former Soviet Union and five Eastern European nations agreed to dissolve the Warsaw Pact. This dramatic event, along with others that marked the end of the Cold War, caused NATO members to reconsider the role of the organization. They discussed the possibility of changing NATO from an alliance focused on collective defense against a specific threat to an alliance based on extending democracy and providing stability throughout Europe. Key episodes during 1994 illustrated how such changes could develop.

1. In April, the NATO alliance carried out its first bombing raid. NATO bombed Serbian positions in Bosnia-Herzegovina to protect UN officials under fire and to protect thousands of people in the town of Gorazde from being attacked.

2. In January, U.S. President Bill Clinton and other NATO leaders proposed a Partnership for Peace program, which was intended to bring about closer ties between NATO and its former Warsaw Pact enemies. It would allow these former communist nations to join military exercises, peacekeeping operations, and other activities without actually granting them NATO membership or security guarantees. As of June 1994, eighteen Eastern European nations and former Soviet republics had signed the partnership agreement. In 1999, Poland, the Czech Republic, and Hungary joined NATO. In April of 1999, NATO intervened in Kosovo after Yugoslav forces began ethnic cleansing of the Albanian majority as a response to violence by the KLA (Kosovo Liberation Army), which demanded the independence of the province from Yugoslavia. Through a massive air campaign against targets in both Kosovo and Serbia, NATO eventually forced the Yugoslav troops to leave the province. As the basis of the peacekeeping force in Kosovo after the withdrawal of Yugoslav troops, NATO encountered problems both with the population and the Russian troops who were serving them. Despite efforts by NATO to create a democratic multiethnic state in Kosovo, a divided state, as in Bosnia, seemed likely.

## Germany

In the years immediately after World War II, the question of what to do about Germany caused much tension between the superpowers. At the end of the war, most of Germany was divided into four occupation zones—American, British, French, and Soviet. The city of Berlin was also divided into four such zones. Some territories in East Germany were put under Polish control. Since the four Allies were unable to agree on a plan for German

GLOBAL
CONCEPTS

**Choice**

CONCEPTS
GLOBAL

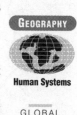

**GEOGRAPHY**

**Human Systems**

GLOBAL
CONCEPTS

**Change**

CONCEPTS
GLOBAL

reunification, the Western nations permitted their zones to come together in 1949 as the Federal Republic of Germany (West Germany), with its capital at Bonn. The Soviet zone became the German Democratic Republic (East Germany), with its capital in East Berlin. West Berlin, although surrounded by East Germany, became part of West Germany. The Soviets tried to cut off access to West Berlin in 1948 and 1949 by imposing the Berlin Blockade. However, the Western Allies sent in food and supplies by plane (the Berlin Airlift). The Soviet Union subsequently backed down and ended the blockade.

1. *The Berlin Wall.* The Soviets again made Berlin a tension spot in 1961 when they built a wall (the Berlin Wall) separating the Western section from the Eastern section. These areas had been used as escape routes for people who wanted to flee from communist rule. The wall was another example of the Soviet policy of restricting the flow of ideas, goods, and people between the free world and the communist world. This restrictive policy became known, in the words of former British Prime Minister Winston Churchill, as the Iron Curtain.

The many historic changes in the European communist world that occurred in 1989 and 1990 can be thought of as cracks in the Iron Curtain. One crack was the destruction of the Berlin Wall

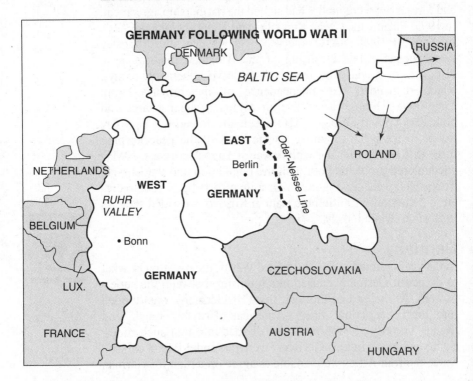

GERMANY FOLLOWING WORLD WAR II

466

by the communist authorities, making Berlin a more open city. From November 1989 onward, when the wall was opened, it lost its significance as a political, economic, and social barrier.

2. *German reunification.* With the end of the Berlin Wall and the friendlier relationship (détente) between the superpowers, the chances of reunifying Germany became a very distinct possibility. In 1990 free elections were held in East Germany. West German political parties, such as the Christian Democrats and Social Democrats, ran candidates and won the support of some voters. In July 1990 an economic merger occurred when the West German mark became the unit of currency in East Germany. This meant that even though Germans were still living in two separate nations, they would use the same money. East Germans were allowed to move into West Germany; West German companies were allowed to set up capitalist-style businesses in East Germany. With these developments, it became likely that German reunification would occur by 1991. Indeed, discussions about a reunited Germany were held throughout 1990. The major discussants were the four victorious World War II Allies, as well as representatives from the two Germanies. These discussions were thus known as the four-plus-two negotiations. Poland wanted to be included in the talks, because it had suffered more from German occupation in World War II than any other European nation. It wanted assurance that a reunited Germany would respect Polish sovereignty and would not seek to retake any land given to Poland after the war. Specifically, Poland wanted to be sure that the Oder-Neisse boundary line between East Germany and Poland would remain intact. A promise to maintain this boundary was made by West German Chancellor Helmut Kohl in the spring of 1990, on the assumption that he would become the first head of a reunited German nation.

A reunited Germany came into being on October 3, 1990. In December 1990 the first all-German elections were held. The winner was the Christian Democratic Union (CDU) coalition party and its leader, Helmut Kohl. To finance the huge cost of reunification and to fight the economic depression that now affected the eastern part of the new nation, taxes had to be raised. The new government also decided to move the capital from Bonn to Berlin by the year 2000. The move was made in 1999. Two events occurred in 1994, to mark the new Germany: (1) In August, all American, British, French, and Russian troops left Berlin; (2) In October, the second all-German elections were held. In 1999, a third election was held with Gerhard

GEOGRAPHY

**Human Systems**

GLOBAL CONCEPTS

**Change**

CONCEPTS GLOBAL

Schroeder winning. Gerhard Schroeder, the leader of the Social Democratic Party (SPD), remained the chancellor of Germany until 2005. In November 2005, Angela Merkel, the leader of the Christian Democratic Union became the new chancellor of Germany after her party won the September elections and all parties later reached an agreement. Ms. Merkel's rise to power is significant, as she is the first woman chancellor and is from the former East Germany.

## Other Key Issues at the Turn of the Century

The consequences of German reunification is one of several political issues that will concern Western European nations in the 1990s. Some of the others are:

### Ireland

The Irish question has been a source of controversy between Ireland and England for centuries. By 1600, Protestant England had gained control over Catholic Ireland. From that time until the 20th century, British imperialist treatment of the Irish was cruel and harsh. During the 17th century, when Oliver Cromwell ruled England, many Irish were killed by British forces; in addition, Protestants from England and Scotland took over large areas of land in Northern Ireland. Until the 1800s, Irish Catholics could not hold political office and were taxed to support the Anglican (Protestant) Church.

In 1905 the Sinn Fein Party was formed as a nationalist group to press Britain for Irish independence. Its leader was Eamon de Valera. Although the Easter Rebellion in 1916 against the British was unsuccessful, the Sinn Fein continued its campaign for independence. In 1922, the southern four-fifths of the island of Ireland became a free nation known as the Republic of Ireland. The remaining one-fifth, Northern Ireland, also known as Ulster, decided to remain as part of the United Kingdom (Great Britain). Catholics in Northern Ireland wanted the area to be united with the Irish Republic to the south, as did the new Republic of Ireland itself. These requests were turned down by Britain, particularly because the majority of Ulster citizens were Protestants and wanted to stay under the British Crown. Extremist groups, both Catholic and Protestant, began to fight an undeclared civil war in Northern Ireland. The IRA (Irish Republican Army) and its political party, Sinn Fein, spoke for many Ulster Catholics and demanded a united Ireland. Militant Protestants, headed by the Reverend Ian Paisley, are against unification. British troops have been sent to Ulster since 1976 to help maintain peace and stop the killings and terrorist actions of both sides. These efforts have not been very successful. A 1985 agreement between Ireland and Britain, the Hillsborough Agreement, attempted to end what has been called the Troubles. It provided for greater cooperation against extremist groups, stopping discrimination toward the Catholic minority in the north, and giving the Republic of Ireland some involvement in the governing of Northern Ireland. The agreement has had mixed results and has been criticized by both Catholics and Protestants.

In December 1993, Prime Ministers John Major of Britain and Albert Reynolds of Ireland signed a declaration of principles in London to encourage talks for a peace plan. The agreement's highlights were: (1) all groups that promise to renounce violence, such as the I.R.A. and Protestant guerrilla organizations, would be invited to join negotiations on the future of Northern Ireland; (2) Northern Ireland would remain a province of Britain for as long as most of its people want it to; (3) the Irish government agreed to amend its constitutional claim to the territory of Northern Ireland. Although little progress toward peace was made in the early months of 1994, there was a reduction in the bloodshed that had claimed over 3,100 lives in the preceding 25 years.

From 1995 to 1998, efforts to end the violence progressed slowly. Due to the efforts of the American Senator George Mitchell, a peace plan was reached on April 10, 1998 (Good Friday). The accord, known as the Good Friday Agreement, set up a timetable in which the British would withdraw and a government made up of representatives of both the Protestant Unionists and the Catholic Nationalists, including Sinn Fein, would share power and the decision-making process.

Ratification of the Good Friday Agreement by the political parties of Northern Ireland progressed slowly as the extremists on both sides found objections. In the summer of 1999, the whole process temporarily stopped over the issue of the IRA disarming before the new power-sharing executive was set up. By the autumn of 1999, due to the efforts of Unionist leader David Trimble and Nationalist leader Gerry Adams, the Good Friday Agreement seemed back on track. Despite good intentions, implementation of the Good Friday Agreement proved difficult from 1999 to 2005. However, in 2005, hopes for peace in Northern Ireland increased when the Irish Republican Army (IRA) officially gave up its armed struggle and agreed to hand in its weapons.

## Political Union and a "United States of Europe"

**GEOGRAPHY**

**Human Systems**

The political unification of European nations is an idea that has been under consideration since the end of World War II. There already exists a European Parliament, a European Court of Justice, and a European Commission. These organizations have limited powers but stand for some attempt at international cooperation. The twelve nation European Union (EU) (formerly known as the European Community), has made great strides toward economic cooperation. At its June 1990 meeting in Dublin, the EU agreed to consider proposals for political union. These have been discussed further in conferences at Rome and elsewhere. French presidents and German chancellors have spoken of a single European currency as well as possible political unification.

One factor that helped to set the stage for consideration of political and economic cooperation was the Helsinki Pact of 1975. This was a treaty signed by the United States, Canada, and 33 European nations, at what was called the Conference on Security and Cooperation in Europe. The signing nations agreed to accept the post-World War II boundaries in Europe. They also agreed to recognize the importance of promoting human rights throughout Europe and to investigate any governmental actions that violated such rights. A Helsinki Watch Committee was established to conduct such investigations.

In 1992, the members of the European Union signed the Maastricht Treaty, which began the process of creating a unified Europe. This included an end to tariffs and passports between members. This process was taken further in 1999, when members of the European Union began to replace their national currencies with the Euro. The EU also began to consider the applications of the Eastern European nations formerly in the Soviet bloc to join. By 2005, the European Union had twenty-five members. In 2007, two additional countries, Romania and Bulgaria, were allowed to join, bringing the EU membership to twenty-seven nations. The new members were primarily nations from Eastern Europe. Other nations, including Turkey, were candidates for membership. The issue of Turkish membership in the EU is complicated by the fact that Turkey is a mostly Islamic nation.

# Part C: Eastern Europe, the Cold War, and the Transition to Democracy

## The Cold War (1953–1990)

As a result of the division of Europe, a cold war (political, economic, and diplomatic conflict without open military conflict) developed. In 1949 the countries of Western Europe and the

THE DIVISION OF EUROPE

**KEY**

NATO Countries
Other NATO members include: Canada, Iceland, and the United States

Warsaw Pact Countries

Neutral Countries

0    200    400

ATLANTIC OCEAN

FINLAND
NORWAY
SWEDEN
DENMARK
BALTIC SEA
U.S.S.R.
IRELAND
UNITED KINGDOM
NETH.
POLAND
EAST GERMANY
BELGIUM
LUX.
WEST GERMANY
CZECHOSLOVAKIA
FRANCE
AUSTRIA
HUNGARY
ROMANIA
SWITZ.
ITALY
YUGOSLAVIA
BLACK SEA
BULGARIA
PORTUGAL
SPAIN
MEDITERRANEAN SEA
ALBANIA
GREECE
TURKEY

United States formed a military alliance, NATO (North Atlantic Treaty Organization), in response to Stalin's takeover of Eastern Europe and his unsuccessful attempts to install communist governments in Greece, Turkey, and Iran. This policy, called Containment (to limit the spread of communism to areas where it already existed), was answered by the U.S.S.R. with the creation of the Warsaw Pact, an alliance of the Soviet Union and the Eastern Bloc or communist satellite countries. The military buildup that resulted from the Cold War put an even greater strain on the Soviet economy, which was still suffering from the devastation of World War II. The U.S.S.R.'s new superpower status was expensive to maintain, and Soviet consumers bore the burden.

With the death of Stalin, there was a period of readjustment from the fear and suffering the Soviet dictator's rule had brought. The "Great Thaw" from Stalinism (1953–1958) allowed some freedom of political and cultural expression (mostly denouncing Stalin). However, this was short-lived. When Nikita Khrushchëv (r. 1958–1964) took power as First Secretary and Premier, these freedoms ended. Khrushchëv attempted to increase industrial and agricultural production through a series of plans, particularly productivity incentives and an expansion of agricultural development into thinly populated areas (Virgin Lands Program). Khrushchëv's policies failed due to the inefficiency of the bureaucratic Soviet system, the lack of incentives to produce in the factories, and the severe forces of nature in Russia. Many conservatives from the Stalinist period resented Khrushchëv. They used his setback in the Cuban Missile Crisis and the failures of his economic reforms to oust him from power in 1964.

Khrushchëv was succeeded by Leonid Brezhnev (r. 1964–1982), who, unlike Stalin or Khrushchëv, did not have complete power and was answerable to top Communist Party officials. Despite the great need for change that had prompted Khrushchëv's programs, Brezhnev feared that reform would undermine the authority of the Communist Party. The policy of concentrating on heavy industry was therefore continued, except for one unsuccessful experiment to expand consumer goods production in the Ninth Five-Year Plan (1971–1975). By 1972 the antagonism between the Soviet Union and Communist China and the fear produced by improved relations between China and the United States forced Brezhnev to adopt a policy of Détente (Understanding) with the United States and Western Europe. This first thaw in the Cold War also resulted in the first of two SALT (Strategic Arms Limitation Talks) agreements, in which both NATO and the Warsaw Pact nations agreed to restrict the development of antiballistic missile systems. These

**GEOGRAPHY**

Use of Geography

**WORLD ISSUES**

Economic
Growth and
Development

GLOBAL
CONCEPTS

Choice

CONCEPTS
GLOBAL

were followed by START (Strategic Arms Reduction Talks) in the Gorbachëv era. Despite Détente, Brezhnev continued to suppress dissent and oppose any domestic reform.

## Gorbachëv (r. 1985–1991)

After the brief period of rule by Yurii Andropov (r. 1982–1984) and Konstantin Chernenko (r. 1984–1985), Mikhail Gorbachëv became General Secretary of the Communist Party. He quickly consolidated his power by removing the older, more conservative members of the U.S.S.R.'s ruling Politboro (chief political committee of the Communist Party) and replacing them with younger reformers like himself. The stagnation of the Soviet economy had reached a crisis, and Gorbachëv proposed sweeping economic reforms known as Perestroika, or "Restructuring." Gorbachëv also adopted a policy of Glasnost (Openness), which was aimed at destroying the secrecy and suspicion of Soviet life. Public criticism and suggestions about national problems were encouraged as well as the expression of opposing ideas, which had previously been censored. Literature, films, music, and art that had been banned were now reinstated as cultural life was given new freedoms. As the Russian Orthodox Church celebrated its millennium (1,000-year anniversary), Gorbachëv lifted many of the restrictions on Orthodox Christianity and the practice of religion in general.

GLOBAL CONCEPTS

**Change**

CONCEPTS GLOBAL

**Human Systems**

From 1988 to 1989, Gorbachëv reorganized the entire Soviet political system. Communist Party control over the government was reduced, a popularly elected assembly (the Congress of People's Deputies) was established, which was a structure for a multiparty system, and a presidency with control over domestic and foreign affairs was created. In March 1989 the U.S.S.R. held its first elections, in which many non-Communist Party candidates were elected. Yet the majority of representatives were Communists who ran unopposed. When the Congress first met in June, it elected a smaller body (the Supreme Soviet) to deal with daily legislation. It also elected Mikhail Gorbachëv as the U.S.S.R.'s first (and only) president.

GLOBAL CONCEPTS

**Political Systems**

CONCEPTS GLOBAL

Gorbachëv also greatly improved relations between the U.S.S.R. and the West. In 1987 the U.S.S.R. and the United States agreed to the I.N.F. (Intermediate-Range Nuclear Forces) Treaty, in which both sides would destroy two classes of nuclear weapons. He also implemented the Gorbachëv Doctrine, a policy of noninterference in Eastern Europe. By the autumn of 1988, he began to reduce the number of Soviet troops in some of the satellite nations, which helped to bring about the collapse of the communist regimes in those countries a year later.

## The Decline and Collapse of the Soviet Regime (1989–1991)

By 1989 Gorbachëv began to retreat from his reforms. The election to the Congress of People's Deputies of dissidents, such as the prominent scientist Andrei Sakharov, and officials who were openly critical of the regime, such as the President of the Russian Republic Boris Yeltsin, was seen by Gorbachëv as a threat to the survival of the Soviet system. Yeltsin had risen to power by promoting Russian nationalism and downplaying the Soviet Union. This gave the population a new pride in their nation and directed their anger at the Soviet government. Gorbachëv, who never understood this, continued to support dominance by the Communist Party. In so doing, he became as unpopular as the system he defended. By 1991 he had backed down from his reforms and appointed conservative Communists to important government positions.

With Gorbachëv's new policies, many of the U.S.S.R.'s republics, beginning with the Baltic nations, demanded independence. Gorbachëv was totally overwhelmed by the rise in nationalism and agreed to sign a union treaty with the leaders of most of the republics that would have given these nations greater autonomy. This frightened the conservative Communists into attempting a military coup d'état (an unexpected seizure of power) in August 1991. Gorbachëv, who was on vacation in the Crimea, was put under house arrest. The coup lacked any public support or the support of the bulk of the military, and it collapsed after three days. Yeltsin, who had defied the takeover, became a national hero. Gorbachëv returned, and the leaders of the coup were arrested or committed suicide. This series of events became known as the Russian Revolution of 1991.

The coup had made Gorbachëv seem weak and incompetent. Rumors circulated that he had actually planned and ordered the coup as a way of undoing his reforms before the Communist Party leadership had completely lost power. The failed overthrow discredited both the Communist Party and the KGB (secret police). Disregarding the unsigned agreement, Yeltsin declared Russia to be an independent state. One by one, the other republics also claimed independence. Unable to stop the swift breakup of the Soviet Union, Gorbachëv resigned on December 25, 1991, from the presidency of an empire that no longer existed. Communism in both Russia and the U.S.S.R. had ended.

GLOBAL CONCEPTS

**Change**

CONCEPTS GLOBAL

**GEOGRAPHY**

Use of Geography

**WORLD ISSUES**

Determination of Political and Economic Systems

# The Commonwealth of Independent States (1991–    )

When the U.S.S.R. disbanded, each republic held its own elections and established its own independent government. Russia, as the largest and most populous of these states, took a leadership position in creating a new federation of autonomous nations, the Commonwealth of Independent States (C.I.S.). The United Nations recognized each new nation, giving them their own representatives in the world body.

Some republics did not make a smooth transition. Civil war flared up in Georgia between the newly elected government and rebels. Fighting between the Christians of Armenia and the Muslims of Azerbaijan, which had started in the last years of the Soviet Union, also continued. From 1992 to 1993, Russia and Ukraine negotiated a compromise over the Black Sea fleet in the Crimea (an area in southern Ukraine that had been a very important naval base for the Russians). The two nations finally agreed that it would belong to Ukraine, but the Russian fleet would be allowed to use it.

GLOBAL CONCEPTS

Political Systems

CONCEPTS GLOBAL

GEOGRAPHY

Use of Geography

Era VII **THE WORLD SINCE 1945**

# Russia and the Transition to Democracy (1991–    )

In the fall of 1993, President Yeltsin dismissed the Congress of People's Deptuies. Composed mainly of Communists from the Gorbachëv period, the former Soviet parliament had blocked all efforts to turn the Russian economy into a capitalist free market. Yeltsin demanded that new elections be held since most of the parliament's deputies had never been elected, but had run unopposed as Communist Party candidates in 1989. Realizing it would probably not be returned to office, the Congress refused to stop meeting and the members barricaded themselves in the parliament building. Yeltsin brought in troops to storm it and arrest rebellious deputies. These decisive actions added to Yeltsin's popularity. He also took steps toward creating a new constitution that would give greater powers to the presidency. While some accused Yeltsin of trying to establish a dictatorship, most Russians still had confidence in him as a strong leader. Yet, the enormous suffering that the economic transformation brought created new problems that threatened the development of democracy in Russia. This became evident in the national elections of December 1993, when ultra-nationalists won an impressive number of seats in the new Russian parliament.

**GEOGRAPHY**

**Human Systems**

The national elections of 1994 confirmed popular support for both Yeltsin and a new constitution. Within the year however, the Russian Army's inability to put down rebellion in Chechnya (a republic within Russia), a rise in government corruption and organized crime, and the hardships created by economic reforms, overwhelmed the Yeltsin presidency. Despite these problems, Yeltsin campaigned successfully on a platform of commitment to reform and a moderate choice over both right-wing nationalists and old-style Communists in the 1996 elections. Soon after both his health and popularity faded as the struggling president continuously shifted ministers.

Yeltsin seemed to recover both physically and politically at the start of 1997. A peace treaty in Chechnya and mild improvements in the economy helped restore confidence in the government. In July, the remains of the last tsar and his family were buried in the Cathedral of Saints Peter and Paul in St. Petersburg. By late 1997, however, the economy declined steadily and with it the standard of living for most Russians. Popular anger forced Yeltsin to remove reformers from his cabinet. The economic relapse continued into 1998, made worse by a decline in the Russian president's health and a rise in organized crime. Facing staggering economic and social problems, the Yeltsin government began to see a slow, but steady improvement in 1999.

Despite these successes, there was resentment and anger towards the Russian president. This was compounded by government scandals involving the laundering of money by Russian banks. On January 31, Yeltsin resigned, making Vladimir Putin acting president until the national elections scheduled for March of 2000. The resignation appeared to be designed to strengthen his current prime minister's position and improve his chances to be elected president. The new support Putin received from politicians in January 2000 seemed to confirm the wisdom of Yeltsin's action.

In the March 2000 election, Putin was elected president with a strong popular mandate. His platform of ending corruption in government and opposing the "oligarchs" (government "insiders" who took illegal advantage of their positions to gain control of newly privatized industries, becoming extremely wealthy and influential) gave him enormous public support. His KGB background gave Putin the image of a strong, decisive leader who would both strengthen internal security against terrorism and restore Russia's declining military power. The election also saw a significant drop in support of the Communist Party, the Ultra Nationalists, and other extreme parties that had done fairly well in the last election because of anger over the economy.

Despite Putin's authoritarian style in implementing his reforms, he has remained popular. Over the next six years he increased the strength of the national government. He greatly weakened the power of local governments by stripping the eighty-nine governors of the Russian Federation of their seats in the Federation Council, creating seven new supraregional governors appointed by the president. Putin also obtained legislation allowing the president to remove any regional leader accused by federal authorities of wrongdoing. He gained greater influence over the Duma by creating federal requirements for political parties.

Putin placed restrictions on the Russian media's ability to criticize the government. While seen by many, especially outside Russia, as censorship of free speech, control of much of the media gave the president surprising popular support. Exposure of the corruption of the oligarchs and their responsibility for the 1998 economic collapse gave Putin the political mandate to make needed economic reforms. In 2001, he designed a new land code allowing the purchase and sale of land in Russian cities for the first time since the Bolshevik Revolution of 1917. It generated a new housing market attracting both domestic and foreign investment. The expansion of privatization and free enterprise resulted in the development of stock exchanges to provide investment capital throughout Russia in the 1990s. The lack of regulation however, as well as the problems the government experienced in tax collecting, resulted in the creation of a small aggressive class of wealthy entrepreneurs, often tied to organized crime, with government connections. Most ordinary Russians with low-paying jobs and the elderly, dependent on small pensions, became extremely resentful of the rise of this group. Social ills, such as crime, prostitution, and alcoholism, combined with high unemployment and government corruption, led to disillusion with the new system and the flight of many young people to the West in search of economic opportunities. On coming to power, Putin took steps to correct these problems by reducing taxes, implementing reforms to curb corruption within the government bureaucracy, cracking down on organized crime, and waging a war on the oligarchs in which the government seized control of their industries.

Despite Putin's use of authoritarian means, which resulted in strong criticism from both within and abroad, by 2002 it appeared that the Russian economy had stabilized. The government's budget showed a surplus, and Russia had paid off all of its foreign debts in full for the first time since 1991. Putin's strong action restored public confidence in the economy, which revived foreign investment. The government seizure of control of the oil and gas industries from the oligarchs, which benefited from the high prices on the international market, contributed greatly to the economic recovery. Finally, the successful humbling of the oligarchs created greater confidence in the government and opened up new opportunities for small, independent entrepreneurs.

In 2004, Putin won reelection and his party, United Russia, took 50 percent of the seats in the State Duma (Parliament). From 2004 to 2007, Putin instituted changes to limit other parties from running candidates. These included creating difficult requirements for candidacy and ending local parliamentary districts replacing them with a system of nationwide closed party lists. In 2007, United Russia won a huge majority in the Duma, giving Putin the ability to pass legislation. In 2008, Putin could not run for reelection due to a constitutional limitation of two consecutive terms. He supported fellow United Russia candidate Dimitry Medvedev, who won the election easily. Putin became prime minister. Many believed that he was still really running the government. During the Medvedev presidency, there was increasing criticism of government corruption and the growth of a wealthy elite connected to United Russia, which was shrinking the newly created Russian middle class.

In 2011, Medvedev chose not to run for reelection, supporting Putin, who could legally seek the presidency again in 2012. This meant Putin remained in power for an additional 12 years (United Russia used its parliamentary majority to extend the presidential term from 3 years to 4). In the parliamentary elections of 2011, United Russia lost a large number of seats, barely retaining its majority. The losses were surprising considering the reports of election fraud and vote rigging by the government from international observers. This was seen as a growing disillusion with both Putin, whose popularity had started to fall, and United Russia. Following the December 2011 elections mass protests began, with citizens demanding an investigation of election fraud and new elections. Despite Putin's election as President in March, popular discontent with United Russia continued into 2012.

The NATO military invasion on the side of the ethnic Albanians of Kosovo and the bombing of Serbia in the spring of 1999 created further strains in relations between Russia and the West and the United States. Russia supported Serbia and was highly critical of the NATO actions in the Yugoslav province. Its role in ending the conflict and the involvement of Russian troops in the peacekeeping force resulted in further tensions and mutual suspicions.

Terrorist attacks in Russian cities during the summer of 1999 were blamed on Chechen separatists. This resulted in a full scale Russian military invasion of Chechnya in autumn. By the winter, Russian troops had captured much Chechen territory and forced thousands of refugees to flee. The international community, including the United States, was critical of Russia's harsh reaction to the terrorist attacks. Yeltsin responded that it was an internal matter and it was hypocritical of the West to criticize Russia's actions after NATO's military interference in Kosovo and bombing of Serbia.

On coming to power in 2001, Putin escalated Russian military action in Chechnya. Although the campaign was successful in crushing rebel resistance and recapturing the Chechen capital city of Grozny, as well as most of the lowlands, it devastated both the country itself and the economy. By 2002, the cost of the war and the continuation of Chechen terrorism within Russia forced Putin to rethink his strategy. A new policy of working with a pro-Russian Chechen president to end the fighting and create a compromise that would allow Chechnya autonomy while remaining part of Russia was adopted. Although this plan has led to a considerable decline in violence, the problems are far from resolved and the threat of new conflict continues.

As the new millenium began, new tensions between Russia and its neighbors were becoming apparent. Each was still struggling to solve its economic problems, especially Russia, in order to make a smooth transition to capitalism and a free market. At the same time, strong nationalist movements within these nations and anger over the poor conditions brought on by the transitions may limit or even prevent the success of their economic reforms.

## Former Soviet Republics

### Ukraine

In Ukraine, Russia's largest neighbor, a political division between the western and eastern regions became clear soon after independence in 1991. The western Ukrainians were highly nationalistic and anti-Russian, favoring stronger ties with Western Europe and joining both NATO and the European Union. Eastern Ukrainians, many of whom were primarily Russian speaking, wanted closer ties with Russia and opposed joining any Western organization. The Ukrainian Duma (Parliament) became a battleground between these opposing political views, often resulting in angry debates and physical violence.

From November to December 2004, a series of mass protests took place in response to charges of massive corruption, voter intimidation, and electoral fraud in the 2004 Ukrainian presidential elections. In late December, Ukraine's Supreme Court ordered a revote. Under the close supervision of Ukrainian and international observers, the runoff election resulted in a victory for Viktor Yushchenko, who became president in January 2010. These events became known as the "Orange Revolution." Initially his main rival, Viktor Yanukovych had won the election. The successor of outgoing president Leonid Kuchma, Yanukovych was very pro-Russian and had his main support in Eastern Ukraine. Yushchenko, who was the candidate of a coalition of nationalist groups (Orange parties) with support in Western Ukraine, ran on a program of reform and pro-Western policies. Orange, the color adopted by Yushchenko's election campaign, became the symbol of political change that Ukrainians hoped his election would bring.

Under the Yushchenko presidency, the Ukrainian constitution was changed to shift power from the presidency to the parliament. The Orange Coalition was unable to make successful economic reforms due to divisions between the parties and the enormous corruption within the government. Creating a rival coalition with the pro-Russian Socialist and Communist parties, Yanukovych became prime minister, which created permanent conflict within the government. In 2007, new parliamentary elections were held in which the Orange parties won a narrow majority, but were unable to push through further reforms or pro-Western policies such as NATO or EU membership.

In the presidential election of 2010, Yanukovych was elected in response to the failure of the Orange parties to push through reform. He consolidated his personal power and began to attack his political opponents, in particular Orange Party rival Julia Tymoshenko, who was arrested, put on trial, and convicted of "exceeding her authority as prime minster." These actions created sympathy for the opposition and brought strong criticism from the West. Yanukovych's policy of pursuing economic integration with the EU hurt his relations with Russia and angered much of his support in Eastern Ukraine. At present, the government of Ukraine seems unsure about what direction to take.

## Belarus

In 1994, Aleksandr Lukashenko was elected president of Belarus. By 1996, he had annulled the constitution and began to rule the nation alone. His popularity with extreme nationalists, less educated farmers, the elderly, and those who were sympathetic to the old Soviet regime gave him a base of support. He began arresting, imprisoning, and killing all political opposition and critics, taking complete control over the mass media. He consolidated control over the armed forces and established a dictatorship. Lukashenko claimed he was "saving" the nation from the problems of capitalism and democracy; he transformed Belarus back into a Soviet-style state. Initially purposing union with Russia, he was able to gain its support to keep the Belarusian economy from collapsing. Lukashenko also reached out to the West for economic integration, trying to play the Europeans against the Russians. These tactics managed to keep him in power despite strong criticism from the foreign press and human rights groups. This policy eventually backfired as the Belarusian economy began to fail when the foreign loans finally stopped in 2010. In November 2011, Lukashenko was forced to give Russia complete control of Belarus' gas pipeline network, including the right to raise prices, in return for a $14 billion rescue plan. Alienated from the West due to his recent crackdown on political opposition, Lukashenko appears to have put his nation under Russian influence. With popular discontent and political opposition rising despite his repressive measures, the government may be headed for collapse.

## Moldova

The nation of Moldova was part of Romania until after World War II when the U.S.S.R. annexed it and made it a Soviet Republic. Repopulating it with Russian-speaking Eastern Ukrainians and ethnic Russians, who became a majority (54 percent), the ethnic Romanians were forced to accept separation from their nation. When Moldova became independent in 1991, ethnic Romanians, especially in the region of Transnistria, demanded reunification with Romania. This led to uprisings (1991–1992) that were put down with the help of the former Soviet military. In 1992, economic reforms and a market economy were adopted by the government. A parliamentary democracy was established. Appealing to the non-Romanian Russianized population, the communists came to power in 2001. Unable to deal with the global economic crisis of 2007–2010 and discredited by government corruption, their victory in the 2009 elections led to civil unrest, forcing President Vladimir Voronin to resign. A coalition of liberal democratic parties, the Alliance for European Integration, formed a new government. Two seats short of a majority, the coalition was unable to elect a new president. Since 2009 there have been three acting presidents as the Parliament and government remained deadlocked. New elections are scheduled for January 2012.

## Baltic Nations

Unlike the other former Soviet republics, the Baltic nations became democratic states with free-market economies after independence in 1991. Lithuania, Latvia, and Estonia quickly established constitutions and parliaments with multiple political parties. Alternating between capitalist and socialist policies, governments struggled to expand their economies. All three joined the European Union in 2004. Resentful of past Russian and Soviet domination, they immediately developed strong economic and political ties to the West. They also had to deal with the problem of large ethnic minorities in each nation. In Lithuania, tensions between the large Polish minority and the Lithuanian government over restitution of prewar Polish property and language rights in Lithuanian schools have developed. In Latvia and Estonia, the large Russian populations have created separate cultural, religious, and social institutions, as well as political parties. Resentful of past Russian control, this has created divisions in Latvian and Estonian society. Despite these problems, the transition from Soviet satellites to free democratic nations has been peaceful and successful.

## Caucasian Nations

The nations in the Caucasian Mountain region have experienced turbulent relations with both Russia and each other. The former Soviet republics of Georgia, Armenia, and Azerbaijan have had difficulties transforming into independent nations.

In 2003, American-educated Mikheil Saakashvili became president of Georgia. Promising economic and institutional reforms, he defeated Eduard Shevardnadze, a Soviet-era leader who had been president since Georgian independence in 1991. Tired of corruption in government and the poor economy, the population hoped the election would bring real change. It became known as the "Rose Revolution." Saakashvili strengthened state institutions, such as security and the military, and made reforms to end corruption in government. He also made economic reforms, which encouraged foreign investment. Saakashvili's pro-Western/American policies, which included proposing to join NATO and the European Union, strained relations with Russia, which wanted Georgia to stay within its sphere of influence.

In 2004, Georgia tried to regain control of South Ossetia and Abkhazia, two regions that had become autonomous (self-governing) after the breakup of the U.S.S.R. in 1991. Both regions has Muslim Turkic populations within Georgian minorities. Fearful of losing influence in the region after Georgian independence, Russia supported both regions' autonomy by providing peacekeeping forces to protect them in 1992. Saakashvili's attempts to restore Georgian control were unsuccessful and led to both regions voting to become independent nations in 2006. This led to tensions between Georgia and Russia, resulting in war by August 2008. Claiming to be protecting the autonomy of South Ossetia and Abkhazia, Russia sent troops to the region and bombed the Georgian capital city of Tbilisi. This forced Saakashvili to end the campaign to restore Georgian control over these areas. The autonomous statuses of both regions were restored and EU peacekeepers replaced the Russians in 2009. Russia was criticized for its actions by Western nations, including the United States, which believed that Russia had used the conflict as a means of regaining control of the Caucasus area and forcing out the Saakashvili government.

Despite much criticism from Georgian opposition parties and the failure to regain South Ossetia and Abkhazia, Saakashvili remained popular and was reelected in 2009. His government continued to make reforms to end corruption, fight organized crime, and transfer more power from the presidency to the Parliament. His success in preventing Russian denomination and developing economic ties with the West brought the nation stability, but also created a potentially dangerous situation with its larger neighbor.

Armenia established a stable and democratic government after independence in 1991 largely due to the economic assistance and support from its larger diaspora (Armenians living in other nations). With limited resources, the nation had a difficult time building its economy.

Armenia's largest problem has been conflict with its neighbor Azerbaijan, which has brought tensions to the Caucasian region. Beginning in the 1990s, the two nations fought over the region of Nagorno-Karabakh, an area with an Armenian majority within Azerbaijan's borders. With Russian support, Armenian forces gained control over the region along with seven additional Azerbaijan provinces, from which the Azeri populations were chased out. Despite a cease-fire agreement reached in 1994, observers fear the situation is a "frozen conflict" that will explode again. A summit between Armenia and Azerbaijan in June of 2011 failed to achieve a negotiated solution.

Armenia also has strained relations with its other neighbor Turkey, which closed its border to Armenia in 1993. The poor relations are due to continued Turkish denial of the Armenian Genocide by the Ottoman and Nationalist Turkey from 1915 through 1922 (in which almost two million Armenians were slaughtered), and its support of the Turkic Azeris over Nagorno-Karabakh.

Despite its relatively smooth transition to a free market democracy, Armenia's economy has been limited by a low population due to high levels of immigration, few resources, and little industry. Dependent on Russia for military support in case of renewed conflict with Azerbaijan, Armenia faces a difficult and uncertain future.

After its independence in 1991, Azerbaijan's economy grew due to its wealth of gas and oil. Instead of becoming a free market democracy, the nation developed into an oligarchy run by wealthy tycoons, organized crime, and corrupt politicians. Oil money created a political system that is inefficient, corrupt, and resistant to reform.

In 1991, former KGB general Heydar Aliyev, communist leader of Azerbaijan under Soviet rule, became president. Ruthless and repressive, he established a personal dictatorship, crushing all political opposition and eliminating his rivals. Aliyev gained control of the mass media and Parliament, placing the nation under his personal rule. Azerbaijan remained under the control of the Aliyev family as the dictator's son Ilam took over as president in 2003. The wealth produced from the oil industry raised the standard of living for most Azeris, making the government popular.

The build-up of Azerbaijan's military and the use of nationalism to gain support for the government has created a dangerous situation. Aliyev's policies have made the tensions between Azerbaijan and Armenia over Nagorno-Karabakh, which were already high, potentially explosive. Russia's strong support of Armenia raises the danger to an even higher level. The Caucasian region remains highly unstable and problematic.

## Central Asian Nations

The Central Asian nations continued to be ruled by one party after independence in 1991. The leaders of the Communist Party became presidents and adopted more nationalist policies, but the Soviet system initially continued. Recently, there has been a movement in Kyrgyzstan to create a more democratic government, but most Central Asian states continue to be ruled by one party and/or one leader.

In Kazakhstan, Communist Party leader Islam Nursultan Nazarbayev, who came to power in 1989, was elected president in 1991 after the nation became independent. Making needed economic reforms to end the Soviet-style system, he began developing the country's oil and hydrocarbon industries. Reaching out to the West while maintaining good relations with Russia and China, Nazarbayev built up the Kazakh economy, creating a middle-class society. This made the leader very popular, despite his repression of political opponents, rigging of elections, control of the mass media, and domination of his Otan Party (former Communists) in the parliament (as a presidential republic, most power is in the hands of the executive). Tolerant of both religious and ethnic minorities, Kazakhstan has avoided the bloody conflicts between ethnic groups in its Central Asian neighbors. Reelected several times, Nazarbayev remains popular. His age and failing health have raised the fear of civil war and ethnic conflict.

In Kyrgyzstan, tension between ethnic Kyrgyz and Uzbeks, which began under Soviet rule with the Osh Riots in the 1990s (in which the Kyrgyz majority tried to take Uzbek farms), threatened to create a civil war when the nation became independent in 1991. Communist Party leader Askar Akayev was elected president and immediately imposed strong central control to create stability. He began economic reforms and limited political freedom. Corruption in government and organized crime made most government reforms ineffective. Akayev's successor, Kurmanbek Bakieyev, encountered similar problems. The corruption in government, poor economic conditions for most people, and brutal repression led to civil unrest in the capital in April 2010. President Bakieyev was forced to resign and flee to Kazakhstan. A transitional government led by former foreign minister Roza Otunbayeva took power. In June, fighting between ethnic Kyrgyz and Uzbeks erupted. Many believed it had been instigated by the supporters of exiled president Bakieyev. The government was able to restore order by August. In 2011, the first free elections were held in Kyrgyzstan in which Otunbayeva formally became president. The current government faces great challenges trying to end corruption, fight organized crime, make economic reforms, and maintain peace between the nation's ethnic majority and minorities.

In Tajikistan a destructive civil war between the nation's clans (1992–1997) after independence in 1991 led to the deaths of over 100,000 people. Unlike the other Central Asian nations, the Soviet-era leaders were not able to keep the nation together. In 1997 a cease-fire was reached, and in 1999 elections were held. President Emonali Rahman, who first came to power in 1994 in a highly controversial election, was reelected. He was strongly criticized from both within and outside the nation for manipulating the election. The Rahman government gained control over the military, mass media, and Parliament repressing all political opposition. Rahman's People's Democratic Party of Tajikistan (PDPT) continues to dominate Parliament as he continues to follow repressive policies. These have led to the rise of Islamic militants in the nation's eastern provinces, which the government continues to fight. Tajikistan has retained good relations with Russia, China, and the United States, assisting NATO in fighting the Taliban in Afghanistan. The Rahman government however, has failed to build up the economy, end corruption, or improve the quality of life for its citizens. It faces a very uncertain future.

In Turkmenistan, Communist Party leader Saparmuray Niyazov, who took power in 1985, was elected "President for Life" after independence in 1991. Promoting policies of traditional Muslim and ethnic Turkmen culture, he established a dictatorship, brutally removing all political opposition. Isolationist and repressive, Niyazov developed a cult of personality (similar to Stalin), making himself "Turkmenbasy" or "Leader of the Turkmens." With his sudden death in 2006, there was a hope for change. In 2007, Gurbanguly Berdymukhammedov was elected president. He began to make political reforms, establishing a constitution and a Parliament. While allowing the creation of multiple political parties, Berdymukhammedov gained control over the mass media, blocked political freedoms, and repressed political opposition, dominating the Parliament with his Democratic Party of Turkmenistan (DPT), which was formerly the Communist Party. While he increased contact with his neighbors and the West as well as developing the nation's largest resource of natural gas, the economy has not grown. Most of the nation's wealth remains in the hands of the DPT and corrupt government officials. Most of the population remains uneducated and poor as the government continues to follow repressive policies.

In Uzbekistan, Communist Party leader Islam Karimov was elected President after independence in 1991. He created a Presidential republic, in which the executive holds most of the power. While multiple political parties are allowed to exist, Parliament is dominated by the President. Karimov has remained in power through manipulating elections, crushing political opposition, controlling the mass media, and exploiting the ethnic conflicts between Uzbeks and other ethnic minorities, in particular the Tajins, both in Uzbekistan and neighboring nations. Most of the nation's wealth remains under the control of the President and his supporters. The Karimov government continues to follow repressive policies.

## The Soviet Bloc (1945–1989)

Unlike the Byzantine Commonwealth or the Pan-Slavic alliances of the 19th century, the creation of the Communist Eastern, or Soviet bloc was forced on the nations of Eastern Europe by Stalin. The bloc consisted of Hungary, Czechoslovakia, Bulgaria, Albania, Poland, Romania, and East Germany. From the start, Yugoslavia under Tito refused to take orders from Moscow. The formation of NATO in 1949 and the subsequent creation of the Warsaw Pact in 1955 once again divided Europe into two camps, the East and the West.

**GEOGRAPHY**

Use of Geography

Starting with riots after Stalin's death in 1953, the nations of the Eastern bloc began to oppose control by the U.S.S.R. In 1956 a revolution overthrew the puppet communist government in Hungary, but Soviet troops were sent in to restore it. In 1961 Albania's extremist communist government, under the leadership of the Stalinist dictator Enver Hoxha, left the sphere of Soviet domination and allied itself with Communist China. In Berlin, the Berlin Wall was built to stop the embarrassing flow of East Germans and Eastern Europeans from the East to the West. In 1968, after the Czechoslovakian government under Alexander Dubček tried to initiate democratic reforms (the Prague Spring), Soviet troops invaded that nation and installed a government more obedient to Moscow. From 1970 to 1980, food riots and worker unrest in Poland grew, as the trade union *Solidarity* was formed under the leadership of Lech Walesa. In 1981, the puppet Polish government began a series of unsuccessful moves (pressured by Moscow) to crush Solidarity. By 1989, Solidarity was legalized. In addition, domestic and international pressure forced the Polish government to hold free elections, in which the Communists were swept out of power. Solidarity formed a new government, with Solidarity leader Tadeusz Mazowiecki as prime minister. Encouraged by Mikhail Gorbachëv's reforms and his policy not to interfere in Eastern Europe (Gorbachëv Doctrine), other countries began to break away from the Communist Bloc.

GLOBAL CONCEPTS

**Change**

CONCEPTS GLOBAL

**GEOGRAPHY**

**Human Systems**

# The Collapse of Communism and the Transition to Democracy in Eastern Europe (1989–    )

In the fall of 1989, Hungary allowed thousands of East Germans to escape through that nation. Faced with enormous protest and pressure, both internal and external, the East German government allowed free travel, and citizens began to dismantle the Berlin Wall. Realizing that their authority had gone when Gorbachëv refused to support them, the East German communists resigned their monopoly of power. A noncommunist government was elected, and the reunification of Germany took place the following year.

**WORLD ISSUES**

Determination
of Political
and Economic
Systems

In the manner of dominoes, Hungary, followed by Czechoslovakia began reforms and free elections. By 1990 both nations had ousted their communist governments and established democracies, electing former dissident writers Arpad Goncz (Hungary) and Vaclav Havel (Czechoslovakia) to lead the new governments.

## Hungary

In 1989, a multiparty system began to develop as negotiations were held between Communist leaders and representatives of the new political parties that had formed to ensure an orderly transition of power. In the October elections, the Communists (who had changed their name to the Hungarian Socialist Party) were badly defeated. In December, the parliament was dissolved. In the 1990 elections, the remaining Communists were swept from power. The new parliament began the transition to a free-market democracy under President Goncz

Throughout the 1990s, Hungary made enormous progress toward transforming itself into a fully capitalist economy, shifting policies between right-, center-, and left-leaning parties. From 2002 to 2006, the Socialist Liberal Coalition under Prime Minister Peter Medgyessy expanded the Hungarian infrastructure and improved the standard of living. In 2004, Hungary joined the European Union. In 2006, the Socialist Liberals were reelected under a new prime minister, Ferenec Gyuresany. The global financial crisis of 2007–2010, however, led to a decline in the economy and a break up of the Socialist Liberal Coalition in 2008. In the elections of 2010, the center-right Fidescz Party won. Under Prime Minister Viktor Orban, strong nationalist, more Eurosceptic policies were adopted. From 2010 to 2011, the Fidescz government restricted the role of the Constitutional Court and adopted the "Basic Law," which replaced the 1989 constitution. This restricted individual rights and gave the government more power. A media council was also created, which would issue fines to material it found offensive. The growing authoritarianism at the Orban government has resulted in strong criticism both within and outside Hungary. It raises concerns about the future of the nation's democracy.

## Czechoslovakia

Tensions, however, soon developed between the Czech and Slovak leadership. In 1992 nationalist Slovak Prime Minister Vladimir Mečiar succeeded in getting his country to vote for independence. On January 1, 1993, Czechoslovakia separated into the nations of the Czech Republic and Slovakia.

## Czech Republic

After the separation, the Czech Republic was able to make the transition to a free market democracy with relatively few problems. Under successive governments ranging from moderately left and right of center, state control of the economy gradually diminished in exchange for employment and social stability. In 2004, the Czech Republic was accepted for membership in the European Union.

Despite its membership in the European Union, the government of the Czech Republic has followed Eurosceptic (distrustful of European integration) policies since 2003 with the election of Vaclav Klaus and the center-right Civic Democratic Party (CDP). A long-time opponent of centrally developed economic policies in the European Union, Klaus has maintained the Czech Republic's independence in financial decisions. He has also developed strong ties with Russia and the West. Reelected in 2008, the CDP and President Klaus remain popular and continue to follow a cautious policy balancing European integration and independence.

## Slovakia

In contrast, Slovakia became increasingly conservative and nationalistic. Under Mečiar (1993–1998) privatization and the transition to a free market economy was slowed down as he built up his own personal power base. His attempts to censor the free press greatly damaged Slovakia's world image as a developing democracy. Mečiar's nationalistic policies hurt the economy, as they discouraged badly needed foreign investment to build industries and relations with Slovakia's neighbors, because of the harsh treatment of its large Hungarian minority. By 1998, Slovakia's health and educations systems were bankrupt, the economy was on the verge of collapse, and privatizations had failed as state enterprises were sold to Mečiar's political appointees at bargain prices.

In the elections of September 1998, Mečiar and his nationalist party were voted out. New democratic and pro-Western parties dominated successive governments that took Slovakia in a different direction. The nationalist policies of the Mečiar era were abandoned, and greater efforts were made to develop a free market economy by encouraging foreign investment, increasing privatization, ending government corruption through reforms, and increasing democratic participation by amending the constitution to provide for direct popular election of the president.

In 2004, Slovakia joined the European Union. Succeeding left- and right-wing coalitions tried to end the problem of corruption in government, which greatly hurt Slovakia's efforts to create an efficient free-market economy. In 2010, a center-right coalition led by Iveta Radicova was elected. An Oxford-educated sociology professor, the new prime minister adopted strong policies to end corruption. Inexperienced politically, Radicova faces tremendous challenges.

## Poland

In Poland, the 1990 elections revealed the great divisions in the post-communist leadership. Despite his lack of education and political experience, Solidarity leader Lech Walesa was elected president as a compromise among the various factions. After the election of October 1991, Walesa formed a series of coalition governments with a variety of political parties from both the left and right. They were unable to make a real transition to a free market economy as the rapid pace of reforms had created great economic hardship for many Poles, especially the elderly and farmers. In November 1995, Walesa was replaced by Alexander Kwaśniewski, a moderate who believed the economic transition had to be slowed down and monitored. Successive Polish governments alternating between right- and left-wing parties managed the nation's transition into a free-market economy. By 2004, Poland had been accepted for European Union membership.

In the elections of 2005, two conservative parties that came from the Solidarity movement emerged as dominant—the victorious Law and Justice (PiS) and the second-place Civic Platform (PO). Led by the twin brothers, Lech and Jarosław Kaczyński, PiS formed a coalition government that promoted foreign investment and a free-market economy. However, by 2007, despite the economic progress, some Poles began to dislike the government's social conservatism and Eurosceptic (distrustful of Europe) foreign policy. As a result in that year's parliamentary elections the more socially moderate PO won a majority of seats, replacing Jarosław Kaczyński with Donald Tusk as prime minister. This created conflicts within the government.

On April 10, 2010, a Russian-built plane carrying President Kaczyński and ninety-five other top Polish officials crashed in Smolensk, Russia, killing everyone on board. The Polish delegation was on its way to commemorate the anniversary of the infamous Soviet genocide of Polish army officers at Katyń during World War II. The tragedy generated great national unity, especially during the week of official mourning. Bronisław Komorowski of the PO assumed presidential powers upon Kaczyński's death, due to a constitutional clause. Although relations with Russia temporarily improved due to Russian sympathy, the ambiguous circumstances of the plane crash prevented a real thaw in relations between the two nations. An independent Polish investigation blamed both the Polish pilots and the Russian infrastructure, whereas a Russian state investigation refused to review the Polish report and put the full blame on the pilots.

In October 2011, the PO won the presidential and parliamentary elections. Komorowski formally became president and the PO became the first party ever to win consecutive elections in post-Communist Poland. The current government under Prime Minister Tusk and President Komorowski continues to follow policies of close economic integration within the EU, as well as promoting progressive social changes. Poland's foreign policy is very pro-Western, as demonstrated by an American military presence on Polish soil, and the Polish economy continues to grow unlike the rest of the EU.

**GEOGRAPHY**

**Human Systems**

## Romania

In Romania, a major uprising in December of 1989 overthrew the communist dictator Nicolai Ceauşescu, executing him and his closest followers. The new Romanian government, the National Salvation Front, led by a former associate of Ceauşescu, Ion Iliescu, came under much criticism as a disguised continuation of the previous dictatorship. Popular discontent to governments run by ex-communists continued until 1996 when a reformist coalition was elected. Disputes within the coalition, corruption within the bureaucracy, and the inability to provide strong leadership resulted in a sharp decline in the economy. The elections of 1998 led to a new, but similar reformist coalition.

The determination to implement free-market reforms led to strikes by miners and other groups adversely affected. As crime and the economy worsened, a disillusioned population brought former leader Ion Iliescu and his right-wing party to power in 2000. While supporting Romania's integration with the Western European democracies and free-market reforms in general, he also pledged to end corruption in government and crime. President Iliescu soon encountered the same problems as their predecessors when trying to balance the need for free-market reforms with the economic hardships they created.

In 2004, Traian Basescu was elected president with a coalition known as the "Justice and Truth Alliance." Under the Basescu government, Romania joined NATO in 2004 and the EU in 2007. As the global financial crisis of 2007–2010 greatly weakened the economy, Basescu was forced to adopt unpopular policies of austerity. He was barely reelected in 2009. Romania faces great challenges in the future as the country struggles to revive its economy.

## Bulgaria

Bulgaria's communist government also started to make concessions to reform following Gorbachëv's lead, but seemed to stop short of making real changes. Bulgarian Communist Party leader Todor Zhivkov tried to overcome criticism by launching a campaign to nationalize by ousting the country's Turkish Muslim minority. However, Zhivkov was forced to resign in 1989, and parliamentary elections were held. In 1990, the Bulgarian Parliament ended the Communist Party's domination of the government. Yet, from 1991 to 1997 governments consisting of ex-communists ruled Bulgaria. Public dissatisfaction with corruption in the bureaucracy and economic stagnation led to the election of the nation's first real reformers in 1997. Under the leadership of Prime Minister Ivan Kostov, a reformist coalition began a program of economic reforms to transform Bulgaria into a free market economy. Under Kostov (1997–2001) crime was reduced, foreign investment began, privatization was implemented, economic productivity rose, and the private sector grew for the first time in the post-communist era. Despite these gains, the standard of living for the average Bulgarian had stagnated. The transition to a free market had been particularly difficult for the urban populations, especially the elderly who depended on pensions.

In 2001, the former Bulgarian King Simeon II and his Simeon National Movement Party seemed to offer a "third way" between Kostov's reforms and the socialists who wanted to reverse the reforms. Simeon became prime minister, forming a government that included many returning Bulgarian émigrés who had been educated in the West. This led to a growth in foreign investment and efficiency in government due to experienced ministers trained outside Bulgaria.

Economic, social, and political conditions improved. In 2004, Bulgaria joined the EU. The global financial crisis of 2007–2010 greatly weakened the Bulgarian economy. Succeeding governments were unsuccessful in stemming corruption and organized crime. In the elections of 2009, the Citizens for the European Development of Bulgaria Party took power. Prime Minister Boyko Borisov instituted policies to end corruption and fight organized crime, as well as building up the nation's infrastructure. Despite early successes, by 2011 Bulgaria saw an outbreak of xenophobic (fear of foreigners) riots against the nation's Roma (Gypsy) and Turkish minorities. The Borisov government faces great challenges in the near future.

**GEOGRAPHY**

Use of Geography

## Albania

Albania, the most xenophobic (fearful of foreigners), isolated, and ruthless communist regime, showed the first signs of change in 1990. Hoxha's successor, Ramiz Alia, was forced to begin political and economic reforms as he saw the rest of Eastern Europe abandoning the communist system. He was forced to allow thousands of Albanians to leave the economically devastated country and hold free elections for the first time. In the spring of 1992, the communists were removed from power in Albania following national elections. The new government, under President Sali Berisha, began to make economic and political reforms to transform Albania from one of the poorest nations in the world to a functioning free market economy and democracy. The popular Berisha government's involvement in a disastrous investment scheme that cost thousands of Albanians their life savings in 1996, created a scandal that resulted in riots and rebellion. By 1997, a state of civil war erupted between forces loyal to the government and those that opposed it. Forcing thousands of Albanians to flee, the fighting brought an international peacekeeping force to restore order. UN-monitored elections were held in April of 1998, bringing to power a coalition of Socialist parties under Fatos Nanos. Fighting, however, continued through the year as the new government slowly regained control of southern Albania, which remained loyal to Berisha. Unable to keep the fragile coalition together, Nanos resigned in September.

Pandeli Majko then became prime minister. A member of the new post-Hoxha generation, he enjoyed great popularity, especially among younger people. Denounced by Berisha as a "Nanos puppet," he faced enormous opposition from a coalition of parties determined to prevent reform toward a free market. Committed to ending government corruption and ending crime, the Majko government found itself overwhelmed as thousands of refugees flooded Albania from Kosovo in the spring of 1991. The crisis had an unexpected positive effect economically, as the arrival of UN troops, foreigners, and Western aid created new employment in the construction and humanitarian service industries, especially in the Albanian capital city of Tirana. The infusion of foreign money to help the nation deal with the cost of the refugees stimulated economic productivity and raised the standard of living, especially in cities. This allowed the Majko government to pursue privatization and reforms toward a free-market economy.

Despite having led the country through a difficult period of crisis, Majko was forced to resign in October 1999. In the elections of 2000, the Socialists won a majority in the Albanian Parliament, allowing the government to pursue its goals of economic reform, fighting organized crime, ending government corruption, and ending civil fighting within Albania.

The Socialists' reforms had limited success as political divisions and entrenched government corruption frustrated their efforts. Succeeding right- and left-wing governments encountered similar problems. Conflict between Prime Minister Berisha and opposition leader Edi Rama paralyzed the Albanian Parliament and divided the population. The situation grew worse after the Republican Guard fired on protesters in December 2011. Having joined NATO in 2011, the present conflict has hurt Albania's hope of joining the EU in the near future. Continued strikes within the government makes the nation's hopes of building up its economy and infrastructure equally unlikely. The inability of any government so far to effectively limit corruption, organized crime, and civil fighting presents serious challenges for the future.

## Yugoslavia

GEOGRAPHY

Use of Geography

After Tito's death in 1980, the independent communist government of Yugoslavia began to allow civil liberties unheard of in the Eastern Bloc. Yet, despite these, a poor economy caused riots and strikes, forcing several of Tito's successors to resign. The forces of local nationalism also reappeared. This became evident in 1990 when the republics of Slovenia and Croatia declared independence from Yugoslavia. This led to conflict between those republics and the Yugoslavian government, which opposed the breakup of the federated nation. Slovenia was able to repulse the Yugoslav government's troops and force recognition of its independence. The Croatian government, however, became involved in a civil war against the sizable Serbian minority, which was assisted by the Serbian-dominated Yugoslav Army. Acts of brutality were committed on both sides, with ethnic cleansing (the violent removal of people) being practiced to drive Serb and Croatian civilian populations out of one region into another. As a truce was finally reached between Croatians and Serbians in 1991, hostilities broke out between the Serbians and the Muslims of Bosnia-Herzegovina, after that republic declared its independence from the Yugoslav federation. The conflict soon became a three-way ethnic war between Bosnia's Serbs, Croats, and Muslims, with the Yugoslav and Croatian governments arming their Bosnian kinsmen. The war was also encouraged by the nationalist politicians of the Yugoslav republics (Serbian President Slobodan Milošević, Croatian President Franjo Tudjman, and Bosnian President Alija Izetbegovič). In late 1992, the former Yugoslav Republic of Macedonia declared independence, leaving only the republics of Serbia and Montenegro. The killing in Bosnia continued into 1994, despite the efforts of the United Nations and European Union to resolve the conflict. In 1995, the Dayton Peace Conference divided Bosnia-Herzegovina into a Serb Republic and Bosnian state. Even though the Dayton Accord reduced the conflict, it did not end it, as an international peacekeeping force remained in Bosnia-Herzegovina. In 1997, U.S. air strikes against military positions violating the ceasefire agreement further helped to keep the peace.

## Croatia, Slovenia, and Bosnia

In Croatia, Tudjman's death in 1999 led to the defeat of his nationalist HDZ party in the 2000 elections. A center-left coalition under Prime Minister Ivica Racan amended the constitution, making Croatia a parliamentary system rather than a presidential one. The Racan government also brought the nation out of semi-isolation under Tudjman and began to transform the economy into a free market. In 2003, a reformed HDS took power under Prime Minister Ivo Sanadar. Reelected in 2007, Sanadar abruptly resigned in 2009 due to charges of criminal involvement (he was later arrested on corruption charges). In the 2010 elections, the HDS lost to the Social Democratic Party of Croatia (SDPC). Under SDPC Prime Minister Ivo Jospiović, the economy was further liberalized. In 2011, Croatia became a candidate for membership in the European Union.

After Slovenia became independent in 1992, the Liberal Democracy of Slovenia Party (LDS) dominated Slovenian politics. Under President Milan Kučan and Prime Minister Janez Drnovsek, who led the LDS government from 1992 to 2002, the nation was transformed into a free-market democracy. That same year, a right-wing coalition led by Janez Jansa came to power. In 2008, a left-wing coalition under Borut Pahor won the election by a narrow margin. Both coalitions were unsuccessful in gaining strong popular support. In 2004, Slovenia joined NATO and the European Union. In September of 2011, the Pahor government was removed after a no-confidence vote in the Slovenian Nation Assembly (Parliament). In December, the centrist Positive Slovenia Party under Zoran Janković was elected.

**GEOGRAPHY**

**Use of Geography**

Since the end of the Bosnian war, the country has remained ungovernable. Bosnia-Herzegovina is divided into two parts; the Serb-dominated Republina Srpsha (Serbian Republic) and the Bosniak-Croat Federation. The two governments function independently of each other and the threat of renewed civil war is constant. Milorad Đodik, president of the Serbian Republic, continues to demand the dissolution of Bosnia-Herzegovina. The government of the Bosniak-Croat Federation is divided as the Croatian political parties refuse to join or recognize the mainly Bosniak government of the Social Democratic Party that won the elections of 2010. The nation is in danger of fresh conflict or breakup and faces great challenges to its survival.

## Kosovo

In 1998, conflict erupted in the Yugoslav province of Kosovo between the Yugoslav police and Albanian separatists demanding union with Albania (known as the Kosovo Liberation Army or KLA). In April of 1999, NATO began a massive air campaign against Serbia. This led to a new campaign of ethnic cleansing by Serbian President Milošević using the Yugoslav military to drive out the Albanian majority from Kosovo. Although NATO claimed that the action was only to stop the ethnic cleansing in Kosovo, the bombing of civilians and foreign embassies in the Serbian capital city of Belgrade as well as Albanian refugee convoys raised questions about the role of NATO after the Cold War. The Yugoslav government and some nations, especially Russia and China, viewed the military action as a violation of national sovereignty. The countries of NATO and other nations saw the military interference as a stand against ethnic cleansing and the violation of human rights. The United Nations, while condemning Milošević's actions, resented NATO's unilateral action as it undermined the UN's authority.

The air campaign and the inclusion of Serbia's traditional ally Russia in the peace negotiations resulted in the withdrawal of the Yugoslav Army by June. This failed to solve the long-term problems as well as creating new ones in Kosovo. The destruction and flood of refugees that resulted from the bombing destabilized the entire Balkan region. Despite his indictment as a war criminal by the International Court and Serbia's exclusion from all Western economic aid until his removal as Serbian President, Milošević remained in power. A weak and divided Serbian political opposition and a population angry at NATO for the bombing of their cities made it possible for the unpopular leader to continue. The NATO/Russian peacekeeping forces came into conflict with both the population of Kosovo and each other. The withdrawal of Yugoslav troops quickly resulted in massacres of Serbs by vengeful ethnic Albanians. Attempts to prevent these by the peacekeepers proved difficult. Serbians fled into Serb-dominated areas in northern Kosovo or Yugoslavia, while the KLA, disregarding NATO demands to disband, took over local administration. The exiled Kosovo Albanian leadership came into conflict with them when they returned.

In December of 2010, flawed elections were held in Kosovo. A government was only formed the following February. The elected prime minister, Hashim Thaci, is reported to be an organized crime leader involved with the sale of heroin and illegal human organs. The continued persecution of Serbians and destruction of their property in Kosovo has raised doubts about the viability of it as an independent state. Despite international efforts, the creation of a stable democratic multiethnic country seems very unlikely in the near future.

## Serbia

The aftermath of the NATO military intervention in Kosovo in 1999 severely weakened Milošević politically. Economic decline in Serbia and growing political opposition led to his defeat in the elections of September 2000. Despite his efforts to contest the election results, public anger against him made it clear that his 13-year rule was over.

Vojislav Kostunica became the new Serbian president. In an attempt to maintain good relations with the West, he sent Milošević to The Hague for trial in the International Court of

Justice for his role in the war crimes committed during the Yugoslav civil war. (Milošević died in 2006 before the court was able to make a decision on his case.) This turned out to be a decision that divided the Serbian population. Kostunica also worked to keep Kosovo as part of Serbia. Finally, he was determined to prevent Montenegro from leaving what was left of Yugoslavia.

Kostunica's preoccupation with maintaining Serbia's borders and the division over Milošević prevented him from dealing with growing domestic problems. Economic assistance from the West in order to prevent further problems in Serbia helped the Kostunica government to spur economic growth.

In the 2004 elections, the center-left Democratic Party (DP) won a majority and its leader Boris Tadić became president. The new government adopted pro-Western policies that included applying for EU membership. This brought much criticism from Serbian nationalists and right-wing parties who felt the Europeans had betrayed Serbia during the wars in Bosnia and Kosovo. In 2006, the Tadić government accepted separation with Montenegro when the nation declared its independence and ratified a new Serbian Constitution, which allowed greater political freedoms. In the 2008 presidential elections, Tadić was narrowly reelected. In the parliamentary election later that year, Tadić's coalition "For a European Serbia" fell short of a majority and needed to work within a leftist coalition to form a new government under Prime Minister Mirko Cvetković. Its hopes of becoming a candidate for EU membership improved after the Serbian government handed over the Serbian general Ratko Mladić to the international war crimes tribunal. This brought further anger and criticism from conservative and national Serbs, especially after the EU granted candidacy to Montenegro and Croatia, but not Serbia, in December 2011. With an economy that was struggling and a growing feeling that the price of EU membership might be too high, the pro-European Serbian government was defeated in the elections of May 2012 and populist Tomislav Nikolić of the Serbian Progressive Party gained the presidency.

In 2002, Serbia and Montenegro agreed to a partnership that would keep them allied but give each domestic autonomy (self-rule). Serbia also came to an understanding with the other former Yugoslav states.

## Montenegro

In 2006, Montenegro declared itself an independent nation. Serbia did not object to the declaration. Since that time relations between the two nations have been good. In December 2011, Montenegro became a candidate for EU membership.

The violence and disorder in Eastern Europe following the collapse of communism presents new challenges to the world community. On July 6, 1990, NATO issued an official statement proclaiming the end of the Cold War. Yet, in its place old ethnic and religious hatreds have reappeared. Many question if NATO, in its new role as the "Policeman of Europe," can or should use its military power to control ethnic and religious conflict within individual nations. While the communist regimes were able to suppress these conflicts, they did not resolve them. In addition, the nations of Eastern Europe must deal with the legacy of communist "progress"—economic and environmental damage. In their new-found freedom, these countries face enormous obstacles that will require all their resources to solve.

# REVIEW QUESTIONS

*Multiple Choice.* Select the letter of the answer that correctly completes the statement.

1. Starting with Brezhnev, the U.S.S.R. followed a policy of détente, or
   A. understanding with the West
   B. openness with the West
   C. standing firm to the West
   D. suspicion of the West

2. Gorbachëv's policy of glasnost was aimed at creating greater
   A. job opportunities and work incentives
   B. efficiency, especially in industry
   C. openness, with an end to the secrecy and suspicion in Soviet society
   D. patriotism and faith in communism

3. The event that led to the Russian Revolution of 1991 and the collapse of communism in the U.S.S.R. was
   A. the elections of 1991
   B. the signing of the Union Treaty
   C. the unsuccessful coup d'etat by the conservative Communists
   D. Gorbachev's election as president of the U.S.S.R.

4. Which of the following former Soviet republics engaged in a conflict after the collapse of the Soviet Union?
   A. Russian and Ukraine
   B. Moldova and Belarus
   C. Georgia and Uzbekistan
   D. Armenia and Azerbaijian

5. Russian President Yeltsin dismissed the Congress of Peoples' Deputies in the fall of 1993 because
   A. he wanted dictatorial powers
   B. it continued to block all economic reforms
   C. it had tried to impeach him
   D. it was making too many reforms too quickly

6. Which of the following leaders dominated Russian politics in the early part of the 21st century?
   A. Mikhail Gorbachëv
   B. Boris Yeltsin
   C. Vladimir Putin
   D. Dmitry Medvedev

7. The formation of NATO in 1949 resulted in the creation of an Eastern European communist military alliance under Soviet domination known as
   A. SEATO
   B. EEC
   C. the Eastern bloc
   D. the Warsaw Pact

8. The two Eastern European nations that unsuccessfully attempted to free themselves of Soviet domination in 1956 and 1968 were, respectively,
   A. East Germany and Czechoslovakia
   B. Hungary and Poland
   C. Hungary and Czechoslovakia
   D. Poland and Czechoslovakia

9. The Polish Communist Party was forced out of power in 1989 largely due to
   A. the Polish Liberation Army
   B. the trade union Solidarity
   C. NATO
   D. détente between the U.S.S.R. and the United States

10. Democratic reform and ethnic struggles began in Yugoslavia after the death of
    A. Josip Broz (Tito)
    B. Nicolai Ceausescu
    C. Joseph Stalin
    D. Alexander Dubček

11. "Ethnic cleansing" is defined as
    A. mass killing of a people
    B. persecution of a minority within a country
    C. violent removal of a people
    D. destruction of a people's culture

12. Which leader is *incorrectly* paired with his nation?
    A. Milošević/Serbia
    B. Tudjman/Croatia
    C. Izetbegovič/Slovenia
    D. Nanos/Albania

13. The Dayton Accord of 1995 reduced the conflict in
    A. Albania
    B. Bosnia-Herzegovina
    C. Kosovo
    D. Croatia

14. The NATO air strikes against Serbia are in response to its
    A. violations of the Dayton Accord
    B. ethnic cleansing of Albanians from Kosovo
    C. attacks on Bosnian Croats
    D. ethnic cleansing of Bosnian Muslims

# Part D: The Middle East

## 20th-Century Nationalism

The desire of a group of people to establish their own nation in a specific territory can be described as nationalism. Nationalist movements in the 20th century have resulted in many new nations in the Middle East and elsewhere.

## The Establishment of Modern Turkey

The Ottoman Empire was divided after World War I. Spheres of British and French influence were created in the Middle Eastern lands. Western Asia Minor, which included the city of Istanbul, was given to Greece while the eastern part was to be the nation of Turkey (despite vague promises from the victorious Allies, nothing was done to restore the Armenian people to their traditional lands in eastern Asia Minor). Angered by the Allied division and the weakness of the Ottoman government, the Nationalist Party was formed by a group of army officers under the leadership of war hero Mustafa Kemal. The Nationalists set up a rival government in the city of Ankara in 1920, proclaiming it the Turkish Republic and rejecting the authority of the Sultan. Kemal was elected president of the new republic as well as commander-in-chief. Gaining the support of the army, the Nationalists invaded Western Asia Minor. Taking advantage of the war-weariness of the Allies (upon whom the Greeks newly established in western Asia Minor depended), Kemal's forces were able to drive the Greek army back into Greece by 1922. Claiming that attrocities had been committed against the Turkish population while under Greek occupation, the Nationalist forces massacred the Greek population (the ancient city of Smyrna was burned to the ground). This began a policy of persecution to drive out non-Turkish populations in order to create an exclusively Turkish state ("ethnic cleansing"). The victory of the Nationalists made Kemal a national hero. In the Turkish Constitution of 1923 he was given almost dictatorial powers. This enabled him to make radical changes that transformed Turkish society:

- There was separation of the state from traditional Islamic law and custom.
- Traditional Islamic clothing, in particular the wearing of the veil by women and the fez (tall brimless cap) by men was replaced by Western clothing.
- The Latin alphabet replaced the Arabic.
- Mandatory public education was established.

- Women were given the right to vote (1929) and encouraged to participate in public life.
- Sunday replaced the traditional Islamic Friday as the state "Day of Rest."
- Western technology was introduced to Turkish society.
- The Turkish army was modernized.

Kemal's role as the "Father of Modern Turkey" earned him the title of "Ataturk" or "Head Turk." His close relationship with the army gave the military enormous influence over succeeding governments after his death in 1938. Seeing themselves as the protectors of the established order, the military have exercised a strong and conservative control over Turkish politics until the present day.

## Arab Nationalism

The nationalistic desires of different groups of Arabs were evident in both the African and Asian parts of the Middle East.

**GEOGRAPHY**

**Use of Geography**

1. *Algeria.* Algeria came under French control in the 19th century. Algerian nationalism grew in the 20th century and posed a problem for France after the end of World War II in 1945. France's refusal to leave Algeria led to a long and bloody war between 1954 and 1962. Peace talks in 1962 finally brought an end to the war, and Algeria became an independent nation. Its first leader was Ahmed Ben Bella.

2. *Lebanon and Syria.* After World War I, France held mandates in Lebanon and Syria. However, after World War II, Lebanon and Syria became free nations when the French left peacefully. Independence came to both nations in 1946.

3. *Iraq and Jordan.* Britain was given mandates over both Iraq and Jordan after World War I. Iraq became independent in 1923, but Britain held on to its mandate in what was then called Trans-Jordan until 1946. This was part of the area that was the British mandate in Palestine.

4. *Egypt and Saudi Arabia.* From the late 1800s until 1922, Egypt was a British protectorate. However, in 1922 Egypt became a free constitutional monarchy, although Britain controlled Egypt's foreign affairs. This lasted until 1936, when Egypt gained more self-government. Saudi Arabia, never formally colonized, became a nation in 1927. Its name came from Ibn Saud, the head of a Muslim sect that had established its power in most of the Arabian Peninsula.

**GEOGRAPHY**

**Human Systems**

## Zionism

This term is used for the nationalistic desire of Jews to reestablish a nation of their own. The Zionist goal was achieved in 1948 with

504

the establishment of Israel, which was located in Palestine, with borders somewhat similar to those of the ancient Israelite kingdoms. The territorial goals of Zionists and Arab nationalists conflicted in Palestine, especially while the area was a British mandate from 1920 to 1948. The conflict continues to the present day, with four major wars having been fought between Israel and the Arabs since 1948. (A brief examination of this conflict follows.)

## Background of the Arab-Israeli Conflict

The conflict between Israel and the Arab nations is over sovereignty (political control) in the land called Palestine. This small strip of land on the eastern shore of the Mediterranean Sea has been inhabited by Jews and Arabs for thousands of years and, as you read earlier, has been under the dominance of different rulers at many times in history. The word "Palestine" refers to a geographical area, not to a nation. There has never been a nation or state called Palestine. Therefore a Palestinian is a resident in the area but not a citizen of any nation called Palestine.

1. *Jewish sovereignty* in Palestine existed for about 1,000 years. However, with the Roman conquest in 70 C.E., many Jews were forced to leave what for them was "the holy land." This dispersion of Jews, with many eventually settling in Europe, North Africa, Asia, and later in the Americas, is known as the diaspora. (The word "diaspora" today can mean any place in the world where a people live outside of its original homeland.) Jews in the diaspora generally led difficult lives, especially in Europe. They were often persecuted for their religious beliefs (such persecution against Jews is referred to as anti-Semitism) and were frequently forced to live in separate areas of cities, called ghettoes. The ghettoes, as well as village settlements, often suffered from violent attacks, called pogroms. By the late 19th century, the majority of Jews lived in the diaspora; yet there was continuous Jewish habitation in Palestine from the Roman conquest into the 20th century. The movement for the restoration of a Jewish nation in Palestine (Zionism) was sparked in the late 1800s by Theodore Herzl, an Austrian Jew and journalist who wrote a book called *The Jewish State.* In the early 1900s, Zionists increased their efforts to help persecuted Jews immigrate to Palestine. At the same time, Zionists tried to get the ruling Ottoman Turks to grant territory for a Jewish state. Jews supported Britain in World War I against the Turks; Chaim Weizmann, an English Jewish chemist, contributed to the British war effort with his scientific achievements.

2. *Arab sovereignty* in Palestine can be traced to the Umayyad conquest in 637 C.E., which began a long era of Muslim control

**WORLD ISSUES**

Political and

Economic

Refugees

**WORLD ISSUES**

War

and

Peace

**WORLD ISSUES**

Political and

Economic

Refugees

**GEOGRAPHY**

Use of Geography

**WORLD ISSUES**

Human

Rights

GLOBAL
CONCEPTS

**Identity**

CONCEPTS
GLOBAL

that lasted until the end of World War I (1918). Different Arab dynasties held power in Palestine from the 7th to the 15th centuries. From 1453 until World War I, sovereignty was held by the Ottoman Turks, who were not Arabs. However, Arab habitation in Palestine was continuous during the period of Ottoman Turkish rule. The Arabs did not like the Turks and wanted to establish their own nation in the area, as did the Jews. Consequently, the Arabs sided with the British in World War I in the struggle against the Turks. With the end of the war, Britain was given temporary control (the British mandate) over Palestine by the League of Nations.

GLOBAL
CONCEPTS
**Political Systems**
CONCEPTS
GLOBAL

3. During the period when Palestine was under the British mandate (1920–1948), Jews and Arabs continued to press their nationalistic claims. Britain had made territorial promises to both groups and issued an important document in 1917, while defeating the Turks in Palestine, called the Balfour Declaration. Named after Lord Balfour, the English statesman, the document proposed that Great Britain would view ". . . with favor the establishment in Palestine of a national home for the Jewish people . . . it being . . . understood that nothing shall be done which may prejudice the civil and religious rights of . . . non-Jewish communities . . ." In 1922, acting on their own, the British also carved out over half the mandate area, almost 70 percent, as a separate Arab enclave to be known as Trans-Jordan. This was the first partition of Palestine.

Encouraged by the Balfour Declaration, Jews began to increase their immigration to what little remained of Palestine, where they bought land from some Arabs and cultivated areas left unused by the Turks. Only 23 percent of the original Palestine remained for what might be a Jewish state. Nevertheless, Arab protests against Jews grew into riots and violent confrontations. Britain found it difficult to maintain peace between the two sides and was further weakened by its involvement in World War II (1939–1945). World War II was also the time when persecution against Jews in Europe reached an unprecedented level, with the killing of 6 million Jews by the Germans and their collaborators in the Holocaust. This tragedy convinced many Jews that the only safe place for them would be their own nation in Palestine.

At the end of World War II, Britain decided to give up its mandate over Palestine and asked the United Nations to resolve the conflict between the Arabs and Jews in Palestine. By a majority vote in 1947 the UN decided to partition the remaining non-Arab 23% of Palestine into two states—a Jewish state and an Arab state. This was the second partition of Palestine. The city of Jerusalem, which was holy to both Jews and Muslims, was to be

**WORLD ISSUES**

War
and
Peace

**WORLD ISSUES**

Terrorism

**WORLD ISSUES**

Determination
of Political
and Economic
Systems

under UN supervision. Jews accepted this decision and declared their state of Israel in 1948. Arabs both in Palestine and in the new Arab nations outside of Palestine rejected the partition plan. In May 1948, six Arab nations—Egypt, Iraq, Trans-Jordan (later to be called Jordan), Syria, Lebanon, and Saudi Arabia—declared war on Israel. Although the combined Arab forces were larger and better equipped, they were unable to accomplish their goal of destroying Israel. A UN-arranged truce in 1949 ended the fighting.

## The Four Arab-Israeli Wars

1. *The War for Independence, 1948–1949.* (This was described above.) Even though the Arabs failed in their goal to drive "the Jews into the sea," they still refused to accept the UN Partition Plan of 1947. In addition, they also refused to recognize the state of Israel even though the United States, the Soviet Union, and most of the world recognized the new state.

Israel is the only democracy in the Middle East, and although it was established as a Jewish state, Israel permits religious freedom to all people within its borders. Nevertheless, during the 1948 to 1949 war, over 700,000 Palestinian Arabs fled from Israel to Arab lands, thus becoming refugees. Some of these people fled because they feared the fighting. Many others were urged to leave by Arab armies, who promised to let the Palestinians return once the expected victory over Israel had been achieved. As another result of the Arab reaction to the Partition Plan, as well as to the fighting, many Jews in Arab nations suffered persecution. Consequently, almost 800,000 of them fled to Israel as refugees.

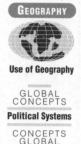

**GEOGRAPHY**

Use of Geography

GLOBAL CONCEPTS

**Political Systems**

CONCEPTS GLOBAL

**WORLD ISSUES**

Political and

Economic

Refugees

The holy city of Jerusalem

507

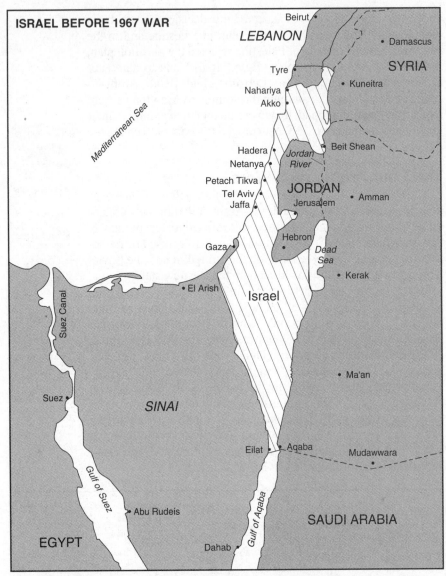

**ISRAEL BEFORE 1967 WAR**

Beirut

LEBANON

• Damascus

Tyre

SYRIA

Nahariya
Akko

• Kuneitra

Mediterranean Sea

Hadera
Netanya

Jordan River

Beit Shean

Petach Tikva
Tel Aviv
Jaffa

JORDAN

Jerusalem

• Amman

Gaza

Hebron

Dead Sea

• Kerak

• El Arish

Israel

Suez Canal

• Ma'an

Suez

SINAI

Eilat • Aqaba

Mudawwara

Gulf of Suez

• Abu Rudeis

Gulf of Aqaba

SAUDI ARABIA

EGYPT

Dahab

The patterned area shows the nation of Israel that existed between 1949 and 1967. At its narrowest point, near the city of Netanya, Israel is only 9 miles wide.

This first Arab-Israeli war also affected the status of Jerusalem. The Israelis gained control of the western part of the city, while Jordan illegally seized East Jerusalem, which contained the city's important holy sites. Jordan promised to permit equal access to these holy Christian, Jewish, and Muslim sites for members of the three religions. (However, Jordan never permitted Jews to visit their holy sites.) Jordan also seized and occupied the West Bank. These actions violated the UN Partition Plan, as this area was supposed to become an independent Palestinian Arab state. The Jordanian occupation received international condemnation and was never recognized by any Arab nation. It lasted for nineteen years, until 1967. The Arab view of the 1948–1949 War is different from the Israeli view. The Arab world labels the war's events as the nakba, or "disaster." This word is used because of the defeat of the Arab armies along with the flood of Arab refugees. (Some Arabs did not flee Israel. Today, they and their descendants make up about 20 percent of the Israeli population.)

2. *The 1956 War.* Under President Gamal Abdel Nasser, Egypt nationalized (took over) from England the Suez Canal in 1956 and prohibited Israel from using it. Moreover, terrorist raids into Israel by Egypt and other Arab nations caused many deaths. As a result, Egypt and Israel went to war again. However, this time France and England joined with Israel and attacked Egyptian forces along the Suez Canal. Israel defeated the Egyptian army in the Sinai Peninsula and occupied the entire region. The UN arranged a ceasefire ending the second Arab-Israeli war. Egypt kept the Suez Canal and demanded that Israel give back the Sinai Peninsula. Israel agreed to give back the Sinai, hoping that in return Egypt would recognize the state of Israel and agree to peace. A United Nations Emergency Force (UNEF) was sent to keep peace on Israel's borders.

GEOGRAPHY

Use of Geography

3. *The Six-Day War, 1967.* Egypt and the other Arab nations continued to refuse to recognize Israel and stepped up their terrorist attacks. Egypt built up its forces in the Sinai Desert, forbade Israel to use the Suez Canal, and closed the Gulf of Aqaba to Israeli shipping. It also ordered the UNEF to leave. These measures, along with Egypt's continued threats to destroy Israel, led the Israelis to strike at Egypt in early June 1967. Although Egypt was well supplied with Soviet equipment and was supported by other Arab nations that attacked Israel, Israel was able to defend itself successfully for the third time in 19 years. Arab armies that attacked Israel from the north, east, and south were thrown back, and Israel took over large amounts of land—the Sinai Peninsula and Gaza (from Egypt), the West Bank of the Jordan River and East Jerusalem (from Jordan, which had illegally taken these areas in the 1948 to 1949 war and was asked by Israel not to attack her in 1967), and the Golan Heights (from Syria). The war lasted for six days. Israel annexed East Jerusalem and the Golan Heights, making them part of Israel. Israel offered to negotiate for the other newly

won territories if the Arabs would sign a peace treaty and recognize Israel's right to exist.

After the war, Israel held occupied territory, such as the West Bank, that contained a large Arab population. The area was also known by its ancient names: Judea and Samaria. As thousands of people fled, the number of Arab refugees in Arab nations such as Lebanon and Syria increased. Many Arab refugees were forced by their Arab host nations to live in camps with poor facilities that served as training grounds for terrorist activity against Israel.

In November 1967, the UN passed Resolution 242 calling for all warring nations to recognize one another and make peace and for Israel to withdraw from some of the occupied lands. The Arab nations continued their refusal to recognize Israel, and Israel refused to return territory until it received recognition.

4. *The Yom Kippur War, 1973.* The fourth Arab-Israeli war began on October 6, 1973 (Yom Kippur, the holiest day of the year to Jews), when Egypt attacked Israel by surprise across the Suez Canal. The war, which the Egyptians call "the October War," lasted almost a month, with Egypt gaining a small amount of land in the Sinai. Syrian troops attacked Israel on the Golan Heights but were beaten back. Several other Arab countries sent troops to fight. The Soviet Union increased its arms shipments to the Arabs, hoping to avoid another victory by Israel. To counter the Soviets, the United States sent military help to Israel. Oil-rich Arab nations pressured the United States not to help Israel and began an oil embargo (a refusal to sell oil). Once again, the UN arranged a ceasefire to end the fighting. In 1973 the UN also passed Resolution 338, calling for "negotiations . . . between the parties concerned . . . aimed at establishing . . . peace in the Middle East."

GEOGRAPHY

Use of Geography

## Developments Between 1973 and 2000

1. In 1977 Egyptian president Anwar Sadat visited Israel to begin peace talks. He was the first Arab leader to visit Israel. Later in the year, Israeli prime minister Menachem Begin visited Egypt.

2. In 1979, at Camp David near Washington, D.C., an Egyptian-Israeli Peace Treaty was signed by Sadat and Begin. President Jimmy Carter of the United States brought the two leaders together. The peace treaty provided that (1) Egypt and Israel would recognize each other and exchange ambassadors; (2) the state of war that existed between them from 1949 to 1979 was over; (3) Israel would return the Sinai Peninsula to Egypt in stages between 1979 and 1982, and a UN peacekeeping force would be reestablished on the border; and (4) negotiations would begin on the status of the Palestinian Arabs.

GEOGRAPHY

Human Systems

3. Many Arab nations were angry at Egypt's actions and broke off relations. In 1981 Muslim extremists assassinated Sadat, and Hosni Mubarak became the new Egyptian president.

4. In 1982 Israel invaded Lebanon in response to repeated terrorist attacks by the Palestine Liberation Organization (PLO) and the inability of the Lebanese government to control PLO actions. The PLO claimed to speak on behalf of Palestinian Arabs and was so recognized by most Arab nations. By 1984 the PLO forces had left Lebanon. The Israeli action in Lebanon stirred much controversy among Israelis, and after the 1984 Israeli elections, its army was pulled back from Lebanon except for a small "security zone" in southern Lebanon.

**WORLD ISSUES**

Terrorism

5. Also in 1982, Israel, in compliance with the peace treaty with Egypt, withdrew completely from the Sinai Peninsula.

6. In 1987 an uprising by Palestinians in the West Bank and Gaza Strip began. This uprising, called the Intifada, was a protest against continued Israeli occupation of the land it had won in war. Many Palestinians supported the PLO and its leader, Yasir Arafat, in its goals of overthrowing Israel and establishing a Palestinian state. However, the PLO was branded as a terrorist group by Israel, because it was one of several Arab organizations that had carried out murderous actions against civilians in the Middle East and elsewhere in the world. Consequently, the Israeli government refused to negotiate with the PLO over the status of the occupied territories.

**GEOGRAPHY**

Use of Geography

**WORLD ISSUES**

Terrorism

Within Israel the question of what to do with the occupied territories created discussion and divisiveness. Many Israelis wanted to keep the territories because they view a Palestinian state as a military threat, and some claim that a Palestinian state already exists in Jordan. Others wanted to meet some of the Palestinian demands.

**GEOGRAPHY**

Human Systems

7. The Arab boycott (a refusal to buy goods from someone) against Israel continued as an economic weapon. It operates on two levels: (1) all direct trade between Arab states and Israel is forbidden; and (2) Arab countries will not do business with any company that does business with Israel. Therefore, many companies, afraid of losing business with Arabs, will refrain from having contact with Israel. Israel has repeatedly asked for an end of the boycott.

**WORLD ISSUES**

Determination of Political and Economic Systems

8. Iraq's threats of nuclear and gas attacks against Israel caused concern about the possibility of a fifth Arab-Israeli war. Iraq's unprovoked firing of Scud missiles on Israel during the 1991 Persian Gulf War almost ignited such a conflict. (Israel was not a participant in the war.)

GLOBAL
CONCEPTS
**Interdependence**
CONCEPTS
GLOBAL

9. The 1991 breakup of the Soviet Union, a longtime supplier of weapons to Arab nations, meant that the flow of arms into the Middle East would be reduced. Another consequence of the breakup was the increased influence the United States, as the world's chief superpower, could now exert in the region. U.S. prestige also increased in some parts of the Arab world based upon the U.S. role, supported by a few Arab nations, in defeating Iraqi President Saddam Hussein's forces during the 2003 Persian Gulf War.

10. A much more dramatic moment in the quest for Middle East peace occurred on September 13, 1993, in Washington, D.C. On that day, with U.S. president Bill Clinton presiding, Israeli prime minister Yitzhak Rabin and PLO chairman Yasir Arafat shook hands and signed a peace agreement. With millions watching on television, the two former adversaries shook hands on the first-ever pact between Jews and Palestinians to end their conflict. Its key features were: (1) Israelis would withdraw from Gaza and the West Bank city of Jericho by April 1994; (2) a five-year period of Palestinian self-rule would begin in these places; and (3) talks on a permanent agreement would start by December 1995, with the agreement to take effect in December 1998. These features were originally agreed upon at talks in Oslo, Norway.

**WORLD ISSUES**

Determination
of Political
and Economic
Systems

11. Another historic event affecting the Middle East occurred in 1993. This was the signing in Jerusalem of an agreement between Israel and the Vatican, whereby diplomatic relations would be established for the first time. The Roman Catholic Church would now recognize the state of Israel, reversing its prior policy.

12. Peace in the region received another boost in July 1994. At that time, Prime Minister Yitzhak Rabin of Israel and King Hussein of Jordan signed a peace treaty that ended forty years of war between them.

## Arab Views of the Conflict

1. The creation of Israel in 1948 was wrong and was another sign of Western imperialism in the Middle East. A. Many Arabs view Israel's creation as illegitimate.

2. Israel was established on land that belonged to Arabs. Any housing and settlements built by Israel on land it had after the 1967 war should be removed.

3. Arabs never accepted the UN Partition Plan of 1947.

4. The majority of people in the Middle East are Arabs. Israeli society and culture represent a threat to Arab values.

5. Israel's creation stemmed from European guilt about what happened to Jews during the Holocaust. It is wrong to take out this guilt on the Arabs. A Jewish state should have been created somewhere, but not in the Middle East.

6. Palestinians deserve a land of their own.

7. The UN has condemned Israeli actions in the occupied territories.

8. Jerusalem is a holy city to Muslims, as it contains the Dome of the Rock and the El Aksa Mosque and is the third holiest city after Makkah and Medina. Jerusalem should be under Muslim authority, not occupied by Israel.

9. Arab sovereignty in Palestine, prior to 1948, was more recent than Jewish sovereignty.

10. Israel seeks to expand beyond its borders.

11. Israel must give back land it gained in wars as a condition for any peace negotiations.

12. The Intifada events showed the wrongfulness of Israeli occupation and the need for a Palestinian state.

## Israeli Views of the Conflict

GLOBAL CONCEPTS

**Empathy**

CONCEPTS GLOBAL

1. Israel is located on land that was the original homeland of the Jewish people and that was promised to them in the Bible.

2. Arabs sold land to Jews prior to 1948; other Arabs fled from the land in the 1948–1949 war.

3. The UN Partition Plan was approved by a majority of the world's nations. Israel is an existing, functioning nation, recognized by 172 of the 193 members of the United Nations.

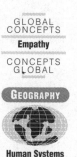

**GEOGRAPHY**

**Human Systems**

4. As a small nation of 7 million people, Israel does not represent a threat to the 100 million Arabs in fifteen nations in the region. Arabs who still live in Israel have a high standard of living and live in the only democracy in the Middle East.

5. A Jewish state is needed as a safe place and refuge, because of the centuries of anti-Semitism in Europe and in Arab lands.

6. Jordan exists as a state for Palestinians. It was created illegally by the British in 1922 from 77 percent of the land that Britain held as a mandate from the League of Nations. There is no need or obligation to create a second Palestinian state. Most Jordanians today are Palestinians.

7. UN votes condemning Israel are signs of Arab ill-feeling and reflect Arab pressure on oil-poor countries to vote with the Arabs or face oil embargoes.

8. Jerusalem was the capital of Jewish kingdoms in ancient times and is a holy city to Jews, containing the Western Wall and the sites of the first two temples. These areas were restricted to Jews when Jordan ruled Jerusalem from 1948 to 1967. Today the

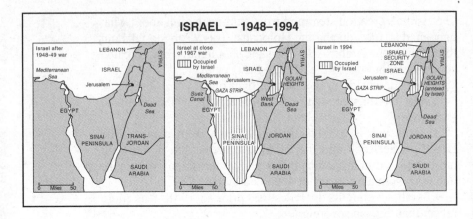

ISRAEL — 1948–1994

Israeli government permits the Muslim holy sites to be watched over by members of the Israeli Muslim community. Jerusalem was never an important Arab political center, as was true of Damascus and Baghdad.

9. Jewish sovereignty in Palestine was earlier in history than that of the Arabs.

10. If Israel had not been attacked so often by the Arabs, it would not have any land other than that given to it under the 1947 Partition Plan. Israel has never intentionally tried to take away land from any Arab nation, whereas the Arabs have tried to take away and destroy Israeli land. Israel has the right to build housing and settlements on West Bank land, as that region was never legally controlled by any Arab nation.

11. Israel is willing to negotiate with the Arabs and return land if the Arabs end the war they have waged since 1948. With the exception of Egypt (since 1979) and Jordan (since 1994), no Arab nation recognizes Israel's right to exist. Israel has shown that it is willing to exchange land for peace (for example, the return of the Sinai to Egypt).

12. The two Intifadas were just other phases of the attempt by Arabs since 1948 to destroy Israel.

GLOBAL CONCEPTS

**Empathy**

CONCEPTS GLOBAL

**GEOGRAPHY**

**Use of Geography**

## Developments in Arab-Israeli Relations in the Early 21st Century

A second Intifada emerged in 2000 similar to the one begun in 1987. This showed continued Palestinian resentment against Israel and its perceived occupation and settlement policies. The resentment was seen in deadly terrorist attacks on Jewish civilians. These attacks on innocent people were carried out by homicide bombers (often labeled "suicide bombers" in the media). One Israeli countermeasure was the construction of a barrier, started in 2004, known as the "security wall" or "separation barrier," designed to stop the penetration of homicide bombers from the West Bank. It has had much success in reducing murderous acts. The Israelis also claim that it was necessary since the Palestine Authority has failed to disarm terrorist groups and to prevent their attacks. However, its erection caused bitterness in the Arab world and harsh criticism from several nations outside the Middle East. Critics condemned it as illegal.

A more hopeful sign of calm was a road map plan for peace formulated in 2002. This plan grew out of the Oslo Accords of 1993 and was to be implemented under the guidance of a quartet consisting of the United States, Russia, the United Nations, and the European Union. The goal, as agreed to by Israel and the Palestinians, was to plan for a future Palestinian state. The Palestinians, in the meantime, would adopt democratic reforms, end terrorist actions, and halt the vicious anti-Semitism prevalent in mosques and schools. Israel would stop settler buildups and withdraw from specific areas in the occupied territories. Unfortunately, throughout the succeeding years, the road map did not appear to be progressing. The ruling Palestinian Authority could not or would not prevent armed terrorist groups from committing atrocities against Israelis. Israel, in response to Palestinian violence, carried out house searches, made arrests of suspected terrorists, closed down border crossings, and targeted assassinations of militant leaders. The cycle of attacks and counterattacks resulted in the deaths of many people. The preaching and teaching of anti-Semitism throughout the occupied areas, as well in most of the Arab world, continued unabated. In the last several years, a number of events have occurred in the Middle East that may likely influence the course of future relations between Israel and the Arab Muslim peoples in the Middle East:

1. *The death of Syrian President Hafez al-Assad in 2000.* He was very anti-Israeli and permitted dangerous radical Arab terrorist groups to maintain headquarters in his country. His place was taken by his son, Bashir al-Assad, who has shown a more willing attitude in working toward better relations with Israel. Yet, he refuses to grant recognition to Israel and has demanded that Israel return the Golan Heights to Syria. He has also allowed terrorist organizations to remain in his country.

2. *The death of Yasir Arafat in 2004.* As the most significant figure among Palestinians, he was involved in high-level negotiations with Israel, the United States, and many other nations in an attempt to create a Palestinian state and to better the lives of his people. By the time of his death he had failed to accomplish

these goals, as he was not seen as trustworthy by the Americans and the Israelis. His place as head of the Palestinian Authority was taken by Mahmoud Abbas, head of the Fatah Party. He faced acute challenges in trying to unify his people and in disarming violent militant groups who want to destroy Israel.

3. *The withdrawal of Israeli settlers from Gaza in 2005.* Under a decision made by Israeli prime minister Ariel Sharon, Israel arranged for the removal of the more than 8,000 Jewish settlers from the Gaza Strip. This entire area would now have limited self-rule under the Palestinian Authority, with the hope of one day becoming part of a Palestinian state. Although some Israelis were against Sharon's decision to evacuate Gaza, the vast majority of the population supported it and hoped it would be seen as a step toward peace by the Palestinians and their supporters in the Arab world and elsewhere. Although the Israelis left behind some manufacturing and agricultural sites for use by the Palestinians, the Palestinians nevertheless destroyed them. Militant groups among the Palestinians also began to fire missiles and rockets into areas of Israel, causing property damage and civilian casualties.

4. *The threat by Iran's President.* In November 2005, Iran's president called for the eradication and destruction of Israel by any means possible. This was seen as a dangerous pronouncement and a violation of the United Nations Charter. Iran is thought to possess nuclear weapons and has supported radical Islamist groups who have carried out homicide bombings in Israel. Although no Middle East Arab nation condemned the threat, it was denounced by the United States and many other nations. The threat continued into 2012.

5. *The impact of Hamas.* The early months of 2006 witnessed some major developments affecting Arab-Israeli relations. In January, the elections held in the Palestinian territories were won by Hamas. This victory was seen, however, as a severe hindrance to the peace process. Labeled as a terrorist group by the United States and the European Union, Hamas has staged several homicide bombings over the years that have killed innocent Israelis and some Westerners. Hamas rejects any negotiations with Israel, refuses to recognize any of Israel's land claims, and vows to destroy Israel. As of April 2006, the quartet (see page 513) stated that financial assistance to the Hamas-controlled Palestinian Authority is likely to suffer. This is because Hamas has not been willing to recognize Israel, renounce violence, and accept previous agreements. Hamas was a Palestinian political party that now controlled Gaza, and disagreed on several issues with the other Palestinian political party, Fatah, which con-

trolled the West Bank area. The continued Hamas shooting of missiles and rockets into nearby sections of Israel, as well as the capture of an Israeli soldier, prompted Israel to stage a series of attacks in Gaza in late 2008 and early 2009. These attacks, seeking to avoid civilian injuries and aimed chiefly at Hamas officials and military personnel, had limited success at first. Nevertheless, Hamas continued sporadic firing and holding Gilad Shalit, the captured soldier, into 2011. (In October 2011, an agreement was reached between Israel and Hamas, whereby Shalit was returned to Israel in exchange for the release of 1,027 Palestinian prisoners. They had been arrested for committing terrorist acts, including murder, against Israeli citizens.)

6. *Protection from nuclear attacks.* Concerned about a nuclear confrontation from hostile Muslim nations, Israeli planes destroyed nuclear weapon sites in Iraq in 1981, and in Syria in 2007.

7. *Lebanon War in 2006.* In order to stop attacks from Southern Lebanon, Israel established a "security zone" in the region from 1982 to 2000. Although Israeli forces left the region in 2000, there was continued rocket and sniper attacks from across its northern border. This was mainly by Hezbollah. Hezbollah was a political party, consisting of Islamic extremists and other Arabs, financed by Iran and anti-Western countries dedicated to Israel's destruction. As the Lebanese government could not or would not curtail Hezbollah's activities, the Israeli army and air force crossed into Lebanon in 2006. A 34-day war took place, leading to a cease-fire arranged by the UN. Hezbollah has gained power and prestige in Lebanon and has increased its arms supplies with help from Iran and Syria. Tension still exists along the Israeli-Lebanese border.

8. *Israeli blockade of Gaza.* In an attempt to prevent arms and weapons from reaching Hamas fighters, Israel imposed a naval blockade on Gaza. In May 2010, a flotilla (group) of six vessels attempted to break the blockade. The vessels sailed from Turkey, containing Hamas supporters. When Israeli commandos boarded one of the ships to check for weapons, they were violently attacked by people on the ship. As the commandos fought to protect themselves, several were injured while nine of the attackers were killed. The other ships were escorted peacefully to Israel, where any humanitarian items they carried were sent to Gaza. The Turkish government, in support of Hamas, was angered over the incident, as some of the dead were Turkish citizens. It demanded that Israel make payment and apologize. Israel refused. Relations between the two governments now became tense and unfriendly. The UN conducted an investiga-

tion and determined that under international law, the blockade was legal.

9. *The appeal by the Palestinian Authority to the UN for statehood, 2011.* In September 2011, Mahmoud Abbas, head of the Palestine Authority, asked the UN to grant statehood to the Palestinians. He hoped that the Security Council would give its approval after studying the request. There were serious problems with this request:

a. President Obama was expected to have the United States veto the request.

b. The UN cannot create a state, but can grant observer status.

c. The Abbas appeal violates previous agreements between the Palestinians and Israel, whereby they would meet by themselves on the statehood issue.

d. The Palestinians are not united and have no fixed boundaries. The Fatah Party controls the West Bank, whereas Hamas controls Gaza.

e. The appeal was rejected.

10. *2011 and after.* As 2011 drew to a close, it was hoped that both the Israelis and the Palestinians would once again meet to discuss vital issues. When he spoke before the UN in September 2011, Israeli prime minister Benjamin Netanyahu echoed this wish and did not want to have preset conditions for any talks. Palestinian president Abbas, however, asked for a halt on settlement building by Israel prior to any talks. The key issues center around the settlements as well as the status of Jerusalem, Arab refugees, Palestinian statehood and boundaries, and Arab recognition of Israel as a Jewish state.

## Other Political Developments in the Middle East, 1979–2011

**Iran-Islamic Fundamentalism and the War with Iraq.** The shah of Iran, Mohammed Reza Pahlavi, introduced many Western and modern practices to his country during the 1960s and 1970s. However, many religious leaders felt that traditional Islamic customs were threatened by Western ideas. These leaders were Islamic fundamentalists, who wanted to keep Islam pure and fundamental, without any "contamination" from the outside world. Known as Islamists, they opposed the shah and were also upset with the dictatorial manner in which he ruled. Riots and demonstrations against the shah forced him to leave Iran in 1979. In his place the country was run by an Islamic Revolutionary Council, led by Ayatollah Ruhollah Khomeini. This Iranian Revolution, also known as the Islamic Revolution,

GLOBAL
CONCEPTS
**Empathy**
CONCEPTS
GLOBAL

caused concern in other Muslim nations in the Middle East. The Ayatollah's government was anti-Western and held fifty-two Americans as hostages from 1979 to 1981. Although Khomeini died in 1989, the new rulers of Iran have followed similar foreign and domestic policies.

In 1980 war between Iran and Iraq broke out when Iraq, under its leader Saddam Hussein, attacked Iran. Known as the Iran-Iraq War, this conflict had several causes. These included: political causes—each nation wanted to dominate the Persian Gulf area; frequent criticism by Hussein and Khomeini of each other; border disputes existed; social causes—Iraq feared the "export" of the Iranian Revolution; there were great religious differences between the Sunni Muslims of Iraq and the Shi'ite Muslims of Iran; and economic causes—the oil fields of the Persian Gulf area are very valuable; the Persian Gulf itself is the most important route for transporting oil from the Middle East. The fighting ended in 1988 under a UN-supervised agreement, but it caused hundreds of thousands of casualties and hurt the economies of both nations. The war ended as a stalemate.

**WORLD ISSUES**

War
and
Peace

Today, Iran is tightly run by the Muslim clergy. As a result, strict limits are placed on basic rights and freedoms. The 2009 elections, with Ahmadinejad winning once again, saw widespread claims of fraud. Protestors were severely beaten by security forces, with many of the beatings recorded on cell phones and then shown on the Internet across the world.

**Lebanon—Civil War and Syrian Occupation.** A civil war broke out in Lebanon that lasted from 1975 to 1990. It can be explained by examining the country's political and religious history. When the French mandate in Lebanon ended in 1943, a government was created that was supposed to strike a balance between Lebanese Christians and Muslims. Since the Christians were then the majority group, it was decided that most of the top government positions (such as president and armed forces commander) would go to Christians. From the 1940s to the 1970s, Lebanon prospered economically and was peaceful. However, Muslims became the majority group, and they wanted changes in the political structure to give them more power. It was also in this period that Palestinian refugees, including PLO leaders, settled in Lebanon as a result of the Arab-Israeli wars. From these settlements, many Palestinians made terrorist raids into Israel. Frequently, Israeli forces attacked these settlements in retaliation. Lebanese Christians, represented by the Phalange Party, were against the Palestinian presence in Lebanon.

**GEOGRAPHY**

Use of Geography

In 1975 Muslims and Christians began to fight each other. In addition, different Muslim groups began to fight one another and different Christian groups also began to fight one another. Each of the groups formed its own private army, or militia. In 1976 Syria, under President Hafez el-Assad, sent in troops as requested by the Arab League (an organization of Arab nations in the Middle East). Although Syria's purpose was to restore order, at various times the Syrians supported different militias in Lebanon. By 1990 there were 40,000 Syrian soldiers in Lebanon, and President Assad began to drop hints of incorporating Lebanon into a "greater Syria."

Other Middle Eastern nations, such as Iran and Libya, also supported one or more of the warring groups. Some of these groups, such as the Islamic Jihad, carried out terrorist activities against foreigners and other Lebanese in order to focus world attention on their political goals. These terrorist activities

WORLD ISSUES

Terrorism

included taking citizens of France, the United States, Germany, and the Soviet Union as hostages and sometimes killing them, hijacking a TWA airliner, and killing American and French soldiers in a suicide bomb attack. Tragically, there was no single government in Lebanon acceptable to all its people and able to bring stability to the nation. The civil war resulted in separated enclaves (closed-in areas) in Beirut and elsewhere under the control of whichever militia proved to be the strongest. The Lebanese economy was ruined by the war.

Syria's role changed in 2005 when its forces withdrew from Lebanon. The withdrawal was mainly the result of the Cedar Revolution. This was the name given to a series of demonstrations following the assassination of Lebanese prime minister Rafik Hariri. The UN began an investigation to determine whether Syria and the Islamic extremist party, Hezbollah, were involved in this incident.

WORLD ISSUES

War
and
Peace

**War in Afghanistan (1979–1989).** In 1979 a Marxist pro-Soviet government came to power in Afghanistan. It faced opposition by the majority of Afghan people, who began an armed struggle against it. The Soviet Union invaded Afghanistan, claiming that it was reacting to a request by the Afghan government. However, many observers believed that the real reasons for the Soviet actions were to gain access to oil and gas deposits in Afghanistan and possibly to reach through Iran into the Persian Gulf. The Soviets also may have been afraid of the impact of Islamic fundamentalism in Afghanistan and Iran on the Muslim communities in the Soviet Union. The Soviet military action was condemned by nations around the

GEOGRAPHY

Use of Geography

globe and caused controversy in the Soviet Union itself. The Afghan fighters, the Mujahadeen, were supplied by the United States and were able to deny the Soviet Union a victory. In 1989 the Soviets retreated from Afghanistan with severe military and political losses.

Afghanistan was not to have political stability, however, as different religious factions fought each other for control. A coup in 1992 was one sign of this instability.

An Islamist government was established by the Talibans. Yet, they experienced difficulty in trying to put down other Afghan groups who were against them.

**Libya and State-Supported Terrorism.** When Colonel Muammar Qaddafi came to power in 1969, Libya began to support terrorist groups. These groups have carried out actions mainly against Israeli and U.S. interests. In 1986 American bombers raided Libya in retaliation for violence directed against Americans in Europe and the Middle East. The worst incident of terrorist violence involving Libya concerned the unspeakable bombing of Pan Am flight 103 as it flew over Lockerbie, Scotland, in 1988. The death toll numbered all 259 passengers and crew members, allegedly due to the work of agents trained in Libya. Libya refused to release the suspects to U.S. authorities, for which the UN imposed sanctions on Libya. In 1998, however under international pressure, Libya finally agreed to release two suspects to stand trial. One of them was found guilty in a trial in 2001.

The Libyan government's connection with such bloody unprovoked acts toward people of other nations is an example of "state-supported terrorism." This term refers to a government policy that supports, trains, finances, and protects organizations that engage in terrorist activities. Besides Libya, other Middle Eastern nations that have provided such support are Iran, Syria, Iraq, and Yemen. Examples of groups that have received their assistance have been Islamic Jihad, Hamas, and the PLO.

**Pan-Arabism.** This term refers to the idea of all Arab nations uniting and standing together on political and economic issues. The movement reached a high point while President Nasser ruled Egypt. However, since his death in 1970, and due to several disputes among the Arab nations, the movement has died down. The movement was tied to the idea of Arab socialism (government control of industry and the attempt to improve living conditions for all Arabs).

**WORLD ISSUES**

Terrorism

## Operation Desert Storm—the Persian Gulf War of 1991.

This war lasted from January 16, 1991, to February 27, 1991. The conflict, whose chief adversaries were Iraq and the United States, had its roots in the Iraqi invasion of Kuwait in August 1990. Iraq, which wanted to take over Kuwait's rich oil fields and have greater access to the Persian Gulf, would probably have then sought to take over Saudi Arabia. Such actions would have given Iraq control over 40 percent of the world's oil reserves. Saddam Hussein refused to leave Kuwait despite UN requests and its eventual imposition of trade sanctions and threat to use force.

**WORLD ISSUES**

| War |
| and |
| Peace |

**GEOGRAPHY**

**Use of Geography**

As Iraqi troops killed, tortured, and raped thousands of Kuwaitis, destroyed much property, and were poised for an attack on Saudi Arabia, U.S. President George Bush assembled a multinational force of 500,000 troops from twenty-nine countries. This coalition, under the command of American General Norman Schwarzkopf and containing 450,000 U.S. troops, went into action in January under the authority of a UN Security Council Resolution when Iraq failed to meet a deadline to withdraw its troops from Kuwait. With the use of high-tech weaponry, the U.S.-led coalition defeated the Iraqis and freed Kuwait in five weeks.

**WORLD ISSUES**

| Human |
| Rights |

The chief consequences of the war for the Middle East were as follows: (1) Saddam Hussein remained in power, still in possession of a large army and many weapons of mass destruction. He frequently failed to cooperate with the UN inspection teams that came to Iraq to check on his weapons program. (2) The ecology of the Persian Gulf area was severely upset by Iraqi soldiers. They burned oil wells and released great amounts of petroleum into the gulf waters. (3) A large split among Arabs occurred. Egypt, Saudi Arabia, Syria, and Kuwait sided with the United States. In support of Iraq, although not sending in any fighters, were Jordan, Yemen, Tunisia, Algeria, Yemen, and the PLO. (4) Kurdish people in Iraq were treated very harshly by Saddam Hussein. Their attempt to break away from Iraqi rule was suppressed, and many were killed or forced to become refugees. Thousands were given "safe-haven" areas in northern Iraq under the protection of the United States and the United Nations.

**WORLD ISSUES**

| Environmental |
| Concerns |

## The Future of the Kurds.

As an ethnic group of approximately 24 million people, the Kurds have spread out during this century to various parts of Turkey, Iran, Iraq, and Syria. Often suffering persecution, they have long wanted to have a nation of their own—to be called Kurdistan. The greatest concentration of Kurds is in Turkey, whose military-dominated government has most frequently and violently persecuted them. This resulted in the creation of the PKK or Kurdistan Workers' Party, which worked to promote Kurdish independence and recruit guerrillas to fight the Turkish authorities. Under Abdullah Ocalan, the PKK led Kurdish resistance to repression and genocide, both physical and cultural, by the Turkish government throughout the 1990s. Ocalan's arrest in 1999 and his subsequent trial were the source of much international controversy and criticism. Found guilty and condemned to death, Ocalan's execution was held up while the Turkish government negotiated with Kurdish rebels in the hopes of reaching a compromise agreement that would give the Kurds some autonomy rather than full independence. Turkey's poor human rights record with the Kurds has also resulted in international pressure on the Turkish government to reach a peaceful resolution of the conflict.

**War in Iraq.** In March 2003, the United States attacked Iraq. Although not supported by the United Nations, but with some help from coalition partners such as Great Britain, the United States was able to defeat the forces of Saddam Hussein in less than two months. The fighting was known as Operation Iraqi Freedom as well as the Second Gulf War. Saddam Hussein was arrested in December 2003 and put on trial in 2005. He was executed by hanging in 2006. The invasion of Iraq was said to be for several reasons: Iraq's possession of weapons of mass destruction (WMDs) and its refusal to comply with demands and requests made by UN inspectors over a number of years after the 1991 Persian Gulf War, Iraq's support of terrorist organizations such as Al Qaeda and its leader Osama bin Laden, and Iraq's possible links to the September 11, 2001, murderous attack on the World Trade Center in New York. Yet, in the two years following Iraq's defeat, several investigations suggested doubt about the WMD issue as well as any link to Al Qaeda and the 9/11 attack. During those years, the United States and its coalition partners faced increasing isolated fighting from small groups of insurgent Iraqis and other Arabs who slipped into Iraq and were known as jihadists. Although the United States lost more than 1,000 troops during this time, it tried to achieve unity among Iraq's different ethnic groups and to promote democratic reforms in the country as well as better living conditions. A new constitution was written and elections were held to select a governing body. Traditional tensions among Sunni Muslims, Shiite Muslims, and Kurds often made these goals difficult to achieve. In late 2005, the United States began to consider the start of gradual troop withdrawals. It was hoped that U.S.-trained Iraqi soldiers and police could help preserve safety and stability. Inside the United States, controversy grew about the American presence in Iraq. U.S. president George W. Bush maintained that the American role in Iraq was vital in the war against global terrorism. In 2007, a U.S. troop surge made an important impact on the war. Iraqi forces took over more of the fighting. Both the American and Iraqi governments finally reached agreement on a withdrawal of U.S. combat forces by December 2011. President Obama announced that after this date, a few thousand U.S. troops would remain as advisers and trainers.

**War in Afghanistan.** The struggle against global terrorism was also a factor responsible for American forces fighting in Afghanistan. Control of that country by the Taliban, beginning in the 1990s, continued into the 2000s. As Islamic fundamentalists, the Taliban government claimed to be anti-American and protected the terrorist group Al Qaeda. Al Qaeda was held responsible by the United States for the horrific aggression in New York, Washington, D.C., and Pennsylvania on September 11, 2001. The United States viewed this unprovoked aggression as an act of war and sent military forces to Afghanistan. The goal was to overthrow the Taliban (who had refused to shut down Al Qaeda and give up its leader Osama bin Laden), destroy Al Qaeda, and capture its leaders. With the defeat of the Taliban in December 2001, the United States helped anti-Taliban Afghans to create a government headed by Hamid Karzai. The year 2004 became noteworthy on his election as president and the writing of a new constitution. Nevertheless, scattered fighting and homicide bombings by Taliban terrorists continued. These were met by the remaining American forces, supported by troops from some NATO countries and from Pakistan. The hunt for Osama bin Laden continued, however, as he was thought to be hiding in the rugged mountainous region surrounding the Afghan-Pakistani border. Finally, in September 2011, U.S. Navy Seals found and executed bin Laden in a house in Pakistan.

Also in 2011, President Obama ordered the withdrawal of 10,000 troops from Afghanistan by the end of the year, and to withdraw another 23,000 by the summer of 2012, part of what he called "the beginning, but not the end, of our effort to wind down this war." He also noted that "by 2014, this process of transition will be complete, and the Afghan people will be responsible for their own security." The president said his announcement was a fulfillment of a commitment he made in December 2009 when he authorized a surge of 30,000 U.S. forces into Afghanistan.

**The Arab Spring of 2011.** The Arab Spring of 2011, also known as the Arab Uprising and Arab Awakening, was a series of political revolts and changes that began in Tunisia. It soon continued to spread throughout the Arab world, from Algeria to Syria. These monumental changes, as with other major events and movements in world history, had causes that were both underlying and immediate (see pages 426 and 428). The basic causes were severe unemployment, government oppression, and corruption. The immediate cause was a tragedy in Tunisia in 2010, a tragedy that was to spark uprisings in other nations.

1. *Tunisia.* In December of that year, a street vendor was beaten up and humiliated by a government official for no good reason. Such an occurrence was frequent in that country. Consequently, the vendor set himself on fire and died. Protests and antigovernment demonstrations erupted all over the nation. Later in the month, the president, a man who had held office for 23 years, fled the country.

2. *Egypt.* News about the rebellious situation in Tunisia reached Egypt and other Arab nations. In January 2011, thousands of Egyptians, mostly young people, gathered in Tahrir Square in Cairo. They were expressing their anger at the many years of harsh and brutal actions by the government against any political opposition. Their protests became violent at times, striking out at police forces, and reflecting resentment at rising food prices and a denial of basic freedoms. By using social networks such as Facebook and Twitter, angry citizens were able to contact other protesters and thus organize massive demonstrations in Cairo and elsewhere in the country. So effective were these actions, that President Hosni Mubarak, who had been in power for 30 years, left the country. Ultimately he returned to Egypt and was put on trial. The chief charge was conspiracy to kill prodemocracy demonstrators whose protests drove him from office. The official death toll was 840.

3. *Syria.* In March 2011, antigovernment riots and protests broke out in Syria. The reasons were similar to those that had led to unrest in Egypt. The target of the Syrian uprising was President Bashar al-Assad and his family's repressive 40 years in power. His government's response to the demonstrations was violent and lethal. In Damascus and other cities, Syrian army units fired on unarmed civilians, including women, the elderly,

and children. Other crimes included torture and forced disappearances. All of these crackdown actions were contained in a UN report, noting that in the period from March to November alone, 3,500 people had been killed nationwide. The UN Security Council called upon the International Court of Justice to consider bringing Syria up on charges of committing crimes against humanity.

4. *Libya.* A movement against the 42 years of harsh dictatorial rule by Colonel Muammar al-Qaddafi began in February 2011. Protesters took up arms and were joined by many soldiers of Libya's armed forces. Libyans who were loyal to Qaddafi fought back. The result was a fierce civil war. In March, air strikes against Qaddafi and his supporters, as authorized by the UN Security Council, were made by European and American warplanes. In October, Libyan rebels tracked down Qaddafi and killed him.

5. *Other Arab nations.* Throughout 2011, protests also occurred in Algeria, Bahrain, Jordan, Morocco, Oman, Saudi Arabia, and Yemen. Except for Yemen, none of these caused as much bloodshed or change as was true in Tunisia, Egypt, Syria, and Libya. Yet, the future political situation in these four nations, as well as the rest of the Arab world, remains uncertain. Possibilities include open elections and other democratic reforms, military dictatorship, control by Islamic extremists, and a return to one-party rule. Whether these or any other developments take place in the current decade, it is clear that 2011 will have proven to be a critical moment in the history of the Middle East.

# Part E: South Asia and Southeast Asia

## SOUTH ASIA

### Political Structure in India

India has existed since independence as the world's largest democracy. It has a parliamentary form of government similar to that of Britain but different from that of the United States.

India has had several important political leaders.

1. Jawaharlal Nehru, the first prime minister (1947–1964). Nehru brought some stability to the new nation and tried to achieve a sense of "unity in diversity." He hoped to build a spirit of nationalism, in spite of the many differences among India's population, including religion, language, and varying loyalties to local states and regions.

2. Indira Gandhi, prime minister (1966–1977, 1980–1984). Mrs. Gandhi, the daughter of Nehru, held power longer than any Indian leader. Although popular when she first took office, she gradually began to govern with an "iron fist" in order to pursue her policies concerning economics, birth control, and other issues. Her proclamation of a "state of emergency" in the 1970s was seen as harming India's democracy and led to her downfall in the 1977 elections. From 1977 to 1980, her successors, Morarji Desai and then Charan Singh, proved unable to achieve their goals. Mrs. Gandhi returned to power in 1980, faced with severe internal problems such as persistent poverty and the desire by Sikhs to have their own nation in the Punjab region. Her strong actions against Sikh militants provoked a harsh reaction and led to her assassination by two Sikhs in 1984.

3. Rajiv Gandhi, prime minister (1984–1989). The son of Indira Gandhi, Rajiv Gandhi tried to obtain foreign help for India in meetings with American President Reagan and Soviet Premier Gorbachev. Although he began his term of office amid much sympathy due to his mother's death, Rajiv proved to be a weak and unpopular leader. He made little progress in solving domestic problems (poverty, Sikh dissension). His administration was criticized for being corrupt. An Indian politician in an opposition party claimed that the mood of the people was "one of extreme disenchantment." Consequently, in the elections of November 1989, Mr. Gandhi and his Congress Party were voted out of office.

GLOBAL CONCEPTS
**Political Systems**
CONCEPTS GLOBAL

GLOBAL CONCEPTS
**Power**
CONCEPTS GLOBAL

**GEOGRAPHY**

**Human Systems**

527

## A COMPARISON OF TWO DEMOCRACIES

| | United States | India |
|---|---|---|
| Basic form | Federal republic; one central government and 50 state governments | Federal republic; one central government and 17 state governments |
| Legislature | A bicameral system: Congress consists of the Senate and House of Representatives | A bicameral system: Parliament is composed of the Council of States (Rajya Sabha) and House of the People (Lok Sabha) |
| Executive | A president indirectly elected by the public (presidential form) | A prime minister elected by the legislature (parliamentary form; the prime minister usually is head of the majority party in the Parliament) |
| Governing document | Constitution of 1787 with subsequent amendments | Constitution of 1950 with subsequent amendments |
| | Both documents describe the political structure, protect civil rights and liberties, and were influenced by British legal traditions. | |
| Political parties | Two main parties: Democrat and Republican | Several parties: Congress, Janata Dal, Bharatiya Janata |

4. Vishwanath Pratap Singh, prime minister (1989–1990). V. P. Singh's Janata Dal Party won 141 of the 525 seats up for election in the Lok Sabha in 1989. Other parties supported the Janata Dal and joined with it to form a coalition (a combination formed of different political parties to run a government when no single party has a majority of seats). The coalition was called the National Front and was headed by V. P. Singh, India's eighth prime minister. Yet he found it very hard to keep this coalition together. One reason was his support of the Mandal report. This report recommended that up to 49 percent of jobs in government and public works be reserved for untouchables and members of low-ranking castes. Singh's decision to carry out the recommendations led to riots and to the withdrawal of the BJP (Bharatiya Janata Party) from his governing coalition. The BJP is a right-wing party that is supported mostly by upper-caste Hindus. As opposition to Singh increased, the

coalition government fell apart and new elections were scheduled for 1991.

.5. P. V. Narasimha Rao, prime minister (1991–1996). Although six political parties entered the 1991 elections, most people believed that the Congress Party would emerge as the winner, with its leader, Rajiv Gandhi, regaining the prime minister post. However, Gandhi was assassinated in May 1991. The assassin was a Tamil woman who was angered by his actions as prime minister in helping Sri Lanka put down a Tamil rebellion there. The Congress Party won the election, and one of its members, P. V. Narasimha Rao, became prime minister. However, since the Congress Party did not win a majority of seats, Mr. Rao had to form a coalition government to run the country. The government has made some progress in boosting India's economy by creating more of a free-market system. In political matters, it has searched for ways to end critical domestic problems as well as to mend relations with neighboring nations.

6. By 1996 Rao's Congress Party, dominant for more than 40 years, had proven unable to govern effectively. After two years of a chaotic coalition, the Bharatiya Janata Party (BJP), promoting conservative social and economic ideas and nationalism, won election to power. Atal Behari Vajpayee, the new prime minister, began his term in office by flexing India's military muscle. In 1998, India conducted nuclear tests, shocking and surprising the world. Vajpayee's popularity and the BJP's prestige rose meteorically, even though India received immense criticism and a decline in foreign investment and trade occurred. His government also fostered modernization of and spending on defense and introduced many important economic reforms, encouraging the private sector and foreign investment. Early in the new century these reforms helped to accelerate GDP growth at record levels. The modernization of public and industrial infrastructures, job creation, and a vigorous high-tech industry raised India's international profile and prestige. Good crop harvests, expanded irrigation and housing programs, and strong industrial expansion increased the confidence of Indians and outside investors alike.

Not all activities of the BJP administration were deemed positive. Vajpayee and his government angered many unionized workers groups and public employees with an aggressive campaign of privatization of government corporations. The BJP was also accused of "Hinduizing" the official state educational system and curriculum. The murder of Christian missionaries by Hindu fundamentalists seemed to some to signal government laxness on the issue of religious extremism. In 2001 communal violence between Hindus and Muslims killed thousands over the issue of a holy place in Northern India. Incriminating videos of BJP officials and Army officers accepting bribes from journalists posing as agents and businessmen caused further criticism. After a terrorist attack on the Parliament building in Delhi, Parliament passed the Prevention of Terrorism Act, allowing police and security forces extraordinary powers to detain and question suspects for indefinite periods and expanding government authority over freedom of speech, assembly, and other fundamental liberties. Human rights activists, minority rights groups, the Congress Party, and others strongly attacked it as a rash, discriminatory, totalitarian law.

7. In India's 2004 elections the BJP was ousted by a comeback of both the Congress Party and its Gandhi "dynasty" under the leadership of the Italian-born widow of former Indian Prime Minister Rajiv Gandhi. Sonia Gandhi, however, declined the prime ministership, instead, asking former Finance Minister Manmohan Singh to lead the new government. As a rather low-key politician, Singh's image was "squeaky clean" and he was a widely respected economist. He has been credited by many with overseeing the beginnings of India's early 1990s economic liberalization that averted a major financial crisis.

In 2007 India celebrated the sixtieth anniversary of its independence from Britain. That same year India experienced its highest ever economic growth rate, evidence of its role as an emerging productive and commercial power. The Singh government, reelected in 2009, continued to pursue globalization of the economy, promoting India's vast labor force as a tool for increasing production of export goods to help relieve the country's widespread poverty. Grass roots efforts included the building of numerous new higher-educational institutions in the technical and management sectors, establishment of extensive rural health and employment initiatives, and providing broadened opportunities for "disadvantaged classes" such as untouchables (officially referred to as Scheduled Castes).

Mr. Singh pursued an aggressively positive foreign policy, exchanging visits with leaders of China, Afghanistan, and the United States in addition to actively participating in and frequently serving in informal leadership roles in international economic summit meetings.

## Political Structure in Pakistan and Bangladesh

Although Pakistan today can be described as a parliamentary democracy with a constitution, its first years after partition were very unstable. Under British rule, the Muslims had had very little experience in politics. Therefore, it is not surprising to find frequent instances of divisiveness and "strong-man" rule in Pakistan since independence in 1947.

Mohammed Ali Jinnah's death in 1948 was a severe blow to the young nation. The ineffective political struggles for power by civilians ended when the military suspended the constitution in 1958 and declared martial law. General Mohammed Ayub Khan ruled the country until 1969. Another example of dictatorial rule by the military occurred in 1977, when General Mohammed Zia took power away from the civilian-elected prime minister, Zulfikar Ali Bhutto. General Zia's rule ended with his death in a plane crash in August 1988. In that year, voters put into power the Pakistan People's Party and its leader, Benazir Bhutto. As the daughter of a former prime minister, Ms. Bhutto became the second woman to head a government in the subcontinent and the only woman ever to govern a Muslim nation. In August 1990 the president of Pakistan dismissed the government of Ms. Bhutto, accusing it of corruption and nepotism (favoring relatives for jobs). Ms. Bhutto claimed, however, that democratic reforms that she tried to institute had angered many army officials. It was they who supposedly caused her downfall.

In October 1990 Mian Nawaz Sharif became prime minister of Pakistan. He helped to boost the nation's economy but was unsuccessful in foreign dealings with India and the United States. Antigovernment demonstrations increased, leading to new elections in 1993, and Benazir Bhutto returned to power as prime minister. Her chief problems involve poverty, corruption, education, and Islamic fundamentalism. Eventually, Sharif returned to power. Sharif himself was deposed in a military coup in 1999. Leader of the coup and subsequently self-appointed president was Army General Pervez Musharraf. Considered a moderate leader by Western governments, Musharraf spoke of "enlightened moderation" and criticized the idea of the inevitability of a 'clash of civilizations' between the Islamic and Western worlds. After the 9/11 attacks and the American ouster of the Taliban in Afghanistan, he was forced to strike a balance between Islamic fundamentalists in Pakistan and Western governments pressuring him to aid in the "war on terror." Musharraf's power was legitimized by several electoral processes. He survived a number of assassination attempts and polls seemed to confirm his popularity among Pakistan's population. Criticism from international sources and domestic women's organizations has been directed against the government's perceived failure to deal with the issue of violence against women, particularly gang

**WORLD ISSUES**

Determination of Political and Economic Systems

GLOBAL CONCEPTS

**Power**

CONCEPTS GLOBAL

Era VII **THE WORLD SINCE 1945**

rapes and so-called honor killings of women and girls who do not adhere to strict social conventions. The Musharraf administration has failed to repeal the harsh Islamic penal code in which a woman's testimony is weighed at half that of a man.

The return of the popular Benazir Bhutto to Pakistan in 2007 created another period of political turmoil. In spite of death threats from radical Islamists she planned to campaign for the election scheduled for January 2008. Enthusiastic crowds and an attempted assassination greeted her arrival—she survived but over a hundred in the crowd were killed. A second suicide bomber's attempt succeeded, however, and fomented further political instability. Victory by her Pakistan Peoples Party in the 2008 election became her legacy, as her husband Asif Ali Zardari became president. The early years of Zardari's presidency proved turbulent—allegations of corruption and favoritism, the fragility of his ruling coalition, and the issuance of an arrest warrant for former president Musharraf, accused of involvement in the assassination of Mrs. Bhutto. Perhaps most damaging were criticisms that his administration did not prevent the American raid and capture of Osama bin Laden in 2011.

GLOBAL CONCEPTS

**Change**

CONCEPTS GLOBAL

Use of Geography

Bangladesh came into existence in 1971. Previously it had been the part of Pakistan known as East Pakistan. It was separated from the western part of Pakistan by 1,000 miles. Political, religious, and economic tensions led to a rebellion by East Pakistan in 1971. A war broke out in which India sided with the East Pakistanis. By December the rebellion was a success, and the nation of Bangladesh was declared.

Bangladesh's first prime minister, Sheik Mujibur Rahman, had led the struggle for independence. His inability to deal with food riots and a growing population as well as a growing perception of corruption were some of the reasons for his assassination. After his death, the country experienced several coups. One of these was led by Lt. General Hussain Mohammed Ershad, who ruled as a military dictator from 1982 to 1990. His resignation was brought on by a series of protests and demonstrations and was followed by elections in February, 1991. Begum Khaleda Zia became prime minister, as her BNP party (Bangladesh Nationalist Party) emerged victorious. A change in the nation's constitution gave her greater power than that of any former prime minister. After being out of office as a result of losing in 1996, the BNP won the 2001 election with a two-thirds majority and Khaleda Zia was once again sworn in as the prime minister. Her administration focused on education, introducing compulsory free primary education, free education for girls up to the tenth grade, stipends for female students, and food for education programs. Corruption issues dogged Mrs. Khaleda Zia's second term and continued after she stepped down in 2006. Both she and her opponent, Sheikh Hasina Wazed, daughter of Sheikh Mujibur Rahman and leader of the Awami League Party spent time in jail on corruption charges. In the 2008 election following their release, Mrs. Hasina became prime minister; her government focused on bringing to justice those involved in her father's 1975 assassination and trying war crimes cases from the 1971 independence struggle. The constant political turmoil of the first 41 years of Bangladesh's existence has had little bearing on the nation's many basic handicaps. There are enormous problems in governing a country plagued by overpopulation, severe natural diasters such as floods, and a declining world market for jute— the country's chief product.

## Current Political Issues in South Asia

**GEOGRAPHY**

**Use of Geography**

Separatist (secessionist) movements were the most dangerous political issues facing India and Sri Lanka in the 1990s. Different groups in both nations have grievances against the national governments and want to break away.

GLOBAL CONCEPTS

**Identity**

In India's Punjab state, Sikhs wanted to form their own nation— Khalistan. Resentment against the central government in New Delhi was fueled in 1984 when Mrs. Gandhi sent troops to attack Sikh militant separatists in the Golden Temple at Amritsar, the holiest shrine to Sikhs. Continued violence by both Sikh terrorists and government forces resulted in many deaths, with over 5,000 people killed in 1991. With an increased police and military presence by the Indian government and a diminished desire for independence, the Sikh rebellion seemed to be over by 1994.

CONCEPTS GLOBAL

GLOBAL CONCEPTS

**Diversity**

India was also concerned about growing unrest by the Muslim majority in the northern state of Kashmir. Kashmir is the larger part of an area that was taken over by India after the 1947 partition. However, Pakistan challenges India's claims to the state, especially as Muslims are in the majority. Early in 1990, efforts by the Jammu and the Kashmir Liberation Front to secede from India led to riots and violence. India claims that Pakistan has been behind these activities. India has also been bothered by antigovernment activity by tribal groups, such as the Assamese in the northeast. In the late 1990s, India and Pakistan exchanged artillery fire in the area. With the election of the Congress Party government of Manmohan Singh in 2004 a concerted reconstruction effort was begun in Kashmir with the

CONCEPTS GLOBAL

**GEOGRAPHY**

**Human Systems**

goal of achieving political and social stability. Despite this, infiltration of Islamic militants and a renewed terrorism campaign had continued to increase by 2009.

In Sri Lanka, the Tamil people, who are of Indian origin, want to have their own state. The Sri Lankan government has had difficulty in putting down terrorist actions by Tamils against members of the majority Sinhalese community. Many Sri Lankans think that people in South India are helping the terrorists. The Colombo government nevertheless welcomed the presence of Indian troops to help keep the peace from 1987 to 1989. The Indian Peace Keeping Force was withdrawn in 1990 after suffering heavy losses in battling the insurgents who referred to themselves as the Tamil Tigers. Their campaign against the Sri Lankan military and leadership as well as the Indian government was highlighted by the suicide-bomber assassinations of a Sri Lankan president and an Indian prime minister. Through the late 1990s government troops slowly pushed the Tigers into smaller areas in the north. A 2001 cease-fire and a period of sporadic negotiations ended with the election of a new Sri Lankan government in 2006, as it undertook a renewed campaign to eliminate the separatists. By 2009, the remnant of the Tamil Tigers either surrendered or fled the country, and by 2011, most of the former insurgents had been "reintegrated" into Sri Lankan society.

Communalism (ethnic tension between Hindus and Muslims) has been a frequent source of irritation in India. Part of this tension stems from the partition of the subcontinent in 1947. Much bloodshed broke out between the two groups, as some Muslims in India wished to migrate to Pakistan, while some Hindus in Pakistan wished to migrate to India. Religious differences between the two groups have been another source of friction. The worst case of communalism in recent years occurred in late 1992 and early 1993, and stemmed from an incident in Ayodhya. Located in north India, this site contained a mosque built in the 16th century by a Mogul ruler. Hindus have claimed, however, that the site is the birthplace of Lord Rama and that the mosque should be replaced with a Hindu temple. After unsuccessful marches on the site in 1989 and 1990, Hindu extremists tore down the mosque in 1992. This led to terrible Hindu-Muslim riots in Bombay and elsewhere in India. Within two months over 3,000 people had been killed and many homes destroyed. Massive violence again erupted relative to this issue in 2001 and 2002.

Relations between the two nations seemed to be easing at the time of the visit of Pakistani president Pervez Musharraf to

**WORLD ISSUES**

Terrorism

**WORLD ISSUES**

Politics and

Economic

Refugees

Delhi in 2005. Just over a year later, however, a three-day terrorist rampage of gun battles and bombings in the western Indian port of Mumbai was carried out by Islamist militants. Allegations that the perpetrators had received support from elements of the Pakistani security agency further soured relations.

Wars have been fought three times between India and Pakistan. While the two nations are now at peace, it remains to be seen whether they can permanently overcome problems over borders, distrust, communalism, and nuclear arms.

The growth and testing of nuclear weapons by both India and Pakistan in 1999 made for a very tense situation. Each nation felt it had to maintain a strong military stance. Shortly thereafter, the two nations initiated a peace process to permanently resolve the dispute over Kashmir and other conflicts, symbolized by the opening of a first-ever bus service between the Indian capital of Delhi and Lahore in Eastern Pakistan. The biggest challenge to this process occurred nearly immediately when thousands of terrorists and Pakistani soldiers infiltrated the Kashmir Valley, capturing control of border posts. Indian military units rushed into Kashmir, and after the brief but bloody "Kargil War" things returned to the previous state of constant tension. Airplane hijackings, an attack on India's Parliament building by alleged Pakistani militants, and military buildups and violence along the borders contrasted with a visit to the Indian capital by Pakistan's president Musharraf and other exchanges of civil and religious leaders as the two nations continued their fractious relationship.

During the Cold War between the United States and the Soviet Union, India tried to follow a policy of nonalignment. In doing so, India hoped to establish itself as a leader of the so-called Third World nations. This policy has come into question, however, since India fought a war with China over a border dispute and had been more friendly toward the former Soviet Union than toward the United States. India was not as alarmed as was Pakistan during 1979–1989, when Russian soldiers were fighting rebels in Afghanistan. Today, however, with the Soviet Union gone, India realizes the importance of establishing better relations with the United States.

The history of South Asia has been carved by its native inhabitants as well as by outsiders. The British dream of having the colony of India become one united nation upon independence did not materialize. The internal (national) and external (international) problems facing South Asian nations will take time to overcome. It should be remembered, nevertheless, that they have done much to improve themselves since independence.

**GEOGRAPHY**

Use of Geography

## SOUTHEAST ASIA

Nationalistic, anticolonial movements began in Southeast Asia in the 19th century and gained strength after World War II. The war was of importance for these nationalistic movements for several reasons: (1) Between 1942 and 1945, the European colonial powers lost much of their territorial control to the Japanese. (2) The Japanese, who took over the colonies, were hated as much as the European colonial powers, and the Southeast Asian people rose up to fight for independence. (3) At the war's end, some of the former European colonial powers took back control of their colonies, but they were weary and drained from the war. They sought to comply with the aims of the United Nations charter, and therefore were willing to grant independence. (4) Other colonial powers who took back control of their former colonies were unwilling to grant independence, and they were confronted by native leaders who had fought against the Japanese.

A peaceful transition to independence occurred in these nations: Myanmar (then Burma), Malaysia, Singapore, and Brunei—from England; the Philippines—from the United States. (The United States gained control from Spain in 1898, after the Spanish-American War.)

Bloody transitions to independence occurred in Indonesia, Cambodia, Laos, and North and South Vietnam. Indonesia, under the nationalist leader Ahmed Sukarno, fought against the Dutch from 1945 to 1949. Cambodia, Laos, and North and South Vietnam were created in 1954, after these nations fought the French for eight years. The major forces defeating France were the Vietnamese Communists, led by Ho Chi Minh. After the French defeat in the battle at Dien Bien Phu, the Geneva Accords were signed. They brought the war to an end and provided for French withdrawal from Indochina.

In the early 1960s fighting broke out in South Vietnam, as North Vietnam attempted to establish one unified nation of Vietnam. Fighting against the South Vietnamese government were the Viet Cong (South Vietnamese Communists) and ultimately the army of North Vietnam. The Viet Cong and North Vietnamese received material assistance from China and the Soviet Union. South Vietnam received help from the United States in the form of material as well as over 500,000 combat troops. In 1973 President Richard Nixon withdrew U.S. forces in the hope that both North and South Vietnam could work out their differences peacefully. The South Vietnamese government, under President Nguyen Van Thieu, grew weak and very unpopular.

**WORLD ISSUES**

War
and
Peace

**GEOGRAPHY**

Use of Geography

**WORLD ISSUES**

Determination
of Political
and Economic
Systems

**GEOGRAPHY**

Use of Geography

**WORLD ISSUES**

War
and
Peace

Fighting resumed, resulting in a North Vietnamese takeover in 1975 and the proclamation in 1976 of a united country. Hanoi became the country's capital, while Saigon, the former capital of South Vietnam, had its name changed to Ho Chi Minh City.

## Independence Period (1963–the Present)

The political structures that have evolved since independence reflect the varied backgrounds of the nations in Southeast Asia. Therefore, it is not surprising to find different forms of government.

| Nation | Form of Government | Current Leader* |
|---|---|---|
| Brunei | Monarchy | Sultan Sir Bolkiah Hassanal |
| Cambodia | Monarchy | King Norodom Sihamoni |
| Indonesia | Military government, republic | President Susilo Bambang Yudhoyono |
| Laos | Communist dictatorship | President General Khamtai Siphadon |
| Malaysia | Constitutional monarchy | Prime Minister Najib Razak |
| Myanmar (Burma) | Military dictatorship | President Thein Sein |
| Philippines | Federal republic | President Benigno Aquino III |
| Singapore | Parliamentary government | Prime Minister Lee Hsien Loong |
| Thailand | Constitutional monarchy | Prime Minister Niwattamrong Boonsungpaisan |
| Vietnam | Communist state | President Truong Tan Sang |

*Given the instability in Southeast Asian politics, these leaders may hold office only for a short time. Each was his nation's leader in 2015.

## Key Issues Since Independence

Local versus central control is a problem in Myanmar, also called Burma, where local tribal groups (Karens) in rural remote areas refuse to obey decisions of the national government in Yangon (Rangoon). In the 1990 elections, Aung San Suu Kyi and her National League for Democracy Party emerged as victors. However, these results were nullified by the military leaders of the State Law and Order Restoration Council (SLORC). Although Aung San Suu Kyi was awarded the 1991 Nobel Peace Prize, she was placed under house arrest, and has been in and out of detention since.

GLOBAL CONCEPTS

**Human Rights**

CONCEPTS GLOBAL

The military junta has exercised a restrictive domestic control and kept the nation isolated internationally in spite of widespread prodemocracy demonstrations, ethnic unrest, and occasional violence. In response to this and the international attention bestowed upon Suu Kyi's peaceful opposition, the regime secretly relocated the government from the traditional capital of Rangoon (or Yangon) to an interior isolated mountain compound. Attempts at reform resulted primarily in increased military control and limitations on political parties. Mismanagement of foreign aid following a destructive 2008 cyclone, continued detention of political prisoners, lack of attention to a rampant AIDS epidemic, closed-down universities—these seemed to be the chief "accomplishments" of a military regime funded and empowered by its control of the lucrative heroin trade.

Sustained diplomatic pressure from a variety of nations—Asian as well as Western—led Myanmar's military leaders to relax political restrictions and plan for elections to be held in late 2010. Though not permitted to participate as a candidate, Suu Kyi was released from detention shortly afterward and in the following months conferred with several prominant world leaders, including American secretary of state Hillary Clinton. A special parliamentary election scheduled for April 2012 was to include candidates from Suu Kyi's political party, the National Democracy League, with Suu Kyi herself registered as a candidate.

**GEOGRAPHY**

**Human Systems**

GLOBAL
CONCEPTS
**Political Systems**
CONCEPTS
GLOBAL

Civil war and invasions have plagued Cambodia since Prince Norodom Sihanouk was overthrown in 1970. The military rulers who took over were unable to defeat the Khmer Rouge, a communist force backed by Vietnam. By 1976 the Khmer Rouge, under its leader Pol Pot, controlled the nation and changed the official name to Kampuchea. (However, the country today is commonly referred to as Cambodia.) The Pol Pot government proved to be harsh and genocidal, killing thousands of people. It tried to impose a drastic social and economic restructure of society between 1975 and 1978. Its actions were the basis for a feature movie titled *The Killing Fields*. The Pol Pot government angered Vietnam, which had long wished to take over the territory. (Historically, the people of Kampuchea and Vietnam have been enemies.) With Soviet encouragement and material aid, Vietnam conquered Cambodia in 1978 and installed a government headed by a native figure, Hun Sen. This government faced a rebellion by Khmer Rouge forces, backed by China. With Vietnamese forces withdrawing in 1989, a coalition government was established that sought to bring together the Khmer Rouge and other warring groups.

A UN-supervised ceasefire agreement was signed in 1991, providing for a UN peacekeeping force and UN-sponsored elections. The elections, held in May 1993, produced a 120-member National Assembly, which promptly drew up a new constitution and provided for the return of Norodom Sihanouk as king. In September 1993, Sihanouk ascended to the throne in an elaborate ceremony. His new government was immediately recognized by the United States. His biggest political problem has been trying to put down the armed resistance of the Khmer Rouge. Although they were a party to the 1991 agreement, the Khmer Rouge boycotted the 1993 elections and have been upset with some of Sihanouk's political actions since he became king. Sihanouk abdicated in 2004 and was replaced by his son Norodom Sihamoni. Trials of former Khmer Rouge leaders commenced in 2006 and ongoing tensions between Cambodia and Thailand regarding control of an ancient Hindu temple complex resulted in it being declared a World Heritage site in 2008. A disputed 2009 election extended the rule of the Cambodia People's Party led by Prime Minister Hun Sen.

Instability and corruption are features in many parts of Southeast Asia. However, they erupted into a striking change of government in the Philippines in 1986. Ferdinand Marcos, who had ruled with strong military backing since 1965, was an unpopular ruler who enriched himself and did little to help the masses of people. Widespread demonstrations, a controversial election, and a declining military enabled Corazon Aquino to come to power in 1986, as Marcos fled into exile. He died in 1989, while in Hawaii. As president from 1986 to 1992, Mrs. Aquino was unsuccessful in dealing with problems concerning hostility from Communist and Muslim groups, corruption in government, and a declining economy. A significant foreign policy decision of her government was to refuse to renew the lease on the naval base at Subic Bay. She did not run for reelection in 1992. Fidel Ramos was the winner in that election, decisively defeating former Filipino first lady Imelda Marcos. During his administration, Ramos began implementing economic reforms intended to open up the once-closed national economy, encourage private enterprise, invite more foreign and domestic investment, and reduce corruption. However, Ramos was himself accused of corruption, and when he proposed amendment of the constitution to allow him to run for a second term, voters rejected him in favor of Joseph Estrada. He, too, was accused of corruption, and impeachment proceedings were initiated. When supporters attempted to undermine the process, the armed forces threw their support to Vice President Gloria Macapagal-Arroyo, daughter of a former president. Despite protests and attempted rebellions questioning the legitimacy of her ascension to the presidency and charges of corruption against her husband, she was elected to a new term in 2004.

GLOBAL CONCEPTS

**Political Systems**

CONCEPTS GLOBAL

**GEOGRAPHY**

**Human Systems**

Concerns about election rigging quickly led to an attempt at impeachment. In 2005 renewed Islamic militancy wracked areas of the southern islands. A coup plot and resultant state emergency in 2006 resulted in the deaths of several hundred political activists allegedly killed by the military. With Mrs. Macapagal-Arroyo constitutionally barred from another term, another "dynastic inheritor" was victorious in the election of 2010: Benigno Aquino III, son of Corazon, and the fourth generation of his family to hold high office under the banner of the Liberal Party assumed the presidency.

There are other tensions that have existed in the region in the post-independence period. They include:

1. Indonesia has had disagreements with Malaysia. It also had riots that caused the death of many Chinese in 1965 in the midst of a strong anticommunist policy and scattered anti-Chinese prejudice. Indonesia has been condemned for its human rights violations, based upon its actions in dealing with protests in East Timor. Political activism in 1999 in East Timor resulted in changes for the better. East Timor, after bloodshed and a vote, was granted independence. In addition, the end of Indonesian President Suharto's one man rule was seen as a welcome sign. An election in 1999 was peaceful, with the selection of a new president, Wahid. Under Wahid and the short administration of his predecessor, Habibie, a process of democratic reform was begun. This continued, in fits and starts, following the 2001 election of Indonesia's first woman president, Megawati. Daughter of former strong man Sukarno (some media call her "Sukarnoputri," indicating that aspect of her status), she appeared to see her role mainly as a symbol of national unity. Former military reformer Susilo Bambang Yudhoyono's reputation for integrity, strong personality appeal, and excellent communication skills enabled him to replace Megawati in the election of 2004. Known as the "thinking general" and popular for his investigation of the 2002 extremist bombing in Bali, he faced further Islamist issues, separatist movements in Aceh to the west and Papua–New Guinea to the east, as well as problems caused by the 2004 tsunami in Sumatra. As a result of its position on the Pacific Rim's tectonically active "Ring of Fire," Indonesia suffered through destructive earthquakes in 2005 and 2007. Heavy rains causing massive flooding displaced over 400,000 people in 2007. The controversy-free presidential election of 2009 returned Yudhoyono to the office, solidifying Indonesia's reputation as a stable democracy. The nation also increased its leadership role in regional and global affairs, and economic growth continued to reduce poverty levels and limit

inflation. Slow-paced anticorruption political reform and increasing religiously motivated violence appeared to be Yudoyono's most trying challenges.

2. Chinese and Vietnamese antagonism surfaced in 1979 with a short-lived border war. Vietnam's withdrawal from Cambodia in 1989 after the ousting of the violent Khmer Rouge soothed Chinese-Vietnamese relations. But there have been renewed tensions over control of small island groups in the South China Sea. But on this and other issues, relations between the two countries have improved significantly in recent years. The two countries are bound by culture—and increasingly by economics. Trade is growing rapidly, and Vietnam has become a popular vacation spot for Chinese tourists. And the Vietnamese Communist Party looks to the Chinese Communist Party as a model for opening up its economy while maintaining tight control over politics.

3. Thailand has been worried about the spread of communism from Vietnam, as well as the problem of coping with refugees from the fighting in Cambodia. Instability caused by corruption and political infighting led to a military-dominated government from 1990 to 1992. In October 1992 a civilian-led government was installed in Thailand for the first time in sixty years. Subsequent elections resulted in several coalition governments emphasizing prudent economic management and political reforms. A new 1997 constitution mandated political change. In the January 2001 elections, telecommunications multimillionaire Thaksin Shinawatra and his Thai Rak Thai Party (TRT) won an overwhelming victory on a populist platform of economic growth and development. After winning an unprecedented second term in 2005, Shinawatra has promised to eradicate poverty by spending $60 billion on new infrastructure and continuing privatization of state firms despite strong opposition from unions. The TRT has also advocated low-interest loans and subsidized health care for Thailand's rural poor. A massive tax-free stock sale of a business in 2006 by family members resulted in antigovernment protests and eventually charges of tax evasion against Shinawatra's wife and children. Removed by a military coup and subject to government-imposed taxes, fines, asset seizure, and arrest, the family fled into exile. Popular opposition to the replacement government led to street protests and a "Million Person March" in 2010; government troops cracked down violently on the demonstrators in what the Thai media labeled "Cruel April" followed by "Savage May." When the military finally permitted elections in 2011, the populist Pheu Thia Party's challenge to the established power elite legitimized the

**WORLD ISSUES**

Political and
Economic
Refugees

earlier protests. Ironically, the new prime minister was Yingluck Shinawatra, younger sister of the ousted former leader. Suspicion that she would be a mere puppet of her exiled brother seemed likely to be the most significant roadblock to her possible success in uniting the fractious elements of Thai society. Mrs. Shinawatra's administration had to cope with Islamic fundamentalism among the Muslim minority in the southwest, which has created antigovernment violence. In recent years, it has been concerned with an alarming spread of HIV/AIDS among the urban population.

4. Singapore, which is inhabited mostly by Chinese, strives to maintain good relations with its two large Malay-dominated neighbors, Indonesia and Malaysia. (The Malays are the majority ethnic groups in these nations.)

## Developments in Vietnam into the 21st Century

Severe economic conditions in Vietnam brought about significant changes in government policy. (1) Many years of fighting within and without the country had drained the treasury. (2) The collapse of the Soviet Union in 1991 led to a drastic reduction in the foreign aid that had long maintained the Vietnamese economy. (3) Centralized planning and a refusal to make needed changes hurt productivity.

High-level contacts with the United States were begun in 1990, stemming mostly from the economic factors described above. Americans have agreed to talks based upon Vietnam's willingness to seek peace with its neighbors and to account more fully for U.S. MIA/POWs (missing-in-action/prisoner-of-war servicemen and women). In 1993 and 1994 American businesspeople and politicians visited Vietnam; normalizing relations between the two former enemies eventually occurred.

Since 2001, Vietnamese authorities have committed to economic liberalization and enacted structural reforms needed to modernize the economy. The goal is to produce more competitive, export-driven industries, making the nation a more integrated member of the international economic community. Vietnam's membership in the ASEAN Free Trade Area (AFTA) and entry into the U.S.-Vietnam Bilateral Trade in December 2001 have led to even more rapid changes in Vietnam's trade and economic regime. Vietnam's exports to the United States doubled in 2002 and again in 2003.

Like that of many nations ruled by a single political party, Vietnam's government faced the challenge of maintaining power in an age of dynamic expansion of communication and information technology. A more open system offered many of the country's citizens an escape from the cycle of poverty, the economy as a whole to continue its rapid growth, and the newly expanded urban middle class to experience a rise in living standards. These trends were somewhat slowed by the global economic downturn of the years after 2008 that resulted in an escalating rate of inflation. Internationally, Vietnam successfully served a term on the UN Security Council and acted as chair nation of ASEAN beginning in 2010.

# Part F: East Asia

## SECTION 1: CHINA

### Long March of the Communist Forces

After Chiang's purge of the Communists in 1927, Mao Zedong, one of the founders of the Chinese Communist Party in 1921, escaped to southeastern China. Mao built up a following among the peasants and organized a guerrilla force called the Red Army.

**Use of Geography**

In 1931, the same year Japan conquered Manchuria, Chiang decided to eliminate the Communists. Finally, in 1934 Chiang's Nationalist Army had the Communists surrounded and blockaded. However, Mao organized his followers, broke through the Nationalist lines, and the Communists began the "Long March." Approximately 100,000 Communists began a 5,000- to 6,000-mile march across some of the most rugged terrain in China. Twenty thousand reached northern China in 1935.

### The Communist Victory

With the Japanese attack in 1937, both the Communists and Nationalists found themselves resisting further Japanese aggression. From 1940 on, however, as the Nationalists fought the Japanese, the Communists extended their influence in China. Mao concentrated on building up the Red Army and extending its control. In the areas of China under Communist control, economic and social reforms were introduced. Land rentals were reduced and education programs were begun.

When World War II ended, both the Nationalists and Communists tried to regain control of the areas in eastern China that had been under Japanese control.

In 1947 the Communists and Nationalists battled for control of Manchuria. After the Communists won, they began to push the Nationalists southward. In 1949 the Nationalists could no longer hold the country, and they fled to Taiwan, an island off the coast of mainland China. They established a government called the Republic of China, with Chiang Kai-shek as president, and claimed that the mainland, which they considered part of their country, was in rebellion.

**Use of Geography**

544

On October 1, 1949, the Communists established the People's Republic of China, with Mao Zedong as the chairman of the Chinese Communist Party and Zhou Enlai (Chou En-lai) as premier. The capital was established at Peiping, and the city was renamed Peking (now Beijing).

GLOBAL
CONCEPTS
**Change**
CONCEPTS
GLOBAL

## Why the Nationalists Lost the Civil War

One of the most important reasons the Nationalists lost the war was that the Communists were supported by the peasants. When the Nationalists ruled, they did little to relieve the burden of the Chinese peasants (80 percent of the population). Mao and the Communists promised an extensive program of land reform and reduced land rents in the areas under their control.

**GEOGRAPHY**

**Human Systems**

The Communist forces did little actual fighting against the Japanese during World War II. Instead, they used the war to spread their influence throughout northern and central China. When the war ended, the Communist forces were strong, fresh, and ready. The Nationalist Army, on the other hand, was war-weary and demoralized. The Communist leaders who survived the Long March had suffered with their people and were seen as popular folk heroes. They were hardened and disciplined. Moreover, the leaders of the Communists—Mao Zedong, Zhu De (Chu Teh), and Zhou En-lai—knew how to appeal to the Chinese people, who were tired of inflation, war, and corruption and blamed Chiang and the Nationalists.

GLOBAL
CONCEPTS
**Empathy**
CONCEPTS
GLOBAL

## Goals of the People's Republic of China in 1949

The three major goals of the Communists in 1949 were to reestablish China's world prominence, to push economic development, and to improve life for the Chinese people. To reestablish their prominence, the Chinese had to control China again and remove the foreign imperialists. Industries owned and operated by foreigners were nationalized, Christianity was banned, and Christian missionaries were expelled from China. The Communists brought under Chinese control border areas that had at one time been part of the Chinese empire or tributary states. Such areas included Xinjiang (Sinkiang), Manchuria, Inner Mongolia, and Xizang (Tibet).

To achieve world prominence, the Communists realized that China must be capable of competing with the Western powers both economically and militarily. Consequently, their early economic goal was to industrialize China as rapidly as possible. They employed five-year plans, which stressed industrial production at the expense of agriculture.

**GEOGRAPHY**

**Human Systems**

The most widespread plan was called The Great Leap Forward. Initiated by Mao in 1959, it was designed mainly to have farms become more productive. The key feature was the establishment of communes, groups of people who lived and worked together. The land they worked on was not owned by them, as Mao's form of communism did not allow for any private ownership of property. Title to the land was held by the commune, whose Communist Party members made all the key economic decisions. The commune also regulated peoples' social lives with regard to such issues as marriage, raising children, housing, and so on. The results of all these efforts were disastrous. Millions died of famine because of poor planning, unrealistic regulations, peasant resistance, and drought. For added information on Mao's economic policies and the contrasting ones of his successor, Deng Xiaoping, see Era I, Part C, Section 3, page 66.

GLOBAL
CONCEPTS
**Political Systems**
CONCEPTS
GLOBAL

To achieve their goals, the Communists had to transform Chinese society and win the loyalty of the Chinese people. To suppress Confucianism and turn the Chinese into supporters of the Communist state, the Communists were determined to replace family loyalty with loyalty to the state and party. The Communists used the education system to do this. The legal system was used to improve the position of women. New marriage laws prevented families from forcing girls to accept arranged marriages. Divorce laws gave women equal rights. Women were employed in all occupations. The Communists also undertook mass campaigns to improve health and sanitation. Rural "doctors" were trained in the combined use of traditional Chinese medicine and Western medical practices.

GLOBAL
CONCEPTS
**Power**
CONCEPTS
GLOBAL

A thought-reform movement was established to eradicate the influence of traditional Chinese ideas and replace them with socialist ideology and the cult of Maoism. Former owners of industries, the intelligentsia, businesspeople, and others were subjected to stringent retraining sessions and indoctrinated in socialist ideology. Mao's "Red Book"—*The Thought of Mao Zedong*—became required reading in schools, in factory study sessions, peasant study sessions, and so on.

## The Cultural Revolution

In the late 1950s, Mao's almost complete control of events in China was challenged for the first time. Conservative party leaders questioned Mao's revolutionary domestic and foreign policies. Mao's opponents, called reactionaries or counter-revolutionaries, were led by Liu Shaoqi (Liu Hsao Ch'i). In 1965 their differences became an actual power struggle. Because the conflict was over economic, educational, scientific, political, and social programs, it became known as the Cultural Revolution.

Mao closed the schools and sent high school and college students into the streets to rout out reactionaries. The students, who were known as Red Guards, attacked, intimidated, and humiliated Mao's opponents and anyone they suspected of being reactionary or influenced by Western ideas. They plunged China into chaos. Factories closed, industrial production fell, and transportation facilities were disrupted. Estimates of the number of people who died ran into the hundreds of thousands. The chaos eventually led to a military crackdown, and by 1969 the Cultural Revolution was over. Mao appeared to have won the struggle.

GLOBAL
CONCEPTS
**Human Rights**
CONCEPTS
GLOBAL

Era VII **THE WORLD SINCE 1945**

## Policies Pursued Since Mao's Death

Following the Cultural Revolution, a power struggle emerged between the moderates led by Zhou En-lai, premier of the People's Republic since 1949, and the radicals, led by Jiang Qing (Chiang Ch'ing), Mao's wife.

After Mao's death in 1976, Jiang Qing and three of her strongest allies, who became known as the Gang of Four, tried to take power. However, they were arrested, charged with plotting to seize power, as well as crimes against the people, and the party during the Cultural Revolution. In 1980 they were tried. All four were found guilty, and Jiang was given a death penalty (which was commuted to life imprisonment in 1983). One of the purposes of the trial was to punish the Gang of Four for the way they treated members of the Chinese leadership during the Cultural Revolution. Another was to decrease the esteem in which Mao was held by the Chinese people. Deng Xiaoping, the real ruler of China after Mao's death, felt it was necessary to remove the cult of Mao to effectively carry out his policies. Mao's support for the Gang of Four was revealed during the trial, and it showed the Chinese people that Mao's policies in his old age were in error.

**GEOGRAPHY**

**Use of Geography**

## United States-China Relations, 1949 to 2000

In 1949 the United States refused to recognize the People's Republic of China as the legitimate government of China. Instead, it recognized the Nationalist Chinese government on Taiwan, under the leadership of Chiang Kai-shek. In 1950 the Communists seized U.S. consular buildings in China, and all direct diplomatic ties were broken off.

The Korean War broke out in June 1950 when North Korean troops invaded South Korea. UN forces were rushed to Korea to support the South Koreans. By autumn of 1950,

United Nations and South Korean forces had pushed north to the Yalu River, the boundary between North Korea and China. Fearing an invasion of Manchuria, Mao sent Chinese forces across the Yalu, and fighting raged until 1953, when an armistice was finally signed reestablishing the Korean border along the 38th parallel. United States troops fought under the UN command.

As a result of the Korean War, the United States recognized Nationalist China (Taiwan) as the legitimate government of all China and resisted all attempts to seat representatives of the Chinese Communist government in the United Nations. The Taiwan policy of the United States was considered by Mao as another humiliating blow from a Western imperialist power.

In October 1971 the United States ended its objection to seating the People's Republic in the UN, arguing instead that both Chinas should be seated. However, Communist China was seated and Nationalist China was expelled from the world organization in 1971. The People's Republic of China was given the permanent seat on the UN Security Council previously held by Taiwan.

Another region in Asia that caused friction between the United States and Communist China was Vietnam. When the Communists began to make inroads in South Vietnam through the activities of guerrillas known as Viet Cong, the United States increased its military aid and sent military advisers. In 1965 the United States began to send combat forces to Vietnam. The Viet Cong were assisted and reinforced by the North Vietnamese, who in turn received aid from the former Soviet Union and Communist China. China objected strenuously to the U.S. role in Vietnam and its invasions of Cambodia and Laos.

In 1971 relations between the United States and Communist China improved when an American Ping-Pong team was invited to China. This was the first time in over twenty years that an American group had been invited to China. In 1972 President Richard Nixon made a state trip to China, and the two nations agreed to reciprocal contact and exchange, and they also agreed to expand trade. In 1973 missions of the two nations were established, and in January 1979 full diplomatic relations were established.

Taiwan continues to be an area of discord. The United States withdrew its diplomatic representation from Taiwan when it recognized the People's Republic. However, the United States still maintains unofficial representation in Taiwan through an American Institute. Both Taiwan and China consider Taiwan a part of China. Their disagreement is over who actually should control China. In recent years, the relationship between the two countries has seen some improvement, in spite of the fact that Taiwan refuses to consider any suggestions from China concerning reunification.

Trade relations between the United States and China were expanded considerably after diplomatic recognition in the 1970s. In fact, Japan and the United States rank as China's top two trading partners. Diplomatic and trade relations between the United States and China were strained by the government's brutal crackdown on the democracy demonstrators in Tiananmen Square in 1989. The United States objected to both the actual crackdown and the arrest and subsequent incarceration of thousands of young Chinese. China now enjoys most favored nation (MFN) status with the United States. The Clinton administration had considered tying the renewal of that status to the question of human rights abuses in China. The United States also had demanded that China stop exporting goods produced by prison inmates who were used as forced labor, that an agreement of some sort be reached concerning political prisoners, and that the Chinese adhere to the UN Universal Declaration of Human Rights, among other things. Although China made only some minor concessions in these areas, President Clinton decided to renew China's MFN status. He felt that the continuation of this status would help the American economy and would ultimately improve human rights conditions in China. It was also considered that China's cooperation is critical in dealing with North Korea and in the area of nuclear nonproliferation and in controlling the spread of nuclear weapons. Clinton's action in renewing MNF however was criticized by many U.S. congresspersons and Chinese human rights advocates. There are indications China has been selling nuclear weapons technology to some Third World nations. The United States has also voiced very strong objections to these actions.

In the spring of 1999, charges that the Chinese had not only spied at U.S. nuclear facilities, but that they had actually stolen U.S. technology secrets, came to light. The then Chinese leaders, Jiang Zemin, the president and general secretary of the Communist Party, and Zhu Rongji, the premier, both deny that the Chinese stole anything. Zhu Rongji visited the United States in the spring of 1999 to hold talks with President Clinton in an effort to improve trade relations and gain membership in the World Trade Organization (WTO). The talks were largely unsuccessful, though China did agree to drop bans on U.S. wheat and citrus. Other agreements on further trade concessions and on human rights could not be reached. In December of 1999, the island of

**GEOGRAPHY**

**Human Systems**

GLOBAL
CONCEPTS

**Human Rights**

CONCEPTS
GLOBAL

**GEOGRAPHY**

**Use of Geography**

**GEOGRAPHY**

**Human Systems**

Macao was returned to China from Portugal. In 2007 China exported many hazardous products, including pet products, toothpaste, tires, and toys. This brought attention to the lack of quality control in Chinese factories and the head of the food and drug committee was executed.

An earthquake in 2008 in Sichuan province revealed shoddy construction of schools and in a reaction harkening back to the days of the early Communist era, the Chinese who repeorted the poor construction were imprisoned. That same year over 300,000 babies were sickened by contaminated milk powder from China and six babies died. In 2008, Hu Jintao was elected president and Wen Jiabao was relected premier. That same year China hosted the Summer Olympics and put on a spectacular display for the world.

## Relations Between the People's Republic and the Third World

Communist China saw itself as the example of revolutionary change for the former colonies of Western powers and also as the leader of the Third World nations. It supported Marxist revolutions in Third World nations, provided technical and financial assistance, and set up cultural exchanges with nations in Africa and Asia.

## Sino-Soviet Relations

GEOGRAPHY

Human Systems

The Sino-Soviet Treaty of Friendship of 1950 seemed to indicate that a long-lasting supportive relationship between China and the Soviet Union had begun. The Soviet Union agreed to assist China against aggressive attacks and provide economic and military assistance. By 1960, however, the Soviet Union had cut off its assistance.

Reasons for the split between China and the Soviet Union included:

1. *Khrushchev's attacks on Stalin.* Mao was a great admirer of Stalin.

2. *Peaceful coexistence.* Khrushchev believed that through peaceful coexistence, the world's people would see the superiority of the communist system, and communism would spread worldwide. Mao believed war and revolution were necessary.

3. *Leadership.* The Soviet Union considered itself the leader of the world communist movement. Mao disputed its claim to leadership.

4. *Soviet support for India.* In 1962, when Indian and Chinese forces clashed over territory, the Soviet Union assisted India.

5. *Border disputes.* The Soviets hold territory in Central Asia and northeastern China that China claims. There have been occasional outbreaks of fighting between troops stationed on the borders.

6. *Afghanistan.* China objected to the Soviet invasion in 1979.

Mikhail Gorbachëv's trip to China in May 1989 was intended to normalize relations, but his visit was upstaged by the student rebellion in Tiananmen Square. In spite of all their differences, China and Russia signed a 20-year Friendship Treaty in 2001, pledging peaceful settlement of border disputes and coordination against threats of aggression from others.

## China's New Status in the Pacific

Chinese diplomatic relations with Japan were reestablished following President Nixon's trip to China in 1972. Since then, the two countries have signed trade agreements, and Japan has become one of China's largest trading partners. Japan imports China's agricultural products and petroleum, and China imports Japanese machinery and technology. Japan has given China millions of dollars in loans for development.

GLOBAL
CONCEPTS
**Interdependence**

CONCEPTS
GLOBAL

In 1984 Great Britain and China reached an agreement to return the island of Hong Kong to Chinese control in 1997 and that return, in fact, did take place on July 1 of that year. Hong Kong became a Special Administrative Region of China. Under the agreement reached in 1984 Hong Kong was to be allowed to maintain its capitalist system for 50 years. In 1996 Tung Chee Hwa was elected by a selection committee to be the first chief executive of Hong Kong. Restrictions have been imposed on demonstrations and voting rights. In July 2004 citizens of Hong Kong protested Beijing's refusal to allow greater freedom. Tung Chee Hwa resigned in 2005 and Donald Tsang was chosen to serve the rest of his term. In 2007 Tsang won a full 5-year term.

**GEOGRAPHY**

**Human Systems**

## China After Tiananmen

In the aftermath of the pro-democracy movement and the military crackdown in 1989, the Chinese government reverted to many policies that seemed to be a reminder of the more authoritarian times of Mao. There were more restrictions on the press, there were political study sessions for workers, films and music were banned, and so on. But these restrictions seem to be loosening again. It appears that the economic changes that the government deems necessary to maintain growth and prosperity cannot be achieved under the social and political restrictions that the hard-liners would like to impose.

GLOBAL
CONCEPTS
**Human Rights**

CONCEPTS
GLOBAL

**GEOGRAPHY**

**Human Systems**

# Developments in the 21st Century

On the domestic front, the most significant development has been the extraordinary growth of China's economy. China has become the most productive economic force in East Asia, outstripping Japan. China's admission into the World Trade Organization (WTO) in 2001 marked a vital milestone. Nevertheless, protests against this admission were held by several human rights and labor organizations throughout the world. In political terms, Hu Jintao has emerged as the overall head of the nation. He was named Communist Party General Secretary in 2002, elected president in 2003, and took over the top military post in 2004.

Other post-2000 domestic issues are as follows:

1. Several health trends have caused alarm throughout China. HIV/AIDS has been increasing at a terrible rate. In 2002, China suffered an epidemic of severe acute respiratory syndrome (SARS), and hundreds died as a result. In 2004–2005, an outbreak of avian bird flu virus worried medical officials. Thousands of birds and chickens were slaughtered in an effort to contain the contagion.

2. Space exploration was evidenced by a major achievement. In August 2003, China became the third nation, after the United States and Russia, to send a man into space.

3. Industrial disasters have accompanied China's economic advancement. These have been due mainly to inadequate regulation, corruption, and human error. Examples can be seen in a gas well explosion in South Central China that killed 233 people. A benzene runoff polluted a river near Harbin, in the north, in 2005, leaving millions without drinkable water for several days.

4. China's treatment of two large minority groups has raised issues of prejudicial and abusive treatment. Tibetans came under Chinese occupation in 1951, with a communist government being installed in 1953. The Buddhist religion was repressed, as 100,000 Tibetans fled to India with their spiritual leader, the Dalai Lama. Muslims living in the northwest, in Sinkiang, fear crackdowns on their rights and freedoms and have considered separating themselves from China.

In the area of international relations, the post-2000 period has been marked by these developments:

1. Relations with Russia have been improving. In November 2005, Russian President Vladimir Putin announced that Russia would build a pipeline carrying oil into China. Russia is the world's second largest oil exporter after Saudi Arabia. Russian trade with China was approaching record levels in 2006.

2. Chinese pride was bolstered in 2001 by two noteworthy international acts of recognition. China was admitted into the WTO and was awarded the Olympic Games for the year 2008.

3. China has taken a larger diplomatic role with regard to situations on the Korean peninsula. She has hosted talks and acted as an intermediary on issues relating to North Korea's nuclear weapons program.

In 2010 a series of school killings occurred in China. All of them involved middle-aged men. Nearly twenty people were killed and hundreds, mostly children, were injured. There appeared to be no connection between the attacks, and some surmised they were a product of too-rapid modernization and lack of mental heatlh care.

# REVIEW QUESTIONS

*Multiple Choice.* Select the letter of the answer that correctly completes each statement.

1. The unequal treaties were the result of a war fought against
   A. Japan
   B. Britain
   C. Russia
   D. Vietnam

2. Which of the following required a high degree of knowledge and education?
   A. the tribute system
   B. the civil service
   C. the foreign service
   D. the military

3. The Chinese considered foreigners to be barbarians. This attitude was an example of
   A. ethnocentrism
   B. cultural diffusion
   C. empathy
   D. interdependence

4. During the 19th century, Western nations were able to gain control over parts of China mainly because
   A. the Chinese had a strong tradition of nonviolence
   B. China lacked the military technology needed to stop these ventures
   C. China was promised aid for its industries
   D. the Chinese lacked a strong cultural identity

5. During the Communist Revolution in China, many farmers supported the Communists because they promised
   A. land reform
   B. a peace treaty with Japan
   C. a federal republic
   D. aid from the industrial nations

6. After gaining control of the Kuomintang (Nationalist Party), Chiang Kai-shek's most important goal in the 1920s was
   A. land reform to assist the peasants
   B. destruction of the Communists
   C. the invasion of Korea
   D. assisting Ho Chi Minh in overthrowing the French

7. Hong Kong
   A. is a British Crown Colony
   B. was returned to the Chinese in 1997
   C. has an economy based on agriculture
   D. was won by the Japanese in the Sino-Japanese War

8. The Communist victory in the Chinese Civil War was a result of all
   the following *except*
   A. the inability of the Nationalists to stabilize the economy
   B. the lack of U.S. aid to the Communists
   C. peasant dissatisfaction with the Nationalist regime
   D. the effective use of propaganda and guerrilla warfare by the
      Communists

9. A study of the history of China would reveal that
   A. there has always been strong central government in China
   B. until modern times a single dynasty ruled China
   C. periods of strong central government alternated with periods of
      internal disturbance, foreign invasion, and government corruption
   D. foreigners ruled China for far longer periods than native Chinese

10. During the early 1800s the relationship between China and the Western
    nations was strained because
    A. the Western nations did not wish to purchase Chinese goods
    B. China insisted it be dealt with through the tribute system
    C. the Western nations wished to purchase opium and the Chinese
       refused
    D. China wished to buy Western armaments and other manufactured
       goods and was rebuffed

11. A country with an unfavorable balance of trade
    A. exports goods of greater value than it imports
    B. imports goods of greater value than it exports
    C. exports natural resources and imports manufactured goods
    D. imports manufactured goods and exports textiles

12. The very existence of the Yuan Dynasty supports the fact that China's
    least effective geographic barrier was the
    A. Himalayan Mountains
    B. Great Wall
    C. Gobi Desert
    D. Tien Shan Mountains

13. Which form of government is most likely to suppress human rights?
    A. constitutional monarchy
    B. democratic republic
    C. parliamentary system
    D. totalitarian regime

14. The ethnocentric attitude of the Chinese
    A. resulted in a reluctance to adopt aspects of other cultures
    B. led to periods of internal strife during famine
    C. prevented the Chinese from expanding their territory
    D. caused student rebellions in the 1980s

15. China's earliest civilizations originated in the
    A. Tibetan Plateau
    B. region of Xinjiang
    C. Huanghe River Valley
    D. Canton delta region

16. The 19th century was China's Age of Humiliation for all the following reasons *except*
    A. China was conquered by the Mongols
    B. the unequal treaties
    C. China's defeat in the Opium War
    D. the granting of spheres of influence to Western nations

17. In the late 1880s Confucian scholars resisted government reform and economic change because
    A. the Empress Dowager wished to hand the reins of government to the peasants
    B. they feared it would erode their own political influence
    C. the Russians threatened to withdraw financial aid if the changes took place
    D. Japan had agreed to help them maintain an isolationist policy

18. During the Manchu Dynasty in China the tribute or tributary system
    A. required foreigners to bring gifts to the Chinese emperor and recognize China's superiority
    B. was used to build irrigation systems in the North China Plain
    C. allowed the Chinese to assimilate the culture of the Manchus
    D. granted extraterritorial rights to the European traders in Hong Kong

19. Sun Yat-sen's Three Principles of the People were designed to do all the following *except*
   A. rid China of foreign influence
   B. establish democratic government
   C. break up large estates and provide peasants with land
   D. bring all industry and mining under government monopoly

20. The Tang Dynasty was known as a Golden Age because of achievements in all the following areas *except*
   A. poetry
   B. porcelain
   C. printing
   D. armaments

# SECTION 2: JAPAN

## United States Occupation of Japan (1945–1952)

**Use of Geography**

The U.S. occupation of Japan led to the diffusion of some American ideas and practices into Japanese culture. United States armed forces, under the leadership of General Douglas MacArthur, the Supreme Commander of the Allied Powers (SCAP), occupied Japan from 1945 to 1952. Japan was stripped of its military conquests, and its territory was restricted to the four main islands. Its armed forces were disbanded and weapons factories were closed. Government and military leaders accused of war crimes were brought to trial, and those who had played a role in Japan's military expansion were removed from positions of power. The emperor renounced his divinity. Nationalistic organizations were banned. MacArthur had a new constitution written for Japan, which went into effect in 1947. It is one of the world's most democratic documents.

GLOBAL
CONCEPTS

**Change**

CONCEPTS
GLOBAL

The American occupation of Japan also brought a number of economic and social reforms. The zaibatsu were broken up; a land-reform program required landlords to sell land cheaply to their tenants; all titles of nobility were abolished; the legal authority of the head of the family over other family members was abolished; and compulsory education was extended for three more years.

## The Impact of the Atomic Bombs of 1945

Japan, the only nation in the world ever to have been attacked by nuclear weapons, is opposed to their development and stockpiling. Major demonstrations have occurred in Japan protesting American storage of missiles and the arrival of American nuclear submarines. Similarly, the Japanese protest the testing of nuclear weapons by all nations.

**Human Systems**

To allay Japanese fears, the United States-Japanese Mutual Security Pact was revised in 1960 to include a clause stating that the United States could not bring nuclear weapons into Japan without the knowledge of the Japanese government, nor could it use its forces based in Japan in military action without the approval of the Japanese government. Japan has developed the peaceful use of nuclear power, but many Japanese also protest the opening of nuclear power plants.

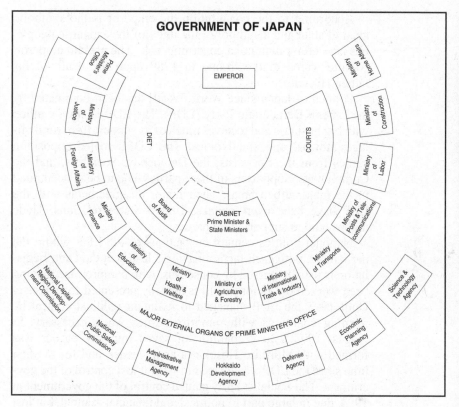

**GOVERNMENT OF JAPAN**

EMPEROR

DIET

COURTS

Prime Minister's Office

Ministry of Justice

Ministry of Foreign Affairs

Ministry of Finance

Ministry of Education

National Capital Region Development Commission

National Public Safety Commission

Administrative Management Agency

Hokkaido Development Agency

Board of Audit

CABINET
Prime Minister &
State Ministers

Ministry of Health & Welfare

Ministry of Agriculture & Forestry

Ministry of International Trade & Industry

Defense Agency

Ministry of Transports

Ministry of Posts & Tele-communications

Ministry of Home Affairs

Ministry of Construction

Ministry of Labor

Economic Planning Agency

Science & Technology Agency

MAJOR EXTERNAL ORGANS OF PRIME MINISTER'S OFFICE

# Democratic System of Government

The 1947 constitution created a parliamentary system with a two-house parliament called the National Diet. The lower house, the House of Representatives, is the more important. The prime minister is elected by the House and is responsible to it. The prime minister and his cabinet can be removed by a "no-confidence" vote, in which case elections will be held for a new house, which then elects a new prime minister. The constitution lists the rights of the Japanese people, which are much like the rights contained in the U.S. Bill of Rights but also include equal rights of women, collective bargaining, equal education, and so on. The right to vote was granted to all citizens over the age of twenty. One of the most well-known provisions of the constitution is Article IX, which renounces the use of war and the "maintenance of land, sea and air forces, as well as other war potential." It does allow the maintenance of defense forces or forces necessary to maintain internal peace.

GLOBAL CONCEPTS

**Political Systems**

CONCEPTS GLOBAL

GLOBAL CONCEPTS

**Human Rights**

CONCEPTS GLOBAL

GLOBAL CONCEPTS

**Citizenship**

CONCEPTS GLOBAL

According to the constitution the emperor is the symbolic head of state and a symbol of the unity of the Japanese people. His is a ceremonial, not a governing, role. The present emperor, Akihito, came to the throne in 1989 upon the death of his father, Hirohito.

Politics in Japan since World War II has been dominated by the Liberal Democratic Party (LDP). The LDP is closely allied with big business and receives much of its support from rural villages, towns, and small cities. The LDP's major opposition comes from the Socialists, the Democratic Socialists, and the Communists. Supporters of these parties tend to be concentrated in the major urban areas. Their major disagreements with the LDP have been over Japanese-United States relations. Trade unions tend to support these parties.

National politics centers on factions of the LDP within the parliament, with each faction having a leader in the Diet. Legislation is usually passed by consensus, with compromises having been worked out before a bill is actually presented for passage. Until 1993 the LDP managed to maintain political control by forming coalitions with minority parties when necessary. In August 1993 a new coalition of seven minority parties was formed with Morihiro Hosokawa as its leader, and for the first time since the LDP was formed in 1955 it lost control of the government. The Socialist Party gained control of the government in 1994, due in large part to political and financial scandal, but lost power to the LDP in 1996.

## Present Military Status of Japan

In spite of the provisions of Article IX of the constitution, Japan does maintain forces for the defense of the Japanese islands. These self-defense forces originated in 1950 when U.S. occupation forces were withdrawn from Japan. They were limited to 250,000 men, and service was voluntary. Japan has sent troops into other areas in nonmilitary roles.

## Treaty of Mutual Cooperation and Security Between the United States and Japan

**GEOGRAPHY**

**Human Systems**

According to the terms of the mutual security treaty between the United States and Japan, the United States agrees to take the major responsibility for defending Japan against aggressors. Many Japanese oppose this treaty because they fear that Japan could be drawn into a United States war against its will and that the presence of U.S. forces in Japan might even provoke an attack on Japan. Japan's military forces have been steadily built up since 1954, but the government maintains that they are only for purposes of self-defense. In recent years Japan has been pressured by the United States to spend more on its own defense. The Japanese people remain opposed to more spending.

## Japan's Role in World Organizations

Japan's role in the United Nations has been affected by Russia's distrust of Japanese-American defense arrangements. Relations between Russia and Japan have sometimes been strained by the presence of American bases in Japan and the close military alliance of the United States with Japan. A dispute over the southern portion of the Kurile Islands and the uneasiness the Russians feel over Japan's close military alliance with the United States caused Russia to block Japan's admission to the United Nations from 1952 to 1956. In 1956 the two nations resumed diplomatic relations, and Japan was admitted to the world organization in 1956.

## Japanese Relations with Other Asian Nations

Many of the nations of Southeast Asia have found it difficult to throw off the image of Japan as the militaristic/imperialist nation that invaded, conquered, and exploited their territories during World War II. Some of the nations feel Japan is still exploiting them economically through trade. To create goodwill in Southeast Asia, Japan paid war reparations to the countries that suffered from Japanese aggression. Japan has also provided economic and technical assistance to developing nations and has contributed large amounts to the Asian Development Bank. Japanese industries have been developed in many areas.

In 1972 the People's Republic of China and Japan signed an agreement. Japan recognized the People's Republic as the official government of China and cut its diplomatic ties with Taiwan. This led to a treaty ending World War II between China and Japan and also to trade agreements.

Increasingly, other Asian nations (South Korea, Taiwan, Singapore, China) are competing with Japan in the world market in such areas as textiles, cameras, electronics, and even cars. But Japan is still by far the leading industrial and economic power in Asia.

Japan became increasingly worried in 1999 about North Korea's hostile nuclear threats. Consequently, many Japanese began to consider the repeal of Article IX of the constitution. South Korea, also worried about North Korea's nuclear capacity, sought to consult Japan about this. An historic moment

GLOBAL
CONCEPTS
**Change**
CONCEPTS
GLOBAL

**WORLD ISSUES**

| War |
| and |
| Peace |

**GEOGRAPHY**

**Use of Geography**

occurred in the summer of 1999 when Japan and South Korea held joint naval exercises.

## Developments in the 21st Century

On the domestic front, the event with the single-most important impact on the average Japanese citizen in the early 21st century has to be the 9.0 earthquake that hit northern Japan on March 11, 2011, and the ensuing tsunami. Tens of thousands were dead or missing and nearly 400,000 were left homeless. In addition, the damage to the Fukushima Daiichi nuclear power plant caused radiation levels to rise as far south as Tokyo and to spike at twenty-three times the normal level. The Japanese have faced this disaster as they have faced other natural and man-made disasters in the past, with resilience and fortitude. They have begun the reconstruction of the area and have thus far contained the damage at the power plant as well as could be done under the circumstances. World donations to relief funds were slow in coming, probably due to a perception that the Japanese economy was strong enough that they could take care of themselves. The people of Japan have also perceived their own government as being slow to react and were severely displeased with the lack of response from Prime Minister Naoto Kan.

The roaring Japanese economy suffered a slump and slowdown in the early 1990s leading to several changes in parliamentary leadership in rapid succession. In the mid nineties the government reaction to an earthquake in Kobe led to accusations against the government for ineffective rescue and relief efforts. In the late nineties the Japanese economy was again severely affected by slowdown and instability and continued to grow worse through the early 2000s. In 2004 the economy rebounded with extensive foreign investment, but in 2008–2009, Japan, dependent on exports, suffered greatly in the worldwide recession when its exports fell by 5 percent. Japan has been replaced by China as the world's second-greatest economic power.

In the field of international relations, Japan has been the focus of many closely watched developments.

1. In November 2003, after the U.S. attack on Iraq in March, the Japanese cabinet approved the deployment of more than 500 noncombatant troops to aid in reconstruction efforts in that country. This was the first time that Japanese soldiers were sent to a combat zone since World War II. The move provoked controversy in Japan, as some feared this might lead to a military right-wing resurgence. Prime Minister Koizumi defended the move as one that was needed to show Japan's importance as a major nation and global power player. Conservatives supported

the move and also spoke of rescinding Article IX. Their efforts received some recognition because of the harsh military stance taken by North Korea. That nation has claimed to have nuclear capabilities and has threatened Japan. Very alarming was the firing by North Korea of a missile over Japan in August 1998, and a missile shot into the Sea of Japan in May 2005. Prime Minister Koizumi has hinted at some form of retaliation should a North Korean missile actually hit Japan.

2. The Chinese are upset, as are the Koreans, about the alleged misrepresentations in Japanese history school textbooks of Japan's role in East Asia during World War II. The war, also called The Pacific War in Asia, is not accurately described, as narrations about it fail to mention many of the Japanese atrocities that took place in China and Korea between 1931 and 1945. Chinese demonstrations against the publication of these government-approved books can seriously affect Japan's relations with China.

3. A continuing source of tension between Japan and Russia is Russia's refusal to return the Kuril Islands to Japan. The Kuril Islands, "discovered" by the Dutch during Europe's Age of Discovery, were ceded to the Japanese by the Russians in 1875. In exchange, Russia was given Sakhalin by the Japanese. At the end of World War II, the Allies gave both Sakhalin and the Kurils to the Soviet Union, the name by which Russia and several other small republics under Russian control were known during the era of communist rule (1917–1991). When the Soviet Union broke up in 1991 and its communist government collapsed, Russia—as the dominant power within the former Soviet Union—retained the international rights and obligations previously held by the Soviets. These rights included possession of Sakhalin and the Kurils. Today Japan still seeks the return of the Kuril Islands, which Russia refuses to cede. Nevertheless, in spite of these tensions, in November 2005, Japan was given a promise by Russian President Vladimir Putin to construct a pipeline that would carry Siberian oil to the Sea of Japan. As Japan has no oil resources, such a promise bodes well for her future energy needs.

4. One positive development affecting Japanese and Koreans occurred in 2002. Japan and South Korea cohosted the international soccer competition known as the World Cup. Previously, Japan had been recognized as the site for international sports competition. Japan had hosted the Winter Games on three occasions. In 1964, Tokyo was host to the Summer Games. Osaka, while never hosting Olympic competition, was host to EXPO '70, the 1970 World's Fair. This was the first time that a world exhibition had been held in Asia.

# REVIEW QUESTIONS

*Multiple Choice.* Select the letter of the answer that correctly completes
each statement.

1. After World War II, Japan was occupied by and aided in its recovery by
   A. China
   B. Russia
   C. Korea
   D. the United States

2. The Tokugawa shogunate was best known for its policy of
   A. isolation
   B. interdependence
   C. education
   D. imperialism

3. The Meiji Restoration was significant for its
   A. military conquest of Korea
   B. enlightened approach to modernization
   C. victory over Russia
   D. return to a policy of feudalism

4. The Kojiki and Nihongi are books dealing with Japan's
   A. economy
   B. politics
   C. history
   D. military

5. Since the early 1970s, Japan's foreign policy has become more
   independent of U.S. policies because
   A. Japan opposed the U.S. policy of ending the Cold War with Russia
   B. Japan has grown as an economic superpower
   C. the United States has failed to honor its commitments to Japan
   D. Japan is so strong militarily that it no longer needs the United States
      to protect it

6. The Diet is Japan's
   A. royal family
   B. legislature
   C. economic control board
   D. army

7. The real power of the Japanese emperors has often been usurped by others, but the imperial family has never been dethroned. A major reason for this has been
   A. the Japanese emperor was revered as a god
   B. the military was controlled by the imperial family
   C. shoguns never remained in power long enough to make important decisions
   D. the strong cultural influence of the Chinese

8. During the 1930s and 1940s Japan practiced a policy of imperialism in order to gain control of the resources necessary to support its industrialization. An example of this was the
   A. opening of trade with the United States
   B. invasion of Manchuria in 1931
   C. signing of the Portsmouth Treaty
   D. expansion of the zaibatsu

9. Japan's feudal period was marked by the
   A. dominance of the samurai
   B. expansion of foreign trade
   C. destruction of the imperial family
   D. weakening of the traditional extended family

10. Real political power in Japan during the feudal period from 1185 to 1600 was actually held by the
    A. emperor
    B. priesthood
    C. shogun
    D. middle class

11. Which of the following statements about the Japanese imperial family is true?
    A. They have most often ruled in name only.
    B. They gained their legitimacy from the shogun.
    C. They control politics in Japan today.
    D. They still claim descent from the gods.

12. Japan's long period of isolation was ended in the 1850s
    A. by the expedition of Commodore Matthew Perry
    B. because the Japanese wanted to renew contact with the European colonial powers
    C. by the occupation by the Allied Powers
    D. in order to gain international relief for earthquake victims in Tokyo

13. The Tokugawa shogunate isolated Japan because it
    A. feared the Mongols would invade Japan
    B. saw European contact as a threat to its control
    C. wanted to end Chinese influence in Japan
    D. was located so close to the Korean peninsula

14. After the Japanese occupation of Manchuria in 1931
    A. the United States placed an embargo on trade with Japan
    B. the League of Nations condemned the attack
    C. China surrendered to Japan
    D. American and British objections forced the Japanese to withdraw
       from the Asian mainland

15. Japan adopted imperialist policies in the 20th century in order to
    A. control the East Asian sea lanes
    B. gain resources for industrialization and militarization
    C. free the Filipinos from U.S. control
    D. maintain its policy of isolation begun under the Tokugawa shoguns

# SECTION 3: KOREA

At the close of World War II, according to an agreement worked out at the Potsdam Conference, the Soviet Union accepted surrender from Japanese troops north of the 38th parallel in Korea, and the United States accepted surrender south of the 38th parallel. Elections for a government of a united Korea were supposed to be held, but efforts to hold the elections were resisted by the Soviet Union, and in 1948 a communist regime was declared in the north with Kim Il-Sung at its helm, and a republic was established in the south with Syngman Rhee as the elected president.

GLOBAL
CONCEPTS
**Political Systems**
CONCEPTS
GLOBAL

## The Korean War
On June 25, 1950, the North Koreans, led by Kim Il-Sung launched an unprovoked attack on the South. The South Koreans suffered terrible losses. Seoul fell in three days. Almost all of Korea, except for a small area in the southeast, called the Pusan perimeter, was overrun in a month. The UN General Assembly decided to send troops to help the South, under the command of U.S. General Douglas MacArthur. They soon forced North Korean soldiers northward, near the Chinese border. China now intervened with her own forces compelling the UN soldiers to retreat. An armistice was signed in July 1953, near the 38th parallel, in Panmunjom. A demilitarized zone (DMZ) separates the two Koreas to this day.

**WORLD ISSUES**

War
and
Peace

The war led to mistrust and hatred between people on both sides. The division of the peninsula has increased political and cultural differences. Millions of people became refugees, separated from their families. In the last 50 years, contact between the two Koreas have been rare. Some family exchanges have occurred; a joint South-North Korean women's Ping-Pong team captured the world title in the 1980s. However, North Korea refused to send athletes to the 1988 Olympic Games in Seoul. Unification has been a controversial issue. The first round of high-level talks between both Koreas on this issue was held in Seoul in 1990.

**GEOGRAPHY**

Use of Geography

## Recent Political Developments
In September 1987 South Korea's constitution was amended to provide for the direct election of a president. In December 1987 the first civilian president of South Korea, Roh Tae Woo, was elected, and he took office in 1988. A second peaceful,

**WORLD ISSUES**

Determination
of Political
and Economic
Systems

democratic election took place in 1992, where Kim Young Sam was chosen president. A continuing sign of political stability occurred with the 1997 election of Kim Dae-Jung as president. Lee Myung Bak won the presidential election in 2007.

In 1993 North Korea threatened to withdraw from the nuclear nonproliferation treaty it had signed nearly ten years before and refused to allow inspection of its nuclear facilities. In mid-February 1994 North Korea agreed to the inspection of its facilities by the International Atomic Energy Agency, but refused to let them inspect the facility at Yongbyon, which has the capacity to produce the enriched plutonium that can be used in the production of nuclear weapons. North Korea maintained that it should establish the boundaries of the inspections. In inspections in other countries, the United Nations has established the boundaries. A CIA report in April 1994 indicated that North Korea might already have at least two nuclear weapons. The United States wished to prevent further development of any nuclear weapons on the Korean Peninsula, and called for a UN resolution threatening sanctions against North Korea. China's plan called for issuing a statement encouraging North Korea to allow inspection of its nuclear sites instead, with the possible use of sanctions later. The Chinese plan had the support of other UN members, even South Korea.

**GEOGRAPHY**

**Use of Geography**

In 2002, North Korea admitted it was engaged in a secret attempt to develop nuclear weapons. China sponsored talks to convince North Korea to end its nuclear weapons program until 2009 when North Korea withdrew from the talks and expelled the International Atomic Energy Agency (IAEA) inspectors. It then tested several missiles and apparently tested two nuclear devices undergound. As a result, the UN Security Council threatened sanctions against North Korea.

In March 2010 a South Korean ship was hit by a torpedo, killing forty-six sailors. South Korea eventually claimed that the attack was at the hands of the North Korean government. In August that same year the United States joined with the South Koreans in military exercises to show their support of South Korea.

In late March and early April of 1994 the armies of both North and South Korea were put on alert, and the United States offered to deploy Patriot missile launchers to help South Korea defend against possible North Korean attack. Kim Il Sung, who had led North Korea since 1946, threatened that the peninsula was "on the brink of war."

South Korea maintains a military defense treaty with the United States, and the U.S. military has over 36,000 troops stationed in South Korea. These U.S. troops were put on a high alert in the late 1990s due to increasing hostile threat on the part of North Korea.

The most dramatic event to occur in Korea in mid-1994 was the death of North Korean leader Kim Il Sung. Known as the "Great Leader," he designated his son Kim Jong Il, known as the "Dear Leader," as his successor. North Korea's economy declined and its people suffered from severe food shortages under Kim Jong Il's command. Kim Jong Il's youngest son, Kim Jong Un, is his successor.

## Developments in the 21st Century

The new century began on a high note for South Korea. Its President, Kim Dae Jung, met North Korean leader Kim Jong Il in June 2000. At this unprecedented meeting in Pyongyang, North Korea's capital, they agreed to seek reconciliation and unification for their countries. In October of that year, President Jung was awarded the Nobel Peace Prize. In December 2000, the peaceful election of a new president, Roh Moo Hyun, was yet a further sign of democratic stability in South Korea.

To support the U.S. military role in Iraq, South Korea sent 3,000 troops there in 2004. Although South Korea's military is mainly concerned about the actions of North Korea, President Roh's government was less fearful of future hostility from North Korea than is the United States. The South's "sunshine policy" toward the North and its attempt to relieve food shortages there by sending shipments of grain and other goods are examples. The United States would adopt a stronger stand toward the North and was more worried about North Korea's potential for nuclear aggression. In 2002, President Bush accused North Korea, along with Iran and Iraq, of being an "axis of evil." That same year North Korea admitted to maintaining a secret nuclear weapons program, an activity that was a violation of past agreements. In the following year, North Korea withdrew from the Nuclear Nonproliferation Treaty. Although the United States then insisted that the North dismantle its nuclear weapons program, the North demanded a nonaggression treaty and economic aid from the United States. Six-nation talks sponsored by China, beginning in 2003, have failed to result in any agreement on the nuclear weapons issue. These talks ended in 2009.

# REVIEW QUESTIONS

*Multiple Choice.* Select the letter of the answer that correctly completes
each statement.

1. South Korea
   A. has a communist government
   B. has more natural resources than North Korea
   C. has had greater economic success than North Korea
   D. signed a mutual defense treaty with China

2. Korea is
   A. a peninsula
   B. an island
   C. a subcontinent
   D. an archipelago

3. The man who controlled North Korea from 1946 to 1994 was
   A. Kim Jong Il
   B. Kim Young Sam
   C. Kim Il Sung
   D. Chu Chang Chun

4. Korea has been divided at the 38th parallel since
   A. World War I
   B. World War II
   C. the Korean War
   D. the Russo-Japanese War

5. Today the majority of Koreans make their living in
   A. agriculture
   B. fishing
   C. manufacturing
   D. lumbering

# Part G: Africa

## African Nationalism and Pan-Africanism

The nationalist movements in Africa varied from region to region and colony to colony. However, for Africans of all colonies, nationalism meant that they wanted to rule themselves and to decide what form that rule would take.

During World War II, many Africans served in the armies of their colonial rulers in Asia, Europe, and Africa. Many others moved to the cities to work in wartime industries for comparatively high wages. In the cities they acquired new skills, learned about life in other parts of the world, joined labor unions and political organizations, and came into contact with the ideas of young nationalists. They began to see that a unified nation might be built and began to transfer their loyalties from traditional groups and authority to these new groups and the idea of a modern nation state.

When the war ended, many of the colonies in Asia achieved independence. Successful independence movements in Asia encouraged the Africans to seek their own independence. Some African nationalists employed the nonviolent methods of Mahatma Gandhi and used passive resistance. Others employed guerrilla tactics. The Europeans, struggling to repair their own economies, industries, and societies, could not afford a prolonged struggle in Africa. They began to prepare their colonies for independence.

In 1957 the Gold Coast gained its independence from Great Britain. It changed its name to Ghana. Guinea gained its independence from France the following year. By 1977 there were more than forty independent nations in Africa. The era of African colonialism was over.

The colonial legacy left a major problem for the newly independent African nations to deal with—rivalries among the many ethnic groups inhabiting their nations. The new African nations must try to unite people with diverse languages, religions, and customs. Many African leaders have met this challenge by outlawing all but one political party and creating single-party states. Most leaders do not see this as undemocratic, because membership in the one party is open to all, and they feel that a single party will ensure a more stable government. Some African nations have approached the problem by not holding elections. In others, elections are so corrupt that they are meaningless.

**GEOGRAPHY**

**Human Systems**

GLOBAL
CONCEPTS

**Change**

CONCEPTS
GLOBAL

GLOBAL
CONCEPTS

**Power**

CONCEPTS
GLOBAL

**WORLD ISSUES**

Determination
of Political
and Economic
Systems

571

In many African nations, the military staged a coup d'etat (overthrow of the government). Sometimes the coup was to overthrow leaders who were thought to be bad, ineffective, or corrupt. Sometimes it was in an effort to improve economic conditions or to subdue rival political factions that had built up their own military. Sometimes it was simply the desire of military leaders for more power.

**GEOGRAPHY**

**Use of Geography**

GLOBAL
CONCEPTS

**Identity**

CONCEPTS
GLOBAL

In about 1960 there was a call for pan-Africanism, a joining together of African nations to improve conditions for all African peoples. The goals of pan-Africanism are to improve economic, political, and social conditions for all Africans. Nationalist feelings in the various African nations have been a stumbling block to pan-Africanism, however.

In 1963 the Organization of African Unity was created to try to foster cooperation and unity in order to achieve progress. It was disbanded in 2002 and replaced by the African Union with a membership of fifty-three nations.

## South Africa

The Dutch established a supply station at the Cape of Good Hope in 1652. Before long, Dutch settlers began to arrive, and the supply station became Cape Colony. (The Dutch settlers and their descendants are known as Afrikaaners. The Dutch farmers were known as Boers.) The Hottentots and Bushmen were pushed north as the settlers took more land for farms. The farmers (Boers) employed black slave labor.

**GEOGRAPHY**

**Use of Geography**

In the late 18th century, the British came to establish their own supply stations, and in 1806 they seized the Cape Colony. In 1836 several thousand Boers began the "great trek" northeastward to escape British rule and preserve their Afrikaaner culture. They were resisted by the Zulu (Bantus), who were defeated at the Battle of Blood River in 1838. By the 1850s the Boers had established two republics in the interior: the Transvaal and the Orange Free State. However, when diamonds were discovered in the Orange Free State in 1871 and gold in the Transvaal in 1886, British miners and businesspeople began to arrive.

Hostilities between the Afrikaaners and the British increased until the Boer War of 1899 to 1902, in which the Afrikaaners were defeated. In 1910 the British united the two Boer republics, Cape Colony and Natal, into the Union of South Africa, which became a self-governing country of the British Empire in 1934.

African and Asian (mostly from the British colony in India) workers were recruited for work in the mines and associated industries. Many Afrikaaners believed in the superiority of the white race and its culture, and the British did little to prevent this attitude or the resulting discrimination and segregation.

In 1948 the Afrikaaner Nationalist Party gained control of the government and began the policy of apartheid (Afrikaans word meaning "separateness"). This policy rigidly defined four racial groups: white, black, Asian, and colored. Under this policy each group was to have its own living areas and develop its own political institutions. Black Africans had to carry passbooks containing information on where they lived and worked and where they could travel. Intermarriage was forbidden, separate education was provided, strikes by black workers were outlawed, jobs were restricted to racial groups, separate facilities had to be maintained, and blacks could not own land outside reservations. Blacks had no vote and no representation in government. They were denied basic human rights. The Bantu Authorities Act of 1951 established ten Bantustans (homelands) for the blacks. Until 1985 a policy of forced relocation of unemployed blacks to the homelands was followed. The blacks were to be allowed "separate but equal" development on these homelands. They were to become independent countries with their own governments and economies.

GLOBAL CONCEPTS
**Human Rights**
CONCEPTS GLOBAL

GLOBAL CONCEPTS
**Justice**
CONCEPTS GLOBAL

### POPULATION OF SOUTH AFRICA

| Official Category | Number of People (millions) | % of Total Population |
|---|---|---|
| Black | 23.9 | 67.7 |
| White | 4.8 | 18.3 |
| Colored | 3 | 10.6 |
| Asian | 1 | 3.4 |

In 1912 the African National Congress (ANC), an organization to unite the South African blacks, to end segregation and to work for the right to take part in government, was created. The ANC was originally a nonviolent organization. They used strikes and employed many of the same methods used by Mahatma Gandhi. After the Sharpeville Massacre in 1960, the ANC turned to the use of sabotage. They blew up power lines and refineries to undermine confidence in the government, disrupt the economy, and bring international attention to their plight. The government banned the ANC and arrested its leaders, including Nelson Mandela.

Beginning with the Soweto riots in 1976, activity against the policy of apartheid increased in South Africa. As more and more nations condemned the policy, some restrictions were relaxed. Petty apartheid (separate facilities) was largely dropped, though some beaches remain restricted. Blacks were allowed to form labor unions, but they still had no voice in government.

As protests and violence escalated, international pressure on South Africa to change its policies increased. The government, under the leadership of P. W. Botha, repealed the pass laws and the Mixed Marriages Act. Many black prisoners were released.

**WORLD ISSUES**

World
Trade and
Finance

In 1974 South Africa lost its voting privileges in the United Nations. In 1986 the U.S. Congress passed sanctions against South Africa. Most American companies sold their interests and left South Africa. The British Commonwealth nations also voted for sanctions.

F. W. de Klerk became president of South Africa in 1989. In 1990 he lifted the ban on the ANC and released Nelson Mandela from prison. By June 1991 the last of the apartheid laws, the race registration law, was repealed, and talks between the white government and representatives of the ANC—including, of course, Nelson Mandela—were begun. In June 1993 the representatives agreed on a date in April 1994 for the first election, in which all people in South Africa would be eligible to vote for a legislature, which would write a new constitution for the country. In September 1993 Nelson Mandela told world leaders that enough progress had been made with the government in South Africa and that the economic sanctions imposed by other nations could and should be lifted.

**GEOGRAPHY**

**Human Systems**

Proposals for the new constitution included guarantees of freedom of speech and fair trial, freedom to choose where to live, freedom from torture, limits on the president's power to declare a state of emergency, and guarantees against the loss of citizenship. In addition, it had been agreed that the homelands will be abolished immediately after the elections.

GLOBAL
CONCEPTS
**Citizenship**
CONCEPTS
GLOBAL

There were a number of groups that condemned the agreements. They included conservative Afrikaaners who did not wish to see any change in the government at all and other white groups that demanded that territory be set aside as a white homeland that would no longer be part of South Africa. There were also black groups that were against the agreements. They included the Inkhatha Freedom Party, which represents the Zulu ethnic group, numbering more than 8 million. The leader of Inkhatha is Mangosuthu Gatsha Buthelezi, who did not wish to cede his political power to Nelson Mandela, who went on to win the presidential election in April 1994. Lucas Mangope, the leader in Bophuthatswana, the homeland of the Tswana people (2.5 million residents), also objected to the new agreements.

GLOBAL
CONCEPTS
**Diversity**
CONCEPTS
GLOBAL

In spite of all the objections, enormous steps have been taken to end the system of apartheid in South Africa and to finally provide political representation for the majority of its people.

In December 1993 Nelson Mandela and F. W. de Klerk jointly received the Nobel Peace Prize for their efforts to work out a plan for the peaceful transition to majority rule and to bring about the end of apartheid in South Africa. The 1994 elections were generally peaceful, and resulted in a multi-party legislature. Nelson Mandela became the nation's new leader in an historic inauguration.

In 1995 President Nelson Mandela appointed a Truth and Reconciliation Commission under the leadership of Desmond Tutu to investigate murders and other human rights abuses under the apartheid government. Elections for a new government were held in the spring of 1999, but Nelson Mandela had no intention of running for office again. His successor proved to be Thabo Mbeki. In 2004, the African National Congress won another landslide victory, and Mbeki was sworn in for another term. South Africa has an extremely high percentage of HIV-positive people (more than 5 million) among its population. Mbeki long denied the link between HIV and AIDS but in 2003 reversed his policy and the government approved a plan to distribute AIDS drugs free of charge. Mbeki resigned in 2008 and Jacob Zuma was elected president in April 2009. South Africa suffered economic setback from the world recession in 2009, but remains the world's largest producer of gold and gem-quality diamonds. In 2010 South Africa gained some international prestige as the first African nation to host the World Cup Soccer Tournament.

## Kenya

In the late 19th century, Kenya came under the control of the British government as part of the East Africa Protectorate. Before long, British settlers came.

The nationalist movement in Kenya began in the early 20th century. Jomo Kenyatta, the leader of the nationalist movement, became president of the Kenya African Union in 1947. Its major goals were to regain control of the land lost to the Europeans, to halt exploitation of Africans by Europeans, and to gain basic civil rights for Africans.

An organization known as the Mau Mau was created in 1952, which used terrorist and guerrilla activities to free Kenya. The British declared a state of emergency and placed thousands in detention camps.

GLOBAL CONCEPTS
**Political Systems**
CONCEPTS GLOBAL

**WORLD ISSUES**

Determination of Political and Economic Systems

**GEOGRAPHY**

**Human Systems**

In 1956 the British began gradual reforms and Africans were allowed some participation in government. However, Africans demanded independence, and in 1963 Kenya was granted independence. In 1964 Kenya became a republic in the British Commonwealth of Nations and Jomo Kenyatta its first president.

There were many problems in Kenya as a result of differences among the many ethnic groups (the Kikuyu, the Luo, the Masai, the Kalenjin, and so on). Kenyatta, a Kikuyu, urged his people to forget their ethnic loyalties and accept a principle he called harambee (pulling together). Kenyatta died in 1978 and was succeeded by Daniel Arap Moi.

WORLD ISSUES

Determination of Political and Economic Systems

Because the major political parties in Kenya represented the major ethnic groups and helped prolong the ethnic rivalries, Kenya was declared a one-party state in 1982. The only legal political party is KANU (Kenya African National Union). In 1991 a constitutional amendment established a multiparty system. Several new parties have emerged since then, but there is much factionalism, and elections have been plagued by electoral fraud. Moi was elected to his fourth term of office December 1992, and in January 1993 he dissolved the multiparty legislature, probably because he feared the legislature would introduce legislation that would limit presidential powers. Moi was re-elected in 1999. Moi was prohibited by the constitution from running for office in 2002. The opposition leader, Mwai Kibaki, won that election. He promised to put an end to corruption but has made little progress toward that goal. Kenya is considered one of the top human rights violators in the world, and in recent years American tourists have been cautioned about traveling in Kenya because of the strife and ethnic conflicts.

GLOBAL CONCEPTS

Human Rights

CONCEPTS GLOBAL

The government began a program to Africanize Kenyan life and economics. Asians were required to obtain work permits and could not be employed unless there were no Kenyans suitable for the job or they had special talents. Many Asians emigrated to Great Britain. In 1968 Britain limited immigration, and the remaining Asians have suffered economically and socially. As part of the program to Africanize Kenya, European ownership of land has also been reduced.

WORLD ISSUES

Political and Economic Refugees

Most of Kenya's people make a living in agriculture, although fertile land is scarce. Kenya has one of the most rapidly increasing populations in the world. The annual per capita income is about $1,000. Major exports are cash crops such as coffee, tea, and sisal. Industrial development is limited, and the unemployment rate is high. The country has two official languages, English and Swahili, and many ethnic languages are spoken by the groups inhabiting the country.

GEOGRAPHY

Human Systems

The global recession in 2009 and one of the worst droughts to hit East Africa in the last 60 years combined to cause a decline in GDP growth of 3.5 percent. Cattle deaths in the north caused by the drought led to widespread hunger and ethnic conflict. Relief for Kenyans suffering from hunger and homelessness was slow in coming. The situation was made even worse by an influx of Somalian refugees also affected by the drought. The Dadaab refugee camp in northern Kenya was housing more than four times the number it was designed for. Nearly 1,400 Somali refugees per day were arriving in the spring of 2011.

## Nigeria

Over 200 different ethnic groups live in Nigeria, but the four largest and most politically dominant are the Hausa and Fulani in the north, the Ibo in the southeast, and the Yoruba in the southwest.

In the mid-19th century, the British began their expansion into Nigeria. By 1914 all of Nigeria was a British colony. After World War I a nationalist movement arose. The British gradually allowed more African participation in government until in 1954 a constitution creating a federal union, ensuring the power of the three major regions—the east, the west, and the north—was accepted. Independence was finally granted in 1960.

Almost immediately, regional differences became obvious. The northern region, with the largest population, controlled the federal government. In 1966 there was a coup led by Ibo military officers, and General Ironsi took control of the government. Later in 1966 violence broke out against Ibo living in the north, and General Ironsi was killed by Hausa soldiers and replaced by Yakuba Gowon, a northerner. General Ojukwu, the leader of the Ibo region, declared eastern Nigeria independent as the Republic of Biafra.

Civil war broke out about two months later. Biafra was unable to hold back the Nigerian troops or to feed its people. An estimated one million Biafrans died as a result of military action or starvation. Early in 1970 Biafra surrendered.

Military coups have occurred frequently in Nigeria since 1970. The country has been under military rule for most of the years since independence. It has been divided into nineteen states, each having its own governor. From 1983 to 1989 all political parties were banned. In 1989 political parties were again allowed to register. Later in 1989 the incumbent president, General Ibrahim Babangida, announced that the government would create two new political parties because, he said, other political parties were linked to discredited groups and had also

GLOBAL CONCEPTS

**Diversity**

CONCEPTS GLOBAL

GEOGRAPHY

**Human Systems**

WORLD ISSUES

Determination of Political and Economic Systems

failed to fulfill registration requirements. Elections were held in the summer of 1993, but the results were voided by Babangida. In August 1993, after much turmoil in the nation, Babangida resigned, and an interim government was named. That government was overthrown by General Sani Abacha, who died in 1998. The new government was headed by General Abdul Salam Abubakar. In 1999, Nigeria returned to civilian government with democratic elections. Olusegun Obasanjo was chosen president. Obasanjo promised reform, but within two years it was obvious they were empty promises. He was, however, reelected in 2003.

Nigeria made a rapid recovery from the civil war, largely because of oil revenues. However, mismanagement and overspending of funds led to an economic decline in the early 1980s. In 1987 the government announced plans for economic austerity and began to encourage a birth-control program. Today Nigeria's stability is threatened by the spread of Islamic law (sharia) across the northern region, which is heavily Muslim. This has caused fighting between fundamentalist Muslims and Christians. Besides petroleum, exports include cash crops such as rubber, palm products, and timber. The annual per capita GDP is less than $800. In 1994, labor disputes continued to weaken Nigeria's economy.

Violent communal conflict spread throughout much of Nigeria in the late 2000s. The government moved against rebel groups in the Niger delta in 2009, killing hundreds, but it did not prevent the rebel groups from expanding their resistance to Lagos, where they set fire to an oil depot and several tanker ships. Christians and Muslims attacked each other in the city of Bauchi. A Muslim militant group called the Boko Haram came under attack by government forces, killing at least 800. In 2010, Muslim herders were attacked in Jos and they retaliated by killing farmers in surrounding villages. Much of the conflict in Nigeria is ethnic and religious and, for the most part, caused by rivalry over distribution of resources and income.

## Ghana

Several civilizations once existed in the area of what is now Ghana. The country's name comes from the ancient empire of Ghana, which was located to the northwest of what is now the modern African country of Ghana. The Ashanti Empire flourished in the area in the 18th and 19th centuries.

British rule in the region was established in 1901, and Ghana became a republic in 1960. President Kwame Nkrumah built hospitals and schools and promoted developmental projects. However, he ran the country into debt, jailed his opponents, and was accused of corruption. Nkrumah was given dictatorial powers in 1964 and created a one-party socialist state. In 1966, he was overthrown by a military coup, and a series of military coups followed. Several of these coups were engineered and led by Jerry Rawlings. Rawlings suspended the constitution and instituted austerity programs that decreased the deficit over the next ten years. In 1992, he returned the country to civilian rule and elections were held. Rawlings was elected president in 1992 and 1996. In 2001, John Agyekum Kufuor was elected president. He set up a National Reconciliation Commission to review human rights abuses during military rule.

Ghana's major exports are cocoa and gold.

## Africa in the Global Context

For the most part, after independence African nations chose to remain nonaligned (choosing to be neither pro-Soviet nor pro-United States). African leaders also feared neocolonialism. For this reason, many were reluctant to maintain strong relationships with their former colonial rulers or with any industrialized Western nation. Others were economically so weak that they had to allow colonial banks and industries to remain in place. In addition, many nations that avoided foreign involvement immediately following independence have since been forced by economic and political crises to accept the presence of multinational corporations.

**WORLD ISSUES**

Determination of Political and Economic Systems

## International Organizations

Many African nations have joined a number of international organizations to promote African unity, improve economics, and strengthen their influence in world markets and world events.

1. *The United Nations.* The African nations now have the most powerful voting bloc in the United Nations General Assembly, with about fifty members, and can influence UN decisions and policies. African nations have received much aid and assistance through various UN agencies.

2. *The World Bank.* The bank, a specialized agency associated with the UN, provides loans and technical assistance to developing nations.

3. *The International Monetary Fund.* The IMF, another specialized agency of the UN, provides loans to members with balance-of-payments problems and provides technical assistance.

4. *The Commonwealth of Nations.* Many of the former colonies of Great Britain belong. It was organized to promote economic cooperation and to coordinate scientific, military, and educational affairs.

**WORLD ISSUES**

Economic Growth and Development

5. *The Lome Convention.* In 1975 a number of African, Caribbean, and Pacific nations voted to associate themselves with the European Economic Community to gain economic benefits through trade and tariff agreements.

6. *Organization of Petroleum Exporting Countries.* OPEC, designed to control world oil prices by coordinating and controlling production, has four African member states: Algeria, Gabon, Libya, Nigeria.

7. *Organization of African Unity.* The OAU was founded in 1963 to promote unity, solidarity, and cooperation among African states. It had little power beyond talking and trying to encourage cooperation. It has enjoyed some success in settling boundary disputes and developing energy sources. The OAU was disbanded in 2002 and replaced by the African Union, which has the same fifty-three members as the OAU. These members include all the African nations except Morocco.

GLOBAL
CONCEPTS
**Identity**
CONCEPTS
GLOBAL

## Foreign Intervention

In certain instances African countries or groups within those countries have been forced to ask for, or have been unable to prevent, foreign intervention in their internal affairs.

1. *The Congo in the 1960s.* After the Belgian Congo became independent in June 1960, the Province of Katanga, under the leadership of Moise Tshombe, seceded and declared its independence. Belgium sent troops to end the rebellions. The prime minister (Patrice Lumumba) of the Congo appealed for Soviet aid, and the Soviets sent weapons, transport equipment, technicians, and advisers. Soviet influence alarmed some Congolese and most Western nations, who encouraged the president of the Congo (Kasavubu) to dismiss Lumumba. An army leader, Joseph Mobutu, ordered the Soviets to leave the country, and in 1961 Lumumba was assassinated. Meanwhile, the Katanga rebellion continued, with Tshombe employing European and South African mercenaries to resist a United Nations peacekeeping force that had been sent into the region. An agreement to end the secessionist movement was finally reached, and UN troops left the Congo in 1964. Tshombe was elected president, but in 1965 he was overthrown in a military coup led by Mobutu. In 1971 Mobutu changed the name of the country to Zaire. Foreign investors were invited back into the country (most fled during the terrorism of the rebellions), but continued conflict in the country has discouraged them. Throughout the 1980s and 1990s, government corruption and economic decline grew worse and worse. Rwandan refugees flooded eastern Zaire in 1994. Rebels from Rwanda attacked the refugee

GLOBAL
CONCEPTS
**Change**
CONCEPTS
GLOBAL

camps in Zaire, and Zairian government troops became involved in the turmoil. Mobutu spent many months in 1996 out of the country for medical care. Meanwhile, a rebel leader, Laurent Kabila, an enemy of Mobutu, began to build up his power and to move toward Kinshasha, the capital. Mobutu returned to Zaire to negotiate with Kabila but was unsuccessful. He went into exile, and Kabila took control of the country and renamed it Congo. Mobutu died in the fall of 1997.

2. *French military involvement in Chad.* Chad gained independence from France in 1960. Chad has a sparse population (being located mostly in the regions of the Sahara and the Sahel). The population is divided between the Christian south and the Muslim north, and tribal differences are also a problem. In 1960 a southerner, Francois Tombalbaye, became president. A rebellion broke out in the northern and eastern sections in 1965 and resulted in civil war. In 1975 a military coup overthrew Tombalbaye's government, but another southerner took control of the government. The conflict between the north and south continued, with France supporting the southern government. Northern forces called on Libya for assistance, and Muammar Qaddafi sent Libyan troops. In 1981 foreign troops were withdrawn, but in 1982 civil war broke out again. Libyan forces entered the war in support of the north, and French and Zairian forces entered the war in support of the south. In 1984 France and Libya agreed to remove their forces, but Libyan troops remained in the north in violation of the agreement. In 1987 the government launched an attack against the northern and Libyan forces and regained control of all but a small strip of land where Libya has an air base. In 1990 a Libyan-supported group overthrew the government, and their leader became president. Libyan troops were said to have withdrawn in May of 1994, and a new constitution was approved in 1996, leading to Chad's first multiparty presidential election.

**GEOGRAPHY**

Use of Geography

3. *Superpower rivalry in Ethiopia and Angola.* Except for a short time during World War II when it was occupied by Italian forces, Ethiopia was one of the only two African nations that maintained their independence. Emperor Haille Selassie ruled Ethiopia from 1916 to 1974. The United States provided the emperor with aid and assistance partly because of the country's strategic location on the Red Sea. In 1974 he was overthrown, and the army began making socialist reforms—land was taken from landowners and turned over to peasant associations. In 1976 a military agreement was reached with the Soviet Union, and United States military advisers were expelled. Ethiopia and

Somalia have had border disputes since Somalia became independent in 1960. Because the Soviet Union was supporting Ethiopia, Somalia turned over a military base to the United States.

Angola received its independence in 1975. After independence, three rival groups fought for control and there was a civil war. The MPLA (Popular Movement for the Liberation of Angola) was supported by the Soviet Union and Cuba; the FNLA (National Front for the Liberation of Angola) was supported by the United States, France, and Zaire; and UNITA (National Union for the Total Independence of Angola) was supported by Portugal, China, South Africa, and white Angolans. By 1976 MPLA had achieved victory. The MPLA established a Marxist state with Soviet backing and Cuban support troops. The United States continued to provide assistance to UNITA rebels, so conflict continued. In 1991, according to the terms of an agreement worked out by President Mobutu of Zaire, the last Cuban troops were withdrawn from Angola. Later that same year UNITA signed a treaty with the government to end the civil war that had gone on for 16 years. UNITA rejected election results in 1992, and fighting broke out again. In 1993 the United States recognized the government of Angola for the first time since its independence in 1975.

4. *Ethnic clashes in Rwanda.* Lingering tensions between the Hutus and the Tutsis in Rwanda exploded in 1994 when the country's Hutu president died in a mysterious plane crash. Hutus blamed the Tutsis. The resulting fighting caused over 500,000 deaths. Refugees seeking to escape Zaire were faced with food shortages and outbreaks of cholera and dysentary. France sent troops to try to stop the fighting and to restore political stability.

GEOGRAPHY

Use of Geography

GLOBAL CONCEPTS

Change

CONCEPTS GLOBAL

## United States/African Relationships

GEOGRAPHY

Human Systems

As part of its policy to contain the spread of communism in the 1960s, the United States began to provide aid and assistance to many African nations.

Americans (government and private citizens) have provided assistance (medical, food, volunteers) to drought-stricken and famine-ridden regions of Africa. Starting in the 1960s, the Peace Corps has helped to develop rural Africa—teaching agricultural techniques, establishing schools, and carrying out many other programs.

WORLD ISSUES

World
Trade and
Finance

The American government has provided millions of dollars in military loans and grants. American multinational corporations have established branches in many African nations, providing employment and infusing some money into the local economy. The United States has on occasion maintained military bases in Kenya, Somalia, and Liberia.

In the past, black African nations have had difficulty reconciling American ideals on human rights with the reality of racial prejudice and inequality in the United States. However, the civil rights gains of the 1960s and the recent change in American policy from constructive engagement to divestment and sanctions against the government of South Africa have done much to improve this situation. The trips to Africa taken by President Clinton in 1998 and Secretary of State Albright in 1999 were signs of continuing U.S. interest in Africa.

## Somalia and the United States

The Somali Republic became independent in 1960. As a result of a coup in 1969 Somalia came under the rule of General Muhammad Siyad Barrah. In 1991 Barrah fled the country, and there was intense fighting between rival clans to gain control of the country. By the late fall of 1992 thousands of people were in peril. Civil war, drought, and famine had already taken the lives of thousands, and the lives of thousands more were threatened. The rival clans interfered with international efforts to relieve the famine by keeping relief supplies from reaching their enemies and also to make the people dependent on them for the supplies. By November 1992 the Bush administration felt that conditions in Somalia had deteriorated to the point where U.S. intervention was necessary. He volunteered U.S. troops for the UN force in Somalia to protect the relief workers, supply routes, and humanitarian-aid distribution points. The UN authorized the U.S. forces to use all means necessary to deliver the relief supplies to the needy. The pressure from the UN and U.S. forces resulted in the signing of a peace treaty by the two most powerful clan leaders in December 1992. Early in 1993, shortly after the agreement was reached, it was broken, and clan fighting broke out again. In June 1993 Pakistani members of the UN peacekeeping forces were killed; General Mohammed Farah Aidid, one of the most powerful clan leaders in Mogadishu, the capital, was considered responsible. Subsequently, several attacks were carried out against Aidid's weapons caches and his supporters' holdings. Aidid was targeted for capture, but he was not caught. In October several members of the peacekeeping forces were killed, including eighteen Americans. Another American was taken captive and interrogated by Aidid's forces, and video excerpts from the interrogation were broadcast worldwide. More American forces and equipment were ordered to Somalia, but it was also

**WORLD ISSUES**

War
and
Peace

**GEOGRAPHY**

Human Systems

announced that all American forces would be withdrawn by March 1994. This was done, amidst concern for the future of Somalia.

By 2011 Somalia had been without a central government for 20 years. One sign of the lawlessness rampant in Somalia is the existence of Somalian pirates who prey on ships in the Indian Ocean. Another was the rise of several Islamist groups that advocate strict Shari'a. One of these groups is the al-Shabab (youth). The al-Shabab has fought the Transitional Federal Government (TFG). The United States has used several means to destroy al-Shabab leaders as they have ties to al Qaeda. The United States declared al-Shabab a terrorist organization. As a result, it became a crime to aid and abet al-Shabab and the United States begin withholding economic and food aid from areas controlled by al-Shabab. These areas are now the areas of Somalia that suffer the most from the drought and famine in Somalia.

## Sudan

On January 9, 2011, a referendum was held in Sudan to determine independence for southern Sudan. The southern Sudanese voted overwhelmingly for independence. On July 9, 2011, South Sudan celebrated its first independence day. After years and years of civil war and atrocities between northern and southern Sudanese, it remains to be seen if Sudan and South Sudan can coexist without warfare and strife. There is hope; South Sudan has resources, but North Sudan has the infrastructure to transport those resources. Perhaps they can create a relationship based on common economics, and end the years of strife. In any case, the newest nation in the world is South Sudan, carved out of the largest nation in Africa.

# Part H: Latin America

## Political Revolutions

The 20th century led to important political changes in many nations in Latin America. Democratically elected governments replaced military-led governments throughout the region. In addition, Mexico experienced a political revolution when the candidate of the ruling party was defeated in the presidential elections of 2000. The long-term effects of all the political changes are not clear yet. However, Latin American and Caribbean nations are faced with increasingly social and economic problems brought on by demographic changes and an unequal distribution of wealth, land, and opportunities for an education and in general a better life.

## Mexico Since 1911

**GEOGRAPHY**

**Environment and Society**

The Mexican Revolution of 1911 led to important changes in that nation. After the fall of Díaz, military leaders succeeded one another as president and created a constitutional government based on a one-party political system. The Roman Catholic Church lost much of its influence and power. The Mexican labor movement was allowed to develop and became an important force. The labor unions competed with the new developing industrial oligarchy to influence the government.

Mexico became more nationalistic, and the nationalization of the petroleum industry in the 1930s by Lazaro Cardenas symbolized the nation's change of direction. In the years after 1940, the leaders of the ruling political party, the PRI, sought to create political stability by allowing a middle class to develop and by encouraging economic change. However, the PRI has continued to hold power despite growing political opposition.

In 1988 Carlos Salinas de Gotari was chosen by the PRI as its official candidate and took office after a disputed presidential election. President Salinas made a number of painful budgetary reductions. There were cuts in spending on education, health care, and other social services. Thousands of government workers were laid off and state-owned industries were sold to private investors. President Salinas also moved toward freer trade, and the Mexican government ratified NAFTA.

In 1994, President Salinas hand picked Ernest Zedillo as PRI's presidential candidate after the original candidate Luis Donaldo Colosio was assassinated. President Zedillo was elected in August 1994 for a six-year term. Salinas promised

**GEOGRAPHY**

**Human Systems**

that the PRI, in power for more than six decades, would not resort to fraud or irregularities to win the scheduled August 1994 elections. In early 1994, a rebellion took place in Chiapas, a poor state in southern Mexico where descendants of the Maya live mostly in poverty. This rebellion is further indication that political, economic, and social reforms are needed. As Mexico entered the millennium the demands of the Zapatistas were still not met by the national government.

In 2000, the free and fair election of Vincente Fox of the National Action Party (PAN) as president for a six-year term ended 71 years of uninterrupted rule by the Institutional Revolutionary Party (PRI). Even though the Mexican two-house legislature remained under PRI control, the fact that the president who was elected was not the PRI candidate was a hopeful democratic sign in Mexico. The Mexican people are increasingly demanding open and fairer elections. The question remains whether a democratically elected government in Mexico can solve problems such as political corruption, drug trafficking, lack of adequate employment, and illegal immigration to the United States. In 2006, Felipe Calderon, the PRI candidate, was elected president of Mexico. President Calderon used the Mexican military to combat narco-terrorism.

## The Cuban Revolution

Cuba remained a Spanish colony until 1898 when independence was established as part of the treaty that settled the Spanish-American War. The U.S. influence in Cuba continued after its military occupation ended in 1902. Between 1933 and 1959 Fulgencio Batista dominated, and although he provided political stability, economic problems led to increased suffering. A rebellion supported by young professionals, students, urban workers, and some farmers was led by Fidel Castro. By 1959 Castro's military forces had defeated Batista's army and seized power.

Castro brought about great political, social, and economic changes. He turned to the communist nations, especially the former Soviet Union, for economic support and protection from the United States. By 1965 Castro's socialist state was officially ruled by the Cuban Communist Party and guided by the principles of Marxism-Leninism.

Castro sought to export the Cuban Revolution by supporting guerrilla movements in Bolivia, Colombia, Nicaragua, El Salvador, and elsewhere. This forced the United States to pay greater attention to the social and economic problems in Latin America. Starting in the 1960s, the United States began to work to isolate Cuba politically and economically.

During the 1990s, the United States continued its trade embargo against Cuba despite opposition from many Latin American and European countries. In the 1980s, the collapse of communism in Europe had ended the massive support of the former Soviet Union and Eastern European nations for Cuba. By the early 1990s, Cuba increasingly experienced economic and social problems. In 1994, Cuba and the United States reached an agreement concerning increased Cuban immigration after another wave of Cubans left the island nation for the United States to escape the harsh economic conditions. Throughout the 1990s, the United States insisted that Cuba make political reforms if it wanted to have the trade embargo lifted. As the new millennium began, Fidel Castro increasingly faced difficult choices as the Cuban economy continued to deteriorate. In 2007, Fidel Castro became ill. Fidel was replaced as president in February 2008 by Cuba's Parliament. In August 2015, the United States reestablished diplomatic relations with Cuba and opened its embassy in Havana.

## Revolution and Political Change in Nicaragua

The U.S. interest in Nicaragua dates from the late 1840s when the American government contested British supremacy in Central America. The United States began a military occupation of the nation in 1912, which lasted until 1933. In the mid-1930s, the national guard, trained by U.S. military officers, took responsibility for maintaining order. The national guard was the instrument for the rise of the Somoza dictatorship, which ruled Nicaragua from 1936 through most of the 1970s. Although there was economic progress under Somoza in agricultural production and then in the industrial sector, there was little real distribution of income.

The assassination of Pedro Chamorro, the publisher of an opposition newspaper, in 1978 sparked an uprising that toppled the Somoza dictatorship and brought the Sandinista Front to power in 1979. The Sandinistas sought to create a socialist-type state in Nicaragua, and Daniel Ortega became the nation's leader. The Sandinistas soon faced opposition from the United States. Moreover, the Sandinista government faced serious economic problems brought on by alienating important segments of the agricultural and industrial sectors.

Hostility toward the Sandinista government because of its ties to Castro's Cuba, the former Soviet Union, and the insurgency in El Salvador led the United States to support the contra military forces, which were seeking to overthrow the Sandinistas. The costly civil war in Nicaragua led to large numbers of

**Human Systems**

casualties, increased emigration, and a further deterioration of the Nicaraguan economy.

In 1990, a democratically elected government headed by Violeta Chamorro, the wife of Pedro Chamorro, took power. The Sandinistas peacefully gave up power but continued as part of the government. In the mid 1990s another presidential election was held and once again the Sandinista Party lost. President Aleman continued the policy of national reconciliation initiated by the previous government. Presidential elections were held in 2001. Enrique Bolanos of the Liberal Constitutionalist Party was elected to the Nicaraguan presidency, defeating the Sandinista candidate Daniel Ortega. President Bolanos promised to reinvigorate the economy, create jobs, fight corruption, and support the war against terrorism. Bolanos took office in 2002. In Nicaragua, political, social, and economic problems remain, but it is hoped that they can continue to be peacefully resolved. In 2007, Daniel Ortega was elected president of Nicaragua.

## Brazil

Getulio Vargas came to power as a result of the Revolution of 1930. Vargas ruled Brazil from 1930 to 1945 and set up programs to promote industrial growth. In the 1950s, Juscelino Kubitschek was elected president. Kubitschek created the new capital city, Brasilia, in the interior of the country. He also began programs to develop Brazil's highways, universities, airports, factories, and hydroelectric plants.

In 1964, the military overthrew President Joao Goulart after the economy faltered and as a result of political disagreements. The military governments that ruled Brazil to the end of the 1980s banned political parties and encouraged economic growth. The generals encouraged foreign investment, and in the 1970s, an economic boom called the Brazilian miracle took place. The upper and middle classes obtained most of the benefits during this time of greater prosperity.

By the late 1980s, Brazil's staggering debt of $110 billion and widespread economic and social problems forced the military to give up power slowly to the politicians. In 1990, Fernando Collor de Mello was elected president. President Collor began a series of drastic economic reforms to control Brazil's spiraling inflation.

In 1993 President Collor was removed from office because of corruption. The vice president, Itamar Franco, took over the presidency. In the 1990s Brazil's leaders tried to find solutions to the problems of high inflation, widespread poverty, malnutrition, lack of adequate health care, and crime in the western hemisphere's second largest nation in terms of territory, population, and economy.

In 1994, Brazil placed its hope in Fernando Henrique Cardoso, the newly elected president, to resolve its many problems. By the 1990s, Brazil had one of the top ten economies of the world. Despite Brazil's economic growth, the problem of inflation made Brazilians live in constant fear that money earned today would be worth much less tomorrow. Cardoso worked to stabilize the Brazilian currency during his first term in office. Brazil became a more reliable trading partner in the expanding global economy, and the nation was able to pay back some of its huge foreign loan debt without devaluing its currency.

Cardoso was reelected in 1998. In his second term in office, Cardoso faced renewed economic problems. The financial crisis that developed in Asia threatened to spread to Brazil. Brazil made an important agreement with the IMF to curtail its budgetary expenses by cutting government employment and eliminating many of the corrupt political practices that made doing business in Brazil so costly. The Brazilian Congress and state governments resisted the call for this type of economic reform, but President Cardoso pushed ahead to bring about needed change.

In the presidential elections of 2002, the Workers Party candidate, Luis Ignacio da Silva ("Lula") was elected to the Brazilian presidency. Lula's election to a four-year presidential term was seen as another step in promoting real democracy in Latin America's largest and most populous nation. Lula is considered to be a man of the people and was a trade union leader and worker. As president, Lula has worked to maintain a balance between his Workers Party supporters and the opposition, which is more procapitalist and favors the idea of economic globalization. This delicate balance is complicated by the fact that resource-rich Brazil with its growing trade-oriented economy has a very unequal distribution of wealth and income.

In 2005, a political scandal erupted in Brazil, and the Workers Party was accused of corrupt political practices. The outcome of the scandal severely weakened President Lula's ability to govern effectively. As the 21st century develops, it is hoped that Brazilian leaders will make their nation a land where political promises become a reality for all the Brazilian people. Brazilian leaders must find solutions that will allow the vast majority of its citizens to live better lives than they do today. In January 2011, Dilma Rousseff was elected as the first female president of Brazil. Brazil has been chosen to host the summer

Olympic games in 2016, which is recognition of the country's increasing political influence and economic importance as one of the rising BRIC nations.

## Argentina

The landed elite, primarily cattle ranchers, were the real source of power in Argentina. Argentinean nationalism developed during the rule of the caudillo tyrant Juan Manuel de Rosas. Rosas ignored the constitution and often used his military power to persecute and terrorize his enemies. Although the provinces of Argentina remained loosely associated under Rosa's federalist control, by the time of his overthrow in 1852, he had, to a large measure, forged national unity. However, the establishment of democratic traditions did not come until later in the 1800s.

In the 1940s a military officer, Juan D. Perón, rose to power. Perón was a populist who used the democratic process to promote a program that favored the middle and labor sectors of society. Perón was elected president twice. Juan Perón and his first wife, Eva Perón, relied on the support of the workers. His program, *Justicialismo*, sought a balance between society's opposing forces. Perón was overthrown in 1955 by the military, with the support of the traditional elite who found his programs threatening. However, Perónism continued to be a political force. In 1973, Perón and his new wife Isabel were chosen as the presidential and vice presidential candidates by the Perónist Party. Perón was reelected but died shortly thereafter. Isabel Perón succeeded him but soon was overthrown by a military coup d'état. A period of harsh military rule followed.

In 1976, as terrorist attacks worsened, the military started a brutal campaign known as the dirty war. As many as 25,000 people, mainly students and workers, were killed or "disappeared" during this time. In 1982 the military launched a campaign to gain control of the Malvinas Islands, also called the Falkland Islands, about 300 miles off the coast of Argentina. These islands had been ruled by the British since the 1830s. The British refused to recognize the Argentine claim and soundly defeated the Argentine military. With this defeat, the military lost all credibility and popular support.

In 1983 voters elected a new president, Carlos Menem. President Menem, who ran for the presidency as a candidate of the Perónist Party, instituted drastic economic reforms, which resulted in curbing a high rate of inflation, pegging the national currency to the dollar to safeguard its value, and selling off government-owned national companies that were inefficient and losing money. Argentina's constitution was amended in

1993 to allow Menem to run for a second term. In the 1990s, President Menem brought political stability and economic growth to Argentina. In 1999, President Menem sought to amend the nation's constitution to be able to run for the presidency a third time; however, the Argentine judiciary refused to sanction this constitutional change.

In 1999, Fernando de la Rua was elected president of Argentina. However, by 2001, he was forced to give up his office because of mounting economic problems that led to increasing social unrest. Argentina's economic situation worsened to the point where its dollar-based currency lost most of its value. In 2002, Eduardo Duhalde became the president, but he too could not reverse Argentina's deepening socioeconomic crises. In less than a year new presidential elections were held.

In 2003, Nestor Kirchner was elected president of Argentina. Since his election, Kirchner has won support from the Argentine people for his nationalist economic policies and his decision to legally pursue the former military leaders responsible for the crimes committed during the period of political repression following the death of Juan Perón. In 2007, Cristina Fernandez de Kirchner succeeded her husband as the president of Argentina.

## Venezuela

Following independence in 1821, most of Venezuela's 19th century history was characterized by periods of political instability, dictatorial rule, and revolutionary activities. In the first half of the 20th century, political authoritarian governments and dictatorships continued to follow one after the other. During the post–World War II years, the Venezuelan economy changed from being primarily agricultural to an economy centered on petroleum production and exportation.

After the overthrow of General Marcos Jimenez in 1958 and withdrawal of the military from direct involvement in national politics, Venezuela began a period of unbroken civilian democratic rule. Until the elections of 1998, the Democratic Action Party (AD) and the Christian Democratic Party (COPEI) dominated political elections and offices on both the national and state levels. Venezuela became one of the more stable democracies in Latin America.

This political calm began to come to an end starting in 1989, when Venezuela experienced riots, the so-called Caracazo, in response to an economic austerity program launched by its then president Carlos Andres Perez. In 1992, a group of army officers led by future president Hugo Chavez tried unsuccessfully to overthrow the government in a military coup. A year later Perez was impeached on corruption charges.

Political instability increased throughout the 1990s, as popular dissatisfaction with the traditional political parties and economic frustrations continued to cause unhappiness and disorder. In the presidential elections in 1998, Hugo Chavez won the presidency after campaigning for broad reform, constitutional change, and a crackdown on corruption.

In another election in 2000, Hugo Chavez and his Fifth Republican Movement (MVR) won control of the national legislature. Chavez now had the power and votes to bring about the political changes that he had promised in 1998. The traditional elites who had ruled the nation organized opposition to what they called Chavez's socialist policies.

The years since 2000 have seen continued political strife. Venezuelans are divided into two political camps. They are either pro- or anti-Chavez. The anti-Chavez forces tried to have the president removed from office by means of a recall vote. In 2002, the opposition to Chavez began a national work stoppage centering on the petroleum industry. The political situation became so heated that the Organization of American States (OAS) created a Group of Friends of the OAS—Brazil, Chile, Spain, Portugal, Mexico, and the United States—to find a peaceful solution to the growing crisis, which threatened civil war.

**Use of Geography**

In 2004, after long negotiations, a recall vote, which was allowed by the Venezuelan constitution, was agreed on. In the recall vote Chavez was supported by the majority of the Venezuelan people, particularly the lower socioeconomic groups, and held onto his office. Since his electoral victory in the recall, and reelected in 2006, Chavez has continued to pursue his economic program, which is designed to assist Venezuela's poorest classes. Venezuela has continued to experience difficulties in its relations with the United States, which opposes Chavez's friendly relations with the Fidel Castro government in Cuba and his ideas about making the nation's petroleum industry more profitable for the Venezuelan government and people by raising crude oil prices.

## Political Integration

In 1823, when Spain threatened to try to regain its colonial empire in Latin America, the United States responded with the Monroe Doctrine. President James Monroe in a statement issued to Congress declared that the American continents were henceforth not to be considered as subjects for future colonization by European nations. The statement also said that any attempt by European powers to extend their system to this hemisphere would be considered dangerous to the peace and safety of the United States. In addition, the United States declared that it would not interfere in European affairs.

The Monroe Doctrine was favorably received by the Latin American nations. Although the United States did not possess the military force to back up this bold statement, it knew that the British navy would protect Latin America because of Britain's commercial interests in the region.

Prior to the 1860s, the United States had done little to protect Latin America from European intrusions. However, in the late 1800s the United States began to play a greater role in the affairs of Latin America. In 1898 the United States defeated Spain in the Spanish-American War and gained control of Puerto Rico and Cuba. Cuba soon gained its independence, but the era of U.S. domination of much of Latin America, especially Central America and the Caribbean, had begun.

President Theodore Roosevelt changed the role of the United States in Latin America from protector to that of an international police power. In 1904 the Roosevelt Corollary to the Monroe Doctrine stated that if the Latin American nations failed to properly maintain their political and financial affairs, the United States would intervene to restore order. This corollary led to interventions in the Dominican Republic, Nicaragua, Haiti, and elsewhere. In addition, the U.S. desire to build a canal to connect the Atlantic and Pacific oceans led it to defend Panama's secession from Colombia in 1903. The Hay-Bunau-Varilla Treaty negotiated with the newly independent nation to build the Panama Canal was very favorable to U.S. interests.

This policy of interference in Latin American affairs caused a growing resentment in the region toward the "colossus of the north" as other presidents continued Theodore Roosevelt's aggressive policy. President Taft supported dollar diplomacy, which encouraged American bankers to make loans to Central America and the Caribbean nations. This led to intervention to protect American creditors.

**GEOGRAPHY**

**Human Systems**

During the 1930s President Franklin D. Roosevelt sought to modify U.S. policy toward Latin America in his Good Neighbor policy. Under Roosevelt, the United States succeeded in its economic and security objectives, but the Good Neighbor policy did little to resolve Latin America's fundamental political, social, and economic problems or reduce the region's distrust of the United States.

After World War II, a new inter-American system, known as the Organization of American States (OAS), was established.

At first, it included twenty Latin American nations and the United States, but it has since admitted Canada, Trinidad and Tobago, Barbados, and Jamaica. The charter of the OAS provides a legal framework for a permanent inter-American organization. In 1967 a series of changes amended the charter. A general assembly of member nations that meets annually was established, and a secretary general elected to a five-year term was approved. The amended charter stresses economic development, social justice, and regional integration.

The OAS record of preserving hemispheric peace has been mixed. The United States has sought to involve the OAS in its attempts to regulate Latin American political affairs. The American-sponsored Bay of Pigs invasion of Cuba in 1961 and the United States' military occupation of the Dominican Republic in 1965 were seen as violations of the OAS charter by many Latin American nations. However, Latin America did support the United States by voting to exclude Cuba from the OAS in the early 1960s.

In the 1980s the United States invaded Grenada and Panama to overthrow dictatorships. The Latin American nations resent these interventions and favor a legal channel for solving international disputes. The Latin American nations also opposed U.S. intervention in Nicaragua. The Contadora peace plan drafted by a group of Latin American nations, most notably Costa Rica, was an attempt to stop armed conflict and to establish regional peace in Central America. The Nicaraguan election in February 1990, won by Violeta Chamorro who ran against the Sandinista candidate Daniel Ortega was the first hopeful sign that electoral politics would replace armed conflict in Central America. During the 1990s, there were peaceful resolutions of the armed conflicts in the nations of Guatemala and El Salvador. The trend towards electoral politics in these nations is another indication that the devastating civil wars that lasted from the 1950s and impacted mostly on helpless civilian populations are a thing of the past in Central America. Today, democratically elected governments rule throughout Latin America.

## Puerto Rico

**GEOGRAPHY**

**Human Systems**

The U.S. rule over Puerto Rico has changed since the Spanish-American War. This evolutionary process transformed the original military government in 1898 into a civilian government under the Foraker Act of 1900. The Jones Act of 1917 allowed the popular election of both houses of the bicameral legislature and a voice in appointing the governor's cabinet.

The Muñoz Rivera and Muñoz Marín political dynasty that dominated Puerto Rican politics from 1900 to the mid-1960s was supported by the United States. The idea of independence did not have much political support in this period. Under Public Law 600 in 1952, Puerto Rico became an associated free state with full autonomy in internal matters and its own constitution. As citizens of the United States, Puerto Ricans share a common currency and the right to defense by the U.S. government. In 1967, a plebiscite (vote) resulted in a large majority favoring commonwealth status rather than statehood. Less than 1 percent of the people voted for independence. In recent years, although some favor independence, the vast majority of the Puerto Rican people favor either statehood or commonwealth status.

In the 1950s reforms initiated by Muñoz Marín led to the development of industry and the growth of tourism on the island. Operation Bootstrap, a United States-sponsored program, offered companies tax savings to build plants in Puerto Rico. Despite economic progress, unemployment in Puerto Rico remained high throughout the past decades. After a vote in 1993, Puerto Rico's political future was determined when the results ended in a victory for the supporters of commonwealth status. In 1998, the issue of whether Puerto Ricans really favored statehood, commonwealth status, or independence was once again put to a vote. The Puerto Rican people reaffirmed their desire to maintain their commonwealth status.

# REVIEW QUESTIONS

*Multiple Choice.* Select the letter of the answer that correctly completes
each statement.

1. The continent that was most affected by the breakup of the European
   colonial empires after World War II was
   A. Africa
   B. Asia
   C. Latin America
   D. Europe

2. Which of the following was not the result of the Cold War?
   A. NATO
   B. SEATO
   C. United Nations
   D. Warsaw Pact

3. Which of the following national leaders adopted a different strategy for
   winning independence from European colonialism than the others?
   A. Jomo Kenyatta
   B. Ahmed Bon Bella
   C. Mustafa Kemal
   D. Mohandas K. Gandhi

4. All the following areas have experienced civil wars in the 20th century
   during the process of becoming independent nations *except*
   A. Western Europe
   B. Indian subcontinent
   C. sub-Saharan Africa
   D. Southeast Asia

5. Select the correct Cold War relationship that shows benefactor and
   recipient.
   A. U.S.S.R. and Greece
   B. U.S.S.R. and Congo
   C. Communist China and Japan
   D. Communist China and South Korea

6. The nation that had become independent of European colonial rule
   before World War II was
   A. South Africa
   B. Israel
   C. India
   D. Vietnam

7. NATO includes the following nations *except*
   A. Great Britain
   B. France
   C. Finland
   D. Canada

8. Identify the leader who is incorrectly paired with his political affiliation.
   A. Mao Zedong/Kuomintang
   B. Yassir Arafat/Palestine Liberation Organization
   C. Jarawaharlal Nehru/Congress Party
   D. Jomo Kenyata/Mau Mau

9. Identify the leader who is incorrectly paired with his policy.
   A. Mikhail Gorbachev/Perestroika
   B. Sun Yat Sen/Three Principles of the People
   C. Nelson Mandella/Apartheid
   D. Ayatollah Ruhollah Khomeini/Islamic Fundamentalism

10. The European Union includes the following nations *except*
    A. Ireland
    B. Spain
    C. Italy
    D. Turkey

# THEMATIC ESSAYS

## Essay #1 Theme: Independence

In the second part of the 20th century, many nations became independent. Some fought for freedom from European colonial empires after World War II while others became independent after the fall of Soviet communism as a result of the Cold War.

**Task:**
1. Define the term "independence."
2. Select one nation you have studied and give one specific historical example showing how that nation became independent.
3. Assess whether independence was either positive or negative for that nation.

## Essay #2 Theme: Globalization

The rapid advance of science and technology since World War II has forced nations increasingly to view the world as a "global village." Globalization poses new challenges and demands.

**Task:**
1. Define the term "globalization."
2. Select one nation you have studied and give one specific historical example showing how globalization has influenced the development of that nation.
3. Assess whether globalization has either been positive or negative for that nation.

## DOCUMENT-BASED ESSAY QUESTIONS

**Essay #1**

This task is based on the accompanying documents (Documents 1–4). Some of these documents have been edited for the purposes of this task. The essay is designed to test your ability to work with historical documents. As you analyze the documents, take into account both the source of each document and the author's point of view.

**Historical Context:** The second half of the 20th century saw the independence of many nations. Some came from European colonial empires after World War II while others became independent after the collapse of Soviet communism as a result of the Cold War. The documents below relate the approaches of various national leaders to independence in the 20th century.

**Task:** Analyze the beliefs expressed in each document in order to evaluate the approach each leader took in shaping his new nation.

**Part A:** The documents below relate the beliefs of four national leaders of countries that became independent from European colonial empires after World War II or Soviet communist rule as a result of the Cold War. Examine each document carefully and answer the question that follows.

**Part B:** Write a well-organized essay that includes an introduction with a thesis statement, several paragraphs explaining the thesis, and a conclusion. Use evidence from the documents to support your position. Do not simply repeat the contents of the documents. You should also include specific related outside information based on your study of history.

**DOCUMENT 1**

"The All Indian Congressional Committee firmly believes in the policy and practice of non-violence, not only in the struggle for independence, but also, in so far as this may be possible of application, in Free India. . . . A Free India would, therefore, throw all her weight in favor of world disarmament, and should herself be prepared to give a lead in this to the world. . . . Effective disarmament and the establishment of world peace by the ending of national wars depend ultimately on the removal of the causes of wars and national conflicts. . . . To that end India will peacefully labor."

—Jawaharlal Nehru (1944)

According to the text, how does the AICC's plan for an independent India reflect the idealism of Gandhi's philosophy?

_____

_____

_____

**DOCUMENT 2**

"I blame the Government because—knowing that the Africans have grievances—they did not go into these grievances: shortage of houses in places like Nairobi, land shortage, and the poverty of the African people both in the town and the Reserves. I believe if the Government had looked into the economic and social conditions of the people, they could have done much good. . . . They wanted—I think—not to eliminate Mau Mau, but to eliminate the only political organization, the KAU, which fights constitutionally for the rights of the African people, just as the Electors Union fights for the rights of the Europeans and the Indian National Congress for the rights of the Asians."

—Jomo Kenyatta (1968),
*Suffering Without Bitterness*

According to the reading, how does Kenyatta justify the struggle against European imperialism?

_____

_____

_____

**DOCUMENT 3**

"The previous (Communist) regime, armed with a proud and intolerant ideology, reduced people into the means of production, and nature into its tools. . . . Out of talented and responsible people, ingeniously husbanding their land, it made cogs of some sort of great, monstrous, thudding machine, with an unclear purpose. . . . For all of us have grown used to the totalitarian system and accepted it as an immutable fact, and thereby actually helped keep it going. None of us are only its victims, we are all also responsible for it. . . . If we realize this, then all the horrors that the new Czechoslovak democracy inherited cease to be so horrific."

—Vaclav Havel (1990),
New Year's Day Address

According to the text, how had communist rule affected Czechoslovak society and its ability to adopt democracy?

_____

_____

_____

**DOCUMENT 4**

"Ultimately, Communism failed because in practice it did not deliver on the material level while its political practices . . . discredited its moral claims. It could not provide a viable socio-economic alternative to the Free Market system . . . Communism . . . by rejecting spiritual values, and by reducing morality to an instrument of politics, made its own success dependent entirely on material performance. And here it could not deliver. . . . As a consequence, Communism's dogmatic self-righteousness reduced idealism to barbaric inhumanity and institutionalized hypocrisy."

—Zbigniew Brzezinski (1993),
*Out of Control*

According to the reading, what was wrong with the communist system itself that made its failure inevitable?

_____

_____

_____

**Essay #2**

This task is based on the accompanying documents (Documents 1–4). Some of these documents have been edited for the purposes of this task. The essay is designed to test your ability to work with historical documents. As you analyze the documents, take into account both the source of each document and the author's point of view.

**Historical Content:** The advance of science and technology since World War II has transformed the world into a global village. The documents below relate how globalization has changed the patterns of human life all over the earth.

**Task:** Analyze the ideas expressed in the documents in order to understand how globalization has affected all people around the world and presented new challenges for the 21st century.

**Part A:** These documents relate opinions on the influence of globalization. Examine each document carefully and then answer the question that follows.

**Part B:** Write a well-organized essay that includes an introduction with a thesis statement, several paragraphs explaining the thesis, and a conclusion. Use evidence from the documents to support your position. Do not simply repeat the contents of the documents. You should also include specific related outside information based on your study of history.

**DOCUMENT 1**

"For 45 years, from World War II's finish to the end of the Cold War, most agreed that the greatest threat to global security was an all-out war between the two superpowers (US and USSR) that would culminate in the use of nuclear weapons. . . . The post-Cold War era, however, is by no means free of the threat of armed conflict, as demonstrated by continuing warfare. . . . While these conflicts do not have the potential to erupt into nuclear holocaust, they do pose a threat of widespread regional fighting. . . . Moreover, as weapons of mass destruction become more widely diffused, a growing number of these regional wars will entail a risk of chemical and even nuclear attack. Preventing, controlling, and resolving these conflicts . . . will, therefore, constitute the principal world security tasks of the 1990s and beyond."

—Michael T. Klare,
"The New Challenges to Global Security"

According to the text, how has globalization changed the concerns in regard to authority of the international community?

_____

_____

_____

**DOCUMENT 2**

"While there remains a range of estimates of what the earth's total population will be in the years 2025–2050, the raw figures are daunting, especially when placed in historical perspective. In 1825 . . . about 1 billion human beings occupied the planet, the race having taken thousands of years to reach that total. By then, however, industrialization and modern medicine were permitting population to rise at an increasingly faster rate. In the following hundred years the world's population doubled to 2 billion, and in the following half century (from 1925 to 1976) it doubled again, to 4 billion. By 1990, the figure had advanced to 5.3 billion . . . Behind the raw statistics lies the reality . . . if we do nothing to stabilize the world's population . . . before very long we will have so overpopulated and ransacked the earth that we will pay a heavy price for our collective neglect."

—Paul Kennedy (1993),
*Preparing for the 21st Century*

According to the reading, how will population impact on globalization and the international community in the future?

_____

_____

_____

### DOCUMENT 3

"Civilization has been through periods of simultaneous political and religious upheaval . . . before. Yet modern communications, modern weapons, and modern anxiety make the current one seem even more bewildering. After all, religion is not dead; religious revivalists thrive in many parts of the world where traditional values clash with modern secular and commercial ones. But the struggle is the more turbulent for not having been resolved. Militant Islam is one answer thrown up by a traditional society's bewilderment at the intrusion of modern alien ideas, but, its repressive answers to them—indeed, its seeming embrace of terrorism . . . adds only to the general sense of anomie (absence of social norms)."

—Craig R. Whitney (1993),
"A World Unhinged Gropes for New Rules"

According to the text, how has globalization created a conflict between traditional and modern cultures?

_____

_____

_____

_____

_____

**DOCUMENT 4**

"To achieve modernization, the Chinese people must first put democracy into practice and modernize China's social system. In addition to being the result of productive forces and productive relations having developed to a certain stage, democracy is also the very condition that allows for the existence of such development to reach beyond this stage. Without democracy, society will become stagnant . . . Judging from history, therefore, a democratic social system is the premise and precondition for . . . modernization."

—Wei Jingsheng (1997),
*The Courage to Stand Alone*

According to the reading, how has globalization led to the creation of new standards in the development of nations?

_____

_____

_____

_____

_____

_____

# ERA VIII

# Global Connections and Interactions in the 21st Century

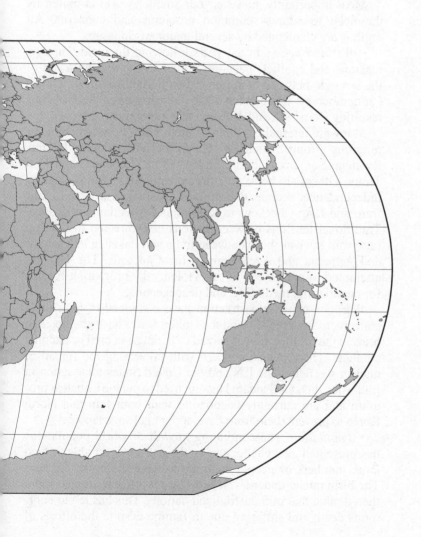

# Part A: World Issues

Today's world could be considered a global village, tied together by the ease of rapid travel and nearly instant communication. These ties create interdependence among culture regions and countries. Examples of this interdependence include trade in agricultural and industrial products, the flow of knowledge and ideas from one region to another, and political alliances that provide mutual help and support.

Most importantly, however, our smaller world is united by the need to address common problems and concerns. All regions are challenged by several major world issues.

• *War and peace.* In the years following the Cold War new tensions and conflicts have developed. Some are the result of the struggle between communist totalitarianism and free market democracy, while others have their origins in the problems resulting from 19th and 20th century imperialism.

Many are internal conflicts within nations between ethnic or religious groups, such as the former Yugoslavia, Ireland, Rwanda, Somalia, Liberia, Sudan, Dafur, Lebanon, and East Timor. Others are between ethnic or religious groups desiring independence, such as Palestinians in Israel; Kurds in Turkey, Iran, and Iraq; Chechens in Russia; and Albanians in Kosovo. Traditional tensions between nations also threaten to develop into wars, such as those between India and Pakistan in Kashmir and Armenia and Azerbaijan in the Caucasus. The UN has attempted to put an end to this violence by promoting forums for negotiating, mediating, and peacekeeping.

Weapons of mass destruction have continued to be a great concern, as both the UN and the United States have attempted to prevent the proliferation or spread of their use in civil or national conflicts. There is also concern with preventing the spread of nuclear weapons. The UN and the United States took action in Iraq when dictator Saddam Hussein tried to pursue a nuclear program and are currently negotiating with both Iran and North Korea to prevent them from developing nuclear weapons.

• *Population.* The continuing growth of world populations has presented new challenges, as the nations least able to feed large numbers of people continue to have the most children. The birth rate in underdeveloped Third World countries is more then double that in industrialized nations. This has led to enormous death and suffering due to famine despite the efforts of the UN and other world health NGOs (nongovernmental organizations) to provide relief. Developed nations, such as India and China, also have problems educating and convincing their people to limit the amount of children they have, to bring down overpopulations (China has taken drastic measures to limit families to two children.) Ignorance and stubborn adherence to traditional practices have hindered efforts of local governments and world health groups to educate people in the Third World to limit their birth rates and bring down overpopulation.

• *Hunger and poverty.* Overpopulation, a lack of modern technology, corrupt governments, and violent conflicts have left much of the world, especially in underdeveloped Third World nations, in hunger and poverty. Populations throughout the world live in primitive conditions with little to eat, no sanitation, a lack of medicines or medical attention, and no means of supporting themselves. Despite the efforts of the UN and world health organizations, hunger and poverty continue to plague people throughout the world.

• *Political and economic refugees.* The global movement of people has increased dramatically throughout the world in recent decades. Often, lack of food, resources, and means of supporting themselves drive populations to move. These are due to natural causes (droughts, floods, disease, natural disasters) or poor government (oppression based on political, racial, ethnic, or religious reasons). Currently there are more than 15 million refugees or people who are forced to move from their homes worldwide. They are often treated harshly in nations that are too poor themselves to support refugees. Wealthier nations, such as the United States, limit immigration of refugees as their own populations are fearful that too many refugees will create strains on their own economies. Many refugees are forced to live in camps under poor conditions and face very uncertain futures.

• *Environmental concerns.* The development of a global economy has led to an increase in the demand for energy. The development of industries and modern technology (electricity, water, sanitation, communication) requires natural resources (coal, oil, gas) to provide the energy needed. This has led to greater development of these resources, which has had a negative effect on the environment. The burning of coal and oil has released much carbon dioxide into the air, which has created health-damaging pollution, and acid rain and possibly contributed to global warming. The chemicals created by the use of refrigerators, air conditioners, and manufacturing processes has damaged the ozone layer that protects life on earth from the sun's ultraviolet rays. This has led to cancer in humans and damaged plant life.

Economic development has also done great environmental damage. Farming has led to large-scale erosion of soil worldwide, and the cutting down of forests has both endangered wildlife and remained a major source of carbon dioxide absorption. Environmentalists, scientists, and economists are looking for ways to reduce the damage done and find a means of "sustainable growth" or ways in which world economies can grow without destroying the environment.

• *Economic growth and development.* The expansion of the world's economies has led to an increase in the production of goods and services. Manufacturing moved from "developed" or industrialized nations to "emerging" nations or those becoming industrialized. These emerging nations could also obtain labor at less cost, as the standard of living in those nations was not as high. This created great hardship for those employed in developed nations.

Technological advances in manufacturing in developed nations had already reduced the need for labor. Demands in other areas of development, such as communications (especially computerization), led to the creation of new careers. "Information industries," such as insurance, financial services, market research, and advertising, developed a need for "knowledge workers" or jobs that focus on information.

• *World trade and finance.* The advances in both transportation and communications led to the development of "globalization" (the creation of a global economy) by the late 20th century. This meant that financial interactions quickly became international. Telephone and computer advances made it possible for business to be conducted as easily on the other side of the globe as next door. Many companies relocated to less expensive and less crowded places, no longer needing to be in large cities. Multinational corporations or companies that operate in many different countries quickly developed as well. This allowed businesses to establish manufacturing plants in nations where the resources were located and/or where labor was less expensive, while maintaining offices in the countries that were the greatest consumers. This made access to more products available to more people in more places for less cost.

The movement for "free trade" or the elimination of trade barriers internationally expanded as a result of globalization. The General Agreement on Tariffs and Trade (GATT), which was created after World War II has been extended throughout the world since the creation of the World Trade Organization

(WTO) in 1995. Greater economic integration between nations regionally has resulted in the European Union or EU (1992) and the North American Free Trade Agreement or NAFTA (1994). Similar organizations are in the process of being created in Asia, Africa, and the Middle East.

There has also been much criticism of globalization, in particular from environmental groups. They believe that expanded industry has accelerated pollution and increased environmental damage. Other opponents argue that while there have been some benefits to all nations, the developed countries have been the main beneficiaries. Stronger critics maintain that globalization has been a disaster for underdeveloped nations and that they are worse off now then before. Most of the opposition agrees that investment practices and trade agreements must include aid packages and policies to assist the poorest countries.

• *Energy: resources and allocations.* Part of the criticism of globalization is tied to the use of resources. Developed and emerging nations are increasingly using the vast majority of resources, as their postindustrial and industrial economies are dependent on energy. These countries have a greater number of machines and a higher standard of living that uses the bulk of natural resources available. Despite attempts to develop and exploit more natural resources, underdeveloped nations cannot get enough resources to industrialize. Alternative solutions such as water or solar sources of energy are not sufficient, and there is a fear that nuclear energy will be used to develop weapons of mass destruction. Many of the sources of natural resources are also being exploited at an increasingly faster pace, creating the danger of their being exhausted in the near future.

• *Human rights.* The concept of human rights was the result of international legislation in 1948 (Universal Declaration of Human Rights) and 1975 (Helsinki Accords) in response to genocide and political repression in the first half of the 20th century. These are the basic rights of all people to life, liberty, security as a person, and freedom of belief and expression. International organizations, such as the UN and Amnesty International, work to identify, condemn, and create pressure to end human rights abuses by governments and groups throughout the world. Violations of human rights range from the suppression of free speech, and persecution because of political, religious or philosophical beliefs, and genocide due to ethnic, racial, religious, or political hatred. Recently, gender equality (equal rights for men and women) and the protection of children have also become human rights issues.

• *Terrorism.* Terrorism is the use of extreme violence to intimidate and create fear in order to force political, social, or religious change. Although the practice is quite old, the creation of more destructive weapons and advanced technology have made it easier for terrorists to kill large groups of people, sometimes from a distance away.

While political or nationalist causes seem to be the reason for terrorism in the 19th and early 20th centuries, most recent motives have been radical religious and/or cultural beliefs. A terrorist does not care who gets killed, and they are so fanatic that the cause is more important then the means. They are willing to use any weapon to kill, even their own bodies, in order to create the fear they believe will force governments and societies to accept their demands. Terrorists target public places where there are many people. This is intended to make people feel unsafe wherever they are. They may also choose to destroy a government or religious site that symbolizes what they hate. An example of this was the attacks on the World Trade Center in New York City and the Pentagon in Washington on September 11, 2001, by Islamic fundamentalists belonging to the Al Qaeda group. As a result of the attacks, 3,000 people died.

The September 11 attack changed the way Americans looked at terrorism. Up until then most terrorist attacks had occurred in foreign countries, often against diplomatic or military targets. The terrorists were living in the United States and had learned to fly the planes they flew into the World Trade Center and Pentagon there. In response, the federal government created the Department of Homeland Security in 2002 to coordinate national efforts against terrorism. The United States also invaded Afghanistan, which was under the control of the Taliban government, which consisted of Al Qaeda leadership. The Taliban was defeated and removed, forcing the Al Qaeda terrorists to flee into neighboring countries. Since 2001, the United States and its allies have declared a "war against terrorism" focusing chiefly on Al Qaeda and the Muslim fundamentalists who have tried to destabilize the Middle East and Southeast Asia.

These issues, icons of which are shown throughout this book in the margins, show that we live in a world of global interdependence. Today, all regions enjoy the potential for sharing and cooperation and the progress that can result.

# Part B: Population Issues and Their Impact

## SECTION 1: POPULATION GROWTH IN DEVELOPED AND DEVELOPING NATIONS

Population growth is the easiest issue to recognize but the most difficult with which to deal. In the year 1800 the world population was 1 billion. By 1900 the world population had doubled, reaching 2 billion, and by 1975 it had doubled again and there were 4 billion people. By the year 2000 the world population had reached more than 6 billion. Current UN projections estimate world population to be 7.5 billion by 2020. Many believe that such a large number of people will strain the earth's "carrying capacity," that is, the ability of its resource base to support people at a reasonably safe and comfortable standard of living.

The changes brought about by the scientific and industrial discoveries have added to this population growth. Increased agricultural productivity has improved nutrition, modern medical knowledge has reduced the number of deaths caused by disease, and improvements in sanitation have bettered health conditions. As a result, more children survive through infancy and more people live longer and healthier lives in both the developed and developing nations.

In the developed nations where the production of material goods has increased and protective social and governmental services have been introduced, people have generally decided to have fewer children. Most of these nations have low population growth rates, and some have even reached zero percent population growth. Demographers (social scientists who study population patterns) and politicians agree that developing nations must make special efforts to control population growth.

Consequently, the governments of many developing nations have begun family planning or birth-control programs. They use many techniques, such as advertising and educational campaigns, economic incentives, and restrictive legislation to convince their citizens to have fewer children. China's one-child family law, India's transistor radios for vasectomies campaign, and Singapore's free education only for the first two children policy are examples of the different approaches that have been used. Reducing the birth rate in many developing nations has proved to be difficult, however. Often cultural factors have worked against limiting population growth. In some cultures, economic and social conditions as well as religious beliefs lead to the desire, even the necessity, for large numbers of children. Children may be needed to help with the family farm or business, to provide care for elders, or to contribute income from outside jobs. They may also be needed for religious ceremonies (especially funerals), to enhance a family's prestige, or to inherit the family occupation and property and carry the family name into the future.

### POPULATION OF WORLD REGIONS 1990–2020

| Region | 1990 | 2000 | 2010 (Estimated) | 2020 (Projected) |
|---|---|---|---|---|
| World | 5,275,000,000 | 6,079,000,000 | 6,812,000,000 | 7,500,000,000 |
| Africa | 635,000,000 | 812,000,000 | 1,022,000,000 | 1,278,000,000 |
| Asia | 2,168,000,000 | 3,675,000,000 | 4,164,000,000 | 4,565,000,000 |
| Latin America/Caribbean | 443,000,000 | 522,000,000 | 590,000,000 | 652,000,000 |
| Europe | 721,000,000 | 728,000,000 | 730,000,000 | 744,000,000 |
| North America (USA/Canada) | 283,000,000 | 314,000,000 | 344,000,000 | 374,000,000 |
| Oceania | 27,000,000 | 31,000,000 | 37,000,000 | 48,000,000 |

Source: Population Division of the Department of Economic and Social Affairs of the United Nations Secretariat, *World Population Prospects: The 2010 Revision*, http://esa.un.org/unpd/wpp/index.htm.

**GEOGRAPHY**

**Use of Geography**

In some areas, other factors also make limiting population growth difficult. Geographic and historical circumstances have created an uneven distribution of population. Fertile river valleys and coastal plains are capable of producing vast amounts of food grain, and such production requires large labor forces. Consequently, dense populations are both possible and desirable. Eastern China, coastal Japan, and South Asia's Indo-Gangetic Plain are examples of this circumstance.

At the same time, modern agricultural technology has made areas that previously provided only small amounts of food extremely productive with small labor forces. The Great Plains of North America and the North European Plain are two such areas, and they help to provide Americans and Europeans with an abundant food supply and a high standard of living.

Urbanization stimulated by the Industrial Revolution has also contributed to uneven population distribution. Today, over 40 percent of the world's population lives in cities. Cities need workers for industries and services. Moreover, urban areas provide many economic and cultural opportunities for their inhabitants. As a result, people migrate from the rural agricultural areas to further crowd and congest urban areas, helping to create squalid, crime-ridden, and unhealthy slums. This trend of rural to urban migration is continuing today.

Population can also be unequally distributed by age. In the developed nations, more people live longer and couples have fewer children. As the population grows older, these societies need to provide services for retired people and care for many elderly. At the same time, there are fewer wage earners to provide tax revenues for such services.

Developing nations, with their growing populations, are faced with large numbers of school-age children. However, they do not have the money to fund education. This deprives young people of the skills and knowledge necessary to compete for jobs in modernized sectors of the economy and results in large numbers of young people being unemployed or underemployed.

As it relates to the network of world trade, the population issue involves developing relationships that promote fairness in the prices paid for natural resources and agricultural products provided by developing nations. Increased prices for these products would help provide money for these nations to improve education, skill training, industrial capacity, transportation, and communication. These items make up a nation's infrastructure, a necessity for improving living standards and

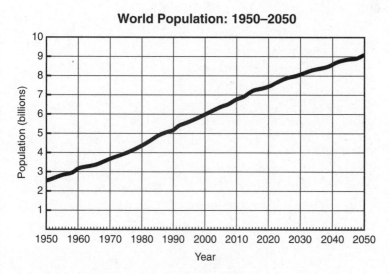

**World Population: 1950–2050**

*Source:* U.S. Census Bureau, International Data Base, April 2005 version.

enabling societies to effectively deal with poverty, hunger, and population growth.

Population pressure is not limited to particular culture regions nor is the issue simply that of numbers of humans or even birth or population growth rates. It involves decisions about fairness and equity and how nations will deal with one another in the future. Developing nations react to criticisms of their high birth rates by criticizing how much of the world's natural resources are consumed by the industrialized countries. Indeed, one citizen of a developed nation may consume twenty to thirty times the amount of resources used by an individual in a developing nation.

# SECTION 2: WORLD HUNGER

Although population growth is an underlying cause of hunger and malnutrition in many parts of the world and the increasing numbers of people put a strain on food supplies, the issue is more complex. Many nations do not grow enough food crops. This is often because of policies carried out by former European colonial powers. In these areas, food production was frequently replaced by the production of cash crops for the European market. Also, in some areas, especially in Africa, borders were drawn without regard to natural and traditional agricultural ecosystems (the living community and nonliving environment working together in a cooperative economic system).

Since independence, the governments of some developing nations have ignored the development of agriculture. Instead, leaders have often emphasized industrialization and the growth of cities, hoping to build political support among city workers, the growing middle class, and the educated elite.

Climatic conditions and changes affect the food supply in some areas. Droughts (a long period of dryness, as in Africa's Sahel) often force people to overuse and damage the environment by digging deeper wells, which lower the water table, or by allowing herds to strip sparse vegetation. Floods and storms (as in Bangladesh) can wipe out harvests, ruin arable land, and destroy storage and transport facilities.

Although the developed nations produce a large enough food surplus to ease shortages in crisis areas, a number of obstacles prevent an equal distribution of these surpluses. Simply giving vast amounts of food to needy nations creates dependencies. It also interferes with agricultural prices in other areas. Political differences and policies may hamper the distribution of both food aid and local food supplies. Moreover, corruption, hoarding, and price fixing are often part of the political and economic systems of developing countries.

A rapid rise in food prices in 2010 and 2011 drove millions of people below the UN-designated poverty level. Production had already failed to keep up with the growing population in some less developed areas. In more prosperous economies increased demand for meat from grain-fed livestock and a growing biofuel industry diverted food grains from many needy areas. Unfavorable weather events, national export quotas, use of former farmland for commercial development, water scarcity, and lack of government investment in agriculture and development all contributed to driving the food/hunger equation to the "brink of disaster," as some experts described it.

Finally, many developing nations do not have or cannot afford to develop the necessary factors to produce the technological innovations (new ideas) that could bring about higher crop yields. They also are unable to purchase those items from more developed countries. New, improved seed varieties, chemical fertilizers, pesticides, and farm machinery are all expensive. Also, prices for fuels used in small engines that power farm machinery have increased.

# SECTION 3: EDUCATION—
# A GROWING GAP

Development in nations depends on information and technical skills. Education is necessary to make use of resources. However, as communication and information technology leap ahead in the industrialized nations, the developing nations are losing ground in gaining access to these essentials. This is due in part to the shortage of funds available for schools, colleges, and educational media. Also, social or economic limitations often take children out of the educational system. For example, they may be needed to contribute to family care or earnings, or tradition may exclude the participation of females. Also, governments sometimes ignore or attempt to eliminate long-standing methods or institutions, which makes it difficult for citizens to adapt to new ways. Birth rates in most nations can be tied to education; more educated populations tend to have more economic options. These greater opportunities often lessen the need for children as economic assets and lead to a desire for smaller families. In developed nations, too, differences in education levels can create gaps between groups, as between those who have only a secondary education or less and those with college and more advanced degrees; on average, those with more education have higher incomes.

# Part C: Economic Development and World Trade

Interdependence brought about by scientific, technological, and industrial progress has carried the message of economic development to every nation on earth. Every government strives to improve the standard of living of its citizens in a variety of ways. Improved health, sanitation, and nutrition; broader educational training and employment opportunities; better housing, clothing, and other basic necessities; affordable entertainment; reasonably priced consumer goods; and more leisure time—all of these are elements of economic development.

Accomplishing these things requires the investment of money and human effort, both of which may be strained by the great need. Political leaders must make decisions and set policies, although there may be differing opinions about how their nation can best develop economically.

Within a nation, even close political partners can disagree about how to achieve economic development. In Mahatma Gandhi's vision of independent India, he saw a nation of cottage industries with skilled craftspeople producing goods in their own homes or small shops. However, his follower and India's first prime minister, Jawaharlal Nehru, promoted industrial development and urban growth.

# SECTION 1: GLOBAL POWER—THE GAP BETWEEN RICH AND POOR

Both developed and developing nations may suffer from an unfavorable balance of trade. Many developing nations earn foreign-exchange capital by selling natural resources at relatively low prices and then must pay high prices for manufactured and consumer goods. In addition, they must borrow capital to finance improvements in their infrastructure, which often leads to massive debts and huge interest costs.

In recent decades this so-called debt bomb has crippled the economies of a variety of developing nations and created problems in the entire world economy. In the 1980s, Mexico's overdependence on oil as a source of income led to a high ratio of debt and economic hard times. In the latter part of the 1990s, the once rapidly growing economies of East Asian nations such as South Korea, Thailand, Indonesia, and even Japan suffered similar difficulties due to overly optimistic investing and producing. As exports and prices fell, so did currency values, reducing the abilities of both governments and private companies to make debt payments.

For the world's poorest nations, sometimes referred to as "basket case" economies, the situation can be even more dire. Although the world economy has generally been growing and diversifying, the share of the least developed countries in world trade has steadily declined in recent decades. Like other developing nations, they have difficulty producing competitive goods and services and often lack the ability to export what they do produce. Also, products and services—and the demand for them—are changing rapidly. Struggling economies often lack the capacity to innovate, to access new markets, or to anticipate new opportunities. Social and political instability discourage foreign companies who are reluctant to risk investing in a climate of uncertainty.

These countries may also be more seriously affected by barriers to international commerce—particularly technical regulations and sanitary measures imposed by international agreements and the standards of more developed nations. Information and communications technologies (ICTs) have become increasingly important in all areas of world trade from agriculture to industrial products, consumer goods, and professional services. The rapid growth of this "e-commerce," disadvantages nations with limited access to Internet facilities.

Some economists have speculated that the cancellation of debts ("forgiving loans") owed by developing nations and their businesses to financial institutions such as the World Bank and private banks would be beneficial to the global economy. This would, in theory, promote economic growth by applying assets to development rather than debt service, strengthening national economies and the global economy.

Developed nations consume large quantities of material goods and provide many services for their citizens; also, their workers earn high wages. Consumers in these countries often find it cheaper to buy goods from other nations whose workers are paid less. Buying goods such as automobiles and TVs that are imported from other nations can lead to large trade deficits. Since the citizens of such countries expect high levels of public services, government borrowing and budget deficits may result. Nations with debts and deficits, whether developed or developing, may find the value of their money weak or declining in relation to that of other nations. This further limits their ability to fund economic development.

Often governments use tariffs (import taxes), which raise prices on imported goods, to protect their own industries. Nations with similar interests often form organizations to promote their own interests. The Organization of Petroleum Exporting Countries (OPEC) cooperates on pricing and other issues, and the General Agreement on Trade and Tariffs (GATT) is designed to benefit the industrial nations that have signed the agreement.

# SECTION 2: RESOURCE AND ENERGY MANAGEMENT

As science and technology find more ways to use up more of the earth's natural resources, managing scarce or declining resources becomes an ever more critical issue. Developing nations with abundant supplies of nonrenewable mineral resources need to sell them to obtain development capital. Developed nations who use such resources strive to keep the prices for them low and to find ways of recycling and using such resources more efficiently.

In industrial countries, financial resources may be spent on excessive amounts of consumer goods or be lost to corruption or inefficiency (as in some former communist nations). Developing countries are often forced to use much of their capital to pay off their debts and the interest on their loans. In developed capitalist nations, dishonest investing techniques and conspicuous consumption may create waste and inequity.

Human resources are also crucial to development. Many African and Asian societies have suffered a so-called brain drain, as many of their educated, skilled, or financially prosperous citizens have immigrated to developed nations for better opportunities. The lack of money for investment in education means that developing nations cannot fully develop the potential of the remainder of their population.

# SECTION 3: GLOBALIZATION

The McDonald's restaurant in Moscow is the world's busiest. Young children in Philippine villages wear Chicago Bulls' jerseys. German skinheads beat up on Turkish "guest workers." Tourists can buy Kodak film and drink Coca-Cola in Katmandu. Often the most exciting players in Europe's top soccer leagues are Africans or South Americans. In recent decades, some of the most famous Americans in the world have been sports stars— Muhammad Ali, Michael Jordan, and Magic Johnson. Disney theme parks have been built in France and Japan. Apples raised in Chile can be found in American supermarkets. Madonna is criticized by Indians for making a video using Hindu religious images. These are all examples of the so-called globalization of human culture and the world economy.

What are the elements of this process? Modern technology, transportation, and communication have interwoven human activities as never before. Consumer goods, even perishable ones, can be moved great distances in a very short time in order to satisfy the changing tastes of customers. Developed nations in need of workers encourage immigration: companies in richer countries "outsource" jobs to economies where wages are lower; firms in the same countries incorporate in places with much lower tax rates; satellite television broadcasts news, sports, and entertainment around the world; and tourists carry ideas and impressions to their destinations and others back home with them.

International organizations such as the World Bank, the International Monetary Fund, OPEC, the World Trade Organization, and the European Union wield ever-wider influence on the world economy through their policies. The World Trade Organization (WTO) deals with the rules of trade among nations. At its heart are the many agreements negotiated and signed by most of the world's trading nations. The goal is to help producers of goods and services, exporters, and importers conduct their business. The vast majority of WTO members are party to the General Agreement on Tariffs and Trade (GATT), a set of policies that covers international trade in goods. Most also belong to one or more regional trade agreements (RTAs), such as the North American Regional Trade Agreement (NARTA), which further regulate economic relations among its member nations. It was estimated that nearly 300 RTAs might be in force by the year 2005.

Multinational or transnational corporations may exercise the greatest influence in the globalization process and control significant percentages of the world's economic assets. The combined revenues of the world's largest automobile manufacturers, General Motors and Ford, exceed the Gross Domestic Product of all of sub-Saharan Africa, and the combined sales of Japan's six largest corporations almost equals the GDP of South America. About half of the 100 largest companies in the world are companies that do business across national boundaries.

Opinions vary as to the consequences of this world-straddling economic pattern. Supporters acclaim its efficiency in promoting economic progress—producing consumer goods, promoting industrialization, creating jobs—but there are also many critics. They claim that it concentrates financial power in the hands of too few nations, most of them in the north and most former colonial powers. Far from creating employment, naysayers decry the loss of jobs to mechanization, especially in developing nations. Population shifts create poverty, prejudice, and conflict; health and equity issues are ignored; while pollution increases; biodiversity decreases; and the diversity and integrity of local and national cultures becomes homogenized. These are other criticisms of a process that to some seems beyond the control of any limiting factors.

As the second decade of the 21st century began, a number issues regarding globalization continued to create a standard-of-living gap between prosperous and less prosperous countries. Among them:

- Steady economic growth is a key factor in reducing the income divide between rich and impoverished regions; the economies of many nations grow only sporadically.
- The worldwide economic slump that started in 2008 slowed international trade, affecting nations dependent on a limited variety of exports.
- Periodic economic slowdowns tend to affect the well-being of less prosperous nations more severely; they become less likely to attract investment capital for industrial, commercial, and infrastructure development.
- Technological progress has been a driving force for income growth in developing nations; access to technology lags in many poorer regions.

# SECTION 4: TRADITION AND MODERNIZATION—FINDING A BALANCE

As developing nations look for ways to improve living standards for their citizens, they often find that modern techniques disrupt or conflict with established cultural patterns. For example, family planning programs may violate religious beliefs (as with the Roman Catholic Church in Latin America); migration from rural areas to urban areas upsets established social structures (for instance, India's caste system); changing roles for women threatens the traditional male-female relationships (as in some Islamic nations); and changing governmental structures may clash with centuries-old economic patterns (China's communes versus family farms).

The Islamic world provides the most obvious example of the conflicting visions of cultural and social change. Fundamentalist Muslims see the influence of modern values and styles (usually labeled "Western" and decadent) as both a threat and an insult to long-established Islamic doctrines and morality. This has, in turn, manifested itself in the violent terrorist actions of a small, but extremely militant and active minority.

# Part D: Changing Political Power Structures

## SECTION 1: THE SUPERPOWERS

During much of the period after the end of World War II, world politics was dominated by the so-called superpower struggle, pitting the communist ideology of the former Soviet Union against the capitalist ideas of the United States. This struggle, which involved military, political, and economic competition, has often been called the Cold War, and each nation attempted to build and extend its power and influence. The Cold War was an icy state of tension and hostility between the former Soviet Union and the United States without direct armed conflict.

Although competition between the superpowers was world-wide, it often focused on Europe, where their two opposing alliances faced one another across the Iron Curtain. Here, the Soviet Union and its allies (the satellite states of Eastern Europe) in the Warsaw Pact confronted the United States and its Western European allies in NATO. The Cold War led to an arms race in which both sides built more sophisticated and destructive weapons designed to maintain a balance of terror, or mutually assured destruction (MAD), preventing all-out warfare between the two sides.

During the Cold War, there were periods of stability when both sides sought peaceful coexistence. These periods of détente alternated with times of heightened tensions, such as during the Cuban Missile Crisis of 1961 and the Soviet invasion of Afghanistan in 1979. From time to time, summit meetings were held between leaders of the two nations in order to improve communication and to seek conflict resolution.

Each of the superpowers attempted to extend its influence to other areas of the world. At times, the United States supported military or dictatorial governments opposed to communism, often at the expense of real democracy in those countries. The Soviet Union supported national liberation movements in some nations, often condoning sabotage and terrorism.

The dramatic political changes in Eastern Europe toward the end of the 20th century greatly changed the Cold War pattern of relationships. The ideology of communism and its reliance on totalitarian control were discredited and found ineffective in meeting people's economic and emotional needs. The desires for self-expression and self-determination of the people of Eastern Europe were coupled with a need for higher material standards of living. The result has been the fragmentation of the former Soviet Union into a number of newly independent nations, a closer relationship between several former Soviet satellites and the nations of Western Europe, and a variety of solutions to the problem of transforming economies from centrally planned socialist to some degree of free enterprise.

Russia itself, the dominant force in the former U.S.S.R., experienced some of the most serious transitional pains, as unscrupulous money men and thuggish enforcers turned a free-wheeling market economy into their personal cash cows at the expense of the prosperity and stability of the economy as a whole. Though some Western investors and lenders have seen Russia as a potential growth area, political corruption has made other investors extremely wary. In politics, too, instability as well as personal health problems plagued the government of former Russian president Boris Yeltsin. The resignation of Boris Yeltsin at the end of 1999 led to his replacement by the Russian prime minister, Vladimir Putin, as acting president. Putin won the presidential election held in March 2000. Putin's popularity was due to the Russian people's desire for greater political and economic security, and the Russian army's retaking of Chechnya after a brutal military campaign. President Putin was reelected in 2004. In 2008, Dmitry Medvedev was elected president of the Russian Federation. Vladimir Putin served as his prime minister. Putin was nominated to run for the presidency in 2012. Putin was elected President in May 2012. Dmitry Medvedev was elected Prime Minister in May 2012.

# SECTION 2: THE DEVELOPING WORLD

Many African, Asian, and Latin American nations have held a different world view, that of a multipolar, or many-sided, pattern of power. The concept of nonalignment for nations that did not wish to be too closely allied with either the West or the Eastern bloc was formulated by Nehru of India. The first meeting of nonaligned nations was held by Sukarno in Indonesia in 1955.

The superpowers often became involved in regional conflicts and disputes. At times, these involvements led to direct superpower confrontations, while at other times, the former Soviet Union and the United States were minimally involved, supplying only weapons or aid. The Korean War pitted communist North Korea and China directly against the United States and its allies. American military involvement in Southeast Asia brought massive Russian support for North Vietnam. The Soviet invasion of Afghanistan brought American weapons and money to aid Afghan *mujaheddin* (freedom fighters) who were resisting Soviet control.

Soviet and American efforts to influence events in the Middle East were frustrated by the ongoing Arab-Israeli conflict. Arab nations used the superpower competition to gain weapons and aid from both sides.

American president Jimmy Carter helped bring about an Egyptian-Israeli peace treaty (Camp David Accords—1979) and President Bill Clinton presided as Palestine Liberation Organization chairman Yassir Arafat and Israeli prime minister Yitzhak Rabin took a major step toward a possible settlement in 1993.

American troops led a UN force in driving Iraq out of Kuwait in 1991 after an invasion by Iraq, but U.S. marines suffered losses to terrorists in trying to stabilize Lebanon in the midst of a civil conflict.

Elsewhere, many conflicts are regional in nature and do not involve the United States or Russia. India and Pakistan have engaged in hostilities over Kashmir, and China and India have clashed along their disputed borders at several places in the Himalayas. Argentina and Great Britain fought a brief but bloody war over Las Islas Malvinas (the Falkland Islands) in the South Atlantic in 1982, and hostilities broke out between Vietnam and China even though both are communist nations.

# SECTION 3: ARMS CONTROL

The large sums of money expended in stockpiling nuclear weapons in their arsenals has led the superpowers to search for ways to reduce the massive budgets allocated for their development and deployment. Likewise, the potential for other nations to develop or acquire such weapons has led to efforts to control their spread.

During the 1960s, the Limited Test Ban Treaty (1963), the Nuclear Non-Proliferation Treaty (1968), and similar agreements were the focus of control efforts. Nations without nuclear capability, however, have claimed the right to it for both peaceful means (energy) and to protect themselves against enemies who already possess such weapons. India's 1974 nuclear test possibly spurred Pakistan's quest for an "Islamic bomb."

The United States and the former Soviet Union had many arms-control discussions, some of which have been successful. The 1970s saw limitations placed on certain types of missiles as a result of the first Strategic Arms Limitation Treaty (SALT), while SALT II set limits on the kinds of warheads, missile weights, and types of delivery vehicles. More recently, discussions focused on Strategic Arms Reduction Treaties (START), designed to "build down" (decrease) the numbers and types of weapons each nation possesses. In 1999, the U.S. senate rejected a treaty to ban nuclear testing.

Arms control issues have taken on a differing emphasis since the breakup of the Soviet Union. Political and economic instability in Russia and some of the other former Soviet republics have raised concerns about the security of nuclear weapons still in place. Could they be stolen, sold, acquired, and used by rogue nationalists, or even terrorist groups?

For other nations with nuclear capability, the key issue has become nonproliferation. In 1998, when India successfully carried out nuclear testing, Pakistan soon developed a nuclear bomb capability. North Korea, too has attempted to "go nuclear."

The other weapons-control issue involves the development of chemical and biological devices for use in warfare and in some nations such as Iraq, for control of domestic populations. Former Iraqi president Saddam Hussein played a cat-and-mouse game with arms inspectors from the United Nations throughout the 1990s.

It has become increasingly difficult to control the spread of nuclear weapons and the expanding military role that some nations have undertaken in recent years. For example, North Korea and Iran are both seeking to develop nuclear weapons systems, which will increase the arms race. In addition, the economic growth of China since the 1990s has been accompanied by its expanding military presence in Asia and the surrounding seas. A number of Asian nations claim the South China Sea as part of their offshore territorial boundaries because of the potential energy resources below the surface. China's rise as the leading military and naval power in Asia will be a crucial issue in the 21st century.

# SECTION 4: TERRORISM AS A POLITICAL WEAPON

Today some groups, frustrated by what they feel to be oppression by their own government or the policies of other governments, often turn to terrorism. They use violence or the threat of it to publicize their grievances or to press their demands. Terrorism involves the use of violence against unarmed, innocent civilians. Its special horror lies in the fact that innocent men, women, and children are killed.

Terrorism can involve kidnapping or hijacking, assassination, random murder, or mass killing. It is usually carried out by small groups of highly dedicated, even fanatical individuals who believe they can obtain concessions, frustrate governments, or just gain revenge. Some believe in violence as the only way to fight conditions they view as evil, but most have specific goals.

Among those who turned to terrorism to publicize their demands are the Palestinians, who have carried out global attacks against citizens of both Israel and its supporters, especially the United States. From the 1960s to the turn of the century, branches of the Irish Republican Army that are against Britain's role in Northern Ireland and groups like the Tuparmaros of Uruguay and the Shining Path (Sendoro Luminoso) in Peru used terrorist tactics to defy the governments of those nations. In the United States, a government office building in Oklahoma City, Oklahoma, was blown up by American anti-government radicals, killing 168 people. Terrorist hatred on the part of Islam jihadists led to the World Trade Center and Pentagon murderous atrocities of September 11, 2001.

State-supported terrorism has also become a problem. Countries such as Libya, Iran, and Syria have been accused of providing money and training for Palestinian and Islamic fundamentalist terrorist groups and have supported their activities. But international pressure has created the possibility that some terrorists can be brought to justice. Libya agreed to hand over for trial two suspects in the 1988 bombing of a Pan Am airliner over Scotland, and a Kurdish leader considered by Turkey to be a terrorist was extradited from Kenya. General Augusto Pinochet of Chile, whose government persecuted and killed opponents, was indicted by a Spanish court and arrested in England. In 1999, a British court ruled that Pinochet could be sent to Spain to stand trial. However, Pinochet was never sent to Spain and finally returned to Chile. Nevertheless, his arrest was a warning to other political and military leaders that they could be held responsible for state-sponsored criminal acts against innocent people.

In the 21st century, the use of terrorism as a political weapon has spread to other countries. Somalia and Yemen have become centers of terrorism. Also individual acts of terrorism have taken place in countries such as Great Britain, Spain, and more recently, Norway. Political terrorism knows no boundaries.

# Part E: Environmental Issues

As humans increase their capacity to use the earth's resources through technology, they also become increasingly capable of destroying and polluting the very environment that sustains human and all other life. Human activities now affect the ecology and even the climate of the entire planet. As Margaret Mead, a noted anthropologist, said, "We won't have a society if we destroy the environment. . . ."

Chief among the environmental concerns are possible climate changes caused by the greenhouse effect. Carbon dioxide and other gases produced by modern industries trap more of the sun's heat and energy within the earth's atmosphere, causing global warming. While scientists disagree on the causes of global warming, many feel that even a slight increase in the earth's temperatures worldwide could melt the polar ice cap, raise sea levels, submerge coastal areas, and change growing seasons and agricultural production.

Associated with possible climate change is the issue of the destruction of forests, especially the tropical rain forests. Increasingly, the developing nations are clearing large areas of tropical rain forests. They are exporting timber to obtain foreign capital, converting forests to farmland to grow cash crops such as rubber, and attempting to develop more land for settlement and to raise food crops. It is estimated that three thousand acres of tropical rain forest are destroyed every hour. At this rate, in a hundred years the rain forests could all be gone.

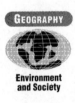

**Environment and Society**

The destruction of the forests add to the greenhouse effect because it decreases the number of trees and plants on the earth that change carbon dioxide to oxygen. In addition, thousands of plant and animal species may become extinct, reducing the earth's biological diversity and possibly its capacity to sustain other kinds of life. If the rain forests vanish, 40 percent of all living species will be destroyed. This means that millions of species, many of which have not yet even been discovered, will vanish. Finally, changing natural patterns can destroy the useful-

**Use of Geography**

ness of the soil and the effectiveness of the water supply, thus defeating the original purpose of the attempted change in land use. The soil of the tropical rain forest is extremely poor in many nutrients and can sustain agriculture for only a short time. As a result, farmers move on and cut down more forest. In 1992, the United Nations Conference on Environment and Development was held in Rio de Janeiro. Five major agreements on global environmental issues were signed. In the following years a number of formal treaties designed to protect the environment were negotiated and signed. Among these formal treaties and agreements were the Framework Convention on Climate Change and the Convention on Biological Diversity, which were legally binding on the signing parties. In 1997, the Kyoto Protocol, a treaty that has legally binding targets to limit or reduce greenhouse emissions became a reality. The majority of industrial nations have already signed, but the United States has refused to accept the provisions of the protocol.

Also at issue is the need to protect endangered species and to conserve the wildlife of the earth. Animals such as leopards and alligators (for their skins), elephants and rhinos (for their tusks and horns), and ostriches (for their feathers) have been hunted almost to extinction to provide luxury consumer goods. The nets used by the tuna-fishing industry have endangered dolphins. Several nations have depleted the whale population for industrial purposes, and the spread of human settlement and recreation areas have reduced the land available for animals and plants.

Increased industrialization means increased pollution and an increased threat to human health. Pollution creates carcinogens that cause cancer. Respiratory diseases result from unhealthful substances in the air we breathe, and chemicals in the water supply and food chain create additional threats. Chlorofluorocarbons used in aerosol sprays and refrigeration units contribute to the depletion of the ozone layer, the part of the earth's atmosphere that filters out some of the most harmful of the sun's rays.

The waste byproducts of energy production are another threat. Acid rain is caused by the burning of fossil fuels and has the capacity to wipe out fish and aquatic plant life when it accumulates in bodies of water. Used-up radioactive fuel from nuclear power plants and other hazardous waste products must be disposed of and their transport across international borders regulated.

Safeguards must be developed to prevent industrial disasters such as those that occurred in Chernobyl in the former Soviet Union and Bhopal in India. Radiation from the accident at the Chernobyl nuclear power plant killed Soviet citizens and spread across northwestern Europe. A poisonous gas leak from an American chemical factory in Bhopal killed and injured thousands. In 2010, in Fukushima, Japan, a nuclear facility was severely damaged because of an earthquake and radiation dangers are still present in areas near to the damaged reactors.

Governments around the world are beginning to cooperate in dealing with these environmental issues, though opinions differ about what to do in specific cases. For example, Brazilians see the clearing of the rain forest as essential to their nation's development. They consider American criticism unfair since the United States has been clearing forest lands for over two centuries. Agreements over the use of the resources of the oceans and areas such as Antarctica may establish patterns for dealing with global environmental issues in the future.

One creative proposal for dealing with environmental issues in developing nations has been related to the debt crises often faced by those countries. Lenders have tied debt cancellation to improved environmental policies on the part of governments, such as slowing the clear-cutting of rain forests.

# Part F: Human Rights

Along with the industrial and scientific revolutions of the past several centuries has come the democratic revolution. Fundamental to this has been the idea that all human beings possess certain political, social, and economic rights. In 1948 the United Nations adopted the *Universal Declaration of Human Rights*, which states the basic right to dignity for all people, as well as the right to freedom of speech, freedom of assembly, and an adequate standard of living.

In 1975, thirty-three nations of Europe, along with the former Soviet Union and the United States, signed the Helsinki Accords. This agreement included a statement of basic human rights. In spite of these documents, however, human-rights abuses continue around the world. Organizations such as Amnesty International and Human Rights Watch monitor and publicize such abuses. Many nations still have much to do with improving human rights and equality for women. Such improvement received global attention in 2011, with the awarding of the Nobel Peace Prizes. Three women were recipients for their promoting humanitarian efforts in their countries: Ellen Johnson Sirleaf and Leymah Gbowee from Liberia, and Tawakul Karman from Yemen

## VIOLATIONS OF HUMAN RIGHTS

### Apartheid in South Africa

For over 40 years South Africa's government denied political rights to all citizens not of European background and attempted to establish homelands for blacks. This policy denied the nonwhite population the use of much of the land and resources of the nation. It severely limited economic opportunities for the majority of the population and preserved the white minority's control of the economy.

The South African system also severely limited the rights of those of Asian or mixed backgrounds and extended full political participation only to those of European ancestry. Efforts by the black majority to gain political rights, including the Freedom Charter of the 1950s as well as demonstrations, often led to violent repression. Several hundred blacks were killed by police at Sharpeville in 1965. Students protesting educational changes were gunned down in 1976, and protests and activism in the 1980s led to continued violence.

Individuals who criticized or campaigned against apartheid suffered banning, that is, restriction in their travel and contacts, or imprisonment. Some, such as Stephen Biko, who died in police custody, were murdered.

When change came, it occurred at a very rapid and surprising pace. Prime Minister F. W. deKlerk, elected in 1990, promised to "dismantle apartheid" and began by releasing revered South African leader Nelson Mandela after 30 years of imprisonment. The formerly outlawed African National Congress was legalized, many rules and laws were changed, and the first free universal elections were held in 1994. Nelson Mandela was inaugurated as the head of the nation.

Though it has struggled with continued racial and ethnic conflict and the resultant poverty and crime, the self-designated "rainbow nation" has made progress both economically and socially. A "Truth and Reconciliation Commission" has been the centerpiece of an ongoing attempt to heal old wounds and set new standards of cooperation.

## Totalitarian Governments

Such governments are known for their violations of human rights. The former Soviet Union suppressed and imprisoned dissidents, those who criticized the Communist Party or the government. Forced labor camps and psychiatric wards were used to punish those who spoke out or wrote critical articles or books.

In the spring of 1989, the democracy movement started by Chinese students and activists was violently repressed by the Chinese communist government. It sent tanks and troops to clear the demonstrators out of Beijing's Tiananmen Square.

Military dictatorships in Latin American countries, such as Argentina and Chile in the 1980s, imprisoned, tortured, and murdered those who opposed them. Central American death squads used terrorist tactics to threaten and eliminate those who disagree with them.

The 1990s saw the replacement of many of the Latin American militarist regimes with democratically elected governments, accompanied by attempts to bring to justice those who perpetrated the human rights violations. There are only vestiges of the totalitarianism of communist Eastern Europe in some of the successor nations, and Western nations continue to criticize the repression of dissidents in China.

Several Arab governments in the Middle East have carried out repressive measures against dissidents and minorities. Egypt, Yemen, Saudi Arabia, Iraq and Syria received condemnations by human rights organizations.

## Genocide

The deliberate extermination of a racial, cultural, or ethnic group is called genocide. The worst-ever example of genocide was the systematic murder of Jewish people in Europe by Nazi Germany during World War II. This policy, which resulted in the death of six million Jews, is known as the Holocaust. There are more recent cases of human-rights violations that warrant special consideration. In Cambodia, Rwanda, and Uganda, an untold number were the victims of genocide.

In Uganda, the issue was ethnic. Colonel Idi Amin seized power in 1971 with the support of an army largely made up of soldiers of his own ethnic group. After declaring himself president for life, he led a bloody campaign against members of other ethnic groups, which resulted in over 300,000 deaths, the emigration of most citizens of Asian background, and eventually an armed invasion of neighboring Tanzania in 1979.

The Cambodian tragedy was even more horrible. The fanatical communist Khmer Rouge, led by Pol Pot, gained control in 1977 after the turmoil of the communist takeover in Vietnam. The Khmer Rouge forced the people to leave the cities and killed the educated, the middle class, Buddhist priests, and anyone else of power, authority, or uniqueness in the society. By the time Vietnam helped establish an opposition government in the capital of Phnom Penh in 1985, it is estimated that some four million Cambodians had died.

Africa, too, has seen its version of near-genocide, or what some have called ethnic cleansing. In the small central African nations of Rwanda and Burundi, the rival Tutsi and Hutu ethnic groups battled for political control and in the process massacred thousands of the opposition. In the Darfur region of the Sudan, Black Christians faced extermination by Arabs during 2004–2005.

The focus for the concept of ethnic cleansing has been the Balkans, where the reassertion of nationalist fervor came with the fragmentation of Yugoslavia into its component republics. First in Bosnia-Herzegovina, then in its own region of Kosovo, the government of what is left of the former Yugoslavia (mostly Serbia) has been accused of attempting to drive out, respectively, the Bosnia Muslims, and the ethnic Albanians (Kosovars).

## Resurgent Nationalism

Events in the Balkans in particular are evidence of a reassertion of nationalist passions, especially in Europe. Ethnic groups from the Baltic republics to Central Asia gained sovereignty as a result of the breakup of the Soviet Union and there are others such as the Chechens who continue to campaign for independence from Russia. Czechs and Slovaks, Croats, Slovenes, and Macedonians, all have established nations based on ethnic and cultural backgrounds, spelling the end of Czechoslovakia and splintering Yugoslavia. Renewed cultural awareness and assertiveness motivates Catalans and Basques in Spain as well as Flemings and Walloons in Belgium. In the United Kingdom, Scots recently voted to form their own parliament, thereby establishing a greater degree of autonomy.

# Part G: Technology

The post-Industrial Revolution refers to changes that have taken place in this century. These changes took place in such fields as the gathering of information technology, communications, and the manufacture of products. These changes have accelerated contact and diffusion among culture regions and promoted global independence. This has, in turn, widened the impact of machines and medical technology on the lifestyles, work patterns, and standard of living of people in all societies.

## The Silicon Chip

Computers have been the key to the changes of the post-Industrial Revolution. The tiny low-cost silicon chip has brought the most important change in human communications since the printing press. A silicon chip makes it possible to perform millions of calculations in a second and to store vast amounts of information. Today's largest computers can perform as many as 800 million calculations a second and store 4 million words. These stored data can be retrieved instantly and transmitted to any location on earth or even into space. Computers today are used in many areas of human activity. These include: international financial and banking transactions and investments; automation of industrial production and product distribution; informational data analysis, sharing, storage, and retrieval; news gathering and spreading via electronic telecommunication; and weapons development, monitoring, and control.

## The Green Revolution

The developing nations need to increase their agricultural production to keep up with the population increases in their nations. The efforts of scientists and government leaders to find ways to do this have produced a Green Revolution, that is, an increase in the amount of agricultural production from land already under cultivation and expansion of farming onto previously nonproductive land.

The basis of these improvements has been the development by agronomists (agricultural scientists) of high-yielding plant varieties. These are seeds that can produce greater quantities of crops (especially food grains such as rice and wheat) from an area of land than traditional seeds can produce. However, the new grains are not always as hardy as the older ones, and they need chemical fertilizers, more water, and pesticides to protect them from diseases and insects. Different farming techniques are also necessary to use them effectively.

The Green Revolution needs government support to be carried out. Governments must provide education and information as well as loans to enable farmers to buy the new seeds and the necessary pesticides and fertilizers. They must also build irrigation and transportation systems and provide price supports to guarantee that farmers can sell their products at a profit. In addition, governments must carry out land reform, distributing land in a more equal fashion. Finally, a technology for the Green Revolution (appropriate farm machines and techniques) that is useful in small areas at low cost must be developed and made available.

Although the Green Revolution has led to increased production, in some areas because of the cost of new irrigation systems, hybrid seeds, pesticides, and fertilizers it has also led to smaller farmers incurring extensive debt and as a result, losing their land. This has occurred in rural areas all over the globe. The increased use of pesticides and chemical fertilziers may also be the cause of increased cancer rates in many rural areas of the developing world.

Without such government support, the risk is too great for most farmers to try the new methods. One of the criticisms of the revolution in agriculture has been its failure to reach poorer farmers. Only those who already make a profit have the money to invest in new methods and techniques. Another criticism is that some of the changes create threats to the environment—irrigation may disrupt normal water systems, internal combustion engines in machinery as well as fertilizers and pesticides pollute the air and water, and overuse of the land can wear it out.

## MEDICAL BREAKTHROUGHS

The advances in medical technology over the past century have prolonged human life and increased its quality. Vaccinations have helped make humans immune to many deadly diseases, while new treatment techniques have increased survival rates for many others. Likewise, improved treatment of wounds and injuries, as well as organ transplants and artificial body parts, have enabled people to live full lives where in the past they might have been severely disabled.

Attitudes have also changed. People are seen as "physically challenged" rather than handicapped and are encouraged to strive to reach their potential. Accessible public facilities and special activities and support groups have helped to enrich the lives of those with physical disabilities.

Preventing diseases has also become an important medical concern. Scientists have researched the effects of most human activities from smoking to jogging, from eating red meat to living near nuclear power plants. Although there is not always agreement on the implications of such studies, the information does provide people with knowledge and possible choices.

Stem cell research has become an extremely controversial aspect of modern medical technology. Stem cells are the first to develop in embryos and are capable of becoming any of the cell types that make up the human body. Scientists have come to believe that embryonic stem cells, especially, may hold the secrets to the cures for diabetes, Parkinson's, Alzheimer's, and spinal cord injuries, among other conditions. At present these embryonic stem cells come from terminated pregnancies, fertility clinics, cloning, and custom fertilization. There are moral and ethical questions concerning all these sources. In 2004 South Korean scientists announced that they had cloned human embryos and harvested their stem cells. In the United States, the Bush administration has severely restricted funding for stem cell research, whereas abroad many governments are generous in their support.

Biotechnology and genetic engineering hold both a promise and a threat for the future. The development of new organisms (biotechnology) may help control diseases or pollutants, but long-term effects may be hard to predict. And the capacity to alter human genes (genetic engineering) that control a person's individual makeup raises ethical as well as medical issues.

Underlying all this is the issue of cost. Medical treatment grows ever more expensive, even in developed nations. In the developing nations, it is one more factor that must be considered in making decisions regarding use of limited financial resources.

# Part H: Transportation and Communication

One aspect of our modern world is increased mobility—of resources, manufactured goods, ideas and techniques, and human beings themselves. The horizons of the average North American, Western European, or Japanese have been expanded by the automobile, the jet airplane, the telephone, and satellite television, whereas in Asia and Africa, the bicycle or motorbike, the train or minibus, and the transistor radio have had a similar impact.

Improved transport systems move oil by supertanker from the Middle East to Japan's industries and move Korean technicians and engineers by jumbo jet to Saudi Arabian oil fields. Paved roads move fertilizer to the rural farms of India's Punjab and rural workers in search of jobs to the cities of Latin America.

China manufactures and uses more bicycles than any other nation. More people ride more trains over more miles in India than anywhere else. Job opportunities for rural Indonesians are increased by their ability to commute to a factory in a nearby town on small Japanese-built motorcycles and bus-vans.

Communication technology also improves people's standards of living. The American investor gathers data using cable TV or satellite and the Internet, and buys and sells using a computer. Cell phones and laptop computers have made it possible for people to work and communicate from the most remote spots on the planet. The Philippine farmer listens to the agricultural and weather reports; the Thai craftsperson watches traditional religious dramas on the government television station.

Mobile phones have become the source of great technological innovation, rapidly replacing traditional land-line telephones. Many are now equipped with Internet access as well as the ability to store video games, films, and music, serving as portable PCs (personal computers). iPads and tablets, portable agenda planners with Internet access and communication devices, are another innovation. These are also capable of storing video games, films, and music, as well as the texts of books. With telecommunication companies competing for customers, the prices of both the equipment and monthly costs for services have become affordable to most people and are rapidly replacing other electronic devices. The iPod, a small device with earphones that stores vast amounts of music, video games, and films, has also become very popular, especially with children and teens. The creation of the e-reader (electronic reader), a portable device for reading books, periodicals, and other texts, has challenged the supremacy of printed material. These inventions have made it possible for people to communicate instantaneously anywhere in the world at any time.

Nearly instantaneous news reporting via satellite not only puts citizens in touch with events around the world, but it also puts pressure on politicians, especially those in democratic nations, to consider their actions and policies in terms of "approval ratings." The Internet gives individuals access to a wealth of information, but much of it may be unreliable or even offensive. By the same token, however, a person can become vastly more self-informed and use the information constructively with careful use of the system. An American teacher, can, for instance, communicate directly with a Serbian citizen cowering in a basement as NATO bombs rain down on his nation, and get a very different picture from that painted by his own media.

However, improved transportation and communications can also have negative effects. The massive oil spill from the ship *Exxon Valdez* in 1989 damaged Alaska's coastline and disrupted its economy. Tokyo commuters wear masks to keep airborne chemicals out of their lungs, and London cab drivers average only 9.2 miles per hour, hoping gridlock will not bring them to a complete standstill.

**GEOGRAPHY**

**Environment and Society**

Terrorists hijack and destroy airliners. Computer hackers develop the potential to disrupt financial, informational, and perhaps even governmental communications systems. Smugglers make millions using boats and airplanes to transport illegal drugs. Each technological innovation also creates the possibility of dishonesty and abuse.

# Part I: Space Exploration

The space race began in 1957 when the former Soviet Union launched *Sputnik*, the first satellite. One of the highlights of the space race was the landing of American astronauts on the moon in 1969. Today the space program continues to be the focus of much attention and requires huge amounts of money and resources. Achievements in this area bring great prestige to the nations involved, but some think that the money could be used more effectively elsewhere. In 2003, China launched its space program.

## Effects on Global Communication and International Relations

Electronic communication by satellite links has had important effects on both civilian and military aspects of human culture. News and entertainment can be shown live or almost immediately, and nations with "spy-in-the-sky" satellites can monitor the actions and movements of potential enemies.

International crises can develop more quickly but can often be dealt with more easily because of rapid communication. Moreover, when emergencies or disasters occur, aid and relief can be dispatched sooner and with greater effect.

## Applications of Space and Space-Based Technology

Both the United States and the former Soviet Union have applied rocket technology from their space programs to the development of intercontinental ballistic missiles (ICBMs) for use as carriers of atomic weapons. The American "star wars," or Strategic Defense Initiative (SDI), was an attempt to apply satellite techniques to the destruction of missiles in flight.

Astronomers have profited from the ability of satellites to look into the depths of space without the interference of the earth's atmosphere. Deep space probes to the farthest reaches of the solar system have extended scientific knowledge in a number of fields. In 2004, the Mars Rovers revealed that Mars was once well watered.

Meteorology and the analysis and prediction of weather patterns have been changed by satellite radar and photography. Such knowledge benefits travelers, businesspeople, farmers, and those threatened by storms or droughts. Other fields, such as medicine, may gain knowledge from the opportunity to conduct experiments in the weightless environment of an orbiting space vehicle. Geographers and geologists have new tools for mapping and analysis of land and water patterns and processes.

## Recent Developments

In 2004, the Cassini-Huygens mission was the first to orbit Saturn. This was a United States–European mission that sent back pictures of Saturn's rings and is scheduled to study several of Saturn's moons.

The International Space Station is the largest cooperative scientific project in history. Sixteen nations, including Canada, Belgium, Denmark, France, Germany, Italy, Japan, Netherlands, Norway, Russia, Spain, Sweden, Switzerland, the United Kingdom, the United States, and Japan, are involved in the project. The first assembly of the station took place in 1998. The *Columbia* disaster, which grounded U.S. space shuttles, led to the loss of the main supply ships to the space station, however, repair and maintenance have taken place since. The plans for the space station include studying the effects of long-term exposure to reduced gravity, growing living cells in a gravity-free environment, and studying long-term changes in the earth's environment by observing the earth from outer space. The year 2011 marked the end of the American shuttle program, but the United States intends to continue unmanned exploration to the moon, Jupiter, and Mars. China plans to begin construction of its own space station with construction expected to be completed by the year 2022.

Both Indian and U.S. scientists published articles in the periodical, *Science*, in 2009, indicating that there is more water on the moon than previously thought.

# Part J: Mutual Impact and Influence: Europe, America, and Africa-Asia

Much of the history of the past 500 years has focused on the relationships between culture regions that experienced the direct effects of the Industrial Revolution and those that received those effects secondhand. The regions that directly experienced the Industrial Revolution, principally the nations of Europe and North America, are also areas whose cultures are based on the Judeo-Christian and Greco-Roman traditions.

The regions that did not directly experience the Industrial Revolution, such as the Native American cultures of the Americas, the ethnic groups (tribes) of Africa, the Islamic, Hindu, Buddhist, and Confucian societies of Asia, have been dominated by the West because of its technical and economic power for many of those 500 years. During this period, there has not been much recognition of the contributions of African and Asian cultures to the development of Europe and North America.

Europe's reaction to the availability of trade and resources in Africa, Asia, and the Americas was colonialism and imperialism. The technology of the Industrial Revolution provided the weapons and tools and the development of capitalism provided the financial resources for Europe to colonize these areas of the world and to dominate them. This dominance profoundly affected European attitudes, resulting in feelings of cultural superiority, prejudice, discrimination, ethnocentrism, and racism.

In time, the cultures that came under European control reacted with an awakening of pride in their own cultures. As nationalism developed, Americans, Africans, and Asians often used European ideas of political revolution, democracy, and self-determination against the European colonial powers.

As the 21st century dawned, the influence and impact seemed to be shifting more from the West to the East than had been the case for much of the previous five centuries. Growing capacity in manufacturing and technology coupled with cheaper costs have meant that Asian nations in particular have been net exporters of goods and services. Profits earned in this way have also been invested by Asian companies and governments in European and American concerns, moving relationships in the direction of greater balance.

Remnants of the colonial economic pattern of raw materials moving from Asia and Africa to Europe and America have been supplemented by the development of new service and industrial capacities, especially in Asian nations. Textiles and other lighter manufacturing industries export goods to the EU and North America. Digital communications and the Internet helped create "outsource" informational giants like India and the Philippines.

In the case of fundamentalist Islam, reaction against Western values and cultural styles has led to expanded campaigns of terrorism against European and American institutions, as well as attempts to establish Islamic theocracies such as that of the Taliban in Afghanistan. The destruction of the World Trade Center in New York, bombings in Turkey, Spain, England, and Indonesia, and other violent acts have been carried out by Al Qaeda and similar or related groups. The expressed goal is a return to basic Muslim beliefs and standards and the destruction of "evil" influences.

Western military "interventions" in Middle Eastern nations earned increased anger and hatred from many Muslims. Among these were American campaigns in Iraq and Afghanistan, the U.S. raid into Pakistan to eliminate al Qaeda icon Osama Bin Laden, and NATO support of rebels who overthrew long-time dictator Muammar el-Qaddafi in Libya.

The Libyan revolt was one element of 2011s "Arab Spring," a series of popular protest movements in nations across North Africa to Syria and the Arabian Peninsula. Some scholars and politicians saw these uprisings as drawing inspiration from western concepts of democracy. Others cited the "Arab street's" disgust with western governments for their support of despotic and corrupt regimes like that of Hosni Mubarak in Egypt.

# REVIEW QUESTIONS

*Multiple Choice.* Select the letter of the answer that correctly completes each statement.

1. People experiencing the revolution of rising expectations today are
   A. eager to accept democracy as the answer to political problems
   B. not interested in receiving assistance from developed nations
   C. dissatisfied with some aspects of their present way of life
   D. determined to follow all their traditional ways of living

2. Rapid population growth in a developing nation is due mainly to
   A. a high standard of living for most families
   B. the availability of medical and health care services
   C. a booming economy and many employment opportunities
   D. the number of marriages among younger teenagers

3. Nations have formed international organizations such as the European Community, the Organization of Petroleum Exporting Countries, and the Organization of African Unity in order to
   A. provide for increased military security and national defense
   B. ensure that they receive a sufficient supply of natural resources
   C. carry out the decisions of the UN Security Council
   D. further their own national interests and improve their situation

4. Political leaders in both the United States and Great Britain have often spoken in favor of peaceful resolution of international conflicts. Yet during the 1980s the armed forces of both nations were involved in military encounters outside their own national boundaries. This observation best supports which of the following conclusions?
   A. Most armed conflicts are deliberately started by one side or the other.
   B. Industrialized nations tend to be more aggressive than developing ones.
   C. A popularly elected government must be warlike to satisfy its citizens.
   D. Nations often place greater value in their self-interest than in peace.

5. "Acid Rain Destroys North American Forests"
   "Chemical Leak in Bhopal, India, Kills Thousands"
   "Nuclear Accident at Soviet Power Plant in Chernobyl"

   These headlines best support which of the following conclusions?
   A. Communist nations produce more pollution than capitalist nations.
   B. Developing nations are responsible for most of the pollution in the
      world.
   C. Protecting the environment is an issue of worldwide importance.
   D. The United Nations is responsible for solving pollution problems.

6. A modern, well-organized infrastructure is necessary for the economic
   development of a nation. Which of the following factors would be
   included in a nation's infrastructure?
   A. network of transportation and communication
   B. written organizational plan for development
   C. technological system for using infrared rays
   D. strong system of family support and unity

7. Nations with a low per capita GNP have
   A. greater life expectancy
   B. greater public expenditure on health per capita
   C. a high infant mortality rate
   D. a high adult literacy rate

Base your answer to question 8 on the chart below.

| What Americans Buy from Africans* | |
|---|---|
| Crude petroleum | $9,900 |
| Coffee beans | $ 599 |
| Platinum | $ 352 |
| Aluminum | $ 292 |
| Diamonds (nonindustrial) | $ 286 |
| Uranium | $ 200 |
| Cocoa beans | $ 137 |
| Iron alloys (for steel) | $ 119 |

* 1982 U.S./sub-Saharan Africa trade ($ value in millions).

8. Most of the goods exported from Africa to the United States can be
   described as
   A. high-tech components
   B. consumer goods
   C. raw materials
   D. agricultural products

9. Global issues such as overcrowding and pollution are a direct result of
   A. high unemployment
   B. an agriculture-based economy
   C. population growth
   D. an imbalance in world trade

10. During the 1970s and 1980s, attempts were made by the United States and the former Soviet Union to
    A. share advances in military technology
    B. bring democracy to Eastern Europe
    C. form an alliance against Israel
    D. limit the build-up of nuclear weapons

11. In developing countries, the major reason that people move from rural areas to urban areas is to
    A. gain more political power
    B. escape dangerous chemical fertilizers
    C. find better job opportunities
    D. enjoy more varied entertainment

12. Terrorism in the 1980s and 1990s was used by certain groups primarily to
    A. find a peaceful way of settling international conflicts
    B. draw the attention of the world to their causes
    C. increase humanitarian aid to their people
    D. put pressure on the superpowers to end the arms race

13. Which is most characteristic of a nation whose economy is dependent upon the production of one commodity?
    A. The economy is self-sufficient.
    B. The nation has a subsistence economy.
    C. Economic well-being is closely tied to world market prices.
    D. Industrialization makes it possible to export a variety of goods.

14. A policy of nonalignment may be attractive to a developing nation because it allows that nation to
    A. become a strong military power in its own right
    B. develop an overseas empire
    C. concentrate on domestic problems
    D. gain benefits from both sides in the superpower competition

15. Which has been an important result of improved means of communication and travel?
    A. Changes in one part of the world can greatly affect other areas.
    B. Countries have become more nationalistic.
    C. Barriers to international trade have been abolished.
    D. There is less need for international organizations.

16. The greenhouse effect may cause a dramatic
    A. increase in the world's food production
    B. reduction in the level of the world's oceans
    C. rise in the temperatures of the earth in the 21st century
    D. decline in industrial pollution in the United States and Europe

17. The destruction of tropical rain forests is most alarming on the continents of
    A. South America and Africa
    B. Europe and Australia
    C. North America and Asia
    D. Africa and Antarctica

18. Demographers would most likely study statistics indicating that
    A. China's Gross Domestic Product grew by 7 percent in the 1990s
    B. educational spending in Italy declined between 1995 and 2005
    C. the world's population exceeded 6 billion by the year 2000
    D. ocean temperatures rose by 1.5 degrees in the 20th century

19. Which of the following is a major reason why it is difficult to lower birth rates in developing nations?
    A. Children often contribute to the economic well-being of families.
    B. Traditional religious values may favor small families.
    C. Some governments encourage people to marry at a later age.
    D. Prosperous and educated people usually favor large families.

20. Most developing nations have opted first to
    A. invest in costly industrial projects
    B. expand the health care system for their people
    C. augment their agricultural production to feed their people
    D. expand programs that safeguard their environment

21. Devastating sexually transmitted diseases are hard to control because
    A. there is a need to control population growth in some areas
    B. no medicines are available for their treatment
    C. developed nations refuse to help poorer countries
    D. it is quite easy to change traditional social behaviors

22. Global economic development has led to
    A. decreased foreign investment
    B. multinational interdependence
    C. increased trade barriers
    D. declining world trade

23. The most recent expansion of the European Union has included
    A. all of the countries of Scandinavia
    B. several former members of the Soviet Bloc
    C. the island nations of Ireland and Iceland
    D. newly independent nations from the former USSR

24. The primary goal of the European Economic Union is to
    A. achieve economic integration of the member nations
    B. form an economic organization along the lines of NATO
    C. prevent nonmember nations from manufacturing in Europe
    D. create a completely self-sufficient trading network

25. In the 1990s, all the world's leading trading nations
    A. increased the volume of their agricultural exports
    B. tried to avoid a disastrous global economic war
    C. erected trade barriers to protect their national production
    D. gave up the idea of forming economic trading blocs

26. All the following are positive effects of multinational corporations *except*
    A. create jobs where they set up manufacturing plants
    B. bring new manufacturing facilities to developing countries
    C. help national industries by increasing competition
    D. contribute to raising the standard of living of their workers

27. Multinational corporations have a tendency to
    A. serve the interests of the nation where their headquarters are
    B. try to remain within the areas of the United States and Western Europe
    C. be increasingly independent and have an international outlook
    D. invest their profits within the nations where they earn them

28. During the 1990s many developing nations
    A. reduced the amount of foreign debt they owed
    B. happily complied with austerity measures called for by the IMF
    C. avoided borrowing to finance infrastructure projects
    D. became more burdened with debts that were not payable

29. The collapse of communism in the Soviet Union and the nations of Eastern Europe
    A. made more financial aid available for developing nations
    B. led to a growth of employment in these countries
    C. caused greater competition for limited financial aid
    D. resulted in more investment capital for Africa and Asia

30. The decline of the United States currency (the dollar) would result in
    A. U.S. goods becoming more expensive in Europe
    B. foreign automobiles becoming cheaper in the United States
    C. no real change because the dollar is still powerful
    D. American products being cheaper in other world markets

31. The global drug trade is a problem for all of the following reasons *except*
    A. huge sums of drug money are laundered by drug cartels
    B. drug money increases political instability and violence
    C. profits from the drug trade are used mostly for philanthropic purposes
    D. some international banks and businesses cooperate with the drug cartels

32. Cultural diffusion has increased because of
    A. increased automation
    B. technological advances
    C. growing materialism
    D. renewed feminism

33. The growth of materialism in the United States and elsewhere has led to
    A. a questioning of values
    B. gender stereotyping
    C. women's liberation
    D. national self-determination

34. New technological advances have resulted in all of the following *except*
    A. increased automation
    B. reduced working hours
    C. declining consumerism
    D. more leisure time

35. In the 1960s, the rebirth of the women's rights movement in the United States reflected
    A. a demand for equal voting rights
    B. the enactment of a constitutional amendment for women's rights
    C. a desire to end all aspects of sexual discrimination
    D. the overall acceptance by men of the equality of women

36. The disappearance of communism in the Soviet Union and Eastern Europe has led to
    A. greater numbers of people being employed
    B. a decline in ethnic and national consciousness
    C. arrival of religious practice in these areas
    D. more people having a better materialistic life

37. The loss of tropical rain forests leads to
    A. animal and plant life being destroyed
    B. a lessening of the greenhouse effect
    C. less carbon dioxide in the atmosphere
    D. the overall improvement of air quality

38. The Bhopal and Chernobyl incidents are examples of
    A. a nation's ability to control its industrial accidents
    B. policies that governments should follow to control pollution
    C. devastating accidents that can happen if safety is ignored
    D. the need to build more chemical and nuclear plants

39. The nation that consumes the greatest percentage of the world's energy is
    A. Japan
    B. Russia
    C. the United States
    D. China

40. The greatest source of the world's energy used today is
    A. natural gas
    B. oil
    C. coal
    D. electricity

41. The post-Industrial Revolution refers to
    A. a growth in mechanized production
    B. the era of airplane travel
    C. increased use of the atomic power
    D. changes in science and technology

656

42. The computer revolution has led to
    A. the increasing high cost of producing silicon chips
    B. a decline in the use of computer-generated stock trading
    C. enormous changes in the gathering of information
    D. a greater independence for industrialized nations

43. All the following are positive effects of the use of computers *except* the
    A. increased use of computer related instructional programs
    B. improvement in the speed of financial and banking transactions
    C. prediction of election results prior to the polls closing
    D. ability to forecast worldwide weather conditions

44. Space exploration began in earnest in the 1950s after the
    A. United States launched the *Columbia* space shuttle
    B. Soviet Union launched the *Sputnik I* satellite
    C. United States developed the Strategic Defense Initiative
    D. Soviet Union developed the first operational space station

45. All the following are accepted medical advances *except*
    A. laser surgery technology
    B. diagnostic services
    C. genetic engineering
    D. organ transplants

# THEMATIC ESSAYS

**Essay #1 Theme:** Science and Technology
Advances made in science and technology in the 20th century will help humans to resolve health problems and communication issues in the next century.

**Task:**
1. Explain how scientific and technological advances help resolve human problems.
2. Select two technological advances and explain how they have helped humankind.

**Directions:** Write a well-organized essay with an introduction to the topic, a body that accomplishes the task, and a summarizing statement.

*Hint:* You may choose health and communication issues that involve you or people you know.

**Essay #2 Theme:** Economic Systems
After the end of the Cold War, capitalism emerged triumphant as the world's leading economic system.

**Task:**
1. Define the economic system of capitalism.
2. Select two capitalist countries and explain how their economic systems are similar and different.

**Directions:** Write a well-organized essay with an introduction, the topic, a body that accomplishes the task, and a summarizing statement.

*Hint:* You may use the United States.

# DOCUMENT-BASED ESSAY QUESTIONS

**Directions:** The following two questions are based on the accompanying documents. Some of the documents have been edited for the purpose of this assignment.

Write two well-organized essays with an introduction stating a thesis, a body of several paragraphs that accomplishes the task, and a summarizing conclusion. Use evidence from all of the documents to support the position you take in your thesis. Do not simply repeat the contents of the document; explain things in your words and relate the information to your thesis. Using the knowledge of the social studies, include related information that is not included in the documents.

**Essay #1**

**Historical Context:** In Latin America, economic nationalism and foreign investment have been interpreted from different viewpoints and influence how nations make economic and political decisions.

**Task:** Discuss how different economic ideas about monetary issues such as foreign investment in Latin America can be defended based on the financial and political interests of those who hold that point of view.

**Part A:** Summarize the main idea expressed in the document.

**Part B:** Respond in an essay. Your essay should be based on a thesis statement. Your essay should explain how each of the statements in the documents reflect a point of view based on economic or political interests. Use all the documents in your essay.

### DOCUMENT 1

"Financial institutions that invest in Latin America have to wrestle with unusual problems to finance their operations. Most of these problems do not plague financial institutions in the developed countries. In Latin America capital is scarce and all business firms suffer from a lack of available cash. Bank rates are high. There is criticism that the automobile business is attracting too much cash to the detriment of other sectors of the economy. National pride is sensitive to the penetration of foreign capital that purchases control of national industries. The price level is under insistent inflationary pressure. Returns to investors have to be correspondingly high."

—M. R. Niefeld (1962), "The American Banker"

## DOCUMENT 2

"Let us examine the reasons that the United States government and financial institutions should be interested in investing in Latin America. With a per capita income which averages one eighth of ours they still consume one fifth of our exports. The nations of Latin America possess one of the world's greatest storehouses of natural resources. Roughly one third of our agricultural and raw material imports come from Latin America. Our private investments bring in healthy returns to the investors. There is a great potential for growth of trade."

—Clement G. Motten (1986), "Reasons for Investments in Latin America"

## DOCUMENT 3

"It is official US policy to encourage investment abroad. This view arises from a desire to reduce direct government investment and the belief that private investment offers the most effective way to achieve economic growth. However, private investment is highly selective. It tends to favor the areas where the greatest returns can be achieved and avoids problems that are too costly if they interfere with the immediate returns on the capital invested. In addition, private investment in Latin America concentrates on petroleum, mineral, and other natural resources."

Marvin Bernstein (1966), "Foreign Investment in Latin America"

## DOCUMENT 4

"The object of foreign investment is to obtain profits for the investors. The first priority of private investment is to select those industries where the returns will be maximized with the least risk and investment in infrastructure. Private investment leads to money being drained from the national economy and sent abroad. Purchase of valuable National industries is a goal of foreign investment. There is no real desire to assist the countries and people in the nation where investments are made by foreign financial interests. The foreign investors often eliminate national competition to gain complete control of a lucrative industry to earn the greatest profits."

—Pablo Casanova (1975), "The Ideology of Foreign Investment in Latin America"

## DOCUMENT 5

"The economic growth and the social prosperity of Mexico must depend basically on the Mexican people. Foreign investment is necessary but must be carefully regulated to prevent from creating problems. Mexico has to guard against the outflow of foreign remittances that are the direct result of making too high of a percentage of profits. The types of investments must be analyzed before they are allowed to be made in order that national interests can be protected. The Mexican workers deserve protection from foreign investors who invest because the wages of Mexican workers are lower than in developing countries. Mexico must protect itself from foreign investment that seeks to take over and dominate a selected industry or national market."

—Mario Roman Betata (1965), Foreign Investment in Mexico

## DOCUMENT 6
## A WEALTHY SALVADORAN GIRL

Ana's ancestors have lived at the family hacienda near Ranchador for generations, ever since the first Spanish families settled in the area. Today Ana and her father and mother and brothers and sisters occupy the large, comfortable farm estate that they inherited. They are proud of their Spanish heritage.

Because of the vast inherited land holdings and his good business ability, Ana's father is very wealthy. . . . The family lives on a lavish scale, entertaining many house guests and enjoying a great deal of activity around the swimming pool. . . . There are numerous household servants, and Ana has no idea how many people are employed on her father's fields.

Ana's mother is interested in helping the poorer people of the tiny town of Ranchador, which is the nearest community to the estate, and also the unfortunate people of Santa Ana, just a few miles to the southwest. . . . Ana's mother has worked to help set up free health clinics at Santa Ana. She and her friends hope to open a training school for nurses. . . . They also want to provide housing for the elderly poor of the area.

Ana does not attend a school; she studies under the watchful eye of tutors employed by her parents. In addition to her regular studies, she is given training in art, ballet, and music. . . . She loves to ride her pony about the estate and play games with her brothers. . . .

The principal crop grown by Ana's father is coffee. His trips to the port city of Acajutla are generally to see about the shipment of his crop from the port. However, he also owns an interest in the large modern cement factory in the port city, as well as its oil refinery and its fertilizer and sulphuric acid plants.

Ana's father also has an interest in the largest coffee mill in the world. . . . Ana is not terribly interested in school. She will probably continue her education . . . taking many general college courses and looking forward to marriage.

---

Adapted from Allan Carpenter and Eloise Baker, *El Salvador* (Chicago Children's Press, 1971), pp. 25, 27. Permission pending.

# ANSWER KEY FOR REVIEW QUESTIONS

**Pages 15–16**
1. C     2. C     3. C     4. C     5. D     6. A     7. D     8. C     9. A

**Page 22**
1. C     2. C     3. B     4. B     5. C     6. D

**Pages 29–30**
1. C     2. D     3. A     4. C     5. B     6. D     7. C     8. B

**Page 36**
1. C     2. C     3. B

**Page 41**
*Fact or Opinion*
1. O     2. O     3. F     4. F

**Page 47**
1. D     2. A     3. C     4. C     5. D

**Page 56**
1. A     2. D     3. B     4. C     5. D     6. A     7. C

**Pages 62–63**
1. B     2. C     3. B     4. B     5. B     6. D     7. B     8. D     9. D     10. C

**Pages 70–71**
1. D     2. C     3. A     4. D     5. A     6. B     7. A     8. B     9. D     10. B     11. C

**Pages 79–80**
1. C     2. B     3. B     4. B     5. C     6. D     7. D     8. A     9. C

**Page 88**
1. A     2. B     3. B     4. C     5. C     6. D

**Page 91**
1. B     2. D     3. B     4. C

**Pages 96–97**
1. C     2. C     3. D     4. A     5. D     6. C     7. A     8. C     9. C     10. C

**Pages 103–104**
1. C     2. B     3. C     4. A     5. B     6. A     7. A     8. B     9. A     10. A

**Pages 112–114**
1. A     2. A     3. D     4. C     5. C     6. B     7. C     8. A     9. C     10. D
11. B     12. D     13. B     14. B

**Page 118**
1. A     2. B     3. C

**Pages 128–130**
1. C     2. A     3. D     4. C     5. C     6. D     7. D     8. B     9. C     10. A
11. B     12. D     13. B     14. C

**Pages 137–139**
1. B     2. B     3. B     4. C     5. B     6. D     7. D     8. A     9. A     10. A
11. B     12. A     13. C     14. D     15. A     16. D     17. A

**Pages 146–148**
1. B     2. B     3. D     4. C     5. A     6. C     7. C     8. A     9. C     10. A
11. A     12. B     13. B     14. C

**Page 154**
1. A    2. A    3. A    4. A    5. A    6. D

**Page 165**
1. A    2. A    3. A    4. D    5. C    6. B

**Page 169**
1. D    2. A

**Page 173**
1. C    2. D    3. A

**Page 179**
1. B    2. C    3. B

**Page 182**
1. C    2. C    3. A    4. B

**Page 187**
1. B    2. D    3. B    4. A    5. D

**Page 190**
1. B    2. B

**Page 195**
1. D    2. A    3. D    4. B    5. A

**Page 199**
1. D    2. A    3. D    4. B    5. A

**Page 205**
1. B    2. C    3. C    4. D    5. D    6. C    7. C

**Pages 254–255**
1. A    2. A    3. B    4. A    5. B    6. C    7. D    8. B    9. C    10. B

**Pages 287–288**
1. C    2. B    3. D    4. D    5. D    6. B    7. B    8. A    9. C    10. A

**Pages 305–306**
1. C    2. A    3. B    4. B    5. D    6. C    7. D    8. D    9. C    10. D

**Pages 350–351**
1. C    2. C    3. A    4. D    5. B    6. D    7. C    8. A    9. C    10. D

**Pages 416–417**
1. B    2. C    3. B    4. D    5. C    6. C    7. C    8. B    9. C    10. C

**Pages 447–448**
1. C    2. B    3. A    4. C    5. C    6. C    7. A    8. B    9. B    10. A

**Pages 500–502**
1. A    2. C    3. C    4. D    5. B    6. C    7. D    8. C    9. B    10. A
11. C    12. C    13. B    14. B

**Pages 554–557**
1. B    2. B    3. A    4. B    5. A    6. C    7. B    8. B    9. C    10. B
11. B    12. C    13. D    14. A    15. C    16. A    17. B    18. A    19. B    20. D

**Pages 564–566**
1. D    2. A    3. B    4. C    5. B    6. B    7. A    8. B    9. A    10. C
11. A    12. A    13. B    14. B    15. B

**Page 570**
1. C    2. A    3. C    4. B    5. A

**Pages 596–597**
1. A    2. C    3. D    4. A    5. B    6. A    7. C    8. A    9. C    10. D

**Pages 650–657**

| | | | | | | | | |
|---|---|---|---|---|---|---|---|---|
| 1. C | 6. A | 11. C | 16. C | 21. B | 26. C | 31. C | 36. C | 41. D |
| 2. B | 7. C | 12. B | 17. A | 22. B | 27. A | 32. B | 37. A | 42. C |
| 3. D | 8. C | 13. C | 18. C | 23. B | 28. D | 33. A | 38. C | 43. C |
| 4. D | 9. C | 14. D | 19. A | 24. A | 29. C | 34. C | 39. C | 44. B |
| 5. C | 10. D | 15. A | 20. A | 25. B | 30. D | 35. C | 40. B | 45. C |

# GLOSSARY

**absolutism** a system of government where a ruler has complete control over the lives of the people

**acid rain** the precipitation or rain that falls through polluted air

**acupuncture** an ancient Chinese practice of sticking needles into certain parts of the body to treat disease and to relieve pain

**adaptation** adjustment to the conditions of the environment or culture

**agriculture** using the land to produce crops and raise livestock; farming

**agronomist** a person who studies soil management and field crop production

**ahimsa** Indian idea of nonviolent action as suggested by Mohandas K. Gandhi

**AIDS** the illness known as acquired immunodeficiency syndrome

**Ainu** among the earliest known people to live in Japan

**Allah** the one God of Islam

**alliance** joining together of groups by formal agreement

**altitude** height of the land above sea level

**animism** the worship of spirits that are part of the natural environment

**annex** to join or add to a larger or more important thing

**anthropologist** social scientist who studies people, their culture, and their different ways of living and behavior

**anti-Semitism** hostility and prejudice against Jews

**apartheid** a policy of segregation and political and economic discrimination against non-European groups in South Africa

**appeasement** satisfying an aggressor's requests in the hope that no more harsh requests will be made

**arable** fertile; suitable for growing crops

**arbitrator** a person chosen to settle a dispute between two groups

**archaeologist** scientist who studies the cultures of prehistoric and historic peoples through their artifacts, such as tools, pottery, building, and writing

**archipelago** a group of islands

**artifacts** objects made by either hand or machine representing a particular culture

**artisan** trained or skilled worker; craftsman

**audiencia** the highest court of Spanish colonial America

**autocrat** one person, who has supreme, unrestricted power over people

**autonomous** self-governing; independent

**balance of payments** a summary of international trade (exports and imports) of a country or region over a period of time

**Bantu** a large group of Africans who speak a common language

**Bedouins** nomadic Arabic livestock-raisers and -herders

**Bible** the holy book of Christians. It contains both the Old Testament and the New Testament. The Old Testament is called the Tanakh by Jews. Jews do not accept the New Testament as a holy book.

**bicameral** a two-house legislature

**bilateral** affecting two sides or parties in any negotiation

**Boers** South Africans of Dutch or Huguenot descent; from the Dutch word for farmers

**boycott** to refuse to buy and use certain goods

**bride price** payment made by a man to a woman's father to be allowed to marry her; bride wealth

**Bunraku** Japanese puppet play

**Bushido** Japanese Samurai Code of Behavior; similar to the feudal code of behavior of the European knights, called chivalry

**cacao** the seeds of a tree from which cocoa and chocolate are made

**caliph** a successor of Muhammed as spiritual and temporal head of Islam

**calligraphy** artistic writing, especially common in China and Japan

**capital** the things used to produce goods and services; money used to develop a country's economy

**capitalism** an economic system based on private rather than government ownership

**cartographer** someone who makes maps

**cash crop** the chief agricultural product raised in an economy in order to sell and obtain income

**caste** social system in which people are grouped according to occupation, wealth, inherited position, or religion

**caudillo** or **cacique** powerful South American leader or dictator

**civilization** level of development of a group; includes food-producing ability, government, and methods of communication

**clan** people within an ethnic group who are descended from a common ancestor

**class** people grouped according to similar social and economic levels

**climate** the general existing weather conditions over an area for a long period of time

**coalition** voluntary union of interest groups, political parties, or nations

**collectives** a system in which a farming community shares ownership of land and farm machinery

**colonialism** a situation in which one group, often a nation, has control over and is depended upon by another area or people

**colony** a body of people living in a separate territory but retaining ties with the parent state

**commonwealth** a nation or state

**commune** often rural community characterized by collective ownership and use of property

**communication** the ability to send or receive information and ideas

**communism** economic system in which a single party controls the means of production with the aim of establishing a classless society

**community** a group living together, having the same laws, and sharing common interests

**confederation** alliance or league

**conservation** protection of natural resources; conserve, to save for the future

**conservatism** a desire to maintain traditional customs and practices, and to make any changes very slowly

**Containment** a policy followed by the United States and the free world during the Cold War, to prevent the spread of communism beyond where it already existed (i.e., China and the Soviet Union)

**continent** a large landmass; one of the seven great divisions of land on the globe

**cooperative** a community system operated by and benefiting all members who contribute to it

**coup d'etat** sudden and violent overthrow of a government by a small group

**Creole (criollo)** a white person descended from French or Spanish settlers of the U.S. gulf states

**crusades** military campaigns and pilgrimages by European Christians to win the Holy Land from the Muslims (1096–1204)

**cultivated** land prepared for the raising of crops

**cultural diffusion** spread of cultural traits from one group to another

**culture** the customary beliefs, social forms, and material traits of an ethnic, religious, or social group

**cuneiform** writing in wedge-shaped characters

**customs** usual ways of acting in a particular situation

**Cyrillic** the alphabet used for Russian and other Slavic languages

**deficit** lacking in amount or quantity

**deforestation** the action of clearing forests of their trees

**deity** a god or goddess

**delta** the land that is formed by mud and sand at the mouth of a river

**democracy** a political system in which the people participate in the making of their own laws or elect representatives to make the laws

**desert** a barren, extremely dry area

**Détente** the friendly relationship between the United States and the Soviet Union during the 1970s

**developed nation** a nation with a stable economy and a modern standard of living for its people

**dharma** the law in the Buddhist religion; correct behavior, virtue in Hinduism

**dialects** a regional or local variety of languages

**diaspora** the lands where people live outside of their original homeland

**dichotomy** a division into two individual groups

**dictator** someone who has taken complete control of a country's government and the lives of the people

**dissident** one who disagrees with the general opinion or actions of a group

**diversity** not alike; variety

**divine right** idea that God has given a ruler the right to rule

**doctrine** a position or principle taught and believed in by a church or government

**drought** a long period of dry weather over an area

**dynasty** a powerful group or family that rules for many years

**economic** relating to the production, distribution, and consumption of goods and services

**ecosystem** an ecological unit consisting of a community and its environment

**elevation** the height of land above sea level; altitude

**embargo** complete restriction or restraint of trade; refusal to buy a product

**encomiendo** a grant of land given by the king of Spain for loyal services

**environment** all of the natural, physical, and cultural conditions that surround and affect people

**equator** an imaginary line circling the earth and equally distant from the North Pole and the South Pole

**ethnic cleansing** act of persecuting members of an ethnic group by killing them or by removing them from an area

**ethnic group** a group of people who have common physical traits, history, and culture

**ethnocentrism** belief that one's own group or culture is superior to others

**Euro** the European currency introduced in 1999

**excommunicate** process of expulsion from the Roman Catholic Church, usually because of disobedience and violation of Church rules and laws

**exploit** to make unfair or selfish use of something or someone

**extended family** a family that includes other members besides mother, father, sons, and daughters; for example, grandparents

**extraterritoriality** existing or taking place outside of the territory of a nation

**extremists** people who go to the greatest extent, including violence, to achieve their goals

**faction** clique; a party or a group

**fallow** plowed land that is not planted for one or more seasons

**favela** a part of a Brazilian town or city where the poor and landless live

**federation** a union of equal organizations that give power to a central group

**fetish** any real object worshipped by people for its supposed magical powers

**feudalism** the political and economic system in which the vassal pledges loyalty and service to a lord in return for land and protection

**genocide** the destruction of a particular group of people

**gentry** people belonging to the upper or ruling class of society

**Ghats** low mountains on the east and west side of the Deccan region in South India

**"global village"** describes the current state of our world, in which events or actions in one part of the world affect other parts of the world

**greenhouse effect** harmful warming of the earth's surface and lower layers of the atmosphere, caused by an increase in carbon dioxide in the atmosphere

**gross domestic product (GDP)** the total value of all goods and services produced in a country during a year

**guerilla** member of a group that carries on raids and fights an established government

**habitat** the natural environment in which people, animals, and plants live or grow

**hacienda** a large land estate or ranch in Spanish America, mainly in Mexico

**Haiku** a Japanese form of poetry

**haj** the pilgrimage to Makkah that all Muslims should take as one of their five obligations

**Hellenistic** Greek culture spread by Alexander the Great on areas he conquered

**heritage** that which is passed from one generation to the next

**hieroglyphics** a writing system using mainly pictorial characters

**Hindi** the major language of India

**Hinduism** the major religion of India

**Hijra** the flight by Muhammed from Mecca to Medina in 622. Sometimes spelled as Hegira, its date is the most important date in Islamic history and begins the Muslim calendar.

**humanism** a belief in the importance of the individual human being, the idea that humans can accomplish great things without regard to supernatural and religious factors. Humanism also emphasized worldly items rather than religious ones. It was a movement that grew during the Renaissance.

**hydroelectric** relating to the production of electricity through the use of water power

**imam** leader of the Shi'ite Muslims; prayer leader of a mosque

**imperialism** a nation's policy of extending its power and dominion over other nations by using force or indirect economic and political control

**inflation** the great increase in the amount of paper money in relation to the available goods for sale; this situation leads to rising prices

**infrastructure** the basic transportation and communication system of a nation

**interdependence** people's dependence on one another

**Internet** a global computer network that links computers together and enables global communication between users

**intervention** the policy of interfering in the affairs of another nation

**irrigation** the watering of crops or other plants by pipes, canals, and ditches

**Islam** a major world religion that recognizes Allah as the only God and Muhammed as his Prophet

**island** a land mass completely surrounded by water

**isolation** separation from others

**isthmus** a narrow strip of land connecting two large land masses and separating two large bodies of water

**jihad** Islamic holy war

**joint family** a family pattern in which two or more generations live together

**Judaism** the oldest of the Middle East religions; the main idea of Judaism is the belief in one God (monotheism)

**junta** a board or ruling body

**Kabbah** a shrine located in the Great Mosque in Makkah and considered to be the holiest site for Muslims

**Kabuki** a form of Japanese drama with song and dance

**Kami** good spirits of nature to the Japanese

**karma** Hindu idea that every human action brings about certain reactions

**kibbutz** an Israeli community of farmers who work together and share all the property and income

**Koran** the holy book of Muslims

**laissez faire** the theory that government should intervene as little as possible in a nation's economic affairs

**landlocked** describes an area or region completely surrounded by land without access to a sea or ocean

**language** a systematic verbal method of communication among a group of people

**latifundia** large farms, ranches, or plantations in Spanish America

**leaching** the washing away of nutrients from the soil

**leftist** a person who favors change or reforms, usually in the name of greater freedom

**liberalism** a belief favoring change and progress in political and cultural traditions

**lines of latitude** imaginary parallel lines running east and west around the globe; these lines measure distance north and south of the equator

**literate** having the ability to read and write a language

**llanos** plains in Colombia and Venezuela; from the Spanish word for "plains"

**mandate** an order or command; a commission set up to rule an area

**Marxist** one who believes in socialism as a method of government

**matriarchal** a family group led by the mother

**medieval** the "Middle Ages" or time between the Roman period and the Renaissance in European history; approximately between C.E. 500 and 1500

**mercantile system** a system in which a colony's only purpose is to provide raw materials for the mother country and act as a market in which products from the mother country can be sold; the colony exists solely for the support of the mother country

**mestizo** a person of mixed European and Native American ancestry

**migration** the movement of people from one area or country to another

**militarism** policy in which the armed forces are made powerful and military interests are most important

**militia** citizens who can be called to help defend a nation; this generally does not include the regular armed forces

**minerals** nonliving materials found on or near the earth's surface, such as gold, silver, and lead

**missionary** person who brings his religion to people who are not members of that religion

**mixed economy** an economy that has both capitalistic (free-market) features and government-directed (command) features

**moderate** not extreme

**moksha** the final resting place for all deserving Hindus

**monarchy** government headed by a king or queen

**monopoly** economic situation wherein one person or group controls the production, pricing, and distribution of a good

**monotheism** the belief in one god or supreme being

**monsoon** a wind in Asia that brings a wet season when it blows from the sea and a dry season when it blows from the land

**mosque** a building used for public worship by Muslims

**most-favored nation** a part of most trade agreements that gives each nation the same rights as all other trading partners

**mouth** the place where a river empties into a sea, lake, or ocean

**mulatto** a person having one European and one African parent, or a person of mixed European and African ancestry

**Muslim** someone who practices the religion of Islam

**myth** a traditional story of supposedly real events that explains a world view of a people or a practice, belief, or natural phenomenon

**nationalism** loyalty and devotion to one's own country, especially placing it above all others

**nationality** a group of people who feel they belong together because of common cultural characteristics like language, religion, history, and traditions

**nationalization** the government take-over of industry and property

**natural laws** laws and rules about human behavior, occurring naturally, without intervention by people

**natural resources** industrial materials and capacities provided by nature

**navigable** deep enough and wide enough for ships to sail on

**negotiate** to confer or bargain in order to arrive at a settlement or solution to a problem

**neutralism** a policy of not taking sides in relation to the great world powers

**nirvana** the stopping of the wheel of rebirth (reincarnation); the goal of all Buddhists

**No (Noh)** a Japanese form of drama developed in the 14th century

**nomad** a member of a group that moves from place to place to secure its food supply

**nonalignment** a policy of not being allied with the great world powers

**nuclear proliferation** the possession of nuclear weapons by more and more countries

**oasis** a place in the desert where there is natural spring or surface water

**ocean** a great body of water that covers three-quarters of the surface of the earth

**oligarchy** governmental rule by a few or a small group

**opium** an addictive narcotic drug

**oral tradition** the practice of passing down stories and information from generation to generation by word of mouth

**origin** thing from which anything comes; source; starting point

**overpopulation** a situation in which an area contains more people than available resources can support

**Pacific rim** refers to the nations of Asia and the Americas that touch both sides of the Pacific Ocean

**pact** an agreement between two or more nations

**paddies** rice fields in Asia

**pagoda** temple or sacred building with many stories (levels) found in India, Southeast Asia, and Japan

**pampas** the large grassy plains of southern Latin American, especially in Argentina

**panchayat** a local council in India

**parliament** a supreme legislative body

**Patois** a local dialect

**patriarch** the highest ranking bishop in the Eastern Orthodox Church, usually ministering over a nation

**patriarchal** a family group led by the father

**patriotism** love and devotion to one's own country

**peasant** a small landowner or laborer

**peninsula** land mass surrounded on three sides by water

**peon** in Latin America, a field worker who owns no land

**per capita GDP** the average value per person of the goods and services a country produces in a year

**petrodollars** money paid to oil-producing countries

**petroleum** an oily, inflammable liquid used in making gasoline and chemicals

**pharaoh** a ruler of ancient Egypt

**pictograph** an ancient or prehistoric drawing or painting on a rock wall

**plain** an extensive area of flat or rolling treeless country

**plateau** a broad land area with a usually level surface raised sharply above the land next to it on at least one side

**pogrom** a violent attack on Jews by non-Jews

**population density** the average number of persons per unit of area

**polytheistic** belief in many gods or deities

**possession** an area under the control of another government

**prehistoric** refers to a period of time prior to written history

**primitive** very simple; of early times in a civilization

**propaganda** the spreading of ideas, information, or rumor for the purpose of furthering one's position or cause to injure another

**provincial** local; relating to a province or district

**quarantine** to blockade in order to prevent the transfer of goods

**Quechua** the language of the Incas, still spoken by the Indians of Peru, Bolivia, Ecuador, Chile, and Argentina

**rabbi** a Jewish religious leader

**race** a division of people having certain similar physical characteristics

**radical** one who favors extreme changes in government or society

**rain forest** a forest of hardwood evergreen trees that requires very heavy rainfall

**rajah** Indian ruler

**realism** a writing style that attempts to portray life as it really happens

**rebellion** armed resistance or fighting against one's government, political system, or culture

**referendum** a practice of submitting to popular vote a measure passed or proposed by a legislative body or by popular demands

**refugee** someone who leaves his or her homeland to seek a safe place to live

**region** an area of land whose parts have one or more similar characteristics

**regionalism** loyalty to local economic and social affairs, customs, and traditions

**reincarnation** the act of returning to some form of life after death

**republic** a type of government in which leaders are chosen by the citizens

**revolution** basic change in or complete overthrow of an existing government, political system, or culture

**rift valley** a split or separation in the earth's crust; the Great Rift Valley extends from southwest Asia (Jordan) to Mozambique in East Africa

**rightist** one who supports conservativism and resists change

**romanticism** a writing style that emphasizes human emotions rather than human reasoning

**rural** having to do with farming and the countryside

**Samurai** the military class of feudal Japan

**Sanskrit** an ancient Indian language; the classical language of Hinduism

**savanna** a grassland in subtropical areas with drought-resistant undergrowth and few trees

**schism** a division or split among people, usually for political or religious reasons

**secede** to withdraw from a group or organization

**sect** a group believing in a particular idea or leader

**sectarian** a member of a sect; a narrow-minded or bigoted person

**secular** concerned more with worldly (earthly) matters than with religious matters

**self-sufficient** able to meet one's own needs without help

**Sepoy** a native of India employed as a soldier by the English

**serf** a member of a subservient feudal class bound to the soil and subject to the will of a lord; serfs had few rights or privileges

**Shi'ite** Muslims who believe Ali and the imams to be the only rightful successors of Muhammed

**Shinto** the original religion of Japan, having gods (Kami) of nature (sea, river, winds, forests, and sun)

**shogun** a military leader of Japan before 1867

**silt** a deposit of sand and mud along a river

**slash-and-burn** a method of clearing land so that it is temporarily usable for farming; used in tropical areas

**social contract** the idea that all people have a right to life, liberty, and property, and that, if a government tries to remove these rights, people also have the right to revolt

**socialist economy** a system in which the government owns the means for production and distribution of goods

**source** origin; place where something begins

**soviet** a worker's council set up by the Bolsheviks in 1917; the term was also adopted by them as the name of the communist government of Russia

**sphere of influence** an area or region within which the influence or the interest of one nation is more important than any other nation

**stable** steady; firm; not likely to fall

**standard of living** the level of comfort enjoyed by an individual or a group

**steppe** flat, treeless plain with short grass found in southeastern Europe or Asia

**strait** a narrow channel of water connecting two larger bodies of water

**subcontinent** a landmass of great size but smaller than a continent; for example, India

**subsidy** a grant or gift of money to assist an enterprise, business, or individual

**subsistence farming** the production of all or almost all the goods required by a farm family, usually without any significant surplus for sale

**suffrage** the right to vote

**sultan** ruler of a Muslim country

**Sunni** the Muslims of the part of Islam that follow the orthodox tradition

**superpower** a nation with greater military and/or economic power than other nations

**suttee** the act or custom of a Hindu widow being cremated on the funeral pyre of her husband

**Swahili** a Bantu language of East Africa used for trade and government; has many Arabic, Persian, and Indian words

**swaraj** Indian term for self-rule

**taiga** a forested area in Russia and other places near the Arctic

**Talmud** books containing Jewish civil and religious law and tradition

**Tanakh** refers to the Jewish bible (called the Old Testament by Christians). Also spelled as

Tanach, it consists of holy books in three categories: the Torah, Prophets, and Writings

**tariff** a tax on goods brought into a country from another country

**terraced farmland** flat shelves of land, arranged like wide steps on a mountainside

**terrorism** the idea of using violence and fear of violence to gain an objective

**textiles** fibers and yarns made into cloth and then into clothing

**Third World** refers to the developing nations of Asia, Africa, and Latin America

**topography** the surface features of a place or area

**totalitarianism** all parts of life—economic, social, political, religious, and educational—are controlled by the state

**trade deficit** when the imports of a nation exceed its exports

**trade surplus** exports of a nation are greater than the imports of that nation

**tradition** the handing down of information, beliefs, and customs from one generation to another

**tribalism** tribal relationships, feelings, and loyalties

**tribe** a group of people who share a common language and religion and are united under one leader

**tributary** the branches of a large river

**tropical** having to do with the hot areas near the equator

**typhoon** a tropical storm or cyclone found in the China Sea and Indian Ocean

**underdeveloped** an area with little industry that is in an early stage of economic development

**unique** one of a kind

**untouchable** a person belonging to the lowest caste of the Hindu social order

**uprising** revolt; rebellion; an act of popular violence in defiance of an established government

**urban** relating to a city

**values** attitudes or beliefs considered to be important by a group

**vassal** a person under the protection of a feudal lord to whom he has vowed his loyalty and service; a subordinate or follower

**veld** South African steppe or prairie

**vernacular** the style of language used in a certain area

**viceroy** the governor of a country or a province who rules as the king's representative

**Yoruba** an African tribe living in present-day Nigeria

**zambo** a person of mixed Native American and African parentage in Latin America

**Zionism** a theory for setting up a Jewish national community in the Middle East and supporting the modern state of Israel

# Examination June 2015

## Global History and Geography

## PART I: MULTIPLE CHOICE

*Directions* (1–50): For each statement or question, write in the space provided the *number* of the word or expression that, of those given, best completes the statement or answers the question.

Base your answer to question 1 on the passage below and on your knowledge of social studies.

... Oral histories are as old as human beings. Before the invention of writing, information passed from generation to generation through the spoken word. Many people around the world continue to use oral traditions to pass along knowledge and wisdom. Interviews and recordings of community elders and witnesses to historical events provide exciting stories, anecdotes, and other information about the past....

—Library of Congress

1 Based on this passage, historians should treat oral histories and oral traditions as

1 persuasive arguments
2 statistical data
3 unbiased sources
4 cultural evidence

1 ____

2 Which academic discipline focuses study on the roles and functions of government?

1 political science
2 anthropology
3 geography
4 economics

2____

3 During the Neolithic Revolution, production of a food surplus led directly to

1 a nomadic lifestyle
2 a reliance on stone weaponry
3 an increase in population
4 a dependence on hunting and gathering

3____

4 Discovery of streets arranged in a grid-like pattern and a system of pipes for moving water in Harappa and Mohenjo-Daro suggest that these ancient river valley cities in South Asia had

1 organized governments
2 subsistence-based economies
3 polytheistic beliefs
4 rigid social classes

4____

Base your answer to question 5 on the passage below and on your knowledge of social studies.

... Monsoons are relied upon throughout the country to provide water for growing crops. Heavy monsoons, however, can bring floods that often have a high death toll. These floods have been exacerbated [made worse] by deforestation of the hills for industrial and agricultural purposes. It is a fine balance between having plenty of water to flood the rice fields and having too much so that crops, homes, and even lives are lost. The alternative to the floods may be famines. However, India's infrastructure can now deal successfully with these: When the monsoon fails in one area, the army is able to move supplies to the drought-stricken area. As a result of this organization, few lives were lost in the Maharashtra famines of 1965–66 and 1974–75, while more than two million people died in the Bengal famine of 1943.

—Louise Nicholson, *National Geographic Traveler:*
*India*, 2007

5 Based on this passage, how have the negative effects of the monsoons been reduced in recent years?

1 The army is building dams to hold back the floods.
2 Farmers have begun to grow crops that require less water.
3 Home construction in flood areas has been controlled by government regulations.
4 An improved infrastructure makes it possible to bring supplies to areas in need of help.      5 ____

6 The Egyptians used hieroglyphics in the same way as the Sumerians used

1 ideographs      3 cuneiform
2 calligraphy      4 letters      6____

7 Which geographic feature served as a barrier to political unity and encouraged the rise of independent city-states in ancient Greece?

1 broad plains      3 navigable rivers
2 mountain ranges      4 numerous ports      7____

8 The Tang dynasty contributed to the development of Chinese culture by

1 creating a shogunate
2 producing porcelain and block printing
3 introducing Hinduism as a major philosophy
4 devising a set of laws and carving them on rocks and pillars      8____

9 A primary goal of European Crusaders fighting in the Middle East was to

1 establish markets for Italian merchants
2 rescue Pope Urban II from the Byzantines
3 halt the advance of Mongol armies in the Asian steppes
4 secure access to Christian holy sites in Jerusalem      9____

10 Increases in trade and commerce that occurred during the late Middle Ages in Europe resulted in

1 lower living standards for guild members
2 the development of more towns and cities
3 a decline in rivalries between kings
4 an increase in the number of self-sufficient manors      10____

11 The writings of both Marco Polo and Ibn Battuta inspired

1 exploration and trade
2 important military expeditions
3 movements for political freedom
4 the spread of Islam to Southeast Asia  11____

12 Nanjing, Venice, and Mogadishu were powerful and influential cities in the 13th century because they all

1 developed agrarian-based economies
2 served as religious pilgrimage sites
3 established democratic governments
4 took advantage of the factors of location  12____

13 The West African empires of Ghana, Mali, and Songhai were able to thrive because

1 they controlled the gold-salt trade
2 their herds of cattle were in demand
3 their armies took control of much of Africa
4 they adopted Christianity as their primary religion  13____

14 What was an immediate result of the Black Death?

1 labor shortages
2 overseas exploration
3 decrease in anti-Semitism
4 improvements in medical science  14____

15 Which statement best expresses the philosophy of humanism?

  1 God selects those to be saved.

  2 The pope expresses the ultimate word of God.

  3 People have potential and can improve themselves by learning.

  4 A person's life on Earth is merely preparation for the afterlife.     15____

16 Which development is most closely associated with early Inca achievements?

  1 inventing the wheel as a transportation device

  2 improving iron weapons

  3 expanding global trade

  4 adapting a mountainous environment     16____

17 What was a major effect of the Columbian exchange?

  1 economic collapse in Europe

  2 introduction of new food crops to Europe

  3 decrease in European population

  4 expansion of democratic rights throughout Europe     17____

18 Which policy is a country using when it regulates its colonies' imports and exports to produce a favorable balance of trade?

  1 embargo         3 mercantilism

  2 outsourcing     4 transmigration     18____

Base your answer to question 19 on the diagram below and on your knowledge of social studies.

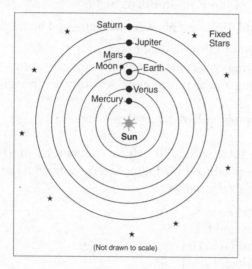

(Not drawn to scale)

19 Which scientist is most directly associated with formulating this view of the solar system?

1 Ptolemy          3 Copernicus
2 Descartes        4 Newton                    19 ____

20 Akbar the Great tried to unify the Mughal Empire and create peace between the different people of India by

1 promoting a policy of religious toleration
2 forcing all people to adopt modern dress
3 building the Taj Mahal to inspire healing
4 establishing Buddhism as the state religion          20 ____

21 • Signing of the Magna Carta
   • Signing of the Petition of Right
   • Passage of the English Bill of Rights

In England, these events were instrumental in

1 supporting a disarmament policy
2 promoting government control of the economy
3 justifying the acquisition of territory in foreign lands
4 developing parliamentary democracy

21 _____

22 Between 1500 and 1750, which commercial products were produced on Latin American plantations using enslaved laborers?

1 corn and squash
2 bananas and tea
3 sugar and tobacco
4 potatoes and wool

22 _____

23 The ideas of Enlightenment philosophers were based on

1 efforts to achieve salvation
2 faith in human reason
3 traditional practices
4 the inevitability of poverty

23 _____

24 Toussaint L'Ouverture and José de San Martín are leaders best known for

1 leading independence movements
2 supporting religious reforms
3 promoting civil disobedience
4 opposing democracy

24 _____

Base your answer to question 25 on the poster below and on your knowledge of social studies.

**The Tsar, the Priest and the Rich Man on the Shoulders of the Labouring People**

ЦАРЬ, ПОП И БОГАЧ

НА ПЛЕЧАХ У ТРУДОВОГО НАРОДА.

Source: A. Apsit, Coloured Lithograph, 1918 (adapted)

25 In early 20th-century Russia, which group may have gained support by circulating this poster?

   1 aristocracy       3 monarchists

   2 Bolsheviks       4 Orthodox clergy     25 ____

26 Which course of action does the theory of laissez-faire suggest a government should follow?

1 providing help for people in need
2 establishing businesses to create jobs
3 letting natural laws regulate the economy
4 controlling the mineral resources of a country          26____

27 One effect of the British landlord system in Ireland in the mid-1800s and in India in the early 1900s was that these landlord systems

1 contributed to famine and suffering
2 allowed local economies to prosper
3 emphasized food crops over mining
4 led to an agrarian revolution          27____

28 Commodore Matthew Perry is best known for taking which action?

1 leading the British East India Company
2 rescuing Europeans during the Boxer Rebellion
3 justifying European spheres of influence in China
4 opening Japan to American and European influences          28____

29 During World War I, developments in military technology led to

1 an early victory by the Allied powers
2 the establishment of industrial capitalism
3 the use of poisonous gas and submarine attacks
4 an increase in ethnic tension in western Europe          29____

30 One major reason the League of Nations failed was that it

  1 was not included in the Versailles Treaty
  2 was controlled by communist Russia
  3 frightened many nations with its large military force
  4 lacked the support of many of the major world powers during crises      30 ____

31 Which geographic characteristic of Japan most influenced its decision to engage in imperialism in the early to mid-20th century?

  1 mountainous terrain
  2 lack of natural resources
  3 abundance of rivers
  4 island location      31 ____

32 Which condition was a result of Joseph Stalin's command economy?

  1 Peasants were encouraged to sell surplus grain for personal profit.
  2 The production of consumer goods increased.
  3 National revenue increased allowing for greater individual spending.
  4 The government controlled agriculture through collective farms.      32 ____

33 After World War I, the rise of Benito Mussolini in Italy and the rise of Adolf Hitler in Germany are most closely associated with

  1 the development of fascism
  2 the desire for containment
  3 an emphasis on democratic traditions
  4 a return to conservative religious practices      33 ____

34 What was a major reason the Soviet Union established satellite states in Eastern Europe after World War II?

1 developing better trade relations with the West
2 creating a buffer zone against future invasions
3 participating in United Nations peacekeeping missions
4 controlling the Organization of Petroleum Exporting Countries (OPEC)                34 _____

Base your answer to question 35 on the excerpt below and on your knowledge of social studies.

...The achievement gap between black and white students in South Africa is enormous. In the province of Western Cape, only 2 out of 1,000 sixth-graders in predominantly black schools performed at grade level on a math test in 2005, compared with 2 out of 3 children in schools once reserved for whites that are now integrated, but generally in more affluent [wealthier] neighborhoods....

—Celia W. Dugger

35 Which underlying historical factor most significantly contributed to this achievement gap?

1 inequalities existing between the races under apartheid
2 economic sanctions placed on school communities
3 lack of governmental support for white educational programs
4 a period of political assassinations and civil war                35 _____

36 **"India Partitioned at Independence"**
**"Serbs Fuel Conflict in Kosovo"**
**"Grievances Divide Hutu and Tutsi"**

Which conclusion do these headlines support?

1 Cultural diversity leads to stable societies.
2 Ethnic and religious differences have been sources of tension.
3 Economic cooperation can overcome political issues.
4 Gender differences are more powerful than differences in social status.          36____

37 Many conflicts in the Middle East during the post–World War II period have directly resulted from

1 the dissolution of the Arab League
2 border clashes between Iran and China
3 disputes related to Palestine
4 the partition of Egypt                          37____

Base your answer to question 38 on the passage below and on your knowledge of social studies.

... More than 30 years after "Year Zero" and more than a decade after the "return to democracy," Cambodia remains in a league of its own—miserable, corrupt and compassionless. Only the toughest and the most unscrupulous can "make it" and get ahead. There is hardly any social net to speak of; the savage insanity of the Khmer Rouge has been replaced with savage capitalism, but often with the same people in charge....

—Andre Vitchek,
"A Tortured History and Unanswered Questions"

38 What does the author of this 2006 passage conclude?

   1 As democracy develops, circumstances will improve.
   2 Though governments change, circumstances often remain the same.
   3 New leadership is determined to replace the Khmer Rouge.
   4 Harsh living conditions have caused people to rely extensively on a social net.           38 _____

---

39 Which action was taken by Deng Xiaoping to improve the economy of China?

   1 discouraging foreign investment
   2 encouraging some capitalist practices
   3 organizing the Red Guard
   4 practicing glasnost           39 _____

40 Which revolution led to increases in global food production as a result of using genetically altered seeds and large amounts of chemical fertilizers and pesticides?

   1 Cultural          3 Scientific
   2 Glorious          4 Green           40 _____

Base your answer to question 41 on the cartoon below and on your knowledge of social studies.

Source: Arend Van Dam, http://www.politicalcartoons.com, July 22, 2010 (adapted)

41 What is the main idea of this 2010 cartoon?

1 Pakistan plays a minor role in the affairs of Afghanistan.

2 The United States and Pakistan will join forces to remove the Taliban.

3 Disputes over water rights between Pakistan and Afghanistan continue to create challenges.

4 The Taliban will pose a threat to Afghanistan when the United States leaves.

41 ____

42 The World Trade Organization (WTO), North American Free Trade Agreement (NAFTA), and European Union (EU) all share the primary goal of

  1 promoting space exploration and maintaining satellites

  2 increasing economic aid to developing nations

  3 encouraging trade between countries and lowering trade barriers

  4 developing regulations to preserve the environment

42 _____

43 The use of the decimal system, advancements in medicine, and construction of Hindu temples are most closely associated with the golden age of the

  1 Abbassid dynasty      3 Gupta Empire

  2 Han dynasty         4 Roman Empire

43 _____

44 One reason the Justinian Code was significant was that it

  1 became the foundation of the modern legal systems of many Western countries

  2 established the basis for the development of the Code of Hammurabi

  3 incorporated laws from all over Asia and Europe

  4 led to the protection of inalienable rights in Roman territories

44 _____

45 Which technological development contributed most directly to the success of the Protestant Reformation?

  1 astrolabe         3 wheel

  2 compass         4 printing press

45 _____

46 "Liberty, Equality, Fraternity" and "Peace, Land, and Bread" are slogans used by revolutionaries to represent

1  frameworks for economic stability
2  political and economic ideals
3  plans for maintaining the social hierarchy
4  methods of political reform                          46____

47 One way in which Otto von Bismarck and Camillo Cavour are similar is that both leaders

1  followed a policy of isolationism
2  adopted papal policies
3  led an African independence movement
4  promoted unification to form a new nation-state     47____

48 Which title best completes the partial outline below?

| I. _____ |
| A. During the early 1800s, Napoleon Bonaparte's grand army sweeps across eastern Europe. |
| B. During World War I, Germany invades France through Belgium. |
| C. During World War II, Germans blitzkrieg western Europe. |

1  Importance of Rivers as Invasion Routes
2  Stalemate of Trench Warfare
3  Use of the Northern Plain for Conquest
4  Role of Naval Blockades in Wars                     48____

49 One way in which the rule of Peter the Great in Russia and the rule of Emperor Meiji in Japan are similar is that both leaders

1 emancipated serfs
2 granted equality to women
3 encouraged modernization
4 ruled according to a constitution          49____

50 One purpose of the Nuremberg Trials and of the Truth and Reconciliation Commission in South Africa was to

1 address human rights abuses
2 support the establishment of democratic governments
3 establish free trade zones throughout the world
4 provide encouragement to people behind the Iron Curtain          50____

**In developing your answer to Part II, be sure to keep this general definition in mind:**

discuss means "to make observations about something using facts, reasoning, and argument; to present in some detail"

## PART II: THEMATIC ESSAY QUESTION

*Directions:* Write a well-organized essay that includes an introduction, several paragraphs addressing the task below, and a conclusion.

**Theme: Belief Systems—Movements**

> Belief systems are an established, orderly way that groups or individuals look at religious faith or philosophical principles. Some belief systems have spread outside their places of origin. The diffusion of these belief systems has affected other societies and regions in various ways.

**Task:**

> Select *two* belief systems that have spread outside their place of origin and for *each*
> * Discuss a central principle of this belief system
> * Discuss how this belief system spread to another region
> * Discuss an effect of the spread of this belief system on a society or region

You may use any belief system from your study of global history and geography. Some suggestions you might wish to consider include Buddhism, Confucianism, Judaism, Christianity, Islam, and communism.

**You are *not* limited to these suggestions.**

**Do *not* use the United States as a region
to which a belief system has spread.**

**Guidelines:**

**In your essay, be sure to:**
- Develop all aspects of the task
- Support the theme with relevant facts, examples, and details
- Use a logical and clear plan of organization, including an introduction and a conclusion that are beyond a restatement of the theme

In developing your answers to Part III, be sure to keep these general definitions in mind:

   (a) <u>describe</u> means "to illustrate something in words or tell about it"

   (b) <u>discuss</u> means "to make observations about something using facts, reasoning, and argument; to present in some detail"

## PART III: DOCUMENT-BASED QUESTION

This question is based on the accompanying documents. The question is designed to test your ability to work with historical documents. Some of these documents have been edited for the purposes of this question. As you analyze the documents, take into account the source of each document and any point of view that may be presented in the document. Keep in mind that the language used in a document may reflect the historical context of the time in which it was written.

   **Historical Context:**

> Throughout history, empires such as the **Roman**, the **Ottoman**, and the **British** have faced various problems that led to their decline. The decline of these empires has influenced changes in societies and regions.

**Task:**

Using the information from the documents and your knowledge of global history, answer the questions that follow each document in Part A. Your answers to the questions will help you write the Part B essay in which you will be asked to

Select *two* empires mentioned in the historical context and for *each*
- Describe problems that led to this empire's decline
- Discuss how this empire's decline influenced change in a society and/or a region

## Part A: Short-Answer Questions

*Directions:* Analyze the documents and answer the short-answer questions that follow each document in the space provided.

### Document 1

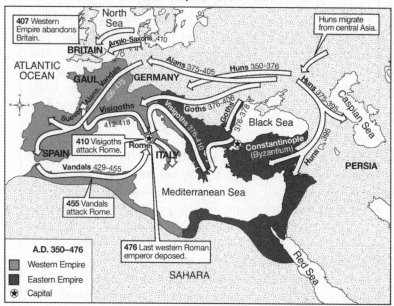

Roman Empire A.D. 350–476

Source: *The Nystrom Atlas of World History*, Herff Jones Education Division (adapted)

1 Based on the information shown on this map, state **one** problem that helped bring about the decline of the Roman Empire. [1]

_____

_____

**Document 2**

... By the middle of the second century Italy [within the Roman Empire] was in a state of decline. By the time of Diocletian, at the opening of the fourth century, decay was apparent throughout the empire. Commerce had largely disappeared owing to the lack of customers, to piracy on the seas, and to insecurity of the roads on land. Generally speaking, purchasing power at that time was confined to the public officials, to the army officers, and to the great landowners. Trade in the everyday objects of daily use had all but disappeared, but trade in luxuries prospered. The cities in the west, omitting the places where government centered, were usually in decline; their commercial and industrial classes had disappeared, the old traders having been replaced by the traveling eastern merchant, of whom the Syrian was the most notorious. Foreign trade was sharply curtailed. At various times the government attempted to prohibit the export of various commodities, among them wine, oil, grain, salt, arms, iron, and gold. With this curbing of exports there was also an effort made to control certain imports such as is evidenced by the state monopoly in silk. These two movements hampered commercial contracts outside the empire and all but killed what was left of foreign trade....

Source: Louis C. West, "The Economic Collapse of the
Roman Empire," *The Classical Journal*, November 1932

2 According to Louis C. West, what were **two** economic problems the Roman Empire faced during its period of decline? [2]

(1)_____

_____

(2)_____

_____

## Document 3

> ... As western Europe fell to the Germanic invasions, imperial power shifted to the Byzantine Empire, that is, the eastern part of the Roman Empire, with its capital at Constantinople. The eastern provinces of the former Roman Empire had always outnumbered those in the west. Its civilization was far older and it had larger cities, which were also more numerous than in the west....

Source: Steven Kreis, *The History Guide: Lectures on Ancient and Medieval European History*, Lecture 17, History Guide online

3 According to Steven Kreis, what was **one** change that resulted from the fall of the western half of the Roman Empire? [1]

_____

_____

## Document 4

> The power of the [Ottoman] Empire was waning [fading] by 1683 when the second and last attempt was made to conquer Vienna. It failed. Without the conquest of Europe and the acquisition of significant new wealth, the Empire lost momentum and went into a slow decline.
> Several other factors contributed to the [Ottoman] Empire's decline:
> - Competition from trade from the Americas
> - Competition from cheap products from India and the Far East
> - Development of other trade routes
> - Rising unemployment within the Empire
> - Ottoman Empire became less centralised, and central control weakened
> - Sultans being less severe in maintaining rigorous standards of integrity in the administration of the Empire
> - Sultans becoming less sensitive to public opinion

Source: "Ottoman Empire (1301–1922)," BBC online, 2009 (adapted)

4a According to the BBC, what was **one** *economic* problem that contributed to the decline of the Ottoman Empire? [1]

_____

_____

b According to the BBC, what was **one** *political* problem that contributed to the decline of the Ottoman Empire? [1]

_____

_____

**Document 5**

> ... In 1875, the Slavic peoples living in the Ottoman provinces of Bosnia and Herzegovina (currently the state of Bosnia-Herzegovina), led an uprising against the Ottomans in order to gain their freedom. The general weakness of the Ottomans led two independent, neighbor Slavic states, Montenegro and Serbia, to aid the rebellion. Within a year, the rebellion spread to the Ottoman province of Bulgaria. The rebellion was part of a larger political movement called the Pan-Slavic movement, which had as its goal the unification of all Slavic peoples—most of whom were under the control of Austria, Germany, and the Ottoman Empire—into a single political unity under the protection of Russia. Anxious also to conquer the Ottomans themselves and seize Istanbul, the Russians allied with the rebels, Serbia, and Montenegro and declared war against the Ottomans....

Source: Richard Hooker, "European Imperialism and the Balkan Crisis," *The Ottomans*, World Cultures

5 According to Richard Hooker, what was *one* problem faced by the Ottomans during the decline of their Empire? [1]

_____

_____

**Document 6**

> ... Mustafa Kemal [Atatürk] was a secular nationalist who believed that all the inheritance of the Ottoman Empire should be abandoned and Turkey should be transformed into a modern European state. This involved less of a sudden break with the past than might appear. The Tanzimat reforms [between 1839 and 1876] had laid the foundations of a secular state, and the Young Turks, even while attempting to preserve the empire, had given a powerful impetus [motivation] to the cause of Turkish nationalism. During the war years [1914–1918], the secularization of education had proceeded and the universities and public positions had been opened to women. Certain of the law courts under the control of the religious authorities had been placed under the Ministry of Justice. A law in 1916 had reformed marriage and divorce....

Source: Peter Mansfield, *A History of the Middle East*, Viking

6 According to Peter Mansfield, what was **one** change that occurred as the Ottoman Empire declined and a new state of Turkey began to take shape? [1]

_____

_____

**Document 7**

The British Empire and Mandates in the Early 1920s

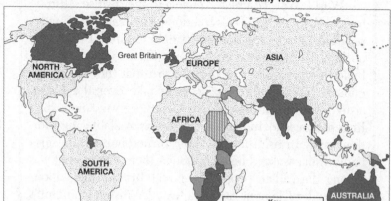

Source: Encyclopedia Britannica Kids (adapted)

7 Based on the information shown on this map, what was a problem the British faced that made it difficult to govern its empire? [1]

_____

_____

## Document 8

> ... World War II greatly changed the British attitude toward the idea of India's freedom. The fear that an independent India would not pay its debt to Great Britain was no longer valid. Great Britain actually owed India over a billion pounds. Nor was the concern that there were not enough Indian military officers to take over the Indian army from the British. As a result of the war, more than fifteen thousand Indian officers were available. In addition, many British soldiers who returned home from serving in India realized how unpopular their government was among the Indian people. In Great Britain, the Labour Party under Clement Attlee defeated Winston Churchill's Conservatives and took charge of the government....
>
> The Labour Party, already sympathetic to the idea of India's independence, faced a great deal of unrest in India. The cold winter of 1945–46 made shortages of food and clothing even worse. Many nationalist leaders, recently released from prison, gave speeches encouraging violent actions to achieve freedom. In Calcutta, demonstrations led to riots in which over thirty people were killed and several hundred injured....

Source: *Indian Independence and the Question of Pakistan*, Choices Program, Watson Institute for International Studies, Brown University

8 Based on this excerpt from *Indian Independence and the Question of Pakistan*, what were **two** factors that made Great Britain more willing to grant India independence? [2]

(1)_____

_____

(2)_____

_____

**Document 9**

> ... During the last 60 years [since 1928], the British Empire has broken apart. Most of the nations that were in the empire demanded and got their independence. With the empire gone, Britain lost a major source of wealth. At the same time, it lost industrial advantages it had enjoyed for many years....

Source: Clare McHugh, *Scholastic World Cultures: Western Europe*, Scholastic, 1988

9 According to Clare McHugh, what was **one** change Great Britain faced with the breakup of its empire? [1]

_____

_____

## Part B: Essay

*Directions*: Write a well-organized essay that includes an introduction, several paragraphs, and a conclusion. Use evidence from *at least* **four** documents in your essay. Support your response with relevant facts, examples, and details. Include additional outside information.

### Historical Context:

> Throughout history, empires such as the **Roman**, the **Ottoman**, and the **British** have faced various problems that led to their decline. The decline of these empires has influenced changes in societies and regions.

### Task:

> Using the information from the documents and your knowledge of global history, write an essay in which you
>
> Select **two** empires mentioned in the historical context and for **each**
> * Describe problems that led to this empire's decline
> * Discuss how this empire's decline influenced change in a society and/or a region

### Guidelines:

#### In your essay, be sure to:
* Develop all aspects of the task
* Incorporate information from *at least* **four** documents
* Incorporate relevant outside information
* Support the theme with relevant facts, examples, and details
* Use a logical and clear plan of organization, including an introduction and a conclusion that are beyond a restatement of the theme

# Answers
# June 2015
## Global History and Geography

## Answer Key

**PART I (1–50)**

| | | | |
|---|---|---|---|
| 1. 4 | 14. 1 | 27. 1 | 40. 4 |
| 2. 1 | 15. 3 | 28. 4 | 41. 4 |
| 3. 3 | 16. 4 | 29. 3 | 42. 3 |
| 4. 1 | 17. 2 | 30. 4 | 43. 3 |
| 5. 4 | 18. 3 | 31. 2 | 44. 1 |
| 6. 3 | 19. 3 | 32. 4 | 45. 4 |
| 7. 2 | 20. 1 | 33. 1 | 46. 2 |
| 8. 2 | 21. 4 | 34. 2 | 47. 4 |
| 9. 4 | 22. 3 | 35. 1 | 48. 3 |
| 10. 2 | 23. 2 | 36. 2 | 49. 3 |
| 11. 1 | 24. 1 | 37. 3 | 50. 1 |
| 12. 4 | 25. 2 | 38. 2 | |
| 13. 1 | 26. 3 | 39. 2 | |

# INDEX

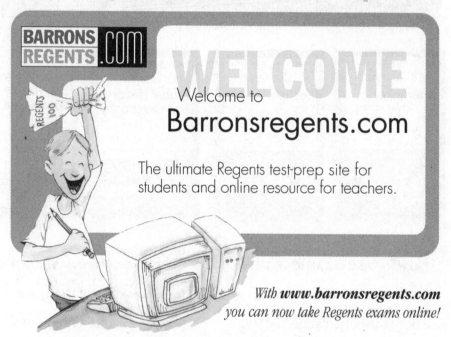

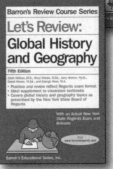

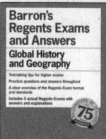

# NOTES

# NOTES